من تو شدم تو من شدی من تن شدم تو جاں شدی
تاکس نگوید بعد ازیں من دیگرم تو دیگری

Mun tu shudam· tu mun shudi,mun tun shudam tu jaan shudi
Taakas na guyad baad azeen, mun deegaram tu deegari

I have become you, and you me,
I am the body, you soul;
So that no one can say hereafter,
That you are are someone, and me someone else.

Ameer Khusro

* Ovee, Abhang, Bharud, Kirtan, pad and devotional songs are the various types of Metaphysical poetry.

Sufism in Maharashtra

(Perspective on Literature of Sufi Saints)

Dr. Kiran Paithankar Ph.D

CLASSY PUBLISHING

First published by Classy Publishing

info@classypublishing.com
www.classypublishing.com

Author Name & Copyright © Dr. Kiran Paithankar, 2021
Title : Sufism In Maharashtra (Perspective on Literature of Sufi Saints)

First Edition : 2021

ISBN Print Book - 978-93-5522-117-9
ISBN eBook - 978-93-5522-122-3

Publishing Services by Abhived Publication, India

Printed in India

Four Words

When we look at the history of the world, we find that the period of almost known history is full of various political upheavals and battles, the rise and fall of different religions and sects. However, during this period, thousands of scholars, and founders of religion as well as various known and unknown saints have contributed on earthly and material fronts with a view to make human life endurable and stable social life. The most close and familiar subject with social life is one's own religious beliefs. In all this, the ultimate goal of religion and faith is social unity, love, and brotherhood. In the course of time, various ideas have become hybrids and new opinions have emerged. In everyday life, the transcendental life of the common man should be happy so that he can fully face the pleasures and sorrows that come with living a material life. It is for this purpose that the saints have come forward in which the Sufi system has a great deal to do, as well as the saints on this bhakti Marg (Varkari/a devotional path). The objectives of both these sects were so similar and goal-oriented that it is not known whether the Sufi saints followed the path of the local saints, and the supporters followed the path of the Sufi saints. Considering this unity, if you study the various literature works and compositions of the Sufi saints, you will find their influence on the local social life and the reflection of the customs of the society in their literature. For this, an attempt has been made in this book to show the place of some Muslim Sufi saints in the land of Maharashtra in the local life by presenting a detailed study of their compositions and literature. The writings of Muslim Marathi saints are of a very high standard. The number of followers of Sufi saints is huge in India especially Maharashtra. But even today, people do not pay much attention to the writings and philosophies of Muslim Sufi saints in Maharashtra. Their bibliography is new to the general public, with the exception of a few disciplines and curious scholars. The work of such great sufi saints and their texts should be introduced. More than half of the general readership in Maharashtra is unaware of the origins of Sufi saints, their propaganda, etc., so that their work can reach the masses. This book deals with the origin, development, propagation, and propagation of Sufi faith as well as the traditions and writings of Sufi saints in Maharashtra. In order to provide useful information to the general readers and practitioners of the Sufi system in a single book, I have taken the approach here. In the first chapter of the book, I have described the concept of religion, in the second chapter analysed the Sufism in the Global concept and in the third section how Sufism spread in India is investigated. In the fourth chapter, Sufi and Varkari from Maharashtra and saints on the path of devotion are depicted. In the fifth chapter, a detailed account of the various prominent poetic compositions of the Muslim saint poets of Maharashtra is presented. It shows the influence of Muslim saints on the issue of social integration as well as spirituality which is another part of the society. In such a detailed book, a unique study of the Sufi faith of the Muslim saint poets of Maharashtra and their works is presented in this book. I think this book will definitely be useful for the general reader, curious, researcher, history student, etc. to satisfy their curiosity and research.

"I am gratefully dedicating this book to the Muslim Sufi saints of Maharashtra and their rich literature. Muslim Sufi saints added value by their literature and enriched Marathi saint literature.

Similarly, the spirit of inter-religious harmony, mutual harmony and unity was enhanced in Maharashtra. They enlightened the society and gave direction to the eradication of superstition and caste inequality. I am offering this book to a well-known and unknown Muslim Sufi saint poet from Maharashtra."

—Dr. Paithankar

Acknowledgement

While composing this research work on Sufism in Maharashtra, I am indebted to a huge number of scholars, sufi saints and I would like to acknowledge here the work of those who have directly or indirectly influenced the writing of what is by its nature an exercise in synthesis. The efforts became possible of writing this book is from the reading, and rich literature work of Muslim Sufi Marathi poets and Warkari saints available in internationally on Sufism. I would like to express my gratitude to every historian, researcher, publisher, the great authors, and editors who have studied, translated, and made Muslim Sufis' literature available to readers. However, I would like to specifically thank my teachers of Persian language in Iran Culture house, Mumbai Mr. Masud Islami and Mrs. Mahnaz Furudi and teachers from Mumbai University of Persian Department Mr. Mohammad Reza Fallah and Dr. Sakina Khan (Head of Department) who have most influenced my understanding of Sufism over my years of study, as well as several colleagues Mr. Shabib Zaidi, Mr. (Adv.) Abdul Azim, Mr. (Adv.) Mustafa Banatwala, Mr. (Adv.) Mohsain Shirazi, Mr. Khan Mahfooz Nisar, Mr.(Adv) Ejaz Ahmed Shaikh and beloved late friend Mr. Zainul Reza Furniturewala who were encouraged and supported me in writing literature on Sufism. My thanks go at the first place to Mr. Zakir Hussain Shaikh for vicariously shaping the development of my ideas on Sufism at different points in my learning and to Dr. Vaibhavi to read through and comment on the manuscript for her exemplary intellectual generosity.

Over the twenty years in which, I have studied the literature of language, history, various religions, philosophies, etc., wholeheartedly. I got the inspiration and a new vision to write this book because of all the Sufi saints and Muslim Marathi Sufi saints from Maharashtra region who preached humanity in their books.

Dr.Paithankar
Maharashtra, India July 2021

Index

Preface

Many introductory books on Sufism already exist, among them several excellent accounts of either specific periods or beliefs and practices which have moved beyond the flaws of the old mysticism model evaluated in this book. There exists no overall survey of Sufism that devotes equal value and emphasis to each period of its history. Aimed at students of history and religious studies, as well as the general reader, this book is just such a general and interpretive narrative tracing Sufism from its period of origins until recent times. In large part, the incrementally global ambit of the narrative presented here reflects the abundance of scholarship that is now available. Since this wealth of scholarship is increasingly difficult to navigate, ample references are provided in the endnotes to allow more committed readers to follow up whichever aspects of Sufi history concern them. More importantly, the attempt to redistribute attention through each period and region articulates a rejection of the idea that Sufism more truly resided in one 'homeland' or 'classical' era than in another. In the Introduction, I discuss that Sufism is better understood through the rubric of 'tradition' rather than 'mysticism'. Since tradition is by definition that which is transmitted through time and space, any genuine attempt to pursue the history of a tradition must accept the temporally diachronic and spatially distributive nature of the exercise. While synchronic or decontextualized accounts of the 'essence' of Sufism have often presented themselves as truer to the spirit of Sufism, I have come to the view, decades of studying the writings of the Sufis, that the struggle with the passing of time and the changing of location is not only central to the concerns of the Sufis but is fundamentally constitutive of their construction of a tradition from that which was or 'handed down' to them. Sufis have not sought communion with God and his Prophet by stepping out of time, but by connecting themselves to chains of knowledge and blessing that shuttle them through the centuries to the moment of Prophet Muhammad's revelation from God's presence. In their much grappling's with the existential dilemmas of human life, Sufis have turned again and again to the lessons of the living masters and the books of the saints whose teachings-in-time have shown them the road to eternity. While I am aware that this may lend a certain methodological un-evenness to certain sections of the book, little opportunity to address the historiographical issues involved and so my evaluations are ultimately implicit in the usage made of particular data. In a relatively, my emphases on conceiving Sufism through the lenses of tradition in Saints and Sufis, society and power has also meant that less attention has been paid than in other introductory writings to the private realms of rapture, love, and experience.

We will also learn more on Sufism which is a process of attaining closeness to the 'Creator' through love, which is attained by purification of the ego. The believer who yearns for something deeper than the promised reward of eternal salvation for good behaviour is faced with a challenge which springs from within. Happiness for him is not achieved by clinging to the hope of endless delights in Paradise, nor is he motivated toward being good in order to avoid the agonies of hell. Consciously or unconsciously, this seeker is after absolute truth. It is the inner man who remembers when he was not separated from his Lord, and now longs to be reunited with his true Beloved. This seeker craves for the conscious realization of what his heart already knows that he is connected very intimately with the essence of Allah, and in fact his true nature lies in the experience of knowing that ultimate reality. The task at hand thus becomes to discover where his 'self' fits in relation to Allah's unlimited Being. Allah defines Himself in the Holy Quran as "…the Light of the heavens and the earth" (24:35). Just as we understand that light is energy, we conceive of Allah as energy. Allah as pure energy is formless but contains the potential to create all forms. Allah's power is at once the energy used to create all forms, and the energy/ substance of forms. For Sufis, Allah's inherent quality of awareness, His comprehensive and eternal consciousness, is another aspect of the 'Light' by which He describes Himself. There can be no god but Allah because the existence of any other power would limit God, who is without any limit whatsoever.

The underlying tenet of Sufism is that human beings were created to know Allah and to manifest His attributes while living on this earth. Tasawwuf is a method and way of life that enables one to become 'insan-kamil', a true human being who has realized intimacy with his Creator. When his or her spiritual potential has been achieved, a human being is fit to be Allah's khalifa (deputy) on earth, as Allah intended, according to the Holy Qur'an. Every human being is equipped with the inner circuitry that joins him with the divine. Many experience moments of truth, when the circuits light up and knowledge of the absolute becomes manifest. While these times of heightened awareness may pass as quickly as they come, the method of Tasawwuf is designed to enable the seeker to forge a pure and permanent connection, to gain eternal life while living on this earth. Allah says in a hadith qudsia (holy tradition, a saying attributed to, or anecdote regarding Prophet Muhammad [peace be upon him], according to traditional eyewitness accounts), "I created some of My servants for my zat (essence; person)". The Sufi's goal in life is to achieve an intimate understanding of and love for God. Tasawwuf, known in the West as Sufism, is a process of attaining closeness to the Creator through love, which is attained by purification of the nafs (egoistic or animalistic nature). Such a loving relationship with Allah, held by many prophets and other saintly individuals throughout history, may be achieved by anyone who sincerely wishes for it and is willing to undertake the discipline necessary to achieve that state. Love is the medium of unity, the process through which the electromagnetic vibrations produced by the heart and mind are working in tandem, thereby setting up the optimum scenario for spiritual learning. The human being's conscience is the voice of the *ruh* (spirit; soul) making itself heard in his heart. For the Sufi, expanding one's consciousness means directing his or her attention to the wisdom of the heart, because knowledge from Allah is broadcast to that centre of his being. The goal of *Tasawwuf* training is to be able to hear Allah's voice in the heart, and for a loving relationship with Allah to develop in that site of spiritual interchange. Sufis wish to serve Allah willingly, knowingly, and lovingly. That is why Sufism is called the way of the heart, designed to bring the human being to his ultimate objective of loving intimacy with Allah. When the heart is clean, the inner spiritual senses come alive to balance the outer senses. The mature Sufi's heart has become identified with Prophet Muhammad's (peace be upon him) heart, which is in constant rapport with the essence of Allah. According to hadith (tradition; saying attributed to, or anecdote regarding Prophet Muhammad, according to traditional eyewitness accounts) the Prophet taught these esteemed individuals how to do zikr (the Sufi practice of repeating the Names of Allah) in two different ways. These methods were passed down through generations and are the foundation upon which the Sufi tariqas were later established.

Likewise, each spiritual seeker has a particular character that can be well served by a tariqa suited to his or her personality. In the dynamic of their loving relationship, as the Prophet scrutinized the purity of his intention, Allah in turn increased his faith. The Sufi *murid* (student) is encouraged to re-enact such a working relationship with Allah, maintaining focus on Allah with the intention to surrender to Him in every way. Intention is the springboard of surrender, the inner aspect which gives meaning to outer deeds. The intention to act in a way pleasing to Allah is the foundation of faith, because in it is the tacit assumption of Allah's complete sovereignty. The acknowledgment *'La ilaha illallah* (There is no god but God)' is implicit in the believer's pure intention. One who knows that Allah holds all power, as our Prophet did, should preface every action by saying, "Bismillah er Rahman er Rahim (In the name of Allah, The One Who Acts with Mercy, The Source of Mercy)." By saying this with sincerity, the believer states that he is acting in Allah's name, with Allah's power and not his own. This is to be in a state of rabita (spiritual connection) with Allah and is the beginning of surrender. Whoever surrenders his whole attention to Allah while doing good, his reward is with his Lord. And for them there will be no fear, nor will they grieve. (2:112)

For a Sufi, being close to Allah is reaching a state of nothingness, whereby one is a fitting vehicle through which Allah may act as He wills. The point of Sufi training is not to gain in spirituality, but to realize one's nonexistence and thus to better know, praise, and serve the One who exists. The Sufi wishes to love and be loved by Allah. In tariqa (the Sufi path) he or she follows in the Prophet's (peace be upon him) footsteps with this single goal in his heart because he knows Muhammad is Habibullah, Allah's lover. He understands that the only way to gain Allah's love is through surrender, for in surrender he denies the selfish urgings of his nafs (egoistic or animalistic nature) in order to secure Allah's good pleasure. Allah created the Prophet as the model of a human being in a state of complete surrender to his Lord. His exquisite state embraced the perfect balance of his inner and outer being. The key to this balance was an unswerving focus on Allah in all things. From the firmness of his faith sprouted his impeccably pure intention to serve his Lord lovingly in thought, word, and deed. That is because Allah never changes the grace He has bestowed on any people until they first change that which is in their nafs, and truly Allah is Hearer, Knower. (Qur'an 8:53) The Sufi's goal is to have an intimate and loving relationship with Allah. Over the centuries techniques have been developed to help the Sufi focus keenly on the goal and steer away from the many distractions that may cloud this relationship. These are the methods of *Tasawwuf* (known in the West as Sufism), which are designed to take the *murid* (student) through the levels of *nafs* (egoistic or animalistic nature), thereby cleaning the obstruction from the spiritual heart, which is the place of connection between Allah and the human being. In other words, everything is a sign from, and pointing to, Allah. Though he may encounter some strange or miraculous occurrences, the *salik*, seeker, learns to regard such incidences as normal episodes in his Sufi trek through life. As he becomes more alert in his broadened scope of observation, his life becomes a Sufi story. This expanded perceptiveness helps to promote the realization that the realms of spiritual and material reality are not mutually exclusive. Please note that the use of the masculine pronouns in some of these writings is purely for convenience. The Sufi path is open to women and men alike. Likewise, there is no gender implication in the Arabic name 'Allah'.

We also look an aspect to understand the medieval Marathi literature which has been enriched by the saintly writings of various religions. Marathi cultures have been enriched by the saint's work of Maharashtra.

The debt of these all-religious and saints has to be acknowledged by the scholars of Marathi language and Marathi culture. The contribution of Jain saints has benefited from the beginning of Marathi literature. Not only that, but many of the tools that we always refer to when helping in the search for the origin of the Marathi language belong to the Jain saints / followers. The first Marathi inscription is carved at the foot of the magnificent idol of Gomateshwara at shravanbelgol. The study and teaching of medieval Marathi literature's contribution to research is often neglected the contribution of Veershaiv Marathi sant kavi is a bit similar. How much attention is paid to the poetry of prominent Veershaiva Marathi saint poets like Manmatha swamy, Laxman Maharaj, Shantilingaswamy, Basavalinga when considering medieval Marathi devotional poetry? I studied the research-projects of all these saintly subjects mentioned above. Indian religions and Islamists from outside India have contributed a lot to the growth and development of Marathi language literature. Similarly, Muslims have a long tradition of Marathi saint poetry. I have been doing a detailed study and research of this tradition for the last few years. Was such a Muslim saint poet only in Maharashtra? The answer to this question is to say that it was all over India because Muslim saint poets have done important work in North and South as well as in different regions of East and West India. This work is for national unity and human welfare. The supernatural work of a saint poet like Kabir is world-renowned. Many Muslim saint poets like Rahim and Raskhan enriched Hindi literature, as well as conveyed the great message of humanity and cosmopolitanism by crossing the barriers of caste. He also introduced the ideal combination of love of religion and tolerance of other religions. If one studies the medieval history of various Indian languages, one cannot help but see the important works of Muslim saint poets in those languages.

If we think of Maharashtra and the Marathi language in the context of the Middle Ages, one can imagine how significant work was done by Muslim saints. In the varakari sector, one of the sayings of Gyanacha eka which is found along with 'Namayacha Tuka' and the phrase 'Kabiracha Sheka'. The varakari sectarianists believe that Namdev-Turkram and Kabir-Sheikh Mohammad are similar to Dyandev and Eknath. The same suffix comes to us when we read the writings of these saints. Just as the varkari sect felt close to the subject of Shaikh Muhammad, so did Shaikh Muhammad become close to the varkari sect. Such intimacy has been felt by various Muslim saints about other sects in Maharashtra as well. They have also become one with these various religions and sects. Surprisingly, from the time the Dharma sect was formed in Maharashtra from its inception (with the exception of the Yadav period), Islamic saints were closely associated with Maharashtrian sects and were absorbed by the

Marhati culture. He also had a heartfelt dialogue with the Marathi people and never allowed the Marathi people to create a line of alienation between him and others (in religion and other contexts). That is why the image of these Muslim saint poets having a noticeable influence on the folklore of Maharashtra, while studying the cultural history of Maharashtra, begins to emerge before our eyes. This Muslim saint poet was associated with which religion in Maharashtra? Most of these Muslim saint poets were particularly associated with Qadri, one of the four branches of Sufism. From the fourteenth century onwards, he was associated with various sects in Maharashtra.

There are many Muslim saint poets belonging to the varkari sampradaya. Shaikh Mohammad was one of them. Shaikh Mohammad Baba of Shrigonda in Ahmednagar district has one major book named 'Yogasangram'. Famous historian-researcher Shri. V. C. Bendre edited this book. Shaikh Mohammad has described in this book in a very succinct language, taking the idea of yoga forts in the sixth chapter of Dnyaneshwari, how one has to fight and do sadhana while making this fort of the body. His other 'Abhangapadadi' compositions include the philosophy of the varakari sector as well as the philosophy of Islam and point to the same objectives in both these philosophies. Although, some devotional poems of Shaikh Mohammad edited by Mr. Bendre, hundreds of his abhangs / poems were still unpublished. In those days, poets like Shaikh Mohammad, who raised their voices against practices and patriarchy like Devdasi, were saints, but in a sense, they were also social educators. Like all religions, he has drawn the attention of various religions. The philosophy of Islam and the philosophy of the noble is based on devotion. A very famous saint of Maharashtra Eknath has mentioned in his "Eaknathi Gatha"that he was blessed by Lord Dattadarshan in the appearance of Malang (Fakir). This also sheds light on some of the interrelationships between Muslim saints and Maharashtrian sects. Many Nath saints are also known by alternative names to Muslim saints. It is a subject of independent study and research.

In particular, it will shed light on the interrelationship of Sufi saints. This Muslim saint poet also had a significant influence on the people of Maharashtra. The adoption of this huge humanitarian role in Maharashtra helped to create an atmosphere of mutual understanding, unity, and harmony in Maharashtra. This picture of cultural harmony and unity in medieval Maharashtra was definitely enticing. This is the first time that such a detailed study of Muslim (Sufi) Marathi saints and their literature is being done in this book. Therefore, new research has to be done in the context of rewriting the cultural history and literary history of Central Maharashtra. It is important to build and promote the new concept of religious harmony so as to meet the challenges posed by religious diversity in a globalized world. On the basis of recognizing religious diversity and differences, all religions should enhance mutual understanding and empathy through dialogue, shoulder the common responsibility of upholding peace and justice through cooperation, and foster intra- and inter-religious harmony and harmony between the religious community and the larger society. It is imperative to promote the principle of "harmony without uniformity" and learn to respect each other and jointly shoulder social responsibilities. The use of religion for ill purposes should be opposed and religious extremism should be guarded against. We have referred many of the topics from the book 'The Sun Will Rise in The West' by Shaikh Taner Ansari. This book is recommended to readers for a detailed and comprehensive explanation of Sufism that is especially tailored to the Western mindset. However, this effort of emphasis from private to public is based on a belief in the explanatory value of these emphases for making sense of the place of Sufism in the surrounding contexts of various sufis and Marathi saint through an eye of global history. In this regard, the aim of this book is to normalize the history of Sufism by placing it into the mainstream of the social, political, and intellectual history of the Sufis and similarities in teaching of Marathi saints to clear the indefinitely suspicious air that has surrounded the study of Sufism. As such, rather than produce an introspectively discrete history of Sufism in Maharashtra, the narrative as a whole aim to link Sufi and Marathi saint's teachings and history to broader contours of world history by pointing to the embeddedness of Sufism in the wider historical experience. the living masters and the books of the dead saints whose teachings-in-time have shown them the road to eternity.

Table of Content

Chapter 5 : Some Prominent Muslim Sufis in Maharashtra 267

List of Appendix

Chapter 1

Religion at a Glance

1. Introduction and History

The word "religion" is an indefinite word with no fixed meaning. It is one word with many meanings. This is because religion has passed through many stages. The concept at each stage is called Religion though the concept at one stage has not had the same meaning which it had at the preceding stage or is likely to have at the succeeding stage. The conception of religion was never fixed. It has varied from time to time. Because most of the phenomena such as lightning, rain and floods, the occurrence of which the primitive man could not explain, any weird performance done to control the phenomenon was called magic. Religion therefore came to be identified with magic. Further in the second stage talks about evolution of religion. In this stage religion came to be identified with beliefs, rituals, ceremonies, prayers, and sacrifices. But this conception of religion is derivatives. The pivotal point in religion starts with the belief that there exists some power which causes these phenomena which primitive man did not know and could not understand. Magic lost its place at this stage. This power was originally malevolent. But later it was felt that it could also be benevolent. Beliefs, rites, ceremonies, and sacrifices were necessary both to propitiate a benevolent power and to conciliate an angry power. Later that power was called God of the Creator. Then came the third stage that it is this God who created this world and man. This was followed by the belief that man has a soul, and the soul is eternal and is answerable to God for man's action un the world. This is, in short, the evolution of the concept of Religion. This is what Religion has come to be and this is what it connotes belief in God, belief in soul, worship of God, curing of the erring soul, propitiating God by prayers, ceremonies, sacrifices, etc.[1]

Religion is a social-cultural structure of designated behaviours and practices, morals, beliefs, worldviews, texts, sanctified places, prophecies, ethics, or organizations, that related humanity to supernatural, transcendental, and spiritual elements.[2] However, there is no scholarly consensus over what precisely constitutes a religion.[3],[4] Different religions may or may not contain various elements ranging from the divine,[5] sacred things,[6] faith,[7] a supernatural being or supernatural beings[8] or "some sort of ultimacy and transcendence that will provide norms and power for the rest of life".[9] Religious practices may include rituals, sermons, commemoration or veneration (of deities and / or saints), sacrifices, festivals, feasts, trances, initiations, funerary services, matrimonial services, meditation, prayer, music, art, dance, public service, or other aspects of human society. Religions have sacred histories and narratives, which may be preserved in sacred scriptures, and symbols and holy places, that aim mostly to give a meaning to life. Religions may contain symbolic stories, which are sometimes said by followers to be true, that may also attempt to explain the origin of life, the universe, and other phenomena. Traditionally, faith, in addition to reason, has been considered a source of religious beliefs.[10] There are an estimated 10,000 distinct religions worldwide.[11] About 84% of the world's population is affiliated with Christianity, Islam, Hinduism, Buddhism, or some form of folk religion.[12] The religiously unaffiliated demographic includes those who do not identify with any particular religion, atheists, and agnostics. While the religiously unaffiliated have grown globally, many of the religiously unaffiliated still have various religious beliefs.[13] The study of religion comprises a wide variety of academic disciplines, including theology, comparative religion and social scientific studies. Theories of religion offer various explanations for the origins and workings of religion, including the ontological foundations of religious being and belief.[14]

2. Origin of Religion

The origin of religion is uncertain. There are several theories regarding the subsequent origins of religious practices. According to anthropologists John Monaghan and Peter Just, "Many of the great world religions appear to have begun as revitalization movement's which is more comprehensive answer to their problems than everyday beliefs. It seems that the key to long-term success and many movements come and go with little long-term effect has relatively little to do with the prophet Muhammad, who appear with surprising regularity, but more to do with the development of a group of supporters who are able to institutionalize the movement".[15] The development of religion has taken different forms in different cultures. Some religions place an emphasis on belief, while others emphasize practice. Some religions focus on the subjective experience of the religious individual, while others consider the activities of the religious community to be most important. Some religions claim to be universal, believing their laws and cosmology to be binding for everyone, while others are intended to be practiced only by a closely defined or localized group. In many places, religion has been associated with public institutions such as education, hospitals, the family, government, and political hierarchies. Anthropologists John Monaghan and Peter Just state that, "it seems apparent that one thing religion or belief helps us do is deal with problems of human life that are significant, persistent, and intolerable. One important way in which religious beliefs accomplish this is by providing a set of ideas about how and why the world is put together that allows people to accommodate anxieties and deal with misfortune."[16]

The social structure of the world's religious traditions can be roughly placed on continuum based on their respective levels of interpersonal involvement and social engagement. On one end of this scale would be the most inwardly directed types, such as the desert saints of early Christianity and the ascetics of Hinduism. On the other hand, one would find the religious traditions that are most firmly entrenched in all aspects of personal, social, and juridical life, such as the medieval Catholic Church and the theocratic regimes of some Islamic states. All other religious traditions could be situated somewhere between these two poles. However, the multivalent interplay between the religious and secular spheres has caused some scholars to question the utility of the term 'religion', as they claim that it presents these traditions in 'a reified, essentialized fashion, isolated from the political, social, economic, and cultural worlds within which they are embedded."[17] The subject of religion can induce a range of responses from love, compassion, and goodwill, to fear, loathing, and xenophobia. Indeed, religion can be seen as something of a paradox, as it simultaneously contains both humanities' most sublime moral and spiritual teachings, as well as grim remnants of intolerance and patriarchy that foster hatred and horror. Thus, despite the growing dangers of religious fundamentalism, the world's religions continue to be treasure chests of spiritual resources for making a positive impact on world affairs. The English word religion has been in use since the thirteenth century, loaned from Anglo French religion (eleventh century), ultimately from the Latin religio, "reverence for God or the gods, careful pondering of divine things, piety, the divine".[18]

The word 'Religion' has been defined in a wide variety of manners, with most definitions attempting to find a balance somewhere between overly restrictive categorizations and meaningless generalities. In this quest, a variety of approaches have been employed, including the use formalistic, doctrinal definitions, and the emphasis experiential, emotive, intuitive, valuational, and ethical factors. Sociologists and anthropologists tend to see religion as an abstract set of ideas, values, or experiences developed as part of a cultural matrix. For example, in George A. Lindbeck's Nature of Doctrine, religion does not refer to belief in 'God' or a transcendent

Absolute. Instead, Lindbeck defines religion as, "a kind of cultural and/ or linguistic framework or medium that shapes the entirety of life and thought... it is similar to an idiom that makes possible the description of realities, the formulation of beliefs, and the experiencing of inner attitudes, feelings, and sentiments".[19] Other religious scholars have put forward a definition of religion that avoids the reductionism of the various sociological and psychological disciplines that reduce religion to its component factors. Religion may be defined as the presence of a belief in the sacred or the holy. For example, Rudolf Otto's "The Idea of the Holy", formulated in 1917,[20] defines the essence of religious awareness as awe, a unique blend of fear and fascination before the divine.

In summary, it may be said that almost every known culture involves the religious in the above sense of a depth dimension in cultural experiences at all levels a push, whether ill-defined or conscious, toward some sort of ultimacy and transcendence that will provide norms and power for the rest of life. When distinct patterns of behaviour are built around this depth dimension in a culture, this structure constitutes religion in its historically recognizable form. Religion is the organization of life around the depth dimensions of experience varied in form, completeness, and clarity in accordance with the environing culture.[21] Other definitions include: "A general term used to designate all concepts concerning the belief in god(s) and goddess(es) as well as other spiritual beings or transcendental ultimate concerns" (Penguin Dictionary of Religions (1997) and 'human beings' relation to that which they regard as holy, sacred, absolute, spiritual, divine, or worthy of especial reverence". Religion and philosophy meet in several areas, notably in the study of metaphysics and cosmology. Distinct set of religious beliefs will often entail a specific metaphysics and cosmology. That is, a religion will generally have answers to metaphysical and cosmological questions about the nature of being, of the universe, humanity, and the divine. Given the generalized discontents with modernity, consumerism, over consumption, violence and anomie, many people in the so called industrial or post-industrial West rely on a number of distinctive religious world views (Zeitgeist). This, in change, has given rise to increased religious pluralism, as well as to what are commonly known in the academic literature as new religious movements, which are gaining adherents around the globe. As suggested above, religious systems (both traditional and modern) are increasing in influence due to the perceived failure of modern and secular ideologies. Some individuals draw a strong distinction between religion and spirituality. They may see spirituality as a belief in ideas of religious significance (such as God, the Soul, or Heaven), but not feel bound to the bureaucratic structure and creeds of a particular organized religion. In this context, the term spirituality is often consciously chosen in opposition to the designation 'religion,' perhaps reflecting a disillusionment with organized religion and a movement towards more 'modern' (i.e., more tolerant, and more intuitive) forms of religious practice. Many adherents of the 'World Religions' do not demarcate between religion and spirituality, as they interpret their tradition as providing access to the spiritual realm. Mysticism, in contrast with philosophy, denies that logic is the most important method of gaining enlightenment. Rather, it is to be attained through non-ordinary states of consciousness, which are, in turn, achieved through psychological and physical processes (such as repetitive prayer, meditation, mantra recitation, yoga, stringent fasting, whirling (as in the case of the Sufi dervishes), and/or the use of psychoactive drugs). From a religious perspective, mysticism it thought of as religious practice meant enable communion with (or conscious awareness of) Ultimate Reality, the Divine, spiritual truth, or God through direct, personal experience (intuition or insight) rather than rational ideation.

3. Religious Epistemology

According to the prestigious Cambridge Dictionary of Philosophy, religious epistemology is "a branch of philosophy that investigates the epistemic status of propositional attitudes about religious claims". Virtually all the extant and current methodologies in epistemology have been employed in assessing religious appeals. Some methods have been more rationalistic in the sense that they have involved reasoning from ostensibly self-evident truth, while others have been more experiential (e.g., empiricism, phenomenology, the stress on passion and subjectivity, the stress on practice as found in pragmatism). Also, some have sought to be ahistorical (not dependent upon historical revelation claims), while others are profoundly historical (e.g., grounded on revelation either known by faith alone or justified evidentially by an appeal to miracles and/or religious experience. Over the past a few years, there has been a growing literature on the nature of religious faith. Amongst many philosophers in the analytical tradition, faith has often been treated as the propositional attitude belief, e.g., believing that there is or is not a God, and much work devoted to examining when such belief is backed up by evidence and, if so, how much, and what kinds of evidence. There has been a famous debate over the ethics of belief, determining what kinds of belief should not be entertained or countenanced when the evidence is deemed insufficient, and when matters of religious faith may be justified on pragmatic grounds (e.g., as a wager or venture). Faith has also been philosophically treated as trust, a form of hope, an allegiance to an ideal, commitment, and faithful action with or without belief.[22] The following examines first what is known as evidentialist and reformed epistemology and then a form of what is called volitional epistemology of religion.

3.1 Evidentialism, Reformed, and Volitional Epistemology

Evidentialism is the view that for a person to be justified in some belief, that person must have some awareness of the evidence for the belief. This is usually articulated as a person's belief being justified given the total evidence available to the person. On this view, the belief in question must not be undermined (or defeated) by other, evident beliefs held by the person. Moreover, evidentialist often contend that the degree of confidence in a belief should be proportional to the evidence. Evidentialism has been defended by representatives of all the different viewpoints in philosophy of religion: theism, atheism, advocates of non-theistic models of God, agnostics. Evidentialists have differed in terms of their accounts of evidence and the relationship between evident beliefs Probably the most well-known evidentialist in the field of philosophy of religion who advocates for theism is Richard Swinburne (1934). Swinburne's projects in the evidentialist tradition in philosophy of religion are in the great tradition of British philosophy of religion from the Cambridge Platonists in the seventeenth century through Joseph Butler (1692–1752) and William Paley (1743– 1805) to twentieth century British philosophers such as A.E. Taylor (1869–1945), F. R. Tennant (1866–1957), William Temple (1881–1944), H.D. Lewis (1910–1992), and A.C. Ewing (1899–1973). The positive philosophical case for theism has been met by work by many powerful philosophers, most recently Ronald Hepburn (1927–2008), J.L. Mackie (1917–1981), Antony Flew (1923–2010), Richard Gale (1932–2015), William Rowe (1931–2015), Michael Martin (1932–2015), Graham Oppy (1960), J.L. Schellenberg (1959), and Paul Draper (1957).[23]

There have been at least two interesting, recent developments in the philosophy of religion in the framework of evidentialism. One has been advanced by John Schellenberg who argues that if the God of Christianity exists, God's reality would be far more evident than it is. The all–too–common insistence among philosophers that proper procedure requires establishing the likelihood of God's existence prior to testing revelatory claims cuts off a huge part of the data base relevant to arguing for theism. Evidentialism has been challenged on many grounds. Some argue that it is too stringent; we have many evident beliefs that we would be at a loss to successfully justify. Instead of evidentialism, some philosophers adopt a form of reliable, according to which a person may be justified in a belief so long as the belief is produced by a reliable means, whether the person is aware of evidence that justifies the belief. Two movements in philosophy of religion develop positions that are not in line with the traditional evidential tradition, reformed epistemology, and volitional epistemology. Reformed epistemology has been championed by Alvin Plantinga (1932) and Nicholas Wolterstorff (1932), among others.

3.2 The Epistemology of Disagreement

The terrain covered so far in this entry indicates considerable disagreement over epistemic justification and religious belief. If the experts disagree about such matters, what should non-experts think and do? Or, putting the question to the so-called experts, if you (as a trained inquirer) disagree about the above matters with those whom you regard as equally intelligent and sensitive to evidence, should that fact alone bring you to modify or even abandon the confidence you hold concerning your own beliefs? Some philosophers propose that in the case of disagreements among epistemic peers, one should seek account of the disagreement. For example, is there any reason to think that the evidence available to you and your peers differs or is conceived of differently. Perhaps there are ways of explaining, for example, why Buddhists may claim not to observe themselves as substantial selves existing over time whereas a non-Buddhist might claim that self-observation provides grounds for believing that persons are substantial, enduring agents. The non-Buddhist might need another reason to prefer her framework over the Buddhist one, but she would at least (perhaps) have found a way of accounting for why equally reasonable persons would come to different conclusions in the face of ostensibly identical evidence. Assessing the significance of disagreement over religious belief is quite different from assessing the significance of disagreement in domains where there are clearer, shared understandings of methodology and evidence.

In Christian-Muslim dialogue, philosophers often share a common philosophical inheritance from Plato, Aristotle, Plotinus, and a broad range of shared views about the perfection of God/Allah. One option would be to adopt an epistemological pluralism, according to which persons can be equally well justified in affirming incompatible beliefs. This option would seem to provide some grounds for epistemic humility. In an appropriately titled essay, "Why religious pluralism is not evil and is in some respects quite good", (2018) Robert McKim presents reasons why, from a philosophical point of view, it may be good to encourage (and not merely acknowledge) ostensibly equally reasonable worldviews. For an overview of the current state of play in philosophy of religion on the topic of religious disagreement.[24] At the end of this section, two observations are also worth noting about epistemic disagreements. First, our beliefs and our confidence in the truth of our beliefs may not be under our voluntary control. Perhaps you form a belief of the truth of Buddhism based on what you take to be compelling evidence. Even if you are convinced that equally intelligent persons do not reach a similar conclusion, that alone may not empower you to deny what seems to you to be compelling. Second, if the disagreement between experts gives you reason to abandon a position, then the very principle you are relying on would be undermined, for experts disagree about what one should do when experts disagree.

4. Mystics about Religion

Mystics speak of the existence of realities beyond perception or intellectual apprehension that are directly accessible through personal experience, arguing that these experiences are genuine and important sources of knowledge. Many religious traditions have mystical elements, though these strands are often marginalized due to their counter-hegemonic nature (in denying the necessity of mediation between the individual and the divine). In an associated approach, esotericism claims to be more sophisticated than religion, to rely on intellectual understanding rather than faith, and to improve on philosophy in its emphasis on techniques of psycho-spiritual transformation (esoteric cosmology). Esotericism refers to 'hidden' knowledge available only to the advanced, privileged, or initiated, as opposed to exoteric knowledge, which is public. It applies especially to spiritual practices. The mystery religions of ancient Greece, the Gnostic systems of the Middle East, and the Hindu path of jnana marga are examples of esoteric religiosity. Philosophy of religion is fundamentally the philosophical examination of the themes and concepts involved in religious traditions as well as the broader philosophical task of reflecting on matters of religious significance including the nature of religion itself, alternative concepts of God or ultimate reality, and the religious significance of general features of the cosmos (e.g., the laws of nature, the emergence of consciousness) and of historical events (like, the 1755 Lisbon Earthquake, the Holocaust). Philosophy of religion also includes the investigation and assessment of worldviews (such as secular naturalism) that are alternatives to religious worldviews. Philosophy of religion involves all the main areas of philosophy and those are metaphysics, epistemology, value theory (including moral theory and applied ethics), philosophy of language, science, history, politics, art, and its significance, with subsequent sections covering developments in the field since the mid-twentieth century. These sections address philosophy of religion as practiced primarily (but not exclusively) in departments of philosophy and religious studies that are in the broadly analytic tradition. A religion involves a communal, transmittable body of teachings and prescribed practices about an ultimate, sacred reality or state of being that calls for reverence or respect, a body which guides its practitioners into what it describes as a saving, illuminating or emancipatory relationship to this reality through a personally transformative life of prayer, ritualized meditation, and/or moral practices like repentance and personal regeneration.[25]

5.   The Evolution of Religion

The use of the term evolution in connection with religion is subject to two objections. On the one side are those who insist that religion is the gift of God and therefore has no historical development. And on the other the biologist may object to the use of the term in any such general sense as a student of social science must adopt. To the first reviewer it may be replied that when he asserts or implies that religion has not developed like other elements in human experience the facts are against him. Whatever may have been its origin, religion exhibits phenomena akin to those observables in social institutions to which the term 'evolution' may legitimately be applied. All religions are phases of religion. To the other class of reviewers, it must be replied that if biologists ever had a monopoly on the term evolution their exclusive rights have long since expired. The conception given the word by the Origin of Species and general biological usage is a particular phase of a view of the world as old as reflective thought. The service which biology has rendered the social sciences at this point has largely been confined to the region of method, vocabularies, and analogies. If these analogies have too often been overemphasized and made to do service in the name of some non-biological science, they have none the less made it possible to realize that whatever precise definition may be given the term evolution, there is a large measure of similarity between certain processes in social history and certain others in the building up of cellular organisms. Outside of the strictly biological sciences the word must be used in a large sense, but it is not identical with mere change or growth. It is possible to trace religion as one of the functional expressions of life itself through increasingly complicated and more highly differentiated activities and institutions, as that life both of individuals and societies seeks to adjust itself more effectively to its environment. The result of such vital activity is to produce, as it were, species of religions, between which, as for example Brahmanism and Mohammedanism, there is only a generic likeness. Furthermore, to justify the legitimacy of the use of the term evolution in a reasonably strict sense, religion, and its development into species of religions according as its expression has been conditioned by its environment, the persistence of vestiges of lower religious forms, concepts, and institutions in the more highly developed and the struggle for the survival of the socially fittest among religions are transcribe.

While talking about the nature of religion, there have been times in which men have endeavoured to arrive at the conception of religion and its characteristics. Other attempts have been made to extend this process of abstraction to all religions and thus to discover that which is, to so speak, a generic concept. The difficulties with such search after a bit of scholastic realism is evident. Generic religion never existed apart from religions, and religions never existed except as interests and institutions of people. There is imperative need that all students of the subject, and especially theologians, should emancipate themselves from scholastic abstractions, and frankly recognize that religion is not a thing, possessed of independent, abstract, or metaphysical existence, but is a name for one phase of concrete human activity. It is only from a strictly social point of view that either religion or religions will in any measure be properly understood. We know only people who worship in various ways and with various conceptions of what or whom they worship. Yet while men possess religions and not merely religion-religions of all sorts, from the simplest custom of the savage to the profundity of Brahmanism and the redemptive gospels of the Buddhist and the Christian the comparative study of human activities expressed in these different religions has, however, discovered within them religion as a common divisor, as it were; viz., a particular functioning of life itself, as truly and universally human as the impulse of self-preservation. If we attempt to formulate this element or describe this functional expression of life expressed in all religions, we must study comparatively both the highly developed religious systems and the simplest type of religion as it exists among primitive people. While not overlooking the more complex systems as a means, so to speak, of determining the direction taken by evolution and thus better fitting ourselves to appreciate religion as never static, we must study the simplest religious organisms to understand the more complicated. To push the biological analogy further, it might be said that the 'cell' of religion is man's conscious attempt to place himself in beneficial relationship with those superhuman forces in his world upon which he realizes his dependence, and which he treats as he would treat persons whom he wished to aid him. It is obvious that the content of such a conventional definition will vary according to the conception of what constitutes this environment; and that this variety of estimate will affect the methods which a man adopts in making that environment propitious. A study of even the most primitive religion leads one-to-two convictions apparently paradoxical religion does not necessarily imply a belief in a supreme person, and yet, in religion, environment is conceived of in the same way that men conceive of persons.

There are several theories undertaking to show how this attitude of mind was induced; but all are majority unsatisfactory. Some find the cause in fear, or dreams, or regard for ancestors, Doubtless there is truth in all these hypotheses, but we are not sure as to just how religion came into existence any more than we are sure how human life itself arose. We can, however, see clearly that the functional significance of religion is an elemental expression of the second of the two elemental impulses of life itself, namely, to propagate and protect itself. Religion is life functioning in the interest of self-protection. It differs from similar functional expressions of life in that firstly it treats certain elements of its environment personally (though not necessarily as a person), and secondly it seeks to make these friendly and so helpful. One or the other of these two elements has almost invariably been overlooked in studies of religion, but both are indispensable to the concept. Religion utilizes personal experience and uncompromisingly pre-supposes personalism not, let it be repeated, in a sense of any systematic worldview, but, in a sense doubtless unconsciously at the first but with ever increasing clearness of conception, it treats the environment as it would treat human beings; and religion is just as uncompromisingly functional, not only in adjusting the individual or the group to its environment, but also in the attempt to adjust the environment personally considered to the person or the community. Thus, Schleiermacher's conception of religion as a feeling of dependence is only part of the truth. To it must be added the conscious effort after reconciliation. It is this two-fold modification of the elemental functioning of life in the interest of self-preservation that distinguishes religion from so many activities with which it has been intimately associated, like hunting and grain planting.

Obviously, the inception of this radically human attitude toward its world is lost in the unrecorded struggles by which humanity raised itself above other forms of animal life with which it is genetically united. But one's ignorance here does not attribute the fact that such a use of experience was made. Sometime, somewhere just when and where it matters not there appeared a man who first living creatures, with the new impulses of a genuine person, attempted to adjust himself consciously to the outer world upon which he saw himself dependent, by an attempt to make that outer world favourable to himself. It makes little difference how he conceived that outer world or which one of its aspects first impressed him. Any one of the various theories of the origin of religion might here suffice. The essential thing is that, in his passion to protect his life and to ensure his continuous existence as a person, he attempted consciously to enjoy or to win the favour of the extra-human environment with which he found himself involved. And that, so far as we know, no animal other than man ever attempted to accomplish. Nor is it necessary to insist that all religions are genetically related in a sense that one has been derived from another. The historic religious method at the present time is in danger of mistaking similarities between religions for genealogical relations. That a certain degree of genealogical relationship in this case may have existed may well be admitted, but a too rigorous application of the comparative genealogical method in the study of religion is certain to distort the facts. If there is anything undeniable in the study of society it is that human nature is essentially the same, and that when facing the same social needs, it functions in a generic sort of way. A striking illustration of the fact that independent activity of individuals produces similar results is to be seen in a study of inventions.

The commonest occurrence is for men subject to the stimulation of similar social need, in absolute independence of each other, to produce instruments and processes practically identical. An even more striking illustration of this general truth is that all civilizations precipitate practically the same moral codes when they arrive at the same stage of complicated social life. So, in the case of religions, the striking similarities which occur between religions belonging to the primitive class and religions belonging to the highly social class are not to be interpreted as necessarily involving imitative, or in fact any, historical relationship. Such similarities both in institution and in process of evolution can often be sufficiently well accounted for by a generic religious impulse in humanity which tends to produce customs, rites, institutions, and creeds in answer to individual and social needs. The evolution of religion viewed historically is nothing than the organization of religions by the differentiation, using social experience, of the practices, institutions, philosophies, by which men have attempted to justify, rationalize, direct, and give value to this phase of the elemental impulse of personality. The essence of religion is not a feeling of dependence, but the impulse toward reconciliation with that which engenders such a feeling. The moment a man thinks that the highest power in his environment is irreconcilable, his relations therewith become utterly passive, i.e., impersonal; he ceases to be religious and simply becomes a fatalist. And fatalism is not religion, for it lacks the fundamental attitude of religion which is the effort to establish favourable relations with the super-environment. In other words, the situation which religion would establish is one of personal harmony between the worshiper and that worshiped, no matter how crude or superstitious that relationship may be.

The evolution of the personal interpretation of environment mainly understood from what has already been said that the term extra-or superhuman environment does not always necessarily involve personality. What the term means is simply some power other and more than human which a man regards as having influence upon his life and fortunes. The fact that such elements of the environment are treated as if they were personal, is only to say that religion involves an extension of experience over into environment as a means of interpreting that environment in the interests of a helpful reconciliation. Such an act is not unlike the way in which, to speak figuratively, a living organism assumes, that its environment discovered by experience can form a part of a dynamic situation. Thus far Ward is correct in saying that religion is in man what instinct is in animals. The essential matter in the evolution of religion as in all evolutions the transformation of the original organism through its relationship with its environment and the nucleating about itself if the figure may be allowed of the cells of other experiences into species of the same genus. And this is accomplished by the transformation of the mass of experience with which humanity adjusts itself to its environment to which it must submit and from which it must derive assistance. Primitive religions generally deal with environment directly.

The primitive gods in the earliest strata of survivals and literature in which we can trace religious concepts were natural forces. The heavens and earth, fire, water, and wind, the sun, moon, and planets these natural objects were worshiped but they were not personified. Man found himself face to face with the awfulness of Nature. He saw how dependent he was upon this nature; how the rising of the river would flood and sweep away his hut; how the rain would come from heaven to give him grass for his cattle, how the sun would drive the animals he hunted into the deep forests. He naturally wanted to make the river and the heavens propitious. If we go even farther back than philology can carry us and study religion as we discover it in the most primitive folk, we find corroboration for this view, although with this difference, there seem to be some tribes that have not risen to the conception of the great natural forces as those that are to be appeased and who therefore concern themselves rather with items in their natural environment. In fact, anything unusual is apt to be regarded by primitive men as a good or a malign influence. In either case it needs to be treated with respect and if possible placated. A rock over which someone has fallen, a cave in the darkness of which someone has been lost, a curious root that was discovered when one became ill, a tree that had been struck by lightning all have been regarded as operative forces in a man's situation which needed in some way to be placated. Here, too, an early step was to regard these natural objects as the residence of some spirit, good or evil. Thus, fetichism arose as a sort of limitation of the lesser nature worship. Not all-natural objects were significant, and even those which might lose their meaning if the spirit abandoned them. It is possible to draw a distinction between magic and religion as soon as religion begins to take on its more social form. The witch is different from the priest if for no other reason than that her arts are antisocial. But despite the weighty names to be quoted against such a view, it would seem to me that no injurious magic may be treated as the vestige of a rudimentary religion preserved and observed by specially empowered persons. For there is in such magic, e.g., rainmaking, that 'will conciliate' as well as to control which, as the complement to the 'will to power,' is the very sign manual of religion. But this is not to say that religion developed from magic. The fundamental difference between magic and religion lies not in that magic was originally anti-social and so nefarious, but that during social evolution it is seen to be so.

As religion develops, certain rites are seen to apply only the impersonal principle that like affects like through the agency of a specially empowered person; but religion seeks to conciliate superhuman influences by means implying personal relations and attributes. This distinction between personal and impersonal is gained through the increased social experience. That practice, which once implied a certain personal analogy, is seen to be irrational and so impersonal, and ultimately anti-social. The primitive religion thus outgrown becomes magic, and although socially condemned, continues as a survival. And the reason why it is condemned is in large measure the development of a knowledge of natural processes. A growing science thus relegates certain elements of a religion to superstition. Similarly, too, in the case of the worship of dead ancestors, a stage in religious development to be found all but universally in simple civilizations. Whatever may have been the origin of such a custom it is sufficiently clear that the dead were regarded as important factors in determining good and evil fortune. To propitiate them is therefore good policy as well as tribal piety.

With the emergence of actual tribal organization, a new phase in this religious interest appeared. A developing civilization does not always, it is true, immediately react upon the conception of the god, but in so far as the religious concept develops it invariably passes through a stage in which these forces which have been treated like persons are treated as persons. Contemporaneously with the development of the clan, religion entered the stage of naive anthropomorphic or anthropopathic religions. Such a development was inevitable for people sufficiently constructive to become a part of the main current of civilization. All others, like the Black Fellows of Australia, preserve the religious ideas in forms as primitive as their civilizations. Such personification, however, does not seem to have proceeded uniformly. In some cases, a tribe would have as its own a god who was the personification of some natural force and would worship him by attributing to him those qualities which, thanks to its social development, the tribe believed to be the most ideal. Without exception these tribal gods are regarded as normally in a state of reconciliation with the tribe. Generally, they are regarded as the fathers of their tribes. In other words, they are believed to participate of the same elemental quality as primitive civilization itself. They are, however, subject to paroxysms of anger evidenced by the defeat of the tribe in battle, by the out-break of disease, and by various other misfortunes.

In such cases they must be placated by gifts. In this we see one of the various contributing influences that made sacrifice a social institution, although there are other influences quite as powerful. At other times, a god appears to be particularly favourable in that he sends good weather and good fortunes. At such times, his kindness needs to be appreciated by gifts. Thus arises the sort of sacrifice which is not intended to appease but to thank the tribal god for his help. But the most essential element in the tribal religion is the conception of the god as the supreme member of the tribe. It is true he is not believed to appear frequently, but at critical moments some member is likely to see him and get some word of encouragement or warning. Further, there have been few peoples who have attained the tribal form of society in which there is not some person or family regarded as in some way the god's special representative. Such persons instruct the tribe as to the will of the god, serve as priests, and, under the god's direction, establish great feasts of which the god partakes. Probably at this point we find the most important contributing source of sacrifice. The social group includes the god, and he shares in the experiences of the tribe, be they sad or joyous. And it should be noted that the rites of religions had their origin in the enjoyment of life as truly as in its misery and fear. Men thought of the gods as their companions as truly as their judges.

In fact, as the tribal civilization develops, in many cases, particularly among the Semites and the Aryans, it would seem as if there were two classes of gods those which represent the material forces more or less personified and constitute a sort of super-divine body of deities to whom worship is to be paid as the final sources of good fortune, and, along with these, so to speak, the working class among the gods. Other tribes carry along with their single tribal god a phase of magic which may be said to be the survival of some more primitive religious practice. Similarly, customs, the meaning of which has long been forgotten, may be carried along as essential elements of a developing religion. So important may these customs become as to give almost its full content to the religion. The fact that the tribal god was regarded as, so to speak, the responsible party in tribal history, led to another phase of religion, the monarchical.

Such a term is at best unsatisfactory but serves to indicate how the thought of God develops by the extension to him of new political conceptions. The national god must be superior to the tribal chieftain. As a chieftain developed in power by conquest to extend the power of the tribe over other tribes, it has been all but uniformly true that the tribal god was regarded as victorious over the gods of the conquered tribes. Thus, as the tribe itself through conquest became the head of a quasination, did the god become a conquering monarch. Only it did not at all follow that the tribe which had been absorbed or conquered would give up its god. It might continue to worship him in the hope that ultimately, he would assert himself and give deliverance to his people. Or, on the other hand, as the tribe was incorporated into a new political entity, its god might become a member of the royal court of the supreme God. There is many a nation whose religious history shows the struggle between the worship of the two sets of deities. Thus, we find, in the history of Israel, a long succession of struggles between the worship of Jehovah and that of the Baalim and the Syrian gods of the high places belonging to the conquered Canaanites. This struggle is likely to be particularly violent when the two sets of gods are brought together, not by war or conquest, but by the intermingling of civilizations. For conquest is not the only source of the development of the king god. Political development as such leads to this more developed conception. It may often be that several tribes have the same god. These may federate, as in the tribes of Israel, religion being the sole or at least the chief bond of the political unity. But even such federation is not necessary for the development of the idea of God. The transformation of the tribe from nomadic to agricultural life has been accompanied by a transformation of the conception of God and has given him new attributes, as in Zoroastrianism.

As the agricultural stage of social evolution has passed into the commercial and urban, the new powers of the chieftains have been used as media for shaping new prerogatives for the god. His relations become less those of the father of the family and more those of the king, increasingly political and forensic. It is not too much to say that in the case of all tribes whose development we can trace across the various stages of social evolution, the idea of monarchy, which, however different its social institutions may have been, has characterized some period of every developed society, has also coloured religions. The god is not subject to the will of the people; the people and their material environment are to obey him. Obedience to his law becomes thus a condition of his rendering his people aid. At this point the great religions have made two important transitions. First, the superhuman monarch of the tribe has come to be regarded as the superhuman monarch of the world, the king of creation. It has not followed that all the other gods have been regarded as non-existent, for in many cases they have been treated as devils or saints. But the passage to genuine monotheism cannot in frequently be traced through this monarchical stage. The divine monarch is supreme over human subjects. He arranges nature. The thunder is his voice, the wind his messenger, the earthquake the creature of his will. Men begin to think of him philosophically, and so transcendental may the thought of him become that the effort to realize the now supreme and increasingly ethical conception of his character gives rise to a genuine if naive theology. The second transition has been the moral elevation of the idea of God. This change has been the work of the prophet.

In primitive religion the prophet in any true sense of the word is unknown. There are only medicine men, necromancers, witches, and the like. But few peoples ever come to the universal monarchy conception of its god without seeing in him the standard of morality. If such a transition is impossible a new god is adopted as the new conscience needs a more sensitively moral God. If, as in the case of classical mythology, gods are past reformation, they are pensioned off with conventional honours and allowed to pass into innocuous desuetude on some mountain where their example will not injure the morals of young people. In the extent of this moral idealism of its idea of God, the Hebrew religion is unique. It seems to have passed through the earlier stages of religious evolution, but as in no other religion did this eventuate in a monarch of absolute righteousness, hating iniquity. That this was the case was due to the work of the prophets who, from an exceptional religious experience, taught an unwilling nation ideal that were to serve as the basis of the non-monarchical ethical religion of Jesus. This monarchical conception has given rise to the most precise theologies. Political experience is so universal, political institutions are so subject to legal adjustment, and legal analogies are so intelligible, that it has been comparatively easy to systematize religious relations under the general rubrics of statecraft. Thus, righteousness has been thought of as the observance of the laws of the god, given through divinely inspired teachers, and punishment has been attached to the violation of such laws in precisely the same way as to the violation of laws of the king. The pardoning of sins has been a royal prerogative, although sometimes needing justification in the way of vicarious suffering by some competent sacrificial animal or person, while the rewards of the righteous have been pictured by figures drawn from the triumphs of earthly kings, just as in primitive societies the future was regarded as the "happy hunting-ground." Thirdly, only a few religions have yet progressed beyond the monarchical stage. In Brahmanism, religion has been denied content and direction by an impersonal cosmic philosophy, and two of the three great religions of Semitic origin Judaism and Christianity have moved over into a quasi-transcendental personal sphere. But the theologies of even these religions have been developed on the monarchical analogy.

All three elements the worldview, and the situation itself are in process of evolution. Paternity can never serve as a synthetic theological and philosophical concept. True as it is for experience it has been too obviously an analogy for theology. Historical orthodoxy is built on divine sovereignty, but there have already begun to appear signs that in the social mind is redescribing that environment upon which men find themselves dependent in terms more consonant with scientific thought than are those derived from monarchy. Here indeed may be said to be the real crisis in which theology finds itself in highly civilized countries. Convinced as are men of scientific temperament that the monarchical conception already anachronistic in a democracy is totally inadequate to express cosmic relations, a rapidly developing scientific thought has not yet reached sufficiently distinct conclusion to enable one to forecast exactly the next stage in the evolution of those of those conceptions by which modern men shall make intelligible to themselves the significance of the religious life. There are those who insist that there is no next stage; that the situation in which religion and science find themselves is not capable of further progress; that the future is to be religion less; that humanity is to replace God, and that ethics is to replace religion as how to regulate the impulse toward reconciliation with a personal environment. But this forecast seems to me untenable. In a certain sense we are back again where religion began its evolution. We can no longer think of God in the way of a naive anthropomorphism. We no longer think of God as sending plagues; we have fastened that indictment upon bacteria. We no longer believe that eclipses are punishments for our sins or that famines and earthquakes are due to divine displeasure. We are really face to face with the Whole. Is religion then to be replaced by natural science, or is it to enter upon a new cycle of development, again starting with nature? Unless all signs fail there is strong probability that this second alternative is to be realized. But modern man will start with a vastly richer experience than that of the primitive man who first endeavoured to adjust himself consciously to the same environment. If we cannot think of the Whole in terms of monarchy, we can yet think of it with Jesus through the discovery within it of the presence of personality. For the fundamental presupposition of any exploration of the universe is that its phenomena can be restated in terms of human thought. But we ourselves must be included in the Whole of things, and we as human personalities are just as truly the expression of the forces resident in that environment as are the laws of physics.

The Whole must at least include those phenomena to which we give the name of personality. And may we not add that, if development of the organism is determined by its environment, these very phenomena argue similar in the whole. For as far as social experience shows, personality is evoked only in personal relations. The modern man as truly as the primitive man is an element in a situation which demands harmony between himself and all its other elements. To attempt such harmony involves precisely the same attitude of mind as that which has found expression in all religion.

The first impression that scientific investigation may make on some minds is that of the doom of religion, but a sober second thought is likely to bring the conviction that, so far from this being the case, our wider knowledge, infinitesimal as it is, of the universe which includes man as well as stars, evokes more strongly than ever that impulse which is the very heart of religion. History cannot be reduced to social processes unaffected by the so-called natural forces. To reinterpret God is not to dissolve him into a mere social survival. To men who are indifferent to some of the elements in the problem, whether on the side of religion or of science, such a recasting of religion may seem impossible. When Socrates endeavoured to free the minds of the Athenians from an erroneous, because imperfect, religious interpretation of their world, they killed him for atheism. Conversely, when earnest Christian men have attempted to utilize the findings of science in the interests of a cosmic conception of God and of religion there have not been wanting those who, in the spirit of Haeckel, have insisted upon a thoroughgoing materialism mitigated only by impersonal social forces. It makes little difference whether a man calls himself a materialist or an idealist so long as he recognizes that there exist in the universe men and women.

The religious man needs to use all the phenomena, to which we have applied for want of a better term the word 'personal'. What we call that synthesis of thought and will and value judgments is of small significance compared to the fact that the actions to which we apply those terms really exist. And whether we get that interpretation of the universe, which, for lack of a better term, we call personal, from reading over into it our experiences, the fact remains that there are phenomena in the extra-human elements of environment which can be so interpreted. To recognize such elements as condition the outcome of the situation in which they and we mutually react is religious. For religion, whatever the interpretation it has given to its environment, has not created that environment. Whatever power social progress may have had to reconstitute situations in which men become religious, ideas have been only a part of environment. A man used fire in precisely the same way when he thought it contained phlogiston as he uses it today when he explains it in terms of chemical dissolution and recombination. So, religion persists in humanity regardless of the magic or the politics or the philosophy with which men have endeavoured to give the rational correlate to the elemental constitutive functioning of the personal life. Fishes did not invent the ocean and religion did not invent God; it has gradually found, understood, and experienced a God who existed as one element of an objective environment which antedated and evoked experience.

Evolution is no more than in a living organism is a matter of ungenetic change. Each new stage in its expression perpetuates in a greater or less degree vestiges of previous stages. Religions have their embryology as truly as their physiology. Just as the human body in its present condition has within it the vestiges which mark the survival of organs which man no longer needs but which were essential to some lower forms of life which humanity has recapitulated, so does each new stage in religious evolution perpetuate those less developed stages from which it has emerged. It could not be otherwise. Religion does not exist by itself, any more than life does. As already has been, strictly speaking there is no such thing as religion in the abstract. There are only people functioning religiously, holding religious ideas and customs, and incorporating them in religion institutions. We have long since passed from thinking of scientific law as doing anything or as being anything except a generalization drawn from experiment and observation. We no longer speak about the state as an entity existing apart from legislators and governors and the other machinery of what we call the body politic. Similarly, it is time to realize that when we speak about religion, we are speaking about the activities of real people acting and reacting in very real social situations from which institutions, customs, and programs evolve.

Now, real people are vastly interesting subjects of study, and no less so because of their inconsistencies. Sometimes we complacently speak as if in the political field the modern man was quite delivered from the crudities of primitive societies; and yet we lynch criminals and plead the 'higher law' for acquitting murderers. It is difficult not to see in such actions the recrudescence of the state of mind of primitive social groups. So, too, in our economic life we cling most vigorously to the formulas of competition when, as a matter of fact, with a rapidity that we deliberately refuse to recognize, we are legalizing a conception of collective bargaining that gives the lie to laissez-faire. It is not abnormal therefore to find that religious people, even highly intelligent religious people, include in their religious thinking and practices some of the elements which were once the dominating characteristics of a religion in its simpler stages. Reference has already been made to magic, but we find non-magical survivals of primitive religion in all stages of religious development. In fact, a superstition may fairly be described as a vestige of some element of religious experience which has come over from a stage in which it was essential to a religion. One might almost say that to be superstitious is to suffer religious appendicitis. There is no cure for it but surgery. Thus, there are women who would not dare say their children are unusually well without knocking three times on wood, and there are men who would hesitate to be one of a party of thirteen at a table. Who would think a wedding complete without rice-throwing? What base- ball club does not have its mascot? Now all these simple-minded practices which presumably intelligently religious people practice are the survivals of some ancient religious custom of our far away ancestors.

As a second thought, religious institutions perpetuate, though generally without the knowledge of their devotees, elements of earlier types of institutionalized religion too. The pious Mohammedan still ties rags to trees to remind genii and saints of his prayers and their duties. Even where a religion develops freely many early elements survive. Modern liberal Judaism presents striking illustrations of such phenomena has possibly even more striking ones. Indeed, so far has the recognition of religious survivals progressed that, if certain tendencies in a modern theological world were to triumph, religion would have to be regarded as little more than history. In fact, much of the cult in any religion is composed of customs, the original meaning of which has been forgotten and which have become sacred or symbolical simply through age. Recall by way of familiar illustration the robes of some of our clergy which perpetuated the dress of the ancient world. Some men will chant creeds they would not otherwise repeat. Almost any religious ceremony is enhanced by this means of linking the modern world with the great course of human history. In fact, he would be a most impracticable iconoclast who would ask the complete elimination of cult from a religion or any institution that stands for the conception of the continuity of human experience. In our religious thinking, these survivals and particularly those intellectual forms which have been derived from social experience, play an important part. As has already been stated, the controlling theological ideas of practically all religions were shaped in the great creative period in which local gods become national and a national religion passed on to monotheism. The monarchical analogies are those which show most pertinacity. In fact, in our modern world there are few men who have thus far deliberately undertaken to set forth a theology that shall embody the changed conception of man's relation to the universe itself. It is, however, altogether unfair to think that such experiments have not been made and are not being made. Religious thought is not nearly so anachronistic as those who know nothing about it appear to suppose. Religious thought can hardly be expected to reshape itself at the behest of every man who has his theory to champion. It, like scientific views themselves, will shape itself slowly, in common with the movement of the social mind; but such reshaping as truly as such a movement is already in progress. Yet, in this retranslation of the situation in which religion is involved because of its appropriation of elements of new social experience, we find our thought and to some extent our experience controlled by the survivals of the monarchical type of religion.

Its nearest group is an academic Brahmanism and neo-Buddhism. In the former the ideal is perfectly distinct, namely, to eliminate and to raise the soul in contemplation as far as possible into the region of the impersonal or at least non-individual. Neo-Platonism somewhat in like fashion attempted to bring man to the Heavenly Vision by ecstasy but was never able to free itself from the control of survivals and was handicapped by an empirical psychology that frustrated its search for its own ideals. Neo-Buddhism, as it is emerging in the universities of Japan, is a restatement of moral ideals common to all highly developed civilizations, under the impetus of Christianity. But for an insistence upon vestiges in vocabulary and thought that come from Japanese Buddhism it would be exceedingly difficult to distinguish one of these modern Buddhists from the radical Christians and liberal Jews who form the ethical culture groups of America. In so far, however, as Christianity is a matter of the experience of the plain people it must be admitted that, on its intellectual side, it is still a modified monarchy. The relations of God to the individual are conceived of in terms of sovereignty. It will be apparent, further, to any student of society that religion without institutions is of small significance. Religion apart from an institution has not succeeded, any more than a state has succeeded without political institutions. If religion is to be socially effective, its institutions require to those who must adapted to the changing social order. There are men who are by temperament anarchic optimists. They believe that institutions are a hindrance to society, and it matters little whether those institutions are those of state or those of religion. Yet even such transcendentalists form societies of anarchists to make anarchy effective. By the same token the man who wishes to make religion a purely individualist matter is not without justification for the maintenance of such a personal luxury, but he overlooks the fact that in a world like our religion always has and always must find social expression, and on both its intellectual and its institutional sides must partake of social evolution. So, it has come about those religious institutions are in process of evolution as truly as are religious conceptions. Mohammedism itself begins to feel the effect of our modern world and, now that it has broken with political autocracy, is likely within a generation or two to break with that religious autocracy which we call fatalism. The movements in Asia and particularly in Japan among the other religions, though not as marked, are none the less of the same general type.

The ancient Chinese education has been abandoned and modern textbooks are being introduced throughout the empire. While it is true that it would be a little difficult to regard Confucianism as more than a system of ethics, it can hardly be doubted that the adoption of the Western school will have decided results in the case of those religious survivals like ancestor-worship which Confucianism embodied and preserved. Protestant churches are already passing through rapid changes as the social aspects of religion and the social, not to mention the medical, opportunities of the church as an institution are becoming more apparent. As a result, social evolution finds expression in an evolution of religious thought and institutions that perpetuate vestiges of simpler and earlier stages. Inevitably such a process is accompanied with struggle, for religious survivals are always a conservative force. Just what will be the outcome of this struggle between the representatives of different stages of social experience in religions only the future can tell. But of one thing we may be sure, there will be no cessation either of the impulse to come into helpful reconciliation with a personally interpreted environment, or of the utilization of social experience to justify, control, enrich, and systematize such impulse. And just here lies the pressing tasks of the apologist and the theologian. For our modern world needs to be reconvinced that religion is more than a survival, and that the appeal to the universe in terms of personalism is justifiable after concepts inherited from less complex social experience have been abandoned.

The concept of the struggle between religions for the survival of the fittest is explained as in what has been said it must have become evident that a distinction is to be made between religion as a functional psychological expression of life, and a religion as a group of beliefs and rites by which this attitude of mind is conditioned and given social expression. The former is as generic as life; the latter is as specific as organisms. The history of religions makes it evident that no one of them can persist unchanged as regulative in a civilization whose moral ideals are superior to its own or whose scientific achievement makes the inherited religious interpretation of existence, outgrown. When a religion has thus found itself out of sympathy with the growing social environment two results follow, either it has been supplanted by another, or the religion has adjusted itself in some fashion as has already in a general way been described, reducing its outgrown elements to vestiges, and becomes a new species of religion, as, e.g., in the evolution of rabbinical Judaism. So, too, in the case of the religion of Greece, the simple original Aryan faith was continuously modified by the artistic anthropomorphism of the Homeric literature as well as by Egyptian and Asiatic influences, the worship of the god Hercules, the rise of the Dionysiac enthusiasm and the mysteries, and the work of Aeschylus, Sophocles, and Pindar. With the rise of the great schools of philosophy the Greek religion grew extremely complicated, a cross-section of Grecian society showing the existence of the survivals of all the elements which had at some time been locally dominant.

In it all, however, there was no actual domination of a single religious conception, and classical religion could not withstand the onset of a distinct, unified, aggressive religio-ethical faith. If the development of a cosmopolitan civilization thus proves fatal to the more primitive stages of a religion, precisely the opposite is true where a civilization stops at a level set by the religion. The two coalesce. Such, for example, is true in the case of Mohammedanism where the development of the political and religious concept seems to have stopped simultaneously at the stage of an imperfectly moral autocracy. In the breakup of Turkish civilization which is already beginning because of the introduction of Western ideals, Mohammedanism will undoubtedly find itself engaged in a life and death struggle with Christianity on the one side and materialistic agnosticism on the other. But such struggle is not likely to extend far below the level of those social strata affected by Western civilization. The great masses of the empire are likely to continue indefinitely under the control of a religion that fits the state of civilization in which they live. Only as Mohammedans are educated will Mahomet cease to be the prophet. The struggle between religions is, then, a struggle not only between theologies and philosophies but between social orders. It may occur within a society which, because of economic growth, is differentiating into classes, or it may be due, as in the case of the Asiatic world, to the introduction of new social and religious ideals into an older order. From such a point of view missions became of the utmost sociological significance. In the light of the past there can be no question that changes in the social order will both be conditioned by and will condition religious evolution, as is strikingly illustrated in Japan. But this change should be sharply defined. The religion best fitted to a social order will not be a religion foreign to that order. Social history seems to argue that it is impossible to annihilate one religion by another. What really will happen will be a biological development of religions through appropriation and assimilation.

In other words, a nation will have several religions, although they may be called by the same general name and have many elements in common. Some of these religions will be so unlike those of earlier stages of social evolution as to constitute a new species. In the struggle which comes between these various embodiments of the religious impulse those elements will disappear which are least in harmony with dominating social conceptions of various social groups, and those will survive which are most in accordance with and can contribute most to the development of superior stages of social evolution. On the one hand it cannot believe in an arthropathic God, but on the other it is not ready to deny personality in terms of purpose and reason to the great process in which mankind finds itself involved. Its sympathies are social rather than individual, and its theology is based not on metaphysics of the Godhead interpreted by human analogy but on those judgments of value and those undeniable facts of science which seem to condition all self-expression. Thus, the vanishing point of religious history is still evolution in the sense that the conscious attempt to bring humanity into helpful relationship with that environment with which it finds itself involved and which possess elements which justify our treating it as we treat persons, will never disappear. It is as real as environment and humanity. But the phases of religion and the modes of controlling the expression of this generic impulse are parts of social history. That religion which best enables religion to express itself in its increasingly complex social environment will survive all others. Other religions will not altogether disappear, but they will become vestiges in the more highly developed religious life. Whatever may be a given society's particular creed, whatever may be its metaphysics, the sense of dependence which science enforces, the need of divine help which human weakness arouses, and the call to sacrifice for social ends that the times demand will be given meaning and justification by the Christian doctrine of reconciliation as it centres about Jesus. And in this doctrine Christianity is but re-expressing the essence of religion itself.

6.   The Field and its Significance

Ideally, a guide to the nature and history of philosophy of religion would begin with an analysis or definition of religion. Unfortunately, there is no current consensus on a precise identification of the necessary and sufficient conditions of what counts as a religion. We therefore currently lack a decisive criterion that would enable clear rulings whether some movements should count as religions (e.g., Scientology or Cargo cults of the Pacific islands). But while consensus in precise details is elusive, the following general depiction of what counts as a religion may be helpful: A religion involves a communal, transmittable body of teachings and prescribed practices about an ultimate, sacred reality or state of being that calls for reverence or awe, a body which guides its practitioners into what it describes as a saving, illuminating or emancipatory relationship to this reality through a personally transformative life of prayer, ritualized meditation, and/or moral practices like repentance and personal regeneration. This definition does not involve counting a tradition as religious if it involves belief in God or gods, as some recognized religions such as Buddhism (in its main forms) does not involve a belief in God or gods.[26] It will be assumed, then, that religions include (at least) Hinduism, Buddhism, Taoism, Confucianism, Judaism, Christianity, Islam, and those traditions that are like them. This way of delimiting a domain is sometimes described as employing a definition by examples (an ostensive definition) or making an appeal to a family resemblance between things. It will also be assumed that Greco-Roman views of gods, rituals, the afterlife, the soul, are broadly "religious" or "religiously significant". From the outset, philosophers in Asia, the Near and Middle East, North Africa, and Europe reflected on the gods or God, duties to the divine, the origin and nature of the cosmos, an afterlife, the nature of happiness and obligations, whether there are sacred duties to family or rulers, and so on. As with each of what would come to be considered sub-fields of philosophy today (like philosophy of science, philosophy of art), philosophers in the ancient world addressed religiously significant themes (just as they took up reflections on what we call science and art) during their overall practice of philosophy. While from time to time in the Medieval era, some Jewish, Christian, and Islamic philosophers sought to demarcate philosophy from theology or religion, the evident role of philosophy of religion as a distinct field of philosophy does not seem apparent until the mid-twentieth century. A case can be made, however, that there is some hint of the emergence of philosophy of religion in the seventeenth century philosophical movement Cambridge Platonism. Ralph Cudworth (1617–1688), Henry More (1614–1687), and other members of this movement were the first philosophers to practice philosophy in English; they introduced in English many of the terms that are frequently employed in philosophy of religion today, including the term 'philosophy of religion', as well as 'theism', 'consciousness', and 'materialism'.

At present philosophy of religion is one of the most vibrant areas of philosophy. Articles in philosophy of religion appear in virtually all the main philosophical journals, while some journals are dedicated especially to philosophy of religion. Philosophy of religion is in evidence at institutional meetings of philosophers (such as the meetings of the American Philosophical Association and of the Royal Society of Philosophy). Firstly, the religious nature of the world population. Most social research on religion supports the view that most of the world's population is either part of a religion or influenced by religion. To engage in philosophy of religion is therefore to engage in a subject that affects actual people, rather than only tangentially touching on matters of present social concern. Perhaps one of the reasons why philosophy of religion is often the first topic in textbook introductions to philosophy is that this is one way to propose to readers that philosophical study can impact what large numbers of people think about life and value. The role of philosophy of religion in engaging real-life beliefs and doubts about religion is perhaps also evidenced by the current popularity of books for and against theism. One other aspect of religious populations that may motivate philosophy of religion is that philosophy is a tool that may be used when persons compare different religious traditions. Philosophy of religion can play an important role in helping persons understand and evaluate different religious traditions and their alternatives. Secondly, philosophy of religion as a field may be popular because of the overlapping interests found in both religious and philosophical traditions. Both religious and philosophical thinking raise many of the same, fascinating questions and possibilities about the nature of reality, the limits of reason, the meaning of life, and so on. Thirdly, studying the history of philosophy provides ample reasons to have some expertise in philosophy of religion. In the West, most ancient, medieval, and modern philosophers philosophically reflected on matters of religious significance.

Among these modern philosophers, it would be impossible to comprehensively engage their work without looking at their philosophical work on religious beliefs: René Descartes (1596–1650), Thomas Hobbes (1588–1679), Anne Conway (1631–1679), Baruch Spinoza (1632–1677), Margaret Cavendish (1623–1673), Gottfried Leibniz (1646–1716), John Locke (1632–1704), George Berkeley (1685–1753), David Hume (1711–1776), Immanuel Kant (1724–1804), and G.W.F. Hegel (1770–1831) (the list is partial). And in the twentieth century, one should make note of the important philosophical work by Continental philosophers on matters of religious significance: Martin Heidegger (1889–1976), Jean-Paul Sartre (1905–1980), Simone de Beauvoir (1908–1986), Albert Camus (1913–1960), Gabriel Marcel (1889–1973), Franz Rosenzweig (1886–1929), Martin Buber (1878–1956), Emmanuel Levinas (1906–1995), Simone Weil (1909–1943) and, more recently Jacques Derrida (1930–2004), Michel Foucault (1926–1984), and Luce Irigary (1930). In Chinese and Indian philosophy there is an even greater challenge than in the West to distinguish important philosophical and religious sources of philosophy of religion. It would be difficult to classify Nagarjuna (150–250 CE) or Adi Shankara (788–820 CE) as exclusively philosophical or religious thinkers. Their work seems as equally important philosophically as it is religiously. Fourth, a comprehensive study of theology or religious studies also provides good reasons to have expertise in philosophy of religion.

7. The Meaning of Religious Beliefs

Prior to the twentieth century, a substantial amount of philosophical reflection on matters of religious significance (but not all) has been realist. That is, it has often been held that religious beliefs are true or false. Xenophanes and other pre-Socratic thinkers, Socrates, Plato, Aristotle, the Epicureans, the Stoics, Philo, Plotinus differed on their beliefs (or speculation) about the divine, and they and their contemporaries differed about skepticism, but they held (for example) that there either was a divine reality or not. In Asian philosophy of religion, some religions do not include revelation claims, as in Buddhism and Confucianism, but Hindu tradition confronted philosophers with assessing the Vedas and Upanishads. But for the most part, philosophers in the West and East thought there were truths about whether there is a God, the soul, an afterlife, that which is sacred (whether these are known or understood by any human being or not). Realism of some kind is so pervasive that the great historian of philosophy Richard Popkin (1923–2005) once defined philosophy as "the attempt the give an account of what is true and what is important". Important philosophers in the West such as Immanuel Kant (1724–1804) and Friedrich Nietzsche (1844–1900), among others, challenged classical realist views of truth and metaphysics (ontology or the theory of what is), but the twentieth century saw two, especially powerful movements that challenged realism: logical positivism and philosophy of religion inspired by Wittgenstein Prior to addressing these two movements, let us take note of some of the nuances in philosophical reflection on the realist treatment of religious language. Many theistic philosophers (and their critics) contend that language about God may be used univocally, analogically, or equivocally.

A term is used univocally about God and humans when it has the same sense. Arguably, the term "to know" is used univocally of God in the claims "God knows you" and "You know London", even though how God knows you and how you know London differ radically. In terms of the later difference, philosophers sometimes distinguish between what is attributed to something and the mode in which some state is realized. Theological work that stresses our ability to form a positive concept of the divine has been called the via positive or catophatic theology. On the other hand, those who stress the unknowability of God embrace what is called the via negative or apophatic theology. Maimonides (1135–1204) was a great proponent of the via negative, favouring the view that we know God principally through what God is not (God is not material, not evil, not ignorant, and so on). While some (but not all) philosophers of religion in the Continental tradition have aligned themselves with apophatic theology such as Levinas (who was non-theistic) and Jean-Luc Marion (1946), a substantial amount (but not all) of analytically oriented philosophy of religion have tended to adopt the via positive, one of the challenges of apophatic theology is that it seems to make the philosophy of God remote from religious practices such as prayer, worship, trust in God's power and goodness, pilgrimages, and religious ethics. According to Karen Armstrong, some of the greatest theologians in the Abrahamic faiths held that God was not good, divine, powerful, or intelligent in any way that we could understand. We could not even say that God 'existed', because our concept of existence is too limited. Some of the sages preferred to say that God was 'Nothing' because God was not another being... To these theologians some of our modern ideas about God would have seemed idolatrous. A prima facie challenge to this position is that it is hard to believe that religious practitioners could pray or worship or trust in a being which was altogether inscrutable or a being that we cannot in any way understand. For a realist, via positive philosophy of God that seeks to appreciate the force of apophatic theology.[27] Let us now turn to two prominent philosophical movements that challenged a realist philosophy of God.

7.1 Positivism

'Positivism' is a term introduced by Auguste Comte (1798–1857), a French philosopher who championed the natural and social sciences over against theology and the philosophical practice of metaphysics. The term 'positivism' was used later by a group of philosophers who met in Austria called the Vienna Circle from 1922 to 1938.

- First, it was charged that logical positivism itself is self-refuting. Is the statement of its standard of meaning (propositions are meaningful if and only if they are about the relations of ideas or about matters that are subject to empirical verification or falsification) itself about the relations of ideas or about matters that are subject to empirical verification or falsification? Arguably not. At best, the positivist criterion of meaning is a recommendation about what to count as meaningful.

- Second, it was argued that there are meaningful statements about the world that are not subject to direct or indirect empirical confirmation or disconfirmation. Plausible candidates include statements about the origin of the cosmos or, closer to home, the mental states of other persons or of nonhuman animals.

- Third, limiting human experience to what is narrowly understood to be empirical seemed to many philosophers to be arbitrary or capricious. C. D. Broad and others defended a wider understanding of experience to allow for the meaningfulness of moral experience: arguably, one can experience the wrongness of an act as when an innocent person feels herself to be violated.

- Fourth, Ayer's rejection of the meaningfulness of ethics seemed to cut against his epistemology or normative account of beliefs, for he construed empirical knowledge in terms of having the right to certain beliefs.

- Fifth, and probably most importantly in terms of the history of ideas, the seminal philosopher of science Carl Hempel (1905–1997) contended that the project of logical positivism was too limited (Hempel 1950). It was insensitive to the broader task of scientific inquiry which is properly conducted not on the tactical scale of scrutinizing claims about empirical experience but in terms of a coherent, overall theory or view of the world.

7.2 Wittgenstein's Philosophy of Religion

Wittgenstein's early work was interpreted by some members of the Vienna Circle as friendly to their empiricism, but they were surprised when he visited the Circle and, rather than Wittgenstein discussing his Tractatus, he read them poetry by Rabindranath Tagore (1861–1941). In any case, Wittgenstein's later work, which was not friendly to their empiricism, was especially influential in post-World War II philosophy and theology and will be the focus here. In the Philosophical Investigations and in many other works (including the publication of notes taken by his students on his lectures), Wittgenstein opposed what he called the picture theory of meaning. On this view, statements are true or false depending upon whether reality matches the picture expressed by the statements. Wittgenstein came to see this view of meaning as deeply problematic. The meaning of language is, rather, to be found not in referential fidelity but in its use in what Wittgenstein referred to as forms of life.

8. Religion and Science

The relationship between religion and science has been an important topic in twentieth century philosophy of religion and it seems incredibly important today. This section begins by considering the National Academy of Sciences and Institute of Medicine (now the National Academy of Medicine) statement on the relationship between science and religion: Science and religion are based on different aspects of human experience. In science, explanations must be based on evidence drawn from examining the natural world. Scientifically based observations or experiments that conflict with an explanation eventually must lead to modification or even abandonment of that explanation. Religious faith, in contrast, does not depend only on empirical evidence, is not necessarily modified in the face of conflicting evidence, and typically involves supernatural forces or entities. Because they are not a part of nature, supernatural entities cannot be investigated by science. In this sense, science and religion are separate and address aspects of human understanding in different ways. The National Academies do seem to be correct in implying that the key elements of many religions do not admit of direct scientific investigations nor rest 'only on empirical evidence'. Neither God nor Allah nor Brahman (the divine as conceived of in Judaism, Christianity, Islam, and Hinduism) is a physical or material object or process. It seems, then, that the divine or the sacred and many other elements in world religions (meditation, prayer, sin and forgiveness, deliverance from craving) can only be indirectly investigated scientifically. First, a minor (and controversial) critical point in response to the Academies: The statement makes use of the terms "supernatural forces or entities" that "are not part of nature". The term "supernatural" is not the standard term used to refer only to God or the divine, probably (in part) because in English the term "supernatural" refers not just to God or the divine, but also to poltergeists, ghosts, devils, witches, mediums, oracles, etc. So, rather than the statement refers to "supernatural forces or entities", a more charitable phrase might refer to how many world religions are theistic or involve some sacred reality that is not directly, empirically measurable. Moving beyond this minor point about terminology, religious beliefs have traditionally and today been thought of as subject to evidence. Evidence for religious beliefs have included appeal to the contingency of the cosmos and principles of explanation, the ostensibly purposive nature of the cosmos, the emergence of consciousness, and so on. According to Steven Pinker, science has shown the beliefs of many religions to be false. To begin with, the findings of science entail that the belief systems of all the world's traditional religions and cultures their theories of the origins of life, humans, and societies are factually mistaken. We know, but our ancestors did not, that humans belong to a single species of African primate that developed agriculture, government, and writing late in its history. We know that our species is a tiny twig of a genealogical tree that embraces all living things and that emerged from prebiotic chemicals almost four billion years ago. We know that the laws governing the physical world (including accidents, disease, and other misfortunes) have no goals that pertain to human well-being. There is no such thing as fate, providence, karma, spells, curses, augury, divine retribution, or answered prayer though the discrepancy between the laws of probability and the workings of cognition may explain why people think there is. Following up on Pinker, it should be noted that it would not be scientifically acceptable today to appeal to miracles or to direct acts of God. Any supposed miracle would (to many, if not all scientists) be a kind of defeat and to welcome an unacceptable mystery.

9. Philosophical Reflection on Theism and Its Alternatives

For much of the history of philosophy of religion, there has been stress on the assessment of theism. Non-theistic concepts of the divine have increasingly become part of philosophy of religion.[28] Theism still has some claim for special attention given the large world population that is aligned with theistic traditions (the Abrahamic faiths and theistic Hinduism) and the enormity of attention given to the defence and critique of theism in philosophy of religion historically and today.

9.1 Philosophical Reflection on Divine Attributes

Speculation about divine attributes in theistic tradition has often been carried out in accord with what is currently referred to as perfect being theology, according to which God is understood to be maximally excellent or unsurpassable in greatness. Divine attributes in this tradition have been identified by philosophers as those attributes that are the greatest compossible set of great making properties; properties are compossible when they can be instantiated by the same being. Traditionally, the divine attributes have been identified as omnipotence, omniscience, perfect goodness, worthiness of worship, necessary of non-contingent existence, and eternality (existing outside of time or a temporally). Each of these attributes has been subject to nuanced different analysis, as noted below. God has also been traditionally conceived to be incorporeal or immaterial, immutable, impassable, omnipresent. One of the tools philosophers use in their investigation into divine attributes involve thought experiments. In thought experiments, hypothetical cases are described cases that may or may not represent the way things are. In these descriptions, terms normally used in one context are employed in expanded settings. Thus, in thinking of God as omniscient, one might begin with a noncontroversial case of a person knowing that a proposition is true, taking note of what it means for someone to possess that knowledge and of the ways in which the knowledge is secured. A theistic thought experiment would seek to extend our understanding of knowledge as we think of it in our own case, working toward the conception of a maximum or supreme intellectual excellence befitting the religious believers' understanding of God. Various degrees of refinement would then be in order, as one speculates not only about the extent of a maximum set of propositions known but also about how these might be known. That is, in attributing omniscience to God, would one thereby claim God knows all truths in a way that is analogous to the way we come to know truths about the world? Too close an analogy would produce a peculiar picture of God relying upon, for example, induction, sensory evidence, or the testimony of others. One move in the philosophy of God has been to assert that the claim 'God knows something' employs the word 'knows' univocally when read as picking out the thesis that God knows something, while it uses the term in only a remotely analogical sense if read as identifying how God knows. Using thought experiments often employs an appearance principle. Some philosophers are skeptical of appealing to thought experiments.[29]

9.1.1 Omniscience

Imagine there is a God who knows the future free action of human beings. If God does know you will freely do some act, then it is true that you will indeed do the same. But if you are free, would you not be free to avoid doing the task? Given that it is foreknown you will do action, it appears you would not be free to refrain from the act. Initially this paradox seems easy to dispel. If God knows about your free action, then God knows that you will freely do something and that you could have refrained from it.

9.1.2 Eternity

In the great monotheistic traditions, God is thought of as without any kind of beginning or end. God will never, indeed, can never, cease to be. Some philosophical theists hold that God's temporality is very much like ours in the sense that there is a before, during, and an after for God, or a past, present, and future for God. This view is sometimes referred to as the thesis that God is everlasting. Those adopting a more radical stance claim that God is independent of temporality, arguing either that God is not in time at all, or that God is "simultaneously" at or in all times. Furthermore, there may be an opportunity to use God is standing outside of time to launch an argument that God is the creator of time. Those affirming God to be unbounded by temporal sequences face several puzzles which I note without trying to settle. If God is somehow at or in all times, is God simultaneously at or in each? If so, there is the following problem.

If God is simultaneous with the event of Rome burning in 410 A.D., and also simultaneous with your reading this entry, then it seems that Rome must be burning at the same time you are reading this entry. The problem is that the more emphasis one places on the claim that God's supreme existence is independent of time, the more one seems to jeopardize taking seriously time as it is known. Finally, while the great monotheistic traditions provide a portrait of the Divine as supremely different from the creation, there is also an insistence on God's proximity or immanence. For some theists, describing God as a person or person like (God loves, acts, knows) is not to equivocate. But it is not clear that an eternal God could be personal.

9.1.3 The goodness of God

All known world religions address the nature of good and evil and commend ways of achieving human well-being, whether this be thought of in terms of salvation, liberation, deliverance, enlightenment, tranquillity, or an egoless state of Nirvana. Notwithstanding important differences, there is a substantial overlap between many of these conceptions of the good as witnessed by the commending of the Golden Rule ("Do unto others as you would have them do unto you") in many religions. Some religions construe the Divine as in some respect beyond our human notions of good and evil.

In some forms of Hinduism, for example, Brahman has been extolled as possessing a sort of moral transcendence, and some Christian theologians and philosophers have likewise insisted that God is only a moral agent in a highly qualified sense, if at all. To call God good is, for them, a quite different from calling a human being good. Here are only some of the ways in which philosophers have articulated what it means to call God good. The latter view has been termed theistic voluntarism.

A common version of theistic voluntarism is the claim that for something to be good or right simply means that God approves of permits it and for something to be bad or wrong means that God disapproves or forbids it. Theistic voluntarists face several difficulties: moral language seems intelligible without having to be explained in terms of the Divine will. Indeed, many people make what they take to be objective moral judgments without making any reference to God. According to one such moderate stance, while God cannot make cruelty good, God can make some actions morally required or morally forbidden which otherwise would be morally neutral. Arguments for this have been based on the thesis that the cosmos and all its contents are God's creation. According to some theories of property, an agent making something good gains entitlements over the property. The ultimate grounding of what makes human motives good is that they are in accord with the motives of God. Zagzebski's theory is perhaps the most ambitious virtue theory in print, offering an account of human virtues considering theism.

Not all theists resonate with her bold claim that God is a person who has emotions, but many allow that (at least in some analogical sense) God may be seen as personal and having affective states. One other effort worth noting to link judgments of good and evil with judgments about God relies upon the ideal observer theory of ethics. According to this theory, moral judgments can be analysed in terms of how an ideal observer would judge matters. The theory receives some support from the fact that most moral disputes can be analysed in terms of different parties challenging each other to be impartial, to get their empirical facts straight, and to be more sensitive for example, by realizing what it feels like to be disadvantaged. The theory has formidable critics and defenders. If true, it does not follow that there is an ideal observer, but if it is true and moral judgments are coherent, then the idea of an ideal observer is coherent. Given certain conceptions of God in the three great monotheistic traditions, God fits the ideal observer description. This need not be unwelcoming to atheists. Should an ideal observer theory be cogent, a theist would have some reason for claiming that atheists committed to normative, ethical judgments are also committed to the idea of a God or a Godlike being.

10. Religious Pluralism

During the new work on religious traditions, there has been a steady, growing representation of non-monotheistic traditions. The Routledge series Investigating Philosophy of Religion with Routledge with volumes already published or forthcoming on Buddhism, Hinduism, Taoism, and Confucianism. The explanation of philosophy of religion has involved fresh translations of philosophical and religious texts from India, China, Southeast Asia, and Africa. Exceptional figures from non-Western traditions have an increased role in cross-cultural philosophy of religion and religious dialogue. There are now extensive treatments of pantheism and student friendly guides to diverse religious conceptions of the cosmos. The expanded interest in religious pluralism has led to extensive reflection on the compatibility and possible synthesis of religions. John Hick is the preeminent synthesizer of religious traditions. They began at different times and in different places, and each expanded outwards into the surrounding world of primitive natural religion until most of the world was drawn up into one or the other of the great revealed faiths. And once this global pattern had become established it has ever since remained stable.

Then in Persia the great prophet Zoroaster appeared; China produced Lao-tzu and then the Buddha lived, the Mahavira, the founder of the Jain religion and, probably about the end of this period, the writing of the Bhagavad Gita; and Greece produced Pythagoras and then, ending this golden age, Socrates, and Plato. Then after the gap of some three hundred years came Jesus of Nazareth and the emergence of Christianity; and after another gap the prophet Mohammed and the rise of Islam. The suggestion that we must consider is that these were all movements of the divine revelation. Some contend that the very concept of "the Real" is incoherent or not religiously adequate. Indeed, articulating the nature of the Real is no easy task. Hick writes that the Real cannot be said to be one thing or many, person or thing, substance, or process, good or bad, purposive, or non-purposive. In addition to the expansion of philosophy of religion to consider a wider set of religions, the field has also seen an expansion in terms of methodology. Philosophers of religion have re-discovered medieval philosophy the new translations and commentaries of medieval Christian, Jewish, and Islamic texts have blossomed. There is now a self-conscious, deliberate effort to combine work on the concepts in religious belief alongside a critical understanding of their social and political roots (the work of Foucault has been influential on this point), feminist philosophy of religion has been especially important in re-thinking what may be called the ethics of methodology and, as this is in some respects the most current debate in the field, it is a fitting point to end this entry by highlighting the work of Pamela Sue Anderson and others. A mark of legitimation of philosophy should be the extent to which it contributes to human welfare.

11. Specific Religion

11.1 Abrahamic

Abrahamic religions are monotheistic religions which believe they descend from Abraham.

11.2 Judaism

Judaism is the oldest Abrahamic religion, originating in the people of ancient Israel and Judea.[30] The Torah is its foundational text, and is part of the larger text known as the Tanakh or Hebrew Bible. It is supplemented by oral tradition, set down in written form in later texts such as the Midrash and the Talmud. Judaism includes a wide corpus of texts, practices, theological positions, and forms of organization. Within Judaism there are a variety of movements, most of which emerged from Rabbinic Judaism, which holds that God revealed his laws and commandments to Moses on Mount Sinai in the form of both the Written and Oral Torah; historically, this assertion was challenged by various groups. The Jewish people were scattered after the destruction of the Temple in Jerusalem in 70 CE. Today there are about 13 million Jews, about 40 per cent living in Israel and 40 per cent in the United States. The largest Jewish religious movements are Orthodox Judaism (Haredi Judaism and Modern Orthodox Judaism), Conservative Judaism and Reform Judaism.[31]

11.3 Islam

Islam is a monotheistic religion based on the Quran, one of the holy books considered by Muslims to be revealed by God, and on the teachings (hadith) of the Islamic prophet Muhammad, a major political and religious figure of the 7th century. Islam is based on the unity of all religious philosophies and accepts all of the Abrahamic prophets of Judaism, Christianity and other Abrahamic religions before Muhammad. It is the most widely practiced religion of Southeast Asia, North Africa, Western Asia, and Central Asia, while Muslim-majority countries also exist in parts of South Asia, Sub-Saharan Africa, and Southeast Europe. There are also several Islamic republics, including Iran, Pakistan, Mauritania, and Afghanistan.

- Sunni Islam is the largest denomination within Islam and follows the Qur'an, the hadith (ar:plural of Hadith) which record the sunnah, whilst placing emphasis on the sahabah.

- Shia Islam is the second largest denomination of Islam and its adherents believe that Ali succeeded Muhammad and further places emphasis on Muhammad's family.
- There are also Muslim revivalist movements such as Muwahhidism and Salafism.

Other denominations of Islam include Nation of Islam, Ibadi, Sufism, Quranism, Mahdavia, and non-denominational Muslims. Wahhabism is the dominant Muslim schools of thought in the Kingdom of Saudi Arabia.

11.4 Indian religions

Indian religions are practiced or were founded in the Indian subcontinent. They are sometimes classified as the dharmic religions, as they all feature dharma, the specific law of reality and duties expected according to the religion.[32] The details discussion is mentioned in the next chapter.

11.5 Indigenous and folk

Indigenous religions or folk religions refers to a broad category of traditional religions that can be characterised by shamanism, animism and ancestor worship, where traditional means indigenous, that which is aboriginal or foundational, handed down from generation to generation. These are religions that are strongly associated with a particular group of people, ethnicity, or tribe; they often have no formal creeds or sacred texts. Some faiths are syncretic, fusing diverse religious beliefs and practices.

- Australian Aboriginal religions.
- Folk religions of the Americas: Native American religions

Folk religions are often omitted as a category in surveys even in countries where they are widely practiced, e.g., in China.

11.6 Traditional African

African traditional religion encompasses the traditional religious beliefs of people in Africa. In West Africa, these religions include the Akan religion, Dahomey (Fon) mythology, Efik mythology, Odinani, Serer religion (A fat Roog), and Yoruba religion, while Bushongo mythology, Mbuti (Pygmy) mythology, Lugbara mythology, Dinka religion, and Lotuko mythology come from central Africa. Southern African traditions include Akamba mythology, Masai mythology, Malagasy mythology, San religion, Lozi mythology, Tumbuk mythology, and Zulu mythology. Bantu mythology is found throughout central, southeast, and southern Africa. In north Africa, these traditions include Berber and ancient Egyptian. There are also notable

African diasporic religions practiced in the Americas, such as Santeria, Candomble Vodun, Lucumi, Umbanda, and Macumba.

11.7 Iranian

Iranian religions are ancient religions whose roots predate the Islamization of Greater Iran. Nowadays these religions are practiced only by minorities. Zoroastrianism is based on the teachings of prophet Zoroaster in the 6th century. Zoroastrians worship the creator Ahura Mazda. In Zoroastrianism, good and evil have distinct sources, with evil trying to destroy the creation of Mazda, and good trying to sustain it. Mandaeism is a monotheistic religion with a strongly dualistic worldview. Mandaeans are sometime labelled as the Last Gnostics.[33] Kurdish religions include the traditional beliefs of the Yazidi[34],[35] Alevi, and Ahl-e Haqq. Sometimes these are labelled Yazdânism.

In today's globalized world, growing exchanges and interactions between religions and a stronger trend towards religious diversity are bringing about new opportunities and challenges to religious relations. On the one hand, as exchanges among different religions are becoming more frequent, more opportunities are provided to religions to conduct mutual learning and strengthen cooperation. In the history of all humanity, particularly in some countries and regions in the east, we have already accumulated ample experience and wisdom regarding cultural diversity. Moreover, the challenges such as religious disputes or even conflicts are rising even as the trend towards religious diversity is driving forward exchanges and cooperation. In some countries and regions, religious distrust is growing almost because of religious diversification, aggravating people's worries over new religious conflicts. Faced with opportunities and challenges, governments, religious communities, and other relevant parties need to shoulder responsibilities and advocate religious harmony, resolve religious disputes and conflicts, promote social harmony, and uphold world peace. By religious harmony, I mean the harmonious and common development within and between individual religions as well as between the religious community and the larger society which is realized through the dialogue generated enhancement of mutual understanding and empathy and the sharing of the common responsibilities of peace and justice on the precondition of recognizing religious diversity and differences. Within a religion, it is important to approach issues of faith and doctrine with tolerance and enhance coordination and cooperation between different denominations. When addressing inter-religious issues, we should respect and accommodate each other, enhance empathy through dialogue and build trust through cooperation. The religious communities should adapt to social progress and development by making self-readjustments, obey secular laws, respect public customs, and contribute to social development by putting into full play their unique advantages.

Freedom of religious belief is a common consensus of the international community and the precondition and foundation for religious harmony. Without it, there will be no religious harmony to speak of. However, we are aware that freedom of religious belief alone does not preclude hatred or conflicts among religions. Religious harmony takes the freedom a step further to offer us a new vision with which to address religious disputes and conflicts. There are many ways to realize religious harmony, among which religious dialogue is an important one. Only when religious harmony is considered the highest spiritual objective can the dialogue have clear direction and inexhaustible drive. We need to start from now, start with ourselves, start with small steps, and push towards this goal in an unyielding spirit. To promote religious harmony, we need to advocate the idea of 'harmony without uniformity'. The idea of 'harmony without uniformity', a high spiritual accomplishment, is the kernel of religious harmony. Many religions have developed in parallel and in harmony for thousands of years. The most important reason is that all religions embrace the culture of harmony. We know that the flourishing of one means the flourishing of all and the demise of one the demise of all. The word 'harmony' is of vital importance in the concept of 'harmony without uniformity', yet it is not realized by way of forced uniformity. Like people, religions also need to show due respect to each other. Religious harmony can be understood as friendly coexistence among different religions. It is not necessary to have winners in every race. One should forgive others whenever it is possible, because one step back earns you a broader way ahead. To promote religious harmony, we should shoulder social responsibilities together. Religion appeared at the very beginning of civilization and constitutes a major part of it. The role played by religion changes as civilization develops. In the face of the trend towards a multi-polar world and economic globalization, all religions need to join hands, share responsibilities, perform good deeds and contribute to world peace, social stability, and people's well-being. The sharing of responsibilities and the experience of working together will generate mutual trust and respect among different religious groups. All religions should protect the purity of faith and give back to religion its original face, to eliminate any room for evil doings by groups or individuals.

Sufism is a form of Islamic mysticism that emphasizes introspection and spiritual closeness with God. Sufism has been a prominent spiritual tradition in Islam deriving influences from major world religions, such as, Christianity, Buddhism and Hinduism (Bhakti movement of Maharashtra) and contributing substantially toward spiritual well-being of many people within and outside Muslim world. The sharing of responsibilities and the experience of working together will generate mutual trust and respect among different religious groups. To promote religious harmony, we need to oppose any use of religion for ill purposes. Sufism may be best described as Islamic mysticism or asceticism, which through belief and practice helps Muslims attain nearness to Allah by way of direct personal experience of God. While there are other suggested origins of the term Sufi, the word is largely believed to stem from the Arabic word suf, which refers to the wool that was traditionally worn by mystics and ascetics. Belief in pursuing a path that leads to closeness with God, ultimately through encountering the divine in the hereafter, is a fundamental component of Islamic belief. However, in Sufi thought this proximity can be realised in this life. The Sufi laid the foundation of communal harmony and peace. They established equality of status, love and brotherhood to the masses and taught people how to respect each other's religion, feelings, and practices. We will see in coming chapter that in the last eight to nine centuries, despite the existence of different religions in a fragmented country like India, Sufi Sampradaya has set a good example on the path of devotional coexistence with society and saints without any religious or social harmony.[36]

Chapter 2
Sufism ~ The Global Concept

1. Definitions

The Arabic word Tasawwuf (lit. being or becoming a Sufi), generally translated as Sufism, is commonly defined by Western authors as Islamic mysticism.[1][2] The Arabic term Sufi has been used in Islamic literature with a wide range of meanings, by both proponents and opponents of Sufism. Classical Sufi texts, which stressed certain teachings and practices of the Quran and the sunnah (exemplary teachings and practices of the Islamic prophet Muhammad), gave definitions of tasawwuf that described ethical and spiritual goals and functioned as teaching tools for their achievement. Many terms that described spiritual qualities and roles were used instead in more practical contexts.[1][2] Some modern scholars have used other definitions of Sufism such as 'intensification of Islamic faith and practice'[1] and 'process of realizing ethical and spiritual ideals'.[2] The term Sufism was originally introduced into European languages in the 18th century by Orientalist scholars, who viewed it mainly as an intellectual doctrine and literary tradition at variance with what they saw as sterile monotheism of Islam. In modern scholarly usage the term serves to describe a wide range of social, cultural, political, and religious phenomena associated with Sufis.[2]

2. Etymology

The original meaning of Sufi seems to have been 'one who wears wool (ṣūf)', and the Encyclopaedia of Islam calls other etymological hypotheses 'untenable'.[3][4] Woolen clothes were traditionally associated with ascetics and mystics.[4] Al Qushayri and Ibn Khaldun both rejected all possibilities other than ṣūf on linguistic grounds.[5] Another explanation traces the lexical root of the word to ṣafā (صفاء), which in Arabic means 'purity', and in this context another similar idea of Tasawwuf as considered in Islam is tazkiyah (تزكية, meaning self-purification), which is also widely used in Sufism. These two explanations were combined by the Sufi al-Rudhabari

(322 A.D.), who said, 'The Sufi is the one who wears wool on top of purity.'[6][7] Others have suggested that the word comes from the term ahl aṣ ṣuffah ('the people of the suffah or the bench'), who were a group of impoverished companions of Muhammad who held regular gatherings of dhikr, one of the most prominent companions among them was Abu Huraira. These men and women who sat at al-Masjid al-Nabawi are considered by some to be the first Sufis.[8][9]

3. History

3.1 Origins

Sufism existed as an individual inner practice of Muslims since early Islamic history.[10] According to Carl W. Ernst the earliest figures of Sufism are Muhammad himself and his companions (Sahabah).[11] Sufi orders are based on the bayāh (بَيْعَة bayāh, مُبَايَعَة mubāyāh 'pledge, allegiance') that was given to Muhammad by his Ṣahabah. By pledging allegiance to Muhammad, the Sahabah had committed themselves to the service of God.[12][13][11] Verily, those who give Baiāh (pledge) to you (O Muhammad) they are giving Baiāh (pledge) to Allah. The Hand of Allah is over their hands. Then whosoever breaks his pledge, breaks it only to his own harm, and whosoever fulfils what he has covenanted with Allah, He will bestow on him a great reward. [Translation of Quran, 48:10] Sufis believe that by giving bayāh (pledging allegiance) to a legitimate Sufi Shaikh, one is pledging allegiance to Muhammad; therefore, a spiritual connection between the seeker and Muhammad is established. It is through Muhammad that Sufis aim to learn about, understand, and connect with God.[14]

Ali is regarded as one of the major figures amongst the Sahaba who have directly pledged allegiance to Muhammad, and Sufis maintain that through Ali, knowledge about Muhammad and a connection with Muhammad may be attained. Such a concept may be understood by the hadith, which Sufi's regard to be authentic, in which Muhammad said, 'I am the city of knowledge, and Ali is its gate.'[15] Eminent Sufis such as Ali Hujwiri refer to Ali as having a very high ranking in Tasawwuf. Furthermore, Junayd of Baghdad regarded Ali as Shaikh of the principals and practices of Tasawwuf.[16] Historian Jonathan A.C. Brown notes that during the lifetime of Muhammad, some companions were more inclined than others to 'intensive devotion, pious abstemiousness and pondering the divine mysteries' more than Islam required, such as Abu Dharr al-Ghifari. Hasan al-Basri, a tabi, is considered a 'founding figure' in the 'science of purifying the heart'.[17] Practitioners of Sufism hold that in its early stages of development Sufism effectively referred to nothing more than the internalization of Islam.[18] According to one perspective, it is directly from the Qur'an, constantly recited, meditated, and experienced, that Sufism proceeded, in its origin and its development.[19] Other practitioners have held that Sufism is the strict emulation of the way of Muhammad, through which the heart's connection to the Divine is strengthened.[20]

3.2 As an Islamic discipline

Existing in both Sunni and Shia Islam, Sufism is not a distinct sect, as is sometimes erroneously assumed, but a method of approaching or a way of understanding the religion, which strives to take the regular practice of the religion to the 'supererogatory level' through simultaneously 'fulfilling ... [the obligatory] religious duties' and finding a way and a means of striking a root through the 'narrow gate' in the depth of the soul out into the domain of the pure arid unimpressionable Spirit which itself opens out on to the Divinity.[21] Academic studies of Sufism confirm that Sufism, as a separate tradition from Islam apart from so-called pure Islam, is frequently a product of Western orientalism and modern Islamic fundamentalists.[22] As a mystic and ascetic aspect of Islam, it is considered as the part of Islamic teaching that deals with the purification of the inner self. By focusing on the more spiritual aspects of religion, Sufis strive to obtain direct experience of God by making use of intuitive and emotional faculties that one must be trained to use.[23] Tasawwuf is regarded as a science of the soul that has always been an integral part of Orthodox Islam.[24] In his Al-Risala al-Safadiyya, ibn Taymiyyah describes the Sufis as those who belong to the path of the Sunna and represent it in their teachings and writings.

3.3 Growth of influence

Historically, Sufism became "an incredibly important part of Islam" and 'one of the most widespread and omnipresent aspects of Muslim life' in Islamic civilization from the early medieval period onwards, when it began to permeate nearly all major aspects of Sunni Islamic life in regions stretching from India and Iraq to the Balkans and Senegal. The rise of Islamic civilization coincides strongly with the spread of Sufi philosophy in Islam. The spread of Sufism has been considered a definitive factor in the spread of Islam, and in the creation of integrally Islamic cultures, especially in Africa [25] and Asia. The Senussi tribes of Libya and the Sudan are one of the strongest adherents of Sufism. Sufi poets and philosophers such as Khoja Akhmet Yassawi, Rumi, and Attar of Nishapur (1145A.D.–1221A.D.) greatly enhanced the spread of Islamic culture in Anatolia, Central Asia, and South Asia.[26][27] Sufism also played a role in creating and propagating the culture of the Ottoman world,[28] and in resisting European imperialism in North Africa and South Asia.[29]

4.   From Mysticism to Tradition: Conceptualizing Sufism

Sufism has often been defined as Islamic 'mysticism' comprising a set of techniques by which Muslims have sought a direct personal encounter with the divine. While it is true that Sufism encompasses many mystical elements, the broad social reach that it acquired over centuries of expansion rendered it much more than the path of an esoteric elite. In recognition of this problem, in his highly influential introduction to Sufism the Cambridge orientalist A. J. Arberry recognized that Sufism comprised the religious way of both the popular Muslim masses and the smaller number of elevated mystics.[30] For Arberry and for many later commentators, the tension in the model of a 'mystical' and a 'popular' Sufism was resolved through a narrative of decline: what had begun as a genuinely 'mystical' movement of individuals seeking personal communion with God was corrupted in the medieval period into a cult of miracle-working saints which held nothing in common with "true" Sufi mysticism. 'It was inevitable', wrote Arberry in scornful tones, 'as soon as legends of miracles became attached to the names of the great mystics', that the credulous masses should applaud imposture more than true devotion." [31] For Arberry as for many others writing in his wake, the consequence of this decline model was that from the later medieval period onwards Sufism was unworthy of study. This was if nothing else ironic, in that the medieval and early modern periods that saw Sufism reach its greatest influence and success were precisely those which were to be overlooked as the ages of post-classical decline. Over the past thirty years, this model of classicism and decline has been thoroughly rejected, and more recent scholarship on Sufism has done much to overturn the grand narrative of Arberry and such later decline theorists as J. S. Trimingham. [32]

Even so, in many discussions of Sufism key aspects of the older tendencies remain, not least the central problem with the earlier school of interpretation that was the model of 'mysticism' itself. As conceived by European and American scholars in the early twentieth century, the notion of mysticism relied on a culturally Protestant, temporally modernist and intellectually cosmopolitan construction of religion in which the authority of the solitary individual's direct, unmediated experience was seen to be the fountainhead of authentic religiosity across all cultures and all periods.[33] In similarly Protestant mode, 'religion' was itself regarded as a category properly (or at least preferably) distinct from the corruptive sphere of 'politics'. When these models were applied to the study of Islam, for many scholars the archetypal Sufi was the antithesis to the legalistic Muslim establishment, whether living in quietist seclusion from the affairs of the world or leading rebellions that ended in passionate martyrdoms.[34]

Prescriptive rather than descriptive, at times this model of mysticism served as a dogma. When applied to more distant cultural or temporal contexts from that where it developed, the model tended to castigate or exclude much of what it was meant to explain. In the case of Sufism, such exclusion or castigation concerned many important dimensions of Sufi history that did not fit the model of the individual God-seeker, from hierarchical Sufi brotherhoods and elaborate rituals of saintly intercession to influence over the decisions of sultans. Yet in contrast to the Western notion of the mystic, many aspects of Sufism were collective and public rather than individualistic and private.

The centrality of the master-disciple relationship that emerged as the keystone of Sufi practice shows that even such "mystical" procedures as the destruction of the ego were not the result of private experiences of direct contact with God but were social processes based on disciplinary relationships with human third parties. As Sufi fellowships grew larger, these relationships (and the joint socio-psychological transformations they fostered) became more and more commonplace, such that their effects became even more widespread and collective. In many regions of the world, Sufism has shaped the configuration of social authority into the authoritarian models explored by the North African anthropologist Abdellah Hammoudi. [35] Along with its neglect of the social, the concept of mysticism also downplayed the physical, placing Sufism firmly within the realms of spirituality when, from their embodied rituals and veneration of relics to their shrine buildings and the blessing powers they were believed to contain in their flesh and blood, Sufis were equally invested in the tangible realms of physicality.

Not so much a universally accessible 'mysticism' based on religious experiences which were democratically available to all, Sufism was in many settings an embodied Islam of authority based on blessing powers inherited through prestigious blood lineages. One anthropologist has thus defined Sufi Shaikh as "those in whose blood (recorded in personal genealogies) the Prophet's grace (baraka) flows." [36] The concept of mysticism also tends to be associated with the spontaneous and unrehearsed rather than the programmatic and political. Yet even the earliest handbooks on Sufi practice showed deep concerns with questions of etiquette and ceremony. Far from being a disinterested spiritual avantgarde, in many regions Sufis were major political players who enjoyed the comforts drawn from vast landholdings and the support of armies of devoted followers. Through the series of developments traced in this book, Sufism became sufficiently authoritarian and anti-individualistic that in the modern period the rise of democratizing and individualizing tendencies among Muslims led millions to desert the teachings of the Sufis in droves. Besides its narrowing and prescriptive tendencies, the model of mysticism also presents challenges to the writing of history. For if as "mysticism" the essence of Sufism lies in transcendental private experience, then historians are inevitably condemned to recording only its trivial outward shells by way of texts, institutions, and actions. There are certainly different ways of tackling this dilemma. One way (most thoroughly pursued by the French scholar Henry Corbin) is to maintain the mystical model by using a phenomenological approach to historical documents in an attempt to interpretively 'represent' the inward character of past mystical experiences. [37] In various degrees and styles, this phenomenological approach has been adopted in several successful introductions to Sufism. [38] Another way is to move away from the model of mysticism and to conceive Sufism in terms that not only fit better with its complex array of characteristics, but also render it more amenable to historical description. Downplaying the notion of Sufism as the mysticism of a marginal party of God-seekers, the approach taken in this book is to conceive Sufism as primarily a tradition of powerful knowledge, practices, and persons.[39] As the following chapters argue, from the very moment of its emergence, Sufism was rooted in a wider Muslim model of reliable knowledge in which the sanction and security of past authority (whether of the Prophet or of the saintly 'friends' of God) was of overwhelming importance. This historical sensibility even shaped a large proportion of Sufi mystical experiences by way of the countless visionary encounters Sufis recorded with past saints and prophets, encounters which fulfilled their desire to connect themselves with the past luminaries of their tradition. [40] This link to the normative and beloved exemplars of tradition is extremely important, for it points not only to the strategy by which the Sufis were able to present themselves as the living heirs of the Prophet. It also points to the axiomatically 'backward-looking' nature of their teachings which emerged because of this need for the sanction of past authority and to the existential desire to return to the state of human being enjoyed by the primordial Adam and Muhammad at the beginning of time.

As Steven T. Katz (a book entitled as 'Mysticism and Religious Traditions') has perceptively explained, far from being instantaneous and inventive, mystical experiences are often acting of conservatism; and we might add, of conservation.[41] This sense of the Sufis' deliberate rooting of their words and actions in the legacy of earlier Muslims also helps us recognize the pervasively Islamic character of Sufism that except in certain cosmopolitan cases has set Sufism apart from the universalist 'mysticism' into which it has sometimes been categorized. As the French scholar Marijan Mole once explained, even if the Sufis un/knowingly adapted elements from other religious groups, 'the Sufis have never wished to be anything other than Muslims; all the doctrines they profess, and all of their actions, customs and usages are based on an interpretation of the Quran and the Prophetic tradition.'[42] This is a key point: Sufism developed as a set of teachings, practices and institutions that emerged as Muslims from the ninth century onwards ruminated on the legacy of the earlier exemplary life of the Prophet Muhammad and the revelatory moment of the Quran. In their attempts to channel the knowledge, comfort, and authority of God (and his prophets and friends) into their private and public lives, Sufis built their tradition firstly by looking back to the time of the Prophet and revelation and secondly by looking back at the teachings and actions of those they identified as the saints who in turn connected them back to the Prophet's own communion with God. Whether in terms of texts they wrote, rituals they inaugurated or brotherhoods they founded, it was the many saintly 'Friends of God' or awliya. Allah who appeared in every century who constituted the tradition that we call Sufism. Except for certain modernist reformulations, without the saints there is no Sufism. Building on their early claim of inheriting the tradition of the Prophet, over time the Sufis gradually developed the wherewithal of their own tradition by way of lineages of saints and teachers whose sanction carried supplementary authority of its own. In the early centuries of Sufi history, this construction of a tradition in some cases involved the retrospective claiming as Sufis pious forebears who lived before the term Sufi was even used.

The emphasis placed here on tradition over mysticism is not to deny that many Sufis underwent mystical experiences which they subsequently held in high value. It is rather to make the point that these private experiences only acquired meaning and credibility through being absorbed into the collective and collaborative venture of different generations of Muslims who over the passage of time remained highly conscious of one another's exemplary actions and teachings. This sense of the historicity of mystical experience does not aim to reduce it, but rather to locate it in the temporal character of human existence. Steven T. Katz, who has written that 'mystical reports do not merely indicate the post-experiential description of an unreportable experience in the language closest at hand. Rather, the experiences themselves are inescapably shaped by prior linguistic influences such that the lived experience conforms to a pre-existent pattern that has been learned, then intended, and then actualized in the experiential reality of the mystic'.[43] As hundreds of Sufi writings make clear, for all the emphasis on spontaneous individual experience in the twentieth century model of mysticism, Sufis were always acutely conscious of their discursive links to past precedent. It was this consciousness of tradition that rendered them Sufi Muslims rather than charismatic lone stars or prophetic founders of new religions. It is ultimately this self-consciousness of individual Sufis as being members of a larger community reproduced across time through the sanction of authoritative past masters that renders them members and perpetuators of a tradition. For as the sociologist Edward Shils has written, tradition is not only that 'which is transmitted or handed down from the past', but also that which has exemplars or custodians.[44] Correspondingly, as with the exemplary models of the remembered Sufi saints of yore, "there is an inherently normative element in any tradition of belief which is presented for acceptance." [45]

In contrast to the older model of a mysticism of lone marginal individuals, this model of a powerful collective tradition is helpful for making sense of Sufi history on several levels. Firstly, it recognizes the crucial roles of third party external and past authorities in valorising individual experiences, decisions, teachings, and writings. Secondly, it recognizes the many nonspontaneous, authoritarian and at times anti-individualistic dimensions of Sufism. Thirdly, it suits the purposes of a historical survey since unlike the temporal collapsing that comes with the emphatic 'now' emphasis of mysticism, the tradition model shows how the recipients of tradition possess their own historical self-consciousness as persons living in a perpetual (if interpretive and often creative) relationship with their past. Fourthly and finally, it allows for the accumulative character of Sufism through its gradual emergence as a multi-generational cultural product that emerges in time, so allowing room for development and diversification. Pointing to this dynamism that is often disguised by the apparent consistency of tradition, Shils describes how "tradition might undergo very great changes, but its recipients might regard it as significantly unchanged." [46] It has been this backward-looking sense of the continuity of the teachings they regard as the legacy of the Prophet Muhammad to his saintly successors that allows us to define Sufism as a tradition in the terms defined by Edward Shils.

5.   From Marginality to Power: Contextualizing Sufism

Having addressed this issue of tradition as both concept and content, we must now turn to this book's contextual emphasis by way of its presentation of Sufis as powerful and influential social actors rather than as conscientious objectors acting from the margins of society. As with the book's switch of emphasis from mysticism to tradition, in its stress on the power rather than the marginality of the Sufis we are dealing with a question of re-emphasis rather than rejection. While there certainly were many marginal (as well as outright antinomian) Sufis, the argument made here is that it was due to its powerful rather than marginal followers that Sufism was able to leave so great an imprint on the societies through which it spread. A result of the historical processes and collective strategies explored in the following chapters, this acquisition of power was certainly gradual. But by the medieval and early modern periods, it was sufficiently real to allow us to speak in many regions of the Muslim world in terms of a Sufi social and religious "establishment." While there were many marginal and deviant Sufis who lived in this period, the Sufi establishment achieved and maintained its status by its members' successful self-presentation as embodiments of the normative Islam of the Prophet Muhammad and indeed as being nothing less than his living heirs. Even where anti-normative and socially marginal Sufi groups flourished (as in the case of the medieval qalandar movement) it is probably fair to say that their ability to get away with breaching social norms was itself a reflection of the power and prestige which Sufism held by their time. In speaking of the Sufis as powerful, we must delineate three main types of power which they will be seen acquiring in the following descriptions: discursive power, miraculous power, and economic power. Discursive power refers to the authority acquired by Sufism as a discourse comprising a legitimate vocabulary of words and concepts, influential models of society and cosmos, and exemplary paradigms of behaviour and morals. This discourse of Sufism was a configuration of tradition since it drew authority from connecting itself to the Quran and the Prophetic Example (or Sunna) of Muhammad. The discursive power which Sufism acquired through its association with the normative Prophetic Example points to the way in which Sufism was not merely a mode of experience or even belief, but a discourse with the power to shape other people's actions through their imitation of the exemplary models it provided. Moving us further beyond the emphasis on unmediated experience in the model of mysticism, this powerful ability to shape behaviour and action was also a function of tradition in the ability of traditions to foster enduring "patterns or images of actions" and "the beliefs requiring, recommending, regulating, permitting or prohibiting the re-enactment of those patterns."[47]

The second type of power which we will see the Sufis acquire was miraculous power through their widely perceived ability to work miracles and wonders as a result of their especial closeness to God. For A.J. Arberry, no less than many twentieth century reformist Muslim commentators, this widespread traffic in the miraculous represented "the dark side of Sufism in its last phase" when "its influence at its most degraded period was wholly evil." [48] Yet in a historical survey such as this, the aim must be to describe and understand rather than to moralize. Even though the twentieth centuries scientifically disenchanted and culturally Protestant model of mysticism drew a firm line of division between mystics and miracle-workers, the historical fact of the matter is that the Sufis' claim of working miracles was inseparable from their claim of mystical proximity to God. Once again, it is the saints whose words and deeds constituted Sufi tradition who must be positioned at center stage: the historical mystic was the saintly miracle worker. While there was always the occasional Muslim who challenged the Sufis' ability to wield such powers, as the following chapters show, from sultans and merchants to peasants and tribesmen, there were many more who sought to draw on these powers by entering relationships with the Sufis. And since, whether about knaves or kings, these were typically relationships of discipleship, the power to wreak miracles was in turn transformed into the currency of social influence. Drawing from and in turn cementing this social influence was the third of the forms of power which the Sufis acquired: economic power. For from the medieval period, prominent Sufis began to receive considerable (and in a few cases vast) endowments of landed property and real estate from disciples drawn from the ruling class as well as smaller offerings in cash or kind from their humbler followers. Despite their rhetoric of pious poverty, these forms of gift-exchange placed prominent Sufis among the tiny, privileged elite of the pre-industrial societies in which they operated till modern times. In this respect too, we see the functioning of Sufism as a tradition, since the need to transfer property through family lineages saw the material heirs of economically powerful Sufis configured in parallel as the heirs of the Sufi tradition.

Family Sufi lineages therefore typically passed down property alongside teachings and blessing power. Since no form of powerful knowledge can exist in isolation from material forms of power, the economic strength of Sufism was crucial to the overall profile it acquired and so ultimately the discursive, miraculous, and economic power of the Sufis were each interdependent. If there was once a tendency to see the emergence of such powerholding as compromising the piety of the Sufi message, to see even religious history in such value-laden terms is sentimental and romantic. Here again it is helpful to think of Sufism as a tradition, for no tradition is ever able to perpetuate and reproduce itself through time without recourse to the material resources that provide homes and stipends for the texts, rituals and remembrancers that constitute ritual as "that which is handed down." If in relation to many earlier presentations of Sufism, the shift in emphasis here towards power and tradition marks something of a Hobbesian turn, then this is perhaps a necessary corrective. For this sense of a powerful tradition not only renders more understandable the following the Sufis acquired, but also the opposition they increasingly provoked as their influence grew, whether from rival religious authorities in the medieval period, state-builders in the early modern period or Muslim reformers in the modern period. It is after all power, influence and privilege that typically garner the strategies of appropriation, incorporation and opposition that have so regularly punctuated the history of Sufism. If as a history of the Sufis rather than their rivals the following chapters inevitably place the Sufis into the spotlight, then the calls of their rivals from the shadows should be seen to echo the high status gained by Sufis proclaimed as the axis around which the whole cosmos turned.

6.   From Contexts to Characteristics: Defining Sufism

In offering an outline of the basic characteristics of Sufism, it is essential in a historical survey such as this to note first that the defining profile we are about to read emerged only gradually through the series of developments. This historicizing caveat accepted, we can now offer a basic definition of Sufism as a powerful tradition of Muslim knowledge and practice bringing proximity to or mediation with God and believed to have been handed down from the Prophet Muhammad through the saintly successors who followed him. From their earliest appearance, Sufis rarely perceived themselves to be anything other than Muslims and as Sufi tradition expanded its influence, for many millions of Muslims Islam appeared to be inseparable from Sufism. While convention prevents it, we might do better speaking of 'Sufi Islam' than of 'Sufism'. For, with the exception of certain antinomian ('rule-breaking') groups, Sufis have generally followed the lifeways of Islamic custom, offering regular formal worship (salah), keeping the fast in the holy month of Ramadan, and abiding by whatever form of Shari'a was observed in their community. Crucially, Sufis have also followed a series of supererogatory ('above what is required') exercises, most importantly the chanted 'remembrance' (dhikr) of God; meditation (muraqaba) on different aspects of the psyche and God; the cultivation of moral virtues (ihsan) through the observance of formal rules of etiquette (adab); and respectful interaction (suhba) with their master. Some (though by no means all) groups of Sufis used the ritualized listening (sama') to music and poetry as a means to reach ecstatic states (ahwal) in which they were brought closer to God or the saints. Sufis have long emphasized that all such practices must be pursued under the direction of a master (murshid) who has been a recipient of the tradition and so (in theory, at least) already trodden this path beforehand. Rituals of initiation into such a 'Path' or brotherhood and its accompanying pledge of allegiance (bay'a) to a master marked the formal entry to discipleship. While such initiations have often been undertaken by adult Muslims seeking spiritual enlightenment, in practice many Muslims received such initiations as children, assuring them of the social and supernatural protection of their masters on their own paths through life. In theory, the purpose of entering a brotherhood has been to learn the practices of adab (etiquette), dhikr (chanting) and muraqaba (meditation) passed down by its masters, with the aim of experiencing the destruction (fana) of the lower self (nafs) that leads to the survival (baqa) of the higherself (ruh). Mapped out as formal "places" (maqamat) on the ascent towards God, such experiences have been seen as lending Sufis the authority to guide to chastise and even punish other Muslims.

The claim to have passed through these 'places' on the way to God has meant that both during and after their lifetimes the most celebrated masters have been regarded as the special intimates or 'Friends' (auliya) of God. The most venerated and feared of these saints have been seen as living 'interfaces' (barzakh) between the human and divine worlds, serving as intermediaries between the ordinary believer and the celestial hierarchy of the saints, prophets, and God. In varying degrees all of the saintly masters have been regarded as having access to God's divine qualities by way of their special knowledge (ma'rifa) and their ability to work miracles (karamat). If claims to predict the future and make protective talismans have in modern times been seen as belonging more to the realm of 'superstition' than 'mysticism', then they have both been important services which disciples have asked of their Sufi masters. Given the centrality of these ties between disciples and masters, far from being the individualistic pursuit of personal liberation, Sufism can be regarded as the sum of similar sets of relationships: between saints and their followers; between the readers and writers of Sufi texts; between the Prophet, the mediating master, and the humble believer; between the subjects and objects of the devotion that has been the emotional heartbeat of Sufi tradition. Insofar as Sufis have pursued personal quests for salvation, they have usually done so by navigating these relationships between the living and the dead, the physical and the textural, the visible and invisible. It is this quintessentially relational profile of Sufism that has positioned its various expressions and exponents at the center of so many Muslim societies, which were themselves bound together by sets of relationships that became infused and intertwined with the blessed bonds of the Sufis.

7. The Narrative in Overview

Following pages present is a narrative history of the emergence of Sufi tradition and the social and geographical expansion that attended its gradual acquisition of power and prestige. The need for a coherent and flowing narrative has meant that there is little explicit evaluation of different primary or secondary source materials, and so for critical evaluations of the historiography students should refer to the recent review articles written by such scholars as myself, Alexander Knysh and Dina Le Gall. [49] To help readers place the Sufis into larger conceptions of Islamic, comparative and ultimately global history, the narrative is divided into four conventional periods, albeit periods which are argued as enclosing distinct developments within Sufi history itself. Further the periods of the early medieval period (800–1100), the medieval period (1100–1400), the early modern period (1400–1800) and the modern period (1800–2000) are described. Yet, unlike in previous surveys of Sufism, approximately equal space is devoted to each of the four periods, though given that the earlier periods have received much fuller synthetic coverage it is fair to say that specialists will find much detailed information.

However, in pursuing the incrementally global expansion of the Sufis, and particularly coverage for regions in Africa, Central, South and Southeast Asia and ultimately Europe that have usually been seen as marginal to the Sufis' supposedly Middle Eastern 'homelands. Even if individual readers do in places find themselves on familiar ground, it is hoped that the scope of coverage and the overall model of a tradition being gradually elaborated and distributed to so many different contexts lend originality to the narrative. The risk of attempting to cover so much material within a single volume is a loss of clarity amid the overall mass of data, especially in the periods which saw Sufism increasingly expand in the early modern and modern eras. For this reason, it may be useful at this point to lay out in the simplest terms the overall interpretation of Sufi history that is embedded in the narrative. The argument in outline is that Sufi tradition was gradually constructed in the early medieval period among the same circles. In the ninth and tenth centuries, a disparate group of thinkers based in Iraq and Iran wrote a series of Arabic works that became foundational in the sense of providing the lexical and conceptual resources that would be passed down to subsequent generations. Adopted as loanwords into various Muslim languages, this Sufi lexicon, and the discursive models it elaborated would still lay the conceptual framework for Sufis in modern times. [50]

From the early eleventh century, the third and fourth generation of Sufis built on the sometimes-contradictory ideas of these early theorists by constructing lineages and pedigrees for their teachings that would link them back in time to the Prophet. From this moment forwards, this backward-looking tendency became crucial to the historical self-consciousness that constituted the teachings of individual Sufis as a tradition that they could present as the higher doctrine passed down unbroken from the Prophet Muhammad himself. While then expanding into new frontier regions in Southeast Asia no less than Africa during the early modern period, the Sufis were able to maintain this establishment status even amid their increasing incorporation into more powerful imperial states and the crisis of conscience that followed the turn of the Muslim millennium in 1591. Amid the tumultuous collapse of Muslim commercial and political power in the modern era, Sufism was among the few premodern Muslim institutions to survive European colonization substantially intact. As the embodiments of Prophetic no less than Sufi tradition in the many societies in which they still possessed landholdings and controlled networks of teaching and initiation, the continued prominence of the Sufis in the nineteenth century saw them pulled in different directions by the demands of both local followers and colonial rulers. Entering the twentieth century in many cases confirmed in their high status by recent alliances with colonial no less than Muslim states, the oppositional politics of Islamic reform rendered this Sufi establishment the natural target of competition and critique. While at the end of the twentieth century many millions of Muslims maintained their ties to the dead saints and living teachers of Sufi tradition, and globalization allowed entrepreneurial Sufi distributors of tradition to find new followers in America and Europe, for educated Muslims in particular Sufism had come to represent corruption, superstition, and backwardness. It is finally worth clarifying what is intended by the book's use of the term 'global'. What is 'global' about the history presented here is not a direct engagement with the literature on globalization theory, but an attempt to provide coverage of each region of the planet to which Sufism expanded over the course of more than a thousand years. This incrementally global coverage is, moreover, pursued as a history of connectivity, showing Sufism to be a cultural technology of inter-regional connection and exchange. Ranging from the Eastern and Western Mediterranean to Central and South Asia in the medieval period to gradually reach into Southeast Asia, China and Africa in the early modern period and ultimately Western Europe, North America and even Australia by the early twentieth century, it is a reasonable claim that the scale of Sufi expansion was indeed global.

More substantially, the narrative attempts to outline some of the processes by which a religious tradition formed in a particular spatial and temporal (no less than linguistic and discursive) context was transformed adapted, vernacularized, institutionalized through its introduction to new environments on an incrementally global scale. And on the other side of the coin, the narrative traces the problems that such global expansion presented to Sufism because of its adaptation to so many different milieux, particularly during its most rapid geographical expansion during the "globalizing" early modern and modern eras. When this global strategy of adaptation combined with the economic and political upsets of the ages of globalizing capitalism and colonialism, it fed into a Muslim crisis of conscience that sought to reform and ultimately suppress the tradition that the Sufis had cherished and promoted over the past millennium. The cultural adaptation of tradition through incorporation of local vernaculars and customs was thence set in reverse by Sufis and ultimately anti-Sufis who sought to strip back the 'accretional' momentum of tradition through a renewed emphasis on Arabic learning and the Prophetic Sunna. By the beginning of the twentieth century, when Muslims came into ever closer contact with European forms of knowledge, a Sufism that had ridden the wave of Islam's early modern global expansion increasingly became a casualty of its own earlier success. There was, then, an inherent push-pull dynamic that reveals itself through such a long-term and globally distributive survey.

8.   Origin, Foundation and Rivalries (850A.D. - 1100 A.D.)

The place is Baghdad, and the year is around 850. It is over eight hundred miles of desert from where the Prophet announced his revelation in Mecca and more than two hundred years since he died. Although the word sufi ('wool-wearer') has been around for many years as a nickname or even a reproach for the hermits of the surrounding wilderness, for the first time it is being used to refer to people in the city itself. And unlike the obscure and self-effacing renouncers in the mountains and desert, these men in the city not only wrote books telling others how to behave, but also achieved enough prominence in the eyes of their contemporaries and successors to have their books discussed and preserved. By the mid-ninth century, eight generations of fathers and sons have lived since Muhammad established his community of Muslims and in its third capital the pious and the scholarly among the heirs of that community were more conscious than ever of the responsibilities of preserving the Prophet's message in his absence. It is a time of unprecedented productivity, legal and moral, spiritual, and intellectual; from the legacy of the Prophet and the first generations of Muslims, the many meanings of Islam are being created (and debated and sometimes suppressed). Over the past generation, the learned have found a new medium to publicize and exchange their ideas, for the city's great trade routes have brought paper from China to replace parchment and papyrus.

Many books are being written and Islam itself is acquiring the meanings, variations, and institutions that later generations will inherit and push back into the lifetime of the Prophet or the words of the Quran he revealed. If the paper trail left by the early Sufis does not take the historian beyond this early ninth century period, then the same can be said for the codification of such other key Islamic institutions as the Law (shari'a) and the Prophetic Example (sunna). The small group of people being called Sufis in Baghdad by around 850 A.D. were not wholly separate in their concerns from the men who thought through the implications of legal principle or sought ways of distinguishing true from false reports of the Prophet's words and deeds. While in later times and other places, to be called a Sufi might mean many different things, here where the term first caught on, it signified individuals who were especially scrupulous in their behavior and piety. Such was their devotion to God, and their distaste for the pleasures of the world, that at first literally and over time metaphorically they donned the hot, coarse, and stinking garments of wool that lent them their name: the Sufis or "wool-wearers. Since the middle of the nineteenth century, academics have sought 'origins' of Sufism in the period prior to that outlined above, it is worth reiterating just exactly what we do (and do not) have in Baghdad by the middle of the ninth century when the earliest reliable data on the Sufis emerged. What we have is primarily a nickname or designator (sufi) being applied to certain people in the Baghdad region (some of whom left written records) and, as we will see below, arguably also far beyond Baghdad (who left no written records). But what we do not have yet is a Sufi movement, a characteristic set of doctrines and still less a tradition, all of which would develop only later. For this reason, it makes little sense to talk about 'Sufism' as though such an entity had any meaningful existence at this time.

Rather, we can say that by the mid-800s there were people being called Sufis whose teachings would gradually (and, moreover, retrospectively) be sifted and appropriated in the following generations as growing numbers of people came to call themselves Sufis and to formulate rituals, doctrines, and dress to distinguish themselves from others and to construct a self-conscious historical pedigree to give weight to their truth claims. By maintaining this distinction between the label and the person, between the word and the referent, we will also be better equipped to navigate the first of the historical problems we need to address the origins of Sufism.

8.1   The problem of Sufi Origins

It would be scarcely an exaggeration to say that more academic ink has been spilt over the origins of the Sufis than over any other question in Sufi history. A good example of this shared symbolic (and indeed linguistic) vocabulary is seen in the term sufi itself. Despite a range of alternative purported etymologies (including the Greek sophia, "wisdom"), the term has now been generally accepted as a derivative of the Arabic word for wool (suf), so as we have seen rendering a sufi someone who wears a woolen garment. The most thorough investigator of the history of the term has argued that it was first used in a Christian rather than an Islamic milieu to refer to a deviating trend that emerged in the late sixth century among the Nestorian Christians of Seleucia-Ctesiphon, around twenty miles south of where Baghdad would be founded in 762.[51] While the official land of the Nestorian Church was Syriac, over the decades after the

Arab conquests of the region in the years after the Prophet Muhammad's death in 632, many Nestorians lost their ability to understand Syriac and so required Church edicts to be made in Arabic. It was this Arabic Christian vernacular that spread the terms labis alsuf ('clad in wool') and in turn Sufi to refer to a particular group of Christian ascetics in Iraq, with whom early Muslim ascetics shared both word and practice as "an identification with a humble, lowly status and a recognition of values other than material."[52]

Initially, there is the question of the degree of importance we are willing to lend to a name and the sub-question of whether that name and its "original" etymological meaning had a direct or arbitrary relationship to the persons, ideas or activities to which it came to refer in later Muslim contexts. In a classic study of seventy eight early Muslim definitions of the terms Sufi and its derivative tasawwuf ("to wear wool" or "to become a Sufi"), only one was found that referred to the wearing of wool and few others that referred to ascetic practices more generally, with the vast majority defining the terms by way of moral values and ethical dispositions.[53] This evidence appears to break the link between the Muslim and purported Christian meanings of the word Sufi so as to suggest that in the different contexts of its usage the things to which the word referred were quite distinct. But the problem here too is that while these seventy-eight definitions are attributed to early ninth century figures, they only survive as quotations in much later sources

Secondly, there is the more substantive problem of whether there was a Muslim adaptation of Christian practices as well as words and the sub-question of whether that adaptation shaped the actual activities of those Muslims being called sufi in the ninth century. Here it is worth returning to the model of a semiotic and in some cases linguistic vocabulary that Muslims and Christians shared rather than exclusively owned. It is important here that we consider the context, in that during the first couple of centuries of Islamic history, the environment in which Muslims lived in such regions as Syria, Iraq and Egypt was one in which they were outnumbered by Christians.

More thoroughly Christianized than even Western Europe at this time, the Middle Eastern Fertile Crescent was a landscape of churches, monasteries, and saintly shrines. These sites and their occupants were not only given legal protection by the new Muslim empires but were also in various ways coopted by their Muslim rulers. Tombs of Christian saints and prophets were recognized as Muslim pilgrimage centers, monasteries served Muslims as wine-serving country clubs for poets and as libraries for literati; and Christian scholars helped translate into Arabic the heritage of Graeco-Roman thought that had been selectively preserved by the Christians forefathers.[54] It has long been recognized that the wearing of wool points to similarities with the ascetic activities of the Eastern Christians, particularly in Syria, where between 661 A.D. and 750 A.D. the Muslims had kept their capital at Damascus before the shift to Iraq with the ascent of the Abbasid dynasty. Reacting to nineteenth century fashions for seeking the origins of the Sufis in Indian thought, scholars in the 1930s uncovered detailed evidence on the similarities between Christian and Muslim 'ascetics' and it was argued that this common ascetic heritage prepared the way for the Sufis' development into fully-fledged 'mystics' more concerned with experience and knowledge than with punishing the body.[55]

In its simplest form, the method has been to place evidence on Christian and Muslim activities side by side, to point to simi larities and wherever possible evidence of direct contact between them, and to use this as evidence for the influence of the Christians on the Muslims, pointing to such similarities as prayer patterns, sayings and attitudes as well as clothing.[56] But here the debate on origins moves in two directions whose different implications need to be carefully For scholars writing in the 1930s, in both the Muslim and Christian case the isolation and self-mortification of asceticism was a natural (indeed, universal) cradle for the development of 'mysticism'. The latter was regarded in turn as a universal urge aimed at "a knowledge of Ultimate reality, and finally at the establishment of a conscious relation with the Absolute, in which the soul shall attain to union with God".[57] In other words, this interpretation presents a developmental model of history in which asceticism is not an end in itself but must mature and blossom in to mysticism, which is what the author cited the Sufis as being involved with.

In recent decades, closer investigation into the discussions that surrounded early Muslim 'asceticism' (zuhd) has cast seri ous doubt on this notion of a seamless flow between the zahid 'ascetic' and the sufi 'mystic' by showing the degree to which self-mortification, seclusion and above all celibacy were denounced as deviations from the sunna or Prophetic Example.[58] Zahid 'ascetics' did not maturely blossom into Sufi 'mystics': instead the voices of the zuhhad were muted by the more successful Sufis' marginalization and eventual replacement of them. Through a form of historical structuralism, it has been argued that the Sufi debt to Nestorian Christianity could thereby be traced through the repetition of doctrinal or biographical patterns found first in Christian works and later in Sufi writings.[59] One example is the writings of the seventh century Iraqi Christian, Isaac of Nineveh, whose threefold model of the soul's ascent through a series of triad clusters of activities and virtues has been interpreted as reappearing in later Sufi elaborations of their own path.[60] The fullest exercise in this vein has been carried out on the biographical accounts of

Rabi'a (d.801), the celebrated female Muslim ascetic of Basra in southern Iraq whom the Sufis would claim as one of their forerunners, and here the method has shown with some success how the Muslim legends of Rabi'a drew on older Christian narratives of penitent prostitutes.[61] But even if we accept that certain configurations of ideas were transmitted, ultimately we are left with no clearer understanding of how this happened and for historians this need for a clear explanation of how something happened is as important as the evidence that it did. As in the older type of intellectual history that once dominated the study of Sufism, without an understanding of process we are presented with texts which are supposedly connected, but with no sense of the readers who are meant to have connected them.

As we will see in more detail below, the problem is that the chief sources on these forebear's date from much later (in many cases, several centuries later) than their own lifetimes. As in the case of Rabi'a, the biographies of such other purported Sufi forerunners as the Central Asians Ibrahim-ibn-Adham (d.777), Fudayl-ibn 'Iyad (d.803) and Bishr-ibn-al-Harith (d.841) and the Egyptian Dhu'I-Nun (d.861) became enmeshed with tropes and motifs that drew on folklore as much as fact.[62] As we have already seen, in the middle 800s there was as yet no Sufi tradition, nor even a coherent movement, merely a group of often quite distinct individuals being nick named Sufis. The point is therefore not so much whether men such as Ibrahim-ibn-Adham existed, nor even whether they were part of an earlier trend towards asceticism. It is rather a question of, first, whether they can be seen as having constituted in any way a coherent group over such vast distances and, second, whether they can be seen as having constituted a trend or trajectory that the Sufis inherited rather than suppressed. In historicist terms, these problems concerning the origins of the Sufis are therefore magnified by an emphasis on the vertical transmission of cause and influence, which stresses the inheritance of ideas over their rejection and the transformation of movements over their suppression. The fact of the matter is that, as in the early history of Christianity, the first centuries of Islam were a period of intense competition between producers of often radically contrasting versions of the faith in which patterns of political allegiance, economic activity, everyday etiquette, and legal restraint were subjects of intensive and at times violent debate. Rather than search for a neat and multi-generational transformation from asceticism to mysticism that has long characterized the study of early Sufi history, by looking at each stratum of time we can see the discontinuities and differences that allow us to assess whether the ideas and actions of the previous generation were perpetuated or rejected.

Following the later biographies written by the Sufis themselves, historians have traditionally taken the zuhhad to have been "Sufis-in-waiting." But by putting the ascetics into the circumstances of their own time, we can see how they served very different purposes and sought very different goals from the Sufis who emerged in later centuries. The eighth century heyday of the zuhhad was a period in which Muslims were still a minority group in their own imperial domains and in which the consolidation of their conquests left frontier regions under the perpetual threat of reconquest.[63] It was in these border regions that many zuhhad ascetics such as Ibrahim ibn Adham flourished, serving in frontier wars in which their religious devotion and robust asceticism brought them not only success in battle but the renown that would pass on their names to future generations. Of course, not all the early Muslim zuhhad ascetics were frontier warriors and many of them probably did spend more time conversing with than fighting with Christians. But what becomes clear by looking at these figures in their own troubled times is that the Muslim ascetics of the eighth century were not only more complicated figures than the teleological role of the 'protomystic' would make them: they were also plainly distinct figures with quite different social roles and moral agendas from the people who from the mid-ninth century would be called Sufis in the more peaceable cities of Iraq rather than the frontiers in Syria or Central Asia. As the subsequent historical writings of the Sufis themselves show, in which the Sufis sought to present the earlier ascetics as their own forebears, the search for antecedents often tells us more about the quest for legitimacy than the processes by which ideas and movements take shape. Rather than attempt to trace the developments of one period in the quite distinct circumstances of its predecessors, let us instead remain in the "horizontal" period and circumstances in which a small number of Muslims acquired the nickname Sufi and see if we can do better explaining their origin in their own stratum of time rather than in those that preceded them.

8.2   The Sufis of Iraq (800 A.D. – 900 A.D.)

By the early ninth century, asceticism was falling into widespread dispute among the urban scholars who were becoming an increasingly important voice in Muslim society. This was a period in which the early Islamic model of a community led by a single figure belonging to the family of Muhammad (alternatively a caliph or an imam) was being replaced by new notions of authority whose different formulations lent varying weight to reason and piety, mastery of the scriptures and charismatic closeness to God. Taking their lead from their readings of Graeco-Roman philosophy in the championing of reason, the Muslim philosophers called falasifa in imitation of the Greek and the rationalist theologians called Mu'tazilites were particularly influential in Baghdad in the ninth century.[64] In the early decades of the century, the rationalist party was sufficiently influential in its championing of reason over revelation to persuade the leader of the Muslim empire, the Caliph al-Ma'mun (r.813–833), to initiate an 'inquisition' or mihna which for eighteen years sought to enforce the doctrine that the Quran was not a pre-eternal text but was created in the contextual time of history.[65] On the other side of the debate were various scholars who sought to uphold the authority of revelation, not least because it seemed to offer firmer (as it were constitutional) grounds for law-making, which struck many as less amenable than reason to manipulation by the ruling class. Based on the premise that Muslims constitute a moral rather than a political community united by their commitment to the message of the Quran and the Example or sunna of the Prophet as recorded in the Hadith, this 'constitutional bloc' nonetheless maintained a special place for the 'ulama ('men of learning') who had the textual expertise to decide on what the message of the Quran and Hadith actually was.[66] On the other side were those who remained loyal to the older Muslim notion of authority and religious knowledge being vested in a single person and, though their ideas too took many decades to develop, they kept their old nickname of the 'partisans' or Shi'a of their first leader, the Prophet's son-in-law, 'Ali.

This context of contentious debates and cultural resources is important because it prevents us from falling prey to the notion that as 'mystics' the Sufis were primarily people who sought a direct relation- ship with God and thereby had little need for the guidance of scripture and Prophetic Example. It will also prevent us from assuming that the Sufis were from their inception in a position of rivalry with the scholars or 'ulama.[67] Given that in this period much of these figures' dealings with the Quran and Hadith were through oral memorization rather than regular resort to written codices, the term 'discursiveness' would be more accurate than 'bookishness', but the overall point remains that the Sufis and 'ulama were likewise invested in the discourses of oral and written texts, with the Sufis debating the degree to which experience shed light on the true meanings of these texts.[68] There were probably many people in this period who had direct encounters with God that had nothing to do with scripture and there were certainly those among the early Sufis who claimed that their experiential pursuit of tahqiq ('realization, verification') rendered their knowledge claims superior to those relying solely on scripture.

In situating the earliest Sufis in their own 'horizontal' time, then, we need to recognize their emergence as belonging to the development of a wider scholar class that was not only equipped with knowledge of Quran, Hadith, and the specialist skills of interpreting them, but was also gaining increasing social authority by dint of both possessing such textual or discursive knowledge and putting its righteous example into practice.

While there would be exceptions, the general rule would remain through future centuries that whether as lawyers, poets, metaphysicians or moralists, successful Sufis were rarely far from pen and paper or from the Hadith and Quran that laid the foundations of Muslim learning. And yet the early Sufis were not only men of the pen and their claims to experiential knowledge should be seen as placing them not wholly distinctly from the emergent scholarly class but as a special sub-or-even splinter group with much in common with the scholars but with an additional claim to the authority of direct contact with the divine realms. Crucially, they also adopted the Quran's vocabulary to create a scripturally sanctioned terminology for the spiritual exercises and forms of experience that they added to the religious repertoire of other members of the scholarly class. This was therefore not a passive form of knowledge and if we have emphasized the Sufis' relationship with books, then we must be clear about their way of using books those were tools for contemplation on the one hand and for action on the other. These material factors fed into the culture of reading that developed around them, albeit with the proviso that religious texts took longer to be committed to paper than such secular texts as poems, scientific works, and cookbooks. As in other manuscript societies in which book use existed within a larger framework of oral forms of learning, books were read deeply and repeatedly, a process sometimes compounded by the requirement of either writing out one's own copy of a text or wholeheartedly memorizing it to acquire it. This sense of reading as an active engagement with the scripture enables us to tackle another of the key debates around the origins of Sufism. Often seen as the 'internalist' counterpart to the 'externalist' of Sufi origins in Christian or other non-Muslim influences, the idea that Sufism originated in the Quran has found its greatest proponents among Francophone and more recently American scholars.[69] Tracing the origins of the technical vocabulary or Sufi lexicon that the first generations of Sufis developed in their writings has demonstrated that this was overwhelmingly a vocabulary of Quranic origin. Critics of the theory have used what they see as the dry, sectarian or narrative tone of the Quran to argue that even on its own evidence, the Quran cannot have been the source for the doctrines of the Sufis: "the [Quranic] text is noteworthy for its rigour and severity, and the mystics of Islam have had to work hard to produce inner meanings which reflect personal communion with God."[70]

So, the question becomes not whether Sufism 'originated' in the Quran in the passive sense of the verb, but whether the Sufis of the ninth century used the Quran as a resource to understand the world around them and to create ways of morally, intellectually and practically interacting with it.[71] There is nothing wrong with asking whether the Sufis made their ideas originate from the holy book, since this is precisely how scriptures are read. The Hadith was used in similar ways, with different groups using the many thousands of often contradictory reports of the Prophet's words or deeds to defend or criticize their own and others' actions. Like the Quran, the Hadith was not an "agent" or necessarily even a "source" of religious movements, but rather a resource which like their other contemporaries the Sufis deployed in the elaboration and defense of their teachings. Finally, the Quran also found use among the Sufis as a source of the chanted phrases that made up the Sufi practice of chanted "remembrance of God" or dhikr (a term itself taken from the Quran). In such contexts, its words functioned not so much as purveyors of linguistic meaning than as sonic provokers of altered states. In this way, we can see how the early Sufis used the distinct discursive resources of the past (scripture and the Prophetic Example) to create their own "way" and to root it in the legitimate sources of authority which were recognized by their contemporaries. Words have histories and so change meaning over time, and in the different times and places in which they are read, the preserved words of scripture are used to point to different referents in the world than those to which they pointed in the time and place in which the scripture was written. So, in the Baghdad of the middle 800s, the Quran was used as a lexical source for a terminology which had different meanings and referred to different activities, virtues, and emotions than it did for the Muslim readers of earlier generations.

Since the Iraq of this period was a far more complex and cosmopolitan society than the Arabia in which the Quran had taken shape, the actions, and ideas to which its vocabulary was attached at that later time were necessarily different. Given the day-to-day cultural exchanges that went on in ninth century Iraq, it would be surprising if some of the actions or ideas to which the Quran's words were attached were not adapted from the many non-Muslims of the region. This is the way scripture operates. When a modern American Christian responds to the Biblical recommendation of charity by writing a check, she is not being any less Christian because such banking procedures were invented in the Dutch Republic rather than Roman Palestine. Ultimately, then, the problem of whether Sufism originated in the Quran or in Christian borrowings is a false one that simplifies the way in which scripture was read and religious ideas and actions were produced.

Among the circles of specialist interpreters of the Quran and Hadith, the early Sufis were closer to the trend defending revelation and tradition over reason. Far from being rule-breaking libertines or spirit- filled radicals, we should probably picture them as a broadly conservative crowd. Instead of fleeing from society like the earlier ascetics, they were often fierce upholders of the emerging moral and legal order. Perhaps the most important certainly the best known among these figures who rejected the showiness (riya) of the ascetics in favor of the mastery of the moral rather than the physical self was Muhasibi of Baghdad (857A.D.).[72] A case has been made that Muhasibi could not have been a Sufi because he was a moralizing theologian rather than a mystic, and indeed in his extant writings he never referred to himself as a Sufi.[73] Muhasibi was also important in terms of providing intellectual resources for the construction of Sufi tradition, for the Sufis of subsequent generations would claim Muhasibi as one of their own. This was a crucially important part of the process we are tracing of the development of a Sufi "tradition" that was at times a retrospective act of claiming prestigious persons and respectable or otherwise useful ideas. For these purposes, Muhasibi was important for developing the key idea and practice that would gradually set the Sufis apart from the other pietists among whom we have positioned them. This practice which lent him his name as the 'self-reckoner' (Muhasibi) was the scrupulous inspection of the lower, carnal self that the Quran referred to as the nafs (note the resort to Quranic vocabulary).[74] Here in discursive as well as practical terms was the 'inward turn' that set Sufis apart from their more externally demonstrative rivals, whether the ascetic zuhhad or the moralizing People of the Hadith. Since the doctrines of the Baghdad Sufis of the ninth and tenth century would form the foundations of subsequent Sufi tradition, the following pages trace these doctrines in some detail, since the key concepts and the Arabic vocabulary to which they were attached would later be transmitted to Sufis as far away as the oases of the Sahara and the spice islands of the Indian Ocean.

8.3   Kharraz of Baghdad (899A.D)

By the middle of the ninth century, in Baghdad as well as in Basra to the south, there were many people being called Sufis. But in terms of both contemporary fame and posthumous emulation, one of the most important was Abu Sa'id, known as al- Kharraz ("the cobbler").[75] We know very little with certainty about the life of Kharraz, except that he travelled widely, visiting not only the holy cities of Jerusalem and Mecca (where he remained for eleven years), but also Egypt and one of the cities named Tunisia. His name tells us that at least at some point in his life he worked as a cobbler, pointing towards the urban artisanal milieu that we will see recurring among other early Sufis. Kharraz's main work was the Kitab al-Sidq (Book of Truthfulness), which seems to have been composed for a broader scholarly than a narrowly sectarian readership, though he also penned several shorter treatises or risalas devoted to more specific and complex questions and probably intended for a smaller and more like-minded readership. Given the tendency of many accounts of Sufi thought to strip away the cultural shell in search of the mystical kernel, it is worth first pointing out the distinctively Islamic character of Kharraz's writings. As in countless other Sufi works of future generations, Kharraz proved his points by presenting supporting quotations from earlier Muslim authorities, whether from the Quran and Hadith or from the scholars and ascetics of the previous two centuries, so using the past that we have already described as a resource for such writers to draw on. Although there was not yet a distinctly Sufi tradition to draw on the writings of Kharraz's generation would themselves serve as the earliest resources for such a distinct tradition to be created over the next few generations there was already an abundant Islamic tradition to draw on in support of one's ideas. Recognizing this Islamic, discursive context is important because it prevents us from falling too easily into line with older tendencies in understanding the early Sufis as mystics in search of raw experience.

On the one pointer, keeping in mind the Islamic content of Kharraz's writings prevents us from too easily stripping away what were to Kharraz and his readers the Islamic foundations of his teachings to present his work as a naked structure of ideas in order to make possible the claim that "his work reads very much like the [Christian] treatises of Isaac of Nineveh".[76] On the other hand, recognizing the intertextual process by which Kharraz and other Sufis constructed their own texts by drawing on (and in some cases, as we will see later, by baldly plagiarizing) authoritative earlier texts, we can avoid the assumption that as 'mystics' the Sufis constructed their writings primarily from the raw material of their own transcendental experiences. The experience was interpreted and gained its meanings through resort to the vocabulary and concepts developed through the Sufis' active reading of Quran and Hadith, such that experience, and text formed part of a creative range. By the same token, Kharraz defended the authority of the Prophets (who were dead) over that of the self-proclaimed awliya allah or 'Friends of God' (many of whom were living). While drawing on and positioning himself within this normative background, Kharraz did make important contributions to the development of what would soon become the distinct proprietary method of the Sufis. In the Kitab al-Sidq, he outlined a series of moral attributes that the sincere Muslim must acquire if (in the words of the Quran as cited by Kharraz) he "hopes to meet his Lord".[77] Kharraz's concern with 'truthfulness' (sidq) was an echo of the critique of ostentatious asceticism we have already seen emerging and as he recorded it himself his aim was to show truthfulness as at once a 'theoretical knowledge' (Urn) and a 'practical science' (fiqh), both of these designations conceived within the framework of Islamic categories that were emerging at this time among Muslim scholars of all persuasions, including the law-makers.[78] Although we are now more used to speaking in terms of 'spiritual development', we are perhaps better off thinking of the principles Kharraz outlined as moral conditions, in that to speak of 'spiritual' devel opment in the absence of action in the world would be to misconstrue the whole tenor of his message in which spiritual development was meaningless if not accompanied by good action. In doing so, Kharraz used what would become the central metaphor of Sufi doctrine: that the Sufi method can be understood as a 'Path' (tariqa) that guides one safely on the journey towards the state of harmony with God that is Islam. Despite arguing for the existence of seven elite classes of humankind, in other respects Kharraz sought to reduce the status of persons whose proximity and absorption in God led them to be considered his special 'Friends' (auliya).[80] While like other Muslims of his day, Kharraz certainly accepted the existence of such saintly figures, he was adamant that their status did not exceed that of the Prophets (anbiya). The implication was that whatever God revealed to his Friends was lower in authority and status to what he revealed to his Prophets: even a Friend of God could not command one to break the laws or deny the revelations brought by the Prophets. While expanding the ways and numbers of people who might have direct contact with God, Kharraz was therefore at the same time restricting the authority that such contact granted over other members of society.

8.4   Tustari of Basra (d.896)

By the second half of the ninth century, the question of the relationship between Prophets and Friends (and thence of the ordinary Muslims in fealty to them) was already a pressing one. Around three hundred and fifty miles to the south of Baghdad in the city of Basra, the question was also being addressed by Kharraz's contemporary, Sahl-ibn-Abdullah Tustari (d.896). Like Kharraz and many other Muslim scholars of the period, Tustari traveled widely in his lifetime and, though he grew up in the Iranian town of Tustar that gave him his name, he made the pilgrimage to Mecca, resided in several towns in Iraq and possibly traveled through Egypt as well.[81] While as evidence historians have the texts that such men as Tustari left behind, it is much harder to assess the impact on their thought of the conversations and meetings that must have taken place during their travels. Later claims that Tustari learned from the semi-legendary Egyptian master, Dhu'l Nun ('He of the Fish', 861A.D.), are not intrinsically unlikely, but simply hard to verify. We do know rather more about the development of ideas in Basra over the decades prior to Tustari's arrival there in 877A.D., when he was already an old man approaching sixty, even if it seems likely that his ideas were already mature by this stage.[82] What is most fascinating about the source of Tustari's creativity is its appearance in the fertile interpretive ground between the Quran and his own experiences. It is important that we do not lose sight of either side of this balance of input, for Tustari was neither solely a freethinking mystic drawing on his own sublime thoughts nor a derivative exegete dealing in simple paraphrases of scripture.

Instead, he was a Muslim for whom the Quranic words of God provided an inexhaustible source of knowledge for the contemplative reader in active engagement with his scripture. With the Quran as his guide, Tustari explored the meaning of his own experiences that came from years spent in the intense chanting of incantatory formulas such as those he learned during his youth from an uncle, a well-known scholar of Hadith. While parallels and sources for this practice of chanting have been sought in the lengthy Jesus prayers of the Nestorian Christians, for Muslims such as Tustari and his uncle, the source was wholly Islamic. Not only did the formulas themselves often consist of words from the Quran, the generic term for such exercises dhikr or 'remembrance' was itself taken from the several Quranic recommendations to remember God. Tustari was the first person we know of who connected this practice of chanting dhikr with the notion of the heart as the organ of knowledge, the purification of which allowed it to become host to God's primordial light.

Although Tustari openly taught that there were four levels to the meanings of the Quran (literal, symbolic, ethical, and eschatological), it was only the friends who could truly understand it. While we see again the concern for ranking and enumeration that also characterized the writings of Kharraz, there is no doubt that the friends loomed far larger in the cosmos of Tustari. While many Muslim scholars were forming an egalitarian (or at least a meritocratic) Islam in which knowledge and authority were acquired through mastery of scripture and concordance with the Prophetic Example, in the circle of Tustari we see the reemergence of an older hierarchical Islam in which knowledge and authority were vested by divine election in a small number of people. Because this was not an elite defined by bloodline, as it was in the Shi'i formulation of authority lying solely in the family descendants of Muhammad, it was a more protean and thereby a more manipulable model that was likely to attract more supporters as a result. Since only the Friends themselves knew they were Friends, there was in principle no method of verifying whether a self-proclaimed Friend was really such a one or not. Unsurprisingly, Tustari claimed to be himself the qutb or 'axis' of the universe who stood at the center of this cosmic hierarchy of Friends whom God had selected in pre-eternity.

Even though Tustari's commentary of the Quran abounds in extraordinary visions and insights, his teachings also therefore provided an ideological resource for the highly authoritarian trends which we will see flowering as the Sufis sought greater influence in centuries to come. In his own lifetime, Tustari's claims to friendship won him as much approbation as support and he seems to have been forced to flee at least one city, therefore. While he was able to gain a considerable following in Basra, after his death his followers moved in different directions, some founding what became seen as a distinct theological rather than Sufi school called the Salimiyya and others moving to Baghdad to join the circle gathering around the next Sufi we must examine, Junayd the 'sober'. What we are seeing is therefore not quite yet a coherent Sufi movement, but rather a series of distinct but intersecting circles gathered around individual masters. As we see with the followers of Tustari and Junayd, in Iraq at least these cir cles had a fair degree of social interaction with one another and it was this interaction which during the ninth and tenth centuries would gradually create a more coherent Sufi movement sharing common ideas and practices. By around 900, we have certainly moved beyond a position where Sufi was merely a nickname for an assorted medley of seekers, and many of the foundational ideas, terms and practices that would constitute a proprietary Sufi method were being formulated. But, as we will see with the next few figures we examine, the debates and disagreements were such that we are still short of a coherent movement, still less a tradition.

8.5 Junayd of Baghdad (910A.D.)

Unlike Kharraz and Tustari, who traveled widely despite spending the most active parts of their careers in Iraq, Junayd was very much a long-term citizen of the imperial capital at Baghdad.[82] Junayd's nick name of al-Khazzaz tells us that he earned his living as a silk merchant, pointing again to an urban occupational background. Even more than the other figures we have discussed, his early training in the emerging discipline of Islamic jurisprudence placed him squarely in the intellectual mainstream of the Baghdad of his day. These scholarly credentials are clear from both the number of treatises he wrote over thirty according to one Junayd account and the familiarity with wider discussions they reveal. Like Kharraz and Tustari, sought to ground his teaching in (indeed, to draw it from) the very same sources being used to create the legal restraints of Shari'a, namely the Quran and Hadith. Just as scores of later Sufis writing in his wake would emphasize the harmony between the internal/esoteric (batini) and external/exoteric (zahiri) dimensions of existence, so Junayd's teachings on the nature of the soul were a counterpart rather than an alternative to the rules of Shari'a. For Junayd, the 'Path' or method was no more and no less than the full realization of the basic principle of Islam as announced in the call to prayer: 'there is no god other than God'. Known as the doctrine of tawhid the 'oneness' or unity of God as opposed to the 'thereness' or trinity of the Christians for Junayd this most fundamental of Muslim principles laid the basis for all Sufi endeavor. It was not sufficient to merely attest to God's unity with the tongue, or accept it with the intellect, but to live or experience it as a reality. Drawing on the same Quranic notion of a covenant being discussed by Tustari in Basra at the same time, Junayd claimed that human souls longed for this original state of being in which their souls were in a state of pre-individual existence in God.

Like Tustari again, he taught that the way to recover this original state was through a process of dying to oneself through the fana or destruction of the lower individual soul. Speaking of his own experience of such self-destruction, Junayd described how "an overpowering vision and a refulgent brilliance took possession of me and induced in me a state of fana, creating me a new in the same way. He had created me when I had no existence". But in the doctrine that would mark Junayd out for future generations of Sufis, he also taught that while states of ecstasy and bewilderment were part of the Path, the seeker who experienced 'surviving' (baqa) after having destroyed himself in God did not remain in that transient state of excitement but passed beyond it into a higher and abiding condition of 'sobriety' (sahw). The highest state of communication with God was therefore accompanied by conformist outward behavior that ordinary Muslims could clearly distinguish from the raving ecstasies or austerities of those less close to the Almighty. At one extreme of the debate was the Baghdad based preacher Ahmad Ghulam Khalil (888A.D.), who in 877 is reported to have brought formal charges of heresy (zandaqa) against over seventy followers of the Sufis such as Junayd, so providing major disincentives against teachings that appeared to contradict the words of the Quran or particularly the Hadith.[88] Many of these rumors of mysterious and charismatic spiritual giants concerned a certain Abu Yazid (d.875) from Bistam, in the distant Iranian countryside far to the east of Baghdad. We know relatively little about Abu Yazid (also known as Bayezid), though many of the 'ecstatic utterances' (shath) he purportedly exclaimed while in blissful understanding with God were collected by his followers, passed on to travelers on the trade route through Bistam, and eventually discussed in the refined religious circles of Baghdad.

The story that Abu Yazid was taught by a man called al-Sindi ("from Sind," in North India) would lead one modern scholar to argue not only that Abu Yazid's teachings was 'monism' derived from Indian sources a 'Vedanta in Muslim dress' but also that this Indian influence permanently changed the direction of Sufi thought. Likely, the Baghdad Sufis were very much men of their own minds and (in the case of Junayd especially) realized that the wild man of Bistam was hardly going to help them in their cause among the urban intelligentsia. If the idea popularized by later Sufis that Abu Yazid and Junayd founded two distinct schools of 'drunkenness' and 'sobriety' was certainly an overstatement, then we can at least see differences emerging by way of doctrinal trends and modes of behavior. Here again we are reminded that the Sufis were not merely mystics basing their teachings on sublime experience, but also public intellectuals participating in the leading debates of the day. The written records the early Sufis bequeathed us were discursive productions shaped by their participation in spoken debates and their borrowings from written authorities. But they were also the result of attempts to map the words and ideas of that discourse onto individual experiences in a way that made sense of that experience but (for conformists like Junayd at least) refused to allow private experience to shake the legal and political foundations of collective social life. But for Junayd the very moderation of the state of 'remaining' in God rendered the accomplished Sufi externally identical to the teacher of Sharia. He is one of the experts in religious law, and in what is permitted and what is forbidden and one of the best informed in all matters pertaining to Islam. He walks in the footsteps of the prophets and follows the way of life of the saints and righteous, he does not stray after those innovations (which, though contrary to tradition, have gained a measure of currency in Islam), nor does he refrain from accepting the agreed tradition of Islam. He holds the view that authority must be obeyed, nor will he separate himself from his community. This conformist stance is not to say that Junayd's career was without its controversies. But rather than seeing the early Sufis' development of their method as intrinsically in opposition to the proponents of law and 'orthodoxy', we should recognize that few positions on anything were beyond debate (even the methods by which Sharia was being constituted were highly variant). Far from being introspective and self-absorbed mystics, Sufis like Junayd were active participants in the creation of a Muslim society and as such participated in vigorous public debates on the nexus between authority and responsibility, behaviour, and fulfillment. But as we will see as we turn to some of Junayd's less sober contemporaries, the experience of feeling intimate with God and the sense of election it imbued was not in all cases so easily socialized.

8.6   Hallaj of Baghdad (922A.D.)

The most famous demonstration of this emerging tension between personally inspired and collectively consulted authority is seen in the life of Husayn ibn Mansur, known as al-Hallaj ("the wool sifter"). Born in southern Iran in around 857, Hallaj became a follower of Tustari and then of another Sufi, 'Amr-ibn-Uthman-al-Makki, in Basra, before entering Junayd's circle in Baghdad. He seems to have been unable to commit to the discipleship of any one master, perhaps through ambitions to attract a following in his own right. Even by the standards of his most mobile contemporaries, Hallaj traveled extremely widely, wandering not only through Iran but also venturing into the far reaches of Muslim expansion in Central Asia and India. On these journeys he disappears from the limited historical horizons of documentation, and he is chiefly known to us through his presence in the literary and intellectual capital of the Islamic world at this time, where he openly courted controversy for his opinions in Baghdad and was finally executed there in 922. Like other victims of untimely deaths, his execution was the crowning of a career, for it ensured his immortalization by scores of Sufi biographers and poets in later centuries for whom he would be remembered as the great believer for speaking the truth of divine love. As we have seen, in the Sufi circles of Baghdad and Basra that he frequented, the idea of being destroyed in God enjoyed wide circulation, as did the notion that God had a special relationship with an elite known as the Friends or auliya. We have already seen how the doctrine of friendship created a special model of authority by portraying the friend as being in such close proximity to God as to have knowledge that no amount of memorizing of the Quran or Hadith could bring. But in terms of the social exploitation of the doctrine, thus far self-proclaimed friends like Tus tari had only used their elect status to gather around themselves small circles of like-minded seekers. With Hallaj, we start to see the playing out of the full social potential of the doctrine through the amplification of the claim to Friendship by its outward demonstration through the performance of miracles (karamat). When it came to winning larger number of disciples, such performative proofs of special status had great potential and Hallaj's public performance of such miracles precisely achieved.

Unsurprisingly, the crowds of followers whom Hallaj attracted brought him to the attention of the state authorities in Baghdad, who own by now rather tired claims to legitimacy were being whittled away with each generation of new ideas. While the reasons for Hallaj's arrest and eventual execution involved an explosive blend of court politics and intelligentsia rivalry, the gravity of the situation was worsened by his own outrageous statements, some of which survive in his own writings and others in quotations in the works of others. Here, Hallaj went beyond the earlier discussion of the ego as being destroyed in God to claim that, since there was now nothing left of Mansur al-Hallaj, it was God who spoke through his lips. The ego of Hallaj had passed away to leave only the spirit of God inhabiting his body as it walked among the streets and peoples of Baghdad. In his most infamous claim, more important through the later belief that he did say it than through any absolute evidence that he did Hallaj used one of the ninety-nine names of Allah to declare 'I am the Real (ana al-haqq)' in effect declaring himself identical with God. Even more extraordinarily, he expressed sympathy for the plight of Satan, whose refusal to bow down before Adam in Islamic legend Hallaj saw as an act of heroic loyalty to God by Adam's refusal to swerve from his absorption in worshiping the divine unity. Even so, the official reason for Hallaj's execution lay in his purported teaching that the pilgrimage to Mecca that was incumbent on all Muslims able to perform it could just as well be performed symbolically around a table at home. By implication, Hallaj was arguing that the symbolic or esoteric dimension of religious duties was more important than their actual or exoteric performance.

8.7   Iraqi Sufism by the Late Tenth Century

As the tenth century wore on, more and more teacher's called Sufis were attracting followers in Iraq and writing works in which they elaborated on the terms and concepts we have seen developing in the writings of Kharraz and others. As with the teachers we have already examined, in showing how the seeker could come close to God, partake in his knowledge and in some cases in his power, these were doctrines with immense socio-political potential, even if this potential had yet been scarcely realized except in the negative sense with the execution of Hallaj. A case in point is a biographically obscure Iraqi called Muhammad-ibn-Abd al-Jabbar, known as al-Niffari ('from Nippur') who died after 977. Building on the Sufi tendency we have already seen emerging to elaborate the many 'places' (maqa-mat) or 'states' (ahtval) on the Path, in his Kitab-al-Mawaqif ('Book of Staying Places'). Niffari developed the idea that the Path also contained 'staying places' (mawaqif, sing, tvaqfa), as it were, stop over points, which though they might be bypassed by some travelers were places in which God revealed different aspects of himself to the patiently thorough going seeker. Implying that other seekers had missed these 'staying places', Niffari went on to describe in astonishing detail the revelations which God gave to him at each of no fewer than seventy-seven places, beginning his discussion of each of these tvaqfas with the frank claim that "God stayed me and said to me....".

Before we move on to explore the other main geographical region in which Sufism developed, it is worth ourselves staying a moment to look over the developments that had taken place in Iraq by the end of the tenth century. Firstly, we have seen a development from a period in which sufi or "wool- wearer" was merely a nickname for a vague assortment of seekers to a period in which the term was used to denote a distinct method of acquiring knowledge which was now termed tasawwuf, which we can fairly translate as Sufism. In other words, the terms have acquired a more substantive and specific meaning: where there were previously only people called Sufis, now there is a practical and theoretical method being called Sufism. The most visible factor was the production of texts in which the Sufis developed a conceptual vocabulary that not only explained their ideas and made sense of their own and their disciples experiences, but also rooted them in the legitimate sources of knowledge by way of the Quran and Hadith. By around the year 1000, the types of Sufi texts being produced ranged from commentaries on the Quran to treatises on individual topics, emotive poetry, admonishing letters, suggestive aphorisms, and accounts of visionary experiences. Often extremely complex and allusive, these were in many cases the creations of an intelligentsia writing for its own members. In a period in which legal and moral authority over the Muslim community was being acquired by precisely those men who called themselves the ulama or 'learned', this social location of the new Sufi method was extremely convenient. The writings which the Iraqi intellects produced were themselves agents in the process by which Sufism expanded and survived, not only transmitting ideas through time (where with each passing generation they grew in stature as the products of a spiritually gilded age), but also transmitting them through space (where they publicized the fashionable new method of Baghdad in the provinces of its empire).

8.8   Competition and Incorporation in Khurasan

The Sufis were by no means the only Muslims formulating esoteric and mystical models of knowledge in Iraq. But what we have seen is the beginning of their gradual and calculated ascendance there as they replaced a fringe ascetic movement (of authority via bodily mastery) and aligned themselves with a mainstream scholarly movement (of authority via textual mastery). When we turn to the eastern region of the 'Abbasid Empire known as Khurasan ('the land where the sun rises'), we see what were at first a set of parallel and quite discrete religious developments gradually encountering the Sufi movement emanating from the imperial center in Iraq and eventually being absorbed by it. It is important that we make a distinction between these different movements and recognize the processes of competition and collusion by which they interacted, since otherwise we will fall into the trap which led many earlier accounts to portray Sufism as appearing at the same time in a wide range of geographically disparate places. Encompassing regions which we would now consider as eastern Iran, Afghanistan, and the Central Asian republics, Khurasan had fallen into Muslim hands during the early decades of conquest that followed the death of Muhammad in 632. Unlike many of the western regions of the Islamic 'Abbasid Empire, which had previously been under Byzantine

Christian rule, Khurasan had been subject to Persian Zoroastrian rule and contained pockets of Buddhist and Christian presence. As in the west, the process of conversion and resettlement was lengthy, and despite the arrival of a new ruling elite of Muslims, in the countryside many of the old Persian-speaking landowners still maintained their influence.

Although later biographical texts from the twelfth century onwards absorbed many early Khurasani masters into the Sufi tradition that they were attempting to construct for their region, modern research has shown that in the tenth century hardly anyone was being called a "Sufi" in Khurasan itself and the few who were had either migrated from or traveled through Iraq.[83] If the early Khurasani renunciants of the ninth century did not call themselves Sufis, then given their distance from the westerly places in which this nickname circulated it is not at all surprising, particularly if we accept the proposition that the term sufi was originally used as part of the vocabulary of Iraqi Christians.[84] In their anti-social tendencies, the two most important of the early Khurasani movements resembled (though were not connected to) the ascetic zuhhad of Syria and Iraq. Called Karramiyya after the name of their founder Abu 'Abdullah Muhammad-ibn-Karram (874A.D.), the members of the first movement were often taunted on account of their rigorous asceticism by their contemporaries with the nickname 'mortifiers' (mu-taqashshifa).[85] Their doctrines combined a literalistic reading of scripture with the claim that work, and material gain were obstacles on the path to God. The third of the Khurasani movements to distinguish from the early Iraqi Sufis was that of the Hakims or 'Wise Men' of the oasis towns around Balkh and Tirmiz around what are now the northern borders of Afghanistan. Given the success with which the Sufis subsequently incorporated the leading Hakims, the claims that the Hakims were straight forwardly Sufis rather than a distinct local movement have usually been taken at face value by modern scholars. But there is reason to classify the group of men known by the title Hakim as a separate movement in its own right, albeit one with less impact and reach than those of the Karramis and Malamatis.[86] While broadly speaking the former were peasant and artisanal movements, from what little we know the Hakims seem to have been of a more 'aristocratic' character, their leaders being not only hereditary landholders but self-declared friends of God as well. Indeed, only the leaders were considered Hakims, which was clearly a title of authority rather than fellowship. For our purposes, the most interesting figure among them was Abu 'Abdullah Muhammad, known as al-Hakim al-Tirmidhi ('the Wise Man of Tirmiz'), who died sometime between 905 A.D. and 910 A.D.[87]

One of the reasons Tirmidhi looms so large in later memory was for the sheer fact that he was able to stamp his own personality on history through writing an autobiography, something not only considered poor form among premodern Muslims but also in striking contrast to the self-abasing strictures of his Malamati and Karrami contemporaries.[88] Like the leading Sufis of Baghdad, Tirmidhi had memorized the Quran early in life, mastered the study of Islamic jurisprudence and Hadith, and also visited Basra and Mecca. Like the Kitab al-Mawaqif of Niffari in Iraq a generation later, Tirmidhi's Arabic autobiography depicts his personal visionary experiences in fascinating detail, beginning with a dream of the Prophet Muhammad leading him through his home city.[89]

Indeed, in providing foundational resources for the subsequent development of Sufi tradition, Tirmidhi was most important for his elaboration of the formal theory of wilaya or 'Friendship with God', that is, the Muslim doctrine of sainthood. Displaying the same taxonomic logic as that seen in the Baghdad Sufis' treatment of the places and states on the Path, in his Kitab Sirat al-Awliya ('Biography of the Friends') Tirmidhi set out to classify and rank the different classes and kinds of God's Friends. He introduced the idea that just as there was a Seal of the Prophets (khatm al-anbiya, a rank occupied by Muhammad), so was there a Seal of the Friends (khatm al-awliya, a rank apparently occupied by Tirmidhi himself). In the writings of Tirmidhi, we see how claims of visionary experience were not simply testaments of personal salvation but evidence on which to build a starkly hierarchical model of humanity and its rightful leaders.

To examine how this process of competition and incorporation occurred, we must turn to another key time and place in Sufi history: the city of Nishapur between the tenth and twelfth centuries.[90] Nishapur was a major trade and oasis city in what is now the northeastern corner of Iran and, with the impoverishment of Baghdad after its fall to the Shi'i Buyyid dynasty in 945, became increasingly important as a center of moral and religious production. Like the imperial capital in its heyday, the great desert emporium was a marketplace in which the producers and pliers of different models of Islam found themselves in keen competition with one another. One broad process we can arguably see at work here is the replacement of what we might term frontier expansion movements by interior consolidation movements. In some ways, this picture of the eastern frontier reflects what we have already seen in the west, where at least some of the ascetic zuhhad settled in the troubled frontiers with Byzantine territory. As the external frontier moved further east and the internal social frontier evaporated at the tipping point of conversion and acculturation to Islam, space was opened in the social fabric for new consolidation movements concerned with the deeper Islamization of society through a 'permanent settlement' emphasizing law, economic production, and maintainable social life for which the renunciant Karramis and the holy warriors of the frontier were no longer appropriate. While the precise contours of these larger rural processes remain unclear, the fuller character of the urban sources means that we have a clearer picture of developments taking place in cities like Nishapur. Here we are looking at two separates but interwoven processes, one discursive and one institutional.

The Quran and the Hadith were common resources; the language of 'Friends' and the 'Path' was in widespread use; and formal prayer, the chanted 'remembrance of God' (dhikr) and for some 'listening to music' (sama') were shared practices. The point is not that all the indigenous Khurasani seekers shared all these commonalities, nor even that when they did that they agreed on the precise meaning of a common term or the proper performance of a common technique. What was important was rather the mutual intelligibility of the various methods on offer, an intelligibility that enabled productive discussions and interactions between members and perhaps more importantly between the 'swing voters' of potential members of the different movements. Despite the vast distance between Iraq and many of the cities of Khurasan (the distance from Baghdad to Nishapur is almost as far as from London to Warsaw), these communication tools enabled the learned from these very different regions to share ideas vicariously through writing. As with the role of Latin in medieval Christendom, we must be careful not to take these common communicative tools for granted: when the Sufis later sought to expand in other geographical and social contexts, they would need to acquire other cultural tools such as vernacular languages and popular songs. But in the present context of interaction between the townsmen of Khurasan and Iraq, we are looking at a process by which Iraqi Su fis traveled or dispatched writings east and Khurasani 'swing voters' traveled west (typically enroute to Mecca) and returned home, in both cases carrying what we might now term portable communication devices in their baggage by way of the books they bought (or more likely copied) on their travels.[91] Since individual motivations are notoriously difficult for the historian to assess, the evidence presented for the incorporation and replacement of the Malamatis and Karramis is one of more general antagonisms and alliances. In perhaps the most convincing overall theory, the Sufis in Nishapur and its surrounding cities are seen as having attached themselves to the Shafi'i school of Islamic law, which lent them "an institutional framework in which mysticism could be taught and practiced".[92] But before moving on to the 'hard' dimensions of this institutionalization, let us first address its 'softer' or discursive dimensions.

As we have seen, from the period of their earliest emergence in Baghdad, the Sufis were very much part of the circles of Quranic, Hadith and even legal expertise. For this reason, we must be wary of older interpretations which saw the developments we are now examining as a process which saw the Sufis finally entering the 'mainstream', since this interpretation depends on the double fallacy that the Sufis were outside the 'mainstream' to begin with and that there even was any such single 'mainstream' that flowed evenly through different places during the preceding centuries.[93] The nature of this efficiency lay in the way in which Shafi'i legal scholarship offered scholars a 'diploma' or ijaza system in which their authority was socially testified by writ ten certification from their teachers and a clear legal methodology to employ in place of memorizing vast numbers of Hadith and constructing idiosyncratic personal methods for making sense of them.[94] This new efficiency, which not only made the practice of law easier but also ensured that the rulings of legal decision-makers were taken seriously, was the product of system wide prestige rather than personal reputation and drew various individuals and parties to adopt the Shafi'i method, with the result that both Sufis and Malamatis converged in adhering to the Shafi'i law school and the social settings of its schools and study circles.

Having attracted these parties, Shafi'ism provided them with further discursive tools. One of these was the model of knowledge transmission through master-to-disciple lineages that the Sufis called the silsila ('chain'), which we will discuss further below. This in turn, encouraged disciples to model their behavior on that of their masters in a way that echoed the notion of the Prophetic Example or sunna.[95] The mastery of Hadith also became increasingly important as Shafi'i Sufis of the period such as Sulami (d.1021) wielded this expert knowledge to create compilations and interpretations of Prophetic traditions in support of the Sufi rather than the Karrami method.[96]

Ultimately it was the consequences rather than the causes of this development that were more important. For what we see emerging in and around Nishapur and spreading from there not only around Khurasan but also west wards into Iraq and as far as Islamic Spain, was a new master disciple relationship that would permanently transform the nature of the Sufi method and tie it to a powerful set of new social relationships. This 'Nishapur model' has been described as one in which 'the Shaikh, by means of a pact, binds the novice to practice unquestioning obedience, to carry out every order and to reveal all his secret thoughts and inner states without exception while…. the shaikh is not to pass over any mistake on the part of the novice and can assign him whatever punishments he wishes'.[97] It seems historically crass to follow an older moralizing interpretation which contrasted a 'healthy' early period in which the followers of the Sufis of Baghdad were like students attending the lectures of their professors with a 'corrupt' later period of slavish adherence to superstition and master worship. Any sharp dichotomy between a 'teaching master' (Shaikh alta'lim) and a 'directing master' (Shaikh al- tarbiya) is probably a simplification, though there is little doubt as to the increasing intensification of the master/disciple relationship.[98] This binding of the disciple to the master was now accompanied by a solemn, designated as a bay'a ('oath') after the formal pledges of allegiance made to Muhammad by the first Muslims. And as we will see below when we turn to the more concrete forms of this institutionalization, for many disciples the new 'apprenticeship' model involved giving up their family lives for a period of the master's choosing to live in a Sufi hospice, as well as cutting their hair and donning special robes that distinguished them as Sufis.[99]

As Sufism came to mean things that it had not meant before its transformation in Khurasan, demanding formal requirements of both participation in a method and membership in a movement found expression in two new types of books that emerged chiefly in Khurasan during the eleventh and twelfth centuries. Further examples produced in the following century included the Risala al-Qushayriyya film al-Tasawwuf ('Qushayn's Treatise on the Science of Sufism") of Abul-Qasim al-Qushayri (d.1074) and the Kashf al- Mahjub ('Revelation of the Hidden') of Ali-ibn-Uthman al-Hujwiri (d. circa 1075).[100] All of these handbooks were produced by writers either in or from Khurasan. Since one of the clearest common characteristics of the handbook was the legitimacy of the Sufis emphasized through stressing the conformity of their doctrines and practices to the Quran and the Sunna, it was once common places to describe them as 'defensive' works whose great achievement was to convince the guardians of Islamic legal orthodoxy that the Sufis were not heretics. This apologia was seen as having been more pressing after the execution of Hallaj in 922. It is here that our contextual picture of competing movements and abundant religious productivity proves its worth, especially when combined with what was in the tenth century at least the newness and unfamiliarity of the Sufis in Khurasan compared to the more familiar and better established Karramis and Malamatis. For with their self-justifying rhetoric, abundant explanations of doctrine and detailed expositions of practice, the handbooks are probably best seen as advertisements and manifestos intended for Muslim scholars throughout Khurasan who were unfamiliar with and even wary of the Sufi newcomers.

As with the move to socialize the frontier warrior-ascetics and the world-renouncing Karramis, in the Sufis' attempt to redirect the lower class violence of the futuwwa and related 'ayyar gangs of the Khurasani towns and countryside, we can see a reflection of the moralizing middle ground sought by the Baghdad Sufis that fits well with the fact that many of Khurasan's chief Sufis were members of the urban legal and property owning establishment.[101] The other important new type of book which emerged in this period was the biographical compendium or 'book of generations' (kitab al-tabaqat).[102] Whether as a separate book or a section within a larger book, it was in this genre of text that we can finally see the emergence of a fully-fledged Sufi 'tradition' defined by the historical self-consciousness of its members. For the 'book of generations' served as a textual means by which present forms of Sufi knowledge and their practitioners gained legitimacy and prestige through being presented as heirs to a lineal tradition that reached in an unbroken 'chain' through every generation to the person of Muhammad. In textual terms, what this involved was the col lection (and in some cases we must assume the creation) of biographical notices on the linking figures of every 'generation' or tabaqa.

Here was a process of the invention of tradition which required that the semi-legendary ascetics and pietists of the seventh and eighth centuries be presented as Sufis and that Sufi teachings themselves be seen as the original doctrine of Muhammad as transmitted through the ages. This repeatable procedure allowed tradition to serve as a form of transferable symbolic capital that could link the Prophet and the early Sufis of Baghdad to eleventh century Khurasan as easily as to nineteenth century India or to whichever time and place in which the biographical handler of tradition happened to be writing. But back in the eleventh and twelfth centuries, when, at the hands of Abu 'Abd al-Rahman al-Sulami in Khurasan and Abu Nu'aym al-Isfahani (d.1038) in central Iran, the earliest extant Sufi biographical compendia were written, the 'book of generations' performed two main operations. First, in a consequence of the Sufis familiarity with the techniques of scriptural learning, it borrowed from Hadith scholarship the method (or rhetoric) by which authentic knowledge of Muhammad's words was verified by means of a chain (sanad) of transmitters linked back to the Prophet himself. Second, the book of generations genre performed a back-projection into the venerable past of the more recent development of master disciple bonds of allegiance and initiation. Through creating biographical chains which connected the Sufis of later times and distant places with men considered as their pious ancestors, the biographical compendium afforded the Sufis the comfort that their beliefs and practices were those recommended by none other than the Prophet himself. And between Muhammad in Mecca and men like Sulami in Nishapur, there stood the likes of Junayd in Baghdad a few generations earlier, whose remembered lives and books of advice now served as resources in the construction of a Sufi tradition.[103] As a result, Malamati masters were inserted into the lineages of the Sufis and their distinct history was elided as the Malamatis became textually remembered as only a sub-group of the Sufis.[104] They were helped in this process of expansion and incorporation by the fact that there was now a more tangible Sufi social 'body' into which new followers might be incorporated by way of the madrasa and khanaqah. It is to this 'hard' aspect of the Sufis' institutionalization that we must now turn.

While the earliest madrasas appear to have been associated with the Karramiyya, as colleges for the study of the 'Islamic sciences', madrasas effectively owed their expansion to the collusion of the Muslim scholarly class with the nomadic Saljuq Turks who in the middle of the eleventh century steadily conquered the cities of Khurasan before finally subduing Baghdad in 1055.[105] Needing not only a literate and legally informed bureaucracy to manage their vast conquests, but also the sanction of legitimacy that came through the public support of Muslim social norms, the Great Saljuq dynasty (1037–1157) channeled part of their material resources into constructing a large network of such colleges right across their domains, so aligning themselves to a trans-regional religious establishment that they themselves substantially (or at least institutionally) created.[106] With the books and treatises it comprised by the eleventh century, 'the science of Sufism' or 'Urn al- tasawwuf could now itself be conceived as one of the religious sciences alongside the mastery of Arabic grammar, the interpretation of scripture and the techniques of jurisprudence. As such, it was able to find a place in the readings of those associated with the new madrasa colleges, if probably not being formally taught within them. Of course, this professorial version was very much a bookish brand of Sufism. But in being connected to a salaried official class of bureaucrats and lawyers, this respectable Sufi method of knowledge (respectable by now through its prestige as a 'tradition') received the impetus that would finally enable it to incorporate or suppress its competitors.[107] The leading light of this 'college Sufism' was Abu Hamid al-Ghazali (d.1111), a public intellectual whose mastery of academic politics and intellectual trends saw him elevated to the position of rector of the great Nizamiyya madrasa founded in 1065 in Baghdad.[108] While not the most original Sufi book, his massive lbya 'Ulum-al-Din ('Revivification of the Religious Sciences') did perform the important function of systematizing many of the ideas developed by earlier Sufis into coherent and intelligible form. As a result, it was read for centuries after his death down to the present day. Among his many other works (which included a short influential commentary placing the Quranic Verse of Lights into line with Sufi ideas of the cosmic Light of Muhammad), the most effective in the propagation of Sufism was a shrewd Arabic autobiography in which this most famous scholar of his day described his own journey towards truth as one in which he pursued every branch of philosophy and book learning before finally realizing that it was the Sufis who held the true keys to wisdom.[109] While the madrasa was certainly an important area for Sufi influence, the most characteristically Sufi institution which would develop in Khurasan during this period was that of the khanaqah or residential

Sufi lodge, which in the later eleventh and twelfth centuries the Saljuqs also came to patronize. Although on both the eastern and western limits of Islamic rule, frontier ascetics had previously dwelt in fortified compounds known as ribats (a term which in some areas would also later be adopted for Sufi lodges), for the most part the early Sufis of Iraq and Khurasan had met either in the homes of their masters or in public mosques.[110] Their gatherings, like those of the scholarly 'ulama from whom they were not clearly distinguished, were typically conceptualized through the notion of the balqa or 'circle' that gathered around a particular master. Over the centuries between approximately 1000 and 1300, this picture would change radically and the first step in this direction was the creation of propertied institutions specifically earmarked for Sufi activity. This is the tenth century ribat that was excavated in the late 1980s from the coastal sand dunes at Guardamar in the modern Spanish province of Valen cia, what was at the time of the ribat's construction part of the Muslim caliphate of Cordoba. Established in 944 according to the Arabic inscription on its foundation stone, the ribat at Guardamar comprised a communal mosque, a large reception area, lodging rooms for pilgrims, and thirteen cells for the residential hermits. In a pointer to the religious exercises that were practiced there, each of the cells contained its own prayer niche, while Arabic graffiti survive from the late eleventh/early twelfth century in which pilgrims ask for prayers to be said on their behalf. There is considerable debate over the extent to which such ribats spread across Islamic Spain and the regions of North and Saharan Africa to which Spain was connected. However, Arabic sources from Muslim Spain do point to the existence of an extensive network by the eleventh century, ranging from Denia and Almeria on the eastern coast to Toledo and Badajoz in the interior and to Silves on the western fringes of the Iberian Peninsula.

An eleventh century ribat has even been in the Balearic Islands now better known for sunbathing saturnalia than ascetic retirement, as well as in Sicily. According to some scholars, the ribats were linked to a militaristic spirituality that was distinctive to Islamic Spain, though we have already noted the presence of such warrior ascetics on the eastern Byzantine Christian and Buddhist Central Asian frontiers of Islam. It remains unclear how this frontier jihad of the ribats was linked to other religious currents in Islamic Spain, including Sufism. However, Arabic biographical dictionaries from Islamic Spain do frequently refer to ribats as places of ascetic and other pious practices and these clearly formed the day-to-day life of their residents even if they were at times involved in holy war. As in the emergent khanaqahs of Khurasan religious literature was also being created in the ribats, as in the case of the renunciant poetry of Ibn Tahir al-Zahid ('the ascetic', d.988).

In another echo of what we will shortly see of the commercial links of the Sufi lodges emerging in Iran around the same time, it has also been argued that the coastal ribats of Spain and Morocco were multi-purpose institutions that served maritime traders as well as ascetics. This would reflect the fact that Sufism followed a different pattern in Spain (or al-Andalus) more generally, where its theorists were often attacked for straying too far from the legal literalism of the Maliki school. However, even if we cannot be sure how closely the 'militaristic spirituality' of the early ribats related to the many Sufis of al-An-dalus, the archaeological excavations of the ribat at Guardamar do allow us to examine in detail at an architectural level what an early Muslim ascetic (and perhaps by inference a Sufi) lodge looked like. For as time passed, the ribats did lose their early militaristic dimensions and became predominantly places of Sufi retreat. Turning back to the Middle East, the earliest significant individual figure whom we can connect to the development of the new expressly Sufi 'lodges' lived in southern Iran, which with its closer proximity to Baghdad in the tenth century had developed a brand of Sufism with much in common with the sober moralizing of Junayd. This figure was Abu Ishaq al-Kazaruni (d.1035), named after the southern Iranian city of Kazarun in which he lived and whose deeds were recorded in a Persian biography composed by the son of his successor. While, like other early Sufis in Iran, his teachings do seem to have laid somewhat more stress on the theme of love between humans and God, Kazaruni was also very much a moralist. Kazaruni left no such system of rules, but even so, his network of lodges does point towards an important development in the Sufis' relationship with wider society in which we see one of the first of the many reciprocal exchanges by which Sufis negotiated to mutual benefit with different social groups. Since Kazaruni's lodges lay on some of the most important trading routes of the Middle East, many of his traveling guests were merchants (here echoing Spain), who in return for his hospitality made the donations that rendered further expansion of the network possible.

Within in a short time, Kazaruni lodges reached all the way from central Iran to the port cities of eastern China. With Kazaruni, the Sufis were for the first time attracting significant capital investment to themselves as Sufis, investment which in turn funded further publicity for their movement. Given Kazaruni's characteristic moralism, and his upbringing among Muslim preachers to local Zoroastrians, it seems fair to consider his network as a form of social outreach in which supper came at the price of repeating a few prayers. As the cultural frontier receded, here was another interior consolidation movement deepened the Muslim commitments of the rural inhabitants and passing traders in the deserts and mountains of Iran. A no less interesting figure who contributed to these "hard" institutional developments was Abu-Said-ibn-Abi'l-Khayr (d.1049), a Khurasani master who resided for some time in Nishapur but spent most of his life in the semirural setting of Mayhana in present-day Turkmenistan. There he established a khanaqah which unlike those of Kazaruni held the spiritual training of its inmates as its central purpose. In themselves, the rules were not at all novel to remain ritually clean, to follow all the formal prayers and perform additional orisons at night, to recite the Quran and perform dhikr daily, for example but placed together they signaled a shift to the more formalized institution of Sufi 'training' that we have already seen developing. The shift was even more significant because with Abu Said, these training rules were also attached to a residential institution. Even currently, Abu Said's was not a unique case in Khurasan. Further south in the city of Herat in what is now Afghanistan, his contemporary Abdullah Ansari (d.1089) issued a similar set of rules in local Persian dialect which seem to have been intended for easy memorization by his followers. While Abu Said was happy to borrow the institution of the khanaqah from the Karramiyya, his enjoyment of the good life stood in direct opposition to their vehement stress on poverty. And while in compiling a set of pious rules for the khanaqah's residents, he reflected the outward Sunni conformism we have seen among the Sufis of Nishapur no less than of Baghdad, his emphasis on musical performances and sumptuous dinner parties placed him into disrepute with many of his contemporaries.

Although some of the libertine poems on wine, pretty boys and sing songs may be spurious attributions, there is no doubt that Abu Said laid great emphasis on the practice of 'listening' (sama'), which in this context involved love songs set to drums and lutes which sent audiences into ecstasies expressed through wild dancing. For example, while the word and concept of sama' was discussed much earlier in Baghdad, the actual practices we see developing around the likes of Abu Said in eleventh century Khurasan were likely not borrowed from Iraqi Sufis at all but from the secular hobbies of the rural Khurasani aristocracy who in lifestyle and status Abu Said so closely resembled. This process of the grafting of a linguistic and conceptual superstructure onto the deeper social structures of life in different environments helped Sufism to embed itself into the new communities to which it expanded from the tenth century, first in Khurasan and later in India, Anatolia and elsewhere. Dwelling in the lodge of which he was master; surrounded by a band of men who had sworn to obey his every command; protecting the poor who sought the safety of his shadow; receiving grandees and princes as though he were one of their rank, enjoying the courtly pleasures of music and verse: all of these activities are found in abundance in the two biographies of Abu Said written in the century after his death. On the one hand, in the biographies many stories of miraculous aid to the poor, we see a new appeal of Sufism or at least of powerful Sufis to peasant social groups.

Once again, essential to this development was the interaction of texts with the concrete resources of their contexts. In biographies written by those who inherited the capital and status of the founders of lodges, Sufis like Abu Said and Kazaruni were venerated in the language of Friendship with God, and their spiritual rank and miraculous power were presented in turn as no less inheritable than their property. Teaching lodges did not become saintly shrines by a process of long decay and 'spiritual malaise' as an earlier generation of historians once had it but were from their beginning interdependent aspects of the same institutions. Men like Abu Said, Kazaruni and Ansari were buried in the lodges they founded and even in their own lifetimes in the eleventh century their contemporary Hujwiri could describe his pilgrimages to the tombs of the earlier Sufis in his cautiously conformist handbook on Sufi practice. What we see in the creation of the lodges, then, was the heady fusion of the symbolic capital of Friendship with the material capital of real estate. In the following chapters we will trace the vast repercussions of this development as these shrine-lodges spread from Khurasan to every corner of the Islamic world.

8.9   Summary

What we are left with from the earliest centuries of Sufi history is almost exclusively textual evidence, much of it highly arcane and containing little reference to the specific contexts in which it was written. In finding ways in which we can connect this written evidence to the world from which it emerged, our task has partly been one of trying to understand the appeal of writings that allowed Sufism to develop and spread beyond its early core of supporters. To do so, over the previous pages we have traced the series of developments which between around 850 and 1100 ensured that the term sufi referred to a much larger range of persons, ideas, activities, and institutions by the beginning of the twelfth century than it had when it was first used by Muslims three centuries earlier. The first major development we have seen is what we can call a discursive one, by which the early Sufis used scriptural resources to develop a respectable Sufi lexicon with which to label the ideas and activities they promoted. Whether referring to specific persons as 'Friends of God' (auliya allah), specific activities as 'Remembrance' (dhikr) or specific social attitudes as 'Reliance on God' (tawakkul), this Sufi lexicon connected the Sufis from the outset to wider developments in the mainstream of Islamic thought. As we have seen, this lexicon and the different types of text that used it to elaborate doctrines on the Path and the Friends were intelligible in Khurasan no less than Iraq, helping what was originally an

Iraqi movement to gain followers in eastern regions that had previously developed their own religious movements. It was in these eastern regions that we have the fullest textual evidence for the consolidation of Sufism from a teaching into a tradition, a process in which we have seen a central role played in the late tenth and early eleventh centuries by biographical works that used a genealogical framework to present Sufi doctrine as having been passed down the 'generations' (tabaqat) from the time of Muhammad to the time of the author in question.

In this, we see a process by which the writings and remembered lives of the early Sufis of Iraq (as well as the semi-historical ascetics of an earlier period) served as the 'usable past', as history that could be strategically employed to create a prestigious and legitimizing tradition. Not only did this prestige and legitimacy help Sufis win further supporters and shield them from the potential criticism of having committed deviating 'innovation' (bida'). It also placed their methods squarely into a dominant epistemological framework in which tradition and revelation were considered as superior to invention and reason. The Sufis' repeated attempts to link themselves with the authoritative past whether articulated through their use of Quran and Hadith or through their own lineages of master's points again to the danger of the notion of the Sufis as 'mystics' engaged primarily in the pursuit of experience. While the pursuit of experience what by the end of this period many Sufis were referring to as 'tasting' or dhatvq was an important feature of Sufi activity, we must remember that the Sufis were engaged in a perpetual struggle to connect these experiences with the authorized concepts of tradition denoted in the early lexicon. In the process of competition and incorporation through which they expanded from their early arena in Iraq, the Sufis would also be helped by their integration into the institutional frameworks of wider Sunni scholarship (such as the Shafi'i law school and the madrasa college) and by their development of institutional mechanisms of their own (such as the authoritarian master-disciple relationship and the khanaqah lodges). By the end of the period between 850 and 1100, we are also seeing the notion of the Sufi as a Friend of God with special access to God's power enabling Sufis to gain a larger following among the ordinary people for whom miraculous intercessions in their ordinary lives was of more pressing importance than a direct vision of God. This expansion of the franchise was arguably the most important development in Sufi history. While we have therefore by no means reached the end of the story, for present at least we can say that over all the period between around 850 and 1100 saw Sufism develop from being merely a locally used word designating 'wool wearers' to a method of knowledge elaborated in increasing numbers of texts and finally to a tradition enabled by institutional mechanisms of collective affiliation and reproduction.

9.   An Islam of Saints and Brothers (1100 A.D. -1400 A.D.)

9.1   Changing Contexts

In the centuries between 850 A.D. and 1100 A.D., we have seen the Sufis emerge as only one among many Muslim groups operating in Iraq and gain a following, as well as a conscious sense of tradition and a more institutionalized mode of organization, through their easterly expansion into Iran and Central Asia. While the last chapter focused on the two main regions of early Sufi productivity in Iraq and Khurasan, by 1100 A.D. there was also a substantial Sufi presence in the Islamic west of Spain and North Africa, as well as the beginnings of their tremendously influential expansion into India. Having recognized their institutional footholds across a wide region, the period between 1100 A.D. and 1500 A.D. to which we now turn saw the Sufis achieve an extraordinary ascent to a position in which, from Morocco to Bengal, they acted as the social and intellectual linchpins of the very different communities that they penetrated across this vast area. By 1500, not only were Sufis at once the patrons and clients of kings, but they were also central to the lives of lower-class groups in town as well as country, a position consolidated by their role in the conversion of nomadic and cultivator groups to Islam in expanding frontier regions. We have already seen how the study of Quran and Hadith was the formative discipline of the early Sufis and how, as time passed, the Sufis ensured their alliance with the emerging norms of Sunni Islam. With the mainstream as their natural environment, rebels like the executed Hallaj were the exceptions rather than the rule. But if the Sufis were rarely far from the norms of the period, in their early centuries they were unable to become dominant religious authorities. It was almost a century before the new Mongol rulers of the central Islamic lands converted to Islam, but when they did it was among the Sufis that they found their proteges and teachers. If these centuries of turmoil ushered in very different societies from those in which Sufism had first emerged, they also offered opportunities for Sufis to connect themselves to much larger constituencies than had ever been the case, winning the hearts and purses of not only nomadic khans but also of the townsmen and peasants they ruled over. By diversifying their spiritual method and vernacularizing their means of communication, and by founding brotherhoods and saint cults, the Sufis reached a point at which Islam became effectively inseparable from the persons, ideas, and institutions of Sufism.

9.2   The Diversification of Sufi Doctrine

Success breeds success and the establishment status that the Sufis had achieved by the twelfth or thirteenth centuries encouraged even more Muslims to voice their religious ideas through the respectable idioms Sufis had created over the previous centuries. Sufism was now itself a tradition with a lineage pushed back into the time of the Prophet, while the ties to the ruling class of many of its leading representatives cemented their influence in the present and their role of shaping the future of their societies. This 'establishment' status did not mean that their movement had run out of steam and if anything, we can see the respectability achieved by the Sufis of the first period as having enabled the diversification process that we see in the centuries between 1100 A.D. and 1300 A.D. For the Sufis, these were centuries of extraordinary textual productivity, because there were not only many more Sufis in existence, but they were now also widening their literary ambit beyond Arabic. The panorama of ideas explored in this period was tremendous, without even speaking of the rejoinders and responses, the ruminations, and commentaries, that each significant work triggered. To make sense of what was new amidst this voluminosity, we will look at the way in which the inheritance of the first centuries was diversified by examining such key themes as light, being and friendship, along with the main figures with whom they were associated. Each of these themes and doctrines, and the texts in which they were elaborated, became important materials in the discursive consolidation of Sufi tradition The first of these themes was that of light (nur). Everything in the universe existed as light and every act of knowledge was an expression of light.[111] Born in northern Iran, Suhrawardi saw himself as the heir to several traditions of 'wisdom' or hikmat and presented his system as the elucidation of what was previously known to the pagan Greeks and Zoroastrian Iranians as well as to the early Sufis.[112] Although it is open to question whether he can be considered a Sufi himself, he certainly spent much time in the company of Sufis, drew on their earlier ideas and influenced their later ones.[113] Suhrawardi's magnum opus was his Kitab Hikmat al-'lshraq ("Book of Oriental Illumination"). In this he laid out the framework of what (in a pointer to the central theme of light) he termed "oriental" wisdom in the sense that the east is the place where the sun rises over both the inner and outer horizons where the light of knowledge dawns.[114]

For Suhrawardi, the universe and its inhabitants consist entirely of light that emanates from God, who is Himself nothing other than pure self-existent light. Beneath God, the universe exists as a hierarchy of light-beings, whose own light (and so being) is merely contingent in emanating from God. These light-beings are what ordinary people call angels, and the most important among them was the angel whom Suhrawardi identified with both the Gabriel who delivered the Quran to Muhammad and the Active Intellect discussed by the philosophers. Here was a refiguring of the Sufi model of a Path with places along the way into a journey through stages of existence which were themselves forms of the increasingly pure light described in the Quranic Light Verse on which we have seen Ghazali writing a commentary less than a century earlier.

Between the physical and the angelic worlds, Suhrawardi placed an intermediary realm which he called the "World of Likenesses" ('alam almithal). It was this realm, possessing shape but not substance, which acted as the meeting place between human and angelic beings; it was also here that humans moved when experiencing visions and dreams. This crepuscular meeting ground between angels of light and the shadowy souls of men was of central importance to Suhrawardi's system. For it was here that humans could begin to gather the 'experiential knowledge' ('iln al-huzuri) that he considered superior to 'acquired knowledge' ('Urn al-husuli) gathered from books and lessons, because in visions knowledge was not data that was passively learned, but experience that actively happened.[115] Lying somewhere between descriptions of his own experiences and allegories of his philosophical system, in some of the earliest examples of Persian prose writing Suhrawardi penned a series of 'visionary treatises' in which he described his meetings with the angelic beings of light.[116] Although his remarkable writings contributed to disciplines as varied as logic and ophthalmology, what is most significant is his elevation of knowledge by mystical experience over the lesser knowledge acquired from books, a potentially radical realignment of the mainstream Sufi attempt to subject personal experience to the authority of tradition as manifested in the Quran, Hadith and their textual elaboration by way of Shari'a. Some earlier Sufis had described their mystical experiences, as we have seen in Iraq with Niffari's Book of Stopping Places and with the dream accounts of Tirmidhi's wife. But these descriptions were typically either brief (Tirmidhi) or highly allusive (Niffari), and the rare bolder accounts (such as that of Abu Yazid's heavenly ascension) were tainted with controversy. Yet from the twelfth century, we find descriptions of such experiences not only becoming more explicit but gaining sufficient prestige as to serve as proof of the visionary's Friendship with God. Such dream and vision accounts have been aptly described as a new 'rhetoric of sainthood' which fed into the larger process of sanctification explored be low.[117] In the Kashf al-Asrar ('Unveiling of Secrets') that Ruzbihan Baqli (d.1209) wrote in southern Iran, for example, readers were presented with a series of startlingly anthropomorphic visions. In one, God appeared before Ruzbihan in the guise of a fair-skinned Turk who played such tunes on his lute that Ruzbihan cried at their loveliness.[118]

In another vision, he met the Prophet Muhammad, whom Ruzbi-han saw wearing a golden suit and turban and sitting drunk amid a red sea of wine; scooping up cup after cup, the Prophet supped Ruzbihan till they both sat drunk together.[119] Many other such dream and vision diaries were written, among which were the hundred and nine dreams described two centuries later by the Algerian Sufi, Muhammad al-Zawawi (d.1477).[120] What is fascinating about al-Zawawi's dreams is their relationship to the physical world through which he moved, for their most intense period occurred during a journey to Egypt in which al-Zawawi's dreams served to sublimate and somehow accentuate the reality of his waking experiences of the places he was visiting. By this period, Egypt's was a geography dotted with Sufi tombs and after visiting these by day, by night al-Zawawi returned in his dreams to converse with their dead inhabitants, who assured him of his exalted status and invested him with robes of celestial rank. As increasing numbers of Sufis would testify in their writings, it was possible to meet any of the Sufis' past masters and even prophets through such visionary means. What we see developing here is the dream and vision as a cultural technology enabling Sufis to transcend the barriers of time and evade the ambiguities of scripture to plainly ask questions to the face of God's messengers. The epistemological problem of dreams that the personal nature of such experiences rendered the knowledge claims they made inherently difficult to verify was in turn overcome through widespread resort to a hadith in which the Prophet Muhammad had said, 'Whoever has seen me has seen me truly', which was taken to mean that Satan cannot imitate the Prophet's form. In other words, any vision or dream of Muhammad was necessarily authentic, such that by this recourse to the textual authority of Hadith dreams and visions became self-affirming. This was especially true of the most influential of the Sufi theorists of the medieval and probably any other period: the Spanish-born Muhyi al-Din Ibn al-'Arabi (1240A.D.). Born in Murcia to an elite Arab family in court service, Ibn al-Arabi spent his formative years among the Sufis of Spain and the culturally contiguous zone of North Africa, before moving to the eastern Mediterranean in his late thirties.[121]

There he was received with controversy among scholars and with largesse among princes; reaching Syria a decade after the execution of Suhrawardi, Ibn-al-Arabi was more fortunate in his friendships, dying in Damascus at the ripe old age of seventy-five. This grandest of all Sufi visionaries claimed the ability to summon the presence of any of the souls of the dead before him at any moment and spoke regularly with the souls of Jesus, Muhammad, and Moses. In a conscious echo of the Quran's revelation to Muhammad, Ibn-al-Arabi had his own master work, al-Futuhat al-Makkiyya ('Spiritual Conquests of Mecca'), revealed to him while circumambulating the Ka'ba in the holy city.[122] Such audacity sounded throughout his ideas and, as we see below, his protracted outwriting of Muhammad's own revelation was echoed in his claim that Friendship was superior to Prophethood, a theory which served well the need to reproduce religious authority in an age when prophethood was seen as having permanently ended.[123] For his own part, Ibn al-Arabi saw himself as the Seal of the Friends (khatm al-awliya) in whose oceanic being God's exploration of his infinite creativity was fully realized.

While Suhrawardi had been important for systematizing ideas of light a generation earlier, it was this notion of being (tvujud) that represented Ibn-al-Arabi's great contribution. Under his influence, the earlier Sufi emphasis on public morals, supererogatory piety and the search for certain knowledge were subsumed into a grander vision of cosmic existence in which the infinite realizations of creative being now took center stage. Ibn-al-Arabi did not necessarily introduce new concepts and, like other Sufis before and after, he wrote within the discursive framework of Islamic tradition: the raw materials of his work were the Quran, Hadith and the technical lexicon developed by the first generations of Sufis. Using these resources, he explored the implications of the 'sacrosanct hadith' (hadith quasi) in which God himself had declared, 'I was a jewel that was undiscovered and so I created the world'. Using the Quranic term barzakh which, for Ibn-al-'Arabi at least, took on the meaning of an 'interface' or 'isthmus' he developed the idea that human being was itself this interface between the matter and spirit that were the farthest axes of creation.[124]

Human being, then, was, the place of the Quranic 'meeting of the oceans' (majma-al-bahrayn) in which all levels of existence, all forms of knowledge, and all possible experiences, could be united in a way that was impossible even for the angels (which was why God had commanded the angels to bow down before Adam).[125] While not all humans contained such lofty possibilities this is what separated the masses from the Friends and Prophets those who did were the very reason for creation, for in the words of the sacrosanct hadith, it was they who discovered the divine jewel by realizing all of the possibilities of the Hundred Names of God. Drawing on Suhrawardi's notion of a World of Likenesses that mediated the mystic's encounter with other realms of being, Ibn al-'Arabi dwelt much on the idea that it was through the creative power of imagination (khayal) by which God and humanity reached out to one another.[126] Given that he was said to have filled a notebook every day of his adult life and that the Futuhat al-Makkiya alone takes up over 15,000 pages, Ibn 'Arabi's own career was no small expression of this faith in the creative power of the imagination.

This vision came to be summarized as that of the Unity of Being (wahdat-al-wujud), a form of cosmic monism which many a Persian Sufi would subsequently sum up in the epithet, 'All is He'! (bama ustl). Arcane as such ideas might seem, there were many potentially concrete social benefits to them. For example, the notion of the Unity of Being has been seen as serving as an enabling mechanism for inter-religious harmony with the different groups whom Muslims encountered. As many a poet (including Ibn al-'Arabi himself) put it, if God was everywhere, then he could be found in the idol temple as much as the mosque.[127] Of course, the clear danger in the idea that humans were made of the same stuff as God was that it broke down the divide between creator and creature and with it the threat of divine retribution that underpinned moral order. And so while to his followers Ibn al-'Arabi was the 'greatest of masters' (al-Shaikh al-akbar), to his critics he was the 'master of infidels' (al-Shaikh al-akfar).[128] Yet Ibn al-'Arabi's thought spread incredibly widely, partly through the piece meal trickles of influence and partly through the efforts of a studious corps of followers who ranged from Sadr-al-Din Qunawi (1274) in Anatolia, Fakhr al-Din 'Iraqi (1289) in India, Mahmud Shabistari (1340) in Iran, Muhammad Wafa (1363) in Egypt, 'Abd al-Karim al-Jili (1408 or 1428) in Iraq, and Muhammad ibn Sulayman al-Jazuli (1465) in Morocco.[129] The early life of the other great diversifier of Sufi thought in this period was similarly marked by the retraction of Muslim power. For in counterpart to Ibn al-'Arabi's flight to the east, Jalal al-Din Rumi (d.1273) as a boy undertook a westward flight from the Mongol advance into Khurasan to the safety of the Saljuq capital of Konya in Anatolia. If Ibn al-'Arabi is often seen as the greatest theorist of Sufism, then Rumi is usually seen as the Sufis' greatest poet.[130]

9.3   The Institutionalization of the Path

We have already seen how the early Sufis presented their method as a 'Path' or tariqa and how over the eleventh century that Path became more formalized through the elaboration of rules and more institutionalized through the foundation of khanaqah buildings. Here we will turn to the process by which these developments were both consolidated and expanded, specifically to the related organizational and conceptual developments which allowed Sufi leaders to address the basic obstacles of reproduction through time and space while at the same time maintaining a degree of consistency through developing mechanisms for standardizing practice and doctrine.[131] We have already seen how the creation of a sense of 'tradition' encouraged Sufis to conceive of their Path as something inherited from masters who had lived in earlier times and other places. But a sensibility of the traditional is not the same as an actual mechanism of tradition: one can believe one is transmitting the teachings of the ancients without doing so. What we see emerging between around 1150 and 1400 are these more formal mechanisms of tradition. This is not to say that such mechanisms were entirely absent among the Sufis beforehand, who were often very much immersed in the methods of knowledge transmission developed by memorizers of scripture and collectors of Hadith. But these latter were not distinctly Sufi mechanisms of tradition. While the more formal methods of teaching, initiation, and organization we have seen emerging around Nishapur were somewhat more (though by no means entirely) distinctive, they were still relatively restricted methods confined to teachers in particular places.

They had not yet developed into mechanisms of tradition capable of reproducing the standardized and proprietary method of a given Sufi across time and distance. To do so, the Sufis would need to develop a more formal geographical distribution network and a cross-generational system of inheritance, as well as more distinctive 'branding' mechanisms capable of distinguishing the tradition of one master from that of another. It was the development of such mechanisms that underlay what historians have usually seen as the creation of 'brotherhoods' or 'orders', a development which is obscured by the fact that the Sufis them-selves continued to use the term tariqa with reference to both the loosely formulated Path of the early centuries and the organized brother-hoods of the later periods. For while some aspects of these mechanisms were organizational and corporate in the sense that the term brotherhood usually suggests, they were both enabled by and subject to the intangible but ultimately more weighty operations of tradition as a conceptual and symbolic mechanism. We should not then expect the brotherhoods of this period to comprise complex organizations with card carrying members and efficient managerial hierarchies.

The absence of such complexity does not mean that we cannot speak of brother-hoods at all in the centuries between 1100 and 1400, nor does it mean that there were no organizational developments in these years. But it does mean that we must recognize that what held the members of such brotherhoods together over the generations and geography that divided them were conceptual as much as concrete bonds of connectivity. In the medieval period, brotherhoods operated as organizational communities largely on the level of locality or region in which legal or face-to-face authority had a realistic chance of success. When it came to bridging larger distances of either time or space they were forced to operate largely as conceptual communities in which fellowship was built on bonds of memory and imagination rather than bureaucratic ties and direct communication.

Indeed, between the twelfth and fifteenth centuries the lodges and shrines from which the Sufi brotherhoods gathered their followers in town and country acted very much as the hardware of Sonification, rendering permanent the religious policies of the Saljuq, Ayyubid and Mamluk rulers who from Anatolia to Egypt sought to cement their conquests of the territory of Byzantine Christians and Fatimid Shi'is through the patronage of durable and axiomatically Sunni institutions that included Sufi lodges.[132]

What began in Khurasan as a temporary alliance between arriviste Saljuq nomads and an ascendant head, wearing earrings or carrying recognizable paraphernalia.

In this way, the lack of impersonal and formal methods of group organization was compensated for through acts of personal and informal identification by members of a particular brotherhood. In similar acts of self-identification, disciples inserted themselves into lineages of initiation that stretched through their own masters back through the generations described in the 'Book of Generations' genre and so to the Prophet himself. Boundaries with other brotherhoods were marked not only by physical appearance but also by different attitudes towards money, music or even drug use. Properties acquired through patronage were linked to specific brotherhoods, forming residences or meeting houses for fellow initiates, which in larger cities came to include special lodges for female Sufis.[133] Masters began to appoint 'deputies' (khalifas) to further disseminate the proprietary Path of their brotherhood. With the symbolic capital of authority and the mate rial capital of property, inheritance systems also began to emerge in which birthright competed with initiation as the proper channel of bequest. These developments afforded the Sufis mechanisms of both horizontal and vertical reproduction that allowed them to expand into new geographical areas and to survive the death of masters. The creation of networks of deputies allowed brotherhoods to spread into new regions, while the recognition of heirs allowed them to continue from one generation to the next. In principle if by no means always in practice, the method of master disciple learning and the reading of training texts ensured some degree of standardization in the doctrines and practices held by fellow members of the same brotherhood at generations and geography. Once again, what we are seeing here is the ongoing evolution of a self-conscious tradition in which precedent and community were far more important criteria than originality and individuality.

Even when mystical experience was sought, it was sought and understood through what the Sufi understood to be long established practices and conceptual frameworks. None of these developments took immediate effect and emerging in different times among different brotherhoods, none can be given a single date at which they appeared. As primarily mechanisms of tradition, the brotherhoods necessarily developed through time and so their consolidation and expansion were an inherently multi-generational process in which different generations relied on one another to play distinct but nonetheless necessary roles as founders and perpetuators, heirs and distributors. It would be easy to see the men after whom the major brotherhoods were named as genuine founder figures and so date the emergence of the brotherhoods to their actual lifetimes:

Abu Najib al-Suhrawardi (1168), 'Abd al-Qadir al-Jilani (1166), Ahmad ibn alRifa'i (1182), Ahmad al-Yasawi (1166?), Najm al-Din Kubra (1221), Mu'in al-Din Chishti (1236), Abu'l Hasan al-Shadhili (1258), Jalal alDin Rumi (1273) and Baha al-Din al-Naqshband (1389).

In the case of some of these men, we do have evidence for new kinds of organizational activity, but overall, we are looking at men who, through writing or preaching, achieved a fame and following in their lifetimes which their disciples and very often their families inherited and perpetuated after their deaths.[134] They did not simply found brotherhoods whose continued existence then simply rolled on through the ages. Rather, the 'founders' are better seen as men who amassed resources whether patrons and property or teachings and charisma that could be inherited and used by their successors to find the brotherhoods which were named after them. They thus only became founders through time when that which was developed from their legacies and survived after their lives was connected back to them by later generations who saw themselves as the followers of the 'founder's' Path.[135] This was the Suhrawardi brotherhood which was named after Abu Najib al-Suhrawardi (d.1168), one of several important Sufis who originated in the Iranian town of Suhraward. While Abu Najib's own public career was more checkered than Ghazali's, he still occupied an important position teaching jurisprudence in Baghdad's great Nizamiyya madrasa and, after losing his appointment through a dispute at court, continued to teach legal and Hadith studies in a madrasa which he founded next to his own Sufi lodge in the city.

Entitled Kitab Adah al-Muridin ('Book of the Disciples' Etiquette'), Abu Najib's introduction to the Sufi life showed little concern for Sufism as metaphysical doctrine and mystical experience and instead focused on the outward behavior the 'etiquette' or 'manners' (adab) which the disciple was expected to display.[136] Inheriting something of the public profile of his uncle, 'Umar likewise entered the circles of the court and became so close a confidante of the 'Abbasid caliph, al-Nasir (r.1180–1225), as to serve as his official ambassador and work on his project to socialize the boisterous young men of Baghdad into futuwwa or 'chivalry' clubs, whose character bore much in common with the emerging Sufi brotherhoods themselves.[137] Gathering a circle of followers, and patronized by his admirers at court, like his uncle, 'Umar also wrote a book of rules, in which the prescribed duties and beliefs of the disciple were laid out in far greater detail than had been the case with the nascent rules of Abu Sa'id and Ansari a century and a half earlier in Khurasan.[138] From among these disciples, it was the nephew 'Umar rather than the uncle Abu Najib who laid the organizational and conceptual foundations of the brotherhood by founding a network of lodges and arguing for the Sufis as the sole legitimate heirs of the

Prophet.[139] Even then, the founding was only beginning, and it needed the next generation of his followers, particularly Najib al-Din Buzghush (d.1279) and Baha al-Din Zakariya (d.1262), to distribute the Suhrawardi proprietary version of the Path eastwards into Iran and northern India.[140] Each successive generation would play its part in consolidating and contributing to the symbolic and material resources of the brotherhood, inflating the charisma of the founder and gathering the patronage to found new lodges. When after six centuries the institutionalized inheritance of the 'deputies' or caliphs of Muhammad was extinguished by the Mongol sack of Baghdad in 1258, Suhrawardi's initiatory network of brothers was already spreading far and wide. While the context of the 'founder' was an important shaper of any brotherhood, the contexts of the first few generations of heirs who reproduced and effectively shaped his legacy were therefore even more important, pointing to the way in which trans-regional and transgenerational brotherhoods like the Suhrawardiyya emerged out of an organizational and conceptual interplay between different times and places. In setting up shop in the distant north Indian city of Multan, 'Umar's disciple Baha al-Din Zakariya brought with him not only the prestige of a Baghdad that was even more powerful at so great a geographical remove.

Through the apparatus of the brotherhood, he also brought the initiatory and pedagogic mechanisms to reproduce the blessing and behavior of its lin eage's most famous holy men. To transform the brotherhoods from the creation of individual genius into the collaboration of communal process is not to reduce them. It is rather to point to the collective nature of the investments of emotion and action that allowed the brotherhoods to function so effectively in the expansion of Sufism into new areas. For the initiation, rituals, and teachings by which any new disciple entered and identified with a brotherhood were intrinsically portable and reproducible, allowing deputies to move into new areas and establish new 'franchises' of a brotherhood. Once again, we are reminded that in this period the brotherhoods offered a conceptual cultural mechanism as much as a concrete organizational apparatus. By similar means of multi-generation collusion, the Qadiri brotherhood named after another Sufi public moralist, 'Abd al-Qadir al-Jilani (d.1166), emerged from a Baghdad that was imagined as much as it was real to spread, in the century after the caliphate's end, into Syria, Egypt and Yemen and in later centuries to India, Southeast Asia and Africa.[141]

Our picture of a Sufi brotherhood looks rather different if we turn to the case of the Khwaj agan-Naqsh-bandi brotherhood in Central Asia.[142] Whereas the Chishtiyya emerged in India during a period of the expansion of Muslim rule, the Khwajagan masters (whose traditions would later be subsumed into the more famous Naqshbandi brotherhood) by contrast emerged after the death of the 'founder' figure 'Abd al-Khaliq al-Ghijduwani (d.1220) during the century of pagan Mongol rule over Central Asia between the 1220s and the early 1300s. While the Chishtis were establishing socially prominent formal lodges sponsored by the Muslim elites of the towns of India, the early members of the Khwajagan brotherhood, acting in a region governed by non-Muslims, were more likely to consist of the 'decent poor' who were taught to abhor possessors of wealth and high office and follow the far less socially visible practice of 'retreat within society' (khalwat dar anjuman).[143] The Khwajagan sought to increase their following through a stern critique of other Sufi groups, presenting their rivals as morally lax and arguing that possession of khanaqahs was proof of a concern with material things.[144]

Of course, we must be aware that such Khwajagan-Naqshbandi representations of their rivals were strategic uses of rhetoric rather than objective factual descriptions and historians have struggled to piece together a sequence of events from the mutually contested sources on the period. However, in outline it appears that as conditions changed after the Mongols' conversion to Islam, and amid the rise and fall of a tumultuous series of tribal Muslim dynasties, a more organized and socially engaged brotherhood emerged which gradually co-opted the following and prestige of the Khwajagan and absorbed it in a similar way that the Sufis had previously absorbed the Karramis in Khurasan.[145] Under the leadership of the brotherhood's 'second founder', Baha al-Din Naqshband (d.1389), and more particularly under his own heirs in the next few generations, this new Khwajagan Naqshbandi brotherhood radically shifted its doctrinal position to one of actively seeking connections with political leaders and encouraging the acquisition of wealth, which now came to be seen as a sign of God's favor to his Friends.[146] Through a series of affiliations with Central Asia's fragile rulers, whose own traditions and legitimacy were by now far shallower than those of the longer-established Khwajagan-Naqshbandi masters, the branch of the brotherhood led by 'Ubaydullah Ahrar (d.1490) reached the extraordinary status of being the largest landowner in Central Asia. At the same time, both brotherhoods shared the basic organizational and conceptual fabric of a chain of charismatic descent from the Prophet Muhammad.

In both cases, this was used to create an association of 'brothers under the master' through rituals of initiation and sworn allegiance to the living representative of the Prophet and the Friends whose grace, across hundreds of years and thousands of miles, flowed down their respective chains to reach their initiates in either India or Central Asia. Between 1100 and 1400, the Sufi brotherhoods had penetrated societies as far apart as Spain and Mauretania in the west and Bengal and Turkestan in the east, with a firm concentration in the wealthy mercantile middle regions of Egypt and Syria.[147] In the many regions in which they flourished, local circumstances led them to adopt methods and techniques as varied as those of the Khwajagan-Naqshbandis and the Chishtis. But each of them shared the same basic characteristics we have described, mechanisms of reproduction and standardization that allowed the brotherhoods to endure and expand while maintaining the meaningful consistency that they cherished as their proprietary traditions. While the history of each brotherhood varied greatly, it is fair to say that between the twelfth and fifteenth centuries the multi-generational process of the formation of the brotherhoods led to an overall pattern of greater and more centralized organization by the 1400s than had existed four centuries earlier.

9.4   The Sanctification of God's Friends

It was once common for historians to discuss the evolution of Sufi teaching and the brotherhoods and lodges through which it occurred without reference to the transformation of leading Sufis into saints. Indeed, the latter process was once considered a quite separate one belonging to a later period of decline from 'mysticism' to 'superstition'.[148] However, because of new research over the past few decades, neither dichotomy nor decline fit the facts as they now appear. The doctrinal fabric of Sufi teaching, the notion of certain Sufis being God's special 'Friends' (auliya) a relationship possibly preordained and certainly bringing special knowledge and powers had been a matter of controversy from the earliest period, with the sometimes fierce debate suggesting that there was already a great deal at stake in gaining such status in the earliest period.[149] Even as sober and mainstream a figure as Junayd of Baghdad had written on the theory of friendship (wilaya) and we would do well to note that, of all the early Sufis, it was Junayd who was most commonly incorporated into the chains of forerunners later developed by the brotherhoods.[150] In terms of the institutional fabric of the Sufi brotherhoods, the notion of the Friend was central to the brotherhoods as both conceptual and concrete entities, through the veneration of the past masters of the tariqa chains and the construction of mausolea in the midst of the lodges. Given the existence of so many Chris tian saintly institutions in the Islamic west, and their recognition as pilgrimage sites by Muslims from an early period, it is possible that the existence of such saintly practices had a much earlier existence in Islam.[151]

New work on the early history of Islam shows that the veneration of graves, relics and holy persons has a much older history among Muslims than was once thought.[152] In understanding how this came about, we are once again confronted with the role of the Sufi brotherhoods as mechanisms for re production. For, as chains of descent and capital gathering institutions, the brotherhoods were able to both reproduce new masters in every generation and provide them with public spaces to be buried in on their deaths. There were, of course, several sets of components involved in this process. One set comprised the conceptual components by which a given Sufi was initiated into a chain of descent (silsila) and afforded recognition as a Friend of God: the latter status was either achieved through personal accomplishments (preaching, praying, writing) or simply inherited through the emergence of family dynasties of brotherhood leaders. Another set of components comprised the spreading of rumors of miracles, which were frequently lent official sponsorship through the writing of hagiographies whose narratives spread into the oral sphere through the work of professional guides who escorted pilgrims through expanding numbers of shrines.[153] A third set of components comprised the development of cult rituals by which pilgrims were able to access the blessing power or baraka that the saint transmitted, rituals which, depending on the integration of a given shrine into wider networks of pilgrimage (ziyara), might be trans-regional or local in character. A final set of com ponents comprised the financial mechanisms by which money was raised for the construction of the mausolea that served as the focus of cultic activity mausolea which by 1400 were coming to rival those built for courtiers and rulers. Possessing abundant access to the necessary components of charisma, commemoration and capital, the brotherhoods thus operated as highly effective institutions for saint-making. After our earliest detailed evidence for the development of these components around such men as Abu Sa'id in eleventh century Khurasan, with the expansion of the brotherhoods over the next few hundred years the pattern was re-produced to reach a point at which the cult of the saints had sponsored whole suburbs for the holy dead al-Qarafa in Egypt, Shah-e Zinda in Central Asia, Khuldabad in South India where the wealthy competed to build their own mausolea close to the shrines of the saints.[154] While by no means every venerated saint was a Sufi in medieval Islam any more than every Sufi was a saint, the ideas and institutions of Sufism nonetheless became inextricably interwoven with the saintly practices that came to play a central part in the Islam of the ordinary believer. As with the brotherhoods own creation, this process of sanctification was typically a multi-generational project, seeing shrines acquire increasing prestige and capital as the centuries passed.[155] While the organizational and conceptual structure of the brotherhoods played a central part in the spread of this culture of Sufi saints, they were not the only enabling factors at work. Two other factors were of crucial importance, namely, the further elaboration of doctrine, which created a powerful ideology of a divinely ordained hierarchy of mankind, and the making of political contacts, which brought major Sufi's access to capital through relationships of patronage. For present purposes, Ibn al-'Arabi is important for promoting the ideas that sainthood was ultimately more important than prophethood and that the universe was held together by a hierarchy of saints and, indeed, it continued existence to the existence of a saintly 'axis' or qutb known as the Perfect Man (insan-al-kamil).[156] Ibn-al-Arabi was by no means the only person promoting such ideas, and over the next century his ideas on sainthood and the Perfect Man were publicized and elaborated by many other Sufis, particularly Muhammad Wafa (d.1363) in Egypt and 'Abd al-Karim al-Jili (d.1408 or 1428) in Iraq. In many respects, this was a continuation of the Saljuq practice of patronizing scholarly Sufis with madrasas and charismatic Sufis with khanaqahs.

When the Mongols finally converted to Islam in the 1330s, they too recognized the prospective dividends of such patronage.[157] It was in the eastern regions of the Islamic world in Iran and Central Asia ruled by the Mongols and their tribal successors that some of the largest and most stunningly decorated Sufi shrines ever constructed were built in the fourteenth and fifteenth centuries, shrines that in some cases served as the only sedentary institutions with which nomadic groups had any interaction.[158] One of the most impressive and stylistically typical surviving buildings the Mongols patronized for the Sufis was the shrine complex of Shaikh Muhammad ibn Bakran (d.1303, also known as Pir-e-Bakran), which was completed around 1312 around twenty miles from the Iranian city of Isfahan.[159] As these associations with ruling groups became more and more commonplace, and the Sufis claims of cosmic el evation became ever more grandiose, the mausolea of the Sufi saints came to borrow the style of royal tombs. In some cases, rulers even began to abandon their own ancestral burial sites to be interred at the feet of the saints.[160] From one group among many Muslim claimants to religious leadership before the eleventh century, the Sufis became, between 1100 and 1400, not only God's spokesmen on earth but also the confidantes of kings. This becomes clearer when we look at the kinds of belief, action and emotion that the sanctification of the Sufis made possible, not just for the ruling elite but also for the ordinary people of their time.

Let us turn to these consequences of sainthood in turn, first by looking at how the lives of the elite and then the lives of the masses were shaped by their relationships with the Sufis as saints. As we have seen above, from the Saljuq period onwards, the Sufis entered bonds of patronage with the rulers of the time through which they acquired the mate rial resources necessary to build concrete institutions in which to live and teach. Yet it is important to grasp the two sides of this relationships and, to see what sultans and other elites received in return for their patronage, we must turn to the special type of resources that leading Sufis, both in life and death, were believed to possess. For the Sufis were not merely meant to act as propagandists channeling religious legitimacy to the state through publicly serving in its madrasas or receiving gifts in its khanaqahs. The relationship between saint and sultan was, then, one of reciprocal exchange, albeit an exchange of the dissimilar resources of cash and land for miracles and blessing. In almost every corner of the Islamic world, from the twelfth century on we begin to hear more and more stories in which the Sufi saints were seen to use their baraka as a means of intervention in what in secular terms would be seen as political affairs. We have already seen this developing in the saintly biographies written by the family of Abu Ishaq al-Kazaruni (d.1035), stories which were successful enough to attract local dynasts. As a result, the ruler of southern Iran, Sharaf al-Din Mah-mud Shah (d.1336), named his younger son Abu Ishaq after the saint and in 1334 the dynasts paid for a madrasa to be built beside Kazaruni's tomb.[161] Such traffic with kings was nothing to be ashamed of: the family of Abu Sa'id ibn Abi'l-Khayr (d.1049) in Khurasan recorded with pride dozens of stories of their saintly ancestor's supernatural dealings in affairs of state.[162] More interesting, perhaps, is the spread of such stories away from the histographical productions of the saintly families and into the realm of the books of 'history or tarikh sponsored in the royal palace rather than the Sufi lodge. This is not to suggest a clear divide between courtiers and Sufis, because the richer picture researchers are building of social interaction in such medieval capitals as Shiraz, Herat, Konya, and Delhi suggests that, aside from a hard corps of fulltime Sufis, there existed larger bodies of followers who drifted between court and khanaqab?[163] Magnified by gossip and expectation, the stories spread by this growing number of influential fellow travelers served to increase the prestige of the Sufis and the belief in their powers.

The consequences of this belief in the Sufis as saintly wonder-workers comprised not only the production of stories. As with 'Umar Suhrawardi in Baghdad no less than among the fissiparous tribal polities further east, the saintly status of Sufi families rendered them inviolate blessed men perfectly suited to act as diplomats and go-betweens.[164] Elsewhere, as with the migrant Iranian Ni'matullahi family in the south Indian capital of the Bahmani Sultans (1347–1527), we find Sufis acting as symbolic king-makers in rituals of royal investiture. United in death as in life, both the Bahmani sultans and their saints were buried in grand neighboring mausolea on the outskirts of the capital at Bidar.[165] Between the twelfth and fifteenth centuries, the ties established in Central Asia between powerful Turkish tribes and the saints of the Yasawi brotherhood were introduced into Anatolia as the descendants of both saints and tribesmen rode westwards, although this twin-migration interpretation has recently been challenged.[166] The same process saw the ties established in the fifteenth century between the Naqshbandi saints and the Timuri rulers of Central Asia reproduced over distance and time, a branch of the Timuri dynasty (known commonly as the Mughals) conquered India in 1526 and invited the saintly protectors of its forefathers to join them in their new dominions.[167]

Through their links to these larger communities, miracle stories fueled the wider mechanisms by which Sufism was able to perpetuate itself through time, since such stories of past saints served no purpose if there were no living inheritors of their power through future generations, no permanent site of pilgrimage at which it could be accessed, or no surviving community or dynasty to which a saintly lineage was attached. All such heirs had an interest in ensuring that those stories were remembered and passed on. But for those Sufis who swore to abhor the company of kings, the basic fact of their institutional existence meant that they needed at least a basic operational budget.[168]The theoretically court avoiding Chishtis of medieval north India thus found themselves developing complicated ethical guidelines by which they hoped (perhaps vainly) to avoid compromising their principles. Earning a living (kasb) was denigrated in favor of a system of gifts (fu-tuh) that might even be accepted from kings so long as they were not asked for and were channeled into the shared activities of the khanaqah.[169]

Even so, kings were not the sole source of material support for the expanding Sufi institutions of the period and while the process is, yet little understood there is good evidence of at least some khanaqahs growing wealthy through the patronage of merchants. According to the North African traveler Ibn Battuta, in the mid-1300s Muslim house rules obliged these merchants to stay a minimum of three days, during which they were fed delicious keskek stew made with meat, wheat and the rich flavors of lamb's fat. Offered a form of supernatural insurance for the safe passage of their wares, the merchants pledged the saint sums of money which, on their safe arrival home, they dispatched to Kazarun with the next merchant going there.[170] While such techniques of attracting merchants were probably widespread, more seems to have been made in the written sources of royal than mercantile patronage. Again, there is no need to pass moral judgment on the matter, because no religious institution can survive long without a regular source of material support and, in the period, we are looking at, wealth was concentrated in small portions of society. Of course, there were Sufis who avoided any contact with elite groups, and whose tombs were chiefly the resort of the urban poor and peasantry. But such limited constituencies lacked the literacy for text producing and the wealth for shrine-building, and so unless one of the saints attracted a new following, such patrons of the poor emerge rarely from the shadows of history. Even when we do know of individual Sufis from this period who wrote themselves into history by their own literary efforts whether it was Shihab al-Din al-Suhrawardi (d.1191), Ibn al-'Arabi (d.1240) or 'Ala al-Dawla al-Simnani (d.1336) this was often through their acceptance of royal patronage and protection.[171] Even if such help was neither sought nor accepted, it was a rare Sufi who dared to openly defy the rulers of his day. One case was that of 'Ayn al-Qudat (d. 1131) of Hamadan in western Iran, who from his imprisonment on grounds of heresy wrote his Shakwa al Gharib ("Stranger's Complaint") in defense of his teachings.[172] While the precise origins of the practice are unclear, from the fifteenth century in the region stretching between Anatolia and India we find more and more saints being described through the terminology of kingship. Saints were termed 'emperors' (shah), their shrines called 'royal courts' (dargah), and their headgear considered 'crowns' (taj), designations which may have begun among the followers of 'Shah' Ni'matullah Wali (d.1431) in eastern Iran.

As over a period of generations the great medieval shrine complexes acquired more and more status, in many regions saintly dynasties became a more permanent and long lived 'establishment' class than the shorter-lived dynasties of kings. It seems likely that beneath the common theory and terminology of Friendship across wide areas, there lay substantial differences in the way in which saints, their descendants and their institutions functioned in the Turco-Persian east and the Turco-Arab west, with the former regions seeing the saints reach their greatest social and economic impact. Yet no substantial comparative work has been carried out between the process of sanctification in the Islamic east and west. To some degree at least, part of the explanation for this variation lies in the greater impact on the societies of the Islamic east of the tribal and nomadic groups for whom Sufi saints were so important. This was most clearly seen through the conversion of whole tribes because of the alliance between a tribal leader and a Sufi. Of particular importance here are the conversion narratives through which a whole range of tribal groups across Central Asia, Iran and India constructed their ethnic identities around stories of the conversion to Islam of their founding ancestor at the hands of a Sufi.[173] Even in agrarian settings in such regions as Egypt, Sufi saints were looked on as founding ancestors by the villagers who lived around their shrines.[174] Moving from saintly narrative to saintly action, what evidence we have suggests that such interactions between saints and tribesmen were far from purely 'spiritual' and in many cases comprised the physical interactions of marriage, sex and procreation. Although the process is not fully understood not least because tribes did not generate written documents until they settled, came under urban influences, and sponsored others to write their histories for them we find many tribal groups recounting their ethnic origins as lying in the offspring of either a tribal elder and the daughter of a Sufi saint or a Sufi saint and the daughter of a tribal elder. The Timuri branch of the Chahar 'Aymaq tribe of what is now western Afghanistan thus considered themselves as descendants of the union of the Naqshbandi Sayyid Amir Kulal (d.1370?) and a daughter of the great tribal conqueror Timur (d.1405), a tradition in this case bolstered by its appearance in the medieval Persian hagiography, Maqamat-e Amir Kulal[175] ('Spiri tual Stations of Amir Kulal'). Among the Mongol tribes of the Golden Horde in what is now southern Russia and Kazakhstan, a similarly obscure fourteenth century Sufi by the name of Baba Tiikles was considered to have been the convertor or even ancestor of the Golden Horde.[176] In such ways, Sufis were sanctified through their integration into myths of ethnogenesis and structures of tribal life, becoming saints through the commemoration and veneration of tribesmen who considered themselves their collective descendants. However, while the theory certainly has its appeal, closer inspection of the kinds of Sufis connected with the tribes has shown that many of them were in fact formal initiates of the Sufi brotherhoods, suggesting that there Islam was more than the cosmetic camouflaging of shamans.[177] Even among the more sedentary polities of the Islamic west, we find the notion of baraka ('blessing power') being transferred through blood being eventually drawn into the social structure of the agricultural land lords along the rim of the Sahara, for whom such blessed bloodlines served to bolster the ethnic boundary between Arab landowner and African slave.[178] If saintly charisma is often seen as an intangible and symbolic resource, through connecting baraka to blood in many such settings from Central Asia to Africa, baraka became a physical and reproducible asset. Looking beyond the elite to the masses, the sanctification of the Sufis had its greatest impact in laying the foundations for a devotional Islam in which the veneration of saints deemed more accessible than a distant God provided a vehicle for popular religious expression. What we have seen of the formation of the doctrines and institutions of sainthood scholar and sultan suggests that, if anything, saint veneration emerged at the top of the social spectrum and trickled down from there. Nonetheless, the reproductive mechanisms of the Sufi brotherhoods enabled the gradual expansion of an immense network of shrines built to venerate the local representatives of the various brotherhoods. The development of these shrines allowed the God of Islam to be accessed through interactions with physical spaces and not solely with written scripture: it created an Islam that was immanent and tangible in its local environments. In the country if not always in the town, Islam effectively was Sufism; and Sufism was in turn an Islam in which access to Allah was mediated through God's local saintly representatives. In such contexts, the veneration of saints took on distinct local forms through the fusion of pan-Islamic concepts with more local idioms of language and ritual. Although such veneration of the saints was surely expressed in vernacular languages, little if anything survives of this folk literature before 1400. But from what is known, it appears that the saints were imagined in ways that fitted closely to the folkways of their clients. In southern India, for example, we find devotion to the saints being expressed through rustic vernacular lullabies and cheerful work shanties for grinding wheat.[179]

In other cases, the close proximity in which Muslims lived with Christians and Hindus saw the development of 'syncretistic' idioms of ritual and speech that enabled non-Muslims to participate in saint-veneration without formally accepting Islam.[180] As Anatolia fell from Byzantine to Saljuq rule in the twelfth and thirteenth centuries, Sufi lodges acted as spaces of mediation between older Christian communities and newly arrived Turkoman nomads.[181] In sites connected to other regions by busy trade routes, we typically find such syncretism and localization being expressed without losing sight of the saints' connections to the wider practices of Islam. But in regions which were more remote or poorly connected, it was not uncommon to find high levels of variation from trans-regional Islamic norms and, as the Sufis spread into such rural settings, they or their followers at times lost their earlier Sufi commitment to the Shari'a and scripture. In some cases, as with the veneration of Shaikh Adi by the Yezidis in the mountains of Kurdistan, such disconnected localization saw the veneration of Sufi shrines gradually fuel the creation of new and independent religions.[182]

9.5 The Vernacularization of Sufi Teachings

Till now we have looked at two processes by which between 1100 and 1400 the Sufis were able to massively expand their status and following through developing the conceptual and organizational institution of the brotherhood and becoming the focus of saintly veneration. In reflection of the vast geographical and social range on which the Sufis were now operating, the medieval period also saw a third important development by way of the increasing vernacularization of Sufi ideas into the regional languages of the many regions they had now entered. Clearly, if Sufism was to evolve into something more than the Islam of the elite, it would need to develop inroads into the vernacular language worlds in which most Muslims east of Iraq in South and Southeast Asia especially lived and thought. Throughout this process of translating Sufi teachings into the range of languages being spoken by new Muslim communities, a core vocabulary of religious terms was passed on either in the original Arabic or in a modification of the Arabic according to local phonology, so creating 'a transregional, standardized Islamic vocabulary across South and Southeast Asian Muslim societies'.[183] Given that Sufis were instrumental in the creation of new Muslim communities in various regions in this period, it has recently been argued that these acts of vernacular translation should be seen as integral to the parallel process of conversion as 'through translation' new communities gradually created, adopted, and accumulated the cultural resources that made memories of an Islamic past and a lived Islamic presence possible.[184] Even so, this process of vernacularization was by no means the unique achievement of the Sufis. If in some regions the Sufis do seem to have been literary pioneers of the vernaculars, then in other regions they were copying the fashions of the court in adopting local tongues. Overall, we can therefore posit three broad modes of vernacularization: a courtly one emerging through the patronage of polished literary productions by regional dynasts; a scholarly one of Sufis translating works of doctrine and etiquette for local followers; and a folkloric one emerging through the adaptation of low status folk genres.

In the centuries before 1500, the courtly mode effectively meant Persian (and, in one brief period, Hindi); the scholarly mode Dakhani Urdu and possibly Malay; and the folkloric mode various other languages in which at least some Sufis interacted with their followers but from which the only surviving evidence is in certain forms of Turkish and again Dakkhani Urdu and possibly Malay. By the year 1010, the poet Abu'l Qasim Firdawsi (d.1020) had completed his epic Shahnama ('Book of Kings') in which he recounted the heroic deeds of the ancient rulers of Iran in easily memoizable Persian couplets. Although Persian poetry developed first, prose soon followed. Sufis in Iran and Khurasan were already using Persian in Firdawsi's lifetime: In the previously mentioned the earliest Persian prose manual in the Kashfal Mahjub ('Revelation of the Hidden') written by Hujwiri in the new Turkish capital of north India at Lahore.

With the validity of this pioneering vernacular having been recognized, more and more Sufis over the following centuries chose to write in Persian, borrowing both the genres and the technical language of their Sufi predecessors who had written in the more prestigious Arabic of the scripture and the other religious sciences. While the development of a Persian prose literature widened the social reach of Sufi ideas and provided a more accessible means with which Sufis from the eastern Islamic world could contribute ideas, in terms of explaining the growing success of the Sufis in the medieval period we must turn to the more popular and memoizable medium of verse. Although Sufis were surely already composing poems in Persian in Firdawsi's day, we have relatively little evidence except for the collections of quatrains (ruba'iyyat) attributed to such figures as Baba Tahir (d.1020?) of Hamadan in western Iran and Abu Said (d.1049) of Mayhana, whom we have earlier seen organizing musical soirees at his Khurasani khanaqah.[185] Such poems are what we would now think of as lyrics, since they were intended to be sung to musical accompaniment and formed the basis of the Sufi practice of 'listening' (sama'), whose legitimacy we have already seen being debated. Comparing the themes of worldly pleasure that characterized the first generations of Persian poetry with the esoteric themes that subsequently came to dominate all but panegyric genres of Persian verse, one scholar has gone so far as to speak of a Sufi 'colonization of Persian literature'.[186]

In social terms, such poetry served to justify the at times aberrant behavior of the Sufi poets by draping their actions in the obscuring but none the less respectable rhetoric of metaphysics.[187] The larger point is that such poems owed their aesthetic as well as social power to the multiple ways in which their meanings could be understood. For the very ambiguity and double-entendre of the passionate performance of such sung poetry lent the Sufis a highly effective means of community outreach and propaganda. Here we must bear in mind that in preindustrial societies, in which music necessarily meant live performance, for most people the opportunity to hear music was a rare pleasure and so the increasing tendency of khanaqahs to sponsor musical concerts or mahfil-e sama' formed an important attraction for their surrounding communities.

In Iran and Khurasan, between the twelfth and thirteenth centuries, the Sufis adapted from the courts the genre of the secular love lyric or ghazal in which the relationship between the Muslim and God was presented as one of lover and beloved, allowing poets to imagine the Almighty in vivid physical terms: a fair-skinned slave, an androgynous beardless boy. Borrowing from the romance poetry popular at court, the Sufi himself was painted in similarly new guise, as lover, fool or madman, alternatively teased and tortured in the alternating presence and absence of his lover. Increasingly, the Sufi was depicted in the form of the qalandar, a shady and rule-breaking figure of whom we will have more to say later.[188] Such was the earthiness of the imagery that in the finest examples of such 'Sufi' ghazals in the work of poets such as Sana'i (d.1131) of Ghazna and Saadi (d.1292) and Hafiz (d.1390) of Shiraz, it is hard to say whether their verses were intended for esoteric interpretation or plainly for the pleasure of young princes. In other cases, as with the lyrics produced by such thorough going Sufis as Fakhr al-Din 'Iraqi (d.1289) and Jalal al-Din Rumi (d.1273), there is less ambiguity as to the poet's intentions. Ultimately, though, the question of authorial intention is less important than the fact that the Sufis coopted the genre and imagery of the court poets for their own purposes.

Once again, we see how the Sufis could incorporate people and their writings into their own tradition and in so doing to lend meanings to others' works that were in line with their own doctrines. Just as the earliest Sufis had made mystical meanings from the Quran, so later did they find similar affirmation in the intoxicating love songs of medieval Persia. From the time of Rumi in the thirteenth century, the ambiguous possibilities of the Persian lyric became well-established as the preferred medium for daring ideas. In Rumi's case, this included nothing less than the declaration that the glory of God shined from the face of his beloved boon pal, Shams al-Din of Tabriz. But despite the ardor and excitement of Rumi's ghazals, in which the Sufi path was presented as one of the be wilderment and ecstasies of love, it was in his vast and rambling narrative poem or mathnawi ("rhyming couplets") that he made his greatest contribution to the spread of Sufi ideas. Like other forms of Persian poetry, narrative verse emerged in the courts of Khurasan and in terms of the development of the religious and more specifically Sufi narrative the key figure was again Sana'i at the court of the Turkish sultans of Ghazna (modern Afghanistan) in the early twelfth century.[189] While Sana'i is better viewed as a court poet than a mystic singing to the moods of his patrons, his poems ranged from celebrations of drinking to moralizing homilies on good conduct his extended poem laid the foundations for verse as a didactic vehicle. In such works as his Hadiqat al-Haqiqa wa Shari'at al- Tariqa ('The Garden of Truth and Law of the Path') and Sayr al-'lbad ila al-Ma'ad ('Journey of God's Slaves to the Place of No Return'), Sana'i rendered rhymes into allegorical maps of the cosmos, revealing the journey of the soul through the various cosmic spheres.[190]

In perhaps the most famous pun in all Persian literature, the thirty birds (si murgh) who made it to their destination realized that they were themselves identical to the fabulous griffin (si murgh) who was their bird-king: when the Sufi destroys his lower self through following the Path, at journey's end all that remains is God. In terms of measuring the successful expansion of the Sufis that was so central a feature of medieval Is lam, the main point to grasp about such poems is that in their preindustrial cultural contexts they were a form of entertainment. Committed to memory by professional bards, such poems formed hours of entertainment that could be easily transported and reproduced for audiences who would be edified no less than amused. As in the case of lyrical poems set to music, through the jokes and stories they wove into their poetry, the Sufis were able to tie their message to vehicles that the ordinary and unlettered would welcome to their villages. Compared to the dogmatic handbooks, and even to the heady but complicated treatises, these poems had a more immediate appeal and accessibility. If the Arabic prose literature we have seen the Sufis developing from their early days in Baghdad helped them maintain their position in the religious establishment, then it was through their co-option of such vernacular entertainments that the Sufis were able to reach a more general audience. If sanctification brought the Sufis a mass following based on power and respect, then vernacularization ensured that it was also a relationship which was warmed with affection and informed by at least a measure of understanding. The actual lives of such poets as 'Attar and Rumi point us to another important feature of the spread of Persian in the exodus of refugees fleeing Khurasan in the wake of the Mongol invasions.[191] 'Attar was not so fortunate, and like thousands of his fellow townsmen in Nishapur, some-time around 1220 the poet disappeared in the anonymity of the general massacre. As a child growing up in the Khurasani towns of Vakhsh and then Balkh, the young Rumi was more fortunate, and his scholarly father had the connections to find a position in the new capital of the Turkish Saljuqs in the Rum (literally "Rome") or Anatolia that was to lend Rumi his name. When the Sufi theorist of light visions and 'founder' of the Kubrawi brotherhood, Najm al-Din Kubra, was slaughtered by the Mongols, some of his followers also fled to Anatolia, where in the city of Kayseri his disciple Najm al-Din Razi (d.1256) summarized his master's teachings in his Persian prose treatise, Mirsad al-'lbad min al-Mabda ila al-Ma'ad ('The Path of God's Slaves from their Origin to their Return').[192]

In such ways, the Mongols did not put an end to either the Sufis or their new fondness for Persian. As we have seen, when the Mongols began to convert to Islam from the end of the thirteenth century, they too became assiduous patrons of the Sufis like the former Saljuq nomads before them. Whether to the west in Anatolia or to the south in India, many thousands of people fled the Khurasan that had not only reared its distinct traditions of Sufism but had also pioneered the literary use of Persian. While Persian was already present in north India, the role of Delhi as the protective 'canopy of Islam' (qubbat al-islam) protecting these refugees saw the city develop a rich Persian prose literature cast very much in the clay of Khurasan. Even so, the Indian heirs to this Khurasani exodus did push the genres they inherited in new directions, not least in expanding the older practice of quoting masters verbatim into a whole new genre of the 'recorded conversation' or malfuzat. From the time of the Delhi-based Chishti Sūfi Nizam al-Din Awliya (d.1325) onwards, malfuzat served as a paper technology for reproducing the precise living words of the inspired master long after he died. As the Sufis of the Delhi Sultanate spread into southern and east ern as well as northern India, they too became vigorous producers and judicious popularizers of Persian. By inspiring such court poets as Amir Khusraw (d.1325), the Sufis succeeded in bending the literary fashions of the Delhi court to their own purposes in a way that echoed what had happened earlier in the courts of Khurasan before the Mongol invasions.[193] In doing so, they laid the foundation for a rich body of literature that, from saintly biographies to technical treatises and collections of letters (maktubat), recreated for a new environment the forms of Persian Sufi expression that had developed earlier in Iran and Central Asia.[194] Although in literary terms the period before 1100 belonged mainly to Arabic, and the centuries between 1100 and 1500 mainly to Arabic and Persian, there were certain situations in which other languages were put into writing. For if Persian served as a vernacular in large parts of Central Asia and Iran and was widely understood among the educated or immigrated in Anatolia and India, in the latter regions it was never truly a vernacular. Just as, under the shadow of Arabic, Persian took several centuries to establish its credentials as a literary language, so did the various forms of Turkish and Hindi/Urdu need time to emerge from the shadows of Persian. While this second phase of vernacularization was certainly under way in the medieval period, it would not be completed until as late as the seventeenth century. Of course, it had taken the patronage of royal courts to give Persian the status of a written language and it would ultimately be sultans and states rather than Sufis and peasants that were responsible for properly putting Turkish and Hindi into ink. Nonetheless, if usually only as interpolations in Persian texts, we do possess enough examples of Sufis using these less prestigious vernaculars to suggest they were willing to adopt any language necessary to reach a larger audience. In India the earliest evidence relates to the master of the Chishti brotherhood, Farid al-Din Ganj-e-Shakar (d.1265), whose verses in an early form of Punjabi were transmitted orally for generations before eventually finding an incongruous home in the Sikh holy book, the Adi Granth.[195] By now the Sufi quest was being seen not only through 'Attar's Persian allegories of birds, but also through tales of romance and adventure that appealed not solely to the warring lords of the palaces but were also intelligible to the ordinary folk of the countryside, where we can assume Da'ud's poems circulated secondhand with all the cachet of the court.

Although no other Hindi mathnawis have survived from this period, in the sixteenth and seventeenth centuries many other Sufi romances would be written in Hindi.[196] Steeped in the landscape, the heroes and the fantasia of India, by the 1400s the Sufis were vernacularizing their teachings to an extraordinary degree. For many Sufis, such rustification appeared to be diluting Islam with paganism. But with the greater accommodation the Chishti brotherhood afforded to their cultural environment, this was a risk which the likes of Amir Khusro and Mulla Da'ud were willing to take. The third major move towards the vernaculars that we find in this period was in Turkish. Nonetheless, some evidence does survive of medieval Sufis using Turkish, even though these verses were not written down for several centuries. The most important examples are the quatrains known as hikmet ('wisdom'), attributed to the Central Asian Sufi Ahmad Yasawi (d.1166?), which championed the life of the ascetic and celebrated the miracles of the saints. If much of the so-called Yasawi corpus of poetry was probably of later date and falsely attributed to the saint, the collective purpose of these verses still seems to have been to spread Islam (albeit in its Sufi version) among the unconverted nomadic Turks of the steppe, a process in which the poems were aided by their links with the great pilgrimage shrine built round Ahmad Yasawi's grave in what is now Kazakhstan.[197] A century and a half later, when the Turks were well established in Anatolia, the poetry of Yunus Emre (d.1321?) served to transmit a Sufism of humility and love through the often complex oral verse forms Yunus Emre introduced to Anatolian Turkish.[198] Another important case was 'Ashiq Pasha (d.1333), whose monumental Gharib-name ('Book of the Poor') comprised around 12,000 Turkish verses which served to transmit complex theological doctrines into the vernacular arena.[199] Although Yunus Emre seems to have been a wandering dervish rather than a settled master of high formal status, Turkish was also occasionally used by the wealthy custodians of the shrines being founded in Anatolia as part of the Saljuq and early Ottoman sponsorship of Muslim institutions. The most important example was that of Sultan Walad (d.1312), the son and impresario of Rumi, whose recorded output included several dozen poems in Turkish and a smaller number of verses in the Greek still spoken by most of the region's Christians.[200] Although the number of Sultan Walad's Turkish poems pales beside his almost forty thousand lines of Persian verse, its very existence is proof of the deliberate attempt the medieval Sufis made to reach audiences with no command over Arabic or Persian. And the strategy was a success, for through their move into vernacular forms of expression, especially into the oral and performative genres of poetry and song, the Sufis were able to reach a far larger audience than would otherwise have been possible, shifting their following beyond the towns and the learned to the unlettered nomads and peasants who first found Islam through their words.

9.6　Summary

While Sufis were increasingly using the more accessible vernaculars to explore the finer implications of their ideas, learned Sufis in all regions continued to use Arabic. From an earlier period dominated by short treatises and lengthier handbooks, after 1100 we enter a period in which Sufi Arabic literary production expanded in terms of both length and genre. In Arabic and its Persian handmaiden, the expansion into the unwritten vernaculars was therefore matched by a massive literary profusion by way of biographies, pilgrimage manuals, letter collections, recorded conversations, epic poems, and dream diaries, to name just a few examples. In genre and complexity no less than temperament and theme, between 1100 A.D. and 1400 A.D. the core vocabulary of terms and concepts developed in the first period of Sufism became a far more diversified idiom in which a much wider range of Muslims from across the geographical and social spectrum found their needs answered and their worlds reflected.

Yet in expanding from their early use of Arabic into Persian and more local vernaculars, the Sufis effectively shifted the entry requirements to their fellowship from close knowledge of the Quran and specialist methods of chants (dhikr) and retreats (khalwa) to a far more accessible curriculum that progressed from singing the vernacular melodies of Yunus Emre to pondering renditions of the allegories of Attar. Like the rumors of miracles that circulated among pilgrims to the shrines of Sufi saints, over time these orally transmitted verse forms were able to penetrate and shape the imagination of the masses in a way that the Quran could not. As with each passing century the Arabic of the Quran became ever more distant from the many spoken languages of Islam, the songs and the shrines of the Sufis served to bridge the growing distance between the believer and the moment of Muhammad's revelation. And for increasing numbers of Muslims in their farflung locales, what they knew of Islam was what was brokered through the tongues and tombs of their community's Sufis. The cult of the saints by which Sufis were venerated in architecture, ritual and narrative therefore served as the crucial bridgehead between Sufism as an esoteric method belonging to an inevitably limited movement of committed spiritual aspirants and Sufism as an everyday idiom appealing to the religious needs of a mass clientele.

As approachable grandees in their accessible shrines, the 'sanctified' Sufi saints could act as intermediaries between the limited reach of human agency and the limitless power of God. Reproduced in shrine buildings from Morocco to Turkestan, this was an arrangement that was as useful to peasants as it was to sultans, each of whom contributed to the coffers of the shrines, placing Sufis into the patterns of reciprocal exchange that tied them to their communities of clients by a mutual web of favors. Given the distance of these developments from a model of Sufism as a personal mystical quest for union with God, they were once seen as heralding a medieval end of 'true' Sufism. But such an interpretation is to miss both the internal logic of friendship and the social strategies by which the Sufis were able to survive and reproduce their tradition through time. For shrines were not separate institutions from the teaching rooms, lodges, and retreats in which 'mysticism' took place but were rather one element in larger complexes shared by day visiting pilgrims and permanently resident Sufis. It makes sense to think of the holy graves in such complexes as the pilgrim-gathering public interface to the wider societies on which the Sufis depended for material support. The public services of the Sufis as saints were matched by their more private services to the new brother-hoods in which sanctification occurred as part of the corollary of institution-building, whereby the founders of brotherhoods were sanctified through the veneration of the brotherhood members.

The mechanisms of sanctification and of tradition operated hand-in-glove as the prestige of the knowledge and blessing passed down through the brotherhoods' chains of descent required each figure in the chain to be regarded as a Friend of God, because otherwise the chain of saints was incomplete and the knowledge and blessing it transmitted rendered worthless. The logic of tradition and its use for the conceptual foundation of the brotherhoods was thus in itself an engine to produce saints. Linked to popular and wealth generating shrine complexes, as both organizational and conceptual institutions the brotherhoods formed a means of attaching Sufi ideas and practices to the actual communities whose membership could be expanded and reproduced through simple rituals of initiation at the hands of a master. While it would be anachronous to see such brotherhoods as akin to modern organizations with integrated hierarchies of efficient communications between their many geographical outposts, in functioning as conceptual if not always organizational networks they were able to construct parallel (if not necessarily interconnected) institutions in the many different environments in which medieval Muslims were living. By reproducing such parallel institutions across distances of thousands of miles, the Sufi brotherhoods created mechanisms of interaction, coherence and fellowship between Muslims who were otherwise increasingly separated by political disunity and ethnic difference. By making such saints and brothers and labeling them with the same Arabic lexicon in regions as far apart as the Bay of Bengal and the North African coast of the Atlantic, the Sufis rendered Islam both tangible in their local settings and consistent across the wider world. In so doing, for many millions of medieval Muslims, these developments rendered Sufism inseparable from Islam itself.

10. Empires, Frontiers and Renewers (1400 A.D. -1800 A.D.)

10.1 Introduction

The influence and reach of the Sufis expand in a multitude of directions, social no less than geographical. In ranging from cycles of metaphysical systems and vernacular songs to social networks and miraculous protection, the different things that Sufism came to mean in the medieval period assured its reception among princes and peasants, nomads, and townsmen, the lettered and unlearned. Of course, such an influential proliferation of personnel no less than practices meant that there were critics of certain forms of Sufism and their practitioners, most famously by the Syrian scholar Ibn-Taymiyya (d.1328). But such criticisms were largely of (and especially popular) aspects of shrine devotion rather than of the entire metaphysical and moral edifice connected to the saints. Ibn-Taymiyya was especially vehement in his castigation of festivities around the tombs of Sufi saints, seeing them as 'innovations' from the Prophetic Example.[201] Nonetheless, he may still have been a Sufi himself and was an admirer of the great Baghdad Sufi, 'Abd al-Qadir al-Jilani (d. 1166).[202]

The critiques made by others tended to be ad hominen attacks on individual Sufis rather than on corporate groups of Sufis at large, taking the form of attacks by Muslims (often Sufis themselves) against other particular Muslims. While in a few cases such attacks came from sufficiently influential corners to draw on the powers of the state (as in the execution of Shihab al-Din Suhrawardi in Aleppo in 1191), for the most part the medieval period saw representatives closely supporting the persons and institutions of Sufism. This triggered massive investment in the shrines and lodges that through the medieval era saw Sufism become physically embedded in landscapes and townscapes from the Atlantic coastline of Africa to the Bay of Bengal. If criticism of certain Sufis was part of the tempo of medieval religious debate, then there was no wholesale attack on Sufism. Despite the customary usages of both academics and publishers, 'Sufi Islam' is probably a more helpful term than 'Sufism'. Although it would be simplistic to offer a single trajectory for the fortunes of Sufism in the very different regions to which this 'Sufi Islam' spread, certain common or otherwise large-scale developments can be observed in the centuries between 1400 A.D. and 1800 A.D.

In large part, these relate to major changes in the relationship between Sufism and the state, changes which were themselves dependent on the emergence of new kinds of 'early modern' state which were more bureaucratized, centralized, and confident of their own authority. With such a rapid turnover of dynasties in the centuries of tribal incursions between around 1100 and 1500, state interactions with religion were not only of a stop/start character. Along with their palaces and policies, tribal dynasties rose and fell in rapid succession, but the endowed shrines and lodges of the Sufis out-lived them as the more permanent feature of the physical and social landscape. Through their often grandiose and durable shrine architecture, Sufis acquired a kind of petrified immortality, their flesh turned into the stone of shrines that became a permanent part of the urban and rural landscapes in which more mortal Muslims lived and died. The comparative permanence of Sufis compared to sultans was also manifested in dynastic terms. We have already seen the Sufi brotherhoods promoting the model of a 'chain' or 'lineage' of masters, each inheriting his blessing, knowledge, and authority from his predecessors. In an age in which lineage (whether manufactured or genuine) was essential to any claim of authority, whether political or religious, the great families of saints that emerged in the medieval period could claim lineages of impeccable descent. These were articulated through the same vocabulary as that used by sultans, for the Sufi term silsila could be applied to a royal no less than a religious 'dynasty'. Wealthy in property and feared for their strange powers, the great Sufi families and brotherhoods that emerged through the medieval period were major players in their societies.

Although each of the early modern empires pursued these policies towards different ends, in each case they affected a change in the relationship between the Sufis and the state. In coinciding with a concomitant deepening of the previously weak ties between state and society compared with the previously stronger ties of the Sufis and society, these changes effected a gradual shift in the balance of power between religious and state elites. This did not necessarily weaken the Sufis, who, as we will see, in many cases became major beneficiaries of the states more efficient command of its resources. Since these resources included the employment of larger numbers of civil servants, in several contexts we will see Sufi brotherhoods becoming closely identified with selective organs of state. An important dimension of this process is seen in the increasing role of Sufis as frontiersmen, expanding and settling new territories on the fringes of state control. This not only occurred on such medieval frontiers as the mountains of southeastern Europe and the jungles of Bengal, but now spread to expanding new frontiers in Africa and Southeast Asia as the new Muslim states that emerged as the brokers of the growing global trade in gold, spice and slaves employed Sufis as settlers and administrators of their new territories. If the new picture was therefore more one of realigning the Sufis position between state and society than. As even emperors strove to model themselves as Sufis, it is probably fair to say that the sixteenth and early seventeenth centuries witnessed the zenith of Sufi influence to date, with the English loanword 'sophy' (derived from the name of the Safawi brotherhood) trickling even into the vocabulary of Shakespeare and the authors of 'The Travels of the Three English Brothers' as a title for Persian kings rather than religious figures.

But this very success contained the need for its own dilution as those outside these cliques of the Sufi establishment chafed at the Sufis' access to state coffers and contacts. So as time passed, this collusion between royal and Sufi authority was viewed as counterproductive and even threatening to the longer-term maintenance of state power as opposed to the original seizing of power. This manifested itself through the growing ability of certain states to construct a model of Islamic 'orthodoxy' and impose it on their citizens. The cultural agency of this latter event was magnified through its connection to a longstanding discourse hailing the religious 'renewal' (tajdid) and 'renewers' (mujaddid) who were meant to accompany each passing century, and especially the millennium.[203] Of course, this turning of the millennium marked a point in cultural time rather than in the more neutral or processual time of the historian. But what made the millennium significant was that the century that followed it the first century in the second millennium of Muslim cultural time coincided with a host of developments in the processual time of the historian. Affecting different Muslim regions in sundry but nonetheless significant ways, these developments included increases in population that shifted the demographic relationships between different social groups; growing urbanization that increased contacts between towns men, peasants and nomads; expanding trade that empowered merchant communities and heightened interactions with non-Muslim peoples; natural or man-made ecological changes that resulted in migrations and the settlement of new regions; a renewed bout of military encounters with pagan and Christian polities in Eurasia and Africa; and, by no means of least importance, the formation of new imperial states with bureaucratic agendas that increasingly brought religious leaders and discourses into the remit of government. Each of these developments in social history had its effect on developments in religious history, creating a sense among certain Sufi individuals or groups acting in a wide variety of regions that the Muslims around them had lost their moral or spiritual grounding.

Even as the new Muslim millennium's occurrence was uneven and its unfolding complex, the coincidence of the cultural time of the new Muslim millennium with the processual time of early modernity was of vast significance. However problematically, the phrase "crisis of conscience" is therefore used in this chapter to recognize at a general and comparative level the significance of this broad if multifarious coincidence of temporalities. In most cases, the crisis of conscience that accompanied the manifold social changes of the early modern era was not explicitly voiced in millennial terms but in the multiple calls for self-reflection or renewal that were heard from Southeast Asia to West Africa. Nor did the crisis of conscience occur in a single moment in all regions: its timing depended on local factors of social change and individual action. And when the millennium was explicitly invoked, its semantic weight was used for strategic ends in the pursuance of agendas. Even so, certain broad trends can be discerned. In almost all areas, this crisis of conscience saw attempts to diminish the influence of individuals or movements increasingly being considered 'unorthodox' in the eyes of the state, especially charismatic movements that had the potential to fuel rebellions against the ruling power. In broad terms, what we will see in this chapter is a picture of the early modern Islamic empires first associating themselves with charis matic forms of Sufism in the sixteenth century and then increasingly distancing themselves from them in favor of a more legalistic Islam (whether Sufi or otherwise) in the seventeenth century.

Nonetheless, by looking through the opposite end of the telescope from this "state's eye" perspective, there is much to be learned from the smaller scale perspective of small group and individual Sufi actions. While the early modern era saw states become more influential players in Sufi history than in previous centuries, this did not mean that Sufis ceased to be historical agents. Finally, in a context of imperial contraction and widespread social disorder from the mid-eighteenth century, we will trace in this chapter the emergence of a series of new sub-brotherhoods that sought to impose order on societies they saw as collapsing. Their success in doing this was itself the result of the increasing mobility of the early modern era and the legitimacy carried from the medieval period of the continuous tradition that the Sufis claimed to transmit into an uncertain eighteenth century. Once again, the notion of Sufism as an adaptable mechanism of 'tradition' capable of reproducing itself over time and space helps us understand how Sufism acted as a highly efficient response to the collapse of other logistical and ideological forms of social organization.

10.2   Empires - Brotherhood, 1400–1600 A.D.

The period between around 1100 to 1400 was one in which much of the Middle East and Central and South Asia saw state-making dominated by mobile tribes or tribal confederations. Most of these tribal groups had their distinct affiliations with Sufi families or brotherhoods. However, there was a difference between the types of Sufis with whom these tribal rulers chose to associate at different points in their careers. Through their connection with the two 'career stages' of the successful state-making tribe, we can loosely designate these types as 'tribal' and 'settled' Sufis. The most famous example of such a literate and learned 'settled Sufi' being patronized by a tribal polity in its settled period in Jalal al-Din Rumi (d. 1273), who rose to prominence with the support of the Saljuq Turks after they had settled into their capital at Konya. The association was a convenient one, in that many such Sufis specialized in deploying their supernatural powers for typically tribal demands, such as discovering water sources or intervening in skirmishes over pastureland.[204] Given that successful tribes were rich in the portable wealth of livestock, slaves and bullion, such association were beneficial to both parties. In numerous cases, we find tribesmen pledging allegiances of loyalty to these Sufi protectors, who as a result were able to oust the authority of tribal elders. As much product of the fissiparous social structure of the tribes than a result of the independent operations of 'charisma', this process was particularly important through its ability to unify different tribal groups under a common Sufi leader. For the Sufis position as an 'outsider' born out of the folds of tribal genealogy allowed him to unite the members of different tribes more effectively than any 'insider' who belonged to any one of the rival tribal groups in question could. Even where tribal Sufis did not attract such coalitions, many of them emerged as leaders of the nomadic tribal bands or the semi-pastoral highland communities that populated the steppes and mountains between Anatolia and Central Asia.

While the rhetoric (indeed, the purpose) of tradition is to present its content as unchanging, tradition is in fact a highly flexible resource, as sociologists have long recognized. When we put this into the mobile and fissiparous tribal societies beyond the towns, what such a model suggests is that while the holy men of the tribes did partake in Sufi tradition using its terminology, adapting its rituals, giving initiations into its brotherhoods they did so on their own terms rather than under the command of a master elsewhere and in accordance with the needs of their tribal clients. After all, in such 'anarchistic' milieu there was no one to prevent tribal Sufis from creating their own idiosyncratic medleys from the resources of tradition they inherited, just as there was no Sufi 'Vatican' to ensure a common catechism to abide by.[205] While many scholars have described tribal Sufis as 'unorthodox' or 'heterodox', the fact is that in their own period there was no centrally empowered 'orthodoxy' with which to compare them. As we will see later in this chapter, such 'orthodoxies' (with the terms of orthodoxy varying in each imperial state) were only to emerge as products of the centralization of the early modern empires that followed the more fluid tribal era of the 1400s. From the Balkans to India, the half-century either side of 1500 saw the tribal founders of new states struggle to transform themselves from conquerors to rulers. This transition also involved a transformation of the kinds of Islam they supported, as they became responsible not only for the fortunes of their tribal kinsmen but also for the more complex and diverse populations they now ruled over. The ruling elites of the Safawi, Ottoman and Mughal empires each had to make this transition and the different ways in which they did so had important consequences for the fortunes of Sufism in their dominions.

With its abundance of ambitious tribes, and its rapid turnover of settled polities, it was the mobile, fractious, and religiously anarchistic environment of the steppes and mountains that gave birth to both the Ottoman and Safawi empires. While the case of the Mughals is more complex, in that their rise to power saw them move out of the mobile steppe to conquer the settled agrarian society of India, when they came to rule over the more pluralistic domain of India, the Mughals too faced the problem of how to divorce themselves from their old steppe loyalties to the Naqshbandi brotherhood.

10.3 The Mediterranean: The Early Ottoman Empire

To see how this uneasy transition was made from the support of 'tribal' to 'settled' forms of Sufism, let us first turn to the Ottoman case. Between the fourteenth and sixteenth centuries, the rise of the Ottoman state from a petty tribal chiefdom to a complex bureaucratic empire joining southern Europe with Anatolia, Egypt and ultimately Arabia involved a precarious transformation from tribal and settled forms of religious loyalty. Like the Saljuq, Ayyubid and Mamluk rulers before them, the Ottomans considered the institutional fabric of the Sufi brotherhoods in the towns to be an important fillip in the maintaining of social order.[206] As a result, Ottoman expansion saw a reaffirmation of the role of the learned and orderly brotherhoods in urban life, whether through support to pre-existing brotherhoods or through the introduction of new brotherhoods or sub-brotherhoods with closer ties to the Ottomans themselves. The Khalwatiyya ("Seclusionist") brotherhood is a case in point as an example of a legally-conformist brotherhood with little previous connection with Anatolia.[207]

The Khalwatiyya developed close connections with both the Ottoman sultans and their highest officials, leading to the establishment of a grand convent for the brotherhood in 1574 in the heart of Istanbul by the grand vizier, Sokollu Mehmed Pasha.[208] The new em pire also sponsored the expansion of Rumi's Mevlevi brotherhood of 'whirling dervishes', which became the favored affiliation of the Ottoman bureaucracy. This in turn saw the Mevlevi brotherhood's organization become more efficiently centralized around the shrine complex constructed around Rumi's grave in Konya. The Ottoman conquest of Syria and Egypt from the Mamluk dynasty in 1516–1517, for example, saw the gradual replacement of the Sufi notables linked to the Mamluks with a new Sufi order with closer affiliations to the new regime.[209] This 'colonizing' agenda was no less apparent when, after moving from Anatolia to Egypt in the wake of the Ottoman conquest, Hasan al-Rumi dictated the terms of the endowment for a new lodge built in Cairo in the Ottoman style: he specified that none of its employees should be local Arabs.[210] By sponsoring the construction of new Sufi lodges and mausoleums, even the sacred geography of these areas of conquest was gradually 'Ottomanized'.[211]

Indeed, the imperial patronage of new Sufi foundations in the newly conquered territories of the Ottomans in southeastern Europe no less than the Levant has led several historians to describe Sufis as playing the roles of colonists and settlers. In such urban contexts as Aleppo or Cairo, this effectively entailed a privileging of one set of Muslims over another, as in the case we have seen of Sufi brotherhoods or individuals affiliated to the Ottomans replacing those favored by the Mamluks. This was not a policy directed solely at Christian areas and, as in the case of the Bektashi brotherhood's outposts in Anatolia, it was also used to control rural areas with unstable populations of tribal Muslims.[212] The imperial patronage of Sufism was therefore not only a question of supporting institutions whose role in the 'civilizing process' made for a more orderly and governable population. It was also a question of supporting institutions that helped settle new territories in the wake of conquest. It would be a mistake to see such settlements as part of a long-term trajectory of Muslim/Christian opposition. While there were presumably in many cases Christians who became unhappy and even disenfranchised by the arrival of Sufis with friends in high places, as had already happened in the case of earlier Sufi settlements in the medieval period, over time the different religious communities came to accommodate one another and create new syntheses of religious practice.[213]

It has been suggested that the Ottomans encouraged the settling of legally-inclined Naqshbandi Sufis in their domains as part of their attempt to disseminate a more standardized and legally-codified adherence to Sunni Islam among the Turkoman tribes of the countryside.[214] While more recent research has questioned this, there is little doubt that the patronage given to Naqshbandis did contribute to the more staunchly Sunni character of Ottoman society that emerged over the longer term.[215] On an individual level, the career of Niyazi-e Misri (d.1694) showed that there remained Sufis who were willing to use their social influence to voice explicit denunciation of the Ottoman rulers.[216] While the ruling powers decided it was un wise to execute such a critic, they did have the power to do so: in Niyazi's case they chose to exercise their power through the more discreet mechanism of exiling him to the island of Rhodes. The sheer resources, organizational acumen and longevity of the Ottoman state therefore meant that it did overall bring an unprecedented degree of state control over the hierarchical Sufi assemblies of the towns and the lodges by which it could reach out to the country. It is little wonder that Bali Efendi (d.1553), an eminent Khalwati Sufi with close ties to the imperial order, acquired the nickname 'the spy of the Shaikhs' (jasus almasha'ikh).[217]

The Ottomans were not the first dynasty to sponsor a literate and orderly Sufism in the lands they governed. Much of the Ottoman conquest of the Balkans and Rumelia (that is, modern central Greece and European Turkey) was sub-contracted in precisely this fashion.[218] Such freebooting

Sufi warriors drew on the notion of ghaza or 'raiding' the lands of Christian infidels, an ideology of legitimate violence that was more flexible than the more legally restricted doctrine of jihad.[219] In some cases, we hear of a formalization of these Sufi raids into the more structured armies of the Ottomans, with particular Sufis being attached to regiments through the office of 'army Shaikh'(ordu Shaikhi).[220] Those Sufis were not only influential frontier figures in their own lifetimes but also after death, as their legends were written down and their tombs transformed into pilgrimage centers. This helped spread their fame beyond the time and place of the frontier societies in which they served their original imperial purpose, so perpetuating their disorderly and idiosyncratic visions of Islam into the period of settlement in which the state was promoting a more orderly Sufism that was substantially standardized throughout its domains.[221] This attempt to contain the very forces that had helped to establish their empire was one of the lasting dilemmas of Ottoman history. It was by no means unique to the frontier with Christian Europe and the most vivid illustration is seen in the history of the Bektashi brotherhood that was named after a classic tribal Sufi, Hajji Bektash Wali (d.1337).[222] Like the frontier cults of such similar figures as San Saltuk (d.1298) in the Balkans, the cult of Hajji Bektash was initially only associated with new Turkish speaking settlers, whether warrior tribesmen or newly settled agriculturalists.[223]

As time progressed, from the late sixteenth century onwards the cult of Hajji Bektash maintained (or acquired) its military association through connections with the more regularized Ottoman army. However, attempts to then centralize and control the Bektashis began as early as 1501 with the state appointment as head of the Bektashis of the Ottoman loyalist Bahm Sultan (d.1516), who was designated the 'second master' (pir-e sani) in the manner of an official heir to the 'founder', Hajji Bektash.[224] While earlier sultans had been generous and enthusiastic patrons of Hajji Bektash's shrine, after the reign of Bayezid II (r.1481–1512) such imperial support was far less regular.[225] Somewhat ironically, in a period in which the Ottoman state was attempting to promote a more standardized and orderly Islam, this policy ensured that many features of the old anarchistic Islam of the tribes were spread and perpetuated through the Bektashi lodges established in every city of the empire. But in the larger picture of Sufi history, the intervention of the centralizing Ottoman state in Sufi affairs meant that the Bektashi brotherhood was transformed from an eclectic blending of tribe and tradition into a more bureaucratic organization of tradition.

While the fifteenth century had seen tribal Sufis lead many successful expansions of Ottoman territory, it had also seen rebellions led by the same kinds of figures (most notably that of Shaikh Badr- al-Din in 1416) and as the century progressed such rebellions became more frequent.[226] The physical mobility and anarchistic religiosity of such movements meant that they were as likely to resist as assist imperial objectives. In 1493, a Sufi of the antinomian Haydari brotherhood even attempted to assassinate the emperor, Bayezid II.[227] So, for a centralizing government, the idea of appointing Sufi leaders and promoting firmer structures of brotherhood organization beneath them was therefore clearly attractive. Even if such attempts remained partial and incomplete, over the course of the sixteenth and seventeenth centuries they did bring the brotherhoods into closer relations with the Ottoman state, even if those relations were never characterized by outright fealty. longevity of the Ottoman state therefore meant that it did overall bring an unprecedented degree of state control over the hierarchical Sufi assemblies of the towns and the lodges by which it could reach out to the country.

While Ismail's ideas were certainly like those of earlier times, the rural and tribal context in which they were deployed was quite distinct from that in which we have seen the terminology and ideas of Sufism previously emerge. The unregulated religious environment in which the Safawis emerged was one that allowed such intellectual resources of Sufi tradition as the idioms of the master's authority and the powers of God's friend to be deployed towards such self-aggrandizing ends without effective challenge. Indeed, several near contemporary accounts report how on several occasions the Qizilbash tribesmen cannibalized the enemies of their master Ismail.[228] According to an Indian Muslim ambassador to the Safawi court, 'it was decreed that whoever was a convinced believer [mu'taqid] among the great fighters of faith [ghazis] must partake a morsel of the roasted [human] body as his share. A terrifying crowd of man-eaters swarmed in and ate the body up such that not a trace of flesh or bone remained'.[229]

Here was a physical demonstration of the tribesmen's unswerving loyalty to a God who in incarnating himself in the body of Ismail was himself no less material in form. Here the early Safawis had much in common with the early Baktashi and similar tribal movements we have seen in the territories of the Ottomans. And this was precisely the problem. For the Safawi brotherhood not only emerged on the fractious eastern fringes of Ottoman territory, but its appeal to tribes' men nominally loyal to the Ottomans found expression in anti-Ottoman uprisings in support of the Safawis. Since in 1501 Ismail had also declared that his state would follow the ordinances of Shi'i rather than Sunni Islam, the rivalry between the Ottomans and Safawis also afforded each empire the rhetoric of defending the true version of Islam against its Sunni or Shi'i corrupters. The effectiveness of the Safawi family in channeling the loyalty of the Qizilbash tribesmen into the founding of a new state led to a corresponding attempt to suppress not only direct sympathizers but any similar movements among the tribesmen of Ottoman Anatolia.

As part of their policy to contain the Safawi threat, the Ottoman sultans Bayezid II (1481–1512) and Selim I (1512–1520) made several attempts to suppress the Qizilbash tribesmen present in their own domains.[230] Yet when we com pare the trajectories of Sufism under the Ottoman and Safawi empires, what emerges is not a simple picture of the triumph of a tribal Sufism realms a corresponding suppression of tribal forms and a patronage of settled forms of Sufism in the Ottoman Empire. For just as we have seen the Ottoman state itself struggling to contain the bands of tribal Sufis that had contributed so effectively to their every expansion, so did the creation of a stable state structure require the Safawis to reassess the usefulness of their own tribal Sufi followers. In the Safawi case, the result would be immeasurably more catastrophic for the Sufis than the Ottoman attempt at simply regulating the brother-hoods through greater organization. At the beginning of the Safawi period, the Qizilbash were secure in their special status as the spiritual disciples of the man they made king. But over the following decades, for their part the Safawi.

10.4   Iran: The Early Safawi Empire

The fortunes of Sufism in the Ottoman domains were not only a reflection of internal concerns but were also shaped by the need to respond to developments in neighboring regions. In this respect as in others, no single event in the early modern period was of greater importance than the rapid conquest of Iran by a tribal Sufi group who originated in the mountainous eastern frontiers of Ottoman rule. In 1501, with the help of an army of tribal followers, a teenaged hereditary Sufi master conquered the Iranian city of Tabriz. Over the next decade, he conquered the remainder of Iran to lay the foundations for an empire which at its greatest expanse would stretch from eastern Anatolia to the borders of India. Right up to its collapse in 1722, the imperial dynasty that the teenage Ismail Safawi (1487–1524) had founded bore the name of his own Safawi (or Safavid) Sufi family. The Safawi family and brotherhood originally garnered its following among the tribes of the regions around the mausoleum of the brotherhood's founder, Safi-al-Din (1334), in the highlands of what is now north-western Iran, though its wealth and prestige also lay in landholdings and influential urban followers.

However, it was the Safawis' tribal following that was to prove most influential in its rise. As in the case of other tribal Sufi movements, in the fifteenth century Safi al-Din's descendants Junayd and Haydar gained the following of increasing numbers of Turkoman tribesmen, whose energies they channeled into the kind of religiously-sanctioned raiding or ghaza that we have also seen characterizing the Ottoman frontier in the same period.[231] Referred to as the qizilbash or 'red-turbaned', the tribal followers of the Safawi Shaikhs were fiercely loyal to their masters. While, as in the case of other tribes men, we have no record of their side of the story, from the poetry of the founder of the Safawi Empire, Shah Ismail, they appear to have venerated him as a living incarnation of God.[232] Given that the logistical and emotional enterprise of founding a new state and binding its peoples together around the charismatic person of the ruler was hardly unique to Muslim states of the early modern period, it is perhaps worth comparing the 'political theology' of the early Safawis with European formulations of the king's sacred body from the same period.[233]

Against the view that Shah Ismail claimed to be God in human form, the objection has been made that his poetry invoked less a deliberate new doctrine of incarnation (hulul) than the poetic license lent to dispensation, Sufis played an active role in enabling and then ultimately disabling the Afghan inter regnum that followed.[234] If the beginning of Mughal rule therefore presented a picture of continuity of Sufi saints being on a comparable footing with sultans, as the Mughals' hold over India settled, the balance of power shifted in favor of the state. While the Mughals were never to attempt anything like the centralizing organization of brotherhoods seen under the Ottomans, important parallels do appear with both Ottomans and Safawis in the ways in which the Mughals came to interact with the personnel and the symbols of the Sufis. As in the case of other early modern states, the tradition of the Sufis presented a valuable resource for the state to appropriate.

Nowhere is this sense of Sufism as a state resource more apparent than in the great Mughal gazetteer of empire 'A'in-eAkbari (1590) in which the Sufi shrines and holy men in the territories of the Mughals were catalogued alongside every other category of imperial possession.[235] Akbar (1556–1605), the emperor who commissioned this work, represents the Mughals' most audacious attempt at channeling Sufism towards imperial ends. This was first seen in his decision to build a new imperial capital at Fatehpur Sikri around the home (and, shortly, the tomb) of Salim Chishti (1572), the Sufi who had miraculously granted him a son and heir.[236] As the conqueror of Bengal, Rajputana, Gujarat and Kashmir, Akbar's ambitions were even grander than this, leading him (or his chief courtier, Abu'l Fazl) to promote a new socio-religious organization in which elements of Muslim and Hindu religiosity were synthesized to form a new 'divine religion' or din-e-ilahi.[237] At heart, the din-e-ilahi was an imperial cult in which the now long-established idioms of the Sufis were co-opted for the emperor himself, who was designated as the perfect man (insan-e kamil) and spiritual director (murshid) of a circle of loyal Sufi disciples (murids) who were none other than his courtiers.[238] Given Akbar's varied millenarian concerns, there is also reason to connect his inception of the din-e-ilahi with the turning of the Islamic millennium in the middle of his reign. Even so, there was a series of precedents for the Mughals' imperial Sufi ideology, particularly in Iran. A century earlier a poetic Sufi parable entitled Salman-va-Absal addressed by Jami of Herat (d.1492) to his Aq-Qoyunlu patron Sultan Yaqub (1490) had similarly presented the tribal ruler in the guise of the Sufi 'perfect man' who was as such an ideal ruler over other, existentially-lesser Muslims.[239] Another precedent was the courtly chub-e-tariq ('rod of the way') ritual of the early Safawi rulers of Iran in which Qizilbash tribesmen were symbolically beaten into submission to their royal and spiritual master.[240]

Even if the short lifespan of the din-e-ilahi has seen it belittled as a princely caprice, the Sufi language of the emperor as the murshid and the courtier as murid would continue under subsequent Mughal rulers.[241] In the reign of Akbar's successor, Jahangir (r.1605–27), for example, the courtier 'Abd al-Satar collected the emperor's conversations in the form of a malfuzat text of the kind usually reserved for the speeches of Sufi Shaikhs.[242] In Sufi language, 'Abd-al-Satar expressly referred to this conversational compendium as the malfuzat-e jahangiri, in addition to describing Jahangir as a miracle-worker bearing the Sufi titles of 'master and guide' (pir-u-murshid).[243] Nor were the Mughals the only early modern rulers in South Asia to adapt these models of Sufi authority to their own courtly purposes. From his small mountain kingdom to the north of Delhi, a century after the reign of Jahangir the Indo-Afghan ruler Muhammad Khan Bangash (r.1713–1743) formulated a similar persona that blended the imagery of the Sufi master (pir) and the holy warrior (ghazi) and encouraged his courtiers to think of themselves as his Sufi disciples (chelas). Sufi models of authority were therefore highly transferable.[244] Overall, the dealings of the Mughal court with Sufism reflected the different roles that Sufism played in Indian society at large during the Mughal era.[245]

Even more than the other empires of the period, that of the Mughals brought together a variety of ethnic and religious groups, and though their identities were subject to change over time, there existed vivid senses of difference and factionalism between them. On the one hand, we find that the people who gathered around a given Sufi were predominantly of the same ethnic group as the Sufi himself, a factor which emerged from a context of the migration and displacement that was a feature of imperial society.[246] On the other hand, we find many cases of living Sufi masters or their shrines acting as vehicles of social integration by bringing together members of different ethnic and even religious groups.[247] In the Indian context, the doctrine may have served as an enabler of social unity that allowed Muslims and Hindus to recognize their different gods and practices as part of a greater cosmic unity.[247] While it is difficult to know how to prove such a generalization, the doctrine of wahdat-al-wujud did enable many Muslim poets (and their listeners) to imagine themselves entering temples and bowing down before their statues. In so far as such an ideological role can be granted to wahdat-al-wujud in India, it is significant that the doctrine also enjoyed state support in the similarly multi-religious empire of the Ottomans. But it was not only the message but also the medium that afforded such accommodation between members of different religious groups. Looking beyond Persian, we have already seen how vernacularization spread Sufi teachings through various local languages and this was no less the case in India. In the case of such Punjabi poets as Shah Husayn (1599), Sultan Bahu (1691) and Bulleh Shah (1757) and such Sindhi poets as Shah 'Abd al-Latif (1752), the Mughal period saw the trickling down to the rural level of Sufi idioms that before 1500 were largely the preserve of the urban classes.[248] This rural outreach not only brought religious ideas to a rural audience, but also mechanisms of arbitration and control, for whether in admonishing law breakers, settling disputes or teaching seemly behavior, the Sufis became important pillars of the rural social order. If in Mughal India they never became as closely connected to the state as in the Ottoman Empire, and even if it was at a greater distance from the state, the Sufis did much to maintain social order and harmony in India.[249]

Another important parallel between Sufi-state relations in the Ottoman and Mughal domains is seen in the Sufi role in expanding the imperial frontier. We have already seen the importance of Sufi 'settlers' to Ottoman expansion in southeast Europe and the Levant and there was a parallel process in Mughal India. The process in itself was not new to India and Sufis had helped expand Muslim settlement along the fertile Ganges plain throughout the period of the Delhi Sultanate (1206–1526), whether as self-helping frontiersmen or as recipients of lands granted by the sultan.[250] While this in part expanded the reach of formal Islamic learning, it also pushed the process of vernacularization to new levels of fusion, with Middle Bengali Sufi literature cross-fertilizing themes drawn from Tantrism and the old legends of the forests.[251]

This pattern of early modern states appropriating and redirecting either the personnel or idioms of Sufism was not unique to the three great empires of the period and can be seen in a variety of other settings. In many cases, this involved the mobility of elite Sufi families, moving from prestigious older centers to frontier environments in which the symbolic capital of their learning and existential status as friends were scarce resources. The incorporation of such mobile holy men into new states on the maritime frontier of the Indian Ocean helps us tie together the history of Sufism in different areas. The regional sultanates of the south Indian Deccan region are one example. As part of a larger policy of sponsoring immigrant over local elites, the Deccan's Bahmani sultans attracted the family of the sanctified Iranian Sufi, Shah Ni'matullah (1431), to their capital at Bidar.[252] Continuing these ties between saint and sultan into the following generations, the great south Indian historian, Firishta (1620) repeated the story, while another biography of Shah Ni'matullah was dedicated to the next Bahmani ruler, 'Ala' al-Din Ahmad Shah II (r. 1436–1458), who was described in the dedication as the 'sultan of Gnostics' (sultan al-urafa).[253] Other south Indian sultanates also saw a tightening of the relationship between Sufis and the state, as in the case of the great increase in the bestowing of land-grants (inam) and pensions (yawmiyya) to Sufis by the Adil Shah sultans of Bijapur in the seventeenth century.[254]

10.5   Southeast Asia: The Malay Sultanates

If the Deccani picture most closely resembled the Ottoman model, then there were also examples of smaller regional polities following the more radical cooption of Sufi idioms seen under Shah Ismail in Iran and Akbar in India. Such presentations of the king as 'Friend of God' and Perfect Man also occurred in the sultanates of Southeast Asia, making rots thaumaturges for the spice islands of Java and Sumatra. Early Malay sources such as the Hikayat Raja-Raja Pasai ('Tales of the Kings of Pasai') show how even in the earliest Islamic sultanates established in the region, sultans were being presented as sharing the power to work miracles (karama) in common with the Sufis.[255] Not only devotional hyperbole, but such imaginative associations also point to the interdependence of religious and trade networks that allowed the Sufi 'imports' of the early modern era. While the process can only be glimpsed through miraculous narratives preserved in royal chronicles, the conversion of the Malay rulers of the new mercantile states that emerged in Southeast Asia in the fifteenth and sixteenth centuries was widely attributed to the charisma and teachings of such mobile Sufis who sailed to the region from such older centers as Baghdad, though more recent research suggests India to have been a more likely source for these holy men.[256]

From sixteenth century Southeast Asia, evidence survives of writings by Sufis themselves, whose works testify to what was already a highly sophisticated grasp of metaphysical subtleties on this oceanic frontier. This sophistication reflected the emergence of a class of peripatetic Sufi scholars in the region.[257] In the case of Hamza Fansuri (d.1527 or 1590), we find a Sufi who was born in Southeast Asia travelling to Mecca,

Baghdad and even Palestine before returning to teach in his home region, again suggesting a model of two-way circulation more than simple center-to-periphery transfer.[258] By Fansuri's lifetime a century later, Pasai had developed into a religious no less than a commercial carrefour from which Fansuri and his disciples transmitted Sufi tradition to new geographical areas.. Poetic as well as doctrinal, Fansuri's own abundant writings in Malay are the great early example.[259] At the same time that Fansuri sought Malay equivalents for Sufi terms, in the midst of this vernacularization, his loaning into Malay of key terms from the original Arabic lexicon of the early Baghdad Sufis helped maintain the continuity of this new Malay Sufism with earlier tradition.[260] Somewhat later, such key words as wali ('Friend of God') were also borrowed into Javanese from the Arabic Sufi lexicon. In line with the larger early modern picture of state-Sufi interaction, the adaptation of Sufi tradition to this new Malay cultural context occurred in partnership with larger ideological agendas. Given that Su fis such as Fansuri were supported by royal patrons, it is scarcely surprising that the Sufism these patrons supported bolstered rather than undermined their own authority. Even so, it must be said that the circumstances and even date of Fansuri's career remain contested and so, as we see below, it is only in the seventeenth century that we can speak more clearly about the interactions between Sufi and state in Southeast Asia.

10.6 Central Asia: Shrine Societies

If the picture in Southeast Asia is hazy during the sixteenth century, we possess much fuller documentation of the traffic between Sufi brotherhoods and the state in Central Asia. The case of the Naqshbandiyya is a valuable one, since it shows how the same brotherhood became very different in its various settings, pointing to the interactions between a tradition, its participants, and its environment. If in the Ottoman domains the Naqshbandis remained only loosely organized through the early modern period, in the oasis towns of Central Asia the case could not have been more different. After forming a more centralized organization structure under the leadership of Ubaydullah Ahrar (1490), the brotherhood (or more concretely the followers of Ahrar) effectively constituted a state in their own right, operating a system of 'protection' or bimayat through which the brotherhood's members not only received spiritual blessings but also the more tangible aid of employment on Ahrar's vast agricultural landholdings.[261] This policy of agrarian expansion through using waqf endowments to grant under used arable land to saintly families was promoted was by the Timuri sultans (particularly Husayn Bayqara (1469–1506), and when the state itself collapsed, the saintly families held onto their rich agrarian resources.[262]

Through the fifteenth and sixteenth centuries, the Naqshbandi brotherhood offered its vast membership among settled peasants and townsmen such state-like services as protection from nomadic raiders or such privileges as immunity from taxation.[263] Having emerged in the 1100s as a quietist, poor and loosely organized brotherhood, by 1500 the Naqshbandiyya had become a vastly wealthy and highly centralized organization with close ties to every dynasty it encountered. Surviving letters written by Ubaydullah Ahrar and the members of his organization document the operation of a highly effective bureaucracy which paralleled and in certain cases outreached the authority of the formal rulers of the region. Startlingly practical in character, the many surviving letters show the brotherhood as a mechanism for solving property and legal disputes, offering 'passports' to travelers, giving cash grants to peasants and tax breaks to merchants. While Ubaydullah Ahrar and his Naqshbandi heirs were the most successful operators of this system of 'shrine societies', they were by no means the only ones. The early modern period saw the system expand throughout the vast Central Asian steppe lands, with the Sufis' institutional longevity enabling them to manage a fragile agricultural ecosystem far more effectively than the ephemeral dynasties of sultans.[264] Further east along the silk road, Ubaydullah's Naqshbandi descendants were even more successful in their state-making ventures. One of 'Ubaydullah's own sons, Ahmad Kasani (1543), expanded the reach of brotherhood as far as Kashgaria in modern western China and ultimately to Tibet, attempting to replicate there the earlier Naqshbandi success in bringing the moral restraints of Shari'a to the Turkic tribesmen of the steppes. In 1531, in what appears to have been a convenient marriage of the missionary expansiveness of the Naqshbandiyya and the attractions of the wealthy trade routes that crossed through the Himalaya, one of Kasani's disciples from the Shaybani dynasty even launched a jihad against Tibet.[265]

10.7 North Africa: Marini & Sadi Kingdom

Under the Marini (1215–1465) and Sadi (1509–1659) dynasties of Morocco, North Africa saw the Sufis in similarly elevated positions. While Sufism had previously faced many detractors in North Africa, the Marini period witnessed steady gains in the status of the region's Sufis. In part, this came about through the Sufi affiliations of lawyers trained at the great Qarawiyy in madrasa that the Marinis funded in their capital of Fes to provide their government with administrators.[266] When the Portuguese conquered Tangier, for example, the Shadhili Sufi Muhammad al-Jazuli (d.1465) helped lead a jihad in defense of Muslim territory that brought together twelve thousand Sufis and tribesmen under his leadership.[267] Not all Sufis were happy with the rise of the Wattasis, particularly those who held positions in the Marini administration, leading such non-Qadiri Sufis as Ahmad al-Zarruq (d.1493) to leave Fes for a long exile in Cairo.[268] Developing the idea that the Sufi was the 'substitute' or badil who rightfully held authority in the absence of the Prophet, al-Jazuli and his successors carved out an influential place for themselves not only at court but in North Africa's rural communities as well. Like the Safawis at the same time in Iran, in its ascent to power the Sadi dynasty made use of the millenarian expectations of the period, drawing on eschatological themes in the writings of Jazuli in partic ular. As in other regions, the decades around the turn of the Islamic millennium in 1591 witnessed millenarian anxieties in Morocco that both Sufis and sultans sought to channel to their own messianic claims.[269] The legitimacy of the early Sadi's was framed in precisely such terms. Their dynastic name of al-dawla- al-Sadiyya ('the salvific state') drew on the notion oisada ('bliss, salvation') in the teachings of Jazuli. It encapsulated the millenarian promise to find a perfect Muslim community based on the expulsion of the Portuguese infidels and the shared rule of dynastic descendants of the Prophet and the Jazuli saintly axes.[270]

Early on in their reign, the importance the Sadi's lent to the Sufis was seen in the devotion the Sadi founder Muhammad-al-Qaim (1509–1517) held for Jazuli himself; the dynasty's founder even asked to be buried beside the Sufi. This led al-Qaim's successor Ahmad al-Araj (1517–1544) to exhume al-Jazuli's body and rebury it in a specially constructed mausoleum in the Sadi's capital of Marrakech in which saint and sultan were interred together in a vivid symbol of their unity. The rise of the Sadi also involved a struggle to control the semi-Islamized southern frontier of Berber tribesmen and prosperous caravan trails. The many teaching centers which Jazuli's followers established in the countryside no less than the towns not only spread literacy through the importance they lent to scriptural and legal studies, but also gave Jazulis the qualifications to enter the Sadi bureaucracy in a manner that echoed the place of educated Sufis in the Ottoman bureaucracy.[271] As with the fate of the Safawi Sufis and their Qizilbash followers in Iran, after around 1550 the Sadi rulers viewed the lofty Jazuli claims to authority as more threatening than advantageous and so moved to persecute their former Sufi partners. Even so, such expanding state Sufi authority was not only achieved in the urban settings of the Moroc can 'realm of government' (bilad-al-makhzan), but also through the establishment of rural lodges among Berber tribes in the frontier 'realm of dissidence' (bilad al-siba'). In the process, they brought abandoned and previously uncultivated land under cultivation, developments which, as with the Naqshbandi role in the unsettled tribal/agricultural zones of Central Asia at the same time, made Sufis leaders of what amounted to agrarian Sufi frontier fiefdoms.[272] In time, this early modern development policy would also see African slaves purchased to work the land, forging an enduring religious economy of Arab saints and African slaves that survived into modern times.[273]

10.8   The Songhay Empire and Funj Sultnate

The fifteenth and sixteenth centuries also saw the introduction of Sufism to new Muslim states emerging in Saharan Africa. This was probably already the case in the earliest African Islamic state of the period, the Songhay Empire (1464–1591) of west Saharan Africa, where Islamic symbolism was used to support a royal cult in which the emperor was endowed with miraculous powers.[274] While the role of Sufis in these developments is unclear due to the lack of early sources on the Songhay Empire, we do know of various North African Sufis settling in the key scholarly and trading outpost of Timbuktu during the Songhay era. As a result, brotherhoods with a strong presence in North Africa such as the Shadhilis and Qadiris were also those which were taken south.[275] The early presence of Shadhili and Qadiri Sufism was therefore in terms of affiliated individual migrants rather than structured brotherhoods. As a result, what we see emerging in Africa were family-tariqas, that is, locally powerful holy families affiliated by lineage to but organizationally independent from the wider trans-regional brotherhoods such as the Qadiriyya from which they gained prestige in their local settings.[276] As with the Islamization of other regions of the world in the early modern period, especially important in this process were Sufi migrants belonging to prestigious Silsila lineages associating them with the brotherhoods of the Muslim Mediterranean, particularly Morocco and Egypt. As one historian has described the matter, the characteristic Islamic presence in the Funj and Darfur states (of early modern Sudan) was the holy lineage, which usually traced its origins to an immigrant who intermarried locally. The lineage gains a monopoly over education, medical and magical practice in its locality and frequently con solidates its power by receiving tax-exempt status (job) or landed estates (hakuraiqta) from the rulers.[277]

In Saharan Africa, then, as in other regions in the same period, kings and Sufis negotiated workable alliances. Partly in reflection of the juridical Sufism we have seen flourishing in North Africa in this period, and partly in reflection of the rarity of literacy in an African context at this time, Saharan Sufism was also characterized by a strong emphasis on written learning. In many regions, Sufis were termed faqihs or 'jurisconsults' in reference to the prestigious legal learning in which they also specialized. While certain legends survive of Sufis moving into the Sudan region during this period, it is only with the emergence of the Funj sultanate (1504–1821) that the picture of Sufi activities becomes clearer. Islam had first appeared in Nilotic Sudan through the influx of Arab pastoralists in the thirteenth and fourteenth centuries which led to the collapse of the Christian kingdoms of Maqurra and 'Aiwa. By the Funj period, scholars from the madrasas of Egypt and North Africa to the north of Sudan were widely affiliated to Sufi brotherhoods; and, for scholars willing to make the southward journey through the desert, the establishment of the Funj sultanate created rich opportunities of patronage. Funj patronage was typically given in the form of abundant unused land and so, as in the other imperial attempts, we have seen at settling frontier regions, in Sudan Sufis similarly received land grants and founded agricultural villages known as khal was ('retreats'). From there, through employment and inter marriage, they brought about the gradual conversion of their surroundings to an Islam that was inseparable from the Sufis who transmitted it.[278] As in other regions, this pattern of the gradual acculturation of Africans to Muslim lifeways was accompanied by a parallel process of the adaptation of Islam to African ways.[279] With their miraculous powers, their skills in writing Arabic talismans and their posthumous transformation into sacred shrines, the Sufis were central to this two-way pattern of Islamization.

10.9 Legalists and Renewers 1600 A.D.-1800 A.D.

Such was the permeation by the early modern period of Sufi ideas and institutions through all levels of society across most of the Islamic world that it is often difficult to decide who was and was not a Sufi. Whether by paying homage to a shrine, reciting a popular song, or taking formal initiation at the hands of a living master, ordinary Muslims were exposed to a Sufism that had largely become indistinguishable from Islam in general. By 1600, the tradition fostered by the Sufis a tradition they claimed was transmitted from the Prophet Muhammad through such early Sufis as Junayd and the founders of the brotherhoods down to their own time had sufficiently diversified that there now existed a confusing variety of Sufi practices, doctrines, and organizations. There are many reasons why the seventeenth century 'crisis of conscience' occurred when it did. As we have already seen in the introduction to this chapter, while its timing can partly be explained by the turning of the Muslim millennium in 1591 (the year 1000 in the Islamic calendar) the cultural time of the Islamic calendar was not the only factor. The processual time of the historian must also be considered. As we have already seen, the last century of the first Muslim millennium and the first century of the second Muslim millennium coincided with the processual time of a panoply of social, economic, and political changes that have led historians to refer to the period as one of early modernity. It is the considerable effects of this coincidence of cultural and processual time that allows us to speak of the period as characterized by a crisis of conscience which affected many groups and not only the Sufis.

This was part of a gradual and cumulative conscience driven critique that emerged in the seventeenth to blossom most vividly in the eighteenth century when the heightening pressures of early modernity saw the collapse of many Muslim states. Whatever its theological dimensions, in historical terms the crisis of conscience can be understood as a response to the abundant success of Islamization rather than its failure, as many of the clerical critics of the Sufis claimed in their accusations. Such increasing awareness of the troubling diversification of tradition itself occurred as growing numbers of Muslim scholars travelled to other Muslim regions (particularly outside the Middle East) as part of the larger interactions between different regions that characterized early modernity. A connection can also be made between the rise of the innovation critique and the increasing interaction between regions that also characterized the period. For as country people moved to the growing cities of the early modern empires, they brought with them their distinctive vernacularized Islams. And as literate urbanites were dispatched on government service to provincial or rural areas, they were in turn confronted with the variations of Sufi Islam in the countryside.

Rather, in the first century of the new Muslim millennium, the crisis remained one of questioning which aspects of Sufi tradition were beneficial and which obstructive to the proper Muslim life. It would have to wait until the great Muslim Reformation in the late nineteenth and early twentieth centuries until large numbers of Muslims saw Sufism in all its forms as failing to connect them to the intentions of the Prophet. Even so, in the seventeenth century, there did emerge a new emphasis on legal compliance in each of the early modern empires. But rather than looking for innate tensions between abstract moralistic and mystical pieties representing legal and mystical authority, in historical terms it is more fruitful to conceive this shift towards legalism and the crisis of conscience behind it as involving groups re acting to circumstances. By seeing mystical knowledge and legal book learning as forms of authority which might alternatively be united in a single person or separately championed by rivals, this contextual approach helps us reckon with the inconsistencies of the older static picture of mystics versus lawyers. For what we are mostly looking at is a picture of Sufis using the law to either criticize one another or else criticize the common people (though we will see important instances of legal specialists with no Sufi affiliations using the law to criticize the Sufis in a masse). In the following years, we understand what amounted to a widespread seventeenth century challenge by the lawmakers in almost all corners of the Islamic world. If many of these legalistic challengers were themselves Sufis seeking to undermine brethren who took the law more lightly, in other cases we will see the increasing status of a scholarly class with no Sufi affiliations at all.

10.10 The Mediterranean: The Later Ottomans

In this survey of the seventeenth century crisis of conscience, let us again turn first to the Ottoman Empire. There, despite the state's investment in training a class of legally expert 'ulama, the period between around 1620 and 1685 saw a faction of these scholars use the prestige of their learning not in the service of social integration but in sowing discord in a society they regarded as morally bankrupt. Known as the Kadizadelis, this faction criticized the Sufis who were an integral part of Ottoman society. As such, the polemics the Kadizadelis exchanged with their Sufi opponents represented a struggle between different parties within the Ottoman system.[280] The eponymous founder of the Kadizadeli movement, Kadizade Mehmed (d.1635), was the son of a minor provincial judge who came to Istanbul in search of employment in the imperial religious bureaucracy or ilmiyye. Having scaled the ladder of the official waiz or 'preacher' hierarchy (one of the 'ilmiyye's lowest tiers), Kadizade Mehmed used his influence as preacher in the largest mosques of Istanbul to disseminate his vision of a decadent age needing a renewal of faith (tajdid-e-iman). The scope of his critique was wide, taking on not only the doctrine of the Unity of Being but also Sufi musical concerts, the popular rituals of the Sufi culture of saints and a range of degenerate activities (smoking tobacco, drinking wine or coffee) for which he regarded morally lax Sufis as responsible. As we have already noted, the key critical tool was the notion of bid'a or 'innovation' from the Prophetic Example, which he used to recast the tradition of the Sufis as a deviation of the true faith. Of course, the Sufis answered back and defended the practices the Kadizadelis condemned. But nothing could hide the fact that, after centuries of increasing Sufi influence in both society and state, a new social faction or even party was emerging which used the charge of innovation and the authority of law to place its members in a position to challenge the authority of Sufis who were in many cases privileged pillars of the Ottoman establishment.[281]

Moreover, as far as the ruling elite was concerned, the task of the religious bureaucracy was not to strictly enforce Islam but to maintain social order through the pragmatic rather than literal interpretation of Islamic law. Far from maintaining social harmony, the Kadizadelis were at first regarded as upsetting it, though as time went by, the significant following they acquired rendered them political players, with some high palace officials attempting to use Kadizadelis for their own purposes. Sufis did, after all, hold many of the most comfortable sinecures in the Ottoman system. Statistics show that the Kadizadeli heyday between 1621 and 1685 also saw almost half of the preacher positions granted to members of those Sufi brotherhoods favored by the higher officials who made the appointments.[282] Even so, there was more at stake than government jobs. The resonance the Kadizadelis found in the streets suggests they were more than a disgruntled fringe and tapped into a wider conscience brooding on the twin concerns of moral decline and the need for renewal. For many, the Sufis were regarded as the root of the problem. The popularity of the messianic movement centered on the self-proclaimed Jewish messiah Sabbatai Sevi (d.1676) among Ottoman Jews in the 1650s and 1660s suggests that the desire for renewal was not unique to Muslims and may have sprung from deeper socio-political tensions that affected all groups in the empire.[283] Even after the Kadizadelis petered out in the 1680s, this conscience resurfaced in various Ottoman domains. This dissemination may have been connected to the other Muslim regions in which this conscience spread through networks of texts and teachers which historians have not yet traced. In 1711, for example, a preacher in Cairo declared Sufi saints unable to perform miracles and lacking any special knowledge that was hidden to other Muslims and so encouraged his listeners to prevent Sufi dhikr chants, destroy saintly shrines and turn Sufi lodges into madrasas.[284] Yet, while legalistic critiques on Sufi 'innovations' and 'excesses' were by no means unique to this period, from the seventeenth century they were finding a deeper social resonance as certain groups in society chose to identify themselves with a theological critique that had tangible consequences by way of the distribution of influence, competition and opportunity.

By the eighteenth century in Egypt, the Ottoman Khalwatiyya Sufis were promoters of a Sufism in which the experience of ultimate reality (haqiqa) was in scrupulous harmony with the injunctions of the law (shari'a).[285] Far from seeing a divorce between Sufis and 'ulama, by the mid-eighteenth century this resulted in the rise of the Khalwatiyya to the favorite affiliation of the teachers at al-Azhar, the most important seminary for Sunni ulama in the Middle East.[286] The crisis of conscience was not restricted to cities like Cairo and Istanbul and, on the tribal periphery of Ottoman rule in the Najd region of Arabia, the second half of the eighteenth century also saw the emergence of ultimately the most influential critic of Sufi 'innovations' Muhammad-ibn Abd-al-Wahhab (1787).[287] The central concern of Ibn Abd al-Wahhab was to attack all forms of 'innovation' and 'idolatry' that divorced Muslims from what he saw as Muhammad's original teachings. This in turn led him to denounce such practices as shrine veneration and the treating of Sufi holy men as intermediaries between man and God. While the modern rise of the Saudi family as the rulers of Arabia would see the development of Ibn Abd al-Wahhab's ideas into a wholesale anti-Sufi agenda, in his own period Ibn Abd-al-Wahhab was part of the wider conscience calling for a return to the Prophetic Example and the rejection of innovations. If Ibn 'Abd al-Wahhab stood at the furthest extreme of this spectrum (bringing him as many critics as supporters), he was still a man of an era in which Sufism might be reformed but rarely completely rejected.

10.11 Iran: The Later Safawis

If the Ottoman seventeenth century saw the influence of anti-Sufi 'ulama wax and wane according to the alliances they fostered against Sufis they identified as enemies, then parallel developments were at work in Iran at the same time. We have already seen how, after coming to power as a tribal Sufi movement backed by Qizilbash tribesmen, the Safawi dynasty found the model of the Sufi brotherhood too restrictive to bind together the varied peoples of their empire. Over subsequent decades, the Safawis 'imported' Shi'i legal experts from the Jabal Amil mountains of Lebanon, who spread their critique of the Sufis widely through Iranian society by attracting students and writing legal guidebooks in simple Persian.[288] The shrines that were so central to the Sufis' popularity and wealth lost their patronage and pilgrim traffic and were gradually replaced by rival and specifically Shi'i shrines known as imamzadas ('descendents of the imam').[289] Those brotherhoods with the firmest Sunni commitments (such as the Qadiris and Naqshbandis) were either suppressed or exiled to the fringes of the empire. While for most of the sixteenth century these new Shi'i Sufis managed to survive and occasionally flourish in Iran, during the reign of Shah 'Abbas I (r.1587–1629) they became less and less politically useful and so the cycle of their suppression was completed. By building an army of slaves, the Safawis freed themselves from their military dependence on Sufi-affiliated Qizilbash tribesmen, while the importing of Shi'i clerics from Lebanon brought the dynasty authority that no longer depended on the Sufi origins of their Safawi family. While the Ottomans continued to find Sufi brotherhoods useful aids in governance and expansion, in Iran the same organizations became superfluous. In 1593, matters came to a head when followers of the Nuqtawi movement, which a created a millenarian synthesis from elements of Sufi tradition and the incarnationist tendencies of the frontier, rebelled against Safawi's rule. While the shahs held onto their Sufi title of murshid-e-kamil or 'perfect master', from then on their authority was mainly as Shi'i sovereigns allied with legalistic clerics who were only too willing to denigrate their Sufi rivals.[290] Around the turn of the eighteenth century, the rise of the fanatically anti-Sufi jurist Muhammad Baqir Majlisi (1699) and his successor Muhammad Husayn Khatunabadi (1739) as the chief state jurist saw Sufis banned from the capital at Isfahan.[291] Even so, the collapse of the Safawi Empire in the 1720s afforded new opportunities for the Sufis and the last decades of the eighteenth century saw the migrating return to Iran of several Ni'matullahi masters almost three centuries after their ancestors sought patronage at the Bahmani court in India.[291]

10.12 The Central Asian Frontier and China

Faced with the westward expansion of the Chinese Qing dynasty from the 1640s and the disintegration of the Mongol khanate of the Chaghtais, Afaq Khwaja drew on the older Naqshbandi role as political mediators to travel to Tibet and enter negotiations with the fifth Dalai Lama, Ngawang Lobsang Gyatso (1682), whose own military power base had rendered him the ruler of a united Tibet.[292] With diplomatic support from Buddhist Tibet and military support from Qalmaq tribesmen, Afaq Khwaja was able, in 1680, to seize power from the Chaghtai rulers and establish a system of Naqshbandi political rule over the region of Kashgaria that would survive until its fall in 1760 under the conquests of the Chinese Qing Empire. Known as the ishanat after the respectfully indirect 'they' by which its leaders were known, during its day the Sufi ishanat state managed a 'veritable economy of spirituality' in which the hierarchy of the brotherhood directed taxes and land-holdings at the same time as administering to the moral and spiritual guidance of its followers through the characteristically Naqshbandi format of the séance (suhbat) around the master.[293] By the seventeenth century, Chinese Muslim scholars working further east in the cultural heartlands of China proper were not only translating such Sufi works into Chinese but also writing original texts on Sufi theory in literary Chinese. In a Chinese playing out of the process of vernacularization we have already seen at work in Turkish, Malay and Indian settings, Wang Taiyii (d.1657/1658?), from his residence in the Southern Ming capital of Nanjing, grappled with the use of such existing Chinese conceptual terms as chen to express such Muslim notions as divine unity (Arabic tawhid) and the unique revelation of the Quran. In addition to writing his Chen-ching chaowei ('Displaying the Concealment of the Real Realm'), a Chinese version of the Persian Lawa'ih ('Flashing Lights') of the Naqshbandi poet Abd-al-Rahman Jami (1492), Liu Chih also wrote a celebrated biography of the Prophet Muhammad in Chinese.[294]

10.13 India: The Later Mughals

Turning to Mughal India, in the seventeenth century we saw certain aspects of Sufi thought (the doctrine of Unity of Being in particular) opening the possibility to interpret non-Muslim religious ideas as part of God's limitless manifestation. In his Haqa'iq-e Hindi (Indian Truths), for example, Abd-al- Wahid Bilgrami (1608) compiled a dictionary of devotional songs to the god Vishnu in which Hindu hymns were given Islamic meanings to render them fit for Sufi musical concerts. In the Mirat-al- Haqa'iq ('Mirror of Truths') of 'Abd-al-Rahman Chishti (1683) a century later, there appeared a sympathetic Persian rendering of the Sanskrit Bhagavad Gita in which Krishna's message was seen as no less compatible with the teachings of Islam.[295] Various other Sufis, including the Mughal Prince Dara Shikoh (1659), took interest in the teachings of the Hindu sages they regarded as the 'Indian unitarians' (mutvahidun-e hind). Yet such mystical accommodation to the Indian environment created tensions of its own and was widely attacked by the later part of period. For in India, too, we see the rise of a legalistic critique presenting certain Sufi practices as 'innovations' from the Prophetic Example. Over five hundred of the letters were collected into an epistolary compendium or maktubat from which scholars have struggled to reconstruct a coherent overall doctrine. Nonetheless, certain key themes are apparent. One which we have already encountered elsewhere is the criticism of innovation and the need to return to the Prophetic Example, a theme related to the wider importance to the law. The present age, he thought, was one in which morals had become tax through the abandoning of Sunna and Shari'a and so required a renewer to bring Muslims back to the path of salvation. Sirhindi had no qualms about declaring himself to be this renewer and his claim to this grand role brought him many disciples.

Another major theme of Sirhindi's letters was the danger of misunderstanding the teachings of Ibn-al-Arabi. Although Sirhindi saw himself as properly interpreting rather than disproving Ibn al-Arabi's work, he was mindful of the dangers of their misinterpretation. This was particularly the case with the doctrine of Unity of Being which he correctly claimed encouraged some Muslims to minimize the difference between Islam and other religions or the difference between God and themselves. Instead Sirhindi argued for a doctrine of Unity of Witnessing (wahdat al-shuhud), which held that while in his highest ecstasies the mystic might feel as though he had become united with God, for those who (like Sirhindi) traveled further on the Path, it was clear that God was always other than his creatures and that the Unity of Being was merely a lofty illusion on the way to the fuller realization of God's otherness. Unlike figures whom we have seen equating Muslim teachings with the higher doctrines of the

Hindus, for Sirhindi there always remained a clear division between Islam and the religions of infidels. Based on the letters that Sirhindi wrote to the members of the Mughal court, it was once thought that he was responsible for a shift in imperial policy which saw the inter-religious experiments of Akbar replaced by the renewed commitment to Shari'a seen in the reign of Awrangzeb (1658–1707).[296] As in the case of the Kadizadelis in the Ottoman Empire, in the first century of the new millennium the Naqshbandi critique of a society which had gone astray found resonance among a significant segment of India's Muslim elite. Awrangzeb's reintroduction of various aspects of Shari'a in to Mughal governance has been shown as having more to do with court politics than Sirhindi's influence.[297] Even as there were many Muslims in India who gravitated towards a Sufism which accommodated Islam to the religious pluralism of the Indian environment, there were also those who found attractive Sirhindi's demand that the Hindus be treated like dogs and insulted through the slaughtering of their sacred cows and the imposition of the jizya poll tax.[298] Yet, despite Sirhindi's criticisms of Sufis who failed to up hold the law, he still remained committed to the notion of Sufism itself as a tradition that connected Muslims to the Prophet's teaching, reflecting larger trends in other parts of the Muslim world. In part, this was because the diminishing of the state as a provider of social order magnified the importance of sub-state providers of social control.

In part, this was because the collapse of an empire controlled by a Muslim elite was interpreted as divine punishment for Muslim immorality. But if the Muslims were seen to be astray, then the Sufi Path was still seen as offering the solution, albeit the legally conscientious form promoted by the heirs of Sirhindi, 'Abd al-Haqq and their heirs. As the eighteenth century saw the old imperial capital pillaged by a sequence of invaders, Hindu as well as Muslim, prominent Sufis such as the Naqshbandis Shah Waliullah (d. 1763) and Mirza Mazhar Jan-e-Janan (1781) in Delhi and the Chishti Nur Muhammad Maharawi (d.1791) in Punjab pushed forward the legalistic critiques of the seventeenth century, not least through the establishing of madrasas to spread their teachings.[299] The same logic was found in the Delhi circles of Muhammad Nasir Andalib (1759) and his son Mir Dard (1785), who in founding a form of Sufism they referred to as the 'Path of Muhammad' (tariqa Muhammadiyya) likewise sought to redirect Sufi practices into harmony with the authority and Example of the Prophet. In line with the increasing focus on the study of Hadith, the Prophet himself came to play an increasing role in spiritual practice: the disciple now sought annihilation in Muhammad before reaching Allah.[300] Developments in India were again part of the larger international picture, which also saw the notion of as tariqa Muhammadiyya being spread in North

Africa by such figures as Ahmad al-Tijani (d.1815) a few decades later. But rather than a new eighteenth century phenomenon, a distinct 'neo-Sufism' as some scholars have called it, the focus on Muhammad and his Prophetic Example was the culmination of the general conscience of renewal that emerged in the previous century.[301] It is therefore important not to overstate the influence of the legalistic Sufis, especially in the vernacular sphere of Sufism which continued to develop in India throughout this period. In rural Sindh and Punjab, the rustic vernacular verses of Shah 'Abd-al-Latif (1752) and Bulleh Shah (1757) included many satirical jibes at the Muslim law makers. As Shah 'Abd al-Latif sang in mockery of those who studied the classics of law and grammar, if you have read Kanz, Quduri, Kafiya and understand all of them, It is as though a lame ant, fallen into a pit, would regard the sky.[302]

10.14 Southeast Asia: Renewal in the Malay States

We have already seen Hamza Fansuri spreading the ideas of Ibn al-'Arabi in Malay at the court of Aceh at the western end of the Indonesian archipelago. In the seventeenth century, his disciple Shams al-Din (d.1630) of Pasai in northern Sumatra received the post Shaikh al-islam (placing him second only to the sultan in rank) at the court of Sultan Ala al-Din Riayat Shah (1588–1604) and acted as the Sufi master of Sultan Iskandar Muda (1607–1636), whom he regularly accompanied on state occasions.[303] In sources from Aceh itself, we find the notion of the Perfect Man or insan al-kamil, which featured in the teachings of Ibn-al-'Arabi and Hamza Fansuri alike, being used to aggrandize Sultan Iskandar Muda.[304] Already seen in Iran and India, this royal co-option of Sufi idioms can be seen at work in a Malay court poem to Iskandar Muda which borrowed from the original Arabic lexicon of the Sufis to describe the sultan as 'Royal Axis, completely perfect / Friend of God, in complete union/Gnostic King (Raja qutub yang sampurna kamil/ Wali Allah, sampurna wasil/Raja arif)'.[305] Just as Iskandar Muda seems to have been influenced by the Sufi titles of his Mughal contemporaries Akbar and Jahangir, in the course of the 16th and 17th centuries this presentation of the king as Sufi cosmic axis (qutb) or 'Friend of God' (wali) was also put to work in the new Muslim states developing on the archipelago frontier, whether at Mataram in Java or Gowa on Sulawesi.[306]

As one of the earliest Sumatrans to have written in Arabic, in his own writings Shams al-Din similarly showed the influence of Indian Sufi ideas on the Malay imagination, particularly the ideas of Muhammad ibn Fadlullah (1620) of Burhanpur in central India, whose Tuhfat al-Mursalaila Ruh al-Nabi ('Gift Addressed to the Spirit of the Prophet') subsequently spread even deeper into Southeast Asia through its translation into Javanese.[307]

Nur al-Din's upbringing in the Indian region of Gujarat suggests that his ideas should also be seen in relation to the larger currents we have seen washing through India in his lifetime. Nur al-Din's critique of the teachings of his Sufi predecessor in Aceh, Hamza Fansuri (particularly in relation to Fansuri's version of Unity of Being) may even have drawn on the attack on the same doctrine we have seen carried out by Ahmad Sirhindi in the India of Nur al-Din's youth.[308] More clear is the evidence connecting Nur al-Din to the 'Aydarusi brotherhood from the Hadramawt region of Yemen, whose diffusion through the Indian Ocean consistently disseminated a legally-oriented Sufism.[309] 'Aydarusis such as Nur al-Din were not the only itinerant Sufis preaching this legalistic Sufism in Southeast Asia during the seventeenth century. The early modern intensification of Southeast Asia's connections to Arabia during the eighteenth century saw this legalistic Sufism spread further through the movement of more Sufis from the Hadramawt and the transmission of their teachings as far as North Africa. It was these mobile Sufis who connected Malay Muslims to the wider currents of the age.[310] It seems possible that this more intensified circulation of ideas was linked to the increased sea traffic that accompanied the growth of early modern trade. The rise of mercantile Dutch power in Southeast Asia even brought about the introduction of Islam to South Africa through the deporting of a renowned Malay Sufi, Yusuf al-Maqasari (d.1699), to the Dutch outpost at Cape Town.[311] Even in the shackles of Europeans, the Sufis continued to breach new frontiers in the spread of Islam.

10.15 Shari's in the Sahara

Comparable patterns can be seen in North and Saharan Africa during this period. We have already seen how the fifteenth century saw the emergence in Morocco of a self-consciously legalistic Sufism through the efforts of such figures as al-Jazuli and Ahmad al-Zarruq. In such writings as his Aqida ('Creed'), Jazuli had likewise displayed concern for outward propriety, calling for the community to raise its moral standards. While he had his definitions of what it meant, Jazuli was among the several Sufis of the period who spoke of a tariqa Muham-madiyya or 'Path of Muhammad' in which the practices of the Sufis were to be constrained by the example of Muhammad's actions. In seventeenth and eighteenth-century North Africa, these attempts at a union of mystical and legal claims to authority continued through the model of the 'juridical Sufi' whose knowledge and behavior combined the traditions of the Sufis and the Prophet. By initiating travelers who came to his teaching center in the Moroccan city of Fes, al-Tijani expanded his following southwards into West Africa, where it would form one of the most influential Muslim organizations of the nineteenth century.[312] In North Africa itself, this expansion of a legally conformist Sufism with no place for 'innovations' was echoed in the policies of the Moroccan rulers Sidi Muhammad ibn 'Abdul-lah (1757–1790) and Mawlay Sulayman (1792–1822), with the latter seeing many Sufi brotherhoods as obstacles to the religious renewal he sought for his kingdom.[313]

Even so, the early modern period in North Africa saw Sufi brotherhoods gain new wealth by becoming major players in the expanding trade between Europe, North Africa and the Sahara, rendering their leaders among the most wealthy and influential figures in their communities. Whether with the Nasiriyya in the northern Sahara or the Qadiri-affiliated merchants of the Kunta clan in the southern Saharan regions, by providing wide-reaching networks of trust, communication and credit, Sufi brotherhoods acted as enabling mechanisms for the growing trans-Saharan trade that connected Africa to Europe.[314] At the same time, these trade routes were also knowledge routes by which Sufis carried Arabic learning and the Nasiri brother-hood's syllabus of legal and mystical study into the oasis settlements of what is now Mauretania, Mali, Niger and Sudan.[315] Even as somewhat haphazard networks, they were still able to connect Saharan Africa to practices and debates that were emerging in North Africa, Egypt and Africa. During the mid-seventeenth century, African affiliations to the Qadiri brotherhood were spread by Taj al-Din Bahari, who was originally from Baghdad and who attempted to bring members of existing Sudanese holy families into the Qadiri fold.[316] Another autonomous branch of the Qadiriyya was established around this time by Idris-ibn-Muhammad al-Arbab (1650), who successfully attracted the elite of the Funj sultanate, while also acting like other Sufis of the period as a diplomatic mediator, in this case in disputes between the Funj and their enemies.[317] In the spread of the sanctification process to Africa, a mausoleum was built over Idris's grave at al-Aylafun to the south of modern Khartoum in Sudan, turning it into a pilgrimage center for the semi-Islamized people of the region. Over a period of several generations, these villages in the heart of Africa became little Sufi worlds of Islam as their inter-related inhabitants were bound together by common descent from the Shaikh and his early followers. In other cases, the brotherhoods created new patterns of sociability that transcended ethnic barriers.

In all cases, the brotherhoods tied people together into communities based on a common vision articulated by their Shaikhs. Many of these leaders belonged to the same holy families, allowing the brotherhoods to act as mechanisms of domination in which families or ethnic groups were able to perpetuate their status through time. In Islamic Africa as elsewhere, the leading Sufis constituted an established class, made wealthy by their land holdings and the gifts of their followers. In such ways, Sufi tradition offered the peoples of the Sahara an adaptable set of resources for the construction of social order, from models of authority and organization to unifying communal rituals and the sanction of a historical legacy that connected an African Sufi establishment to such prestigious urban centers as Cairo, Baghdad and Mecca. As in other regions at the same time, many major Sufis in Saharan Africa during the seventeenth and particularly eighteenth centuries laid especial emphasis on the law. In the Funj Sultanate of Sudan, the seizure of power by Hamaj noblemen in 1762 triggered a crisis of legitimacy that the Hamaj tried to solve by a policy of promoting Shari'a. This in turn required them to offer positions in the court and bureaucracy to Sufis or other scholars qualified to carry through the policy.[318] As a result, legalistic Sufis ascended in influence and by the end of the eighteenth century there spread through Sudan a sustained attack on Sufi or other popular practices that smacked of 'innovation'. In a manner that echoed the agendas of Naqshbandi Sufis among the oasis dwellers and tribesmen of Central Asia, Arabic manuscripts which survive from the Sahara's urban enclaves show the period's Sufis as key proponents of Shari'a. By the second half of the eighteenth century, these developments reached new levels as such major North African Sufis as Ahmad al-Tijani (1815) and Ahmad ibn Idris (1837) reached beyond the Arabized peoples of the Sahara to initiate large numbers of black Africans into their new brotherhoods. At the western end of Saharan Africa in what is now Mauretania, the period also saw Muhammad al-Hafiz (d.1830) travel to Mecca and Fes, where he was initiated by al-Tijani before returning through the Sahara to propagate a form of Sufism in which the study of Hadith and the Prophetic Example were given central place.[319]

Even though it has been argued that dan Fodio regarded Sufism as a means of personal purification which was separate from the sources of his political vision, the fact remains that Sufis if not always Sufism was responsible for the establishing major new states in Africa.[320] However, we should not only see this as a picture of the Sufi impact on Africa, but also as one of the African impacts on Sufism. More specifically, we should recognize the process by which Sufism afforded Africans a religious idiom, organizational model and means of transferring knowledge that enabled them to export elements of African religious practice to the wider Muslim world. In large part, this was made possible by enforced slave.

10.16 Summary

In a period in which Islam was still expanding in large parts of the globe, Sufis also acted as frontiersmen and their institutions served as state surrogates as Muslim societies developed around them. While among the Sufis there naturally remained significant numbers of impoverished wandering dervishes, the larger mark on history was left by mobile Sufi elites whose learning, prestigious lineages, miraculous powers and in some cases ethnic backgrounds enabled them to muster the resources to either found states or acquire important offices within existing policies. While developments were gradual, the first two centuries of the new millennium saw an emphasis on the law-abiding moral rectitude of the Sufi as a social role model that was attractive to state administrators. If Sufis and sultans had first entered alliances in the medieval period, then the early modern centuries saw Sufis settle into the security of being indispensable players in the social no less than the political order, especially in the more durable empires. If the period saw increasing attempts to regulate the more capricious dimensions of Sufi behavior through uniform standards of law, except in such exceptional settings as Shi'i Iran this was ultimately a sign of the extraordinary influence Sufis had acquired by this period by pointing to how much was at stake when Sufis morally misled their followers. Taken as a whole, the early modern period saw Sufi tradition being taken in two opposing but interrelated directions. After all, with its claims to authority and its mechanisms of loyalty and affiliation, Sufism had developed into a powerful idiom of collective organization and communal solidarity. In the other direction, the period saw the opposing (but ultimately related) process of the increasing consolidation of these powerful idioms and symbols of tradition into organized and regularized brotherhoods, whose behavior thereby became more predictable and stable.

While the process was certainly patchy, from this period the brotherhoods resembled more networked organizations rather than the mechanisms for reproducing tradition of the medieval era. Even in the major case in which Sufism was suppressed in Safawi Iran, the chief factor was the replacement of an older, fissiparous tribal Sufism with a standardized, legalistic model of Shi'i Islam which, unlike even the largest brotherhoods, could unite an entire population. The eighteenth century has often been presented as a distinct 'age of reform' in which 'neo-Sufi' brotherhoods pushed a new, Prophet centered agenda of legally circumscribed Sufism. What we have instead seen in this chapter suggests that the millennium of 1591 marked the more significant turning point. Of course, the conscience of decline and the critiques of 'innovation' that resounded through almost every Muslim region were not triggered by the calendar alone and in each region the legalists success was reliant on local social and political circumstances. Although such groups as the Kadizadelis wielded the slur of 'innovation' from the Prophetic Example as a way of criticizing their privileged Sufi rivals, it was usually Sufis themselves who used Sunna and Shari'a to criticize other Suis. In some cases, this was part of longer-term doctrinal brands nurtured by brotherhoods that had always upheld the primacy of obeying the religious law no matter how intoxicating one's private communions with God.

11. Sufism under Establishment 1800 A.D - 2000 A.D.

11.1 Resistance to Accommodation

Since the colonial impact on Sufism can most effectively be traced through imperial interactions with Sufi institutions and personnel, the following chapters largely focus on these more tangible exchanges before turning to the attitudes of both the Europeans and Muslims who came to variously appropriate, reject or reinvent Sufism in the post-colonial era. In broad outline, the history of colonial interactions with Sufis can be seen as a two-way pattern of anti-colonial rebellions and pro-colonial alliances, a pattern which can in many cases be seen as a processual development of failed rebellions giving way to negotiated alliances.[321] At different moments, the European empires therefore not only suppressed but also at times patronized Sufis. In a pattern of continuity with the eighteenth and early nineteenth centuries, such rebel Sufis also tended to belong to the legalistic trend which was often as critical to the Muslim as the colonial establishment. By contrast, alliance and accommodation policies tended to be pursued by well-established Sufis who already possessed authority and status among their host communities, along with property granted them by precolonial powers. At times, a process of transition can be observed amid these two parties as the heirs of Sufis who acquired followers and status through leading what were ultimately unsustainable rebellions entered alliances with the same colonial powers who had defeated their fathers or grandfathers.

11.2 A Crumbling Establishment: 1800 A.D. - 1950 A.D.

While colonization had a tremendous impact on both the Sufis and their rivals during the nineteenth and the first half of the twentieth centuries, we should be wary of exaggerating the global reach of colo nial power. In the remote high mountains of the Pamir on the borders of Russian rule, the Sufi poet Mubarak-e-Wakhani (1840–1903) lived in such isolation that he had to invent a huge nineteen stringed rubab lute to accompany the singing of his poems and was forced to develop his own papermaking machine to write the poems down. Russian colonialism was far from his mind and his struggles are instead reflected in such verses as "My senses and thoughts are preoccupied by paper".[322] While it is certainly the case that members of Sufi brotherhoods who entered alliances with colonial rulers were kept under surveillance by the authorities, ultimately this did not prevent the Sufis from making use of the new travel networks on which European rule and commerce was also dependent. The opening of trans-colonial routes put Muslims in distant regions of the world into easier and more regular global contact with one another.[323] In the case of the Rashidi-Ahmadi brotherhood, we find the Sudanese Shaikh Ibrahim al-Rashid (1813–1874) reinvigorating the tradition he had inherited from his own teachers through a new brotherhood that quickly spread to Arabia, Syria, Egypt, Sudan, Libya, West Africa, the Malay states, Borneo, Singapore and ultimately Thailand and Cambodia.[324]

In part, these wide disseminations were enabled by access to printing presses, through which the new brotherhoods' books could be mass produced for international distribution. Often these presses were in such transport hubs as Istanbul, Bombay or Singapore and their books distributed at such global pilgrimage destinations as Mecca.[325] Such trans-colonial movements show that Sufism offered sufficiently robust forms of inspiration and organization to with stand colonial pressures. Perhaps more important than such trans-colonial diffusions of new brotherhoods were the fact that there also remained Muslim parts of the world which Europe did not colonize. It is important to set what we have seen of the colonial experience beside the fortunes of Sufis in these uncolonized regions. For looking at the history of nineteenth and early twentieth century Sufis in the Ottoman Empire, Iran, and Afghanistan there emerge several general patterns that bear certain similarities with the policies of colonial states. This suggests in turn that the colonial scenarios we have examined need to be situated in the longer historical patterns of interaction between powerful Sufis and state powers, whether the latter were 'colonial' or 'indigenous'. In the most important of all Muslim regions to at least avoid colonization until after the First World War, the shrinking but none the less vast Ottoman Empire remained a crucial arena for the Sufis. It was also one in which the interactions of Sufis and the state show parallels with regions under colonial control. In the early nineteenth century, the most important Sufi event was the official abolition in 1826 of the Bektashi Sufi brotherhood, along with the janissary military corps that had been its main support base for over three hundred years.[326] In the wording of the imperial fireman order that announced the joint abolition, birisi-dús mam din ('the one is the enemy of the state, the other the enemy of the faith').[327] Given that the Bektashis' rituals had long incorporated such suspicious practices as wine drinking, the abolition can partially be seen as part of the longer term promotion of legally conformist forms of Sufism. This perspective is confirmed by the coincidence of the Bektashis' demise with the rapid rise in elite Ottoman circles of the new legalistic branch of the Naqshbandi-

Mujaddidi brotherhood founded by the itinerant Kurdish master, Shaikh Khalid (d.1827).[328]

For what directly prompted the Bektashis' suppression was the outbreak of the Greek Revolution in 1821 and the subsequent series of defeats of Ottoman armies that culminated in Greece's independence a decade later. Given that parts of Greece had been under Ottoman control for four hundred years, the sudden loss of the western portions of the empire triggered tremendous anger against not only the armies but against what was widely perceived as a moral malaise that had weakened the empire from the inside. Their abolition also had the advantage of allowing the state to seize the many waqf endowments which the brotherhood had accrued over the centuries.[329] In an Ottoman reflection of responses to European expansion in other Muslim regions, the following decades saw the rise of Sufis who publicly denounced the lapse morals of the Bektashis, members of Shaikh Khalid's Naqshbandi Mujaddidi brotherhood. Right through to the 1870s, Shaikh Khalid's heirs occupied the chief religious rank of Shaikh al-islam in the imperial bureaucracy, as well as preaching positions at the major mosques of Istanbul.[330] In the 1850s, another Ottoman crisis this time of the Crimean War helped the rise of another group of reformists for whom not even law abiding Sufis offered a solution to the scientifically empowered victories of Europe.[331] But the brief heyday of these Tanzimat ('Re-ordering') reformers between 1839 and 1876 by no means signaled the demise of Sufi influence in the Ottoman realms. For defeat by the Russians in the war of 1877–78 discredited the Tanzimat reformists in turn, leading to the reactionary reign of 'Abd al-Hamid II (1876–1909 The master of ceremonies in this policy of legitimization through the patronage of the old Sufi Islamic institutions was the Rifa'i Sufi master, Abu al-Huda al-Sayyadi (1850–1910). He oversaw a highly effective mobilization of Sufis through an 'integration politics' in which the Sultan 'Abd al-Hamid was able to draw on the earlier Ottoman centralizing religious develop ments.[332] Overseeing a so called 'black cabinet' comprising three other Sufi Shaikhs with links to North Africa and South India, Abu al-Huda orchestrated a trans-national propaganda project in which the Sultan 'Abd al-Hamid was presented as the caliph or leader of all the world's Muslims.[333]

Another of the leading figures in this renewal of the old alliance between Sufi and sultan was the Palestinian Qadiri Sufi, Yusuf al-Nabahani (1850–1932), who after spending two years at the court in Istanbul in the 1880s rose quickly through the Ottoman judicial service.[334] From his office in Beirut, al-Nabahani wrote propaganda pieces in celebration of the sultan's achievements and in defense of his autocratic goals, while denouncing anti-Sufi and modernizers as the thin end of a Europeanizing wedge that would undermine the Muslim foundations of Ottoman society. In a series of polemical works, al-Nabahani denounced the intellectual leaders of the emerging anti-Sufi Salafi reform movement: Jamal al-Din al-Afghani was an 'apostate', Muhammad 'Abduh an 'active devil', and Rashid Rida a 'perpet uator of evil'.[335] Al-Nabahani's was no lone voice. Supported by state appointments or stipends in various provincial cities through-out 'Abd al-Hamid's reign was a larger conservative block of late Ottoman Sufis, for whom tradition was not simply a status be defended at all costs: it was a body of doctrinal and institutional resources that might confront the challenges of the modern age just as well as the modernists teachings. Nor did such conservatism put a stop to new developments. From the 1880s in Damascus, the followers of the exiled former Algerian rebel Abd al-Qadir were at the forefront of the revival of literary and historical interests that would culminate in the Arab or 'renaissance'.[336] In the case of the Salafl ('Fore runners') movement that emerged in Ottoman Syria and Egypt and around the turn of the twentieth century, the Sufi upbringings of men like Muhammad 'Abduh (1849–1905) in Tanta and of the followers of 'Abd al-Qadir in Damascus were renounced in maturity in favor of a rationalized Islam in which the rituals and miracles of the Sufis were denounced as incompatible with a modern world of scientific knowledge in which religion should be based on the rational exegesis of scripture rather than on the acceptance of distorting tradition.[337] The resulting rapid replacement of Sufi Islam by Salafi Islam in many regions of the world (the Middle East especially) has been one of the major social and religious changes in modern Islamic history. From their Middle Eastern headquarters, the Salaf is spread their anti-Sufi critique far and wide through the travels of their students and the publishing of such journals as al-Manar ('The Lighthouse').[338]

The oppositional politics of an agonistic era meant that when the reformists gained the upper hand with the Young Turk Revolution of 1908, they viewed the Sufi more than ever as self-serving enemies of progress and destroyers of the Prophet's true teachings. In 1909, al-Nabahani was dismissed from his post in the judiciary. Still, even as full blooded a modernizing Turkish nationalist as Ziya Gökalp (1876–1924) was able to view the intellectual if not the social dimensions of Sufism as valuable assets, arguing that the teachings of Ibn al-'Arabi (d.1240) anticipated the philosophy of Berkeley, Kant and Nietzsche.[339] By 1918 every Sufi Shaikh in Istanbul had been sent a printed questionnaire in which they were asked to detail their qualifications, employment history, number of followers and pledges of allegiance.[340] When the Ottoman Empire was formally disbanded in 1922 as a corollary of fighting on the losing side in the First World War, the founder of the Turkish Republic, Mustafa Kamal Atatürk (1881–1938), finally took the drastic step of banning the Sufi brotherhoods altogether in 1925.[341] However, the very last years of the eighteenth century saw the return to Iran from India of the heirs to the Ni'matullahi brotherhood that we previously saw spreading from Iran in the sixteenth century to the Bahmani Sultanate of south India.[342] Through such itinerant teachers as Nur Ali Shah (1797), and their followers in the next generation, these migrant Sufis over saw a considerable Sufi revival in Iran. To do so, they propounded an appealing theology centered on ecstatic experiences of rarefied emotions of love (hubb), passion ('ishq), devotion (wadd) and ardor (hawa) which could be summoned by the singing to musical accompaniment of the old Persian love poems of Rumi and Baba Tahir.[343] Such was their appeal that by the 1830s the Sufis even gained a following among the Jewish community of Mashhad. There Jewish Rabbis brought Sufi ideas into their readings of the Torah and made visionary connections with the medieval Sufi tradition of the surrounding Khurasan region through visions of Abu al-Qasim al-Qushayri (d.1074).[344] By the mid nineteenth century, the Sufis had also found support at the Iranian royal court, most crucially through the rise of the Ni'matullahi Sufi, Hajji Mirza Aqasi (1783–1848), to the position of grand vizier of the Qajar ruler, Muhammad Shah (r.1834–1848). Under Aqasi's patronage, the dilapidated shrines of the great medieval Sufis of Iran such as Abu Yazid Bistami and Shah Ni'matullahi Wali were restored and extended, while individual Sufis were granted stipends or endowed with landholdings.[345] Through such strategic alliances with the new Qajar dynasty of erstwhile Turcoman tribesmen that was not entirely dissimilar to the colonial powers in its lack of legitimacy, the Ni'matullahis won back for the Sufis a stake in Iranian society that they had not held for two hundred years. As the century progressed, the Ni'matullahis held onto this renewed profile by maintaining ties with Iranian merchants, not least the rich community of Iranian traders that emerged in colonial Bombay.[346] After a provincial upbringing in Isfahan, Safi Ali Shah (d.1899), the leading Iranian Ni'matullahi of the later nineteenth century, launched his career through a period of residence in Bombay, where he not only won the support of its Iranian merchant diaspora, but also printed the book-length poem Zubdat al-Asrar ('Quintessence of Secrets') that established his reputation on his return home.[347]

In the new age of printing, Safi 'Ali's verse represented both an appropriation and an extension of earlier Sufi tradition by self-consciously imitating the style of the medieval verses of the great Jalal al-Din Rumi[348]. Through the charity dinners of the anjuman-e-ukhuwwat and through such other modernizing venues as magazines and philosophical academies, the Iranian Sufis of the early 1900s in an era of modernization linked themselves to the aspirations of a new national elite. Through reconfiguring their legacy of writing in Persian to the new ideology of Iranian nationalism, and through adapting the old Sufi role of moral admonition to address modern anxieties about drug consumption and women's rights, right up until the Islamic Revolution of 1979, the Sufi masters of Iran continued to find patronage at the highest levels of state, including the Empress Farah.[349] In South and Central Asia, meanwhile, the survival of princely and 'buffer' states on the fringes of British India allowed the old alliance between Muslim rulers and establishment Sufis to survive well into the twentieth century. In Hyderabad (an Indian princely state about the size of France), the existence of a ruling Muslim class afforded the continued patronage of Sufi activities, particularly by the ruling Nizam Mahbub 'Ali Khan (1869–1911), whose generosity saw Hyderabad hosting Sufis from far beyond the shores of India. Sheltered from the colonial upheaval of the old social order, Sufis in Hyderabad continued their old literary tradition by writing such biographical compendia as the Arabic Mishkat al-Nabuwwa ('Lantern of Prophethood') of Ghulam 'Ali Qadiri (1842), which through textual chains of initiate descent connected the living Sufis of Hyderabad to the ancient saints of Khurasan and Baghdad.[350]

If the anti-Sufi reform movements of British India slipped across the border into Hyderabad, then with the support of local mill-owners such Hyderabadi Sufis as Mu'inullah Shah (1926) were able to adapt themselves to the new idiom of reform and pass on their teachings even after Hyderabad was absorbed into independent India in 1948.[351] In Afghanistan, just over the northwestern frontier of British India, the struggle of the modernizing Afghan rulers of the early twentieth century to assert their fragile authority over unruly tribesmen and oppositional clerics led Afghanistan's rulers into a familiar pact with leading Sufis.[352] In 1919 this royal quest for power also involved the declaration of a holy war against a British Empire that, in the wake of the First World War, was too weakened to fully respond. When King Amanullah (r.1919–1929) publicly announced this unlikely jihad after a family power struggle that followed the assassination of his ruling father, he made sure he had the celebrated Naqshbandi master, Shah Agha (d.1925), standing by his side before then dispatching the Sufi and his brother Sher Agha to accompany his troops in battle.[353] In return for their support, the brothers received large land-grants on the outskirts of Kabul and honorific titles (such as Shams al-Masha'ikh, 'Sun among Shaikhs'). When King Amanullah was toppled in a coup, his successor Nadir Shah (1929–1933) ap pointed Sher Agha as head of a new national committee of religious scholars and sent the third Sufi brother, Gul Agha, as ambassador to Egypt.[354] While Sufi influence was still high in the 1930s, the fol lowing decades saw a retraction of Sufi influence in Afghanistan. As in other regions, the last Afghan king Zahir Shah (1933–1973) preferred a secularizing modernism to alliances with living saints, while the intellectuals of the small Afghan middle class were coming under the influence of communist ideas from neighboring Soviet Central Asia and so regarded the Sufis as royal stooges. Nonetheless, the mountainous countryside of Afghanistan preserved many aspects of the vernacularized regional forms of Sufi tradition that had by then disappeared under the modernizing or reforming pressures that had re shaped other Muslim countries in the twentieth century.[355] In the northern Afghan town of Tashkurgan (also known as Kholm), there survived vernacularized versions of tradition passed down by bilingual Persian/Uzbek pocket books which connected carpenters, tanners and other craftsmen to the rituals and lineage of particular patron saints, with halva cooks being allied to Baba Farid of Multan.[356]

11.3 Expansion and Rejection: 1950 A.D. – 2000 A.D.

We have seen how in certain regions by the early twentieth century Sufism was for the first time being suppressed in the service of nation-making. As we have already seen, in the Central Asian regions of the Soviet Union no less than in Republican Turkey, Sufism was suppressed in the name of a socialist or nationalist modernity. In other regions, particularly the Arab Middle East, modernists heightened their ideological attacks on Sufis as corruptors, collaborators or charlatans, while in institutional terms the nationalization policies of various postcolonial Arab states saw a further expansion of the long-term process of state regulation of Sufi brotherhoods.[357] In the new Saudi regime in Arabia, the teachings of the eighteenth century reformer Ibn 'Abd al-Wahhab were interpreted as wholly condemning the Sufis and installed as the ideology of the new state. We have already seen how the term 'Sufism' itself was invented by European scholars in the colonial period and in their discussions came to the acquire meanings which in many cases were at odds with the Sufis' own understanding of their tradition. Thus, in late colonial India, in creating what was by any standards an inspirational body of poetry in Persian and Urdu, the reformist poet Sir Muhammad Iqbal (1877–1938) absorbed the colonial critique of modern day. Sufis as lazy charlatans while accepting the same European scholars praise of medieval Sufis as Islam's last true mystics.[358]

Like many other postcolonial attempts to reappropriate a precolonial heritage, the project of re-Islamizing Sufism involved more a reinvention than a simple transmission of tradition. For before colonial scholars had suggested Hindu or even Buddhist sources for Sufi ideas, the notion of an 'Islamic Sufism' (al-tasawwuf al-Islami) was an unnecessary tautology. Moreover, in all corners of the Muslim world, the twentieth century witnessed an unprecedented pluralization of religious authority and doctrine through increasing access to education (whether secular or religious), new media technologies (whether printing or broadcasting) and new organizational forms (whether religious associations or political parties). The increasing range of Islams made available to believers served to relativize the Sufis' teachings and marginalize their brotherhoods in regions where they had long been dominant or major players. In short, by the mid-twentieth century, there were far more ways of being Muslim available. Faced with many more choices than following a Sufi master, millions of Muslims across the world elected to follow either one of the many new non-Sufi teachers or abandon external authority to follow their own conscience alone. While the scale of Sufi influence undeniably declined, there remained many different forms in which the tradition of earlier centuries was passed on, albeit at times in distinctly modern forms.

As we have seen earlier, there were reformist Sufis who adapted their teachings in response to their anti-Sufi critics. In situations where such critics had labeled many aspects of Sufi tradition nothing more than 'superstition' (khurafa), Sufi reformers jettisoned many aspects of Sufi practice, particularly practices such as amulet making or faith-healing for which the rise of modern medicine had anyway reduced demand. In more modernized and wealthy Muslim regions, Sufi activities were substantially truncated as a whole host of practices from shrine veneration to miracle stories and talismanic objects were discredited as the disjecta membra of modernity. Yet whatever the confident expectations of the secularization theories that shaped discussions of Sufism in the mid-twentieth century, modernization has not brought about a thorough going disenchantment of Muslim religiosity. In various regions, particularly those in which Sufis managed to maintain their social status and institutional capital, Sufi tradition continued to be passed on, albeit under the increasing attacks of anti-Sufi reformers. Even in the most modernized regions of the world, the second half of the twentieth century saw Sufis respond to the transformations of self and society by creating new organizational formats or conceptual models by which to transmit their teachings. Let us look at a few case studies of these different ways in which Sufism developed from the 1950s onwards. While in India and Pakistan, postcolonial governments weakened the old Sufi establishment by seizing control of many Sufi landholdings, tradition continued to be passed down in a far less truncated way than in the Middle East, where secular nationalism and religious reformism gained greater social ground.[359] Even so, in both India and Pakistan, Sufism was drawn into the postcolonial formation of new national identities. In

India, certain forms of Sufism (particularly the musical performances and ecumenical shrines of the Chishti brotherhood) were promoted as tolerant forerunners of the multi-confessional secular Indian Republic, with their festivals receiving coverage on national television and their history being championed by university teachers. According to the varying ideologies of the political parties in question, Sufis were alternatively presented in Pakistan as missionary preachers of Islam or socialistic champions of the rural peasantry, with research centers or medical outlets being built as appendages to medieval shrines as the concrete expression of the new alliance of the Sufi and the President.[360]

In the writings of the former Pakistani army officer and Sufi master, Captain Wahid Bakhsh Rabbani (1995), the memory of the medieval saints was turned even more explicitly towards national service. As in Egypt, where we have seen European models of Sufism triggering a defensive 're-Islamization' of Sufi ideas, in Pakistan Rabbani similarly responded to European images of Sufism in his English work, Islamic Sufism. Here he argued against Orientalist notions of the external origins of Sufism to show the harmony of Sufi teachings with the Quran and Shari'a, while also drawing on an eccentric selection of French scientists and American New Age writers to prove the harmony of Sufism with science.[361] In Southeast Asia, parallel projects of modernizing nation-making had their impact on Sufism in new postcolonial states such as Indonesia and Malaysia. After achieving independence from the Dutch in 1949, between 1965 and 1998 Indonesia was pushed through an uncompromising 'New Order' which saw the emergence of an educated modern population. Sufism moved in distinct directions during these years, whether moving into the new public sphere of Muslim political parties or withdrawing into the private sphere of the kebatinan or 'esoterist' groups that promised their followers occult rather than political power.[362] Combined with the critiques of anti-Sufi reformists, such modernization rendered Sufism's old organizational format unappealing to the new generations of Indonesians, who came to regard the old brotherhoods as suspiciously secretive, anti-democratic and authoritarian.[363] In response, since the 1970s Indonesia's Sufi teachers have made radical breaks with their old institutions by creating new organizational formats to reach their modern educated compatriots, setting up seminars, workshops and retreats. As a result, despite anti-Sufi polemics, increasing numbers of middle class and female Indonesians were won back to a form of Islam that promised an attractive combination of personal happiness and professional success. Such 'lifestyle Sufism' also held the attraction of avoiding the stigma of political Islamism associated with Indonesia's other religious organizations.

Even in Central Asia, where as an 'Islamic feudalism' Sufism had been brutally suppressed during seven decades of Soviet rule, the creation of new republics in the 1990s saw a massive revival of Sufi activity that was both state sponsored and individual.[364] Since imperial Russian and then Soviet rule had brought about a decisive break with earlier tradition, what resurfaced in the 1990s was a curious hybrid of remembered rural folk traditions and nationalistic reinventions of patron saint cults.[365] This rupture with tradition had been reinforced by the Soviet replacement of Arabic script by Cyrillic and the promotion of Uzbek as a national language, which as in modern Turkey rendered earlier Sufi writings from the region in the Persian language and Arabic-script inaccessible except through the occasional translation. Since most of the old Sufi families had been persecuted and disinherited into obscurity, the new post-Soviet Sufi revivers were pious university professors such as the Uzbek writer Sadr al-Din Salim Bukhari, who under Soviet rule had established his career as an expert on the German poet Goethe.[366] In Turkey, the period since the 1970s in particular saw a resurgence of the Naqshbandi brotherhood in Turkish life, not least under the institutional guise of socially conservative political parties.[367] In Turkey, Fethullah Gülen (1941-) managed a more open rapprochement with Sufism through preaching the importance of Sufi doctrines but not institutions.[368] Linked to pious industrialists rather than the imperial stipends and land grants of old, and founding schools in which a Sufi Islam was seen as being wholly compatible with a scientific education, the Gülen movement had by the 1990s outgrown its national origins and ventured into the religious markets opened in Central Asia by the collapse of the Soviet Union and its seventy year suppression of Sufi ways.[369]

The success of his movement was viewed with ambivalence by Turkey's leaders and in 1998 Gülen emigrated to the United States, a decision that marked a new global moment in the expansion of his teachings. If, as in the Indonesian examples, the Gülen movement is in its concrete forms an entirely different entity to the brotherhoods and shrines of previous ages, in its appeal to a liberal and educated Muslim middle class, it represents a highly effective transmission of a truncated Sufi tradition to the present day. Despite predictions during the heyday of Arab nationalism of the inevitable demise of Sufism in the Middle East, and the long reformist project of the individualization of religious authority, by the end of the twentieth century. Middle Eastern Sufi masters still held sufficient esteem to attract followers from various backgrounds. In northern Syria, Sufi disciples range from university professors and wealthy industrialists to poor manual workers, whose Shaikhs conduct them through grueling rites of passage that include handling live snakes, eating burning coals and piercing their bodies with skewers.[370] While in Egypt state regulation has sought to banish such dramatic practices from the saintly 'birthday' festivals or mawlids, the Mubarak government still uses the festivals as platforms for political broadcasts and public orderliness, entering pacts with reformist Sufi leaders who own chemical factories and hold science degrees from communist Eastern Europe.[372] Albeit behind closed doors, ecstatic Sufi performances remain an important part of Egyptian Muslim life. As in the new brotherhood founded in 1952 after the Prophet Muhammad appeared in a dream to the civil servant Jabir Husyan Jazuli (1913–1992), there continue to emerge new organizations that now pass on tradition through cheap audio tapes, DVDs and home study materials designed to accompany the collective dhikr chanting sessions that first emerged over a thousand years earlier.[373] Throughout the Middle East, Sufism has managed to maintain an appeal through recordings of its music, which despite involving a commodification of tradition has allowed the poetry of earlier centuries to reach young urban audiences, some of whom in turn take the step of formal initiation into a Sufi brotherhood.[374] In some cases this has seen new vehicles of Sufi tradition emerge, which like other examples elsewhere play down the 'Sufi' label to present themselves in more plainly Muslim or else modern guises.

A Lebanese example is the Jam'iyyat al-Mashari' al-Khayriyya alIslamiyya ('Society of Islamic Philanthropic Projects'), founded by the exiled Ethiopian Shaikh 'Abdullah al-Habashi, which has had considerable appeal among Lebanese Muslims tired with political Islam.[375] Competition with Islamist organizations has also been a feature of Sufi history in postcolonial Africa. We have already seen prominent Sufis taking a leading role in political life in the years after independence in 1956 in Sudan. But since the 1970s the rise of such Islamist organizations as the Muslim Brotherhood and the National Islamic Front has marginalized Sudan's Sufis from public life. While Sudanese Islamists have attracted rich investments of oil money through the new global mechanisms of Islamic banking, the Sufis who had flourished under the Funj and British empires alike were left with the depleting resources of agricultural landholdings and economically marginal followers.[376] In West Africa, heirs to pre-existing Sufi brotherhoods have continued to flourish through making strategic alliances with modern political organizations. Elsewhere in the region, recent decades have seen the followers of the former colonial French prisoner Amadu Bamba keep pace with changes in West African society by appealing to a new following among rural migrants to the growing cities of Senegal.[377] Under his family successors, Amadu Bamba's Senegalese Mouride movement has also kept pace with developments in communication technology to maintain its followers' loyalty even in the extensive Senegalese trading diaspora that globalization has created in Europe and America.[378]

While in Sudan, Sufis declined in relation to their Islamist rivals through comparative underinvestment, in Senegal the Mouride brotherhood attracted expanding financial flows through the promotion of a pious business ethic that encouraged followers to see their international business travels as inseparable from their spiritual progress.[379] By the 1990s Sufism remained no less alive in neighboring Mali, through the rise of charismatic young Sufi leaders who, in such cities as Bamako and Ségou, were highly successful in promoting themselves among other urban young people.[380] In the case of Shaikh Soufi Bilal, this involved growing fashionable 'rasta' dreadlocks, self- publishing booklets of his teachings and buying advertising airtime on local radio stations. As in other postcolonial environments, where modern citizens have been divorced from the literary traditions of their ancestors by colonial language policies, the writings of such Sufis as Soufi Bilal are in French rather than in the Arabic of the Saharan Sufis of former ages. But if this certainly involves a recasting of tradition, the pragmatic fact of the matter is that it is through French rather than Arabic that such Sufis can appeal to their mass urban audiences. As a kind of postcolonial vernacularization, such languages as French and English have followed where Persian and Turkish once led the way as new languages of Sufi Islam.

Chapter 3

Histrography of Indian Religion and era of Sufism

1. Periodisation

James Mill (1773–1836) distinguished three phases in the history of India, namely Hindu, Muslim, and British civilisations in his 'The History of British India' (1817). This periodisation has been criticised, for the misconceptions it has given rise to. Additional periodisation is the division into "ancient, classical, medieval, and modern periods", although this periodisation has also received criticism.[1] Romila Thapar noted that the division of Hindu-Muslim-British periods of Indian history gives too much weight to "ruling dynasties and foreign invasions",[2] neglecting the social-economic history which often showed a strong continuity. The division in Ancient-Medieval-Modern overlooks the fact that the Muslim-conquests took place between the eight and the fourteenth century, while the south was never completely conquered. According to Thapar, a periodisation could also be based on 'significant social and economic changes', which are not strictly related to a change of ruling powers. Smart and Michaels seem to follow Mill's periodisation, while Flood and Muesse follow the 'ancient, classical, mediaeval, and modern periods' periodisation. An elaborate periodisation may be as follows:[3]

- Indian pre-history including Indus Valley Civilisation (1750 BC)
- Iron Age including Vedic period (1750–600 BC)
- Second Urbanisation (600 BC–200 BC)
- Classical period (200 BC-1200 A.D.)
  - Pre-Classical period (200 BC-320 A.D.)
  - "Golden Age" (Gupta Empire) (320 –650 A.D.)
  - Late-Classical period (650 –1200 A.D.)
- Medieval period (1200–1500 A.D.)
- Early Modern (1500–1850 A.D.)
- Modern period (British Raj and independence) (from 1850 A.D).

## 2.	Pre-Vedic religions (before 1750 BC)

### 2.1	Pre-history

Evidence attesting to prehistoric religion in the Indian subcontinent derives from scattered Mesolithic rock paintings such as at Bhimbetka, depicting dances and rituals. Neolithic agriculturalists inhabiting the Indus River Valley buried their dead in a manner suggestive of spiritual practices that incorporated notions of an afterlife and belief in magic.[4] Other South Asian Stone Age sites, such as the Bhimbetka rock shelters in central Madhya Pradesh and the Kupgal petroglyphs of eastern Karnataka, contain rock art portraying religious rites and evidence of possible ritualised music.

### 2.2	Indus Valley civilisation

The religion and belief system of the Indus valley people have received considerable attention, especially from the view of identifying precursors to deities and religious practices of Indian religions that later developed in the area. However, due to the sparsity of evidence, which is open to varying interpretations, and the fact that the Indus script remains undeciphered, the conclusions are partly speculative and largely based on a retrospective view from a much later Hindu perspective.[5] An early and influential work in the area that set the trend for Hindu interpretations of archaeological evidence from the Harrapan sites[6] was that of John Marshall, who in 1931 identified the following as prominent features of the Indus religion: a Great Male God and a Mother Goddess; deification or veneration of animals and plants; symbolic representation of the phallus (linga) and vulva (yoni); and, use of baths and water in religious practice. Marshall's interpretations have been much debated, and sometimes disputed over the following decades.[7][8]

One of the Indus valley seals shows a seated, possibly ithyphallic and tricephalic, figure with a horned headdress, surrounded by animals. Marshall identified the figure as an early form of the Hindu god Shiva (or Rudra), who is associated with asceticism, yoga, and linga; regarded as a lord of animals; and often depicted as having three eyes. The seal has hence come to be known as the Pashupati Seal, after Pashupati (lord of all animals), an epithet of Shiva.[9] While Marshall's work has earned some support, many critics and even supporters have raised several objections. Doris Srinivasan has argued that the figure does not have three faces, or yogic posture, and that in Vedic literature Rudra was not a protector of wild animals.[10][11]

Herbert Sullivan and Alf Hiltebeitel also rejected Marshall's conclusions, with the former claiming that the figure was female, while the latter associated the figure with Mahisha, the Buffalo God and the surrounding animals with vahanas (vehicles) of deities for the four cardinal directions.[12][13] Writing in 2002, Gregory L. Possehl concluded that while it would be appropriate to recognise the figure as a deity, its association with the water buffalo, and its posture as one of ritual discipline, regarding it as a proto-Shiva would be going too far. Despite the criticisms of Marshall's association of the seal with a proto-Shiva icon, it has been interpreted as the Tirthankara Rishabha by Jains and Dr. Vilas Sangave[14] or an early Buddha by Buddhists. Historians like Heinrich Zimmer, Thomas McEvilley are of the opinion that there exists some link between first Jain Tirthankara Rishabha and Indus Valley civilisation.[15][16]

Marshall hypothesized the existence of a cult of Mother Goddess worship based upon excavation of several female figurines and thought that this was a precursor of the Hindu sect of Shaktism. However the function of the female figurines in the life of Indus Valley people remains unclear, and Possehl does not regard the evidence for Marshall's hypothesis to be 'terribly robust'.[17] Some of the baetyls interpreted by Marshall to be sacred phallic representations are now thought to have been used as pestles or game counters instead, while the ring stones that were thought to symbolise yoni were determined to be architectural features used to stand pillars, although the possibility of their religious symbolism cannot be eliminated.[18] Many Indus Valley seals show animals, with some depicting them being carried in processions, while others show chimeric creations. One seal from Mohen-jo-daro shows a half-human, half-buffalo monster attacking a tiger, which may be a reference to the Sumerian myth of such a monster created by goddess Aruru to fight Gilgamesh.[19]

In contrast to contemporary Egyptian and Mesopotamian civilisations, Indus valley lacks any monumental palaces, even though excavated cities indicate that the society possessed the requisite engineering knowledge.[20][21] This may suggest that religious ceremonies, if any, may have been largely confined to individual homes, small temples, or the open air. Several sites have been proposed by Marshall and later scholars as possibly devoted to religious purpose, but at present only the Great Bath at Mohen-jo-daro is widely thought to have been so used, as a place for ritual purification.[22] The funerary practices of the Harappan civilisation is marked by its diversity with evidence of supine burial; fractional burial in which the body is reduced to skeletal remains by exposure to the elements before final interment; and even cremation.[23][24]

2.3   Dravidian culture

The early Dravidian religion constituted of non-Vedic form of Hinduism in that they were either historically or are at present Āgamic. The

Agamas are non-Vedic in origin [25] and have been dated as post Vedic texts or as pre-Vedic oral compositions. The Agamas are a collection of Tamil and later Sanskrit scriptures chiefly constituting the methods of temple construction and creation of murti, worship means of deities, philosophical doctrines, meditative practices, attainment of six-fold desires and four kinds of yoga.[26] The worship of tutelary deity, sacred flora and fauna in Hinduism is also recognized as a survival of the pre-Vedic Dravidian religion.[27] Ancient Tamil grammatical works Tolkappiyam, the ten anthologies Pattuppāṭṭu, the eight anthologies Eṭṭuttokai also sheds light on early religion of ancient Dravidians. Seyon was glorified as the red god seated on the blue peacock, who is ever young and resplendent, as the favoured God of the Tamils.[28] Siva was also seen as the supreme God. Early iconography of Seyyon and Siva and their association with native flora and fauna goes back to Indus Valley Civilization.[29] The Sangam landscape was classified into five categories, thinais, based on the mood, the season, and the land. Tolkappiyam, mentions that each of these thinai had an associated deity such Seyyon in Kurinji the hills, Thirumaal in Mullai the forests, and Kotravai in Marutham the plains, and Wanji-ko in the Neithal the coasts and the seas. Other gods mentioned were Mayyon and Vaali who were all assimilated into Hinduism over time.

Dravidian linguistic influence[30] on early Vedic religion is evident, many of these features are already present in the oldest known Indo-Aryan language, the language of the Rigveda (500 BC), which also includes over a dozen words borrowed from Dravidian.[31][32] This represents an early religious and cultural fusion or synthesis between ancient Dravidians and Indo-Aryans, which became more evident over time with sacred iconography, traditions, philosophy, flora, and fauna that went on to influence Hinduism, Buddhism, Charvaka, Sramana, and Jainism.[33] Throughout Tamilakam, a king was considered to be divine by nature and possessed religious significance.[34] The king was 'the representative of God on eart' and lived in a 'koyil', which means the 'residence of a god'. The Modern Tamil word for temple is koil. Ritual worship was also given to kings.[35] Modern words for god like 'kō' (king), 'irai' (emperor), and 'āṇḍavar' (conqueror) now primarily refer to gods. These elements were incorporated later into Hinduism like the legendary marriage of Shiva to Queen Mīnātchi who ruled Madurai or Wanji-ko, a god who later merged into Indra.[36] Tolkappiyar refers to the Three Crowned Kings as the 'Three Glorified by Heaven'.[37] In the Dravidian-speaking South, the concept of divine kingship led to the assumption of major roles by state and temple.[38] The cult of the mother goddess is treated as an indication of a society which venerated femininity. This mother goddess was conceived as a virgin, one who has given birth to all and one, typically associated with Shaktism.[39]

The temples of the Sangam days, mainly of Madurai, seem to have had priestesses to the deity, which also appear predominantly a goddess.[40] In the Sangam literature, there is an elaborate description of the rites performed by the Kurava priestess in the shrine Palamutircholai.[41] Among the early Dravidians the practice of erecting memorial stones Natukal or Hero Stone had appeared, and it continued for quite a long time after the Sangam age, down to about 16th century.[42] It was customary for people who sought victory in war to worship these hero stones to bless them with victory.[43]

3.   Vedic period (1750–800 CE)

The documented history of Indian religions begins with the historical Vedic religion, the religious practices of the early Indo-Aryans, which were collected and later redacted into the Samhitas (usually known as the Vedas), four canonical collections of hymns or mantras composed in archaic Sanskrit. These texts are the central shruti (revealed) texts of Hinduism. The period of the composition, redaction, and commentary of these texts is known as the Vedic period, which lasted from roughly 1750 to 500 CE. The Vedic Period is most significant for the composition of the four Vedas, Brahmanas and the older Upanishads (both presented as discussions on the rituals, mantras and concepts found in the four Vedas), which today are some of the most important canonical texts of Hinduism, and are the codification of much of what developed into the core beliefs of Hinduism.[44] Some modern Hindu scholars use the 'Vedic religion' synonymously with 'Hinduism'.[45] According to Sundararajan, Hinduism is also known as the Vedic religion.[46] Other authors state that the Vedas contain 'the fundamental truths about Hindu Dharma' which is called 'the modern version of the ancient Vedic Dharma'.[47] The Arya Samaj is recognize the Vedic religion as true Hinduism.[48] Nevertheless, according to Jamison and Witzel, ... to call this period Vedic Hinduism is a contradiction in terms since Vedic religion is very different from what we generally call Hindu religion at least as much as old Hebrew religion is from medieval and modern Christian religion. However, Vedic religion is treatable as a predecessor of Hinduism.

3.1   Early Vedic period – early Vedic compositions (1750–1200 CE)

The rishis, the composers of the hymns of the Rigveda, were considered inspired poets and seers. The mode of worship was the performance of Yajna, sacrifices which involved sacrifice and sublimation of the Havana sámagri (herbal preparations) in the fire, accompanied by the singing of Samans and 'mumbling' of Yajus, the sacrificial mantras. The sublime meaning of the word yajna is derived from the Sanskrit verb yaj, which has a three-fold meaning of worship of deities (devapujana), unity (saògatikaraña), and charity (dána).[49] An essential element was the sacrificial fire the divine Agni into which oblations were poured, as everything offered into the fire was believed to reach God. Central concepts in the Vedas are Satya and Rita. Satya is derived from Sat, the present participle of the verbal root as, 'to be, to exist, to live'. Sat means 'that which really exists the really existent truth; the Good', and Satya means 'is-nesses.' Rta, 'that which is properly joined; order, rule; truth', is the principle of natural order which regulates and coordinates the operation of the universe and everything within it. 'Satya (truth as being) and rita (truth as law) are the primary principles of Reality and its manifestation is the background of the canons of dharma, or a life of righteousness'. Satya is the principle of integration rooted in the Absolute, rita is its application and function as the rule and order operating in the universe. Conformity with rita would enable progress whereas its violation would lead to punishment. Panikkar remarks: Rita is the ultimate foundation of everything; it is 'the supreme', although this is not to be understood in a static sense. It is the expression of the primordial dynamism that is inherent in everything. The term rita is inherited from the Proto-Indo-Iranian religion, the religion of the Indo-Iranian peoples prior to the earliest Vedic (Indo-Aryan) and Zoroastrian (Iranian) scriptures. 'Asha' is the Avestan language term (corresponding to Vedic language rita) for a concept of cardinal importance to Zoroastrian theology and doctrine. The term 'dharma' was already used in Brahmanical thought, where it was conceived as an aspect of Rita. Major philosophers of this era were Rishis Narayana, Kanva, Rishaba, Vamadeva and Angiras.[50]

3.2   Middle Vedic period (1200–850 CE)

During the Middle Vedic period Rigveda, the mantras of the Yajurveda and the older Brahmana texts were composed. The Brahmans became powerful intermediaries. Historical roots of Jainism in India is traced back to 9th century BC with the rise of Parshvanatha and his non-violent philosophy.

3.3   Late Vedic period (from 850 CE)

The Vedic religion evolved into Hinduism and Vedanta, a religious path considering itself the 'essence' of the Vedas, interpreting the Vedic pantheon as a unitary view of the universe with 'God' (Brahman) seen as immanent and transcendent in the forms of Ishvara and Brahman. This post-Vedic systems of thought, along with the Upanishads and later texts like epics (namely Gita of Mahabharat), is a major component of modern

Hinduism. The ritualistic traditions of Vedic religion are preserved in the conservative Śrauta tradition.

4. Sanskritization

Since Vedic times, 'people from many strata of society throughout the subcontinent tended to adapt their religious and social life to Brahmanic norms', a process sometimes called Sanskritization. It is reflected in the tendency to identify local deities with the gods of the Sanskrit texts.[51]

5. Shramanic period (800–200 CE)

During the time of the shramanic reform movements "many elements of the Vedic religion were lost". According to Michaels, "it is justified to see a turning point between the Vedic religion and Hindu religions".

5.1   Late Vedic period Brahmanas Upanishads: Vedanta (850–500 BC)

The late Vedic period (9th to 6th centuries BC) marks the beginning of the Upanisadic or Vedantic period.[52] Deussen: "these treatises are not the work of a single genius, but the total philosophical product of an entire epoch which extends [from] approximately 1000 or 800 BC, to 500 A.D. but which is prolonged in its offshoots far beyond this last limit of time".[53] This period heralded the beginning of much of what became classical Hinduism, with the composition of the Upanishads,[54] later the Sanskrit epics, still later followed by the Puranas. Upanishads form the speculative-philosophical basis of classical Hinduism and are known as Vedanta (conclusion of the Vedas).[55] The older Upanishads launched attacks of increasing intensity on the ritual. Anyone who worships a divinity other than the Self is called a domestic animal of the gods in the Brihadaranyaka Upanishad. The Mundaka launches the most scathing attack on the ritual by comparing those who value sacrifice with an unsafe boat that is endlessly overtaken by old age and death.[56] Scholars believe that Parsva, the 23rd Jain tirthankara lived during this period in the 9th century BC.[57]

5.2   Rise of Shramanic tradition (7th to 5th BC)

Jainism and Buddhism belong to the sramana tradition. These religions rose into prominence in 700–500 BC in the Magadha kingdom., reflecting "the cosmology and anthropology of a much older, pre-Aryan upper class of north-eastern India", and were responsible for the related concepts of saṃsāra (the cycle of birth and death) and moksha (liberation from that cycle). The shramana movements challenged the orthodoxy of the rituals. The shramanas were wandering ascetics distinct from Vedism.[58][59]

Mahavira, proponent of Jainism, and Buddha (563 B.C.-483 B.C.), founder of Buddhism were the most prominent icons of this movement. Shramana gave rise to the concept of the cycle of birth and death, the concept of samsara, and the concept of liberation. The influence of Upanishads on Buddhism has been a subject of debate among scholars. While Radhakrishnan, Oldenberg and Neumann were convinced of Upanishadic influence on the Buddhist canon, Eliot and Thomas highlighted the points where Buddhism was opposed to Upanishads.[60] Buddhism may have been influenced by some Upanishadic ideas, it however discarded their orthodox tendencies.[61] In Buddhist texts Buddha is presented as rejecting avenues of salvation as 'pernicious views'.[62]

5.2.1 Jainism

Jainism was established by a lineage of 24 enlightened beings culminating with Parsva (9th century BC) and Mahavira (6th century BC). The 24th Tirthankara of Jainism, Mahavira, stressed five vows, including ahimsa (non-violence), satya (truthfulness), asteya (non-stealing), and aparigraha (non-attachment). Jain orthodoxy believes the teachings of Tirthankaras predates all known time and scholars believe Parshva, accorded status as the 23rd Tirthankara, was a historical figure. The Vedas are believed to have documented a few Tirthankaras and an ascetic order similar to the shramana movement.[63]

5.2.2 Buddhism

Buddhism was historically founded by Siddhartha Gautama, a Kshatriya prince-turned-ascetic, and was spread beyond India through missionaries. It later experienced a decline in India, but survived in Nepal and Sri Lanka, and remains more widespread in Southeast and East Asia. Gautama Buddha, who was called an 'awakened one' (Buddha), was born into the Shakya clan living at Kapilavastu and Lumbini in what is now southern Nepal. The Buddha was born at Lumbini, as emperor Ashoka's Lumbini pillar records, just before the kingdom of Magadha (which traditionally is said to have lasted from 546–324 BC) rose to power. The Shaikh claimed Angirasa and Gautama Maharishi lineage,[64] via descent from the royal lineage of Ayodhya. Buddhism emphasises enlightenment (nibbana, nirvana) and liberation from the rounds of rebirth. This objective is pursued through two schools, Theravada, the Way of the Elders (practised in Sri Lanka, Burma, Thailand, SE Asia, etc.) and Mahayana, the Greater Way (practised in Tibet, China, Japan, etc.). There may be some differences in the practice between the two schools in reaching the objective. In the Theravada practice this is pursued in seven stages of purification (visuddhi); viz. physical purification by taking precepts (sila visiddhi), mental purification by insight meditation (citta visuddhi), followed by purification of views and concepts (ditthi visuddhi), purificaion by overcoming of doubts (kinkha vitarana vishuddhi), purification by acquiring knowledge and wisdom of the right path (maggarmagga-nanadasana visuddhi), attaining knowledge and wisdom through the course of practice (patipada-nanadasana visuddhi), and purification by attaining knowledge and insight wisdom (nanadasana visuddhi).[65]

5.3   Spread of Jainism and Buddhism (500–200 BC)

Both Jainism and Buddhism spread throughout India during the period of the Magadha empire. Buddhism in India spread during the reign of Ashoka of the Maurya Empire, who patronised Buddhist teachings and unified the Indian subcontinent in the 3rd century BCE. He sent missionaries abroad, allowing Buddhism to spread across Asia. Jainism began its golden period during the reign of Emperor Kharavela of Kalinga in the 2nd century BC.

6.   Epic and Early Puranic Period (200 BC – 500 A.D.)

Flood and Muesse take the period between 200 BC and 500 A.D. as a separate period, in which the epics and the first puranas were being written. Michaels takes a greater timespan, namely the period between 200 BC and 1100 A.D., which saw the rise of so called 'Classical Hinduism', with its 'golden age' during the Gupta Empire. According to Alf Hiltebeitel, a period of consolidation in the development of Hinduism took place between the time of the late Vedic Upanishad (500 BC) and the period of the rise of the Guptas (320–467 A.D.), which he calls the 'Hindus synthesis', 'Brahmanic synthesis', or 'orthodox synthesis'. It develops in interaction with other religions and peoples: The emerging self-definitions of Hinduism were forged in the context of continuous interaction with heterodox religions (Buddhists, Jains, Ajivikas) throughout this whole period, and with foreign people (Yavanas, or Greeks; Sakas, or Scythians; Pahlavas, or Parthians; and Kusanas, or Kushans) from the third phase on [between the Mauryan empire and the rise of the Guptas]. The end of the Vedantic period around the 2nd century CE spawned several branches that furthered Vedantic philosophy, and which ended up being seminaries in their own right. Prominent among these developers were Yoga, Dvaita, Advaita, and the medieval Bhakti movement.

6.1 Smriti

The smriti texts of the period between 200 BC-100 A.D. proclaim the authority of the Vedas, and "non-rejection of the Vedas comes to be one of the most important touchstones for defining Hinduism over and against the heterodoxies, which rejected the Vedas". Of the six Hindu darsanas, the Mimamsa and the Vedanta "are rooted primarily in the Vedic sruti tradition and are sometimes called smarta schools in the sense that they develop smarta orthodox current of thoughts that are based, like smriti, directly on sruti". According to Hiltebeitel, "the consolidation of Hinduism takes place under the sign of bhakti". It is the Bhagavadgita that seals this achievement. The result is a universal achievement that may be called smarta. It views Shiva and Vishnu as "complementary in their functions but ontologically identical".

6.2 Vedanta – Brahma sutras (200 CE)

In earlier writings, Sanskrit 'Vedānta' simply referred to the Upanishads, the most speculative and philosophical of the Vedic texts. However, in the medieval period of Hinduism, the word Vedānta came to mean the school of philosophy that interpreted the Upanishads. Traditional Vedānta considers shabda pramāṇa (scriptural evidence) as the most authentic means of knowledge, while pratyakṣa (perception) and anumāna (logical inference) are considered to be subordinate (but valid). The systematisation of Vedantic ideas into one coherent treatise was undertaken by Badarayana in the Brahma Sutras which was composed around 200 BC.[66] The cryptic aphorisms of the Brahma Sutras are open to a variety of interpretations. This resulted in the formation of numerous Vedanta schools, each interpreting the texts in its own way and producing its own sub-commentaries.

6.3 Indian philosophy

After 200 A.D. several schools of thought were formally codified in Indian philosophy, including Samkhya, Yoga, Nyaya, Vaisheshika, Mimāṃsā and Advaita Vedanta.[67] Hinduism, otherwise a highly polytheistic, pantheistic or monotheistic religion, also tolerated atheistic schools. The thoroughly materialistic and anti-religious philosophical Cārvāka {charvaka} school that originated around the 6th century BC is the most explicitly atheistic school of Indian philosophy. Cārvāka {charvaka} is classified as a nāstika ('heterodox') system; it is not included among the six schools of Hinduism generally regarded as orthodox. It is noteworthy as evidence of a materialistic movement within Hinduism.[68] Our understanding of Cārvāka {charvaka} philosophy is fragmentary, based largely on criticism of the ideas by other schools, and it is no longer a living tradition.[69] Other Indian philosophies generally regarded as atheistic include Samkhya and Mimāṃsā.

6.4 Hindu literature

Two of Hinduism's most revered epics, the Mahabharata and Ramayana were compositions of this period. Devotion to deities was reflected from the composition of texts composed to their worship. For example, the Ganapati Purana was written for devotion to Ganapati (or Ganesh). Popular deities of this era were Shiva, Vishnu, Durga, Surya, Skanda, and Ganesh (including the forms/incarnations of these deities). In the latter Vedantic period, several texts were also composed as summaries/attachments to the Upanishads. These texts collectively called as Puranas allowed for a divine and mythical interpretation of the world, not unlike the ancient Hellenic or Roman religions. Legends and epics with a multitude of gods and goddesses with human like characteristics were composed.

6.5 Jainism and Buddhism

The Gupta period marked a watershed of Indian culture: the Guptas performed Vedic sacrifices to legitimize their rule, but they also patronized Buddhism, which continued to provide an alternative to Brahmanical orthodoxy. Buddhism continued to have a significant presence in some regions of India until the 12th century. There were several Buddhistic kings who worshiped Vishnu, such as the Gupta Empire, Pala Empire, Malla Empire, Somavanshi, and Satavahana.[70] Buddhism survived followed by Hindus.[71]

6.6 Tantra

Tantrism originated in the early centuries CE and developed into a fully articulated tradition by the end of the Gupta period. According to Michaels this was the 'Golden Age of Hinduism' (320–650 A.D), which flourished during the Gupta Empire (320-550 A.D.) until the fall of the Harsha Empire (606-647 A.D.). During this period, power was centralised, along with a growth of far distance trade, standardization of legal procedures, and general spread of literacy. Mahayana Buddhism flourished, but the orthodox Brahmana culture began to be rejuvenated by the patronage of the Gupta Dynasty. The position of the Brahmans was reinforced, and the first Hindu temples emerged during the late Gupta age.

7.　Medieval and Late Puranic Period (500–1500 A.D.)

7.1 Late-Classical Period (650–1100 A.D.)

After the end of the Gupta Empire and the collapse of the Harsha Empire, power became decentralised in India. Several larger kingdoms emerged, with countless vasal states. The kingdoms were ruled via a feudal system.

Smaller kingdoms were dependent on the protection of the larger kingdoms. 'The great king was remote, was exalted and deified', as reflected in the Tantric Mandala, which could also depict the king as the centre of the mandala. The disintegration of central power also leading to regionalisation of religiosity, and religious rivalry. Local cults and languages were enhanced, and the influence of 'Brahmanic ritualistic Hinduism' was diminished. Rural and devotional movements arose, along with Shaivism, Vaisnavism, Bhakti, and Tantra, though 'sectarian groupings were only at the beginning of their development'. Religious movements had to compete for recognition by the local lords. Buddhism lost its position and began to disappear in India.

7.1.1 Vedanta

In the same period Vedanta changed, incorporating Buddhist thought and its emphasis on consciousness and the working of the mind. Buddhism, which was supported by the ancient Indian urban civilisation lost influence on the traditional religions, which were rooted in the countryside. In Bengal, Buddhism was even prosecuted. But at the same time, Buddhism was incorporated into Hinduism, when Gaudapada used Buddhist philosophy to reinterpret the Upanishads. This also marked a shift from Atman and Brahman as a 'living substance' to 'maya-vada', where Atman and Brahman are seen as 'pure knowledge consciousness'. According to Scheepers, it is this 'maya-vada' view which has come to dominate Indian thought.

7.1.2 Buddhism

Between 400 and 1000 A.D. Hinduism expanded as the decline of Buddhism in India continued[72] Buddhism subsequently became effectively extinct in India but survived in Nepal and Sri Lanka.

7.1.3 Bhakti

The Bhakti movement began with the emphasis on the worship of God, regardless of one's status whether priestly or laypeople, men or women, higher social status or lower social status. The movements were mainly centered on the forms of Vishnu (Rama and Krishna) and Shiva. There were however popular devotees of this era of Durga. The best-known devotees are the Narayan from southern India. The most popular Shaiva teacher of the south was Basava, while of the north it was Gorakhnath. Female saints include figures like Akkamadevi, Lalleshvari and Molla. The 'alwar' or 'azhwars' those immersed in god were Tamil poet-saints of south India who lived between the 6th and 9th centuries CE and espoused 'emotional devotion' or bhakti to Visnu-Krishna in their songs of longing, ecstasy and service.[73] The most popular Vaishnava teacher of the south was Ramanuja, while of the north it was Ramananda. Several important icons were women. For example, within the Mahanubhava sector, the women out numbered the men and administration was many times composed mainly of women. Mirabai is the most popular female saint in India. Sri Vallabha Acharya (1479–1531) is a very important figure from this era. He founded the Shuddha Advaita (Pure Non-dualism) school of Vedanta thought.

7.2 Early Islamic rule (1100-1500A.D.)

In the 12th and 13th centuries, Turks and Afghans invaded parts of northern India and established the Delhi Sultanate in the former Rajput holdings.[74] The subsequent Slave dynasty of Delhi managed to conquer large areas of northern India, approximately equal in extent to the ancient Gupta Empire, while the Khalji dynasty conquered most of central India but were ultimately unsuccessful in conquering and uniting the subcontinent. The Sultanate ushered in a period of Indian cultural renaissance. The resulting 'Indo-Muslim' fusion of cultures left lasting syncretic monuments in architecture, music, literature, religion, and clothing.

7.2.1 Bhakti movement

During the 14th to 17th centuries, a great Bhakti movement swept through central and northern India, initiated by a loosely associated group of teachers or Sants. Ramananda, Ravidas, Srimanta Sankardeva, Chaitany, Mahaprabhu, Vallabha Acharya, Sur, Meera, Kabir, Tulsidas, Namdev, Dnyaneshwar, Tukaram, and other mystics spearheaded the Bhakti movement in the North while Annamacharya, Bhadrachala Ramadas, Tyagaraja, and others propagated Bhakti in the South. They taught that people could cast aside the heavy burdens of ritual and caste, and the subtle complexities of philosophy, and simply express their overwhelming love for God. This period was also characterized by a spate of devotional literature in vernacular prose and poetry in the ethnic languages of the various Indian states or provinces. The Bhakti movement gave rise to several different movements throughout India During the Bhakti movement, many Hindu groups regarded as outside the traditional Hindu caste system followed Bhakti traditions by worshipping/ following saints belonging to their respective communities. In their lifetimes, several of these saints even went to the extent of fighting conversion from foreign missionaries, encouraging only Hinduism within their communities. In Assam for example, tribals were led by Gurudev Kalicharan Bramha of the Brahmo Samaj; in Nagaland by Kacha Naga; and in Central India by Birsa Munda, Hanuman Aaron, Jatra Bhagat, and Budhu Bhagat.

7.2.2 Kabir Sect

The Kabir Panth is a religious movement based on the teachings of the Indian poet saint Kabir (1398-1518).[75] Kabir, the legendary saint of India, descends directly in this tradition of mysticism-singer-critic. Kabir, father of bhakti movement, leading in the 15th century (fall between 1398 and 1518), Kabir upturned the religious conceptions and social principles of that period.[76] Saint Kabir, who insisted on the devotional singing of praises of lord through his own compositions.[77] Kabir sermonized a monotheism that appealed clearly to the poor and convinced them of their access to god with no liaison. He denied both Hinduism and Islam, as well as meaningless religious rituals, and condemned double standards.[78] This infuriated the orthodox aristocracy. No one could frighten Kabir who was bold enough to stand up for himself and his beliefs.[76] The Kabir Panth considers Kabir as its principal guru or even as a divinity truth incarnate. Kabir's influence is testimony to his massive authority, even for those whose beliefs and practices he condemned so unsparingly. For Sikhs he is a forerunner and converser of Nanak, the originating Sikh Guru (spiritual guide). Muslims place him in Sufi (mystical) lineages, and for Hindus he becomes a Vaishnavite with universalist leanings.[79]

7.2.3 Lingayatism

Lingayatism is a distinct Shaivite tradition in India, established in the 12th century by the philosopher and social reformer Basavanna. The adherents of this tradition are known as Lingayats. The term is derived from Lingavantha in Kannada, meaning 'one who wears Ishtalinga on their body' (Ishtalinga is the representation of the God). In Lingayat theology, Ishtalinga is an oval-shaped emblem symbolising Parasiva, the absolute reality. Contemporary Lingayatism follows a progressive reform-based theology propounded, which has great influence in South India, especially in the state of Karnataka.[80]

7.2.4 Unifying Hinduism

The tendency of 'a blurring of philosophical distinctions' has also been noted by Burley. Lorenzen locates the origins of a distinct Hindu identity in the interaction between Muslims and Hindus, and a process of "mutual self-definition with a contrasting Muslim other", which started well before 1800 A.D. Both the Indian and the European thinkers who developed the term 'Hinduism' in the 19th century were influenced by these philosophers.

7.2.5 Sikhism (15th Century)

Sikhism originated in 15th century Punjab, Delhi Sultanate (present day India and Pakistan) with the teachings of Nanak and nine successive gurus. The principal belief in Sikhism is faith in Vāhigurū represented by the sacred symbol of ēk ōaṅkār [meaning one god]. Sikhism's traditions and teachings are distinctly associated with the history, society, and culture of the Punjab. Adherents of Sikhism are known as Sikhs (students or disciples) and number over 27 million across the world.

8. Modern period (1500 A.D.– present)

8.1 Early modern period

According to Gavin Flood, the modern period in India begins with the first contacts with western nations around 1500 A.D. The period of Mughal rule in India saw the rise of new forms of religiosity.

8.2 Modern India (after 1800 A.D.)

8.2.1 Hinduism

In the 19th century, under influence of the colonial forces, a synthetic vision of Hinduism was formulated by Raja Ram Mohan Roy, Swami Vivekananda, Sri Aurobindo, Sarvepalli Radhakrishnan and Mahatma Gandhi. These thinkers have tended to take an inclusive view of India's religious history, emphasising the similarities between the various Indian religions. The modern era has given rise to dozens of Hindu saints with international influence.

For example, Brahma Baba established the Brahma Kumaris, one of the largest new Hindu religious movements which teaches the discipline of Raja Yoga to millions. Representing traditional Gaudiya Vaishnavism, Prabhupada founded the Hare Krishna movement, another organisation with a global reach. In late 18th century India, Swaminarayan founded the Swaminarayan Sampraday. Anandamurti, founder of the Ananda Marga, has also influenced many worldwide. Through the international influence of all these new Hindu denominations, many Hindu practices such as yoga, meditation, mantra, divination, and vegetarianism have been adopted by new converts.

8.2.2 Jainism

Jainism continues to be an influential religion and Jain communities live in Indian states Gujarat, Rajasthan, Madhya Pradesh, Maharashtra, Karnataka and Tamil Nadu. Jains authored several classical books in different Indian languages for a considerable period.

8.2.3 Buddhism

The Dalit Buddhist movement also referred to as Navayana[81] is a 19th - and 20th century Buddhist revival movement in India. It received its most substantial impetus from B. R. Ambedkar's call for the conversion of Dalits to Buddhism in 1956 and the opportunity to escape the caste-based society that considered them to be the lowest in the hierarchy.[82]

9. Summarization on learning from Religion

Religion in India is characterised by a diversity of religious beliefs and practices. The preamble of the Indian constitution states that India is a secular state, although there were please going on Supreme court of India to remove the words secular and socialist from the Preamble to the Constitution of India.[83][84][85] The Indian sub- continent is the birthplace of four of the world's major religions: namely Hinduism, Buddhism, Jainism and Sikhism collectively known as Indian religions that believe Moksha is the most supreme state of the Ātman (soul).[86] According to the 2011 census, 79.8% of the population of India practices Hinduism, 14.2% adheres to Islam, 2.3% adheres to Christianity, 1.72%! Bookmark not defined. Throughout India's history, religion has been an important part of the country's culture. Religious diversity and religious tolerance are both established in the country by the law and custom; the Constitution of India has declared the right to freedom of religion to be a fundamental right.[87]

Today, India is home to around 94%[88] of the global population of Hindus. Most Hindu shrines and temples are in India, as are the birthplaces of most Hindu saints. Prayagraj hosts the world's largest religious pilgrimage, Prayag Kumbh Mela, where Hindus from across the world come together to bathe in the confluence of three sacred rivers of India: the Ganga, the Yamuna, and the Saraswati.[89] The Indian diaspora in the West has popularized many aspects of Hindu philosophy such as yoga, meditation, Ayurvedic medicine, divination, karma, and reincarnation.[90] The influence of Indian religions has been significant all over the world. Several Hindu-based organizations, such as the International Society for Krishna Consciousness, the Ramakrishna Mission, the Brahma Kumaris, the Ananda Marga, and others have spread Hindu spiritual beliefs and practices. The Indian subcontinent also contains the largest population of Muslims in the world, with about one-third of all Muslims being from South Asia.[91][92][93] India is also the cradle of Ahmadiyya Islam. The shrines of some of the most famous saints of Sufism, like Moinuddin Chishti and Nizamuddin Auliya, are found in India, and attract visitors from all over the world.[94]

10. History of South Asian Sufism

The tenth century is very significant in the history of Islam. This period witnessed the rise of Turks on the ruins of the Abbasid Caliphate, as well as striking changes in the realm of ideas and beliefs. The domination of the Mutazila or rationalist school of Islam was terminated by the emergence of orthodox schools that put emphasis on the Quran and Hadith. The period was also marked by the rise to prominence of the sufi mystics and silsilahs (orders).[95] The Mutazilites or rationalists received the patronage of the Abbasid Caliphs and used their power to persecute their rivals. They also tried to systematize theology by applying reason (aql). The orthodox elements however, condemned them as religious skeptics and persecuted them. It is not surprising that famous sufi saint Mansur Hallaj was also executed in the tenth century A.D. for his unorthodox views. The collapse of rationalist school strengthened the hands of the 'traditionalists' which culminated in the advent of four schools of Islamic law. Of these, the Hanafi school was the most liberal. The eastern Turks who later migrated to India were the followers of this school, this partly explains why the Muslims in the subcontinent, unlike their counterparts elsewhere, were often comparatively flexible in matters of faith. The decline of the Mutazilites also contributed to the ascendancy of the sufi mystics. The Sufis emerged in Islam at a very early stage. Most of them were highly spiritual persons who were disgusted by the vulgar demonstration of wealth and degeneration of morals in the aftermath of Islam's politico-military triumph. Some of the sufi pioneers such as Hasan Basri and his disciple, the woman sufi Rabia (8th century A.D.) reiterated the importance of prayer, continual fasting and unconditional love of God. The term sufi originated from the Persian word suf meaning coarse wool.

The Islamic mystics of Central and West Asia used to wear a long garment (khirqa) manufactured by suf which caused constant pinching. Such discomfort kept them awake throughout the night and reminded them about their spiritual duties such as zikr (reciting the name of God).[96] Wearing of a patched garment of wool (suf) also indicated that the Sufis tried to follow the legacy of the prophets, and Christian apostles and ascetics who believed in simple living and high thinking. Simple and austere lifestyle made the Sufis very much acceptable to the poor Indian masses. At the same time their sophistication in terms of cultivating literature or theology enhanced their status among the aristocracy in general and Muslim aristocracy. The sufi concept of fana or spiritual merger of the devoted with Allah antagonized the orthodox ulama. Mansur Hallaj's proclamation of the doctrine Anal-Haq (I am Truth/God) reflected the sufi belief that unification with Allah was the highest stage of enlightenment.

Sufi movement got its martyr when Mansur sacrificed his life for his beliefs. The tragic death of Mansur earned the Sufis the reputation of being men who were pure hearted, sincere, and indifferent to worldly gains. This was how an essentially quietist movement based on love, devotion and contemplation gradually became inclined towards ecstatic love with the potentiality to challenge existing social norms, religious beliefs, and practices.[97] Between the tenth and twelve centuries various sufi orders or silsilah's emerged. During the same period khanqahs (sufi hospices) were also being established by the renowned Sufis. Apparently, the practices and organization of the khanqahs resembled the Buddhist and Christian monastic systems. The ambulatory Nath Panthi Yogis, with their markaz (headquarters) at Peshawar, familiarized the Sufis with the practices of hath-yoga. The translation of Amritkund, the Sanskrit book on hath-yoga, into both Arabic and Persian confirms the interaction between the yogis and Sufis which strengthened the composite nature of Indian culture in the medieval period.[98] Like the wandering Yogis, the wandering Islamic mystics, popularly known as Qalandars had to encounter various religio-cultural groups in course of their traveling and became liberal and unorthodox.

However, they were denounced as be-shara (those who do not act in conformity with the sharia) Sufis by the orthodox elements. Many present-day qawwali singers show their respect to these qalandars and thus reflect their appreciation for India's multiculturalism. There are also Sufis who function in tune with the sharia (canon law of Islam) and are known as ba-shara. This is one of the reasons why sufi movement should be studied as a heterogeneous movement. [99] Sanai (1131), Rumi (1273) and many other Persian poets spread the sufi message of mystic union and love far and wide. Imbued with the spirit of humanity and tolerance, their verses created ripples in the Indian subcontinent. It is not surprising that the eclectic Mughal Emperor Akbar was a great admirer of Rumi. Some of the Sufis were fond of musical gatherings (sama) in which a state of ecstasy was created. This created consternation among the orthodox ulama who argued that music is not permitted in Islam.[100] The Chishti Sufis were amongst earliest Islamic mystic migrants to south Asia. This sufi silsilah tried to appropriate various aspects of Indian cultural traditions, such as music, and became extremely popular in the subcontinent. They supported Sama.

In the thirteenth century, Delhi emerged as one of the major centres (markaz) of the Chishtis. This was possible largely due to the activities of the illustrious Chishti saint Khwaja Qutbuddin Bakhtiyar Kaki, who left his birthplace in Trans oxiana and arrived in Delhi in the early 1220s. He was warmly welcomed by Sultan Iltutmish.[101] It is useful to note that following the Mongol devastations of Central and West Asia, Delhi emerged as an inviting place before many eminent scholars, religious divines, and fugitive princes. After coming to Delhi, Kaki met the challenge both ulama and the Suhrawardis. The former wanted to oust him from Delhi and condemned Kaki as a heretic on the ground that the mystic was fond of Sama. This criticism had no impact upon Sultan Iltutmish who wanted to use sufi influence to counter the ulama. Once Kaki was about to leave Delhi for Ajmer, which is also an important centre of the Chishtis. But a huge crowd accompanied him outside the city for miles and he had to settle in Delhi. The magnitude of popularity the Chishti saints enjoyed in South Asia is amazing. However, the Suhrawardi silsilah, because of their orthodox approach, could not enjoy such popularity among the Delhiites.[102] Why some of the Sultans of Delhi, such as Iltutmish, favoured charismatic Sufis like Kaki, should be studied in its broader historical perspective.

The Turko-Afghan Sultans were trying to build up their empires in the Indian subcontinent where Muslim population was overwhelmed by the non-Muslim population. Particularly during the embryonic stage of 9 empire building, strict observance of the sharia (canon law of Islam) would have antagonized the majority population. Establishment of the sharia rule in tune with the advice provided by the ulama, was not possible in the Indian environment. Many sultans who excelled in statecraft realized that an empire derives its strength from heterogeneity. Now many sufi saints epitomized India's composite culture in the sense that they had Hindu, Sikh, and Muslim followers. Many Chisti and Qadiri Sufis believed in the policy of sulh-i-kul or 'peace with all'. Later, Mughal Emperor Akbar could emerge as a great empire builder largely because of his capacity to translate this concept into practice. So, offering patronage to some Sufis implied strengthening of the symbols of multiculturalism. Thus, many Sultans were able to win the confidence and loyalty of the subject population who represented diverse linguistic and cultural backgrounds. The two most prominent sufi orders in south Asia during the Sultanate period were the Chishti and the Suhrawardi. The Chishtis flourished in Delhi and in the surrounding area, including Rajasthan, parts of Punjab and modern UP. Bengal, Bihar, Malwa, Gujarat and later the Deccan also experienced the waves of sufi movement. The Suhrawardis were influential mainly in Punjab and Sindh. Territories were divided between different pirs (leading sufis of different orders in such a way that Sufis of various orders could maintain a cordial relationship amongst themselves. Indeed! the modern religious sects have much to learn from these predecessors. Muinuddin Chishti, the doyen of the Chishti movement in South Asia moved to Ajmer around 1206 A.D. when Turkish hegemony was firmly established there and a sizeable Muslim population of Turkish ghazis and prisoners of war who had to embrace Islam under duress, came into being. The saint selected

Ajmer as his centre because like Chisht (in Central Asia), it was a small town and away from the epicentre of political activity, Delhi. The saint believed that the environment in a small town was favourable for spiritual experimentation. Similarly, great saint Hamiduddin settled down at Nagaur another small town in Rajasthan. Khwaja Muinuddin was married but led the life of an ascetic. His principal object was to enable the Muslim piety to lead a life of devotion to Allah. He was not interested in conversions, since he believed faith was an individual concern. This same spirit was reflected in the activities of rulers such as Sultan Muhammad bin Tughluq and Emperor Akbar who used to venerate this saint. It should be mentioned that many sufi saints became famous after their demise. Muinuddin was no exception. His image as a saintly man became larger after his death in 1235 A.D. Muhammad bin Tughluq visited his grave. Canonization of a sufi is marked by the erection of structures like dome or mosque on the tomb of the deceased sufi. For example, a mosque was built near his tomb by Mahmud Khalji of Malwa during the 15th century.

However, Muinuddin's stature as a saint reached its apex under Akbar who nurtured deep respect for him. Akbar could grasp the political importance of Ajmer. This far-sighted ruler also identified Muinuddin as the symbol of India's composite culture who was respected by all irrespective of religious beliefs. Akbar knew that in the volatile situation of Rajasthan such positive elements required strengthening. Muinuddin advised his followers to "develop river like generosity, sun like affection and earth like hospitality".[103] River, sun and earth are sacred among the Hindus. In this way the sufi saints reflected their appropriating nature while addressing the common people in a language they understood. Such an approach increased the popularity of Chishti saints in medieval south Asia. It brings us to another great Chishti saint Baba Fariduddin Ganj-I-Shakkar, the most famous disciple of Kaki. Farid lived at Hansi in modern Haryana, then moved to Ajodhan which was on the Sutlej on the main route connecting Multan and Lahore.[104] He put emphasis on poverty emulating the Prophet Muhammad who used to say, "I take pride in my poverty." It is useful to note that many sufi saints used the image of the Prophet as a source of authority. This was a natural legitimizing process as they had to encounter the challenges of Islamic orthodoxy.[105] Farid also put stress on renunciation of worldly goods and attachments, control of the senses by fasting and other austerities, humbleness, and service to others.[106] He was a saint of broad outlook and some of the verses, ascribed to him were included in the Guru Granth Sahib of Nanak. Nizamuddin Auliya (1325A.D.), a chief successor of Baba Farid was the most illustrious Chishti saint of Delhi where he worked for fifty years during a period of great political turmoil characterized by the collapse of Balban's dynasty and the ascendancy of

Alauddin Khalji, volatility following the demise of Alauddin Khalji and the rise of the Tughluqs. He survived those frequent changes of dynasties and rulers because of the Chishti philosophy of keeping politics at bay and not associating with the rulers and nobles.

The Chishti saints laid emphasis on a life of simplicity, poverty, humility, and selfless devotion to God. Many of them were so obsessed with the notion of poverty that they lived in mud covered thatched houses, wore patched clothes, and encouraged prolonged fasting. Like the yogis, they considered that control of senses was necessary for spiritual uplift. Muinuddin Chishti interpreted the highest form of devotion to Allah in terms of redressing the misery of the miserable, helping the helpless and feeding the unfed. Nizamuddin Auliya regarded altruistic services as more important than obligatory prayers. At a time when the Turks turned a blind eye to the Islamic concept of brotherhood and looked down upon the ordinary people, the sufi attitude of non-discrimination helped to reduce social tensions. The principal concern of the Sufis was the amelioration of the condition of Muslims. However, their care and concern did not exclude the Hindus. The Chishti saints freely interacted with Hindu and Jain yogis and discussed with them various matters, particularly yogic exercises. Once being greatly impressed by the devotion of a group of Hindus, Nizamuddin Auliya remarked before his friend poet Amir Khusro "Every community has its own path and faith, and its own way of worship," Bahauddin Zakariya, the founder of the Suhrawardi silsilah in India, did not believe in starvation or self-mortification.

Unlike the Chishtis, the Suhrawardis accepted royal grants and believed that money was necessary to help the poor. They also put emphasis on the external forms of religion, i.e., namaz (prayer), roza (fasting), hajj (pilgrimage to Mecca) or zakat (charity). Though Bahauddin prescribed restricted visits to sama (sufi music), the orthodox ulama became hostile towards him on that issue. When the Chistis tried to distance themselves from politics, Bahauddin believed that visits to royal courts enabled the saint to help the poor through royal support. On the other side, such visits enabled the Sultans and their associates to receive the spiritual blessings of saints. The Suhrawardi order had the credit to be the first Sufi order that was introduced to Bengal by Shaikh Jalaluddin Tabrizi (d.1225), a saint of India-wide fame. However, the Persian and Urdu works provide no information about his activities in Bengal. Shaikh Abdul Haqq Muhaddis Dihlawi (1642 A.D.) had devoted a few pages to Shaikh Jalaluddin in his famous work Akhbar ul Akhyar (in Persian), but is silent about the Shaikh's birth place (watane paidaish), and as regards Bengal, he only mentions that Shaikh Jajaluddin has started to move towards Bengal.[107] According to Akhbar ul Akhyar, Jalaluddin Tabrizi was initially a disciple of Shaikh

Abu Said Tabrizi, and then after the latter's death, of Shaikh Shihabuddin Suhrawardi.[108] Now the silence of the Persian sources in connection with Shaikh Jalaluddin's activities in Bengal have led some scholars to depend on Shek Subhodaya, a later work in Sanskrit wrongly attributed to Halayudh Misra, a court poet of the last Sena king Lakshmana Sena. According to this book the birthplace of Jalaluddin Tabrizi was Etawa (in modern U.P., India), the name of his father was Kafur and he had received education with the help of Ramadan Khan, a merchant. This book also mentions that Shaikh Jalaluddin arrived in Bengal before Bakhtyar Khalji's conquest of Nadia and foretold the impending Turkish invasion of Lakshmana Sena's kingdom. But according to modern scholars the stories in Shek Subhodaya are fictitious. The saint was born at Tabriz in Persia and not at Etawah.[109] Secondly, he could not have come to Bengal before Bakhtiyar Khalji's conquest. According to Fawaid ul Fuad (in Persian) the saint came to Delhi when Sultan Shamsuddin Iltutmish was reigning.[110] Now Sultan Iltutmish ascended the throne in 1210 A.D. So the saint could not have come to Delhi before 1210 A.D, not to speak of his arrival in Bengal before that date (Lakshmana Sena died in 1206).[111] The original shrine was built by Sultan Alauddin Ali Shah (BC 742-43/1341-42 A.D.) at the order of the saint in dream.[112] Probably the original mosque was also built by him, which was repaired in 1664 A.D. by Shah Nimatullah.[113] The Bhandar Khanah was erected by one Chand Khan in 1673 A.D.[114] The inscription attached to the Lakshmana Sena Dalan shows that Muhammad Ali of Burji had repaired the astanah (place of meditation) of Shaikh Jalal Tabrizi in the year 1722 A.D. The inscription in Tanur Khanah records that it was built by one Sadullah in 1682 A.D. The endowment to the shrine of the saint is known as Bais Hazari, its income having been twenty-two thousand tankas. From the developments mentioned above we can deduce that building activities around the tomb or shrine of a saint used to commence decades and sometimes more than a couple of centuries after his demise. Similar thing happened with Muinuddin Chishti's shrine.

As a result, these saints sometimes became more famous after their deaths. Secondly, the sultans and nobles often contested among each other in showing their respect to the deceased saint through their involvements in building activities. It is useful to note that mainly the important influential and popular shrines received the patronage of the sultans and nobles in medieval India. It was a common legitimizing process through which the rulers and aristocrats tried to enhance their images among the nobility and the subject population. Thirdly, the existence of mosque at the site was in conformity with the Suhrawardi preference for the external rituals of Islam. The discovery of Tanur Khanah (kitchen) at the site confirms the fact that the Suhrawardis were keen to sustain the sufi ritual called langar. The latter became a symbol of Islamic egalitarianism as the nobles and the commoners received the same food served at the sufi center. Interestingly this practice is also common among the Sikhs.[115] Another great Suhrawardi Sufi of Bengal was Shah Jalal Mujarrad-i-Yamani (1346A.D.). This reputed saint was also a great warrior and was largely responsible for the propagation of Islam in the whole of Eastern Bengal and Western part of Assam.[116] The Chishtis also consolidated their position in Bengal. Shaikh Akhi Siraj (d.1357) was one of the most famous saints of this order who flourished in Bengal. Because of his sound knowledge, his spiritual guide Nizamuddin Awliya used to call him Aina-i-Hindustan (Mirror of India). Another illustrious Chisti saint of Bengal was Nur Qutb Alam (d.1415 A.D.). His tomb is in the town of Pandua (Malda). The Naqshbandi and the Qadiri Sufis flourished in Bengal after the collapse of the Delhi Sultanate. The Naqshbandis were orthodox and expressed their hostility to the mystical folk songs of Bengal. Bijapur in the Deccan flourished as an important centre of the Chishtis from 1300A.D. to 1700A.D. Apart from the Chishtis, the Qadiris and the Shattaris exercised their control in Bijapur. Another important Sufi centre in the Deccan was Gulbarga which was graced by the presence of Bandanawaz Gisudaraz (d.1422A.D.), the famous Chishti saint, who migrated there from Delhi. Bidar also emerged as an important markaz (centre) of the Qadiri silsilah, many of whom were Arab migrants. In course of time many successors of Gisudaraz became landed gentry or inamdar Sufis who received land as inam (grant) from the kingdom of Bijapur. In return for this patronage the Sufis had to pray for the perpetuity of the Kingdom.

However, after Aurangzeb's campaign in that region, many of these Sufis switched over their allegiance to the Mughal Emperor who did not terminate the practice of offering inam to secure the loyalty of local Sufis. The mutually beneficial relationship between the Kingdom of Bijapur and the sufi saints confirmed the fact that the latter did not always function in conformity with the Chishti concept of keeping politics at bay.[117] Apart from the Chishtis, the Naqshbandis also had their base in the Deccan. However, they were not as popular as the Chishtis. Awrangabad became an important centre of the Naqshbandis. The most illustrious Naqshbandi Sufis of Awrangabad were Baba Palangposh (1699) and Baba Musafir (1715). Baba Palangposh was born in a place near Bukhara. He permanently came to Deccan in 1683 and is lying buried in Awrangabad. Baba Shah Musafir was also of Central Asian origin. His father hailed from the Kubrawiyya sufi order and his mother belonged to a family of Sayyids (descendants of the Prophet).[118] Particularly the Naqshbandi Sufis used genealogy as a source of authority.[119] Thus, in the Weberian sense, Baba Musafir could successfully combine hereditary charisma with acquired charisma. If the focus is shifted towards western India, it would be interesting to note that the commercial city of Ahmadabad can also be described as the city of dargahs because more 15 than a dozen major dargahs are located here. Among the important dargahs of the city are those of Piranpir, Shah Abu Turab Shirazi, Shah Abdul Wahhab, the Senior and Junior Airdrus and Pir Muhammad Shah.[120] We shall discuss the dargah of Pir Muhammad Shah for its representative value. He came to Ahmadabad from Bijapur in the eighteenth century. This renowned sufi hailed from a Qadiri background and was known for his profound scholarship and literary bent of mind. He was groomed under the paternal care of his uncle Sayyid Abdurrahaman who not only exposed him to formal education in traditional religious lore but also initiated him into the basic tenets of the Qadiri silsilah from quite a young age. He visited Mecca and Medina and engrossed himself in the study of various religious sciences such as Quranic exegesis, hadith (tradition), and tasawwuf (Sufism) under the guidance of illustrious teachers. It can be deduced from the above description that in those days many erudite Muslims regarded scriptural and mystical knowledge as complimentary to each other.

This to a large extent buttressed their endeavours to accommodate diverse cultures and different interpretations. Logically this broadened the mental horizons of many medieval saints and contributed to the sustenance of India's composite culture. Pir Muhammad Shah died in May 1750 A.D. and was buried within the walled city, near the haveli of Salahuddin Khan, where his disciples from the town of Kadi (District Mehsana) constructed his tomb, a mosque, and a garden close by. The saint's mausoleum is a large domed building resembling a degenerate Mughal style. The glory of the Mughal Empire was waning fast during that period particularly after the Persian and Afghan invasions spearheaded by Nadir Shah and Ahmad Shah Abdali respectively. Signs of decay could be visible in the external material and masculine world. The internal spiritual world was still untouched by the ravages of wars and political intrigues that characterized the declining phase of the empire.[121] Apparently the vacuum in the external world was being compensated by the developments in the spiritual world. But still the Mughal Empire and the symbols which represented it were regarded as legitimizers. Hence the Mughal architectural pattern could be emulated while building a mausoleum for a deceased sufi saint such as Pir Muhammad Shah. This process and the magnitude of its success determined the spiritual position of a particular shrine or tomb or mausoleum in the hierarchy of similar buildings. Gujarat was also famous in the Mughal era as a revenue rich province largely due to its long tradition of maritime trade. Seen from that angle it would be relevant to study the material implications of sufi establishments of Ahmadabad. Pir Muhammad Shah has a considerable following among the affluent trading community of Sunni Bohra Muslims domiciled in Ahmadabad and other important towns such as Surat, Patan and Baroda.

Through the munificent offerings of these wealthy businessmen murids (disciples), the sufi establishment has, over the years, amassed huge, landed property in and around the dargah (shrine). The value of these lands has risen considerably, and the entire estate is maintained by a registered Board of Trustees known as the Dargah Pir Muhammad Shah Committee. Its members and those of its sub-committees are elected from among the members of the community.[122] The saint's Urs (death anniversary) is celebrated on a grand scale when hundreds of devotees from the city and distant places throng the mausoleum. In its spacious premises board and lodging facilities is offered to the pilgrims. On the first day the usual sandalwood ceremony is held. On the second day, the Quran is recited by a group of thirty trained people. This event challenges the stereotyped notion that Sufis do not function in conformity with the sharia (canon law of Islam).

Indeed! At times the Sufis can play a significant role in popularizing the basic tenets of Islam among the common people. During a special dish of pulao called in popular parlance Pir Muhammad Shahi pulao is served among the participants. It is useful to note that in a dargah complex more than one sufi saint can be venerated. For example, the death anniversaries of Pir Muhammad Shah's uncle and first preceptor Sayyid Abdurrahman, of Shah Wajihuddin Alawi, and of the founder of the Qadiri order Sayyid Abdulqadir Jilani of Baghdad (d.1166A.D.), are also celebrated with the fatiha ceremonies and the distribution of sweets and eatables. In the month of Ramadan, a special dish, halim, is prepared and served to fasting pilgrims who come to stay for tarawih (additional night prayers during Ramadan) prayers in the mosque.[123] The Dargah Trust is also involved in welfare and social service activities such as organizing training classes for girls and women, promoting education by offering scholarships, books, and similar facilities. There is a spacious building attached to the dargah. In one wing of that building is a large library open to the public.

There are some 3000 printed books in that library available in different languages such as Arabic, Persian, Urdu, Gujarati, and English. Availability of books in so many languages is significant. It implies that many sufi centres by reflecting their broad and liberal outlook contribute to the nourishing of India's cultural pluralism. By making knowledge available in both oriental and occidental languages this particular sufi centre serves as a bridge between the east and the west. When the peace of our planet is being threatened by religious fundamentalism, sectarianism and cultural chauvinism, the UNESCO would do a great job by giving publicity to such sufi establishments in a meaningful manner. Besides, the library has a fine collection of about 2000 valuable Persian, Arabic and Urdu manuscripts covering different branches of Islamic learning and literature.[124] Pir Muhammad Shah was a poet by his own right who composed verses with 'Aqdas' and 'Shahid' as his poetic names. He has to his credit several tracts in Persian and Gujari or Dakani verse. These priceless manuscripts are also preserved in the library. Many of his murids (disciples), both male and female, have composed verses in Persian and Urdu, as also mourning his death. Collections of these poems are also available in the library. These are extremely useful materials to assess Gujarat's contribution to Urdu language and literature.[125] The Piranpir's dargah in the Jamalpur quarter of the city was built in the seventeenth century over the grave of Shah Abdulkhaliq whose origin was traced from the illustrious saint of Baghdad, Shaikh Abdulqadir Jilani (d.1166). Linking genealogy to the famous saints of Middle East is regarded as a form of legitimizer by the sufi silsilahs (orders) of South Asia. So far as its architectural pattern is concerned, the usual tomb style of perforated stone-screen walls has been adopted. Many visitors throng the dargah on certain weekdays. It attracts a larger number on the anniversary of the buried saint, as well as of the founder of the silsilah (the Qadiri order), which falls on Jumada. It is useful to remember that veneration of illustrious sufi saints who never visited India is not unique among the pious Muslims of Gujarat. It is common in Bengali Muslim piety as well. Availability of their tazkiras particularly the tazkira of Abdulqadir Jilani in the Bengali language confirms this fact. Majority of such biographies appeared during a period when the external, masculine and material world was being dominated by colonial presence. In the era of socio-economic and political challenges, Indian Muslim piety often used the world of the Sufis as the bastion of Islam from which they could derive peace, solace, and inspiration. Like the Prophet Muhammad, the sufi pirs also emerged as their friends and their role models. However, it is useful to remember that all the pirs (sufi saints having many disciples) did not enjoy similar respect in the spiritual hierarchy. Some saints such as Abdulqadir Jilani, were regarded as the universal symbols of Islam who can be surpassed only by the Prophet Muhammad.

These universal symbols of Islam got priority over the local symbols of Islam (such as local pirs) in the nineteenth and twentieth centuries when resurgent and reformist Islam was moving from strength to strength. This was to facilitate the process of community solidarity among the Indian Muslims.[126] The rauza (tomb, mausoleum, shrine)[127] of Shaikh-al-Aidrus is situated in the Jhaveriwada locality and is a fine mausoleum of stone of the domed and perforated stone-screen-walls variety. Shaikh-al-Aidrus hailed from a renowned saintly family of Hadramout in southern Arabia.

The saint migrated to Gujarat in the fifteenth century. The tomb attributed to his son Shaikh Abdulqadir al-Aidrus is not very far from his own tomb. Junior Aidrus is better known for his prolificity as a writer and poet of Arabic. He authored many books including Al-Nur al-Safirli Ahl al-Qarn al-Ashir which is regarded as an important source for the cultural and literary history of sixteenth century Ahmadabad.[128] Junior Aidrus's case is unique from the linguistic point of view. Generally, the sufi writers and poets in South Asia manifested their creative faculties in the Persian language. There were also occasions when many sufi poets and writers expressed themselves in the vernacular languages which contributed to the growth of those local languages.[129] But Junior Aidrus used Arabic as his medium of expression.

Unlike Persian, Arabic was not the official language in medieval India. Nor was it a spoken language in India. But original Quran and hadith are available in Arabic. Considering this religious dimension of the language, the saint perhaps tried to legitimize his place in the spiritual hierarchy by cultivating this language. The dargah of Shah Abu Turab, a scion of the Salami Sayyid family of Shiraz, rose to prominence at the time of Emperor Akbar's conquest of Gujarat in 1573.[130] It has been indicated elsewhere that like any other pragmatic ruler, Akbar understood the importance of maintaining a cordial relationship with the leading sufi establishments which were popular among both the Muslims and Hindus to enhance the stature of the Mughal Empire. Such legitimization was particularly necessary in a province like Gujarat which was being exposed to Mughal military and administrative mechanisms. Akbar trusted Shah Abu Turab who carried out negotiations with the nobility in Gujarat on behalf of the Mughal Emperor. In 1578, he was appointed as the amir-i-hajj (one who leads the hajj pilgrims) by Akbar. After performing hajj, Shah Abu Turab returned to Fatehpur Sikri with the qadam-i-rasul (the footprint of the Prophet), which was reverently received by Akbar. The eclectic Emperor Akbar knew how to resolve the underlying tension between the veneration of a local pir (who at times may be interested in international networking as manifested in the case of Shah Turab who led the hajj pilgrims.) and the emphasis on the universal symbols of Islam such as the qadam-i-rasul or the hajj. Thus, qadam-i-rasul and hajj could be used as source of authority both by the Sufis and the sultans in medieval south Asia. This hypothesis is confirmed by the fact that Shah Turab's dargah, which is situated in the old Asawal locality, to the south of the Calico Mills, seems to have been venerated mainly on account of the qadam-i-rasul, which was there until the middle of the eighteenth century. It is stated that during the Maratha insurgence, it was removed to the walled city. It has been argued that later the descendants of Shah Abu Turab, shifted it to Cambey, to which place they belonged.[131] Majority of the Sufi saints in South Asia accepted the concept of wahadat al-wujud or 'Unity of Being'. They believe that "The world is so closely related to Him that everything is He".[132] (Hama Ust or 'Everything is He').

In other words, God is reflected in everything. It implies that God is also reflected in a Hindu, so a Hindu should not be denounced as a kafir (infidel). Such an inclusive approach contributed to the strengthening of India's composite culture and further enhanced the popularity of many Sufi saints. It should be mentioned that there were also Sufis who did not share this liberal approach and embarked on a policy of exclusion. They believed in the exclusion of Hindus from important administrative and military positions and expected the Muslim rulers to administer the state in strict conformity with the sharia (canon law of Islam). That is why it is often difficult to draw a demarcating line between a section of Sufis and the orthodox ulama. The Sufis played a significant role in the growth and efflorescence of vernacular literature such as Urdu, Hindi, Bengali, Deccani and other regional languages. The classical language Persian continued to receive patronage from the court as the language of power and administration. The Sufis massively contributed to the spread of poetry and music. The Chishtis used song and dance techniques of concentration and for creating spiritual ecstasy.[133] Some of the early Bengali poets had been sufi-poets such as Sayid Sultan, Shah Barid Khan and Alaol. Bengali folk music, such as the baul and jari songs also owed much to Sufism.[134] Sufis also appropriated ritual dynamics prevalent in a region or locality.[135] For example mention can be made about votive offerings at dargah (burial place of a Muslim saint), burning incense and tying bricks at holy places with the expectation of securing fertility among women. In this way Sufism significantly contributed to the formation of regional identities in different parts of South Asia. If Sufis learnt from non-Muslim traditions, the local, Indic, traditions (local, foreign, Indic are sensitive categories which must be handled with care), were also influenced by the principles of Islam as represented by the Sufis. The dynamics of Sufi Islam was resonated in the teachings of Kabir and Nanak as they criticized idolatry, and meaningless rituals and laid emphasis on monotheism and egalitarianism. In the case of Sikhism, important sections of the Guru Granth Saheb are borrowed from Sufi poetry. The proximity of the Sufis to non-Muslim traditions helped the former to play an important role in conversion and Islamization, even if many of them may not be working with a concrete agenda of this sort. Yet the presence of charismatic Sufis was the principal factor in the conversion of large sections of south asian population to Islam. Sufi institutions, khanqahs (sufi dwelling) and dargahs, emerged as centres where Muslims and non-Muslims assembled for worship and sought blessings and benediction. The process of conversion commenced with devotion towards a particular Sufi, leading to the emergence of syncretic sects, symbolizing only half conversion. Eventually, there emerged communities of Muslims who professed Islam formally, but continued with their practice of local customs and traditions, which invited the criticism of puritanical, reformist Islam. Reformist movements gathered momentum from 18th -19th centuries onwards.[136]

11. Sufism – the theory of Divine Love

Anyone acquainted, however slightly, with the mystical poetry of Islam must have remarked that the aspiration of the soul towards God is expressed, as a rule, in almost the same terms which might be used by an Oriental Anacreon or Herrick. The resemblance, indeed, is often so close that, unless we have some clue to the poet's intention, we are left in doubt as to his meaning. In some cases, perhaps, the ambiguity serves an artistic purpose, as in the odes of Hafiz, but even when the poet is not deliberately keeping his readers suspended between earth and heaven, it is quite easy to mistake a mystical hymn for a drinking song or a serenade. Ibn al-'Arabi, the greatest theosophist whom the Arabs have produced, found himself obliged to write a commentary on some of his poems in order to refute the scandalous charge that they were designed to celebrate the charms of his mistress. Here are a few lines: "Oh, her beauty the tender maid! Its brilliance gives light like lamps to one travelling in the dark. She is a pearl hidden in a shell of hair as black as jet, A pearl for which Thought dives and remains unceasingly in the deeps of that ocean. He who looks upon her deems her to be a gazelle of the sand-hills, because of her shapely neck and the loveliness of her gestures". It has been said that the Sufis invented this figurative style as a mask for mysteries which they desired to keep secret. That desire was natural in those who proudly claimed to possess an esoteric doctrine known only to themselves; moreover, a plain statement of what they believed might have endangered their liberties, if not their lives. But, apart from any such motives, the Sufis adopt the symbolic style because there is no other possible way of interpreting mystical experience. So little does knowledge of the infinite revealed in ecstatic vision need an artificial disguise that it cannot be communicated at all except through types and emblems drawn from the sensible world, which, imperfect as they are, may suggest and shadow forth a deeper meaning than appears on the surface.

'Gnostics', says Ibn al-'Arabi, 'cannot impart their feelings to other men; they can only indicate them symbolically to those who have begun to experience the like'. What kind of symbolism each mystic will prefer depends on his temperament and character? If he be a religious artist, a spiritual poet, his ideas of reality are likely to clothe themselves instinctively in forms of beauty and glowing images of human love. To him the rosy cheek of the beloved represents the divine essence manifested through its attributes; her dark curls signify the One veiled by the Many; when he says, "Drink wine that it may set you free from yourself", he means, "Lose your phenomenal self in the rapture of divine contemplation". I might fill pages with further examples. This erotic and bacchanalian symbolism is not, of course, peculiar to the mystical poetry of Islam, but nowhere else is it displayed so opulently and in such perfection. It has often been misunderstood by European critics, one of whom even now can describe the ecstasies of the Sufis as 'inspired partly by wine and strongly tinged with sensuality'. As regards the whole body of Sufis, the charge is altogether false. No intelligent and unprejudiced student of their writings could have made it, and we ought to have been informed on what sort of evidence it is based. There are black sheep in every flock, and amongst the Sufis we find many hypocrites, debauchees, and drunkards who bring discredit on the pure brethren. But it is just as unfair to judge Sufism in general by the excesses of these impostors as it would be to condemn all Christian mysticism on the ground that certain sects and individuals are immoral. "God is the Saqi {Cupbearer} and the Wine: He knows what manner of love mine is", said Jalaluddin. Ibn al-Arabi declares that no religion is more sublime than a religion of love and longing for God. Love is the essence of all creeds: the true mystic welcomes it whatever guise it may assume.

"My heart has become capable of every form: it is a pasture for gazelles and a convent for Christian monks, And a temple for idols, and the pilgrim's Kaba, and the tables of the Tora and the book of the Koran. I follow the religion of Love, whichever way his camels take. My religion and my faith are the true religion. We have a pattern in Bishr, the lover of Hind and her sister, and in Qays and Lubna, and in Mayya and Ghaylan. Commenting on the last verse, the poet writes: "Love, quā love, is one and the same reality to those Arab lovers and to me; but the objects of our love are different, for they loved a phenomenon, whereas I love the Real. They are a pattern to us, because God only afflicted them with love for human beings in order that He might show, by means of them, the falseness of those who pretend to love Him, and yet feel no such transport and rapture in loving Him as deprived those enamoured men of their reason and made them unconscious of themselves".

Most of the great medieval Sufis lived saintly lives, dreaming of God, intoxicated with God. When they tried to tell their dreams, being men, they used the language of men. If they were also literary artists, they naturally wrote in the style of their own day and generation. In mystical poetry the

Arabs yield the palm to the Persians. Anyone who would read the secret of Sufism, no longer encumbered with theological articles nor obscured by metaphysical subtleties let him turn to 'Attar, Jalaluddin Rumi, and Jami, whose works are partially accessible in English and other European languages. To translate these wonderful hymns is to break their melody and bring their soaring passion down to earth, but not even a prose translation can quite conceal the love of Truth and the vision of Beauty which inspired them. Listen again to Jalaluddin: "He comes, a moon who's like the sky never saw, awake or dreaming, crowned with eternal flame no flood can lay. Lo, from the flagon of Thy love, O Lord, my soul is swimming, and ruined all my body's house of clay. When first the Giver of the grape my lonely heart befriended, Wine fired my bosom and my veins filled up, but when His image all mine eye possessed, a voice descended, 'Well done, O sovereign Wine and peerless Cup'. The love thus symbolized is the emotional element in religion, the rapture of the seer, the courage of the martyr, the faith of the saint, the only basis of moral perfection and spiritual knowledge. Practically, it is self-renunciation and self-sacrifice, the giving up of all possession's wealth, honour, will, life, and whatever else men value for the Beloved's sake without any thought of reward. I have already referred to love as the supreme principle in Sufi ethics, and now let me give some illustrations. 'Love', says Jalaluddin, "is the remedy of our pride and self-conceit, the physician of all our infirmities. Only he whose garment is rent by love becomes entirely unselfish". Nuri, Raqqam, and other Sufis were accused of heresy and sentenced to death. "When the executioner approached Raqqam, Nuri rose and offered himself in his friend's place with the utmost cheerfulness and submission. All the spectators were astounded. The executioner said, 'Young man, the sword is not a thing that people are so eager to meet; and your turn has not yet arrived'. Nuri answered, 'My religion is founded on unselfishness. Life is the most precious thing in the world'. I wish to sacrifice for my brethren's sake the few moments which remain'.

On another occasion Nuri was overheard praying as follows: "O Lord, in Thy eternal knowledge and power and will Thou dost punish the people of Hell whom Thou hast created; and if it be Thy inexorable will to make Hell full of mankind, although art able to fill it with me alone, and to send them to Paradise". In proportion as the Sufi loves God, he sees God in all His creatures, and goes forth to them in acts of charity. Pious works are naught without love. "Cheer one sad heart: thy loving deed will be More than a thousand temples raised by thee. One freeman whom thy kindness hath enslaved Outweighs by far a thousand slaves set free". The Moslem Legend of the Saints abounds in tales of pity shown to animals (including the despised dog), birds, and even insects. It is related that Bayazid purchased some cardamom seed at Hamadhan, and before departing put into his gaberdine a small quantity which was left over. On reaching Bistam and recollecting what he had done, he took out the seed and found that it contained several ants. Saying, "I have carried the poor creatures away from their home", he immediately set off and journeyed back to Hamadhan several hundred miles. This universal charity is one of the fruits of pantheism. The ascetic view of the world which prevailed amongst the early Sufis, and their vivid consciousness of God as a transcendent Personality rather than as an immanent Spirit, caused them to crush their human affections relentlessly. Here is a short story from the life of Fudayl-ibn-Iyad. It would be touching if it were not so edifying. "One day he had in his lap a child four years old, and chanced to give it a kiss, as is the way of fathers". The child said, 'Father, do you love me?' 'Yes', said Fudayl. 'Do you love God?'. 'Yes'. 'How many hearts have you?' 'One'. 'Then', asked the child, 'how can you love two with one heart?' Fudayl perceived that the child's words were a divine admonition. In his zeal for God, he began to beat his head and repented of his love for the child and gave his heart wholly to God". The higher Sufi mysticism, as represented by Jalaluddin Rumi, teaches that the phenomenal is a bridge to the Real. "Whether it be of this world or of that, they love will lead thee yonder at the last". And Jami says, in a passage which has been translated by Professor Browne: A student came craving counsel on the course before him, Said, 'If thy steps be strangers to love's pathways, Depart, learn love, and then return before me! For, should though fear to drink wine from Form's flagon, though cannot drain the draught of the Ideal. But beware! Be not by Form belated: Strive rather with all speed the bridge to traverse. If to the borne though fain wouldst bear thy baggage, Upon the bridge let not thy footsteps linger". Emerson sums up the meaning of this where he says: "Beholding in many souls the traits of the divine beauty and separating in each soul that which is divine from the taint which it has contracted in the world, the lover ascends to the highest beauty, to the love and knowledge of the Divinity, by steps on this ladder of created souls". "Man's love of God", says Hujwiri. "Is a quality which manifests itself, in the heart of the pious believer, in the form of veneration and magnification, so that he seeks to satisfy his Beloved and becomes impatient and restless in his desire for vision of him, and cannot rest with anyone except him, and grows familiar with the recollection of him, and abjures the recollection of everything besides. Repose becomes unlawful to him, and rest flees from him. He is cut off from all habits and associations, and renounces sensual passion, and turns towards the court of love, and submits to the law of love, and knows God by His attributes of perfection".

Inevitably such a man will love his fellowmen. Whatever cruelty they inflict upon him, he will perceive only the chastening hand of God, "whose bitters are very sweets to the soul". Bayazid said that when God loves a man, He endows him with three qualities in token there of: a bounty like that of the sea, a sympathy like that of the sun, and a humility like that of the earth. No suffering can be too great, no devotion too high, for the piercing insight and burning faith of a true lover. Ibn-al-'Arabi claims that Islam is peculiarly the religion of love, in as much as the Prophet Mohammed is called God's beloved (Habib), but though some traces of this doctrine occur in the Quran, its main impulse was unquestionably derived from Christianity. While the oldest Sufi literature, which is written in Arabic and unfortunately has come down to us in a fragmentary state, is still dominated by the Koranic insistence on fear of Allah, it also bears conspicuous marks of the opposing Christian tradition. As in Christianity, through Dionysius and other writers of the Neoplatonic school, so in Islam, and probably under the same influence, the devotional and mystical love of God soon developed into ecstasy and enthusiasm which finds in the sensuous imagery of human love the most suggestive medium for its expression. Dr. Inge observes that the Sufis "appear, like true Asiatics, to have attempted to give a sacramental and symbolic character to the indulgence of their passions". I need not again point out that such a view of genuine Sufism is both superficial and incorrect.

12. Devotional practices

Love, like gnosis, is in its essence a divine gift, not anything that can be acquired. "If the whole world wished to attract love, they could not; and if they made the utmost efforts to repel it, they could not". Those who love God are those whom God loves. 'I fancied that I loved Him', said Bayazid, 'but on consideration I saw that His love preceded mine'. Junayd defined love as the substitution of the qualities of the Beloved for the qualities of the lover. In other words, love signifies the passing away of the individual self; it is an uncontrollable rapture, a God sent grace which must be sought by ardent prayer and aspiration. 'O Thou in whose bat well curved my heart like a ball is laid, nor ever a hairbreadth swerved from them bidding nor disobeyed, I have washed mine outward clean, the water I drew and poured; Mine inward is Thy demesne do Thou keep it stainless, Lord!". Jalaluddin teaches that man's love is really the effect of God's love by means of an apologue. One night a certain devotee was praying aloud, when Satan appeared to him and said: 'How long wilt thou cry, 'O Allah'? Be quiet, for thou wilt get no answer'. The devotee hung his head in silence. After a little while he had a vision of the prophet Khadir, who said to him, 'Ah, why has thou ceased to call on God?' 'Because the answer 'Here am I' came not,' he replied. Khadir said, "God hath ordered me to go to thee and say this: "Was it not I that summoned thee to service? Did not I make thee busy with My name? Thy calling 'Allah!' was My 'Here am I,' They are yearning pain my messenger to thee. Of all those tears and cries and supplications I was the magnet, and I gave them wings." Divine love is beyond description, yet its signs are manifest. Sari-al-Saqati questioned Junayd concerning the nature of love. 'Some say', he answered, 'that it is a state of concord, and some say that it is altruism, and some say that it is so-and-so'. Sari took hold of the skin on his forearm and pulled it, but it would not stretch; then he said, "I swear by the glory of God, were I to say that this skin hath shrivelled on this bone for love of Him, I should be telling the truth." There upon he fainted away, and his face became like a shining moon. Love, the astrolabe of heavenly mysteries, inspires all religion worthy of the name, and brings with it, not reasoned belief, but the intense conviction arising from immediate intuition. This inner light is its own evidence; he who sees it has real knowledge, and nothing can increase or diminish his certainty. Hence the Sufis never weary of exposing the futility of a faith which supports itself on intellectual proofs, external authority, self-interest, or self-regard of any kind. The barren dialectic of the theologian; the canting righteousness of the Pharisee rooted in forms and ceremonies; the less crude but equally undisintegrated worship of which the motive is desire to gain everlasting happiness in the life hereafter; the relatively pure devotion of the mystic who, although he loves God, yet thinks of himself as loving, and whose heart is not wholly emptied of 'otherness' all these are 'veils' to be removed.

A few sayings by those who know will be more instructive than further explanation. 'O God!' whatever share of this world Thou has allotted to me, bestow it on Thine enemies; and whatever share of the next world Thou hast allotted to me, bestow it on Thy friends. Thou art enough for me. (RABIA.) 'O God! if I worship Thee in fear of Hell, burn me in Hell; and if I worship Thee in hope of Paradise, exclude me from Paradise; but if I worship Thee for Thine own sake, with hold not Thine everlasting beauty!'(RABIA.) "Notwithstanding that the lovers of God are separated from him by their love, they have the essential thing, for whether they sleep or wake, they seek and are sought, and are not occupied with their own seeking and loving but are enraptured in contemplation of the Beloved. It is a crime in the lover to regard his love, and an outrage in love to look at one's own seeking while one is face to face with the Sought". (BAYAZID.) "His love entered and removed all besides Him and left no trace of anything else, so that it remained single even as He is single." (BAYAZID) "To feel at one with God for a moment is better than all men's acts of worship from the beginning to the end of the world". (SHIBLI) "Fear of the fire, in comparison with fear of being parted from the beloved, is like a drop of water cast into the mightiest ocean". (DHULNUN) "Unless I have the face of my heart towards Thee, I deem prayer unworthy to be reckoned as prayer. If I turn my face to the Kaba, for love of Thine; Otherwise, I am quit both of prayer and Kaba". (JALALUDDIN RUMI.) Love, again, is the divine instinct of the soul impelling it to realise its nature and destiny.

The soul is the first born of God: before the creation of the universe, it lived and moved and had its being in Him, and during its earthly manifestation it is a stranger in exile, ever pining to return to its home. "This is Love: to fly heavenward, to rend, every instant, a hundred veils; The first moment, to renounce life; The last step, to fare without feet; To regard this world as invisible, not to see what appears to oneself". All the love romances and allegories of Sufi poetry the tales of Layla and Majnun, Yusuf (Joseph) and Zulaykha, Salaman and Absal, the Moth and the Candle, the Nightingale and the Rose are shadow pictures of the soul's passionate longing to be reunited with God. It is impossible, in the brief space at my command, to give the reader more than a passing glimpse of the treasures which the exuberant fancy of the East has heaped together in every room of this enchanted palace. The soul is likened to a moaning dove that has lost her mate; to a reed torn from its bed and made into a flute whose plaintive music fills the eye with tears; to a falcon summoned by the fowler's whistle to perch again upon his wrist; to snow melting in the sun and mounting as vapour to the sky; to a frenzied camel swiftly plunging through the desert by night; to a caged parrot, a fish on dry land, a pawn that seeks to become a king. These figures imply that God is conceived as transcendent, and that the soul cannot reach Him without taking what Plotinus in a splendid phrase call 'the flight of the Alone to the Alone'. Jalaluddin says: "The motion of every atom is towards its origin; A man comes to be the thing on which he is bent. By the attraction of fondness and yearning, the soul and the heart Assume the qualities of the Beloved, who is the Soul of souls". A man comes to be the thing on which he is bent: what, then does the Sufi become? Eckhart in one of his sermons quotes the saying of St. Augustine that Man is what he loves and adds this comment: "If he loves a stone, he is a stone; if he loves a man, he is a man; if he loves God, I dare not say more, for if I said that he would then be God, ye might stone me."

The Moslem mystics enjoyed greater freedom of speech than their Christian brethren who owed allegiance to the medieval Catholic Church, and if they went too far the plea of ecstasy was generally accepted as a sufficient excuse. Whether they emphasize the outward or the inward aspect of unification, the transcendence or the immanence of God, their expressions are bold and uncompromising. Thus, Abu Said: "In my heart Thou well else with blood I'll drench it; In mine eye Thou lowest else with tears I'll quench it. Only to be one with Thee my soul desire's else from out my body, by hook or crook, I'll wrench it!" Jalaluddin Rumi proclaims that the soul's love of God is God's love of the soul, and that in loving the soul God loves Himself, for he draws home to himself that which in its essence is divine. 'Our copper', says the poet, 'has been transmuted by this rare alchemy', meaning that the base alloy of self has been purified and spiritualized. In another ode he says: 'O my soul, I searched from end to end: I saw in thee naught save the Beloved; Call me not infidel, O my soul, if I say that thou thyself art He'. And yet more plainly: "Ye who in search of God, of God, pursue, Ye need not search for God is you, is you! Why seek ye something that was missing never? Save you none is, but you are where, oh, where?" Where is the lover when the Beloved has displayed Himself? Nowhere and everywhere: his individuality has passed away from him. In the bridal chamber of Unity God celebrates the mystical marriage of the soul.

12.1 Dhikr

Dhikr is the remembrance of Allah commanded in the Quran for all Muslims through a specific devotional act, such as the repetition of divine names, supplications and aphorisms from hadith literature and the Quran. More generally, dhikr takes a wide range and various layers of meaning.[137] This includes dhikr as any activity in which the Muslim maintains awareness of Allah. To engage in dhikr is to practice consciousness of the Divine Presence and love, or "to seek a state of god wariness". The Quran refers to Prophet Muhammad as the very embodiment of dhikr of Allah (65:10–11). Some types of dhikrs are prescribed for all Muslims and do not require Sufi initiation or the prescription of a Sufi master because they are deemed to be good for every seeker under every circumstance.[138] The dhikr may slightly vary among each order. Some Sufi orders[139] engage in ritualized dhikr ceremonies, or sema. Sema includes various forms of worship such as recitation, singing (the most well-known being the Qawwali music of the Indian subcontinent), instrumental music, dance (most famously the Sufi whirling of the Mevlevi order), incense, meditation, ecstasy, and trance.[140] Some Sufi orders stress and place extensive reliance upon dhikr. This practice of dhikr is called Dhikr-e-Qulb (invocation of Allah within the heartbeats). The basic idea in this practice is to visualize the Allah as having been written on the disciple's heart.[141]

12.2 Muraqaba

The practice of muraqaba can be likened to the practices of meditation attested in many faith communities.[142] While variation exists, one description of the practice within a Naqshbandi lineage reads as follows: He is to collect all of his bodily senses in concentration, and to cut himself off from all preoccupation and notions that inflict themselves upon the heart. And thus, he is to turn his full consciousness towards God Most High while saying three times: 'Ilahī anta maqsūdī wa-ridāka matlūbī my God, you are my Goal, and Your good pleasure is what I seek'. Then he brings to his heart the Name of the Essence Allāh and as it courses through his heart, he remains attentive to its meaning, which is 'Essence without likeness'. The seeker remains aware that he is Present, Watchful, encompassing of all, thereby exemplifying the meaning of his saying (may God bless him and grant him peace): "Worship God as though you see Him, for if you do not see Him, He sees you". And likewise, the prophetic tradition: "The most favoured level of faith is to know that God is witness over you, wherever you may be".[143]

12.3 Sufi whirling

The traditional view of the more orthodox Sunni Sufi orders, such as the Qadiriyya and the Chisti, as well as Sunni Muslim scholars in general, is that dancing with intent during dhikr or whilst listening to Sema is prohibited.[144][145][146][147] Sufi whirling (or Sufi spinning) is a form of Sama or physically active meditation which originated among some Sufis, and which is still practised by the Sufi Dervishes of the Mevlevi order. It is a customary dance performed within the sema, through which dervishes (also called semazens, from Persian سماعزن) aim to reach the source of all perfection, or enur. This is sought through abandoning one's nafs, egos or personal desires, by listening to the music, focusing on God, and spinning one's body in repetitive circles, which has been seen as a symbolic imitation of planets in the Solar System orbiting the sun.[148] As explained by Mevlevi practitioners:[149] In the symbolism of the Sema ritual, the semazen's camel's hair hat (sikke) represents the tombstone of the ego; his wide, white skirt (enure) represents the ego's shroud. By removing his black cloak (hirka), he is spiritually reborn to the truth. At the beginning of the Sema, by holding his arms crosswise, the semazen appears to represent the number one, thus testifying to God's unity. While whirling, his arms are open: his right arm is directed to the sky, ready to receive God's beneficence; his left hand, upon which his eyes are fastened, is turned toward the earth. The semazen conveys God's spiritual gift to those who are witnessing the Sema. Revolving from right to left around the heart, the semazen embraces all humanity with love. The human being has been created with love to love. Mevlāna Jalāluddīn Rumi says, "All loves are a bridge to Divine love. Yet, those who have not had a taste of it do not know!"

12.4 Singing

Musical instruments (except the Daf) have traditionally been considered as prohibited by the four orthodox Sunni schools,[150][151][152][153] and the more orthodox Sufi tariqas also continued to prohibit their use. Throughout history Sufi saints have stressed that musical instruments are forbidden.[154][155] Qawwali was originally a form of Sufi devotional singing popular in South Asia and is now usually performed at dargahs. Sufi saint Amir Khusro is said to have infused Persian, Arabic Turkish and Indian classical melodic styles to create the genre in the 13th century. The songs are classified into hamd, naat, manqabat, marsiya or ghazal, among others. Historically, Sufi Saints permitted and encouraged it, whilst maintaining that musical instruments and female voices should not be introduced, although these are commonplace today. Nowadays, the songs last for about 15 to 30 minutes, are performed by a group of singers, and instruments including the harmonium, tabla and dholak are used. Pakistani singing maestro Nusrat Fateh Ali Khan is credited with popularizing qawwali all over the world.[156]

13. Saints

Walī (Arabic: ولي, plural 'awliyā' أولياء) is an Arabic word whose literal meanings include 'custodian', 'protector', 'helper', and 'friend'.[157] In the vernacular, it is most commonly used by Muslims to indicate an Islamic saint, otherwise referred to by the more literal 'friend of God'.[158][159] In the traditional Islamic understanding of saints, the saint is portrayed as someone 'marked by [special] divine favor ... [and] holiness', and who is specifically 'chosen by God and endowed with exceptional gifts, such as the ability to work miracles'. The doctrine of saints was articulated by Islamic scholars very early on in Muslim history,[160] and particular verses of the Quran and certain hadith were interpreted by early Muslim thinkers as 'documentary evidence' of the existence of saints. Since the first Muslim hagiographies were written during the period when Sufism began its rapid expansion, many of the figures who later came to be regarded as the major saints in Sunni Islam were the early Sufi mystics, like Hasan of Basra (728 A.D.), Farqad Sabakhi (729 A.D.), Dawud Tai (777-81 A.D.) Rabi'a al-Adawiyya (801 A.D.), Maruf Karkhi (815 A.D.), and Junayd of Baghdad (910 A.D.). From the twelfth to the fourteenth century, "the general veneration of saints, among both people and sovereigns, reached its definitive form with the organization of Sufism into orders or brotherhoods". In the common expressions of Islamic piety of this period, the saint was understood to be 'a contemplative whose state of spiritual perfection permanent expression in the teaching bequeathed to his disciples'.[161]

13.1 Visitation

In popular Sufism (i.e., devotional practices that have achieved currency in world cultures through Sufi influence), one common practice is to visit or make pilgrimages to the tombs of saints, renowned scholars, and righteous people. This is a particularly common practice in South Asia, where famous tombs include such saints as Sayyid Ali Hamadani in Kulob, Tajikistan; Afāq Khoja, near Kashgar, China; Lal Shahbaz Qalandar in Sindh; Ali Hujwari in Lahore, Pakistan; Bahauddin Zakariya in Multan Pakistan; Moinuddin Chishti in Ajmer, India; Nizamuddin Auliya in Delhi, India; and Shah Jalal in Sylhet, Bangladesh. Likewise, in Fez, Morocco, a popular destination for such pious visitation is the Zaouia Moulay Idriss II and the yearly visitation to see the current Sheikh of the Qadiri Boutchichi Tariqah, Sheikh Sidi Hamza al Qadiri-al-Boutchichi to celebrate the Mawlid (which is usually televised on Moroccan National television).[162][163]

13.2 Miracles

In Islamic mysticism, karamat (Arabic: كرامات karāmāt, pl. of كرامة karāmah, lit. generosity, high mindedness) refers to supernatural wonders performed by Muslim saints. In the technical vocabulary of Islamic religious sciences, the singular form karama has a sense like charism, a favor or spiritual gift freely bestowed by God. The marvels ascribed to Islamic saints have included supernatural physical actions, predictions of the future, and "interpretation of the secrets of hearts".[164] Historically, a "belief in the miracles of saints (karāmāt al-awliyā', literally 'marvels of the friends [of God]')" has been a requirement in Sunni Islam.[165]

14. Impact of Sufism Movement in Contemporary India

Sufism was characterized in the one hand as a phenomenon of expressing love towards almighty and on the other hand spreading the message of truth. The Sufis in India became the Ambassadors of cultural integrity and social harmony. It is a mystic dimension of Islam formally originated in the Middle East between ninth and tenth centuries A.D. Safa means wisdom or Purity. 'Suf' refers to Wool. It was said that the development of Sufism was highly influenced by various mystic philosophies of Judaism, Christianity, and Hinduism. The early spread of Islam to India was strongly influenced by the Arab traders who were responsible to the arrival of Sufi saints to Western and Eastern cost of Indian Sub-continent. The political situation in North India was in favour of the spread of Sufism in these regions. Later the political changes in the Caliphate empire paved the way for the vast migration of Sufis in the land of South India and Ceylon. The Qadiriyya and Chistiyya orders of Sufism were the prominent Sufi orders of having many Dargahs throughout India. The Sufi Saints have contributed a lot for the Literature, philosophy, and theological ideas. The main objective of this book is to identify and analyse the impact of Sufism movement in Contemporary India. I have followed the descriptive and analytical research methods as a methodology and consulted the secondary source materials as main sources to write this book. Sufism was characterized in the one hand as a phenomenon of expressing love towards almighty and on the other hand spreading the message of truth. The Sufi doctrines and practices were brought into India have a long and chequered history. Sufism in a mystic dimension of Islam which formally originated in the Middle East between ninth and tenth centuries. (Mysticism: a religious practice in which people search for truth, knowledge, and closeness to God through meditation and prayer). The first Sufi arrived in India towards the close of the eleventh century.[166] The Sufis in India, became the Ambassadors of cultural integrity and social harmony. They brought with them, the religious fervour devotion and piety. They also had brought with them the discipleship with spiritual leaders in those lands. They had a long experience in travelling, fasting and pilgrimages to the shrines of Saints and to Holy Mecca. The origin of the word Sufism can be traced from many roots. The lexicon root of the word is traced to 'Safa' which in Arabic means 'purity'. Another origin is 'Sufi' refers to wool, the simple cloth worn by early ascetics (simple and strict way of life through religious beliefs). It was said that the development of Sufism was highly influenced by various mystic philosophies of Judaism, Christianity, and Hinduism.

Migration of the Sufis to India: The trade in the Indian Ocean was influenced by the Arabs. The early spread of Islam to India was strongly influenced by the Arab traders who were responsible to the arrival of Sufi Saints to Western and Eastern Coast of Indian Sub-continent. The political changes in the Caliphate Empire paved the way for the vast migration of the Sufis in the Mainland of South India and Ceylon. The political situation of North India was also in favour of the spread of Sufism in these regions. The social behaviour and philosophical synthesis were in practice by the Sufis. The Sufi Shaikh's (evolved at the spiritual level) came to occupy a pride of place in the society; most of them were patronized by the kings. Because of their powerful spiritual attainments, noble deeds and liberal out looking, they left an indelible imprint on the socio-religious set up (milieu) of India. Emergence of Sufism (Why did Sufism emerge?) The rise of Sufism could be associated with the disenchantment among some Muslim Ulama (scholars) and disintegration of the Caliphate after the death of Hazrat Ali, the fourth Caliph. This period witnessed intense power struggle, bloodshed, and empowerment of the ruling class. Many Ulama were also killed in process. Due to these tragic and anarchic incidents, the situations were completely shocked. Some scholars who were inspired by the Prophet and the early Caliph began to follow the habit of meditation and spirituality with the purpose of having a direct experience of God. They embraced poverty and started leading a life full of piety and love for fellow humankinds. In the beginning, Sufism did not exist in a properly organized form, but, at the same, one cannot underestimate or overlook the contributions made by the early Sufis (8th, 9th, and 10th Centuries) to the development of Sufi thought. The earliest Sufi was Hasan of Basra who had a fear of God and very cautious that not to commit any sin or mistake in his life. He represented a tendency towards other world liners, piety and asceticism and considered hunger and poverty as symbols of righteousness. Al Hashim Sufi of Kufah is regarded as the first mystic to have used the nomenclature 'Sufi'. He believed that inner transformation (of heart) was the essence of Sufism. Ibrahim-ibn-Adham was the king of Balkh who gave up his throne and all worldly possessions and became an ascetic. Of the many Sufi orders (Silsilas) that have arisen in the world of mystic Islam.

India became the hospitable home for many Sufis. The arrival of Shaikh Muinuddin in India just before the Sultanate period heralded the beginning of a new era in the religious ethos of the country.[167] During the Sultanate period of three hundred years, Sufism had spread every nook and corner of the country. Early Sufis and their orders Khwaja Muinuddin, the founder of Chishtiyya order in India was considered as an early Sufi Saint of North India. He was born about 1142 A.D. at Sistine. The Sufi mystic traditions became more visible during the rule of Delhi Sultanate.[168] The Saint figures and mythical stories had made inspiration on Hindu Communities. The medieval North Indian Society was highly influenced by the Cosmopolitan Culture of Bahadad and Persia. The Ghaznavi and Ghorid Courts accelerated Sufi-intellectualism in India. During the thirteenth Century A.D. the Sufi brotherhood became firmly consolidated in Northern India.[169] The political scenario in Northern India was in favour of the spread of Sufism in India. After the Mongol invasion of Bahadad, the Sufi Saints had chosen India, as their safe abode and destination for settlement.[170] The court of Delhi Sultanate had occupied with Persian intellectuals. Sufism became the main ingredients in all mediums.[171] They acted as advisers to Sultans, bridge between the commoners and rulers. But most of the practicing Sufis rarely had political aspirations. Among the religious elite of Medieval India, Ulamas and the Sufi Mystics or Fakirs had tolerated with non–Islamic traditions. They had mingled with poor people and spread their faith through community services. There were number of Sufi Saints who had led a very popular and discipline life in North India. Sufi Saint Shaikh Nizamuddin-Awliya

(1238–1325 A.D.) had stressed love as a means of realizing God. It implied the love of humanity.

Amir Khusro, the noted scholar, and the royal poet of Delhi Sultanate who accepted the mission and became the disciple of the Sufi who is also buried at Dargah of Nizamudin Awliya. He was responsible for the Mass conversion of the people to Islam. He founded the Chisti Nizami order. He saw the reign of seven rulers of Delhi Sultanate. There were 70 branches of Sufi orders. The famous Suhrawardi order Sufi Saints were Shaikh Sadrudin Arif, Amir Husayan and Ruknuddin. Saint Ruknuddin was highly respected by the Delhi Sultans, from Alauddin Khilji to Muhammad–bin–Tughlaq. This order got spread to Tiruchirappalli and Andhra pradesh in South India.[172] Another order Naqshbandiyya, became an influential factor in Indo–Muslim life and for two centuries it was the principal spiritual order in India. Khwaja Baqi Billa was an influential Sufi personality and protested the state policies of Mughal emperor Akbar.[173] The four different Sufi orders were highly responsible for the spread of Islam in North India. The Hindu rulers of India needed Arab traders and provided them with all facilities and treated them like other subjects. These early missionaries and their progress enabled the spread of Sufism all over Tamil country.[174] Many new Sufi centers were emerged in coastal regions as well as central parts of Tamil country. Dargahs became prominent tombs of Saints. The disciples of early pioneer Sufis were responsible to spread of Sufi movement in the neighbouring states. They became the ambassadors of Sufism and social integrity.

We can see the impact Sufism and noticeable development of Literature and Poems. Secondly, stressed the importance of 'fana' or annihilation in seeking God and believed in Unity of Existence was the ultimate truth. Thirdly, active role in politics and Indian religion was seen. Princess Jehanara of Mughal dynasty was a notable female Sufi Saint of Qadiriya Order and authored two Sufi Manuals. Munis al Aswah or the confident of sprits and an incomplete biography of her spiritual mentor Mulla Shah. The Subcontinent Sufi orders embraced local traditions from ascetics belonging to other religions. Inter religious dialogues were held. The situation of Indian Sufism has been historically summarized by Evelyn Underhill as follows the Muhammadan Mysticism appearing in the eighth century with the beautiful figure of Rabia, the Muslim female Saint (717–831A.D.) and continued by the Martyr Al-Hallay, attains literary expression in the eleventh century by Ghayali (1055–1111 A.D.) and has its classic period in the thirteenth century in the work of mystic poets Atlar (1140–1234 A.D.) Saadi (1184–1263 A.D.) and Jalaludeen Rumi (1207–1273 A.D.). Its tradition is continued in the 14th century by the rather erotic mysticism of Hafiz (1300–1388 A.D.) and his successors and in the 15th century by the port Jami (1414–1492 A.D.).[175] The most remarkable feature of the medieval and contemporary period of Indian History was the emergence of various schools of thoughts. Sufism played a twin role spreading loves towards almighty and spreading the message of truth. The Sufi saints performed an important role in the Indian Contemporary Society. The Arabian trade influenced them to settle in the coastal parts of India. Due to their preaching and profess, there were many religious, social, and political changes had taken place. Therefore, Sufism had a great impact in the Contemporary India.

Chapter 4

Saints and Sufis of Maharashtra

1. Introduction

From the thirteenth to the seventeenth centuries Maharashtra saw a great number of saint-poets, whose songs in simple Marathi continue to inspiring people. The most important among them were Dnyaneshwar (Gyaneshwar), Namdev, Eknath and Tukaram as well as women like Janabai and the family of Chokhamela, who belonged to the "untouchable" Mahar caste. This regional tradition of bhakti focused on the Vitthala (a form of Vishnu) temple in Pandharpur, as well as on the notion of a personal god residing in the hearts of all people. These saint-poets rejected all forms of ritualism, outward display of piety and social differences based on birth. In fact, they even rejected the idea of renunciation and preferred to live with their families, earning their livelihood like any other person, while humbly serving fellow human beings in need. A new humanist idea emerged as they insisted that bhakti lay in sharing others' pain. As the famous Gujarati saint Narsi Mehta said, "They are Vaishnavas who understand the pain of others." The presence of Islam in the Deccan as a set of ideas, ideals, and practices has a history of many centuries. At least from the times of the Khalji and Tughluq sultans, it took a variety of forms in terms of organization, the evidence for which is abundant. These forms may be the result of state patronization of what has been understood to be Islam and Islamic, or the result of the more disparate individual efforts of those concerned, whether pious, learned, or saintly.[1]

Viewing saints historically means a thorough engagement with a variety of sources where different people for different reasons are called holy, and consequently remembered, invoked, and worshipped by different means. Overall, the process of sacralization, or of making a Muslim saint, displays the agency of devotees. This does not mean that the state and its elites have had no say in constituting and representing holiness. The Deccan does indeed have a rich history of kings and other potentates being very close to those understood as holy, including some of the kings being proclaimed holy too. For instance, Indo-Persian writings speak about

Ahmad Shah Wali [2], the Bahmani and Lingayats see him as an avatar of saint Allama Prabhu. Marathi narratives remember another Bahmani king turned into a saint, Shah Bahmani Muntoji alias Mrutyunjay, and they also associate several other royal figures with the saints (e.g. king Shivaji with Ramdas).[3] The holiness of any of these, and of many other figures, is perpetuated by continual worship, belief in their miraculous powers, as well as narratives and memorialization that are firmly set in the concrete and the local and enable the category to exist meaningfully in time. This chapter will also try to evaluate the approaches of historians to the processes that create the saints and will make some preliminary observations about how the history of holiness could be done in a still different manner. Obviously, a variety of different localities where the living worship of the real saint has its own history poses a problem for any attempt to generalize and find some characteristics common to the process itself across time and space. When trying to grasp the localized variety in general and analytic terms several obstacles appear. They blur the dynamic richness of the localness, and its local connections as has been epitomized in the above-mentioned relationship of the powerful and saintly and hence disengage the analytical work from the basis on which the saintliness is formed, produced, and on which it continually relies for decades or centuries.

The most obvious obstacles that discursively fuel the forms of disengagement from saintliness as it is socially practised are the well-known historical processes of nationalism and religious nationalism. Without going too much into the particulars of its historical appearance this chapter states transcript to understand nationalism as perhaps the strongest form of collective identity that globally overshadows other ways of conceiving collectively (family, social strata, or gender to name but a few examples). By religious nationalism, following Peter van der Veer,[4] the ways which supply the idea of collectively with the content of one undivided religious community constituting a nation. In simple, not to say oversimplified, terms nationalism has enabled some idealized collectives to be studied with more fervour than others. Religious nationalism, in turn, has enabled religious collectively to be preferred over religious diversity. This has also conditioned how the saints, historical figures sacralised from below, came to be viewed to homologize them with the prevailing constructions of the national and religious collectives. With respect to the Marathi Deccan (that corresponds roughly but not exactly to the current Indian state of Maharashtra), the history of the Islamic presence that made Muslims and their saints a firm part of the region has been to a considerable extent nationalized by the histories of power and in that by the nationalistic narrative of Maratha historical success. This occurred for a few reasons. Perhaps the most important reason for the popularity of the Marathas[5] among Maharashtrian intellectuals commenting on the past lies in the Marathas own and admirable capacities to assert themselves politically and socially over a huge part of the South Asian subcontinent throughout the eighteenth century.

However, the sentimental attachment to Maratha glory should not be overstated. There is another important factor that framed what was remembered from the past and what was forgotten. It can be seen in the efforts of the British colonial administration to ideologically substantiate its dominance and critically dismiss the claims of the previous rulers of India, who somewhat simplistically were associated with the so-called Muslim period of Indian history.[6] This, in the context of the Marathi Deccan and apart from practical questions of the transformation of the Peshwa's state into the British Raj, could lead many to favouring those historical narratives that were seen as constructing opposition, again in simplistic terms, to the noted period. It is in this context that the narrative of the Marathas' struggle against the Mughals (seen essentially as Muslims) gains its academic and certainly also its increasingly popular prominence in the early part of the twentieth century. This development, to a great extent, reflected the period of a two-nation struggle on the whole of India level, and later derived fresh impetus from the Samyukta Maharashtra movement,[7] and it still has its current societal repercussions. Yet another important factor explaining the overwhelming presence of the Maratha narrative in regional historiographical writing and imagination relates to the processes of modernization of Indian society throughout the nineteenth century that accompanied its nationalism. Increased use of the printed word, the spread of new knowledge via new media, and their embeddedness in the public culture that set as its priorities to shed the shackles of national suppression played their part in imagining the equally constituted and ever-present community (of ethnic Marathas and exclusively Maratha Hindus).[8] There may be still more factors to list, yet what emerges is that the pre-Maratha, i.e. Bahmani and Nizamshahi periods in the Marathi Deccan received much less public attention from Indian and foreign scholars compared with the period of the Marathas. This is not to say that the Bahmani and Nizamshahi were somewhat deliberately overlooked in academic production, far from it.

There certainly exists a considerable body of academic literature discussing one or other aspect of the pre-modern Deccan. Hereby the suggestion is stated which is complex, and not only academic, process of constructing, publicizing, and preserving the memory of Maratha glory [9] historically overshadowed the other pasts and kept them solely, and even there marginally, in the discursive realm of academia.[10] Now, this has had an important influence on how figures such as saints, who certainly could be idealized in the national imagination, were treated historically. Positing the Maratha/Hindu period as a boundary meant searching for this division in other societal categories, religion notwithstanding. But before I delve into explaining in greater detail how increased attention to the Maratha past rather than other pasts conditioned the interpretations of precolonial holy people, it is necessary to point out more factors that are directly connected to what may be described as marathizing/hinduizing the past of the Marathi Deccan.[11] With respect to the method used, one attribute of the aggrandizement of national narrative, and in my opinion an important one, is 'logocentrism'[12] an orientation to text as the main source of knowing the past. Criticizing historians for engagement with texts may well be a futile exercise given that their method is textualist par excellence.

But given that it is literary and epigraphic studies that dominate our knowledge of pre-modern Deccan,[13] and this holds particularly true when its holy figures are concerned, one wonders whether all means of understanding the people who are said to be holy lie only within the realm of the texts. True, this is a complex question and one in which the scarcity of other than written materials also plays its role, yet often the written narratives of the saintly lives (e.g. caritra, tadhkira) have been utilized as direct sources of historical knowledge about the personas concerned.[14] The saintliness of the saint, presupposed in these kinds of texts, was taken for granted and often uncritically recounted within the traditional framework of the stories and woven into the national, collective narrative of the particular religious group. Another result of the logocentric approach to the past that helps the collective identity agenda to permeate the approach of historians is the lines along which the history-oriented writings seem to be divided. The political and cultural aspects of the Deccan sultanates tend to be seen as compartmentalized with their boundaries by language and religion, both of course being strong collective markers. But since languages are employed across religions, it is problematic to seek any direct association between the language employed and the religion followed. Recent research has convincingly shown that language and the ideas of religious/ethnic collectively in South Asia do not automatically follow the Herderian monolingual nationalistic model.[15] It certainly makes sense to approach the study of the Deccan's Muslim society via Persian or Dakhani texts. Yet, it is much more fruitful to see these texts as part of a polylingual functioning on the sanctioned or preferred ways of communication rather than as representative of the Muslim voices heard from the pre-colonial times. This holds particularly true for those, such as some saints, who opted for a different medium of communication than solely Dakhani or Persian and let us admit that this choice does not make such people any less Muslim. The same may be said for those who became their followers and, in many ways, participated in sustaining the saintliness of the saints but through the medium of a different language.[16] With respect to the forms of precolonial religion and its saintly representatives as they are conceived of and examined in the variety of Maharashtrian localities of the rural-urban continuum, it is then rare to find works on the saints of the Marathi Deccan that would attempt to historicize what has been termed as 'sant (or Sufi-sant)-paramparā'. The result is to be seen, for example, in the fact that it is often forgotten (or overlooked) that for instance the Varkaris, the mainstream Maharashtrian tradition that, so to speak, 'lives on saints' can historically trace their development precisely to the periods of the Bahmanis, Nizamshahs and Mughals. As if the postulation of Maratha/Marathi/Hindu identity hampered the meaningful inclusion of the pre-Maratha period in the narrative of regional history. The concentration on the ethnicity-language-religion nexus also causes a lack of detailed historical research that would enable us to historicize the creation of such important works as the canon of those who were popularized as particularly important Marathi saints.

There exists an overt attention to the saint-poetry and hagiographies and their contents rather than to say, social conditions and relations at the time of the creation of these texts, their patronization, transmission, variation across the different manuscripts, and contact with the oral world of the transmission of knowledge. For instance, the 'well-known' Sakala Santa Gāthā (Songs of all the saints) has been reprinted several times and in various editions, and its later texts also include poetry by a few Muslims (Shaikh Muhammad, Kabir, Kamal, Dadu, Latif Shah and Sajjan Kasai).[17] However, we know much less about how these 'words of saints' historically came to be. There do exist recent counterforces to this prevailing current of understanding the saintly heritage of the Marathi Deccan. Ernst's, Novetzke's, Keune's, Green's and Naregal's works[18] may be cited as examples of the increased attention paid to the historical contexts of the people whom others sanctified, although close ethnographic observations of the current re-presentations of the precolonial saintly heritage, which could be enriched for instance by learning from studies in historical architecture, are totally lacking. An important factor, particularly as far as Muslim saints of the Marathi Deccan are concerned, is that all too often the conundrum of ethnicity-language religion causes them too to be easily compart-mentalized under the category of Sufism mainly in regional Marathi scholarship. This has two easily observable results. One is seeing all those numerous differently honoured and known saintly figures, whose graves are to be found all over Maharashtra, as Sufis. However, this is arbitrary and unsystematic. It is one thing to convincingly show that a certain holy figure of a certain locality had indeed connections to the religiosity that defines itself as Sufi (say in the transmission of religious knowledge, in religious practice and philosophy, in a body of followers, or well-known Sufi interregional networks.[19] After all, we need certain identifiers for distinguishing a Sufi; otherwise, the term completely loses its descriptive power). It is quite another to imagine one along the lines of a recently conceived ethnicity-language-religion nexus.

A good example in this respect is the well-known publication by S. M. Pagdi from the early 1950s called "Sūfī Sampradāya" which drew heavily on Malkapuri's early 20th century Tadhkira-ye-awliyā-yedakan.[20] There Mr. Pagdi grouped together under the category of Sufi Chishti's of Khuldabad, for whose lives and teachings there exist numerous historical sources, other rather obscure figures whose only Sufi qualification was their being Muslims, having a tomb and an alleged Sufi 'silsila'. His approach is in a different fashion mirrored in the studies in which we again meet the uncritical acceptance of Sufism as one uniform expressive mode of Muslim religiosity, which is compared to the philosophy of the 'advaita vedanta'.[21] However, it would be much more fruitful to ask what criteria and historical evidence allows us to view certain saintly figures as Sufi than simply assume them to be Sufis. The second result of the uncritical extension of a Sufi denominator to any Muslim saint lies in the attempt to project Sufism as a kind of lighter and more peaceful version of Islam. It reflects the Orientalist search for different facets of Muslim religiosity vis-à-vis the uncompromising monotheism accompanied by militarized agitation around which the West has constructed an ideology of its own historical experiences with Muslim societies. Such a view then translates into attempts to interpret Muslim saintly figures according to the categories of syncretism, or communal harmony. The former is often seen as representing those forms of religious beliefs and practices that combine elements coming from different religions whereas the latter corresponds to a higher social ideal. Beyond these efforts sincere no doubt in the main with respect to the time of their appearance, which roughly corresponds to the increased sensitivity to the political pronouncements of imagined religious nations and the memory of partition, however, linger once more the premises that operate with the variable of monolithic, timeless collectives. In this context it is perhaps the constraints posed by the ethnicity-language-religion nexus that caused so called syncretic figures to have been rarely seriously approached by scholars whose works are situated along the lines of Muslim-Dakhani-Sufi collect activities and their constructed pasts.

Therefore, there exist only a few complex works dealing with Muslim saints in the Marathi socio-linguistic environment. Among the most influential should be mentioned R. C. Dhere's "Musalmān marāṭhī santkavī (Muslim Marathi saint-poets)" republished as 'Ekātmateche śhilpakār' (Shapers of Unity) and Y. M. Pathan's "Musalmān (sūfī) santāñche marāṭhī sāhitya" (Marathi literature of the Muslim [Sufi] saints). However, Dhere's and Pathan's studies adopt a synthetic rather than an analytic approach, even though this means that in their texts we have what is up to now the best and most detailed collection of information also on those Marathi Muslim saintly figures who, from the perspective of a neglected pre-Maratha past, could have served as examples of how to connect historically and meaningfully the so called Muslim Shahi and Maratha periods. They do try to show these connections, but Dhere's effort especially is overwhelmed by concerns that lead him to prefer collectivistic contexts of unifying Hindus and Muslim rather than seeing his materials as evidence of a pre-colonial composite world, which was not in all cases necessarily struggling for religious unity. Engaging in the unity agenda then prevents him from discussing the contents of Marathi Muslim poetry side by side with the history of its authors, transmitters, patrons, and audiences. Also, Dhere's and Pathan's somewhat easy adoption of Sufism without providing the term with historicity in connection with researched saintly figures makes an otherwise great collection of information slightly more problematic. Similarly, just as Mr.Pagdi essentialized all Muslim saints with Sufis, Dhere's and Pathan's Muslim Marathi saint-poets are arbitrarily given Sufi identities without questioning why saints such as Muntoji Bahmani, Shaikh Muhammad, Alamkhan, or Shaha Muni are largely unknown to any of the Sufi networks active in the Deccan, or why it is rather Marathi (and predominantly Vaishnava) discourse that accommodates them. Moreover, the evidence on those saintly figures is often the product of later canonization. Therefore, without excluding the Sufi option, it is still worth asking whether local Muslim religiosity could not be articulated differently and what the Sufi networks, ideas and practices contributed to that articulation.

2.   The Medicant Saints

Till now the discourse has been chiefly about the saints belonging to the main silsilas and attached to khānqāhs. Some of them, like Baba Farid, Nizamuddin Auliya and Shah Madar were throughout their life bound to one place, like veritable muqīmān. Others spent many years travelling, like Data Ganjbakhsh, Khwaja Muinuddin Sijzi or Shah Jalal and only in their declining years did they become 'settled'. The posthumous fame of the awliyā of both the categories and the cult of their tombs are closely connected with the places where they led the life of a hermit or preached in their lifetime, hence the abundance of local legends and toponomy, coming into being around one or another mazār or dargāh and in the aggregate making up a peculiar 'sacred' geography of the sub-continent. However, in

South Asia there were quite a lot of saints and mystics who did not belong to any ṭarīqa, and who spent their entire life on the journey. The most common name for them was the word qalandar (literally 'a rough unshaped block or log').[25] The term qalandar was historically applied to various categories of mystics. Up to the fourteenth century it was synonymous with the concept of dervish and denoted a wandering mystic-ascetic, who did not have personal property or a definite place of residence. In early mystic poetry qalandar is a wanderer who has renounced everything temporal and is absorbed only in love for God. The Persian Sufis of the eleventh century, Abu Saʻid Maihani, 'Abdullah Ansari and Baba Tahir 'Uryan, called themselves qalandarsin precisely this sense. The last-mentioned said: 'I am mystic gypsy called Qalandar; I have neither fire, home, nor monastery. By day I wander about the world, and at night I sleep with a brick under my head.' (Rizvi 1986: 301) And, finally, the word qalandar denoted a member of the mystic ascetic movement in Khurasan, which in the course of time took shape as the Qalandariyya fraternity and by the thirteenth century reached the borders of India.

The teaching of Qalandariyya differed from the doctrines of other Muslim fraternities by virtue of the serious influence of Hindu and Buddhist practices on it. Its fundamental tenets were the rejection of the mystic-ascetic practice of seclusion and life together in a cloister; an indifferent and negligent attitude towards the mandatory injunctions (farāid) and rituals of Islam; the avoidance of participation in common prayer and public worship; a refusal to observe the fast obligatory for all Muslims; subsistence by means of collecting alms; the absence of any property; and a nomadic way of life. Some members of the Qalandariyya fraternity also used to make a vow of celibacy. The Qalandariyya movement came into being based on the early teaching of Malamatiyya (from Arabic malāmat, 'blame'), to which al-Hujwiri has devoted a separate chapter of his Kashf almahjub. After giving an account of different kinds of malāmat incurred by the mystics of the past, al-Hujwiri wrote ironically of his contemporaries: In those days it was necessary, for incurring blame, to do something disapproved or extraordinary; but in our time, if anyone desires blame, he need only lengthen a little his voluntary prayers or fulfil the religious practices which are prescribed: at once everybody will call him a hypocrite and impostor. (al-Hujwiri 1992: 65) The malāmatī used to assert that 'blame is abandonment of welfare' (al-malāmat tark as-salāmat) and in their aspiration for 'belittling themselves' and dissolving themselves in God intentionally attracted people's censure and contempt by their scandalous escapades.[26] In so doing they were guided by the āyat: 'They fear not the blame of anyone; that is the grace of God which He bestows on whomsoever He pleases; God is bounteous and wise' (5: 59).

Conscious of their own insignificance before God and to avoid the attention of others, the malāmatīs rejected everything superficial and ostentatious, including collective dhikr and tarawih (supererogatory prayers), which were widely practised amongst Sufis, their special dress and mode of life, because they considered that these manifestations of piety were meant for the public. However, moderate mystics did not give too much credence to them, remembering that self-abasement was worse than pride. Al-Hujwiri, speaking of people who take refuge in the status of malāmatī after having committed an evil deed, concludes: In my opinion, to seek Blame is mere ostentation, and ostentation is mere hypocrisy. The ostentatious man purposely acts in such way as to win popularity, while the Malāmatī purposely acts in such a way that the people reject him. Both have their thoughts fixed on mankind and do not pass beyond that sphere. The dervish, on the contrary, never even thinks of mankind. (al-Hujwiri 1992: 67)

Abu Hafs Suhrawardi in 'Awārif al-ma'ārif makes a distinction between malāmatī and qalandar. The former, in his opinion, are truly sincere, but do not want outsiders to get to know about their ecstatic state and mystic experience. He regards the movement of qalandars as an anti-social phenomenon, considering that they consciously violate the injunctions of sharat and defy religion and society. The term qalandariyya is applied to people so possessed by the intoxication of tranquility of heart' that they respect no custom or usage and reject the regular observances of society and mutual relationship. Traversing the arenas of tranquility of heart' they concern themselves little with ritual prayer and fasting except such as are obligatory (farāid). Neither do they concern themselves with those earthly pleasures which are allowed by the indulgence of divine law. The difference between the qalandarī and the malāmatī is that the malāmatī strives to conceal his mode of life whilst the qalandarī seeks to destroy accepted custom. (Trimingham 1971: 267) Indeed, qalandars in every way possible used to flaunt their special mystic status both in their outward appearance and in their conduct. They wore a short khirqa which came down only to their thighs, a shaggy fur-cap, a heavy iron necklace, earrings, looking like massive rings worn on the fingers, and wide bracelets, generally called 'qalandar's implements' (ālāt-i-qalandarī).

Undoubtedly these 'implements' were a sign of humble resignation to God's will and of repentance since they reminded one more of a slave's attributes than of a free person's ornaments. Qalandars used to shave their heads and beards, sometimes leaving the moustache untouched. All-knowing Ibn Battuta explained the outward appearance of qalandars by an episode from the biography of Muhammad b. Yunus as-Sawaji (who died in 1232), the founder of the Qalandariyya fraternity.[27] A certain woman living in Sawa (Iran) enticed him into her house on a plausible pretext, and having failed to win his love, locked him up in the pantry. The ingenious qalandar, having been locked up, shaved his head and beard clean, not leaving even his eyebrows. When the temptress saw what her object of passion had turned into, she lost all interest in him and set him free. In gratitude for his deliverance from sin as-Sawaji retained this new appearance throughout his life and entrusted his followers never to part with a razor. The Chishti malfūzāt often refer to the shocking behaviour of the qalandars. Qalandars and those congenial souls the juwāliqs were inimically disposed to the settled ones. They did not recognize their sainthood and considered them to have been secularized and 'turned into bourgeoisie'.

However, at the same time they constantly visited khānqāhs and had the brazenness to ask for gifts and money. The scandals which they in the process perpetrated let us recall the breached wall in Baba Farid's jamā-at- khāna or the riot in Baha'uddin Zakariya's khānqāh can be only partly explained by the qalandars' 'programmatic' endeavour to incur censure. The gentle and patient Nizamuddin Auliyaconsidered a visit by qalandars to be a peculiar penance or at least a sobering agent, which God granted to the shaikhs, so that they did not get too conceited in the atmosphere of general adoration: A juwaliq entered the room. And he began to utter some shameful remarks that are inappropriate for a saintly assembly. The master may God remember him with favour said nothing. In short, he lived up to the expectations that the juwaliq had on him. After that he turned to those present and emphasized: 'This is what has to be done (in such circumstances). Just as many persons come, place their head at my feet, and offer something, so there ought to be people like this who come and speak unabashedly. It is through such acts that the saint can offer penance for those other acts. (Amir Hasan 1992: 136) Qalandars did not confine themselves only to shameful words: in the year 1353 a wandering dervish called Turab, who was dissatisfied with the reception accorded to him in the Delhi khānqāh of the Chishtis, inflicted with a dagger thirty wounds on the great Shaikh Nasiruddin Chiragh-i Dihli.[28] Earlier in the year 1290 a qalandar of the Hyderi sect[29] played a fatal role in the case of the conspirator Sidi Maula: when he appeared for trial in the court of Sultan Jalaluddin Khalji, of an attempt on whose life he was accused, a Hyderi present in the courtroom slashed Sidi Maula's throat with a razor, which, as we will recall, qalandars always kept handy. At the same time Sidi Maula himself belonged to the sect of muwallihs related to the qalandars. Elephants trampled the dervish, who had been fatally wounded by a member of his own brotherhood.

A contemporary researcher of South Asian Sufism, Simon Digby, has called qalandars and similar sects of wandering dervishes with other self-appellations, deviants, that is groups deviating from social and religious conduct (Digby 1984). Moderate 'sober' mystics, let alone 'ulamā, regarded qalandars and similar groups of dervishes as zindīqs. The testimony of Muhammad Gesudaraz in this respect is interesting: People keep on saying that haqīqat is the divine secret, but I, Muhammad Husaini, say that sharī at is the divine secret, because I have also heard talk of h″aqīqat from the mouths of muwallihs, Haidaris, Qalandars, mulhids and zindīqs (heretics of sorts); may, I have even heard it from the mouths of Yogis, of Brahmans and of Gurus. But talk of the sharīat I have not heard from the mouth of anyone other than the people of true faith and belief, i.e., Sunni Muslims. Thus, it is evident that the sharīat is the divine secret. (Schimmel 1980: 53) This quotation proves that, first, such an authoritative Sufi as Gesudaraz did not differentiate between qalandars, muwallihs, Hydaris and other sects of wandering dervishes and, second, equated their irresponsible utterances with the words of kāfirs (Yogis and Brahmans). Gesudaraz's stand is more understandable, since the 'calculated deviation' of qalandars and their like was in the first place directed against the authority of the shaikhs of the main silsilas and against the deep-rooted methods of transmission of baraka.

The qalandars rejected both the basic forms and methods of Sufi practice and the established relations between pīr and murīd, which presupposed movement on the Path only under the leadership of a spiritual preceptor. Generally, speaking the Muslim poetry of the subcontinent is full of scornful, even mocking remarks about hypocritical and hidebound shaikhs, ignorant of the true profundity of mystic enlightenment. Thus, one of the pioneers of poetic tradition in rekhta Urdu, Muhammad Wali (1668 - 1707), in many respects reflects the point of view of malāmatīs or qalandars, when he says: Shaikh yahāñ bātterī pesh na jāyegī kabhū Zuhd kī chor, ke mat majlis-i rindān men ā Shaikh! Nothing you say will ever have any effect here. Abandon your counsels of asceticism and come and join the company of pleasure-seekers. (Matthews and Shackle 1972: 24-5) True, attacks on shaikhs early on turn into a stable semantic motif of the genre ghazal and lose any connection with critical sentiments in Sufi circles. That is why when Mir Taqi Mir depicts the image of an impudent shaikh in a highly intoxicated state distributing the attributes of his affiliation to the fraternity amongst fellow revellers and boon companions, he is only paying homage to the convention of the genre: Shaikh jo hai masjid meñ nangā, rāt ko thāmeikhāne meñ Jubba, khirqa, kurtā, t'opī mastī meñ inām kiyā The Shaikh, who is naked in the mosque, was in the winetavern last night. In his drunkenness he pledged his coat, his patched cloak, his shirt, and his hat. (Matthews and Shackle 1972: 62-3) Denying the role of living spiritual preceptors, qalandars at times declared themselves to be murīds of already dead shaikhs and took the oath of loyalty (bai'a) at their graves, which called forth condemnation and resistance on the part of the heads of silsilas. Thus, one of Shakh Farid's sons, fancying himself to be a qalandar, shaved his head and took the oath at Qutbuddin Bakhtiyar Kaki's tomb, after which he proclaimed himself to be a disciple of this saint. Shaikh Farid was indignant at such a violation of the laws of initiation and declared: 'Shaikh Qutb-u'd-din is my spiritual guide and master, but this form of initiation is not proper. Initiation and discipleship mean that one should grasp the hand of a Shaikh [i.e., is in direct contact with him A. S.]' (Nizami 1955: 95). Qalandars did not recognize khilāfat-nāmas and walāyat the limits of a saints' spiritual jurisdiction, which accounts for their hostile on slaughts on khānqāhs. Shaikh Jalaluddin Tabrizi, notable for his bellicose disposition, once tied up hand and foot and imprisoned a wandering qalandar, who had taken it into his head to cure people of diseases and work wonders in his walāyat in the region of Lakhnauti. Complaints to the effect that juwāliqs lived by begging and deceiving people in the regions around Delhi which were 'under his rule' are to be found even in Nasiruddin Chiragh-i Dihli's malfūz at. At the same time juwāliqs did acknowledge some authority, if one may give credence to the story of how they prostrated themselves before Shaikh Baha'uddin Zakariya on hearing Abu Hafs 'Umar Suhrawardi's name. Baha'uddin Zakariya, being, in principle, an opponent of wandering dervishes, could not deny that amongst them also one could come across quite pious and mystically gifted people. Thus, he came across a juwāliq who could during two cycles of prayer recite the entire Qur'an. However much the Spiritual Sovereign of Multan wished to emulate this, he failed and was compelled to declare: 'Now have I witnessed the truth of this axiom that in the midst of every group of people there is indeed one of God's elects!' (Amir Hasan 1992: 85).

Not liking the qalandars as a particular social group, Baha'uddin Zakariya nevertheless found his chosen ones amongst them. His favourite disciple Fakhruddin 'Iraqi lived the life of a typical malāmatī and the shaikh of Multan initiated another of his favourites, Lal Shahbaz Qalandar (1177–1267 A.D.), into the Suhrawardiyya order and gave him his own khirqa. May be Baha'ddin Zakariya's contradictory attitude towards qalandars is explained by the fact that amongst them there were several gifted poets, and the head of the Suhrawardiyya had always had a weakness for poetry. The earliest qalandars found their way to the subcontinent from Khurasan. Having well got on the nerves of Baba Farid, Baha'ddin Zakariya and the other saints of Punjab, they moved towards Delhi and Bengal, perpetrating scandals in each khānqāh which they came across on the way. From Gorakhattri, a small town in the neighbourhood of Peshawar, where there was the 'transhipping point' of wandering ascetics of various persuasions, they used to make their way along the main highway of the subcontinent extending over one and a half thousand miles, which connected the north-western regions with the capital of the Sultanate. Under the Mughals the highway was called the Imperial Road, whereas under the English it was given the name of the Grand Trunk Road, which later Kipling would call the 'backbone of the entire Hind' and the 'river of life, having no equal in the whole world'.

Along this very 'river of life' there came to the capital of the Delhi Sultanate Shah Khizr Rumi, with whom begins the story of the Qalandariyya fraternity in South Asia. A native of Anatoliya, Shah Khizr Rumi was a disciple of the semi-legendary long-lived saint 'Abdul 'Aziz Makki, whom qalandars traditionally regard as a contemporary and associate of the Prophet. Finding himself in Delhi during the reign of Iltutmish, Khizr Rumi came under the charm of Qutbuddin Bakhtiyar Kaki and took initiation into the Chishtiyya fraternity from him. The great shaikh permitted him to wear the clothes and observe the customs of the qalandars, insisting only that he should refrain from performing 'unclean' miracles. In that way we find Khizr Rumi at the source of the new derivative fraternity of Qalandariyya-Chishtiyya, which was especially popular in Jaunpur and other eastern regions of present Uttar Pradesh. Later, the Jaunpuri branch of Qalandariyya-Chishtiyya became Shia. The fourth successor of Khizr Rumi, namely Qutbuddin b. Sarandaz Jaunpuri (who died in 1518), instituted the dhikr formulae of the order: 'Ya Hasan is forced between the two thighs, Ya Husain on the navel, Ya Fatima on the right shoulder, Ya 'Ali on the left shoulder, and Ya Muhammad in his soul' (Trimingham 1971: 268).

The most widely-known representative of this fraternity is another disciple of Khizr Rumi called Sharafuddin Bu 'Ali Qalandar (who died in 1324), whose tomb in Panipat became a place of mass pilgrimage. Bu 'Ali Qalandar became a very authoritative figure in later Sufi tradition when some authors of the sixteenth century, among them Sayyid Murtaza of Murshidabad, the compiler of Yoga Qalandar, traced the Qalandariyya discipline back to Bu 'Ali of Panipat. As a true qalandar, but 'Ali did not observe the injunctions of sharīat and lived a life devoted to ascetic practices and mortification of the flesh. Wandering throughout the Islamic world, he spent some time in Konya where, according to information in Akhbār-al-akhyār, he became acquainted with Jalaludddin Rumi's son Sultan Weled, the head of the Mawlawi ṭarīqa founded by his father. In any case the verses (a few doctrinal poems and a dīwān), ascribed to Bu 'Ali Qalandar, display a knowledge of Mathnawī and of Rumi's lyrical poetry. Besides verses Bu 'Ali, like many other Sufis, used to elaborate upon his mystic experience in letters (maktūbāt). In one of them he wrote: Recognition of Beauty is a step leading to the understanding of the Beloved. This made the lover and the Beloved identical. Beloveds were created in the form of human beings in order that they might lead people to the righteous path. Both heaven and hell were born of the beauty of the Lover and none of these were meant for anyone but lovers. Heaven was the stage of union; hell was the station of separation and was intended for enemies. (Rizvi 1986: 305) Even from this short passage it is obvious how vulnerable Bu 'Ali Qalandar was to the imputation of zandaqa. By asserting that the Beloved (i.e., God) may be personified in a human being, he verges on h″uluīl, which from the point of view of normative Islam, is a heretical concept of personification of the Divine (i.e., eternal) in something mortal and 'transient'. Huluī together with ittihad (union with God) was the most common accusation on the part of the Muslim theologians against Sufis in general and against Mansur Hallaj, although in his discourses and works he avoided this term. The Chishti mystic Mas'ud Bakk was pronounced guilty of hulul and executed in 1387; even kinship with Sultan Firoz Shah Tughluq could not save him from death. That is why 'moderate' Sufi authors (for example al-Hujwiri, Muhammad Gesudaraz and Ashraf Jahangir Simnani) criticized this dangerous concept in every way possible.

Gradually the main fraternities absorbed qalandars. Thus, for example, Hamid Qalandar, compiler of the malfūz at Khair ul-majāl it was already a typical Chishti mystic, who had spent the greater part of his life in Nasiruddin Chiragh-i Dihli's khānqāh. The head of the Surkh-Bukhari fraternity, as we will recall, was one of the most widely known wandering dervishes Makhdum-i Jahaniyan Jahangasht from Ucch. Although he himself can in no way be reckoned among qalandars on account of the conservation and Puritanism of his views, the Jalaliyya sect of his followers which is under discussion is quite in line with groups of deviant dervishes. The Suhrawardis' connection with qalandars can be traced back to Lal Shahbaz Qalandar, the patron saint of Sehwan, whose tomb is one of the most fascinating sanctuaries of the subcontinent. The real name of this wandering poet, dancer and musician was Mir Sayyid 'Uthman. According to the legend he always dressed himself in red (as did Jalaluddin Surkhposh Bukhari) and hence his nickname Lal (Red). Baha'uddin Zakariya supposedly gave the other part of the nickname Shāhbāz royal falcon to him at the time of his initiation. During his lifetime Lal Shahbaz Qalandar had quite a shady reputation: Barani mentions how once he presented himself at the court of the governor of Multan intoxicated with hashish and surrounded by, who committed such outrages that they were unceremoniously thrown out.

In the legends of popular Islam, Lal Shahbaz Qalandar is depicted as an infernal dancer, in flowing scarlet clothes dancing on burning coals, surrounded by tongues of flame. I have already mentioned that the dargāh in Sehwan came into being at the place of a Shivaist sanctuary. In such instances, as the example of Bahraich shows, some functions and attributes of pre-Islamic objects of worship were imparted to the Muslim saints. It is likely that Lal Shahbaz Qalandar's macabre dance (raqs) was a replica of Shiva's cosmic dance tāndava. It is possible that the cult image of the wandering ascetic took shape under the influence of Shiva Nāṭarāja, the many-handed sovereign of dance, dancing in a fiery circle. There are verses and hymns in Persian ascribed to Lal Shahbaz Qalandar. The key image of his poetry is the dance of death, the convulsions of a person hanged on the gallows (dār) who is a martyr of Divine love. This image is borrowed from the Sindhi folk poetry of the genre hallājiya, which came into being under the influence of Mansur Hallaj's visit to Sindh in the year 905. The dervishes, nowadays performing ritual dances, or dhammal, in the Sehwan dargāh, by the convulsive jerks of their bodies and typical quick movements of their feet, as if they are hardly touching the ground, reproduce both the writhing of the hanged and the gait of those walking on fire.

In general, a visit to Sehwan makes a most powerful impression on a foreigner: inside the dargāh reigns a particularly tense, even hysterical, atmosphere, which is added to by saturated with the suffocating odour of bhāṅg (Indian hemp). The tomb itself, built in 1357 by Firoz Shah Tughluq, is of little interest as far as its architecture is concerned. Apart from that it is difficult to have a close look at it, hidden as it is behind compact rows of stalls and annexes. It was continually in the process of being completed and today it represents a tangled labyrinth of inner courtyards, passages, and galleries. One can reach the central courtyard, where the dhammal dance is performed, only through the 'new' southern gate, built by Zulfiqar 'Ali Bhutto. However, going back through it is for some reason not possible. One has to make a fairly long detour, cross the main courtyard and a connected series of small courtyards, and pass through large, gilded doors, donated by the last Shah of Iran. The 'old' eastern entrance, adorned with dark blue and white tiles and two flanking minarets, leads to the tomb proper. Inside the tomb lamps are placed on high consoles, from which burning hot oil falls in drops into special vessels. The pilgrims, taking the risk of being scalded, dip their fingers in it and smear it on their forehead and lips. The origin of this ritual relates to the fact that in his lifetime the saint, consumed by the flame of divine love, literally used to drink boiling sesame oil, and pour it on his chest. Under the canopy of the cenotaph a big stone is suspended, which seems to be quite heavy and which the saint used to carry on his chest during his lifetime.[30] Going round the mazār, the faithful reverentially touch this stone with their hand.

At six thirty in the evening the thunder of the big drums heralds the commencement of the daily dhammal. On weekdays the dervishes and pilgrims dance for only half an hour, apart from on Thursdays when they dance for a whole hour. Men and women sit down on different sides of the courtyard; for the time being they interchange remarks, but in only a few minutes they will be in the grip of wild excitement, turning into a somnambulistic trance. At first the dervishes come to the centre of the courtyard. From time to time, they jump high, bending their legs in the air at the knees, while performing lezginka (a lively Caucasian folk dance). They touch down not flat on the whole foot, but on their toes, and then till the next jump they jig at a fast tempo, as if performing a toe dance, with the only difference being that they are barefoot. The heads and hands of the dancers twitch abruptly in time with the quickening roll of the drums; faces are distorted with the grimace of ecstasy. Gradually the pilgrims sitting around join the dancing dervishes. Men get up and clumsily jump, mark time, and go into a spin; often amongst them hījr,as (transvestites) are to be seen who move with affectedly dainty steps. Women, on their knees, rotate their heads in a state of frenzy, and their long, loose, flowing hair cuts the air with a whistling sound. Some of them fall into a deep trance and sit slumped on the ground in a catatonic stupor. Everywhere one can see crooked hands and legs, mouths wide open, eyes coming out of their sockets, like a living visual aid for a psychiatrist learning his trade. However, with the stroke of the gong this entire frightening dance of death abruptly comes to an end. First to leave are the dervishes, the instigators, and then the pilgrims also collect their belongings, disperse, and go home. The woman who was just now rolling on the ground, having gone mad in ecstasy, tucks her hair under her black chaddarin a business-like manner, wraps herself up in a shawl, takes her child in her arms and goes home with modest dignity. The industry of pilgrimage in Sehwan-i Sharif is organized on a large scale: following in the saint's footsteps, one must make payment at each step. Entry to the grotto, where Lal Shahbaz used to meditate, costs ten rupees in all. It costs slightly more to crawl under the felled khabar tree, by the side of which he used to pray in his lifetime, and in the process be cured of all diseases. On separate payment one is allowed to collect medicinal water from the spring where the saint in his time used to drink, and so on and so forth. At the same time the dargāh every day receives one and a half thousand pilgrims and feeds them free of cost, whereas at the time of 'urs, celebrated on the 18–20 of Sha'bān, the number of visitors reaches twenty-five thousand, whose reception requires considerable resources.

Dances on burning coals, walking through fire and other ordeals, accompanied by mutilation, made up the rituals, common for many deviant groups. In the preceding chapter it was mentioned how the followers of Zinda Shah Madar used to perform this rite. Another sect of fiery dancers was the wandering Hyderi dervishes, whose eponym was yet another disciple of Muhammad b. Yunus as-Sawaji, Qutbuddin Hyder from Nishapur (died 1221). Shaikh Nizamuddin Auliyahighly praised him as a person who had possessed great spiritual powers and clairvoyance: according to him Qutbuddin Hyder predicted the victory of the Mongols over India.[31] As it is told in Fawā'id al-fu'ād: in that spiritual state he could pick up burning hot iron and shape it around his neck into a necklace or around his hand into a bracelet; the iron in his hand became like wax. The Hyderis still exist, and their members still wear such necklaces and bracelets, but where is that spiritual state (which the founder possessed)? (Amir Hasan 1992: 100–1) The Hyderis not only continued to wear these iron accessories, but even used to pass round iron rods through their male organs and because both ends were sealed called them 'rods of the seal' (sikh-i muhr) of celibacy. Ibn Battuta who often met Hyderis in his travels wrote that they 'place iron rings in their hands, necks and ears, and even their male members so that they are unable to indulge in sexual intercourse' (The Travels of ibn Battuta 1962: 279–80). It is quite possible that the Hyderis borrowed this custom from the Hindu Nāgā sanyāsīs (Rizvi 1986: 307). From a sect of Indian ascetics Kānphatā (a variety of Nath Yogis) they had learnt to make incisions in ears at the time of initiation, inserting heavy iron rings in them. Ibn Battuta described in detail one of his meetings with Hyderis near Amroha in 1342: There came to me a company of poor brethren who had iron rings on their necks and arms, and whose chief was a coal black negro. They belonged to the corporation known as the Haidariya and they spent one night with us. Their chief asked me to supply him with firewood that they might light it for their dance, so I charged the governor of that district, who was Aziz known as al-Khammar to furnish it. He sent about ten loads of it, and after the night prayer they kindled it, and at length, when it was a mass of glowing coals, they began their musical recital and went into that fire, still dancing and rolling about in it. Their chief asked me for a shirt, and I gave him one of the finest textures; he put it on and began to roll about in the fire with it on and to beat the fire with the sleeves until it was extinguished and dead. He then brought me the shirt showing not a single trace of burning on it, at which I was greatly astonished. (The Travels of ibn Battuta 1962, 2: 274–75)

Although many modern researchers tend to perceive the predominant influence of the Indian substratum in the practice of Hyderis and other deviant groups, Ibn Battuta saw in it a similarity with the rituals of the Rifa'iyya dervishes active in Egypt, Iraq, and Syria, in the region between Basra and Wasit, i.e., in the cradle of the Arab Sufism. Ibn Battuta often used to stay in the cloisters of Rifa is he called them Ah-madī by the name of the fraternity's eponym Ahmad b. 'Ali ar-Rifa'i (1106–82) and knew their rituals well. So, Ibn Battuta wrote about Rifai dervishes in Wasit:

They had prepared loads of firewood which they kindled into a flame and went into the midst of it dancing; some of them rolled in the fire, and others ate it in their mouths, until finally they extinguished it entirely. This is their regular custom, and it is a peculiar characteristic of their corporation of Ahmadi brethren. Some of them will take a large snake and bite its head with their teeth until they bite it clean through. (The Travels of Ibn Battuta 1962, 2: 274) Ibn Battuta's last phrase reminds one of the customs of the Jalaliyya fraternity, whose members, as we remember, also swallowed snakes and scorpions. The most widely known of the South Asian Hyderis was Shaikh Abu Bakr Tusi Qalandari, who in the middle of the thirteenth century founded a khānqāh on the banks of the Jamna in the suburb of Delhi. Even from his name in India Hyderis were finally absorbed in the qalandarī trend. According to Amir Khurd, Abu Bakr Tusi was held in respect by the Delhi mystics and used to visit Sultan Balban's court. Sama were often held in his cloister, which were at times attended by Nizamuddin Auliyaaand Jamaluddin Hansawi. The latter gave Abu Bakr Tusi the nickname Bāz-i Safīd (White Falcon), as if by contrast with the Red Falcon, Lal Shahbaz Qalandar. It turns out that the great Shaikhs of both the main fraternities had their own chosen 'falcons' amongst the deviant dervishes.

However, warm relationships with meek Chishti shaikhs did not exert an ennobling influence upon Abu Bakr Tusi: his relations with other contemporaries were not so cordial. He was rather harsh with his neighbour Nuruddin Malik Yar Parran who planned to build a khānqāh near Abu Bakr's; he took an active part in the conflict between the sons of Jalaluddin Khalji, supporting one royal prince Arkali Khan against his rival Khan-i Khanan. But those who really disgraced Abu Bakr Tusi were his disciples, rioters and troublemakers representing the most aggressive detachment of wandering dervishes, with an extremist frame of mind. It was one of Abu Bakr Tusi's murīds, and that too on his instigation, who attacked Sidi Maula with a razor before sentence had been passed upon him.[32] In the khānqāh of the Hyderiyya refuge was given to thieves and murderers hiding from punishment; bringing this to an end was the official reason for the persecution of the sect and its leader during the reign of the stickler for law 'Ala'uddin Khalji.

After Abu Bakr Tusi's death Hyderi dervishes no longer had a centralized leadership or their own cloister. Sultan Firoz Shah Tughluq, favourably disposed only to the 'ulama and moderate 'sober' Sufis who had facilitated his accession to power, banished deviant groups of dervishes from the capital, and wandering mystics had to find refuge in the Sharqi Sultanate and in Muslim Bengal, where the traditions of religious syncretism and programmatic tolerance were deep-rooted. However, with the ascension of the Afghan clan of Lodi to the throne of

Delhi in 1451 fortune once again smiled upon qalandars, and they became welcome guests at the court. This is accounted for by the true prediction of an unknown qalandar who presented himself in Sikandar Lodi's camp and foretold that he would gain victory over the Sultan of Jaunpur. Since then, many rulers of India have been favourably disposed to the presence of qalandars in their vicinity.[33] Even the 'settled' muqīmān Sufis, despite their strained relations with qalandars, sided with them when they faced danger from the authorities. Thus, in the beginning of the fifteenth century the well-known Chishti mystic from Rudauli, Shaikh Ahmad 'Abdul Haqq (died 1434), stood up for the reputation of qalandars and other wandering dervishes, whom the Sultan of Bengal Ghiyathuddin A'zam Shah had decided to banish from his capital, Pandua. This action also had the purpose of getting rid of an excess of 'religious' migrants. Since 1398–9, when Timur's troops had devastated Punjab and the region of Delhi, thousands of wandering ascetics and mystics had moved over to Bengal. To evict 'God's own people, however, some pretext had to be found, and the Shah found it, accusing qalandars of unseemly behaviour and comparing them with Hindu jogis: One night the king visited a camp of qalandars disguised as a beggar. They were just about to start eating and rudely ordered him to leave. Then the king visited the camp of yogis. They were also taking food together and gave him an equal share. To his question why they had fed a mere stranger they replied that this was in accordance with their custom of sharing all food equally, even with dogs. Next morning the king ordered the Muslim mystics to leave Pandua. All were arrested and escorted to boats, which took them to exile. This action led to great unrest in the town. So, Shaikh Ahmad 'Abdu'l-Haqq, accompanied by a dervish (majdhūb) friend went to the palace to test the king's reaction to their presence. They remained unnoticed for quite some time, then left, returning to the house of their host. The Shaikh declared that the king did not expel dervishes and qalandars, only ignorant mystics. (Rizvi 1986: 270–1)

Although the version set forth by 'Abdul Quddus Gangohi in his Anwār al-'Uyūn is quite improbable because it is doubtful whether yogis (or jogis), by which name, as we will recall, Naths were usually referred to, would have so willingly shared food with a Muslim faqīr, the yearning of Shaikh Ahmad 'Abdul Haqq to whitewash his wandering fellow-qalandars and lay the blame on anonymous 'ignorant' charlatans is obvious. Many 'respectable' mystics often travelled in the guise of an indigent qalandar, whose status partly protected the wayfarer from the hazards of the highway. Thus, in the year 1492 Jamali Kanboh, being by then a famed poet, visited the great Abdur Rahman Jami in Herat. The later tadhkira, Afsāna-i-Shāhān by Muhammad Kabir b. Shah Isma'il relates that Jamali was dressed as a wandering ascetic, his head was shaved, his body was smeared with ashes and begirt with a donkey's skin around the waist. Jami, who at first took the visitor for an ordinary cadging qalandar, decided to mock at his appearance and rather impolitely asked what the difference was between him, i.e., Jamali, and a donkey. The guest also replied with a joke that the difference was in the skin because the donkey wore it all its life and the qalandar to sit on it. Then Jamali, bearing in mind that the guise of a qalandar conceals the piety and intensity of mystic experience, recited his celebrated line: 'The dust of thy lane has settled on my body like a garment' ('Marā zi khāk-i kūyat pīrāhan ast bar tan'). Here Jami at last understood that his visitor was Jamali himself, and treated him with great respect, asking him to explain some Hindi words in the verses of Amir Khusro and Amir Hasan.

Although Abdullah Ansari asserted in the treatise 'The Book of Qalandar' (Qalandar-nāma) that wandering mystics are endowed with great virtues: modesty, meekness, self-abnegation and unselfishness, popular hagiographic literature always warned neophytes and mystics against the difficulties and hazards lying in wait for the dervish who chose the qalandarī mode of life. Hence, probably, the image of the handsome qalandar tempting the Sufi and enticing him away on futile wanderings appeared behind him, an image which is widespread in medieval ṭabaqāt al-awliyā and tadhkiras. Meeting with this sort of tempter-qalandar had suddenly changed Fakhruddin 'Iraqi's fate. He left the madrasa in Hamadan, where he was teaching recitation of the Qur'an, and having arrayed himself in the rags of a wandering dervish and shaved his head clean, he followed a handsome young man to Khurasan, and from there to Multan. When the group of qalandars which 'Iraqi had joined was about to move further, a sandstorm started raging, in which the wanderers lost each other. The handsome qalandar mysteriously disappeared and nothing else was left for Fakhruddin 'Iraqi, but to linger on in Multan for an indefinite period. Here he was given refuge and shown much kindness by Baha'uddin Zakariya, under whose influence, which was as powerful as any storm, 'Iraqi managed to forget the fatal qalandar, or rather, to sublimate earthly passion for him into the 'true' transcendental love with which his poetry is imbued. Later the Spiritual Sovereign of Multan gave one of his daughters in marriage to the poet and made up his mind that he had once and for all settled down. However, as we have already seen, after the Shaikh's death 'Iraqi once again set off on his wanderings.

The romantic theme connected with the image of the wandering dervish resounds in the life of Shah Husain, generally known as Madho Lal Husain (1539–93). He is one of the major patron saints of Lahore and his modest tomb on the territory of the Mughal Park of Shalimar became the place where the popular festival Melaī chirāghān (Fair of lights), coinciding with the 'urs, is held every year. This talented poet, dancer, and musician, who was the first to make use of the subjects and artistic devices of Punjabi folklore in spiritual lyric poetry, cannot be reckoned among the qalandars, as he was formally initiated into the Qadiriyya fraternity (like most mystic poets of the north-western part of the subcontinent). However, in his habits and tenor of life he differed little from qalandars: he dressed in red rags, as did his predecessor Lal Shahbaz Qalandar, and over many years he wandered about the streets of the town, living by begging, dancing, singing his verses, and by night finding shelter in Dātā Darbār.

Shah Husain belonged to the caste of Punjabi weavers who converted to Islam relatively later, in Firoz Shah's times. His educator and spiritual preceptor were the Qadiri mystic Shaikh Bahlul Darya'i. Possibly Husain would have become a respectable Shaikh, had he not met a Hindu youth called Madho, the offspring of a Brahman family, residing in the Shahdara locality. At that time Husain was already an elderly person in his verses he complains that his face is wrinkled, and his teeth have darkened: Shah Hussain, you are so old, with wrinkles e'n in your teeth, and yet you are in search, of those, at close of day, who went ahead at morn. (Fakhar Zaman 1995: 80; translated by Ghulam Yaqoob Anwar) However, he went mad with passion for the young man. As if the hero of a romantic mathnawī, in the daytime Husain followed on Madho's heels and at night wandered near his house. Madho, like the heroine of the same kind, over several years ignored his ardent admirer. Since adherence to different religions prevented companionship with Madho, Husain, wishing to see the beloved more often, participated in Hindu festivals holi and basant, sang the Hindu devotional hymns (bhajans), and wore the clothes of a sadhu, thereby showing how porous was the dividing line between a vagrant Hindu ascetic and a wandering dervish. Finally, having experienced fana, he transformed his personality, merging himself totally in his beloved, and, having combined his name with his own, started calling himself Madho Lal Husain. In the tradition of the great mystics like Jalaladdin Rumi and Fakhruddin 'Iraqi the boy's beauty was a witness (shahid) of the Divine Beauty and the 'worldly love' toward a handsome youth was 'a pedagogical experience, a training in obedience toward God, since the human beloved, like God, has to be obeyed absolutely' (Schimmel 1975: 291). Shah Husain learnt the lesson of dissolving his self in the self of Madho as a prelude to his final annihilation in the Absolute.

The kāfīs, in which the suffering Shah Husain, speaking on behalf of Hir, the heroine of Punjabi folk legends, pined in separation from the handsome youth Ranjha, were sung everywhere on the streets of Lahore: Let me be called, by each, By the name of 'Ranjah', dear and none address me as 'Heer'. I have become the 'Ranjah', By calling so oft on Him. (Fakhar Zaman 1995: 70) Madho, on recognizing himself in the image of Ranjha, at last condescended to pay attention to his adorer, and then even shared his passion. As to how this love affair proceeded and how the people in the vicinity reacted to it can be judged from a passage from the Persian poem by Shaikh Mahmud of Lahore 'True Essence of Faqirs' (Haqīqat-al-fuqarā, 1662), which is an account of Shah Husain's life in verse: Qaum-e ū shud pas azdo saī āgāh kīn pisar az husain shud be-rāh Ki chu pesh-e husain bishtābad shab dar āghosh-e ū hamık ͵hwābad Ham may-e nāb mīk ͵hwarad ba-husain 'āshiqāna basar barad ba-husain Pas badīn sīrat-o badān sānash chi 'ajab gar kunad musalmānash ... "His kin in two years saw the truth Husain had quite misled the youth E'er to Husain he'd swiftly race to spend the night in his embrace, with him he'd even drink pure wine And as his lover spend the time - This way of life must surely lead Him to embrace the Muslim creed". (Shackle 2000: 55–73)

Indeed, the culmination of this amorous relationship between Shah Husain and Madho was conversion of the latter to Islam and this fact transformed the heroes' deviant behaviour (the homosexual relations and drinking of wine) into a manifestation of 'true love': Hama-rā tark dāda dar pay-e ū gasht mast-e muhabbat az may-e ū Ba-ṭufail-e husain shud dīndār badar āmad zi zumra-e kuffār for him all things aside he laid on his love was he drunken made, Joining the faithful through Husain with infidels not to remain. (Shackle 2000: 55–73) A Muslim's love for a Hindu girl and her conversion to Islam, symbolizing the annulment of the 'Turk–Hindu' opposition, is the main theme of a large corpus of Indo-Muslim texts, the so-called 'ballad-like' mathnawī, or poems about the mystery of love, which were analysed extensively in my book (Suvorova 2000: 29–43). These poems in Persian and Urdu had an obvious proselytizing orientation and in the descriptions of obstacles in the path of the Muslim hero and the Hindu heroine, of which the most insurmountable was the opposition of the social environment represented by the girl's relatives, they 'codified' the social and psychological trials faced by a missionary Sufi and a neophyte. Shaikh Mahmud's poem is unique not because it exhibits on the stage the same story with scenery of homosexual love, but rather because it organizes in accordance with the laws of classical literary genre the life of a popular saint, who was in addition a historic personality.

Proselytizing poems always concluded with the tragic death or suicide of the heroes and their union after death. Shah Husain's story, however, has a happy end: he lived many years with his friend and passed away in his arms. After the saint's demise Madho became the makhdūm of his tomb and continued to compose songs under the poetic pseudonym of his lover so that Madho Lal Husain's kāfīs available now are the fruit of collective creative work of two 'lamps' (chirāghān) illuminating Lahore. Madho (who died in 1646) was buried by Shah Husain's side. At the close of the eighteenth century the Maharaja of Punjab, Ranjit Singh's wife, erected over the grave of the saints a mausoleum together with a small mosque. Madho Lal Husain's 'ursis observed in February–March and coincides with the celebration of Holi. The rituals of melā-i chirāghān have retained many features of this Indian festival of the vernal equinox: jumping through fire, playful bouts between men and women, and the sprinkling of participants with coloured powder. The unorthodoxy and syncretism of Madho Lal Husain's cult have turned him into a beloved character of folklore, whom latter-day tradition ascribed opposition to the rule of the Mughals and struggle for establishment of an independent state of Punjab. As an anti-authoritarian hero, he became a character of the plays of some contemporary Pakistani play wrights.

At the same time Madho Lal Husain's life, and the poem Haqīqat-al-fuqarā devoted to him, demonstrate that the shockingly scandalous behaviour of wandering dervishes served as a screen to conceal the 'true essence' (haqīqat), and could show a heathen like Madho the way to God and of inspiring the heart of a sinner like Shah Husain with the emotional and passionate experience of faith. The unending road on which qalandars made their way, turned out to be the Path of Love, leading to that very goal, just like the ṭarīqat of 'regular' mystics. All absorbing passion for the Divine Beloved, referred to by Madho Lal Husain, was, of course, not a privilege of those who were part of a silsila and lived in a khānqāh: Rabba mere hal da mahram ton Andar ton in bahar ton in rom rom vich ton Inside is He, and outside also He, in every hair of mine; So intimate is He, With this condition fine. (Fakhar Zaman 1995: 91) The ambivalent image of the wandering saint, that of an impudent ragamuffin and an enigmatic handsome man, a be scandalizing society and an ecstatic visionary, is one of the least studied in the corpus of South Asian awliyā. The qalandars and related groups of dervishes are personages of popular religion of the lower strata of the society and that is why their veneration is rooted in popular magical cults, which have undergone only superficial Islamization. Possibly, in the conflicts of qalandars with 'settled' saints, upon which the hagiographic literature is never tired of dilating, one can discern the echo of the resistance offered by the essentially syncretic popular religion to the expansion of 'pure' normative Islam.

3. Political Condition of India in the early sixteenth century

During the early sixteenth century the political condition of India was unstable due to the fragmentation of the northern India into snail kingdoms. The Political condition of India during the period suggests the tendency of fissiparous outlook. The main territory of northern India comprising the fertile plains of river Indus and its tributaries along with Ganga and Jamuna was under the rule of Lodi sultans of Delhi. All central power similarly Gujrat, Malva, Rajputana, Jaunpur, Bengal were ruled by different independent rulers. According to Babur's memories the Political condition of first quarter of the I6th century suggest political fragmentation. Babur found in the first quarter of the 16th century five Muslims and two Hindu kingdoms of note.

Viz.

1. The Lodi Kingdom extended from Bhera to Bihar
2. Gujrat under Mussafar Shah
3. Malva under Mahmud Khalji
4. Bengal under Nusrat Shah
5. The Bahmanis in the Deccan
6. Mewar under Rana Sanga
7. Vijaynagar under Krishnadeva Raja"[34]

Based on Baburnama accounts Rush brook William clearly divides political condition of Northern India into four groups.[35] In the early 16th Century there was a Paramount power in northern India, strong enough to enforce its will on the numerous independent states or even to forge them into a temporary confederacy for the defence of her extensive frontier. The Lodhis who held Delhi and Agra were master of limited territory and though they gave promise under the energetic Sultan Sikandar (1489-1517) of playing the role of sultanate of Delhi. They failed to develop into an imperial Power, Ibrahim (1517-1526) the last ruler of the dynasty was not only defeated by Rana Sanga of Mewar but lost control over his Afghan Peers, some of whom like Daulat Khan Lodhi[36] governor of Lahore threw of their allegiance to the Sultan. The Lodhi Kingdom was therefore a congeries of semi-independent governorship mostly held by Afghans.

In 1525 Babur occupied Punjab and compelled Daulat Khan Lodhi to Submit. Daulat Khan Lodhi's chief object in life was to retain Supreme authority in Punjab. It was his house which had extended the authority of the Afghan's there and disposed the Mughals of the west Punjab. Daulat Khan therefore naturally feared the movements of Babur on the Western side of Indus. After that Babur's next expedition was start. Now Babur proceed against Ibrahim Lodhi the Afghan ruler and met him on the historic battlefield of Panipat on 21st April 1526. Babur wen a decisive victory over the Lodhi Sultan Babur quickly occupied Delhi and Agra. On Friday (Rajab 15th) while we remained on same ground Maulana Mahmud, and Shaikh Zain went with few others into Delhi for the congregational prayers read the Khutbah in my name distributed a Portion of money to the poor and needy and return to camp. [37] After the occupation of Delhi and Agra Babur quickly realised the necessity and importance of the neighbouring region of Rajputana which had begun once more to loom large on the Political front. In the reign of Rana Sangram Singh Mewar reached at the Zenith of her glory. He was controlling directly or indirectly the entire resource of Rajputana. Rana Sangram Singh was a very powerful ruler and according to Shaikh Zain. There was not a single ruler of the first rank in all these great countries like Delhi, Gujarat, and Mandu, who was able to make head against him. In banner of the infidel flaunted over two hundred cities inhabited by people of the faith.[38] This is confirmed by Baburnama, "Rana Sanga who in these latter days had grown great by his own valour and sword. His original country was Chittor in the downfall from power of the Mandu Sultans he became possessed of many of their dependencies such as Ranthambore, Sarangpur, Bhilsan and Chanderi".[39] Rana Sanga the hero of the Rajpur national revival was certainly a more formidable adversary than Ibrahim. Rana Sanga, the Babur in the famous battle of Khanwah on 16th March 1527. Babur won the battle. Babur's occupation of Bihar and Bengal after defeating Afghans in the battle of Ghaghra. Babur-met with the forces of Nusrat Shah in famous battle of Ghaghra on 6th May 1529. Like Rajputs, Afghans were defeated by Babur. Now from river Sindhu (Indus) to Bihar, and from Himalaya to Gwalior. Babur carved out a Kingdom and laid the foundation of future Mughal Empire. Thus, Babur established a vast empire which extended from the river Amu to Bihar, Khunduz, Badakashan, Kabul, Ghasni pandhar were his Western province. In India Multan and the Punjab, the united province, and the portion of Bihar, formed parts of his empire Biyana Ranthambore, Gwalior, Alwar and Chanderi formed the irregular, boundary line between the empire and the Kingdom of Rajasthan and Malva. Humayun succeeded Babur but due to so many reasons could not keep his father's empire. He was defeated by Sher shah Suri and fled to Iran where he took asylums. After a brief period of asylum, he started his recovery of his lost empire and conquered Kabul, Delhi, and Punjab. However, he could not enjoy his recovered entire as he accidently died on January 20, 1556. Humayun's son and successor Akbar became emperor after Humayun's death, who carved out a vast empire and due to his liberal religious policy brought together all his subjects irrespective of religion, caste, or any other suit distinction. Akbar's successors emperor Jahangir, Shahjahan and Aurangzeb ruled over the vast entire of emperor Akbar during the 17th century. The period of Mughal rule in India from Akbar to Aurangzeb is considered a period of Political stability and thus Indian cultural life was enriched during this period.

4. Beginning of Muslim contact with India

Muslim contact with India started from the time of the rise of Islam in the 7th century A.D., due to trade relation between India and Arab countries. However political contact began with Mohn. Bin Qasim during invasion of Sindh in 712 A.D. The frontier areas were occupied by the Arabs. Subsequently Muhammad of Ghazni invaded India several times in the first quarter of the 11th century A.D. Finally, towards the close of 12th century A.D. Shihabuddin Mohammad Ghori was able to establish his power Lahore and Delhi and this laid the foundation of Delhi Sultanat. [40] Sufis came to India many years. Before the extension of Turkish political power, the Muslim traders, merchants' saints, and mystic peacefully entered into India[41] and settled down. These Muslims immigrant lived outside the fortified town amongst the lower section of the Indian people because of caste taboos. The Muslims settled down in India nearly half a century before the Ghurid conquest and they secured permanent settlement in India. Author writes about Banaras, "There are Musalmans in that country since the days of Mahmud Bin Sabuktigin" [42] Sufis came to India many years before the establishment of the sultanate[43] of Delhi (1192 A.D.). However, it was after the foundation of the Turkish rule at Delhi that many Sufis came from Islamic countries migrated to this country and settled themselves in many parts of India. In course of time Sufi hermitage (khangah) scattered over all northern India and they divided the territory into subdivisions for their spiritual upliftment. The history of the development of the Islamic thought shows how in Muslim countries ideas had been evolved which were analogous to Hindu ideas and which could therefore be presented without shocking them. The material of conduct although peculiar was not thus entirely heterogenous.[44] As a result of it two great cultures met each other and a process of give and take took place. Initially there was a wide gap between Muslims and non-Muslim forces. But at the same time Muslim saint (Sufis) started another policy which was based on humanism and quality.[45]

5. Sufism in India up to Fifteenth Century

5.1 Early origin of Sufism

Islamic mysticism, which is a holy Quran, but in its development is generally influenced by other religions, i.e., Hinduism Buddhism, Zoroastrianism, Christianity and Gnosticism of Egypt and Neo Platonism, Yusuf Husain says "Sufism was born in the bosom of Islam.[46] She metaphysical terminology of the Sufis is largely derived from the Quran in expression like fire for the purity of God". Sufism is not a sect in Islam but only a philosophical aspect of that great faith. It has simply sought to interpret some of the most fundamental principles of Islam on the higher plane of thought and is nothing but its intellectual foundation knowledge love and renunciation, form the keynote of Sufism. Owning to the abstruseness of its principles its teaching has always been Kept exclusive and the institution of the preceptor and the disciple has become its permanent feature. Spiritual awakening according to the Sufis is can only be acquired with knowledge. "Real knowledge is the knowledge of God and knowledge of God connotes retirement into innermost recesses of one's soul which alone contains the light".[47] That Sufism like all other philosophical and mystical school of thought in Christianity, Hinduism, and Buddhism, owes its origin to this universal tendency of human mind will be apparent if we study the genesis of this highly interesting and interesting school of thought in Islam.

5.2   Derivation of the word Sufism

European writers who always try to show that all good ideas emanate from the west identify that the word 'Sufi with Sophas', which means was applied to those people who used clothing of woo, i.e., course clothing the cotton fabrics of Dhacca and Calicut being the monopoly of the nobility in those days and avoided every kind of luxury and ostentation. The name of 'pushminaposh' was therefore given to Sufis in Persia. Some writers are of opinion that the word is derived from the 'Ahlul-Luffah' or the people of the bench. However, the popular conception is that it is derived from the 'Safa' which means 'Purity'.[48] Some say 'the sufi were only named sufis because of the purity (SAFA) of their heart' and the cleanliness of their acts (ATHAR) Bishr-Ibn-al-Harith said "The sufi is he whose heart is sincere (Safa) towards God". But if the term sufi were derived from safa the correct form would be 'SAFAWI' and not sufi. Others think that sufi were only called Sufis because they are in the first rank (Saff) before God. But if the term sufi were refers to saff (rank) it would be 'SAFFI' not sufi. Others said 'they were only called Sufis because their qualities resembled those of the people who lived in the tine of God's Prophet (Suffah). But if the tern sufi were derived from 'suffah' (Bench) the correct form would be 'suffi' not sufi. Lastly, they were only called sufis because of their hablt of wearing suf i.e., wool, if the derivation from suf (wool) be accepted the word is correct.[49]

5.3   Basic conception of Sufism

"Sufism teaches how to purify oneself improve one's morals and build up one's Inner and outer life to allain perpetual bliss. Its subject matter la the purification of the soul and Its end or aim is the attainment of eternal felicity and blessedness".[50] Imam Qushayri the author of the great sufi compendium Rasail takes Sufism in the sense of purity, i.e., the purity of inner and outer life and says that 'purity is something praiseworthy' in which ever language it may be expressed, and its opposite impurity is to be eschewed. Thus, Sufism in the words of Abu Ali or Rudhabari is "giving one's lost the taste of tyranny" and journeying in the pathway of the Holy Prophet. Sufis had great faith in God. They believed in his existence. Sufi believed that God is transcendent and immanent. Nothing could be hidden from God since he is always with us. God is near us, God is omnipresent. The Sufis believe in divine presence. God alone is worthy of worship. The Sufis identified the Hao and Khalq. The creator and created. "It means that God is the unity behind all purity and the Reality behind all phenomenal appearance".[51] In other words they believed in the doctrine of Wahadat-ul-wujud or unity of being. There were many orders (silsilaha) of the sufie in India. The main Silsila's were the Chishtia, the Suhrawardia, the Naqshbandia the jadiris, the Qelandaria and the Shattari. The first sufi saint of the Chishti silsila in India was Shaikh Moinuddin Chishti (1143 A.D.-1236 A.D.) settled at Ajmer before the Ghorian conquest of that region. Shaikh Moinuddin was born in 536 A.D /1143 A.D. at Sistan. The live Khwaja adopted a catholic attitude in his dealings with the Hindus. His aim was that the highest form of devotion to God consists of doing service to humanity. Khwaja had many disciples who propagated his ideals and teachings. Two of the most important among them were Shaikh Harnid-ud-din Nagori and Shaikh Qutubuddin Bakhtiyar Kaki[52] Shaikh Qutubuddin Bakhtiyar Kaki (ob. 1235 A.D.) was distinguished Khalifah of Shaikh Moinuddin was a native of Avsh.

Both of the disciple was asked to settle at different places consequently Shaikh Farid-u-din Nagori settled in Nagor while Shaikh Qutub-ud-din Bakhtiyar Kaki at Delhi. Qutub-ud-din Bakhtiyar Kaki adopted Shaikh Farid as his spiritual who settled at Ajodhan. Shaikh Farid-ud-din Masud Ganj-i-Shakar (1175 - 1265) was the famous saint of his time. He worked in Hansi and Ajodhan. Farid-ud-din known popularly as shaikh Farid or Baba Farid. He gave to the Chishti silsilah the momentum of an organised spiritual movement. Shaikh Farid's famous disciple was Shaikh Nizam-ud-din Aulia.[53] (1236-1425 A. D.) It was under him that the Chishti silsilah reached its highest watermark.[54] For nearly half a century he lived and worked in Delhi. Nizanm-ud-din Auliya acquired great fame during his lifetime and became known as Muhbub-i-illahi. His religious activities had a great deal to do with the popularly of the Chishti's order in India. The last great Sufi saint of the Chishti silsilai was Nasir-ud-din Mahmud known as Chirag of Delhi settled down at Lahore. He was born at Ayodhya. When he was 25, he decided to be a mystic and at the age of 45 he became the disciple of Nasir-ud-din Auliya. He was the last great saint of Chishti silsila to have enjoyed an all-India reputation. The Suhrawardy silsilah was the next important sufi order. After Chishti Silsila another important Silsilah of India was Suharawadie Silsila. The founder of this Silsila was Shaikh shahabuddin Suhrawardi who asked his disciple to work in India. Shaikh Shahabuddin's prominent disciple Shaikh Bahauddin Zakaria came to India and settled in Northwestern till his death 1262 A.D.[55] Shaikh Bahauddin Zakari a had seven sons and several disciples. His son Shaikh Sadruddin Arif succeeded him as his Chief Sajjadah Nashin in Multan and his disciple Jalaluddin Surkh Bukhari established a strong suhrawardy centre at {Uch Shareef} Uehch. Jalaluddin Surkh had come from Bokhara and became a disciple of Bahauddin Zakariyya. He acquired influence and converted many Hindus of uch to Islam. His grandson Sayyid Jalaluddin Makhdum-i-Jahamam was one of the most influential Suhrawardy saints of his time. The Suhrawardy Sufis took greater care of their families and devoted more time to the upbringing and training of their sons than the Chishti Saints. A prominent branch of the Suhrawardy silsilah was that of the Firdausia. Shaikh Sharf-uf-din Yahya was a prominent leader of this silsilah. He was a learned man and left behind him a good number of his letters known as his Maktubat in which he tried to recognise the doctrine of Wahadat-ul-wujud (Unity of being). The next order Qadiri Silsilah was founded by Shaikh Abdur Oadir Jilani of Bagdad in the 12th century A. D. Shah Niyamat ullah and Nasir-ud-din Muhammas Jilani who flourished in the middle of the 15th century. Mohaantad Jilan settled at Uch in Sindh. The popularity of the Sufis was due to their understanding of the Indian condition and to their adopting some of the Hindu customs and ceremonies. "According to Sir Jadunath Sarkar the Bhakti movement and Sufi philosophy tended to bring the ruling sect and dominated people close together".[56] Mostly the Hindus of the lower classes came into contact with Sufi, and they had been very much influenced with the number of Hindu associates themselves with Muslim Sufis and they adopted sufistic thought, behaviour and practices.

5.4   Bhakti Movement up to Fifteenth Century

5.4.1 Origin of Bhaktism

The Hindus treat their religion from the point of view of emancipation (Moksha), for the attainment of which they recognise three paths the path of action (karma) of knowledge (dnyan /gyan) and of devotion (bhakti).[57] According to the ancient Hindu thought Salvation or freedom from the bondage of birth and death which is the ultimate end of human life, can be attained by three means (marga) viz, (knowledge) dnyan/gyan, Karma (action) bhakti (devotion).[58] The third path for the attainment of liberation is that of devotion and faith (Bhakti marga). Bhakti has been defined as 'the worship of a personal deity in a spirit of love', as personal faith in personal God love for him as for a human being the dedication of everything to his service, and the attainment of Moksha by this mean rather than by knowledge or sacrifice or works as an affection fixed upon the Lord after acquiring a knowledge of the attributes of the adorable one.[59] The beginning of bhakti may be traced in the hymns of the Rigveda where longing prayers are said to touch Indra who is longing just as a wife with desire get her husband. The word Bhakti is derived from the root bhaj, by the application of the 'tin' suffix which express an action and means among other things, service devotion, attachment, loyalty worship and homage. The traces of Bhakti movement can be found in the philosophy of Gita. The earliest written text of the school of devotion is the Bhagavad Gita.

Bhakti, however, was preached as a doctrine for the first time in the Bhagavad Gita. The Bhakti movement was initiated as a culture of love and devotion based on the Bhagavad Gita and other sacred Hindu texts, by Alvar and Adiyar Brahmins of South India. "The bhakti of Gita has a very close resemblance to the Christian notion of the love of God embodied in the Greek word agape". However, the Bhakti movement in India started in South India during the 7th century A. D. From the eight centuries to Fifteenth the South is the home of religious reform, it is there that Vaishnava and Saivite Saints started the schools of Bhakti and Shankara and Ramanuja Nimaditya, Basava, Vallabhacharya and Madhava expounded their philosophical system.

5.4.2 Basic concept of Bhaktism

Shankaracharya's philosophy was based on dualism. Shankara's philosophy which in so far as thought systems may be causes of events, dealt a fatal below to Buddhism, attempted to rally the Hindu sects together. The one aim of shankara's endeavours was to remove that fatal weakness of Hinduism the fissiparous tendency of its religious sects which all claimed their authority from the sane source namely the Srutis. Shankara had to establish that the sacred scriptures of the Hindus had one consistent teaching to impart and that the differences of schools were due to misunderstanding and lack of true insist. "Monism according to him was the outstanding feature of Hindu theology, a monism uncompromising absolute idealistic". God was one and there was no other besides him. It is said that Shankara was the founder of Bhakti movement. Besides Shankara there were many Bhakti Saints in India till 16th century. Of course, Bhakti movement was systematized by Ramanuja in the 12th century A.D. and propagated all over India. Ramanuja was born in 1016 at Tirupati or prenumber near

Madras. His father's name was Kesava and mother's name was Kantimati. He became at first the pupil of Yadava Prakasa, who was a follower of Shankara. The aim of Ramanuja's teaching was the refutation of shankara's absolute monism and Mayavasa and the establishment of Bhakti within the philosophy of Vedanta and incidentally also to obtain recognition for the non-Vedic panchratra in the Vedic literature."[60] The medieval Bhakti movement in real sense begins with Ramanuja. Ramanuja died in 1137 at srirangam. After Ramanuja the next great Vaishnava philosopher was Nimbarka. He is also known as Nimaditya or Nimananda and is said to be Telugu Brahman of Nima in Bellary district Nimbarka's sect became popular in north India and the success of the Bhakti movement in the north is to a great measure due to him.

The Bhakti movement was spread in the north by Ramananda who was greatly influenced by the teaching of Ramanuja. Ramanuja was born at Prayag in the Kanyakubja Brahmin family. He was educated at Prayag and Benaras. He gave his teachings through Hindi the language of the common people. He ignored the traditional barriers of caste and creed and had among his disciples Raidasa the cobbler, Kabir the Weaver, Dhanna the Jat farmer, Sena the barber and Pipa the Rajput. It is certain that Ramananda came into contact at Benaras with learned Musalman.[61] Ramananda's teaching gave rise to two schools of religious thought, one conservative and the other radical. The legends attached to his disciples show the popular character of the Bhakti movement. Another important Bhakti saint was Madhavacharya who flourished in the 13th Century. Anandatiratha or Madhava (1199-1278) rejected both the theory of unqualified monism of Shankara and qualified monism of Ramanuja. He believed in the theory of district dualism "Madhava conception of God was that of the Sovereign who ruled the world, and whose grace conferred deliverance on man. The next Bhakti Saint Raidas was a worker in leather and thus belonged to a low came social hierarchy. He was born at Banaras; his father's name was Raghu and that of his other Ghurbiniya. His breath a spirit of humidity and self-surrender. He did not indulge in high philosophic speculation about the nature and essence of God and his relationship with the world and man. He believed in a God who was the absolute lord of all. "Hari is in all, and all is in Hari" Kabir (1398 – 1518) was the most important of the disciples of Ramananda. He was a weaver by profession. He lived the life of householder earning his living by weaving. There is in them a denunciation of worldliness, the life of sense pleasure, sectarianism formal religious practices and unrighteous conduct. It is said that Kabir was the son of a Brahmin widow who to hide her shame left him on the side of a tank from where he was picked up by a weaver Niru who adopted him. Kabir was a meditative child and when he grew up, he became disciple of

Ramananda. Kabir himself says "I was revealed in Kasi and was awakened by Ramananda". According to Mohsin Fani 'at the time when he was in search of a spiritual guide, he visited the best of the Musalman and Hindis, but he did not find what he sought, at last somebody gave him direction to an old man of bright genius, the Brahman Ramananda'.

The mission of Kabir was to preach a religion of love which unite all castes and creed. He rejected those features of Hinduism and Islam which were against the spirit, and which were of no importance for the real spiritual welfare of the individual. The God he worshipped was formless one, he called him by number of names, both Rama and Rahima. He sharply condensed caste and religious distinctions and taught the brotherhood of man. He appealed to the conscience, the inner voice of man, and not to scriptures. Hindu or Muslim. He believed that the goal of the human soul was unity with God. Kabir's teachings had a profound effect on the masses. 'The Bhakti movement of medieval India represents the first effective impingement on Hindu Society of Islamic culture and outlook'. It is fact that Bhakti movement was indigenous and was first appeared around the 6th century A.D. in the South Particularly in Tamil country and from there spread throughout much of the country by different saint. The movement not only prepared a meeting ground for the devout man of both creeds it also preached human equality and openly condemned rituals and caste. The main mission of this movement was to unit Hindus and Muslims. The result of this movement was that the two great cultures encountered each other and the process of give and take took place. Initially there was a wide gap between Muslims and Hindus of India. But at the same time Bhakti saints started another policy which was based on humanism.

5.5   Development of Bhakti Movement

Bhakti movement continued during the 16th and 17th centuries in the more detailed form as compared to its early period. During this period, it became unconventional and anti-ritualistic and ignored the old restriction of caste and creed or attached little importance to them. During this period Bhakti movement bifurcated into two divisions i.e., Saguna (God with attributes) and Nirguna (God without attributes). A large number of saints belonged to the Saguna school Which believed that God has many forms and attributes that he manifests himself in incarnations such as Ram and Krishna and that His spirit is to be found in the idol and images worshipped at home and in temples. The most important saints of Saguna school in the 16th and 17th centuries were Vellabhacharya, Tulsidas, Surdas, Mirabai and Chaitanya. Those who believed in Nirguna philosophy categorically emphasised that God is without form or attributes, but nevertheless merciful and responsive to human prayers. This philosophy seems to be the outcome of ancient vedantic philosophy. However, it is also possible that it might have also influenced by Islamic conception of God. The main saints of the Nirguna school were Nanak, Dadu Dayal, Raidas. The saints of both these sections propagated the principles of human love and equality to all without any consideration of caste and creed. The saints belonging to Saguna order. However, tried to retain basic conception of social order. They wanted to bring social-religious reform without breaking the age-old social customs and practices. On the contrary the saints belonging to the Nirguna order strongly preached about social equality by condemning the social customs and practices. The teachings of both the sects influenced the contemporary society and brought peace to all. Further, these teachings also helped in the synthesis of Indian culture and Islamic culture.

5.6   Bhakti saints of Saguna school

5.6.1 Vallbhacharya (1479 – 1531 A.D.)

Vallabhacharya was the next great saint of the Krishna culture of Vaishnavism. He was born in a deep jungle at Banaras in 1479 A.D.[62] Vallabhacharya the founder of the great Vaishnavita sect of Rajasthan and Gujarat was the second son of Lakshman Bhatt a Taliaqana Brahman. Vallabhacharya's early name was Vidharbha Vallabhacharya belonged to a South Indian family known for its learning, scholarship, and deep devotion. He was a very Intelligent and promising child, and it is said that his birth was followed by some miraculous happenings. Vallabhacharya was meant to a life of scholarship and religious meditation and reform.[63] In his early days Vallabhcharya Iearnt four Vedas in four month. The six shastras and eighteen Puranas were finished. He had learnt all scriptures. Vallabheharya's father did when he was hardly ten years old. He wanted his mother's permission to go on pilgrimage. His mother allowed him to go on the holy Journey. He travelled over particularly the whole India more than once. During the long journey the saint was deeply absorbed in the thinking of Vishnu, the Lord of creation and attained enlightment.[64] Vallabhacharya gives special importance to Bhakti (devotion) which according to him can only be conferred by God. Bhakti means spontaneous attachment to God, who himself choose his devotees.

5.6.2 Surdas (1478 – 1580 A.D.)

Surdas was also the most important mystic saint of the Krishna Bhakti culture. Surdas spread and popularise the Bhakti culture in the 16th century. His name was 'surdhwaj', but he is known as Surdas Madan Mohan. There is a controversy among scholars about the place of birth and details of his early life. It is however certain that he was not the same Surdas who is mentioned in the Ain-i-Akbari as the blind bard of Agra and a Poet musician of Akbar's Court. He was in or about 1478 A.D. (Vaishak Shukla 5, 1536 V.S.). Surdas's early childhood and youth spend in caught that and Renuka on Yamuna. Which is 12 miles far from Agra. Here at Renuka he met Vallabhacharya, in 1509 A. D. and became his disciple. According to Abul Fazl Renuka was in the 16th century 'a much-frequented place of Hindu worship'. Surdas must have been born of indigent parents who would not otherwise have forever parted with their gifted though blind son. There is no clear evidence that he was born blind. The study of Surdas's literature suggests that Surdas was probably too born blind because a blind man could not have spoken so well about the shape, form, and colours as well as minute observations of life. Surdas was very much famous for his extraordinary intelligence, native genius, uncommon intellectual and spiritual gift and for his individually. He sang kirtan along with other devotees while he was at Govardhan he frequently visited Mathura and Gokul. it is said that he also met emperor Akbar at Mathura on later's request. Surdas was convinced of the importance of unflinching devotion and profound selfless love over reason an intellectualism and he convey his convictism in a series of charming verses devotional songs and lyrics.

5.6.3 Srikrishna Chaitana (1486 -1533 A.D.)

Mahaprabhu Sri Krishna Chaitanya was a Bhakti saint of Krishna cult of Sanguna sect. He was born on full moon day of Falgun 1407.[65] Saka (16th February 1486 A. D.) at Navadvipa or Nadia in Bengal. His father Jagannath Misra and mother Saichi were very religious and pious. The childhood nana of Chaitanya was Visambhar and Nimai. Chaitanya is known by the name Gauranga. Chaitanya's early education was in Sanskrit texts. At a comparatively young age Chaitanya was married to a beautiful girl named Laxmi, but she died very soon. He married again. Even as a married man passion for devotion was immense. He became disciple of saint named, Ishwarapuri in 1508 A.D. at the age of twenty-two. Ishwarpuri was a famous saint of Gaya. Chaitanya believed in the Krishna culture with Radha and Krishna in unison and because a sincere devotee and passionate lover of God in that form. Chaitanya believed that Bhakti was the only way of salvation.

5.6.4 Mirabai (1498 – 1546 A.D.)

Like Surdas and Tulsidas Mirabai was also Bhakti saint of 16th century. She was the follower of Krishna culture of Saguna school of Bhakti. Mirabai was born to Rajput parents of aristocratic class at the village of Kudki in the Marta district of Rajasthan in 1498 A.D. She was the only daughter of Rao Ratan Sen of Marts and a cousin sister of famous Jaimal.[68] It is said that Mira had devotional instinct from a very tender age. When she was a child of five years, on an occasion of marriage procession asked her mother about her own bridegroom, the mother replied that Girdhar Gopal (Lord Krishna) was her husband since then Mira recognised Girdhar Gopal as her husband and was devoted to her throughout her life. She had now one fine image of Krishna. At the attainment of puberty, she was married to Mewar's Rana Sanga's eldest son and prince Bhojraj in 1516 A.D. But unfortunately, Bhojraj died sometime between 1518 -1523 A.D. After her husband's death she devoted herself entirely to religious pursuits. "In the early stage of her devotion she signed to have been engrossed in her quest of the Lord". In the next stage of her Bhakti, she believed as if she had found him. In the final she seems to have felt as if she had He had become here. She had a pilgrimage of Mathura, Vrindaban and finally settled in Dwarika where she died in 1546 A.D. However, about the date of Mira's death there is controversy and we do not know the exact date. She had firm faith in God and worshipped him in the form of Krishna whom she unstinted love and devotion. The sympathetic colonel Tod says that she was the most celebrated princes of her time for beauty and romantic poetry and that 'her composition was numerous, though better known to the worshippers of Hindu Apollo, than to the ribald bards'. Mira Bai has written many devotional songs. The songs are composed in Brai Bhasha and partly in Rajasthan and some of her verses are in Gujrati. These lyrics are full of love and devotion.

5.6.5 Tulsi Das (1532 -1623 A.D.)

Tulsidas was other important saint of the Saquna school of Bhakti. Tulsidas was born at the village of Rajapur in the district of Banda near Allahabad. He was born in the year 1532 A.D. in the Saryuparin Brahman family. However, in Bhaktmal his birthplace has been mentioned as Ganga Barah (Soron) in the province of Tari. He was born in Sanvat 1589 (1532 A.D.) and his father's name was Atma Ram Dube, his mother's Hulsi. He was married to Ratnavali. At an early age Tulsidas became orphan but was brought up and educated by his father's Guru Narsinghdas He learnt sastras and other religious works. Tulsidas refers to his childhood in his Kavitavali. He also refers to his first teacher Narhari Anand to whom he owned much. It was at Sukar Kheta, writes Tulsidas in his Ramcharitmanas, 'that I was told again and again by my teacher the story of Rama but being a child, I could only follow it partially on account of the limitations of my intelligence'. It is said that due to his wife's rebuke he left married life and decided to spend his life in devotion. He worshipped Lord Rama and thus belonged the Rama culture of Saguna school. He undertook a pilgrimage to important holy places and spent a good deal of his time at Chitrakuta, Ayodhya and Varanasi. He wrote his magnuna opus, the Ramcharitmanas at Ayodhya.[67]

5.7   Bhakti saints of Nirgun school

5.7.1 Guru Nanak (1469 – 1538 A.D.)

Nanak was born at sai Bhoe-ki Talwandi, now known as Nankana Sahib in Shaikhpura district about 65 km. west of Lahore on April 15, 1469, A.D. [68] But the most accepted date of Manak's birth is full moon day of Kartik month of Hindi calendar in 1469 A.D. His father's name was Kalyan Rai or Kalu and mother's Tripta. He belonged to the Bedi branch of Khatris. His father was a shopkeeper as well as the village Patwari or accountant of the local landlord, Rai Bular Bhatti a recently converted Musalman. Nanak learnt Airthmetic and accountancy in Lande Mahajani from his father reading and writing from a Brahmin and Persian and Arabic from a Mawlvi. Being a contemplative mind Manak was happiest in the company of saints both Hindu and Musalman. He wants to serve humanity as a devotee of God. Nanak's bent of mind did not appeal to his worldly-minded father. Nank was married to Sulakhani daughter of Mulchand Chano Khatri of pakhoke Randhawa near Batata in 1487 A.D. 'He had two sons Srichand born in 1491 and Lakshmidas was born in 1496'. Married life did not change Nanak's life. Nanak did not believe in any religion either. According to him 'There was only a change of body produced by a Supreme Miracle'. Nanak gave a practical shape to the idea of the Bhakti movement by coming in close contact with masses. He took up long Journey throughout his pilgrimages he had been spreading the message of love and caste lessness. He did not advocate idolatry either. The advent of Islam has infused new thoughts in Indian philosophy. The sufi had contributed much to the new movement.

5.7.2 Raidas

Raidas was born in Banaras to low caste parents who were chamar or worker of leather as mentioned by him later. His father's name was Ragghu and mothers Ghurbinya. He was a later disciple of Ramananda.[69] Probably after a quite few year of Kabir. He was devoted to saints and spent all the money which he was having. This act annoyed his father's house along with his wife and lived in a small hut. His simple way of life and spiritual knowledge was appreciated by the people. It is said that a Rajput queen accepted him as her Guru. Raidas was basically a saint of Nirgun School like Kabir. His cardinal doctrines are very similar to that of Kabir. Raidas's aim was also to bring about the unity between Hinduism and Islam. His song breath a spirit of humility. He did not indulge in high philosophic speculation about the nature and essence of God and his relationship with the world and nature. Like Kabir he was Rekhta, the Persian language and Sufi terms to show the identity of Hinduism and Islam. It suggested that he might have come in contact of Sufi saint who influenced his thought considerably. Raidas believed in one personal God. According to him there is one supreme being who is the absolute lord of all. Raidas was against the piligrimages, fasts, shaving the heads and dancing in temples and was opposed to idol worship. The teaching of Raidas resulted in removed of distinction between the higher and the lower castes of Hindus and Muslims or our castes in religious field. Both Hindus and Muslims were Hindu Muslim unity in the society and were able to remove old age hatred between the two creeds.

5.7.3 Dadu Dayal (1544 – 1603 A.D.)

Dadu Dayal was one of the prominent saints of the 16th century. He was born in 1544 A.D. at Ahmedabad, but he spent most of his life in Naraina and Bharaina in Rajasthan.[70] Dadu's father was Lodhi Ram a merchant of Ahmedabad, according to some accounts Dadu belongs to the Mahchi, (tenor) caste. Thus, there is controversy about his caste, some believe has was Gujrati, Brahman, other believed as Mochi. According to Mohsin Fani Dadu was Cotton Cleaner. Dadu left his home in quest of knowledge and travelled throughout northern Indian and visited many places of piligrimage and became a devotee. He always enjoyed the company of learned pious and devout persons. At the age of twenty-five Dadu settled down at Sambhar, near the famous Salt Lake in Ajmer suba of then Mughal Empire. Seven years after the arrival in Sambhar Dadu's a son was born to him. He had three sons and two daughters namely Hawwa (Eve) and Shabho. It is said that emperor Akbar was anxious to meet Dadu and sent many nobles to have brought him as his palace. But Dadu replied that he has no skill in the art of flattery, his trust was in God alone. However, with great efforts of Raja Bhagwan Das, Dadu was pursusded to meet the emperor and had an interview with emperor. According to Ain-i-Akbari Abul fzsl and Birbal met Dadu at the initial stage and reported to the emperor the greatness of the saint.

5.7.4 Sundardas (1596 – 1689 A.D.)

Sundardas was born in 1596 A.D. at Deosa near Jaipur.[71] He belonged to Bania family. Once saint Dadu Dayal visited Deosa at that time Sundardas was six years old since then he became Dadu's disciple. Since then, the

Child became known as Sundar (handsome) Sundardas lived with the preceptor Dadu at Naraina. He soon became known for his outstanding genius at a saint. After the death of his preceptor in 1603 A.D. Sundardas came back to his home. He remained at his village for a shorter period and then went to Banaras where he thoroughly studied religious scriptures till the age of thirty. He left Benaras and came back at Deosa. At Deosa, Sundardas was joined by his two disciple paragdas and Rajjab to spread the religion of Bhakti. Sundardas settled at Fatehpur Shekhavati. The Chieftain of Fatehpur Nawab Alifkhan and his two sons Daulat Khan and Tabir were admirers of Sundardas. Sundardas travelled widely and almost all areas of India were covered especially the regions of Rajputana Gujrat and Punjab. Sundardas was a very good scholar of Sanskrit and he learned Persian and other languages. His main work is Sundarvilasa. Sundardas was a man of culture. He was a very good poet. However, he was unable to express his spiritual experience clearly. He did not condemn the existing social order as he was a firm believer of not to injure one's feelings. Though he was a bachelor but praised the virtuous wives. Similarly, warriors were also praised by him. He strengthened unity between Hindus and Muslims through his deeds and sayings.

5.7.5 Pran Nath

Pran Nath was Bhakti saint of the letter part of Urn 17th century. Pran Nath was a Kshatriya by caste and founder of the sect Dharmis in the reign of Aurangzeb. 'He acquired great influence over Chhatrasal Raja of Panna by the discovery of a diamond mine it is said'. Pran Nath was well acquainted with the sacred books of Islam. The mission of Pran Nath was to unite the two religious through his teachings. His aim in life was to reconcile the two hostile communities Pran Nath's thinking represented has vision of communal harmony, sympathy, cooperation, and tolerance. He says there is no Hindu and no Musalman all are creations of the same on almighty. Pran Nath was totally against the caste system. 'His creed proclaims the abolition of the worship of idols, and caste restrictions as well as the supremacy of the Brahmins'. He equally denounced idolatry of Hindus and ritualism of Islam. In his Kulsum Sarup a work in the Gujrati language, he brought together texts from the Quran and the Vedas and showed that they are not incompatible. As a test of a disciple's assets to the real identity of the Hindu and Musalman creeds, the ceremony of initiation consisted in common dinning at the gathering Pran Nath wrote fourteen treatises all in verses some extracts from his Qiyamat name are given 'Go to the followers (Ummat) and tell then rise the faithful ones, for the day of resurrection has come'. He says, 'I tell you in accordance with what the

Quran says and I relate before you the story'. He who is a special leader of the following should stand careful. All of you, whether Hindus or Muslims, will have a common faith. Pran Nath was liberal and made no distinction between Hindus and Muslims. He said both Hindus and Muslims are equal. Prannath's philosophy was under great impact of sufi philosophy. The teachings of Prannath had great impact on the contemporary society, influencing both Hindus & Muslims.

5.7.6 Jagjivandas

Jagjivandas was born at Sardalia in the Barabanki district of Uttar Pradesh in 1682 A.D. He was Chandel Thakur by caste. He belonged to the Nirgun school of Kabir. He spent most of his life at Katwa between Barabanki and Luckhnow. Jagjivan Das spread his teachings all over India through his disciples. He had number of disciples hailing from all castes i.e., Thakur, Chamar, Brahmin and Muslim. His teachings were collected in his three principal works Janan Prakas, Mahapralaya and Prathem Granth. He succeeded in establishing some community of though between himself and Islam. At least two of his disciples were Musalman. Jagjivandas had reorganised the older Satnami sector which has been crushed by Aurangzeb. He preached the doctrine of the unity of God. His God was beyond qualities (Nirguna). He laid great stress upon self-surrender and indifference towards the world. Jagjivandas said that all human beings are son and daughter of the supreme being. Thus propagated the principle of universal brothhood. He held that the goal of human endeavours was absorption in God through the help of a spiritual guide (guru). Truth gentleness and harmlessness were main virtues in his eyes, for attainment of Bhakti. Jagjivandas proclaimed the principal of universal brotherhood. He says all the human beings are equal in this world, The mission of Jagjivandas was to write in Muslims and Non-Muslims. Jagjivandas seems to be much influenced by Sufi philosophy as he used sufis terminology in his preaching's and discourses. His teachings brough tremendous effect on Hindu & Muslim unity.

5.8   Other Saints of Maharashtra

5.8.1 Saint Dnyaneshwar (1275 - 1296 A.D.)

The first, and some say the greatest, of the saints in the Maratha Varkari tradition was Dnyaneshwara, also known as Gnyanadeva. [the variant names are based on three Sanskrit words: Jnana / Dnyan meaning knowledge, ishwar used in the sense of lord, and deva, God. The Marathi can also be transcribed in western (roman) script as Dnyan, thus Dynaneshwara; also, Gyan in Hindi, thus Gyaneshvara, or Gyandeo. Additionally, the ending vara can be transcribed as vara, thus Dnyaneshwara. Born in 1275 in his mother's village, Alandi, near Pune, this young saint achieved much in his short life taking his samadhi in 1296. He was the greatest saint of Maharashtra. He was born in 1275 A.D. in a Brahmin family at Apegaon near Paithan situated on the banks of the river Godavari. He was blessed with divine knowledge and showed signs of greatness from his childhood. He is said to have performed many miracles. It cannot be denied that he was highly learned and talented. He wrote a beautiful commentary in Marathi on the Bhagavad Gita called the Dnyaneshwari at the tender age of 15. Besides his famous work, Dnyaneshwar also wrote Amritanuhhava and Bhavartha Dipika in Marathi. His followers belonged to all castes, as he did not believe in the caste system. He condemned rituals, ceremonies, and sacrifices in religious worship. His followers are known as Varkaris. They believe in attaining the presence of God through religious songs or Bhajans and prayers. They worship Lord Vithoba whom they believe to be the incarnation of Lord Vishnu.

5.8.2 Saint Namdeo

Saint Namdeo was a follower of Saint Dnyaneshwar. There were some twenty saint's contemporary with Namdeo, mostly from the area surrounding the sacred city of Pandharpur, who went on regular pilgrimage to the temple of Vithoba (Vitthala) in Pandharpur. They belong roughly to the period 1250-1350 A.D., with a few from the following century. They came from all strata of society. He was a tailor by caste and was five years older than his guru. He travelled all over Maharashtra with Saint Dnyaneshwar. Following the teachings of his celebrated master, he believed in the equality of all men. He advised people to follow the Bhakti Marga or the path of deep devotion to God. He created in them a strong desire to protect their religion and have a deep love for their motherland! Like Kabir, he condemned idol worship. He carried on the work of Saint Dnyaneshwar after the latters death in 1296 A.D. He composed songs not only in Marathi but also in Hindi and spread the message of equality within and outside Maharashtra. He travelled all over India and went to Punjab. Some of his devotional songs are found in the Granth Sahib and other religious books of the Sikhs. His songs are sung with great love and devotion not only in Maharashtra but also in other parts of the world.

5.8.3 Saint Janabai

Jani (Janabai) was the maidservant from childhood of Damseth and his son Namdeo, caring for the child Namdeo and later the adult Namdeo, being treated more like a daughter. She gained her spiritual realisation from

Namdeo. As a Marathi woman saint, she is regarded as being second only to Muktabai. There are about three hundred abhangas (songs) attributed to Jani which have remained popular in Maharashtra, most of which can be found in the Namdeo Gatha, and some have been translated into English. One of Janabai's most popular verses depicts Lord Vithoba (Vitthal) as a loving parent to his devotees: My Vithoba has many children, a company of children surrounds him. He has Nivritti sitting on his shoulder and holds Sopan by the hand. Dnyaneshvara walks ahead, and beautiful Muktai behind. Gora the potter is in his lap, and with him are Chokha and Jiva. Banka sits on his back, and Namdeo holds his finger. Jani says, look at this Gopal who loves his bhaktas. Banka was the wife of Raka the potter. Jiva is known as a brahmin contemporary of the 15th century north Indian saint, Kabir. Jani's most famous abhanga is the extraordinary text translated into English by the twentieth century Maratha poet, Arun Kolatkar, who conveys the essence of the original through the starkness of his imagery: I eat God, I drink God, I sleep on God, I buy God, I count God, I deal with God, God is here, God is there, void is not devoid of God. Jani says, 'God is within, God is without and moreover, there is God to spare'.

5.8.4 Sawata Mali

Savata mali was a gardener-saint whose Marathi abhangas are sung to this day by those who till the soil in Maharashtra.

5.8.5 Chokhamela

Chokhamela was of the Mahar caste, the untouchables of Maharashtra. His abhangas are full of a deep awareness of his low caste. This translation is by the Marathi scholar S.G.Tulpule. A sugarcane may be crooked, and yet its juice is not crooked. A bow may be curved, and yet the arrow is not. A river may have windings, and yet its water is even.

5.8.6 Narhari Sonar

Narhari Sonar was a goldsmith in Pandharpur who initially differentiated between the gods Shiva and Vishnu, but under the guidance of Dnyaneshwara and Namdeo rose above the relativity of duality and merged himself into the infinite oneness of the Divine. His Marathi abhangas are still sung throughout Maharashtra.

5.8.7 Gora Kumbhar

Gora the potter-saint tested the spirituality of those who professed to be saints in Pandharpur, including Namdeo who he originally judged to be an unbaked pot, i.e., not yet spiritually evolved, sending him to Visoba Khechara. Later Gora and Namdeo were to meet again, and Gora declared in an abhanga (song) that there was now no difference between him and Namdeo. Although there are some 43 surviving abhangas attributed to Gora, most mention later saints in the text and therefore are unlikely to be by Gora himself.

5.8.8 Raka Kumbhar

The kilm was ready, all the earthen pot had been nearly placed in rows upon rows and Raka Kumbhar painstakingly lit the fire and stoked it well. As the fire blazed get shut and sealed the door and let the heat so the job of baking the pots. After some time Raka, hearing persistent mews and 'miaos' around the kiln, went to see what was amiss. To his surprise and horror, he saw a she cat running hither and thither round and round the oven, with eyes wide in terror and calling on helplessly so that Raka understood that unknown to him, she had left her litter of kittens in the interior of the brick oven. By now the fire was roaring in full blaze. It was impossible to put it out at this stage and Raka thought of Panduranga. Raka was one of the numerous saints and devotees who took birth in the land of Manahrashtra, seven centuries ago. A contemporary of Dnyaneshwar, Namadeo and Gora the potter-saints, his heart melted with compassion for all creatures.

5.8.9 Santaji Pawar

During the great wave of religious devotion which swept over Maharashtra, in the days of Saint Dnyaneshwar and Namdeva, there lived in the Ranjana village, Santaji Pawar, a sardar. Santaji was born with the name of the Lord on his lips and relished nothing more than to repeat the name of Narayana, Govinda, at all hours of the day-night. He attended kathas and lectures on philosophy and was completely detached from worldly concerns. It seemed to him that the world was the greatest hindrance to spiritual progress for he was convinced that the world was a transitory creation bound for destruction whereas Vithala's name, the indestructible Sea of Bliss was the only solace of the Bhaktas lost in this maze of samsara. Following his desire to devote his life to the search for Truth and renounce the world to follow the hard disciplines of such sadhana, he placed his head on his monther' feet, seeking her blessings for the fulfilment of his resolve. Trying to deter him, she asked; 'why leave the world, my son? What has it done to you that you must forsake it? What will you gain thereby, tell me?' Pandurangs's ways are unpredictable, and it was to a vani (gracer) in a nearby village that he appeared, ordering him to prepare forthwith a good meal for his devotee. Obeying his instructions, the vani cooked a meal and took it into the forest where he found Santaji seated under a tree and crying inwardly 'O Lord, come to me!' He told him about his dream and how he came on orders of Shri Vithala to give him a good and wholesome meal in the forest. But Santaji's tears flowed anew. 'You too saw the Lord, and I haven't!' Kanta and the vani began to feed him with their own hands as he sat motionless, overwhelmed with longing for the darshan of God. 'I am a sinner, O Lord, I take refuge in Thee! All I desire is to see thy blissful face, just once!' Then Narayan, merciful as ever to his sincere devotes, stood revealed before hi smiling at his beloved child. He lifted Santaji and Kanta and embraced them both, 'Ask', he said, whatever you wish, I shall grant it. But they both has no wish except to see him, love him and serve him. Seeing they were free of attachment, the Lord blessed them: 'Eat now, do not fear, I shall always be with you. Accept madhukari, for food begged this is pure and remember me in your hearts all the time'. Yes, said Namdeva, the great saint of Pandharpur and devotee of Vithala, God takes so many forms to save his children. When the famous Ekadashi yatra of Pandharpur took place, thousands of devotees were unable to cross the river in space, so like the Koli for Santaji and his wife, God took the form of a giant tortoise and ferried them across. So, all could join in the enthusiastic kirtanas of the temple of Vithala.

5.8.10 Saint Janajasawanta

In Namadeva's time, there lived a saint named Janajasawanta who was so imbued with the presence of God that he could see nothing else. To him as others of his time, God permeated all things and so Vithala who loves his devotees entered his humble abode as a servant. 'Put me on to anything', asked the Lord of his devotee, 'all I require in payment is just my kept'. The fortunate home prospered as Vithala's in-fluence filled it and all the work was despatched by him with the greatest ease. As Namadeva wisely remarked good doubles the goof and so his work increased and produced plenty. Whether God laboured in the fields or carried heavy loads of firewood from the forest, Janajasawanta saw Him around him wherever he went. His heart melted with tenderness for his beloved Helpmate: 'Vithala is carrying my plough!' he sang in ecstasy. Vithala indeed worked as no servant would ever have done. He drew endless buckets of water from the well, watered the fields and carrying their young ones on his shoulders, he escorted the saint's wife, daughters, and daughters-in-law home from distant villages. He left no work undone. 'Oh, how shall I describe it?' cried the overwhelmed Janajasawanta, 'Vitho is my sole Caretaker!'. So concluded Namadeva to all who heart him while watching the perfect team of God and his faithful devotee: 'Now remember O my friends, always remember!'

5.8.11 Jagamitra Naga

Jagamitra Naga was a humble, kind-hearted brahmin banker who lived on alms and devoted all his time to singing kirtans with great joy. He was born in Parli Vijanath in the year 1330. Jagamitra was content with whatever he got by begging and seeing Vasudeva in all things. He treated joy and suffering alike and never felt separate from God. Therefore, the villagers respected him and loved him. Some miscreants, envious of his popularity, contrived to set fire to his house in the middle of the night. People came running when the blaze was already consuming everything. With tears in their eyes and shielding their faces from the furnace-like heat they prayed to Panduranga (Krishana). 'O Lord, why did you allow this to happen to such a good soul as Naga?' They pleaded with God to save Nage even as He had saved Prahald and the Pandavas. 'O Panduranga, Vithala, this is the time protect your devotee!' In a faint voice, he pleaded with Jagamitra to spare his life, 'I am an accursed sinner, forgive my pride and the offence I caused you. Remove that tiger and I shall never give you cause to regrate it'. I take refuge at your feet, he added meekly. The tiger roared as it to pounce on his prey, but Jagamitra restrained him and said gently, 'come on now let us go back to the forests', my lord. And he walked beside him into the jungle. The tiger disappeared and with a heart overflowing with love, Jagamitra fell at the feet of the Lord who embraced him. "The lord's devotee has won over the Subendar, said the villagers. Has hari ever forsaken his dear ones?" they added wistfully. Jagamitra left many beautiful abhangas and took Mahasamadhi in Parli, in 1380.

5.8.12 Kanhopatra

Kanhopatra was the beautiful daughter of a dancer who came to the attention of a Muslim king. Rather than submit to his desires, she took her eternal samadhi at the foot of the altar in the temple in Pandharpur. She is buried in the grounds of the temple, where an unusual tree subsequently grew. She left some abhangas of which only a handful have been translated into English. This is her final abhanga: O Lord of the fallen. Why do you torment your devotees so? They are O Lord but your other form. Who else, O Pandarinath, is there to go to? Alas, who is to blame if the jackal has taken the share of the lion? Kanhopatra says, take me from my body which I offer at Your feet! The traditional account of Kanhopatra is given by the eighteenth-century pundit, Mahipati in his Bhaktavijaya. There is uncertainty as to her dates. Tulpule dates Kanhopatra to the mid-15th century in his 1979 survey but places her as a contemporary of Namdev in his 1984 study of Indian mysticism.

5.8.13 Bhanudas

Long ago, when the saints if Maharashtra congregated in Pandharpur to hold Hari Katha and Kirtans in the sacred temple of Vithala, their ecstatic chants of the Holy Name sounded like a gigantic roar of joy. With tears in their eyes and beatific smiles on their faces, they danced and sang in one voice, fully relishing the sweetness of the Name of God, they could go on in this way for days and nights without a break and without feeling the slightest exhaustion. They were in fact most reluctant to end the performance. The extraordinary Kirtans took place regularly, as they do even today, on every Ekadhashi and other auspicious days. Bhanudas born in 1448 at Pratistana or Paithana, he was to be the great grandfather of the famous saint Eknath.

5.8.14 Saint Eknath

He lived in the sixteenth century. Saint Eknaths beliefs and teachings were like those of the great Maratha saints, Saint Dnyaneshwar and Namdev. He advocated social equality and preached the abolition of distinctions based on class, caste, and creed. Thus, he carried on the work started by Dnyaneshwar and Namdev. He preached that one could devote oneself to God by leading a normal family life and discharging all functions of a householder. He did not believe in rituals, ceremonies, and other orthodox ways of worship. He preferred to use Marathi in his religious discourses and composed songs in the language of the common people. He wrote numerous religious songs called Abhangas, Owees, and Bharuds. These songs are still very popular in Maharashtra. Eknath is the link in the Maharashtrian religious tradition between Dnyaneshvara and Namdev in the thirteenth century (CE) and Ramdas and Tukaram in the seventeenth century. He was aware of the work of the earlier saints, writing songs in praise of Dnyaneshvara, Nivrittinath, Sopandev and Muktabai; and composing biographies of Namdev, Gora, Savatamali and Chokhamela. Even more so, he gathered the various versions of the Dnyaneshvari extant in the 16th century and edited what he felt to be the authentic version, which has, for the most part, been followed by later scholars. Eknath's other major work is his translation and commentary in Marathi of the eleventh skanda (or part) of the Sanskrit Bhagavata Purana, popularly known as the Ekanathi Bhagavata. Whilst the full work (of eighteen thousand verses) has not been translated into English, the twenty-third chapter has been translated by Justin Abbott as Bhikshugita: There are many Sufi influences in this work as demonstrated by Van Skyhawk (1992). Eknath also composed a commentary on the ninth chapter of the second skanda of the Bhagavata Purana, known as the Chatu shloki Bhagavata. His Rukmini-svayamvara is a poem on the marriage of Rukmini to Lord Krishna based on the narrative in the tenth skanda of the Bhagavata. His unfinished Bhavartha-Ramayana is a Marathi version of the Valmiki Ramayana.

5.8.15 Saint Tukaram (1608 – 1651 A.D.)

Saint Tukaram was a contemporary of Chatrapati Shivaji, and though he never met the Maratha ruler, Shivaji was greatly influenced by his ideas. Saint Tukaram was born in a Vaishya family in 1608 A.D. in a village near Poona. He was deeply religious even in his childhood and spent his time singing devotional songs in praise of his favourite deity. Lord Vithoba of Pandharpur. Like Dnyaneshwar, Namdeo, Eknath, and other Maratha saints, he believed in the Bhakti Marga or path of devotion to God. He often sang songs in praise of Lord Vithoba. He visited the temple of Lord Vithoba at Pandharpur twice a year in the months of Ashad (June-July) and Kartik (October-November). Saint Tukaram sang devotional songs which he himself composed. He performed kirtans at devotional gatherings and sang his own devotional songs called Abhangas. Thousands of people flocked to listen to him. He preached them the virtues of piety, forgiveness, and peace of mind. He also gave them the message of equality and brotherhood.

5.8.16 Saint Ramadas

Guru Ramdas. His real name was Narayan, but he preferred to call himself Ramdas meaning the servant of Rama. He was a born devotee and was deeply religious from his childhood. He had decided to devote himself to religion and to the worship of Lord Rama. He carried out a great amount of penance (tapasya) at Panchavati (Nasik), a place associated with Lord Rama's life in exile. Ramdas became a great admirer of Hanuman and looked upon him as the god of strength and an apostle of Brahmacharya. Guru Ramdas lived during the period when there was some amount of religious persecution from the Muslim sultans in the Deccan. He advised the people to be strong enough to protect their faith. He made Lord Rama and Hanuman his ideals. He built several temples in honour of Hanuman in Maharashtra. He preached to the people that religion is the most precious possession of man.

6.   Sufism in India during 16th and 19th centuries

As Sufism began in India during the 12th century A.D. which continued, flourished, and patronised by Delhi sultans reached at its Zenith in the 16th century. During 16th and 17th centuries a good number of Sufi saints preached and practiced Sufism in different regions of India. Some of the famous saints of this period were Shaikh Mohd., Sarmad, Shaikh Salim Chishti,

Shaikh Ahmad, Khwaja Baqi Billah, Shah Burhan, Shaikh Nizamuddin of Ambethi, Shaikh Khwaja Abdul. Shahid Shaikh Taha and Imam Waji-ud-din Gujrati. Many Sufis wrote the Marathi literature in Medieval Deccan. Shah Muntoji Bahmani, Ambar Hussain, Chand Bodhale, Shaikh Muhammad Shrigondekar, Alam Khan, Shah Baigh, Bajid Pathan, Latif Shah and Shaikh Sultan are the famous Sufi poets and authors of many books in Deccan. Shah Muntoji Bahmani was the seventeenth century Sufi poet and author. He wrote number of books like, Prakashdip, Siddh sanket, Hindu-Islam Darshan etc. in Marathi. His manuscripts are available at Rajwade Research Center and Shree Samarth Wangdevata Mandir Research Center at Dhule, Maharashtra. Ambar Hussain of Daulatabad wrote Ambar Husaini and Samshlok in Marathi. Shaikh Muhammad Shrigondekar (1548- 1618 A.D.) was another famous Sufi saint from Ahmednager Maharashtra. He was the Guru of Malojiraje Bhosale (the grandfather of king Shivaji). His literature: Yogsangram, Pawan Vijay, Bhakti Bodha and Bharud are available today. Alam Khan wrote in Marathi books; Gurumahatmya and Updeshpad. These all-Sufi authors from Sixteenth to Eighteenth century made the literature in Marathi language. The proposed composition has the special focus on historical study and review of Marathi literature made by Sufis in Deccan with the ideas of harmonious coexistence within it. Previous scholars, Dhere R.C., Padma Shri Prof. Pathan U.M. and Dusan Deak focused on literary aspects of Muslim writings in Marathi. Major part of Deccan region covered by Marathi speaking people today.

6.1 Muinuddin Chishti (1141 A.D- 1235 A.D.)

The Chishti order bears the name of Chisht, a town in Khurasan, which lies about one hundred kilometres east of Herat. The spiritual founder of the order was Khwaja Abu Ishaq Shami (d. 940) who came from Syria and settled for a while in Chisht. He was a disciple and a khalifah of Mimshad Dinwari, (the latter being a khalifah of Hubayra of Basra and a disciple of Junayd of Baghdad). He traced his spiritual lineage through Hasan Basri back to Ali-ibn-Abu-Talib and the Prophet Muhammad and is believed to be ninth after Ali in the line of spiritual succession. Muinuddin Chishti belonged to this silsila and is credited with bringing it to India, where it went on to become one of the most influential orders. Khwaja Muinuddin Chishti (1141-1235 A.D.) was born in Sijistan (Sistan) and brought up in Khorasan. He was only fifteen when his father died leaving him in possession of a garden and a water mill. The economic situation of his family deteriorated with his father's death, so he had to work in the garden himself. One day while he was working, a majzub (ecstatic) named Ibrahim Qanduzi came into the garden. The young Khwaja was polite and well-mannered. Not only did he offer the dervish a seat under a shady tree but also brought him a bunch of grapes to eat. The dervish recognized the spiritual potential of the boy standing in front of him. He took some sesame seeds out of his bag, chewed them, and put them in Muinuddin's mouth.

Once Muinuddin ate the seeds, a spiritual connection was established, and Muinuddin's latent spirituality was awakened. This experience had such an impact on him that he sold his possessions and distributed the money among the poor. This version of the story of how he came to renounce the world is the most authentic. The untimely death of his father might have indeed fostered his serious and introspective temperament and urged him to devote his life to a higher purpose. It might have been the shock of death that took him, a boy immersed in the world, from all that was mundane and brought him into the realm of the spiritual. And, it might have been the visit of Khwaja Ibrahim that finally encouraged him to detach his mind and heart from earthly pursuits and devote himself to the spiritual life he had sought all along. He left his home and began to wander from place to place in search of knowledge. For many years he lived in Balkh, Samarqand and Bhukhara, studying the Qur'an, hadith, fiqh and theology. From there he travelled to Harwan, a suburb of Nishapur, where he met Shaikh Usman Harwani, a Sufi who became his spiritual mentor. Under his tutelage he practiced rigorous spiritual exercises for two and a half years. On completing his training, he was given a khirqa (gown) by the Shaikh and appointed his khalifah. From then onwards he was allowed to train his own disciples.

6.1.1 Khwaja Hamduddin Nagauri (1351 A.D.)

Hamduddin Nagauri was born in Delhi sometime after its conquest in 1192. It is said that his father, Ahmad, came from Lahore and settled in Delhi soon after Muslim rule was established in India. His education was traditional and includedArabic, Persian and the religious sciences. Later, he acquired a good command over the Hindavi dialect used in Rajasthan. He became a disciple of Muinuddin Chishti and stayed with him in Ajmer. Shaikh Hamiduddin was of a highly spiritual disposition and lived a very simple and austere life. Although, the Chishti saints were allowed to receive unsolicited gifts (futuh) to support themselves, he preferred to work for his living. He had a small plot of land in a village called Suwali near Nagaur. He supported himself solely on the income from this land and did not accept any offerings. He followed the principle that no harm should be done to any form of life. His keen sensitivity is evident in the fact that he himself was a vegetarian, and he asked his followers too to follow the same path.

Several Shaikh Hamiduddin's descendants continued his mission and Nagaur developed into a strong centre of Sufism. This was to a great extent due to Khwaja Husain Nagaur, a descendant of Shaikh Hamiduddin. Khwaja Husain followed in the footsteps of Shaikh Hamiduddin and lived a very simple life. He cultivated the land himself and whatever money he received from Sultan Ghiyasuddin Khilji of Malwa (1469-1501) was spent on constructing the tomb of Khwaja Muinuddin Chishti in Ajmer and the gateway of Hamiduddin's tomb in Nagaur. He was also a great religious scholar. He wrote a commentary on the Quran entitled Nur un-Nabi and compiled several treatises on Sufism. He also wrote a biography of Al Ghazali. He attached great importance to education and devoted himself to the religious and spiritual uplift of the people Khwaja Ziyauddin Nakhshabi (d. 1351) was the best-known disciple of Shaikh Farid, the grandson of Hamiduddin. He was a scholar and a Sufi poet. His book, titled Silk us Suluk ('String of Sufism') deals with the basic principles of the Sufi mission in 151 short chapters. He regarded a good knowledge of the shariah as necessary to an understanding of Sufism.

6.1.2 Khwaja Qutbuddin Bakhtiar Kaki

The Chishti order became firmly established in Ajmer and Nagaur, thanks to the efforts respectively of Khwaja Muinuddin Chishti and his disciple, Hamiduddin Nagauri. The disciples who succeeded them worked hard to spread the teachings of the order further afield. One of them was Khwaja Qutbuddin Bakhtiar Kaki, who established a strong Chishti centre in Delhi. By the time Khwaja Qutbuddin came to Delhi, the political scene had undergone a change. Sultan Shamshuddin Iltutmish (1210-35 A.D.) had made the city his capital, for Delhi was the only remaining island of peace in the entire region. The Mongols had invaded Central Asia and Iran, which meant that the Muslims in those areas lost their political power. People therefore flocked to Hindustan and its new capital. These included a large number of princes, nobles, scholars, and Sufis, all of them looking for a safe haven. It was against this backdrop that Qutbuddin Bakhtiar Kaki arrived in Delhi. He was born in Osh,(Kyrgyzstan), in the Central Asian province of Jaxartes. His father died when he was 18 months old, and it fell to his mother to see to his religious education. Legendary accounts tell of his spiritual initiation at the hands of Khizr. When he grew up, his mother arranged his marriage, but he took no interest in family life, so he divorced his wife and left for Baghdad. There, in a mosque, he met Khwaja Muinuddin. Greatly impressed, he became his disciple. After Khwaja Muinuddin left Baghdad, Qutubuddin went to Multan, where he met Shaikh Bahauddin Zakariya. He stayed in Multan for several years and when the Mongols threatened the area, he left for Delhi. Sultan Iltutmish gave him a warm welcome, and many eminent people came to him for spiritual guidance.

6.1.3 Fariduddin Ganj Shakar (1175-1265 A.D.)

Shaikh Fariduddin was the most famous amongst the disciples and khalifas of Khwaja Qutbuddin Bakhtiar Kaki. His ancestors were originally from Kabul but settled near Lahore in Punjab in the middle of the 12th century. His father was a religious scholar and his mother a God-fearing woman who spent most of her time in devotions. Her great piety influenced her son, who did not take much interest in worldly activities, preferring ascetic practices and meditation. People took him to be an abnormal child. When he was eighteen years old, he went to Multan and studied at a seminary in the mosque of Maulana Minhajuddin Tirmizi. It was here that he met Khwaja Qutbuddin Bakhtiar Kaki. He was so impressed by the Khwaja's spirituality that he became his disciple. After completing his studies, he went to Delhi and stayed in the Khwaja's jamaat khana, where he spent much time in ascetic exercises. With the permission of Shaikh, he even performed a chilla, that is, he spent forty days in solitary spiritual retreat, fasting and performing ascetic exercises. When Khwaja Muinuddin of Ajmer visited Delhi, he met Fariduddin and was greatly impressed by him. He prophesied great spiritual attainment as his destiny. Soon his fame spread far and wide and people began flocking to him. With all the attention he received, he found it difficult to engage in his usual devotions, so he left for Hansi in the Hisar district. He was not in Delhi when Khwaja Qutbuddin Bakhtiar Kaki died. On hearing the news, he left immediately for Delhi, reaching it in five days. It was the Khwaja's will that Baba Farid be his successor.

6.1.4 Shaikh Nizamuddin Auliya (1238-1325 A.D.)

Shaikh Nizamuddin Auliya, the celebrated khalifah of Baba Farid, was and remains one of the most popular mystics of medieval India. His grandfather migrated to India from Bhukhara in Central Asia and settled in Badayun. Nizamuddin was born there in 1238. His father died when he was hardly five years old. His mother, a very pious lady, spared no effort in giving her son the best education available in Badayun. First, he learned and memorized the Quran. Then he studied the books of fiqh. Subsequently, at the age of 16, he was allowed to go to Delhi for further studies. There he happened to stay in the neighbourhood of Shaikh Najibuddin Matawakkil, a younger brother and a khalifah of Baba Farid. By then he had mastered the hadith and fiqh. On the strength of these accomplishments, he felt he might be able to secure the position of a Qadi, for his family, now reaching the point of near starvation was in dire need of resources. He therefore requested Shaikh Najibuddin to pray for his appointment, but the Shaikh, well known for his spirituality and austerity, discouraged him from aspiring to a worldly post. Under the influence of Shaikh Najibuddin and after hearing about Baba Farid from him, Nizamuddin finally decided to take up the life of a dervish. He left Delhi for Ajodhan in 1257 to meet Shaikh Fariduddin personally. Baba Farid, quick to gauge his spiritual potential, gave him a warm welcome, and initiated him into the order. Nizamuddin showed great interest in learning ascetic exercises.

6.1.5 Nasiruddin Muhammad Chiragh Dilli (1276-1356 A.D.)

Shaikh Nasiruddin Mahmud was the most prominent of the khalifas of Nizamuddin Auliya. He was also his chief successor in Delhi and was popularly known as the Chiragh-i-Dilli (The Lamp of Delhi). He was born in Awadh in 1276 A.D. His father, who was an affluent wool merchant, died when he was nine years old. His mother wanted him to become an alim, but he was not interested in his studies and his heart was set on asceticism. By the time he was 25 years old, he was already deep into Sufi practices and spent much of his time in self-mortification, fasting and prayers. His favourite retreats were tombs of the saints, isolated spots by rivers and the wilderness of the jungles. Shaikh Nizamuddin had several followers in Awadh, where Nasiruddin Mahmud lived. At their instigation he decided to go to Delhi and become the Shaikh's disciple. He was 43 years old, well versed in ascetic exercises and ready to embark on the way of the Sufis. He was welcomed by the Shaikh and initiated into the tariqa. Nasiruddin's life of prayer, meditation and solitude ill prepared him for an existence in an urban centre such as Delhi. Therefore, he begged his Shaikh to allow him to retire into a nearby wilderness. He was asked instead to remain in Delhi among the people and suffer whatever hardship that entailed as, according to the Shaikh, all kinds of experience were necessary for one's intellectual and spiritual development. Besides, those who had been blessed with the realization of God had a duty to guide the populace along the same path. If they shirked their duty by opting for a life of retirement, it would have amounted to risking divine displeasure. Taking note of the popularity of the Sufis, Sultan Muhammad bin Tughlaq tried to pressurize them into helping him in his ambitious schemes. He wanted both the Sufis and the ulama to move to his new capital and lead the masses there. Those who refused to do so had to suffer the displeasure and the anger of the Sultan. Shaikh Nasiruddin was also one of those under pressure, but somehow managed to escape going to Daulatabad.

6.2 Shaikh Abdul Jilani (1077-1166 A.D.)

The Qadri Order is named after Shaikh Abdul Qadir Jilani, who figures prominently in Islamic spiritual history. For the first fifty years after the Shaikh's death, there was no formal organization to speak of. However, the Shaikh's teachings strongly influenced the thinking and conduct of a considerable number of Muslims during his lifetime. Later, his disciples and followers perpetuated his teachings and saw to their dissemination. The Shaikh eventually came to be regarded as a great saint endowed with miraculous powers, and an embodiment of perfection. Shaikh Abdul Qadir had a highly persuasive way of encouraging people to distance themselves from an obsession with material things and turn instead to matters of the spirit. Having awakened the spiritual side of their nature, he dedicated himself to instilling in them a profound reverence for moral and spiritual values. His religiosity and earnestness made a great impression on men who flocked to his side. He asked his followers to maintain the same strict standard of adherence to all the ramifications of Islamic Law, or shariah, as he did himself, for he looked upon the shariah as the mainspring of all spiritual progress. Insistence upon this point not only forged a bond between the jurists and the mystics (Sufis), but also ensured that there would be a just equilibrium between the varying interpretations of the letter and the spirit of the Quran. In his works and sermons, Abdul Qadir Jilani makes frequent mention of Imam Ahmad ibn Hambal (855 A.D.), and on many issues of religious importance, his stance was certainly influenced by his connection with the Hambali School of Islamic jurisprudence. In fact, he made fiqh (jurisprudence) and tasawwuf (mysticism) complementary to each other, thus bringing jurists and mystics together. In his elaborations on mysticism, he was always careful to keep all legal facets in view and, conversely, in explaining the principles of the law, he emphasized their spiritual implications.

6.3 Shaikh Abdul Qadir Jilani (1078 – 1166 A.D.)

Shaikh Abdul Qadir was born in the village of Nif, in the district of Jilan in northern Iran, south of the Caspian Sea. He was descended from Imam Hasan, the Prophet's grandson. Orphaned early, he was looked after by his maternal grandfather, Sayyid 'Abdullah Suma'i, who was a pious and saintly person. In 1095 A.D., when he was eighteen, he left Jilan for Baghdad, which was then the hub of unparalleled intellectual activity and where the reputed Nizamiyyah College, a seminary founded in 1065 A.D., was at its zenith. However, he chose not to study in this institution and pursued his studies with other teachers of Baghdad. Right from his early childhood, his truthful character had a great impact upon anyone who chanced to meet him. There is a story about his journey from his native place to Baghdad which illustrates this special virtue. When he was about to leave, his mother gave him forty gold coins his share in the patrimony, which she concealed by stitching them into his cloak. As parting advice to her son, she told him always to be truthful and honest; Abdul Qadir promised never to tell a lie.

Twenty-four titles are described to Shaikh Abdul Qadir, of which the most important are:

1. al-Ghunyah li-talibi tariqal-haqq ('That Which Is Sufficient to the Seekers of the Path of Truth'), generally known as Ghunyat al-talibin, an exhaustive work on the obligations enjoined by Islam and the Islamic way of life;

2. al-Fath al-rabbani ('The Revelations of the Divine') a record of sixty-two sermons delivered by him during the years 1150-1152 A.D.;

3. Fath al-ghayb ('The Revelations of the Unseen') a record of seventy-eight sermons compiled by his son, Abdul Razzaq.

He wrote the Ghunyat al-talibin, a detailed account of his religious views, at the request of his followers and friends. It was translated into Persian by Abdul Hakim Sialkoti (1657A.D.). Unlike the two other works, the Futuh alghayb and al-Fath al-rabbani, it is a comprehensive work dealing both with Islamic law and mystical thought. His sermons, however, are less than exhaustive, for his compilers were unable to record his every utterance, resulting in certain inevitable omissions. In the two collections of his sermons, the Shaikh emerges as being of an entirely other-worldly nature, but in the Ghunyat there is a greater equilibrium between spiritual and worldly obligations. His deliberations on faith, charity (zakat), fasting, and hajj (pilgrimage) are followed by an analysis of the propriety of behaviour to be observed in daily life. He also deals with the sects that he considered to have strayed from the true path, ending with an exposition of his mysticism. Overall, the Shaikh set forth his ideas on religion and ethics in the context of faith, devotion to God, and interaction with his fellow men.

The Qadri order was introduced into the Indian subcontinent in the 15th century. Its first centre was established in the Deccan. Later on, independently of it, another centre came to be established in Punjab. The story goes that Shihabuddin Ahmad (1422-1436 A.D.), a Bahamani ruler of Gulbarga, impressed with the spiritual fame and miraculous powers of the descendants of Shaikh Abdul Qadr Jilani, sent his envoy to Kirman where Shah Nematullah Wali, a khalifah of the Shaikh, resided and the Sultan was initiated, from a distance, as his disciple. Later, the Sultan requested his mentor to send his son, Khalilullah to his court to act as his spiritual guide. The Shaikh did not want to part with his only son, so he sent instead his grandson, Mir Nurullah, the son of Khalilullah. The Sultan received him with great reverence and built a town in his honour, naming it Ni'amatabad. When Shaikh Nematullah died in 1431 A.D., Shah Khalilullah joined his son in the Deccan, bringing his other sons as well. The presence The Qadri order 124 of Shah Nematullah's son and grandsons in the Bahamanid Sultanate considerably reduced the influence of the spiritual descendants of Gesu Daraz and the Chishti order in the Deccan, while enhancing that of the Qadri.

6.4 Shaikh Abdul Haqq (1551-1642 A.D.)

Shaikh Abdul Haqq was initiated into the Qadri order by his pir, Shaikh Musa, who was close to Akbar as well as his courtiers, Abul Fazl and Faizi, but he did not share his pir's liking for life at the imperial court. He soon left Agra and returned to Delhi. He stayed there for a while and then travelled to Makkah where he studied under Shaikh Abdul Wahhab Muttaqi al Qadri al Shazili, who taught him the importance of strengthening one's beliefs within the framework of the shariah, following this with an analysis of Sufi works dealing with the concept of wahdat al wujud. This advice seems to have been taken to heart, for all the writings of Abdul Haqq balance the requirements of the law with the practice of mysticism. The list of his spiritual friends and mentors includes, amongst others, Shah Abul Ma'ali Qadri and Khwaja Baqi Billah, the Naqshbandi. He is also credited with writing a letter to his contemporary Ahmad Sirhindi the Mujaddid, his main opponent on the issue of wahdat al wujud.

6.5 Shaikh Abu Najib Suhrawardi (1097-1168 A.D.)

Abu'l Najib 'Abd al Kahir bin 'Abd Allah al Bakri (1097-1168 A.D.) was a Sunni mystic who flourished in the 12th century. He was born in Suhraward in the Jibal region. As a young man he came to Baghdad and studied the hadith, Fiqh and Arabic grammar and literature at the famous Nizamiya madrasa. When he was in his twenties, he abandoned formal studies, turned to asceticism, and returned to Isfahan. There he joined Ahmad al Ghazali (1126), the illustrious mystic and brother of Muhammad al Ghazali, and became his disciple. Later, he returned to Baghdad where he became a disciple of Hammad al Dabbas (1131), an unlettered Sufi of great excellence, who was also the pir of Abdul Qadir Jilani. He taught fiqh and the Suhrawardi Order hadith as well as mysticism in a madrasa and for a while lectured also at the Nizamiya. He wrote a work in Arabic, Adabal Muridin ('The Etiquette of the Disciple'), which several Indian

Sufis subsequently translated into Persian. He had numerous disciples, one of whom, Shihabuddin Suhrawardi, his nephew, went on to give an organizational form to his teachings and doctrines.

6.6 Shaikh Shihabuddin Suhrawardi (1145 – 1235 A.D.)

Suhrawardi was born in Suhraward and came to Baghdad as a youth. He studied theology under Shaikh Abdul Qadir Jilani, but also attended the lectures of other prominent scholars, including those given by his uncle, Abu Najib, both at the Nizamiyya and at the latter's ribat (hospice) on the bank of the Tigris. It was his uncle who initiated him into Sufism. After his uncle's death in 1168 A.D. He withdrew from the world and began to teach in the ribat. His teachings generated great interest and he started to give lectures at other places in the city as well. He was a great orator and could hold the attention of the audience for hours, bringing many to the state of spiritual awakening. He maintained friendly relations with many known Sufis of the day and knew, among others, Muinuddin Chishti, the founder of the Chishti centre in Ajmer and Najmuddin Kubra, the great Sufi of the Kubrawiya order. Legendary accounts speak of his meeting in Baghdad with Ibn 'Arabi and Ruzbihan al Baqli. Shihabuddin Suhrawardi became very close to the Abbasid caliph, al Nasir, who founded a beautiful khanqah for him. He acted as the court theologian and was elevated to the position of Shaikh al Shuyukh within the Sufi circles of Baghdad. On a number of occasions, he acted as the caliph's envoy to the courts of contemporary rulers. This association gave rise to The Suhrawardi order 134 the Suhrawardi tradition of keeping in touch with temporal rulers and the order's approval of the acceptance of lavish gifts. Shihabuddin Suhrawardi wrote a number of books of which 'Awariful Ma'arif ('The Benefits of Knowledge') is the most important. It continued the tradition of the earlier Sufi manuals of al Sarraj and, Kalabadhi but it rearranged the earlier material and supplemented it with new information. The text went on to become the most closely studied piece of literature of the Sufis, with both Suhrawardis and the Chishtis using it as a practical guide. Besides chapters dealing with specific topics, such as the definition of the Sufi, derivation of the term, the concept of tauhid, (Monotheism) the mystic way, prayer, dhikr, (remembrance of God) meditation, sama, (musical assembly) etc., it also talks about the role of the Shaikh and his relationship with his disciples. For the first time it describes the Sufi hospice, (khanqah), and discusses various issues concerned with running it. After his death, he was succeeded in Baghdad by his son, 'Imaduddin Muhammad Suhrawardi (1257) who acted as the custodian of the ribat. Other disciples were ordered by the Shaikh to return to their homelands and establish new centres there.

6.7 Shaikh Bahauddin Zakariya (1182 -1262 A.D.)

Shaikh Bahauddin, whose forefathers probably came to India with the armies of Muhammad bin Qasim and settled in Sind, was born at Kot Karor near Multan. His father died when he was twelve. At first, he studied in the village and later decided to go in search of knowledge to Khurasan. He spent seven years in Bhukhara, and then travelled to Makkah and Madinah. In Madinah he stayed for five years and studied the hadith with a distinguished muhaddith Shaikh Kamaluddin Muhammad Yamani from whom he received a sanad i.e., a formal authorization, to teach the hadith. From there he went on to Jerusalem and then, Baghdad, where he joined the circle of disciples of Shaikh Shihabuddin Suhrawardi, who initiated him into his order and made him his khalifah. One important feature of the Suhrawardi order, which was also upheld by Bahauddin, was that neither the order nor he were against possessing wealth earned by lawful means. After his needs and the needs of his family and the khanqah were fulfilled, what was left of the money received by him as gifts was used for humanitarian purposes for the benefit of the public. This did not, however, imply that everything was to be distributed every day and nothing kept for the next. Not surprisingly, he was criticized for his views on the possession of wealth and property and for his close association with the rulers. But, to him, this was not un-Islamic, for after all, the shariah did not declare property and wealth unlawful. What was condemnable for him was to neglect the higher spiritual and moral values for an involvement in worldly affairs. As long as material things could be kept away from one's heart, there was no harm in possessing them. Another important point to be kept in mind was that worldly resources had to be spent on righteous purposes.

6.8 Qazi Hamiduddin Nagauri:

Qazi Hamiduddin Nagauri was the most learned amongst the khalifas of Shaikh Shihabuddin Suhrawardi. His family migrated from Bhukhara to Delhi at some point before 1200, where his father, Ataullah died. Shaikh The Suhrawardi Order 138 Hamid was appointed the Qazi of Nagaur and served in this position for 3 years. He did not find the service inwardly rewarding, so he left for Baghdad, where he met Shaikh Shihabuddin Suhrawardi and became his disciple. It was also there that he met Khwaja Qutbuddin Bakhtiar Kaki, who later became a renowned Sufi of the Chishti order. Hamiduddin and Qutbuddin became friends. Under the influence of Qutbuddin Bakhtiar Kaki, Hamiduddin started taking an interest in sama', thereby arousing the opposition of the ulama. He was also very close to Qutbuddin's famous disciple, Nizamuddin Auliya. When the latter died, it was Qazi Hamiduddin Nagauri who invested his successor Baba Farid, by presenting him with the relics of his Shaikh. Qazi Hamiduddin was a writer with several works to his credit. Lawaih ('Flashes of Light') was an important Sufi text, but it did not survive the ravages of time. It is attested that Baba Farid used to study it with his disciples. Three other works of Hamiduddin have, however, survived and these are: 'Ishqiyya, Tawali' al Shumus ('Points Where the Suns Rise'), and Risala Min Kalam.

6.9   Shaikh Jalaluddin Tabrezi (1266 A.D.)

Shaikh Jalaluddin Tabrezi was one of the most devoted disciples of Shihabuddin Suhrawardi. Before becoming his disciple, he was, like his father, a disciple of Abu Sa'id of Tabriz. After his death he left for Baghdad and became a disciple of Shihabuddin Suhrawardi. His devotion to his mentor knew no bounds and it is said that he used to carry food for him wherever he went and warmed it on the spot to serve whenever required. He left Baghdad together with Bahauddin Zakariyya and travelled with him as far as Multan, but while Bahauddin Zakariyya remained in Multan, Jalaluddin Tabrezi carried on to Delhi. He stayed there for a while but finally decided it was not the best place for him and continued his journey eastwards. He established himself in Bengal and was responsible for spreading Islam there. At first, he stayed in Lakhnauti, where he built a khanqah, and then moved on to Deva Mahal in northern Bengal. Deva Mahal came to be known as Tabrizabad and became a centre of pilgrimage. Large numbers of Hindus and Buddhists converted to Islam under his influence. His disciples were possessed of a missionary zeal and found many converts among the lower classes, who being persecuted by the zamindars, (land-owners) embraced Islam to share in the equality and human brotherhood they had been denied for centuries.

6.10   Nuruddin Mubarak Ghaznavi (1235 A.D.)

Sayyed Nuruddin Mubarak Ghaznavi was an important khalifah of Shaikh Shihabuddin. His early life is virtually unknown but, when he came to Delhi, he was already famous and Iltutmish appointed him as Shaikh the Suhrawardi order 140 ul Islam. The people of Delhi called him Mir-e-Delhi (Lord of Delhi). According to Ziauddin Barni, he often visited the Sultan and did not hesitate to criticize the non-Islamic customs of the court. He believed that Islam could be protected only when the rulers followed its principles, and that a ruler who followed these principles would be raised with the prophets and the saints on the Day of Judgement. The rulers, he felt, should practice din-panahi or 'the protection of the Islamic way of life' and see to it that the commands of the shariah were observed. Sins, debauchery, and adultery should not be tolerated. Offenders should be ruthlessly punished. The pious should be entrusted with the duty to enforce the shariah and the officers appointed to carry out this task should be well versed in both the shariah and the tariqa. He was against philosophers. He felt that their teachings should be prohibited in the territories under Islam. He believed that justice should be rigorously dispensed and that the tyrants should be overthrown. He seems to have been an extremist who could not tolerate anything but orthodox Islam. He even went to the extent of saying that those rulers who did not follow the principles enumerated by him risked damnation in the Hereafter, and that prayer and fasting alone was not going to benefit them. It is said that he performed hajj twelve times. He was in Delhi during the reign of Sultan Iltutmish when he was offered the post of Sadr us Sudur, which he accepted. But after two years, he resigned and devoted the rest of his life to spiritual exercises.

6.11 Khwaja Bahauddin Naqshband (1317 – 1389 A.D.)

Khwaja Bahauddin Naqshband, the founder of the Naqshbandi order, was born at Kushk-i-Hinduwan, a village near Bhukhara in Central Asia. Later, in his honour, the village came to be known as Kushk-i-Arifan. The title Naqshband that he used literally means a painter or 'an embroiderer'. It is possible that it refers to the profession followed by his family, but it may just as easily have been a metaphorical usage indicative of his spiritual capacity to imprint the name of God upon a disciple's heart. In the mediaeval period, it was not uncommon for children to be sent to the Sufis to receive spiritual knowledge, but this was usually done after they had acquired an education in the traditional disciplines such as the recitation of the Quran and the study of the hadith and jurisprudence. At the age of 18, Khwaja Bahauddin was likewise entrusted to a Sufi saint, Muhammad Baba as-Samasi (1354), who lived in a village called Samas. This saint was as piritual descendent of Khwaja Abu-Yaqub-Yusufal-Hamadani (1140), founder of silsila-i-khwajgan. It is said that Samasi could see the latent spirituality and greatness of Bahauddin and therefore assigned his training to his chief murid, Amir Kulal (1371). It did not take Bahauddin long to achieve mastery in the required spiritual exercises. This made the Shaikh so pleased with his progress that he appointed him his khalifah.

6.12 Abdur Rahman Jami (1414 -1492 A.D.)

Mawlana Nur-ud-din-Abdur Rahman Jami was born in the town of Jam in Khurasan but spent most of his life in the Timurid court at Herat. He was fortunate enough to complete the course in traditional learning at a young age but the study at the madrasa did not satisfy his spiritual yearning. It occurred to him that mysticism might hold the key to ultimate knowledge and thought of the Sufis, who expounded works of tasawwuf to select disciples chosen for their aptitude to grasp the hidden meanings. Therefore, he approached a Sufi saint, Khwaja Saiduddin Kashghari (1459), a khalifah of Khwajah Bahauddin Naqshband, to give him spiritual training. He was accepted and remained under his guidance for several years. After the death of Khwaja Said, he became a disciple of Khwajah Ubaidullah Ahrar, another Naqshbandi Shaikh, who taught him, amongst other works, al-Futuhatal Makkiyah ('The Makkan Revelations') of Ibn'Arabi. As a sign of respect, Jami later wrote a masnavi, which he called Tuhfat-ul-Ahrar ('Present to Ahrar'). Khwaja Ahrar on his part was highly appreciative of his disciple's spiritual attainments and whenever Mawlana Jami sent his own disciples for further training to Khwaja Ahrar, the latter discouraged the practice, saying that there was no need to take the trouble of coming to him after being trained under Mawlana Jami, as the spiritual training given by him was complete. Jami left an enormous body of written work spanning virtually all the genres, from prose to poetry. His Nafahaat-al-uns ('The Breezes of Intimacy from the Sacred Presences'), a collection of over six hundred biographies of Sufis, based on anthologies written several centuries earlier, is an attempt to give the fullest possible picture of Sufism. Together with a book that followed it, Rashahat-i 'Ainul Hayat ('Trickling's from the Fountain of Life') written by his brother-in-law, Fakhruddin Husain Kashfi, it is an important source for the history of Sufism in general and the Naqshbandi order in particular.

6.13 Khwaja Baqi Billah (1563 – 1603 A.D.)

The conquest of India by Babur in 1526 gave a considerable impetus to the development of the Naqshbandi order. Both the new emperor and many his Central Asian soldiers were the spiritual followers of the disciples of Ubaidullah Ahrar. Some eminent Naqshbandiya Sufis followed the military in their move from Central Asia to India. However, during the reign of Humayun the Naqshbandis lost some of their royal patronage, for Humayun favoured a local Sufi lineage called the Shattariya. This changed once again in favour of the Naqshbandis with the ascendance of Akbar. The organizer of the order in India was Khwaja Baqi Billah, who was seventh in the line of succession from Khwaja Bahauddin Naqshband, its founder. Baqi Billah was born in Kabul, which was then a part of the Mughal Empire with Mirza Muhammad Hakim, a younger brother of Akbar, acting as the viceroy. As dictated by the traditon, Baqi Billah first studied the religious sciences with the eminent ulama of Kabul and then, unsatisfied with the knowledge of the learned, travelled to Central Asia to study under the Sufis. Thereafter, he returned to Kabul and from there went on to India. He visited Lahore,

Delhi, Sambhal (in present day UP), and then retraced his steps to Lahore from where he proceeded to Kashmir. His search for spiritual truth took him back to Central Asia where he met many Sufis of Balkh and Badakhshan. The turning point of his life, however, seems to have taken place at Amkina, near Samarkand, where he was received by Khwajagi Amkinagi (1600), a spiritual descendant of Khwaja Nasiruddin Ubaidullah Ahrar.

6.14 Shaikh Ahmad Sirhindi (1564 – 1624 A.D.)

Shaikh Ahmad Sirhindi was the most renowned of the disciples of Baqi Billah. Born in Sirhind, a town in Punjab, he was the son of Shaikh Abdul Ahad Makhdum. Shaikh Abdul Ahad was a man of religion and was fond of the company of devout Muslims. He was, moreover, a religious scholar, and taught his students not only the Qur'an, hadith and, fiqh, but also the books of tasawwuf. He followed the teachings of the Prophet to the letter. For this reason, his mystical leanings led him to develop a special interest in the Naqshbandi order, for the Naqshband is adhered strictly to the teachings of the Quran and the sunnah. It was but natural that Shaikh Ahmad should inherit this interest from his father. In his early childhood Ahmad Sirhindi was given a proper religious education. First, he learnt the Quran by heart and studied at home under his father. After learning Arabic and Persian, and acquiring the basic knowledge of the religious sciences, he was sent to Sialkot to receive education under the guidance of Kamal Kashmiri and other ulama. Yaqub Kashmiri, a great scholar of hadith, was one of his teachers. By the age of 17 he had completed all the required courses and started teaching. Because of his scholarship he was invited to the court of Akbar and stayed in Agra for several years. There, he met Abul Fazl and Faydi, and assisted them in their writings. Soon after he married the daughter of a noble named Shaikh Sultan of Thanesar Shaikh Ahmad believed that a truly faithful Sufi would never transgress the law or the shariah. He criticized the ulama for doing nothing but issuing fatwas (religious decrees), and for taking no pains to affect the internal The Naqshbandi Order 176 purification which was necessary for receiving divine inspiration. Shaikh Ahmad, moreover, did not spare those Sufis who indulged in senseless wrangling. The Shaikh and other Naqshbandi saints, as well as disapproving of music and dance to induce ecstasy, also did not like the loud utterance of God's name, for when God was as close to us as our jugular vein as the Quran said, what was the point of loud recitation? Shaikh Ahmad writes in one of his letters: "with the Naqshbandi Sufis, guidance and discipline depend upon one's submission to and acknowledgement of the prophetic institution. It has nothing to do with external trappings such as the cap or the genealogy of the Shaikh". [72]

6.15 Najmuddin Kubra (1221 A.D.)

The Firdausi order traces its origins to Najmuddin Kubra (1221) through his disciple, Saifuddin Sa'id Bakharzi (1260). Najmuddin Kubra's pirs (spiritual mentors) were all either companions or disciples of Abu Najib Suhrawardi (1168), the spiritual founder of the Suhrawardi silsila and for this reason the Kubrawiya and the Firdausiya are collateral lines of the Suhrawardiya. Najimuddin Kubra called his disciple Saifuddin Bakharzi, 'The Shaikh of Paradise', and hence his spiritual lineage is known as Firdausi. Shaikh Nizamuddin Auliya narrates the story of Bakharzi's conversion to Sufism. In his youth Shaikh Bakharzi was opposed to Sufism, going to the extent of condemning the Sufis publicly in his lectures. Once Shaikh Bakharzi was delivering a lecture full of venom against Sufism, with Shaikh Najmuddin Kubra part of the audience. He never even once contradicted the speaker but while leaving the mosque, he asked, 'Where is that Sufi?' meaning Bakharzi. At this Barkhazi fell at his feet and became his disciple. After giving him spiritual training, Shaikh Najmuddin sent him to Bhukhara, where he died in 1260.

6.16 Sharafuddin Maneri (1381 A.D.)

Shaikh Sharafuddin Ahmad Yahya Maneri (1381) was the best-known saint of this order. He came from Bihar; his ancestors having settled there in the 13th th century. He received a traditional education, which included the study of grammar and language. However, he did not have any religious education, an omission that he later often regretted. When he was about 15 years old, he met Shaikh Sharafuddin-Abu-Tawwama. His coming into contact with a great religious scholar was a God-sent opportunity for him. Shaikh Sharafuddin Abu Tawamma was originally from Bhukhara and was very well educated. He came to Delhi during the reign of Sultan Balban. The Firdausi order 182 but it seems that the local ulama became jealous of his popularity, forcing him to leave Delhi. On his way to Sunargaon in Bengal, he stopped at Maner. The visit of a religious scholar of the calibre of Abu Tawwama was indeed a blessing for Sharafuddin Ahmad. He kept company with Abu Tawwama, accompanied him to Sunargaon and even took to living with his family in order to receive religious education from him. Soon Sunargaon became a popular centre of Islamic learning. After hearing the news of the death of his father, Shaikh Yahya, in 1291, Sharafuddin Ahmad left Sunargaon and returned to Maner to be with his mother. From there he travelled to Delhi and visited Shaikh Nizamuddin Auliya. However, he was not initiated by him. Thereafter he went to Panipat and met Abu Ali Qalandar. But the latter was perpetually in a state of religious ecstasy and was therefore unable to become his teacher. It was then that he met Shaikh Najibuddin Firdausi. He became his disciple and was given written authority to enrol his own disciples in turn. He objected to this, saying that he did not feel adequately qualified. To this his pir, Sheikh Najibuddin, answered that his decision was based on divine inspiration, and he commanded Shaikh Sharafuddin Ahmad to return to Maner.

7.   The Sufi Concept of Meditation

The word meditation is today a much-used word describing a plethora of practices that are sometimes difficult to bring under one common denominator. Hence, the need for a short introduction that will put the subject in its proper perspective. The context in which it is going to be discussed here is religious, and the religion discussed is Islam. Islam, like Judaism and Christianity, is a monotheistic religion, but there are other religions as well which might be described as polytheistic, for example, Hinduism or non-theistic, like Jainism or Buddhism, where meditation too is an accepted practice. Therefore, it is necessary to construct a definition of meditation that would do justice to the whole range of experiences taking place within different religious frames. Meditation might indeed encompass an extremely broad array of practices connected to many of the world's religious and philosophical traditions, but there are certain traits that are common. These generally include refraining from random, disturbing thoughts and fantasies, and aim at calming and focusing the mind on some specific object. Sometimes meditation requires a strenuous effort, while at other times it is an entirely effortless activity experienced as 'just happening'. Different practices involve concentrating one's attention differently. A variety of positions and postures might be involved, for example, sitting cross-legged, standing, lying down, kneeling and walking. At times certain devices like prayer beads (the Islamic tasbih and the Catholic rosary, for example), symbolic representations of the deity, singing and dancing or even consumption of narcotic substances might be used to induce the right frame of mind. The stated purpose of meditation varies almost as much as the practice itself. It is seen as a means of gaining experiential, that is, practical insight into the nature of reality, both in the case of religious and spiritually inclined persons as well as those who profess to follow no religion at all. It is perceived as an effective way of drawing closer or even becoming one with the Ultimate Reality, irrespective of what one might think it to be. Meditation thus requires and, therefore, develops the power of concentration, awareness, self-discipline, and calmness of mind.

Sufism, the form which mysticism has taken in Islam, is not so much a set of doctrines as a mode of thinking and feeling within a specific religious domain. In a way, it represents a reaction against the intellectualism and literalism of the scholars as well as the worldly attitude of the rulers.

Mysticism has been traced to the Prophet and the times of the Pious Caliphs, but it gathered strength during the Umayyad rule (660-750 A.D.) and grew further over the centuries. Islam prohibited its adherents from practicing the mortifying austerity and asceticism of Christian monks or, for that matter, the Hindu yogis. But in spite of the religious injunctions, asceticism kept on gaining ground within the Islamic community, with a large number of pious worshippers seeking to secure salvation through devotional practices (often frowned upon by the orthodoxy), meditation and withdrawing from society. The worldliness and absolutism of the Umayyad caliphs and their regime were yet another factor encouraging pious men to sever their connections with the obviously corrupting world. Turning away from it, they found strength in contemplating the mysteries of God, the soul and Creation. The early ascetics and their spiritual descendants, the Sufis, usually wore, as already mentioned, the undyed coarse woollen mantles like those worn by the Christian ascetics. That is why the term Sufi is usually considered to come from the Arabic word suf, or wool. Gradually 'Sufi' came to designate a very varied group of individuals who differentiated themselves from others by emphasizing certain specific teaching and practices mentioned in the Quran and the traditions of the Prophet of Islam. Though originally Sufism was just a pious mystical trend within Islam with certain individuals being more known than others, there was no attempt to give it any organizational form. But the twelfth century saw the crystallization of several orders. Now, certain chains of lineages through which different Sufis traced their allegiance were put in place connecting them with a spiritual hierarchy going back to the Prophet, mostly through 'Ali and sometimes through Abu Bakr, giving them legitimacy and enhancing their popular appeal through a firm connection with a charismatic and historical predecessor.[73]

The Sufi masters believe that every man has an inherent ability to achieve a release from the self and obtain a union with God. However, this ability being merely latent, the aspirant cannot attain it by himself, without the guidance of a mentor. It is only a mentor who can lead him to the ways of proper meditation so that, finally, he may acquire an insight into spiritual truth. According to Sufism, maarifah, which means gnosis, cannot be reached through intellectual exercise but solely through ecstatic states. A celebrated theologian and theorist of mysticism, Abu Hamid Muhammad al Ghazali (1111), who is famous within the mainstream of Islam as an authority on fiqh (jurisprudence) as well as for his perfectly argued and clearly articulated attacks on the philosophers, writes of his own realization of Truth: "I knew that the complete mystic 'way' includes both intellectual belief and practical activity; the latter consists in getting rid of the obstacles in the self and in stripping off its base characteristics and vicious morals, so that the heart may attain to freedom from what is not God and to constant recollection of Him... It became clear to me, however, that what is most distinctive of mysticism is something which cannot be apprehended by study, but only by immediate experience (dhawq - literally 'tasting'), by ecstasy and by a moral change".[74]

The Sufi who sets out to seek God calls himself a traveller (salik). He advances by slow stages (maqamat) along a path (tariqa) towards union with Reality (Fana'fil Haqq).This path, according to al-Sarraj (d.988), author of Kitab al-Luma' fi'l Tasawwuf [75], the oldest comprehensive treatise on Sufi teaching, consists of the following seven "stages":

1. Repentance (tawbah)
2. Fear of the Lord (wara)
3. Renunciation (zuhd)
4. Poverty (faqr)
5. Patience or endurance (sabr)
6. Trust in God (tawakkul)
7. Satisfaction/contentment (rida). [76]

8. Contact of Bhakti Saints with Muslin saints

The Sufi saint who has settled in India influenced Indian masses with their teachings and way of life. Since the abodes of the Sufi saints were visited by all irrespective of caste and creed, some Bhakti saints also came into their contact. The information regarding the mutual contact between Bhakti saints and Sufi saints is very meagre, but life find occasional evidence of such contacts Dabistan-i-Mazahib mentions that when Kabir was in search of spiritual guide he visited the best of Musalman and Hindus.[77] It is possible that when the best of Musalman, it is he might have visited some sufi saints. The expression of Kabir's teachings was shaped by that of sufi saints and poets. Kabir speaks about cup of love of the lover (ashiq and habib) and the beloved (mashug, Mahbub) of the path and its stations (muqam) etc. Which were derived from Sufism. Like Kabir, Nanak is said to have had long discussions with Shaikh Sharaf of Panipat, the Pirs of Multan and Shaikh Ibrahim, the successor of Shaikh Farid at Pakpattan. Undoubtedly, Nanak enjoyed the company of Sufi saints.[78] We also find evidence regarding Nanak's meeting with Shaikh Abdul Quddus Gangohi and was greatly influenced by the teachings of the Shaikh.[79] It is also said that Nanak also met Shaikh Kohammad Ghaus of Gwalior. Guru Nanak travelled to Baghdad to visit the famous Qadiri centre of Pir-i-Dastgir shaikh Abdul Qadir Jilani. Dadu, another Bhakti saint manifest great knowledge of Sufism that his predecessors probably he was the disciple of shaikh Kamal.

Like Bhakti saints sufi saints also seem to have an urgent desire to meet the Bhaktas. Shaikh Badiuddin Saharanpuri claims to have visited Jadrup Gosain. He relates that it was Jadrup Gosain who told him that Mujaddid is superior to all other spiritual guides. Though we do not find much evidence about personal contacts between the sufi saints and Shakti saints but the interaction of sufi and Bhakti thought suggest that both movements were affected by each other. Shaikh Abdur Rahman Chishti Combined both the bairagi and Miwehid tradition about Kabir in his Mirat-ul-Aarar.[80] Similarly Shaikh Abdul Quddus Gangohi's Rushd-Nama contain comparison between Nath terminology and Dvaidatita Vilakehanavada and the terminology of Sufism and Wahadu-ul-Wugud. Dara Shiakh's Majma-ul-Bahrain contains the mystic truth of Hindu Muwahhids (followers of Wahadat-ue-Wajud) after discovering the secrets of Sufism. The interaction of Sufi aid Bhakti saints is also evident if we study the common practices and common ideas in teachings of both these movements.

9.   Common practices of Bhakti and Sufi saint

As both the bhakti movement and sufi movement flourished in India at the same time, it was but natural that both influenced each other. The result was in the form of adoptation of common practices. Sufis adopted those practices of Bhakti saints which would boost up the working of the Silsila's. The Bhakti saints likewise followed the tradition of the Sufis. There are many instances of adoptation of each other's practices. The main reason of the success and popularity of the Chishti silsilah is India was this, that they understand the condition of India and adopted many Hindu customs and practices, i.e., The practices of bowing before the Shaikh, presenting water to the visitors circulating sanbil, shaving the head of new disciple were very similar to the practices of Bhakti saints. Sama (audition parties) of the Sufi and Kirtan or devotional song and dance are almost same. Bhakti saints practised Kirtan to attain salvation and Sufis practised Sama to attain salvation. Among the Bhakti saints the exponent was Chaitanya who believed that through love and devotional song and dance a stat of ecstasy could be produced in which the personal presence of God would be realised.[81]

Chillah-i-Makus of the Sufis had close resemblance with practice of Bhakti saints. Guru Nanak's conception of Hukum had very close resemblance with the Sufis interpretation of divine will (Risa).[82] But there are many differences between the elder's or silsilah of the Sufis. Such as suhraward is believe in living a normal balanced life, a life in which both the body and the spirit, received equal care. Neither himself fasted perpetually nor did he recommend a life of starvation. The Chishti believed in the control of emotional life as a prerequisite to the control of external behaviour. Similarly, both Bhakti and sufi saints had common approach towards the way of life, they lead. Almost all these saints believed in living a balanced life. For example, Nanak and Dadu opposed to fortune the body to get salvation. The Bhakti saints said that human body was the sublime temple of God. Like Suhrawardy saints many Bhakti saints did not believe in Fasting. Regarding pilgrimage to the holy places both Bhakti and Sufi saints laid emphasis. Bhakti saints largely performed pilgrimage to holy cities of Mathura, Brindaban, Kashi, Prayag, Haridwar etc. Like wise to the Sufi saints the pilgrimage to Macca represent the last stage in spiritual advancement. Caste system was eventually criticising by Bhakti and Sufi saints which they practised in their life. They made their disciples from all castes. Further they tried to bring reconciliation and unity among Hindus and Muslims i.e., 'Shaikh Mohd. Ghaus of Gwalior had intimate relation with Hindus'. [83] "He would stand up to welcome every Hindu visitor. Dadu did not believe in caste and creed distinction and that was the reason that he had both the Hindus and Musalmans among his disciple". He held temples and masques in equal reverence. He used to say that the sun and moon, space the earth, wind, water are all busy in serving him in early one without distinction and that they do not belong to any group or party. Guru Nanak also denounce caste and untouchability. The process of assimilating the Hindu religious thought particularly Tantric practices reached its highest watermark under Mohd. Ghaus, Later Shattari saints followed it they did not odd to it.

Teachings of Bhakti saints and Sufi saints

Both Bhakti saints and Sufi saints who flourished in India in the 16th and 17th centuries influenced the Indian people through their teachings. The Conception of God is almost same in the eyes of Bhakti and Sufi saints. The very conception of loving God and the relation between God and soul as one of beloved and the lover are peculiar to Bhakhtas and were adopted by Sufis in India. Sufis believed in monotheism (believed in one God). The Bhakti saints also believed in monotheism They said that Islam and Hinduism were two different paths leading to the same destination and that Ram and Rahim, Krishna and Karim, Allah and Ishwar were different names of the same Almighty, Indian Sufis like Shaikh Mohd. Ghaus Shaikh Abdul Quddus Gawgohi, Shaikh Salim Chishti etc. were believed in God the real (al Hagg) and he is the creature. In the same way Vallabhacharya's philosophy centered round the conception of one personal and loving God. "He believed in the Marga (Path of Pushti) grace and Bhakti. He looked upon Shri Krishna as the highest Brahma Purshotama (the most excellent of all beings) Parmanand (the highest Joy)".[84]

It is possible to attain the Supreme being by sincere Bhakti. Chaitanya preached the religion of intense faith in one Supreme being by whom he called Krishna or Hari. Dadu says that God Is omnipresent. Is the one alone Real In the world of Unreality, the eternal source from which all beings' conies forth. The treasure house of all excellencies, the lord of creation to whom all creatures bow. He Is still the Doer the merciful the creator the divine companion God alone knows no change. He is Niranjan and Nirgun. This idea of Dadu about God is very similar to that of Sufis. Both Bhakti and Sufi Saints had a strong monotheistic tendency. According to Shaikh Abdul Quddus Gangohl God is only real-being. He only exists and exists for ever. He is eternal (qadim). The Idea that God hidden in everything of the universe and everything of universe hidden in God is found in the teachings of Abdul Quddus. It is very similar to Guru Nanak's conception of God. His God in his primal aspect is devoid of all attributes. He is absolute unconditional. As such he is beyond comprehension. He is unknowable he is unchanging formless or Nirankar. He is without form (rup / and has no material sign (rachna). He is boundless (after). He is unborn (ajanma) etc. Guru Nanak's God is the true Lord (Sat) the creator (Karta Purkh), unborn, self-existent (Saibhang) immortal (Akal) omnipresent, transcendent, and omnipotent.

Guru Nanak emphasised the great less of God as the sole creator and sole sustained and the sole destroyer of his own creation. According to the Sufi saints God is real (Al Haqq), unknowable, unchanging formless and unborn. So, the conception of God for both Bhakti and sufi saints is common. In short, the saints of both the orders believed in unity of one God or unity of one being. They also consider Almighty God as the Supreme creature. Shaikh Ahmad Sirhindi Mujaddid says that God is creature. He believed in Wahadat-al-Shuhud Bhakti and Sufi saint believed that God is transcendent. Many Bhakti saints describe supreme creator as Alakh mat (the incomprehensible or unseeable one) or as Niran gan. Shaikh Abdul Quddus also uses the name Alakh Niranjan in the same sense. He says that his lord is 'unseeable (Alakh Niranjan)'[85]. Like Bhakti saints Shaikh Abdul Juddus attaches great importance to 'omkar'. The term 'SABAD' used by the Shaikh Abdul Quddus identifies mystic contemplation with Shakti as well as Shiva and their union as the course of the existence of three worlds. So, it seems that the union of Shakti the sun and shiva the moon according to the Shaikh Abdul Quddus is the salat-i-Makud of the Sufis. The Idea of both the orders about the relation between God and man is almost similar. According to the Indian Sufis conception the only relation that is possible between God a man is relation of 'Ishq' or love. Love and love alone is the criterion of their creed and the guiding principle of their mundane life. The sufis conception and Bhaktas conception of God and man is that of a master and servant. In the same way many Bhakti saints adopted this Idea of Sufis.

For example, Mirabal consider herself as the lover of Lord Krishna. Like all Sufis Nanak taught that in the soul's Journey towards God, it was necessary to be guided by a Guru. Guru Nanak directed the disciple upon the path which has four stages-sarand Khan, Inan Khand, Karam Khand and Such Khand, which according to the Gurumukh Singh the author of Nanak Prakas corresponds with Sufi Shariat Marifat, Ufaw and Lahut. sufis doctrine of Wahadat-ul-Wujud. They also denounced idolatry as well as polytheism having borrowed so many basic ideas from Hindu religious thought the sufis could not possibly pursue any rigid or fanatic policy towards the Hindus. Their attitude towards conversion comes very near the attitude of hishtis. They had no ambition and were always prepared to give lessons in mysticism to Hindu without demanding formal conversion to Islam. Tansen the famous musician of Akbar's court was a disciple of Shaikh Mohd. Ghaus, Bhakti saints used to visit Shaikh Wajin-u-d-din and learn Sufi practices from him. The mission of Bhakti and Sufi saints was the unification of Hindu and the Musalman. In another word their object was to bring about a compromise between Hinduism and Islam and to foster friendly relation between two communities. But they did not get much success in this object, so from the above interpretation we are confident enough to say that there were many similarities in the practical and teachings of from Bhakti and Sufi saints. So, at last can say that when sufis came to India they adopted those practices which would boost up the working of the silsilah. The Bhakti saints likewise followed the tradition of the sufis.

In the next chapter, we will review in detail the works of some prominent Muslim saints who have made a profound impact on the social life of Maharashtra with their centuries of devotional and Warkari sects.

———————

Chapter 5

Some Prominent Muslim Sufis in Maharashtra

Sufi saints have been around in India since the twelfth century. After the conquest of Devagiri by Allauddin Khilji, the number of Sufi saints increased in Marathwada, Vidarbha and Ahmednagar. At the same time, the existing Warakari and Bhakti sects led to philosophical exchanges between Sufi saints and Warkari saints and social unity was created. Therefore, even the Maratha chiefs who served or worked for the Muslim rulers began to respect the Muslim saints and started helping the happy saints as much as they wanted. Luckily, the common people here also followed in the footsteps of their Maratha sardar and started respecting the sufi saint. The famous powerful families of that time were Lakhuji Jadhav of Daulatabad, Maloji and Vithoji Raje of Verul. The path of devotion to the Sufi saint that he led seems to have been followed by the kings and people of the Marathi Empire for the next few centuries. Let us see some examples of how Shivaji Raja, like his grandfather, had faith in happy saints all his life.[1] One of great example is Maloji Bhosale who was a Maratha sardar (general) who served the Ahmadnagar Sultanate in Malik Ambar's army during Nijamshali dynasty. He was the father of Shahaji and the grandfather of Shivaji, the founder of the Maratha Empire. Maloji was born in 1552 A.D. to Babaji Bhosale (1597 A.D.), a patil (chief) of the Hingni Berdi and Devalgaon villages around Pune.[2][3] Maloji had a younger brother, Vithoji. Maloji and his brother Vithoji migrated away from Pune, and initially served as petty horsemen under the Jadhavs of Sindkhed.[3] The Jadhavs provided military service to the Ahmednagar Sultanate. At that time Maloji Raje was living nearby Elora Daulatabad. His mind was devotional, and he had special faith in Peer Fakir. Therefore, Shaikh Mohammad, who started seeing fame in the atmosphere of Daulatabad, was attracted to it. This incident happened naturally. Sheikh Mohammad accepted his discipleship, both to himself and to his Diwan Balachi Konhere. The Maloji kings built a monastery at Shaikh Mohammad in Chambargonde or Shrigonde (Ahmednagar district) with great reverence. An incident has taken place around 1595 A.D. Shaikh Mohammed must have been around 40 years of

"

old at the time. Makrand is a Sanskrit adaptation of the Persian adjective meaning generous man. The place is known as Makrand Pur Peth, a peth built by Makrand, i.e., Maloji Raja. Shaikh Mohammad started living in a cave in Makrandpur Peth built by his able disciple. After that, his work of spreading Parmarth and Parmarth Vagmayanirmiti continued uninterruptedly till the end. Maloji married Uma Bai (also known as Dipa Bai), the sister of Jagpalrao Nimbalkar, who was the deshmukh of Phaltan. Maloji was childless for a long time. Hazrat Shah Sharif Dargah where Maloji prayed for sons to the Muslim saint. With blessings of a Sufi Muslim pir called Shah Sharif, two sons were born to him in 1594 A.D. and 1596 A.D. Maloji named his sons Shahaji and Sharifji in honour of the pir.[4][5] He also built a reservoir in the name of shah sharif around his tomb.[6][7][8][9][10]

Shahaji was the son of Maloji Bhosale, a soldier who eventually became Sar Giroh and was awarded independent jagir of Pune and Supe districts in the court of Nizam Shah of Ahmednagar. Shahaji married Jijabai, the daughter of Lakhuji Jadhav, another Maratha general in the service of Nizam Shah of Ahmednagar when both of them were children.[11]Shahaji Bhosale (1594 –1664 A.D.) was a military leader of 17th century India, who served the Ahmadnagar Sultanate, the Bijapur Sultanate, and the Mughal Empire at various points in his career. A member of the Bhonsle clan, Shahaji inherited the Pune and Supe jagirs from his father Maloji, who served Ahmadnagar. During the Mughal invasion of Deccan, he joined the Mughal forces and served Emperor Shah Jahan for a brief period. After being deprived of his jagirs, he defected to the Bijapur Sultanate in 1632 A.D. and regained control over Pune and Supe. In 1638 A.D., he also received the jagir of Bangalore, after Bijapur's invasion of Kempe Gowda III's territories. He eventually became the chief general of Bijapur and oversaw its expansion.[12] Shahaji was a father of Shivaji, the Chhatrapati Shivaji Maharaj. Shivaji Bhonsale, also referred to as Chhatrapati Shivaji Maharaj, was an Indian ruler belonged to Maratha family of Bhonsle clan.[13] His paternal grandfather Maloji (1552–1597 A.D.) was an influential general of Ahmadnagar Sultanate, and was awarded the epithet of 'Raja'. He was given deshmukhi rights of Pune, Supe, Chakan and Indapur for military expenses. He was also given Fort Shivneri for his family's residence (1590 A.D.).[14][15] At the time of Shivaji Maharaj's birth, power in Deccan was shared by three Islamic sultanates: Bijapur, Ahmednagar, and Golkonda. Shahaji often changed his loyalty between the Nizamshahi of Ahmadnagar, the Adilshah of Bijapur and the Mughals, but always kept his jagir (fiefdom) at Pune and his small army.[16] Shivaji Maharaj was devoted to his mother Jijabai, who was deeply religious. His studies of the Hindu epics, the Ramayana and the Mahabharata, and Muslim saint also influenced his lifelong defence of Hindu values.[17] He was deeply interested in religious teachings, religious unity and regularly sought the company of

Hindu and Muslim saints.[18] Thus Shivaji had a sense of respect for Hindu saints as well as Muslim saints. Apart from Hindu saints, Shivaji Maharaj used to helped Masjid, Dargah, Muslim saints, church, Christian Father on an equally basis. A notable example of this is his Muslim guru Kelashi's Yakub Baba. Konkan is a clear representative of the religious diversity in India. The temples in Konkan are well known, and so are the beautiful and resplendent Mosques and Dargahs. These places of worship attract and engage Muslims and Hindus alike in numbers amounting to thousands. In Kelshi, the Hazrat Yakub baba Sarvari Rahamtulla Dargah is historically famous and is 386 years old. Legend dictates that Yakub baba travelled from the Hyderabad-Sindh province to Kelshi in 1618. He resided in Kelshi since then and was known for his love for fellow residents and secularism. It is said that this Dargah is built by Chhatrapati Shivaji Maharaj. Some people say that Shivaji Maharaj started the dargah and then Sambhaji Raje completed it. 'Yakub Baba' was the teacher of Shivaji Maharaj. During invasion in Dabhol, Shivaji Maharaj came to know about Yakub baba, and he met him. Maharaj received blessings and guidance from him. Dabhol invasion was successful done. It is told that Yakub Baba had come from Sindh province to Kelshi via Bankot. He had a son with him named Sohail Khan, who was ten years old, who later was known as Himmat Khan. Himmat Khan's Dargah is next to Yakub Baba's Dargah. the Dargah was built with beautiful carvings on stone on a total area of 534 acres. Every year on 6th of December a mega fest 'Urus' takes place here, at the Yakub baba Dargah in Kelshi. Muslims and Hindus attend this Urus in equal numbers to offer their respects and prayers to Yakub baba. The devotees participate with enthusiasm and gusto in the local fests or 'Urus' that take place here. From the above example, we can see that the respect and love of various kings, sardars and common people of Maharashtra towards Muslim saints has been there since time immemorial. Ordinary people want a peaceful life of happiness and contentment. He also considered various Muslim and Hindu saints as his gurus. Saints on the path of devotion and Muslim Sufi saints also helped to increase religious acceptance among the people through their various literature. Here we will consider the texts of these Muslim Sufi saints from different periods in Maharashtra.

Major part of Deccan region covered by Marathi speaking people today. Number of handwritten manuscripts copied texts is available in Bharat Itihas Sanshodhak Mandal Archives Pune, Shree Samarth Vangdevata Mandir Research Center Dhule, Rajwade Itihaas Samshodhan Mandal Dhule and Marathi Department Hastlikhit Samgrah Division, Dr. B.A. Marathwada University, Aurangabad. The Marathi language is attested from at least the eight century A.D., but its major efflorescence coincided with the rule of the Yadavas of Daulatabad in the 13th century. This culminated in the famous 'Dnyaneshwari' (between 1275-1296 A.D.). As Mr. Tulpule and

Mr. Feldnaus observed, such great literary achievements which were made in this period that it had come to be known as the 'Golden Age', in the history of the Marathi language. This period saw the rise and development of the Warkaris and the Mahanubhav as the two sects that produced the bulk of old and middle Marathi literature. Number of dynasties of Hindus and Muslims ruled over the Marathi, Telugu and Kannad language zones of the Deccan region.[19] Many Sufis wrote the Marathi literature in Medieval Deccan. This medieval period of Deccan was not only the development of individual Hindu and Muslim mystical communities but also their interactions with one another. The political stabilities and wealth not only enhanced the administrative capacities of the kingdoms in Deccan but increasing religiously oriented textual productions, religious interactions between Bhakti and Sufi mystical movements in Deccan. In north India, Delhi Sultans and Mughals had very relations with Hindu and Muslim mystical saints and interactions. Humayun was an initiate of the Shattariya Sufi silsila or order and established a close relationship with two of its Shaikhs, Shaikh Phul Bahlul and his brother Muhammad Ghaws Gwaliari. In Deccan, Sabaji Pratapraja, a Brahmin, was a prominent minister in the revenue department of the Ahmednagar kingdom of Burhan Nizam Shah, in the middle of Sixteenth century. He is also the author of Dharmashastra, Parashuram pratapa in Sanskrit. This book was dedicated to Burhan Nizam Shah. Many Muslim and Hindu generals were in job under Deccan sultanates and Mughal during sixteenth to eighteenth century. This era was the era of religious, linguistic, and cultural synthesis. According to Audrey Truschke, under Akbar, Hindus constituted twenty-two percentages of the Mughal nobles. During Aurangzeb period it was increased Hindu participation of the elite levels of the Mughal state by nearly fifty-one percentages.

1. Shah Murtuza Bahamani (1575-1650 A.D.):

Shah Murtuza Bahamanai was originally from the family of Bahamani Dynasty in Bidar of Deccan. Also, he related to the silsila of Qadiriya. He noted in genealogy Sijra-e-Qadiriya in Central Deccan region. Mahipati wrote the history of Shah Murtuza Bahamani with the decline of Bahamani Empire in Deccan. Sahajanand Swami of Anand cult was the friend of Shah Mutrtuza Bahamani. This story noted the Bhaktvijay by Mahipati. He told the story of Sahajanand Swami and Murtuza. Mahipati said that Murtuza read the 'Viveksindhu' of Mukundraj (1128-1200 A.D.), a famous book written in Marathi in early era. Murtuza and Sahajanand were the friends about twelve years. Hanuman Atmaram was the author of 'Purnand charitra' in Marathi. He wrote the stories belongs to the philosophical interactions within Aanand Cult and Murtuza.[20] Shah Murtuza Bahamani had influenced by the number of non-Brahmin cults in Maharashtra and Karnataka border peripheries. In north India, Mir Abdul Wahad Bilgrami (1608 A.D.) wrote a book named, Haqaiq-i-Hindi and noted the many Vaishnavit symbols, term, and ideas with equivalents in Islamic mystical ideas. For example, Murtuza had interactions and friendships with Saint Nageshshaiv, Nath Yogi and Warkari cult from Karnataka and Maharashtra region. That was the main cause to his poetry had the symbolic meaning by Hindu and Muslim theological terms and comparison, commentary with synthetic approach. He had the spiritual co-existence within his writing on the symbolic meaning of the religious terms, practices and spiritualities within the Hindu and Islam theology. Murtuza was noted by name in the Sijra-i-Quadiriyya of Shaikh Muhammad Shrigondekar of Ahmednager.[21] Murtuza was the scholar of Sanskrit, Persian and Arabic also. He wrote the book, "Awindh Punjikaran" or the Hindu Islam Darshan Kosh in Sanskrit-Marathi-Dakhani language. It was the dictionary of religious symbols with comparisons of philosophical terms in both theologies. It was the thesaurus of religious symbols in both religions. He had the very deep knowledge of Shariat and the Quran. "Shah Muntoji Bahamani, Jiname nahi manmaani, Panjikaran ka khoj kiye, Hindu Musalmaan ek kar diye".[22] Shah Murtuza Bahamani is not a selfish man. He discovered / wrote Panjikaran and made the Hindu-Muslim unit / united. He spread the ideology of Sufism and Islamic philosophy by his Marathi poems first time. He had no interest in political affairs. He settled in woods and enjoyed the prayers and meditations (Muraqaba & Yogic practices). He discussed the Hindu and Muslim symbols of spiritual practices and the religious thinking in his Panjikaran book.

Hindu Symbols	Islamic Symbols	Hindu Symbols	Islamic Symbols
Deh (Body)	Wajud (Spiritual Status)	Kaaran (Causations)	-
Jagruti (Enlightens)	Bedari (Haal of Alertness)	Kanth (neck)	Halk (Neck)
Netr (eyes)	Chashm (Eyes)	Hriday (Heart)	Seenh (Heart)
Vedas (Vedic litrature)	Kitab (Islamic Books)	Karm (duties)	Shariat (Islamic Law)
Bhakti (devotion)	Tariqat (Sufi Silsilas)	Dnyan (knowledge)	Ma'arifat (Knowledge)
Prithwi (Earth)	Khaq (Soil)	Tej (Fire)	Aathash
Aakash (Sky)	Hawwa	Guru (Teacher)	Pir (Shaikh, teacher)

Murtuza wrote the ten appendixes on the religious symbols of the Hindu and Islamic philosophies. He wrote in Marathi:

> "Shubdh Waasanaa Anth Karan Hoy taree, Shree Guruche Paawale Drudh Dharee. Taree Thikaanaasi Paawe". "The human being has the number of selfish desires /unlimited requirements, but who catch the feet / guidance of Pir / Guru, he will be the free soul / successful. And he / she enjoyed the successful life."

Dnyansagar Ayya Mrutunjaya (the ocean of knowledge) was the Shaiv Guru and friend of Murtuza in northern Karnataka region. From his influences, Murtuza wrote the poetry on Nagesh and Veershaiv philosophy. His symbols were noted in his poetries as Shiva and his Bhakti. Veershaiv cult was founded by Basaw Swami in northern Karnataka. He was the supporter of caste less society. Also, he was the anti-Brahminism thinker, who had number of clashes with orthodox Brahmin class.[23] Warkari, means a pilgrim, in Marathi Language. These people or groups have a Vaishnava (Vithal Krishna bhakti) religious movement from medieval period in Maharashtra. This Bhakti tradition has the geographical association with the Maharashtra and Karnataka region in Deccan part of south India. Warkari worship Vitthal (God) at Pandharpur temple. Lord Vitthoba or Vitthal was known as the form of Krishna in Maharashtra, an Avatar / incarnation. This Marathi Bhakti movement associated with the movement of Saint Dnyaneshwara (1275-96 A.D.), Namdev (1350 A.D.), Eknath (1533-1599 A.D.) and Tukaram (1608 A.D.). This Warkari tradition has been a part of Marathi devotional movement since, thirteenth century A.D. It formed as a path or way of community, the people, who shared spiritual beliefs and practices during Vari / pilgrim travel visit to Pandharpur. Shah Murtuza presented the ideas and symbols of Warkari cult. He noted the individual sacrifices, forgiveness, simplicity, peaceful co-existence, non-violence, love, and humility in social life of Maharashtra during Bahamani period, in his poetry. Murtuza wrote Siddha Sanket poetry with the influence of Saint Dynaneshwara's famous book Dnyaneshwari. He quoted the number of lines from Dnyaneshwari in his poetries. The Nath cult was a heterodox Siddha tradition cult in Medieval Deccan. It was founded by Matsyendranath and further developed by Saint Gorakh Nath Swami. The cult has faith on Shiva. The aims of Nath Yogi are to enjoy peaceful life, freedom, and happiness in this life. Siddha Sanket poetry collection of Murtuza noted the spiritual symbols of Nath Yogis. Murtuza noted the importance or significance of Yoga and Samaadhi (Muraqaba) in life of Yogis. The shrine or Dargah of Shah Murtuza Bahamani located at the suburb area of Kalyani or Basawkalyan town in northern Karnataka. His Urs festival is celebrated by Hindu and Muslim devotees at Sufi shrine or Dargah at 11th Ramzan (Ramadan) ever year. Due to his deep influence in both communities, the people organized the common feast for poor and all with vegetarian food.

"Ishwarbhakti Keli Jene Bhave, Tyache Man Granthi Sthirave, Aape aap Ugave, Sandeh na pade." Prakashdeep: 15.

"Who devoted himself / herself towards God, he / she will reach to goal of life. He / She rise as a new Morning without any worry." This was the symbols about devoted life of path finder in his life by Upnishad philosophy. Murtuza presented his ideas in his Prakashdeep poetry. "Shudra, Vaishy, Kshatriy, Brahmin, Haa dehaachaachi gun, Tuj Naahi Jaati Varn, Yaasi tu bhulu nako." Prakashdeep:65.

"The Varna system of Vedic religion is on the physical realities, but you (human being) are equal. You are not divided. Do not forget the equality within human being."

Like this, Murtuza presented the Islamic ideology about casteless society. Islam proclaimed equality. It was the great influence of Islamic ideology on the poetry of Murtuza. In Punjikaran thesaurus, Murtuza wrote the comparative study of the religious symbols, terms, practices and beliefs of both Hindu and Islam religion. This book gave the deep knowledge of the Sanskrit, Marathi, and Arabic Persian terms. This was the first book which wrote in Marathi to explain the information of Islamic knowledge in Marathi. And it was the first thesaurus which gave the depth of religious and cultural synthesis by a written text material by a Muslim scholar in regional language of Deccan.

Table of Shah Murtuza Qadiri Bahmani's literature and
religious symbols in poetry: [24]

Sr. No.	Name of the Poetry Collection	Features / influences	Place of Manuscripts/ Name of Archives Ref.
1	Prakaashdeep (Lamp of light) in Marathi	Upnishad, Vedas, Dnyaneshwari etc.	1] Mss, 399 poems, at Sarswati Mahal Manuscript Library, Thanjavur, Tamilnadu. 2] Mss. No. 434, 123-379, V.K. Rajwade Research Centre, Dhule.
2	Siddha Sanket (achieved tokan)	Yoga, Nath Yogis, Samaadhi etc.	1] Thanjavur, Tamilnadu. Mss No. 434:176 (433). 2] Dhule, Rajwade. Mss. No. n.a.

3	Punjikaran (Hindu Islam Darshan Kosh)	Both Religious symbols of Hindu and Islamic philosophy.	1] Samarth Vangdevata Mandir Research Centre, Dhule. 2] Rajwade, Dhule 3] Godatir History Research Centre, Nanded.
4	Jeevoddharan (Search of ourselves)	Guru Mahatmya Importance of Pir in Tariqat	Thanjavur, Tamilnadu
5	Swarup Samaadhaan (Satisfaction of inner soul)	Self-Awareness	Dhule.
6	Adwait Prakash (Vedic Philosophy)	Vedas	Thanjavur Library, 578 Lines poetry.

Shah Murtuza Bahamani wrote about the monotheism and Vedic philosophy also. He discussed the Yog science in Siddh Sanket. He practiced the Vari or pilgrim travel to Pandharpur with his Hindu friends. His Hindu Islam Darshan Kosh or Punjikaran, gave the historic information about the Hindu Muslim symbolism and their dictionary of religious terms in Marathi language, first time. He wrote his book, Prakaash Deep in Bhum or Bhaum, modern Bhum town in Osmanabad District of Maharashtra. His poetry also influenced by the Quranic knowledge. India was likey to be the biggest centre of Sufism in the world.

2. Ambar Hussain (1603-1653 A.D.):

Ambar Hussain was only one Sufi poet who wrote the commentary or Tika on the Geeta, named 'Ambarhusaini'. Amber Khan is the family name of Hassan Amber Khan. His family lived in Daulatabad region. According to 'Vaijyanath' of Thanjavur, Ambar Husain born on Tuesday, Jyeshth Shuddha 11, Shake 1525 / 1603 A.D. He noted the family life of Ambar khan in his 'Chidambar jayanti strotra'. He presented the ideology of monotheism in his 'Geetatika'.

"Jo Brhamadikancha Swami Ek | Jayaa nase aanikha naayak ||"

He explained the Muslim and Hindu ideas in about the monotheism. Ambar khan also noted the importance of Guru and the knowledge (Dnyan) in his writings. Dr. Priyolkar wrote the possibilities about the relations of the Sufi circle of Khuldabad-Daulatabad region to Ambar khan. It should also be noted that a prominent center of Sufi activity was founded near Daulatabad in the town of Khuldabad in thirteenth century Deccan. Already two editions of the 'Ambarhusaini' text were published by Maharashtra Research Parishad, Marathi Sahitya Mandal, Mumbai.[25]

Yawan (Muslim) who is refined in the Gitaganga:

After Saint Dnyaneshwar presented the generous and noble philosophy of Lord Krishna through Marathi language, 'Ithe Marathichiye Nagari', theology flourished and some people of Muslim society, Vaishyas and Shudras of Hindu society also took advantage of it. On the strength of his knowledge, Dnyaneshwar brought Sanskrit Gita and its thoughts in Marathi language. Muslim Sufi saints like Hussain Amber khan also found their way into this ideology. To express his gratitude, Amber Khan also wrote a Marathi lyrical commentary in the song (ovee). At the beginning of this lyrical commentary, Amber Khan mentions his father and grandfather as follows:

आधी अंबर अंबरखान | त्याचा पुत्र याकूत अंबरखान |
त्याचा सुत हुसेन अंबरखान | असे जगद्वंद्य || १.६ ||

First Amber is Amber Khan. His son Yakut Amber Khan.
His son Hussain Amber Khan. Ase Jagadvandya || 1.6.||

From this Amber is the first Amber Khan- Yakut Amber Khan - Hussain Amber Khan leads to family. He has also embodied this line mentioned in a Sanskrit verse-

याकूताम्बरखानोऽभूदम्बराम्बरखानतः |
तत्पुत्रोऽस्ति जगद्वन्द्यो हुसेनाम्बरखानराट् ||

As of today, no definite information is available as to where the Amber Khan dynasty rejoiced. Within a year after of Hussain Amber Khan composed his Gitatika, Balaji Trimala copied it and the copy which is handwritten is available now in the Saraswati Mahal Library of Thanjavur.[26] Amber Khan dynasty might have been in the service of the Nizamshahi at Daulatabad initially. A case of estate dispute of a man named Divakar from Satara district was settled in 1618 A.D. by an authority named Amber Khan from Daulatabad. This suggests that Amber Khan was a government official. From this paper it was certainly understood that, at Daulatabad, around 1618 A.D., an officer named Amber Khan was in power. Whereas the same document also stated that he stayed in Khadki (Aurangabad), Indapur and Mayani villages during his administration. Amber Khan is also included in the character of the famous seventeenth century by saint Ramavallabhadas.[27] Ramavallabhadas's father Ambajipant was from Daulatabad, and he was working with Amber Khan. This is mentioned by one of the followers of Ramavallabhadas in his book 'Birudavali'. Fifteen years later, in 1633 A.D. (June 17), the Mughals conquered Daulatabad, captured Husain Nizamshah and put an end to Nizamshahi. For three years after this, Shahaji established his military camp in Junnar area and flight with Mughals in the name of Nizamshahi. Murtuza, a minor prince of the Nizamshahi dynasty, was imprisoned in the fort of Jeevdhan, thirty miles west of Junnar. Prince Murtuza was released from captivity by Shahaji and was crowned in 1633 with the help of Adilshah's chief Murar Jagdev. On his way back to Bijapur after crowed ceremonay, Murar Jagdev kept five-six thousand troops under the control of Amber Khan to help Shahaji.[28] From this reference it appears that, in 1633, after Daulatabad fell to the Mughals, Shahaji must have had the full support of Amber Khan in his daring attempt to revive the Nizamshahi with the help of Bijapurkar. After Shah Jahan came to the south in 1636 A.D. and shattered Shahaji's dreams, Shahaji went to Karnataka on behalf of Bijapurkar. Hereon, we can assume that Amber Khan also went there with Shahaji at the same time. From this we can assumed that Geetatika was composed by Amber Khan, during his staying at Thanjavur in Karnataka. That is why we can find a copy of this book here in the Saraswati Mahal Library of Thanjavur. While this Amber Khan was an officer at Daulatabad, Saint Chand Bodhale, Janardanaswamy, Ramavallabhadas's father Ambajipant rejoiced in his shelter, and he performed his philosophical activities, spiritual writing without any hindrance. From this fact one can imagine the behaviour of Amber Khan and looks religiously liberal. He was greatly influenced by Warkari and Bhakti Marg and their teaching.

Birth of Hussain Amber Khan:

A very reliable piece of evidence is available regarding the date of birth of Hussain Amber Khan. Vaidyanath, a writer from Thanjavur who was a contemporary of Hussain Ambar khan, was very fond of Amber Khan. He has named his commentary on Ashtavakra as 'Siddhantachidambari' to express his reverence for Amber Khan. Vaidyanathan who performed 'Chidambarajayantistotra' on the birth of Amber Khan. A case called has been written. In this case, it said that 'Mlench Amber Khan is the incarnation of God in Kali Yuga'. (1603 A.D.) Probably, he was the son of Amber Khan, who was ruling in Daulatabad around 1540 A.D., and we have already seen that he is the father of Hussain Amber Khan in terms of spirituality.

Who is the guru (teacher) of Hussain Amber Khan?

Hussain Ambar Khan does not explicitly mention the name of the Guru in his treatise. At the beginning of the book, while reciting Guruman, he says-

जेथुनी हे विश्व होते | जेथे मागुती लय पावते।।
तया सच्चिदानंद श्रीगुरुते। साष्टांग नमस्कार ।। 1.5।।

'My greetings to Sachidananda Guru,
at whose feet this world originates and perishes.'

The word 'Sachchidananda' in this verse is taken as a noun, it cannot be decided in this sense as Sachchidananda. Poet Mr. Oka considered him a disciple of Keshavswami Bhaganagarkar. But there is no definite proof to believe so. Keshavswamy's was roaming in the south with his followers Shah Beg, Bajid Pathan, Shakarganj etc. It is true that many Muslims became disciples. But such support will not suffice. There is another dubious link. The person named as Narayan is the author of Hussain Amber Khan's Geetatika and Narayan is the author of Keshavaswamy's disciple Santraj's 'Chintanivaran'. If these two Narayanas are the same, then there is a possibility that Hussain Ambar Khan and Keshavswami have a philosophical correlation.

The period of Geetatika:

The composition of Hussain Amber Khan is as follows-

शके पंधरासे पंचेहातरि । विजय नाम संवत्सरिं ।
आश्विन शुद्धदशमी सोमवारिं । अंबरहुसेनी टीका संपूर्ण जाली ।।१८.८६।।

Shake fifteen fifteen. Vijay Nam Sanvatsarin.
Ashwin Shuddhadashami Monday.
Amber Husaini's comment is completed.

This comment was completed on Ashwin Shukl 10 Shake 1575 (1653 A.D.). The author of this poem has named his commentary 'Amberhuseni'. Even at the end of the chapter, the name 'Iti Shrimad Ambar Hussain Virchitayan Amber Hussain Amikayam Shri Bhagavad Gita Tikayam ...' is mentioned. At one point he has called his commentary 'Gitabhavarthadipika' (18.84), but it is not the name of the text, but the philosophy of its form. From this it seems that even Muslim Sufi saints like Amber Khan refuted the commentary on Gita as ovee to promote their philosophy and to show that their philosophy is not different from the path of devotion of Hindu saints.

Amberhussaini

Saint Dnyaneshwar wrote the Gita commentary in Marathi, but Hussain Amber Khan read the commentary on the Gita written by Shankaracharya and Sridhar Swami. He had a good knowledge of Sanskrit language. He wrote a commentary in Marathi called 'Gitabhavarthadipika' based on Sanskrit commentary. In this book, he has described the emotions in the ovee in a Marathi language that everyone can understand easily. We see his erudition in expressing the meaning of Sanskrit words with precise Marathi words. He is making this commentary for the common people. Amber Khan has written this commentary in the present language without showing any greatness of knowledge despite his expertise of the Vedas.

Amberhussaini : Appearance and features

Amber Hussain is the first Muslim Saint who wrote the Marathi lyric poem (commentary on Gita is 'Gitatika') in Marathi language. Sachchidanand Baba, was the 'author' of Dyneshwar, as well as Narayan was the author with Amber Hussain while creating this commentary. He mentioned it in the 85ᵗʰ verse of the eighteenth chapter as follows –

हुसेनी अंबराचे कृपेनें लिहिले असे हे नारायणे ।
यांत शुद्ध अबद्ध बिचारणें । संतजनी ।।

This is Narayan who wrote with the grace of Shan Hussain Amber.
This is pure and non-written by any of earlier saints.

So, a humble expression is also revealed. But there is no information available about 'Narayan', as his full name, his village. However, he might be a one of his followers. The writing period of Amberhussaini was 1653. Evidence of this can be found at the end of the 18ᵗʰ chapter of the book Amberhussaini.

शके पंथरासे पंचेहातरि । विचय नामसंबत्सरिं।
आश्विन शुध्द दशमी सोमवारिं । अंबरहुसनी टीका संपूर्ण जाली ।।१८८x८६।।

Shake Pantharase Panchehatari. Vijay namsavantsari।
Ashwin Shuddha Dashmi Somwari. Amberhussaini tika
sampurn zali ||.18x86.[29][30]

The first 14 verses of the first chapter are very important. These included 'Mangalacharan', 'Ganesh-Sharda-Gurubandan' as well as Poet's genealogy, bibliographic purpose, mentioned about predecessors (commentators), inexperience of local commentaries, etc. So many things had come up. Those were very important. The peculiarity of the texts of almost all Muslim Marathi saint poets was also noticed in their Mangalacharans. I would like to mention here the books 'Yogasangram' and 'Siddhantabodh' by Shaikh Mohammad and Shahamuni respectively. Before 'Mangalacharana', Amber Hussain started writing books by chanting 'Ganesha' as 'Shriganeshay Namah'. Later, while worshiping Ganesha, Sharda and Guru, let's see what they have mentioned.

"भेदाभेदाचा आग्रह उरदंड लोचि बिघ्नसमूह प्रचंड ।
तेयाते नाशिता जो वक्रतुंड। तया नमस्कारु ।। १x ।
जो ब्रह्मादिकांचा स्वामी एक । जया नसे आणिख नायक ।
ऐसा जो सर्वोत्तम बिनायक । तया नमस्कारु' । १x २।।

The urge for discrimination is overwhelming.
These were destroyed by Vakratund (Ganesha).
My greetings to him || 1x1 ||
One who is the lord of Brahmadikas (Gods and saints).
There is no own part from him.
The one who is the best Binayak. (Ganesha).
My Greetings to him| 1x 2||

Amber Hussain is a follower of Islam. Islam does not consider caste or stratification. From this point of view, this is the first line (ovee) of 'Amberhussaini'. Amber Hussain found some similarities in the basic tenets of Islam and Hinduism, among them disregard for discrimination, opposition to heterogeneity, reward for equality. Monotheism is the lifeblood of Islam. Even though Indian philosophy mentions many of these obligations, there is only one God, this is the central thought. Ambar Hussain is appealing on the occasion and praise Ganesha. Destroying ignorance and attainment of enlightenment is also an important spiritual goal of Islam and Hinduism.

भक्ती-श्रह्मानंद देती। अवतार, अज्ञान खंडिती।
ऐसी शारदा सरस्वती। तिये नमस्कारु ।। १x३।।

The above verse means I am praising the Goddess Sharada (Saraswati), the Goddess of knowledge and wishing to get guidance for devotion, bhakti, and path of enlightenment. The Indian philosophy tradition holds that the Guru is the Supreme Being. Even in the Sufi sect, the importance of Guru-Pir, Shaikh, is considered as such. God created the world. He is the one who protects and destroys the universe. This idea is present in Islam as well as in Indian philosophy. This idea mentioned by Amber Hussain at the very beginning of the scriptures, the Guru is presented as the Lord –

जेधूनि हैं विश्व होते । जेथे मागुती लय पायतें।
तया सच्चिदानंद श्रीगुरूतें । साष्टांग नमस्कारू' ।। १x ५ ।।

'My greetings to Sachidananda Guru,
at his feet who originates and perishes this world.'

Paramatma means God is the creator of the universe, an idea that is also present in Indian philosophy and in the holy Quran. In the beginning of Amberhussaini's ninth chapter, in the thirteenth verse, poet has explained this idea.

माझिया आधारे प्रकृती । प्रसये चराचर व्यक्ती।
याकारणे सुभद्रापती । जग हे फिरते ।। ९ x १३।।

God has created this nature, every person.
That's why he is only managing and controlling all the activities
of every human being and this moving world. 9 x 13.[31]

The Nirguna principle behind Saguna is important, Amber Hussain insisted the same concept in this chapter. It should also be noted that Nirguna ideology in Islam is centered on Amber Hussain's ideology and he finds it in Indian philosophy and rewards it wholeheartedly. Amber Hussain is well-known, as evidenced by the following observations. In the seventh verse, he wrote as 'Ekashar Nighantu pahon lihile ase'. This means Amber Hussain has read the commentary which was written earlier on the same. However, it is mentioned in the eleventh verse that he has seen the lyric of 'Achutashram' or 'Nivruttinathadika'. 'Aluberuni', an Arab scholar who came to India in the 10th century, had wrote the commentary on the Gita in Arabic language. With this we can say that Amber Husain is the 1st Muslim saint in Maharashtra who has commentary on Gita in Marathi language. Here I would like to give an example of Amber Hussain's very effective interpretations. The example stated in the first chapter is shows the description of 'Kulakshaya' means destroying of whole family or clan which was Arjuna's concern during the Mahabharata war. Amber Hussain has explained the question of Arjuna in very simple language in Ovee number 40-43. Also, in the second chapter of 'Atmanakavivek', Ovee number 40-48 he has beautifully presented it in an analytical manner. The Bhagavad Gita has a background of war. Amber Hussain succeeded in depicting Arjuna's mental state as well as the incidental events in a short but linear way. His dialogues were also effective and reveal effective personalities. Fluent and succinct language style is a feature of Amber Hussain's poetry, and his poignant illustrations also draw our attention. This lyric can be recorded in Marathi literature as a derivative commentary that succinctly describes the 'meaning' of the Gita.

3. Aalam Khan (16th century)

Aalam Khan is the very famous Sufi saint in the region of southern Maharashtra and the northern Karnataka or Gulbarga, Bidar region. His Dargah is situated at village Karali in Umaraga Taluka, Osmanabad District of Maharashtra. Aalam Khan migrated from northern Indian subcontinent. He settled at Mugli village near Bidar. According to Dr. R. C. Dhere, Aalam Khan was the disciple of Nasir-al-din Chishti of Delhi. 'Nagesh Lilaamrut', the Marathi book written by Mr. Trimbak Bhanji Deshpande in 1848 A.D., gave the historical information about the early and later life of Aalam Khan in Deccan.[32] We can find this reference in chapter 39 of 'Nagesh Lilaamrut'. Saint Nagesh was the Marathi name of Nasir-al-Din in Deccan. This book has the forty chapters on the life and poetry of Aalam khan. According to the author, Aalam khan died in the later part of sixteenth century AD. The manuscripts of Aalam Khan poetry are available at Shree Samarth Devata Mandir Archived in, Dhule Maharashtra. Also, the Paad (Marathi poems) of Aalam Khan is available at the Shree Govindraj Baba Maharaj Samsthan, Gulbarga and the Bharat Itihaas Samshodhan Mandl Poona. The poetry of Aalam khan in Marathi has the influence of Quranic and Sufis ideology.

He wrote:

"Kirtan kele ho Mugali gaawi, Shrote milaale virakt nispruhee. Aalam khan babache Sampradaayee, Jyaa babasee naagobaa updeshile. Khanji kashtataa to shuddha hridayee, Nasir ud Din nagobaa bhaale gosaawi. Lay laksha yogee Zaala anubhavi, Mandali tyaachi taisich."

This Marathi poem explained the relation of Aalam Khan with Nasir-al-Din Chirag Dehlawi. Aalam Khan also stated the Kirtan or spiritual lyrics presentation before the mob at Mugali village. Villagers and followers of Aalam Khan had enjoyed these assemblies ever. This poem clearly shows the Sufi practices of Zikr (dhikr) and spiritual assemblies (Bhajan, Abhang, Samaa) with disciples of Aalam Khan. Also, Aalam Khan accept the impressions of Nasir-al-Din Chirag Dehlawi (1274-1356 A.D.) in his life-time spiritual practices.

Aalam Khan wrote another Marathi poem on the Sufi idea of Wujud. Wujud is an Arabic word means existence, presence, being and entity. However, in the religion of Islam, it tends to take on a deeper meaning. It has been said that everything gains its Wujud by being found or perceived by God. For those of the Sufi tradition, Wujud has more to do with the finding of God than the existence of God. Aalam Khan wrote the poem on the lifetime spiritual guidance by him for muridin or shishy":

"Nar deh jaato re, jaato haato haati, Kaahi ek karaa re, karaa Guru Bhakti, Aayushya Molaache, molaache re mudhaa, Antee hosil hosil re, kaalaachaa warpadaa. Putra Kalatra, Kalatra, Nohe re Aapule, Waayaa Bhulale, bhulale re, mokshapadaa chukale. Jyotee asataa, asataa re, thevaavee kari, Jyote maawalalyaa mawalalyaa re, padsil andhakaari Vichaar vivek, vivek re, vairaagya charaare, man halu halu, halu halu re, swarupee laawaawe. Sabaahy antari antari re, swasakshi aatmaaraam jaan, Nagesh paripurn paripurn re, bole Aalam Khan".

The relationship between a spiritual master and his disciple (piri-muridi) has very important thing in Sufi philosophy. Aalam Khan explained the importance of Guru Bhakti or Pir's importance in the spiritual life of the follower or Murid, in his above poem. He stated the significance of Pir in the life of pupil for the Moksha or success life with achievement of final goal. Aalam Khan believed that the death or the end of life is the truth in human being. The human must take the life in serious way. Fanaa is the Sufi term for extinction. It means to annihilate the self, while remaining physically alive. Persons having entered this state are said to have no existence outside of, and be in complete unity with, God. Fanaa is equivalent to the concept of Nirwaan in Buddhism. Aalam Khan discussed the importance of Moksha in his poem. Aalam Khan had the focus on in his Marathi poetic thoughts that, the three concepts, like: Khudi or Swa sakshi (self), Moksh or Fanaa and Vivek (wisdom and/or knowledge). In every poem he noted the name of his Murshid or Pir, Nasir al din Chirag Dehlawi as Nagesh.

Aalam Khan presented the idea of Guru or Pir in his Marathi poem named "Guru Mahaatmya" in Nagesh Darpan manuscript. He quoted in the poem in Marathi-

"Aagamya panth Guruchaa paahtaa Aakal re. Aaj mothaa aanand zaalaa. Maj bhetla Guru Raay. Kaasi Aamhaasi Gurumurti. Gururaaj Dayaa keli, Aantarkalaa Daakhawali. Tuze swarup garuraayaa, paahta nirsale maayaa. Dene Gururaayaache, paawan patitaache. Namo namo Guruwaryaa, aanant viphu krupaanichee, kari maj dayaa. Yaa Gurusi kaay baa dyawe, Amhi kashaane utraayi whaawe. Sadguru Dataraa, krupechyaa saagaraa."

These 1 to 28 padas of Marathi poem of Aalam Khan who is very famous for the importance of Pir in Murid life. Shishy or Murid cannot take the right path in life without the Shaikh's guidance.[33] The Chishti sufis followed practices based on the pir-Murid relationship, such as pilgrimage to tombs of saints (Ziyarat of Dargahs) and the observation of their death anniversaries (urs). Aalam Khan had the spiritual relation with the silsila of Nasir-al-Din Chirag Dehlwi. The poems of Aalam Khan gave the references about the Pirimuridi relations with Nasir-al-Din and Aalam

Khan clearly. This is the unique example of Chishti Sufis writings into Marathi in medieval Deccan. Aalam khan presented the Sufi ideas like Pir Murid relations, Fanaa, Zikr into Marathi in his poems. And even today his both Hindu and Muslim devotees come to Dargah and memorized the spiritual ideas of Aalam Khan. In a village called Karali, which is close to Mugali village, Aalam Khan took Samadhi next to the tomb of Nagesh Sampradayi Agaji Maharaj. On the road from Umarga to Humanabad, at a distance of 6 miles from Umarga, the tomb of Agajhi Maharaj is on a hill. That hill is called Karali Hill. The Samadhi temple is surrounded by a wall. There is the tomb of Alam Khan under the neem tree on the right side of the tomb of Agachi Maharaj.

4.   Shaikh Sultan (18th century):

Shaikh Sultan was a Shahir Poet in Eighteenth century Maharashtra. He village was a carve near Karad. He was famous in Peshwa period within Satara, Karad and Poona region. He was also supported by King Shahu Chhatrapati. His guru Golpanath was living at Triputi near Satara. This Gopalnathan made Shaikh Sultan a great kirtankar who was a shahir poet. He used to chant on Vedas and Upanishads. He came and stayed in Triputi with his Guru and serve him. The remains of his castle are still there today. After hearing Shaikh Sultan's kirtan on Vedas and Upanishads, some orthodox people complained to Bajirao Peshwa that a Muslim saint should be punished for doing kirtan on Vedas and Upanishads. Regarding this complaint, the Peshwas summoned Shaikh Sultan to the Pune court. The Peshwa was very happy to hear that Shaikh Sultan performed kirtan and he was offered an Inam which is a gift a land and garden near Pune. One Inam document had proclaimed by Peshwa ruler Bajirao I in 1728 A.D. to Shaikh Sultan. Today this Inam land belongs to Munjeri Gardan Math near Swargate area of Pune town.[34]

His Guruparmpara or spiritual genealogy as following:

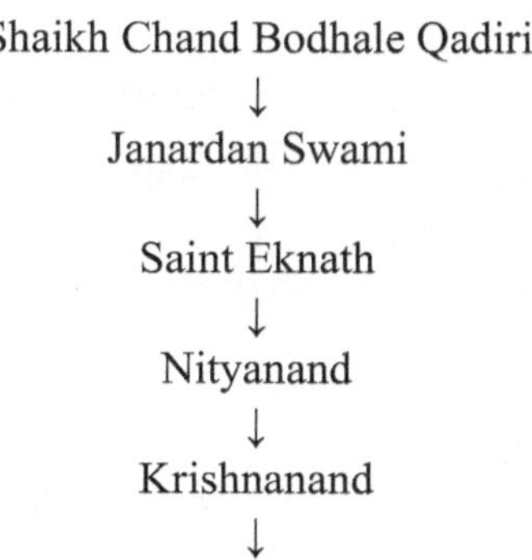

Visobaanand Wishambar

↓

Malharnath Muraarnath Rangnath

↓

Gopalnath

↓

Shaikh Sultan

Shaikh Sultan wrote the poem stories named, 'Ganpati janma', 'Hanuman janma' and 'Shivratrikatha'. His Guru was belonged to Nath culture of Maharashtra. Then Shaikh Sultan's poems and stories influence by Nath ideology. Saheb, Lal, Khayal and Pyari etc. Hindi words used by Shaikh Sultan in his poems. His love poems about God influence by Sufi ideas. Mr. R.C. Dhere stated that, Sultan's poems are both synthesis of the Nath and Sufi ideas of Love with God.[35]

Rajaram Prasadi wrote about Shaikh Sultan in "Bhakt manjari malaa" book, on poem number 47:

"Shishy Mahaabhaavik, Dnyaaatine Yawan hotaa ek. Ekvindh jo upaasak, Sultaan Shaikh naam dayaa".

Above mentioned poem means: "Very polite person and Yawan (Muslim) was the one, whose name was Sultan Shaikh. He was worshiper of God alone and no one else".

Shaikh Sultan wrote following books on mystics' ideas in Marathi:

"Paach Kathaa kavya: Stories of Ganapati Birth, Hanuman birth, Shiv stories etc. Aarati, Pada rachanaa: Hindu ritual worship (pooja) for God by Nath ideology, Jogi, Yogi. Shaikh Sultan called god in his poems as Saheb".

Shaikh Sultan has taken samadhi in 1769 A.D, which was after 3 year from the death of his Guru, Gopalnath. We can visit his samadhi in the meditation room of his palace, which is in his village, Triputi.

5. Shaikh Chand Qadiri (Shaikh Chand Bodhale) (1560 – 1650 A.D.)

Sayyad Chand Saheb Qadiri was the sixteenth century Sufi saint from Qadiriyya silsila or order of Sufism at Nashik – Daulatabad region. Almost all Marathi historians have recorded his important work as well as the disciple tradition created by him. Shaikh Mohammad has mentioned that the guru of Saint Eknath was Saint Chand Bodhale. By Mr. Bendre, Dr. R. C. Dhere and Dr. B. Deshpande has given a scholarly opinion about Saint Chand Bodhale in their books. Saint Chad Bodhale is well known in the Warkari and also in Sufi traditions. In the 40th chapter of 'Mahipati's' book named as 'Bhaktavijay', in the ovee number 76-78, Janadarnapant took Saint Eknath to the darshan of his Guru and this Guru was a yawan means Muslim. Two such stories are found in the book 'Bhaktavijaya'. [36][37][38] He was originally from Chandgiri village, near Tryambakeshwar town of Nashik. He was the murid or follower of Raje Muhammad Qadiri. Shaikh Muhammad Shrigondekar, the murid of Chand Qadiri and son of Raje Muhammad wrote the spiritual genealogy of Qadiri order in Daulatabad region, Shijara-i-Qadiri. In this Shijara spiritual genealogy noted as:

Shaikh Muhammad Gaus
↓
Raje Muhammad Qadiri
↓
Shaikh Chand Qadiri Bodhale
↓
Swami Janardan.
↓
Eknath

Shrisadguru Chand | Tyaani Janopant Angikaarlay ||
Janobaane Eknathaa Updeshileay. | Daasyatwagune. ||15.1||

This means, " Shri Chand is the Guru of Janardan Swami. Janardan teaches to Saint Eknath." This is the harmony of master student relations between Hindu Muslim mystics. Mahipati named Chand Qadiri Bhodale as the Guru of Saints in Daulatabad region. Janardan Swami was the Brahmin Officer of Nizam Shahi of Ahmednagar court. He was also the officer in Daulatabad Fort near Ellora caves. Chand Bhodale taught Chatushloki Bhagawat to Janardan Swami. Eknath also wrote this event in his 'Eknathi Bhagawat' in Marathi language. After the death of Chand Qadiri, Janardan Swami built the Shrine (Dargah) in the front of Daulatabad Fort. Mukundraj wrote in his 'Abhang' about the 'Guru Shishya tradition' of master student relationship of Chand Qadiri and Janardan Swami. Mahipati said about Chand Shaikh that, he was the spiritual leader of coexistence and cultural synthesis in Mughal Deccan.

Mahipati wrote about the Chand Qadiri in his an Abhang as:

"Janardan Mhane Eknathaa, aamuche thayee wolakhi aatta. Te awindh baisoni ashwaaparutaa, aalaa awacheet tyaa thaayaa. Ekrup dekhataa drushtee, Eknaath jaale bhaybhit poti. Pratyaksh yawan disato drushti, asatya goshti maj waate. Vishaalaa dole, aarakt nayan, haati shashtra, ashwa waahan. Sannidhya yeuni utaralaa jaan, mag kele janaardan naman tyaasi".[39]

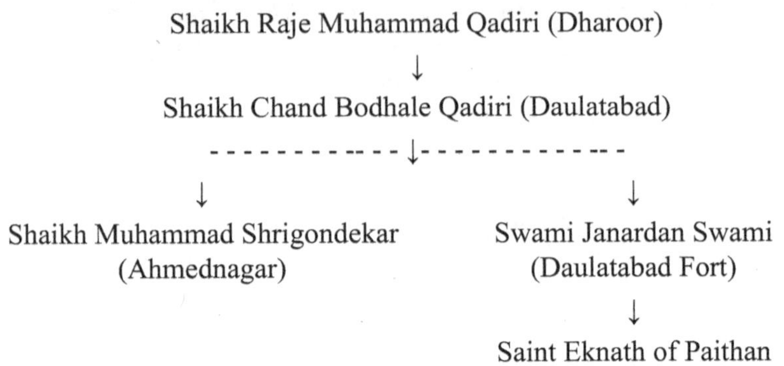

The tomb of Chand Qadiri situated at Daulatabad visited by Hindu and Muslim devotees.

Om Namoji Shree Sadguru Chand Bodhale |
Tyani Janopant Angikarile ||
Janobane Ekaa Updeshile | Das yatwgune ||
"Best wishes for Guru Chand.
Janardan Swami is his pupil.
Janardan teaches to Eknath"-

'Yogsangram', written by Shaikh Muhammad, Shrigondekar. This is the spiritual genealogy of the Qadir Sufi order towards Chand Bhodale. Also, the student of Saint Eknath, Mukundraj noted that, 'Chandra Bodhale Mul Janardan Khod. Shakhaa Paalaw gaod Eknath.' Mukundraj [40] Saint Eknath's literature had influenced by Sufi ideas. His Hindu Turk Samvad dialogue is famous for the spiritual coexistence of the Hindu Muslim thinking. Skyhawk have done the study on Eknath's Bhagavat literature. He insists that the guru of Eknath's guru was not the god Dattatreya as is traditionally believed but rather a Sufi of the Qadiri order. The most recent scholar to write a dissertation on Eknath is the Slovakian historian Dušan Deák, who recently wrote his dissertation on Eknath in the History Department at the University of Pune. Like Skyhawk, Deák focuses on historical points of Hindu-Muslim overlap, and like Skyhawk, his scholarship remains relatively unknown by a wide readership. He also wrote about the Sufi influences towards Saint Eknath's writing. Dusan Deak has studied on the Shah Datta cult of Maharashtra with its Sufi influences. Religious texts from medieval India, sometimes combine teachings of Saints from different religious, western Indian, oral, and scriptural heritage preserved in the Marathi language illustrates a fusion of Hindu Muslim beliefs where the Hindu God Dattatreya appears as a Muslim fakir to convey a spiritual message acceptable to both Hindus and Muslims.

Local imagination, shaped according to the social reality of the times, turned this Hindu deity into a Muslim Fakir.

6. Shaikh Muhammad Shrigondekar (1548-1618 A.D.):

Shaikh Muhammad Shrigondekar was the famous Marathi Muslim Sufi saint in seventeenth century. He was from Dharur village in Marathwada. He wrote 'Yogsangram', 'Nishkalank Bodh', 'Pawanvijay' and 'Dnyansagar'. His devotees are both Hindu and Muslim come to his Dargah (Samadhi) at Shrigonda. Shaikh Muhammad is known as 'Kabir' of Maharashtra. His father was Raje Mahammad and mother Phulai. He was belonged to Qadiri Sufi silsila during Nizamshahi of Ahmednagar.

<u>Spiritual Genealogy of Shaikh Muhammad Shrigondekar</u>

Abdul Qadir Jilani (Baghdada, Iraq)
↓
Sayyad Abdul Razzak Tajoddin Qaudiri
↓
Sayyad Mahammad Gaus Gwalihery Qadiri (Gwaliar)
↓
Shaikh Raje Muhammad Qadiri Sayyad Chand Saheb Qadiri
(Spiritual guide of Swami Janardan of Daulatabad)
↓
Sayyad Shaikh Muhammad Shrigondekar
(Shrigonda, Ahmednagar, Maharashtra)

Shaikh Muhammad wrote in Yogasangram': —

"Namo Shri Chand Bodhale.
Yani Jyanopanta Angikarile. Jyanobane Ekaa Upideshile‖15:1‖

Shaikh Muhammad Shrigondekar said that Chand Bodhale was also the follower of Dnyaneshwar. And both saints (Bodhale and Eknath) were influenced by Dnyaneshwar. King Maloji Bhosale was the Shishy of Shaikh Muhammad. Maloji Bhosale is buried in an Islamicate tomb in Ellora near Khuldabad (Khultabad). Maloji built a 'Math' in 1595 A.D. at Shrigonda in Ahmadnagar for Shaikh Muhammad. Shaikh Muhammad knew the languages like Marathi, Persian, Urdu, and Sanskrit. He wrote in Yogsangram that, Kama (Sex), Krodh (anger), and Alas (laziness) are the enemy of human being. Also, Muhammad Ghaws of Gwaliar, practiced Hath Yoga in his spiritual practices. In Nishkalank Bodh, he did critical analysis on blind faith, rituals, and slavery of religious mediators. Shivswroday, was the Sanskrit book of Shaikh. Also, his 'Rupake'(the way of explaining with examples), 'Bharude'(Bharud is a very old poetic form which was used by 16th century poets like Eknath to compose devotional songs. In his lifetime he wrote around 300 Bharuds on various themes. The Bharuds are narrative songs which carry double meaning. ... Bharud is either sung as a bhajan or devotional song or is enacted by the performer.) and Abhang (type of verse) are famous today in central Deccan Marathi speaking region. Mr. Bendre published 'Santnamavali' of Shaikh Muhammad Shrigondekar, which started by this line: In Yogsamgram, Shaikh Muhammad quoted the oneness of Narayana and Allah.[14] He wrote:

"Shreekaari Om Namo ji Naraayan |
Yaa Allah Mhanti Yawan |
Yawegali Anek Stawane | Saahi Darshnaachee ||"

(Om Narayan of Hindus and Allah of Yawan / Muslims is same.) In Bharud, he quoted:

"Shaikh Mahammad Dharm Jaago |
Nitya Harinaam Uccharow ||"

This is the religious philosophy of Shaikh Muhammad Shrigondekar Maharaj. His tomb or Dargah situated today at Shrigonda, in Ahmednagar District of Maharashtra. Another book of Shaikh Muhammad was Panjeej Musalmaani', in Marathi.

It is about the five basic concepts of Islam:

1. Kalma
2. Namaz
3. Roza
4. Zakat
5. Haj

"Laa ilallah Kalamaa Aawal Cheez ||
Ilallah Wolakhaa | Pe Param Brahm Beej |",

means the fundamental Kalama of Islam in Marathi, quoted by Shaikh Muhammad. There is no God but Allah, and Prophet Muhammad is the messenger of Allah'.

"Dono Aakhyankaa Ekich Dekhtaa |
Do Bhashi Varneelaa Ekachi Jaana || ",

means: " Same vision saw by two eyes. Two languages also described same one"

" Scchaa Pir Kahe Musalmaan |
Mrhate Mhanti Sadguru Purn |
Donhit Naahi Bhinnatwpan |
Aankh Khol Dekh Bhai ||"

"O' brother, Pir of Muslims and Sadguru of Hindus, both are same."
Yogsamgram, Shaikh Muhammad Shrigondekar, 17.3.

The time of Shaikh Mohammad

(1) Fortunately, there is not much controversy about the date of birth and death of Shaikh Mohammad. He was born in 1575 and died in 1674 as concluded by Dr. Modale his dissertation.

(2) The following information is recorded on the plaque on the Dargah at Shrigonde of Sheikh Mohammad-
'Shaikh Mohammad Bali
Born: 1548-1618
Original name - Shaikh Mohammad Raj Mohammad
Accommodation - Punda Bahira (Ashti)'

(3) Dr. Dhere determine their time from their judgment. He says that Shaikh Mohammad had a long life as he was a yogi. Around 1595 A.D., he settled in Shrigonda. Dr. Dhere has given important information about the time that he wrote 'Yoga Sangram' in 1645 A.D. and his decision was made on Falgun Shuddha Navami of 1660 A.D.

(4) Maloji Raje Bhosale's 'Chaknama' is also mentioned an important information which determined the time of Shaikh Mohammad. This is an important part of it. As it contains the date of Hijri year 1005 (August 1596 to June 1597).

Based on the above criteria, especially considering the writing period of 'Chaknama' and 'Yogasangrama', we concluded that Shaikh Muhammad was a saint poet of Shahaji and Shivaji Maharaja period. Considering the time of Chaknama, Dr. Bhima Modale decided that it might be 1575 A.D., However, we need to think more about the birthdate of Shaikh Mohammad. Dr. S. Tulpule considered the period of Shaikh Mohammad to be Shake 1482 (1560 A.D.) to Shake 1582 (1660 A.D.). It should be noted that they have given a balanced interpretation for that. [41][42][43]

Discipleship of Shaikh Mohammad

Mr. Virchand Desai has edited the traditional version of 'Yoga Sangram'. In the preface of this book, it is informed that the disciples of Shaikh Mohammad are in Shrigonda, Alibag, Jalna, Barshi, Belapur and Mumbai-

Pune area. Mudha, Pangul, Azam, Davalji, Hakim, Dayaldas were his main followers. Some of them have also written Aarti of Shaikh Mohammad.

Shaikh Mohammed and various denominations

An important composition of Shaikh Mohammad is 'Santanamabali'. It has been very much ignored by the scholars. Mr. Bendre has mentioned the reference in the preface volume II of his book named 'Kavitasangrah'.[44]

"Jay Jay Aarti Peer Paigambara."|

This is her beginning and this 'Santanamavali' is of 23 verses. It contains the names of saints of innumerable religions. They include Sufi, Nath, Nagesh, Warkari, Dutt, Veershanya (Jangam), Jane etc. Many saints are mentioned, and they are also worth studying in social and cultural contexts. Hafiz, Sarik, Mansoor Qazi Mahmud Jaina, Garib Naval (Nayaz), Hazrat Meera, Kardira Zahira, Sec Farid, Fatima Ibrahim Haruni etc. are also needed to consider. The inclusion of this name in the Marathi Santanamavali is also an indicator of unity. Shaikh Mohammad belongs to the original Sufi sect. They are Warakari from Maharashtra those became particularly one of the sects. The influence of Dnyaneshri on them is highly significant. In the same way, there was also the idea of yoga and "Panchikarana" in the Nath Sampradaya, which was evident from their various compositions. His affection for Jayaramswamy Badgaonkar gives an indication of how close he was to Samarth Sampradaya. They should have a little bit of connection with Datta Sampradaya. In his writings, we feel the confluence and coordination of the Sufism and the Warkari sect's and Advaita sect as well as the Yogasadhana of the Nath sect. Through his writings and speeches, he spread the philosophy of the Sufi and Warakari sects and received a great response during the Shivaji maharaja period. Shaikh Mohammad's literature is also rich and diverse. Like Marathi, he has written in Deccan language. From this literature, one can feel Sanskrit, Arabic, Persian and Deccan languages as well as Marathi. The place of 'Yoga Sangrama' is the best in his entire composition, it is the book king of Shaikh Mohammad. 'Pawanvijay' is his three-part composition. It includes the principles of 'Pawanvijay' and 'Kaljnana'. 'Nishkalanka Prabodh' is also his philosophical composition. Their abhangarachana is diverse. Apart from 'Bhaktibodh', 'Acharbodh', 'Bharud', Vipul Abhangarachana (many of which are still unpublished today), Aartya, 'Gaika'- 'Madalasa' are some of his clear compositions. Ducheshma is his most important dictionary, mainly in Arabic-Persian and Sanskrit-Marathi. Like Marathi, Shaikh Mohammad has written in a significant Deccan language. If we consider this literary wealth of Shaikh Mohammad in detail later, we will come to know the various features of his writing.

Let us consider here an example of the works of Shaikh Muhammad written in the Deccan language. Saints and many Warakari from other sects like Sant Namdeo to Tukoba-Niloba-Bahinabai have written in Deccan language. Shaikh Mohammad is no exception for this. Mr. Bendre has published an independent (eighth) section of this writing called 'Hindustani Poetry' in Deccan language and the second volume as 'Sheikh Mohammad's Kavitasangrah. In this book, this structure is found from page 112 to 118. The Deccan language is a composition of a Persian-Marathi composite. Due to the Farsi multiplicity in this composition many (almost all) scholars have (probably) neglected Persian and Islam and Sufism for such a number of reasons. I felt that Sheikh Mohammad's writings had been ignored by some writers and researchers as it is written in the Deccan language. Sheikh Mohammad's 'Dakshini Kavita' is very useful in understanding his particular point of view, so let us consider it in detail, which no one has done till date. From this point of view, the effect of Shaikh Mohammad's 'Yogasangram' etc. on other works will also be noticed. Mr. Bende has divided the structure into seven parts. (1) Vasudev (2) Lalit (3) Nasihatnama (4) Panjij Musalmani (5) Aarti (6) Sfut Kavita and (7) Dohore. [45]

Some of Shaikh Mohammad's scholars mention 'Nasihatnama' and 'Panjij Musalmani' from time to time but their importance will not be understood without a meticulous study. Panjij Musalmani describes five basic principles of Islam: they are Kalma, Namaz, Roja, Zakat and Hajj. They explain the meaning of 'Mana' of Muslims (Islam) by saying 'Suno Musalmani Ka Cheez Mana' - Muslims say 'Bismillah' and 'Alhamdulillah' when starting anything. Shaikh Mohammad has started his 'Nasihatnama' by writing 'Bismillah Ho Akbar'. 'Panjij Musalmani' is started by writing 'Alhamdulillah'. As a result, Shaikh Mohammad says, the disbelief in our minds disappears and faith in Adveta is created. In 'Panjij Musalmani' he has laid down the following principles: God is one and Hazrat Muhammad is his messenger. The second principle of Islam is 'Namaz' (in the words of Sheikh Muhammad 'Nimaz'). He has also described his two parts 'Sunnat' and 'Farz' in detail. They wash their hands and feet before praying. They are called 'Gusl' and 'Buju' (Baju). The third thing is 'fasting', so a person misses hell. After saying this, they turn to the principle of 'Zakat' (charity) or Chavadhya (Chaharam). Performing Hajj, keeping the fear of God in mind and acting according to His wish and will means that he has mercy on us. Like Shaikh Mohammad's 'Bhaktibodh' and 'Acharbodh' in Marathi language, 'Nasihatnama' which composition is in Deccan language also instructive. The structure of 'Nasihat' meaning 'Teaching' should also be considered very carefully because it contains 'Zikir' (Zikr: Description of God), 'Tasbi' (Tasvih: Namasmaranmala, Japmal), 'Haq' (Final Truth),

'Akhar' (Ultimate Truth) Jag), 'Iman' (Iman = Shraddha means faith on God), 'Peer Ki Yari' along with the terms 'Kufr' of Islam (Kufr) 'Halal-Haram' (Prohibition) Quran (Quran), Hell (Hell), 'Bhisht' (Paradise), 'Bad Amal' (Evil). In this book the emphasis is given on the holiness of conduct. Panjij Musalmani and Nasihatnama are the names of the books that not only describes Islam, but Shaikh Mohammad's 'Vasudev' [Vasudev is a beggar from Maharashtra. Giving alms to them in the morning is a part of Dharmacharana. Prof. Molashe has explained that since Vasudeva is a devotee of Krishna, he has disguised as Lord Krishna.] does the same. [46]

हाजी गा गाजी कुरान पढ़े । नवी रसुल के उफती ।।
हलाल हक समजेगा । वोही अल्ला का प्यारा' ।।

Haji Ga Ghazi read the Quran | Ufti of Navi Rasool ||
Halal Haq will understand | That is the Beloved of Allah'||

In Islam, 'Shara' is an important technical term. Recitation of 'Darood' is an important religious function of a Muslim. It is mentioned in this case as Vasudeva also says the same. This is how Shaikh Mohammad describes the greatness of Islam ('Ajab Cheez Musalmani'). Finally, Shaikh Mohammad has described his Qadri tradition of Sufism in various places in the book. Till today, no one has taken any records about this. Shaikh Mohammad wrote devotional songs on Ganesha and Vitthal in Marathi language, as well as he wrote devotional songs for Allah in Deccan language. These three devotional songs are mentioned by Mr. Bandre in his 'Kavitasangrah' means collection of poems on the page 113-114. The devotional song of Allah is described both "praising of Allah and details about traditions of Islam". Thus, we saw the examples of social harmony mentioned by Shaikh Mohammad in his poetry in the deccan language. From his books, he said that the God of Hindus, Muslims, and all other religions is the same and the path of faith and devotion is the same for all.

Shaikh Mohammad work as Society Enlightenmentor

From the 12th-13th century, the vision of our saints was to awaken the society with religious motivational teaching and spreading the unity conduct to enlighten the masses. This is evident in the literature of Marathi saints from earliest times of medieval era. Great saints like Shrichakradhara Swamy and Dyneshwar-Namdev made a fearless attempt to show the way to the society by discarding the undesirable practices that were prevalent in the society. It resulted into change of mind and thinking of people. By abandoning reactionary thinking, society began to search for signs of progress in time. The thirteenth century was a century in Maharashtra that rewarded the ideas of conscience and intellect. As a result, the mentality of the people of Maharashtra began to change. This incident is auspicious. This did go noticed in later Marathi saint literature including Saint poet Shaikh Mohammad. Discretion and intelligence were establishment in his work. At such times, Kabira's voice becomes clear and broke down on the unwholesome efforts of the society. The same effort does not go unnoticed in the case of Shaikh Mohammad. In fact, being a non-believer, it was not impossible to try to misinterpret his work. It was a natural reaction of the so-called establishment, and such a reaction is possible. We can understand that it is with this mindset that he started writing with confidence. Religious thought is very easy to understand when it described in simple language with example and hence the masses are easily attracted to it and Shaikh Mohammad know this very well because he born and brought up in Maharashtra. He is aware about the mentality, believes of the people of Maharashtra. He had thought deeply about the difficulties encountered in the mental and spiritual upliftment of this society. From that thought, Shaikh Mohammad's ideology is against of hypocrisy, conservational thoughts, evil practices, attacking the pride of knowledge, and caste-tribe, religion inequality. We can see this thought also reflects in his writing. Historians of Marathi literature ignored this author and his progressive role. It would not be irrelevant to say that Marathi historians have done great injustice to this saint poet by refraining from mentioning Shaikh Mohammad's great work. He said that the medium of Sanskrit language was an obstacle, because all the religious texts were in Sanskrit language at that time, and only the priest would tell the meaning of that scripture. Also, there is a strong belief in the society that any religious thing is acceptable only if it is told in the Sanskrit language by the priest. The first attempt to break this deadlock was made by Shrichakradhara Swamy and Saint Dyneshwar and gave Marathi language the status of religious language. It is possible that the so-called well establishment priest class was upset by the opening door of this knowledge to mankind, and they tried to disrupt the process. Even in the sixteenth and seventeenth centuries, Shaikh Muhammad began to face such opposition. This means that even after many centuries from the time of Dyneshwar and Eknath to the time of Shaikh Mohammad, the behaviour of the priest class in the society has not changed. Shaikh Mohammadani has expressed his brief about this in his famous book 'Yogasangram'. He says I am of different religion, and I write in my mother tongue like Marathi language, so some pundits persecuted me, but I did not give up. Shaikh Mohammad's observations were very expressive.

He highlighted the social inequalities created by the Chaturvan system. In his writings, he tried to convince to the established class about the importance of equality, which was corrupted by the egoistic pride of casteism. Many divisive arguments cause confusion in society. There was a believed that gods were not one but many, and that this led to the formation of devotee sects. Due to this, the society is divided. He explained the importance of monotheism to the society in the fifteenth chapter of his book 'Yogasangrama'. In the fifteenth and sixteenth centuries, Shaikh Muhammad also tried to enlighten the society about superstitions like people very easily believe on witchcraft, Blackmagic in the society. This also proves his intelligence from his writings, as we can find his opinion in the fifteenth chapter of 'Yogasangrama', where he elaborated on this topic and had tried to dissuade the society from such things.

Shaikh Mohammad's Unitarianism

There were many Muslim saint poets of the Sufi sect in medieval Maharashtra. Despite being Islamic, these Muslim saints became one of the groups of Warakari, Nagesh, Mahanubhav, Datta and Nath sects and Veershaiva and Jain saints in Maharashtra. Saint poet Shaikh Mohammad has priority in this regard. There were two major challenges in front of these saints in fifteenth and sixteenth centuries. During the Bahamani period, it was a challenge for these saints to defend their religion and culture. And the second question was how to establish a relationship with the foreign Islam, and its followers, its saints, and Islamic culture. If we look at the cultural history of medieval Maharashtra, we can see that these two parties played the role of coordination and harmony instead of struggle. The role of Saint Eknath and Shaikh Mohammad was the ideal symbol in Maharashtra. Saint Eknath wrote 'Bharud' like Bajigar, Siddi, Fakir, Darvesh. He wrote dialogues like Hindu-Turk-Sanvad and Akalgiri. From the writings he has showed that he had played the role of co-ordinator and conciliator. At the same time, Shaikh Mohammad is a Sufi saint poet who is almost a contemporary of Saint Eknath. Considering why Shaikh Mohammad was so united with the Warkari sect and what role he played in his book 'Yogasangram' and other 'Abhangadi' (Abhang etc.) literature, the similarities between the ideologies of these two saints can be easily noticed. Like these saints, other Muslim saints and other Maharashtrian religious saints continue to do so. The role of reconciliation has been instrumental in giving impetus to the idea of unity in Maharashtra. These are some of the common examples of how Shaikh Mohammad of Warakari sect, Shahamuni of Mahanubhav sect, Aalam Khan of Nagesh sect, Shaikh Turab ('Turut Wali') of Samarth sect became one and the same. Shaikh Mohammad gave a special award for this unity. He and Eknath laid the foundation of a pillar of cultural unity.

Similarities of integrations of both religions

Hinduism and Islam are the theistic religions that believe in the existence of God, this is the main formula for this unity. Theology is basically nirguna, formless, it is accepted by all Indian theistic philosophies, as is Islam. Ekeshwarabad is also acceptable to all of them. He also acknowledges the interrelationship between the creation of the universe, the creation of the creatures in the universe and the Supreme Being. The welfare of all creatures in the world is the role of Islam in all Indian philosophies. By cultivating with noble values of life and holy conduct, we should make the journey to prosperity and the hereafter. In this regard too, there is a unity between Indian theistic philosophy and Islam. With so many similarities, even if there are some other differences, we can all live in harmony here, practice according to our religion. You do not have to fight for it. This feeling of unity was spread in the society by the saints of both the religions.

Philosophical similarities

Shaikh Mohammad's writing 'Ducheshma' (two eyes) is included by Mr. Bendre in his collection of poems named 'Kavitasangrah'. It shows the similarities between terminology and terms used in Indian philosophy and Muslim philosophy. Shaikh Mohammad has written important Indian philosophy-critical books like 'Yogasangram', 'Pawanvijay' and 'Nishkalankaprabodh'. Shaikh Mohammad's book 'Muslim Panjij' shows similarities with an Indian text named 'Panchikaran'. This has already been pointed out. He was very much interested in Indian philosophy as well as the fundamentals of Islam and he felt the similarities between the two. Why does Shaikh Mohammad do all this? Their desire for unity by eliminating the differences between the different religions and establishing mutual harmony among them is definitely hidden behind this. This is also the inspiration behind Saint Eknath's writing on 'Hindu-Turk-Dialogue'. This idea can be deduced from the fact that these efforts of the saint poets of the fifteenth and sixteenth centuries were constructive and valuable in terms of creating a rational and sensible public mind.

7.   Saint Bajid Pathan

Saint Bajid Pathan (Bhaganagar-South Hyderabad) was a disciple of Saint Keshav Swami. Despite being a saint, he was a senior officer in the Adilshahi of Bijapur with an army of 25,000 soldiers. Saint poets like Uddhav Chidghan, Jayaram Soot etc. have praised him in their literature. It is known that his time was between 1682 A.D. But since he was a disciple of Keshavswamy, it proves that he was in the 17th century. According to

Saint Mahipati, Bajid Pathan has written 500 verses in Dakkhini (Deccan) language, in which he had mentioned Namasmarana and Virakti. He has also composed many Marathi verses. Not enough research and commentary has been written on his writings yet.

8. Shahbeg or Shambeg

Saint Shahbeg was also a follower of Saint Keshav Swami. He had great faith on his Guru. Some of his verses are found in Keshav Swami's collection of poems. He has expressed his faith for his Guru in his poetry. Our Guru is in the form of Shiva, and by his grace we will be saved from sorrow, danger and life will be meaningful. Like Bajid Pathan's writings, Shahbeg's writings are still neglected and need to be studied by researchers.

9. Shakarganj

He was also the third disciple of Keshav Swami. Only one of his songs is available as his writing. In that song, he is meditating in the cave of the path of knowledge and calling his guru the authority of tradition. Further writings of such Muslin saints who followed in the footsteps of his Guru should be explored.

10. Junglee Fakir (Sayyed Hussain)

After Saint Aalam Khan, another saint poet Sayyed Hussain of Nagesh sect became a saint poet. His real name is Sayyed Hussain, and he used the nickname 'Jangalee Fakir' to write his poems. Prof. Priyolkar has mentioned it in his book named as 'Old Marathi Poetry of Muslims saints'.[47] He has said that an impure poem written by a Junglee fakir has been found in the collection number 1637 A.D. in the Shree Samartha Vagdevata temple at Dhule in Maharashtra and it has been mentioned in many Marathi literary works. Also, Mr. Deshpande has mentioned that he is the Guru brother of Aalam Khan. [48] The Junglee fakir has written long poems based on mythology. Therefore, Dr. Dhere mentioned him as a 'Singer of old stories'. Junglee fakir had also composed some abhangas. Their various compositions need to be researched.

11. Jamal Fakir

The name of the saint poet Jamal Fakir is also found among the Muslim saints belonging to the Nagesh sect. Jamal Fakir was a disciple of Junglee Fakir's guru brother Agyanasiddha. This is mentioned in the 'Srisakalsantagatha' written by Mr. Thaware.[49] He lived in the vicinity of Kumbhaj village in Kolhapur district of Maharashtra. His Samadhi is near Rankala Lake in Kolhapur. In his writings, he used to define the yog-sadhana (practice of Yoga) and his composition also mentions about Padmasana, Samadhi Avastha. In his poetry there are signs of philosophy and meaningfulness. He must have been very popular in his time as manuscripts of his poems are found in various places in the vicinity. His writings can be found in different villages. If research is done on Jamal Fakir and his scattered literature, a lot of light will be shed on Nagesh sectarian literature.

12. Latif Shah

Saint Latif Shah was born in 1679 A.D. and died in 1752 A.D. as mentioned by Mr. Thavare. Latif Shah was born in a Sayyad family in a village called Hal. He was educated by a guru associated with the Sufi saint tradition named Noor Mohammad. You can find these saints mentioned in Mahipati's 'Bhaktavijaya', 'Chandorkar' in the list of saint poetic poems and Mr. Thaware in the 'Sankalsantgatha' and Moropant in his honour. According to Mr. Thaware, he has done a great job in eliminating Hindu-Muslim discrimination.[50] Moropant used the words as 'Tukaramastut', this means the one who was praised by the famous saint Tukaram Maharaj. Saint Latif and Saint Meerabai are mentioned in Latif Shah's literature. He was associated with Saint Eknath of Warkari sect. His writings seem to pay homage to the deities Rama and Vitthal, but in the course of time, their compositions have been destroyed, but among his writings three verse in Dakhani Language and one verse in Marathi language available at Samarth Vagdevata Mandir at Dhule.[51] One of his southern dialects is Bharud and his subject is Garud. He must have made many such compositions under the guidance of Saint Eknath. Garud means the mantra of releasing poison. However, Sant Latif Shah considered caste, inequality, pride in religion, etc., which were rooted in the society, as the nature of poison. And he suggested that the feeling of equality, the search for self-knowledge and self-knowledge, etc., is a healing in the form of Garud. Here we see that the sense of equality, the pursuit of the self and the pursuit of self-knowledge are also found in the mysticism of Sufi philosophy. This means that he had made a lot of efforts for Hindu-Muslim unity. His efforts to establish social harmony and mutual harmony by 'Dharmaprabodhan' and his cultural work are definitely worth noticing. His Samadhi is at Bhuigalli at Mangalvedhe in Maharashtra.

13. Shaikh Sali Mohammad

No information is available about Shaikh Sali Mohammed, only one Kutatmak Abhang (means a Abhang which written in the form riddles) is available. He says:

आम्ही जातीचे ब्राह्मण । आमचे सोयरे मुसलमान ॥
स्नानसंध्या बोळविली । महारासी सोयरिक केली ।।
शेख सली महंमद भला । सुन टाकुनि सासुसी गेला ।।
तिच्या पोटीं कन्या जाली । ते फिरून बाईल केली ।।

We are from the Brahmins caste. Our Relatives Muslims.
Rituals are not performed by us. Formed a relation with Mahara.
Shaikh Sali Mohammad is a great person.
He left daughter-in-law and run away with Mother-in-law.
Mother-in-law delivered a girl child. And he married with her.

This kind of cryptic composition is found in Marathi saint literature by many saints from Dnyansagar to Tukaram. But if we study this riddle carefully, we notice the hidden meaning and it seems that in his abhanga, they had given the message that people should get out of caste discrimination and create a good relationship between themselves.[52]

14. Garib Abdul (Rivayatkar)

'Ghazal' is a type of poetry that has come from Persian to Marathi. Similarly, the song type 'Rivayat' also appeared in Marathi saint literature. 'Rivayat' is a type of mourning song for Muslims which mourns the tragic end of the lives of Hazrat Imam Hassan and Hussain. Even today, 'Rivayati' oral traditions are common in the Bhingar area of Ahmednagar. They are sung in Moharram. Such information was given by the famous historian and former director of Ahmednagar District Museum, Shri. Suresh Joshi to the author Shri U. M. Pathan. Garib Abdul, an eighteenth-century saint, wrote many 'Rivayati'. He was poet in the court of Raje Bhaskar as mentioned by Garib Abdul at the end of his tradition. Mr. U. M. Pathan tried to find the details of Rivayat but did not get much information about it. Only two short stories are available written by Garib Abdul. In the first story, everyone was welcomed, and it was said that they were fakirs of 'Moharram'. We can find this writing in Marathi language and many similes and symbols are used. The subject of his second tale is the story of mother and child separation. In the last line of the 'Rivayat', he mentioned Raje Bhaskar.

15. Shahamuni

Shahmuni was a follower of 'Mahanubhav' Sampradaya. Despite being a Muslim by birth, he made such an impact on the people and society of Maharashtra with his book 'Siddhantabodh' that his book is still read in villages in Maharashtra. His family had inherited the path of devotion. In his book named 'Siddhantabodh',[53] in the beginning of the 36th chapter, he has explained how his family was immersed in the Hindu tradition from last four generations. Along with that, he has given information about his family. His great grandfather's name was 'Shah baba' and great grandmother's name was Amina. Shah baba was born in Prayag. he migrated to Ujjain for business, and there is the famous temple of Lord Shiva Mahakal. They were also immersed in the atmosphere of Shiva devotion of this place. Shahamuni has written that he knows Persian and Marathi language. This means that the period of Shahmuni's great grandfather should be 1728 A.D. after the Ujjain was successfully achieved by the Marathas. Shah Baba's son Janaji was born in Ujjain. He was a devotee of God Vishnu. His wife's name was Madubai. He is God Vishnu's bhakta whose father is God Shiva's devotee; this only shows the individualities of his family. Being in touch with the Marathas, he too was attracted to Bhagwat Dharma in Maharashtra and migrated to Siddhatek in Ahmednagar district of Maharashtra. Siddhatek is famous for its temple of God Ganesha. It was here that Janaji and Mandubai gave birth to a son and named Mansing. Mansing is the father of Saint Shahamuni. After living in Siddhatek, Mansingh had faith in God Ganesha, and his wife Amai and he became a devotee of God Ganesha. This couple gave birth to a son at Ped village, taluka Shrigonde, district Ahmednagar. He named his son Shah baba, believing that his great grandfather was born as his son. This Shah baba means Saint Shahamuni. Shah is his name and Muni is the name of his Guru and he took the name Shahamuni to express his gratitude to his Guru. This is also mentioned in the first chapter of his book 'Siddhantabodh' in the ovee number 151. It is also written in the first chapter of the book that our Guru's full name was Munidra Swami. Dattatraya himself preached to his Guru in Ovee kramankas 353 and 354 in the first 50 and he says that he got blessings from them. This Munindra Swami and Shahamuni had met at Varanasi. Shahamuni also used to roam like their ancestors. He was born at Ped village and met his Guru at Kashi (Varanasi) and wrote the famous book 'Siddhantabodh' at Pathari Mandal near Chambali village in Satara. His tomb is in a village called 'Shahgad' in Beed district of Maharashtra. His samadhi is on a hill near Godavari river outside Shahgad village. He must have lived in this place during his elderly age. Because around five Muslim families those are his disciples still taking care of his Samadhi at that place. Although these families are Muslims, they do not consume alcohol or meat. They also worship Lord Krishna. They get guidance from the Guru of Mahanubhavpantha to pay tribute on the death anniversary day of Shahamuni. The greatness of Shahmuni is well evident from the fact that the monks, priest, and devotees of Mahanubhavpantha stay there.

Shahamuni's Siddhantabodh is a large book with 50 chapters and 9858 Ovees. In the first chapter, he greets God Ganesha, Godess Saraswati, Lord

Dattatraya and Kuldaivata (Family God). In the second verse, he greets the 'Dvaita-dvaita' ['Tattvavada' (also popularly known as 'Dvaita' Vedanta), is a sub-school in the Vedanta tradition of Hindu philosophy. Dvaita is a Sanskrit word that means 'duality, dualism'.[54] The term refers to any premise, particularly in theology on the material and the divine, where two principles (truths) or realities are posited to exist simultaneously and independently.[54][55] Quoting the term 'Advitiyatva', Sharma also says, the term 'Advitiyatva' has been interpreted by Madhva, in the Chandogya Bhashya, in terms of 'absence of peer and superior' to 'Brahman', conceding by implication, the existence, the reality of 'lesser reals' like matter and souls under the aegis of God.] viewpoint and it unmanifest God and present the Nirguna principle of God in Islam and Indian philosophy. He mentioned in the 15th verse that he was writing this book following to the orders of his Guru Munidra Swami. Confusion arises in the minds of the people due to the confusion of different religions, opinions, and deities. Some hypocrites spread false ideas and rituals. Due to the difference in religions, and their opinions and deities, there was lot of confusion had created in people's mind. Some hypocrites spread false religion ideas, rituals. Therefore, Navasayas, Aghori practices, superstitions become common. Shahamuni criticized it in detail. This book has been created to destroy this ignorance and to give true knowledge. That is what the poet says at the end of this chapter.

In the 11th chapter, in Mangalacharan, Shridattas and Godess Sarsawati are first greeted and described interrelationship of life and body by mentioning the God's creation of world and universe. It is necessary to be self-aware about the conciseness of true knowledge which he wrote in the book 'Siddhantabodh', says Shahamuni. From this he has presented the strength of the body and the strength of the soul. This idea in Indian philosophy has also been accepted by the Warkari-Mahanubhavadi sects. (It is the same in both sects.) Islam and Sufism also accept the Nirguna Ishwartatva, and his creation of living beings, the consciousness poured into it in the form of 'Ruh' (soul) etc. Shahamunin must have felt the same view in Islamic philosophy and Indian philosophy. Islam and Warakari-Mahanubhav sects state that one should worship the main (nirguna) God, not polytheism, this idea is presented by Shahamuni in this chapter of 'Siddhantabodha'.

Chapter 13 is important from a theoretical point of view. The first verse mentions the nirguna-nirakartva of God and this role is accepted by Islam and Indian theistic philosophies (Warakari-Mahanubhavadi sects as well). God created the Pruthvi, Aap, Tej, Vayu, Aaka Panchmahabhutas [Pancha Bhoota or Pancha Maha-Bhoota (Sanskrit: पञ्चभूत, पञ्चमहाभूत; pañca-mahā-bhūta), five great elements, also five physical elements, is a group of five basic elements, which, according to Hinduism, is the basis of all cosmic creation.[56] These elements are: Prithvi/Bhudevi (Sanskrit: पृथ्वी:, Earth) Apas/Varuna/Jal (Sanskrit: अप:, Water), Agni (Sanskrit: अग्नि, Fire), Vayu (Sanskrit: वायु:, Air), Akasha/Dyaus (Sanskrit: आकाश, Space/Atmosphere/ Ether). These elements have different characteristics, and these also account for different faculties of human experience.] for human beings, to make their lives happy. The Quran also has a similar interpretation of the creation of the universe and the creation of animals. Considering that Shahamunis are Muslim, it is clear why they felt this similarity between Islam and Indian philosophy. He has said in Ovee number 152 that if we think in this way with common sense and conscience, the differences between religions will disappear. In chapter 13, Shahamuni describes the five great beings created by God to make human life happy. But the 14th chapter discusses how to use those Panchmahabhutas for happiness. In 35th chapter, after Ganesh Vadana, Shahmuni has greeted Brahma-Vishnu, Mahesh. From this, it is known which deities the poet had faith in. The 'Santanamavali' (Index of saints) of this chapter is very important section and None of the scholars, researcher has given attention for the study. The 'Santanamavali' included some of the saints from Nath sect like Matsyendra, Gorakhnath. Saints like Ramanand, Kabir, Nanak, Rohidas, Shaikh Mohammad, Chand Bodhale, Bajid Pathan, Shah Hussain, Raghav Keshavchetanya, Tukaram-Ramdas, Meera, Janabai, Kanhopatra and Shantilin (from Virshaiv) are also mentioned.

From this we can see that Saint Shahamuni carried on the legacy of social wealth of his earlier and contemporary saints.

Shahamuni's social contemplation and social enlightenment

Shahamuni's social observation and social thinking is very subtle and detailed as well as scholarly. Here are some key points to consider. Religion is the place of worship of the society, so there should be no misconceptions in the society about the basic philosophy of religion. The reality and conscience of this philosophy should be imprinted in the mind of the society, so that there will be no ideological confusion in the mind of the society. That was his firm opinion. The principle of God is one. The names of the deities are different but there is only one God. Shahamuni has presented the first, important foundation of his social enlightenment in the very first chapter of the book by presenting the pure role of this monotheistic intellect. The concepts of the philosophy of religion should be clear and not vague, that is, the society should not be engrossed in polytheism and should not be discriminated against. Due to the practice of religion, some norms are formed in the society. They are also caused by superstition. Therefore, the original good religious concepts are affected in a way. The naive and illiterate society starts running after superstition. In a way, it was a loss to the society. Devadasi practice, Aghori practice, ghost ideas etc. Shahamuni has sharply criticized on this in his writing. Society should understand the importance of such noble values of life. With this in mind, Shahamuni gives his detailed thoughts in many places in 'Siddhantabodha'. He also preaches that by practicing this way of life, we should all become 'gentlemen' so that the welfare of the entire society will be ensured. There is enlightenment in the name of Shahamuni's book 'Siddhantabodh'. The purpose of the enlightenment is clear, and they expect the same result.

Chapter 6

An Epilogue

Sufism, as we have seen, is a very complex phenomenon. In India it took root in both the rural and urban areas. In some cases, the deep impact of Sufism and its popularity among the masses transformed rural regions, such as, Nagpur and Sylhet, into flourishing urban centres. In the region of Muhammad bin Taghluq, while in Damascus Shihabu'd-Din Ahmas al-Umari was told that in Delhi there were two thousand large Khanqahs. The number may have been exaggerated, but be that time khanqahs exercised a deep social, political, economic, and cultural influence in India. Sufi disciples gathered round their Murshids, Shaikhs or pirs to learn the rites, rituals, and rules of each order, which were designed to stabilize their emotional and intellectual faculties and to enable them to realize reality or the direct intuitive recognition of God. Sufi disciples tended to deify their pirs, even though the latter were totally disinterested in turning themselves into Godheads. The reliance of Sufis on God, particularly in the material sense, attracted both people form poor classes and members of the oppressed elite into orders. Khanqahs gave to most people a feeling of hope and a vision of a bright future, both in this world and the one to come.

R.C. Majumdar suggested in the book entitled as 'The Delhi Sultanate', second edition, Bombay, 1967, on page 555 and Aziz Ahmad also endorses Majumdar's view in Studies in Islamic culture on page 134, as "......the role of both medieval mysticism and Sufism in the history of Indian culture is often exaggerated beyond all proportions. Whatever might have been the value of either as a distinctive phase of Hinduism and Islam, from moral, spiritual, and philosophical points of view, their historical importance is considerably limited by the fact that the number of Indians directly affected by them, even at their heyday which was short-lived, could not be very large. The number dwindled very appreciably in (the) course of time, and the two orthodox religions showed no visible signs of being seriously affected by this sudden intrusion of radical elements. They pursued their even tenor, resembling the two banks of a river, separated by the stream that flows between them. Attempts were made to build a bridge connecting the two but ended in failure. Even if there were any temporary bridge, it collapsed in no time'. This is not the place to discuss the circumstances which may have made, as Majumdar suggests, the so-called temporary bridge collapse, however, two observations should be made. Firstly, the influence of Sufism was not short-lived; secondly, members of the orthodox sections of both Hinduism and Islam moved in different spheres, while both sufis and Hindu saints (bhaktas) remained unconcerned with the activities pursued by the orthodox. As we have seen, the Suhrawardis and other dervishes, such as Shaikh 'Aiyub and Sidi Maula, played an important role in the power struggles and political upheavals of the ruling classes and the aristocracy. They also amassed large fortunes and tried to pressurize the government into taking an especially narrow view of the world. Through the Suhrawardis petition from the people were presented to rulers and the withdrawn and ascetic Chishtis who has turned their backs on the world was also sought to avert such calamities as drought and panic, for example, during times of political crises. They offered consolation to the masses and reminded them as well as members of the ruling classes, through their own advice and example, of the ethical side of Islam. Until the death of Shaikh Nizamu'd-Din Auliya', the Chishtis has also refused to play any role in the conversion of Hindus to Islam. They believed that contact with the saintly was the only means by which people would renounce evil or adopt Islam. Large numbers of Chishtis continued to follow this policy, but some eminent members of the order, such as Gisi Daraz, unsuccessfully tried to convert Brahmans to Islam. What is noteworthy is that both Chishtis and Sihrawardis only managed to convert high caste Hindus.

The theory that the influence of Sufism and of Islamic egalitarianism were significant factors which led members of the Hindus lower classes to embrace Islam is unfounded. The Muslim conquests did not unleash forces of liberation or change the position of the exploited castes of Hindus and of the untouchables. The social and economic position of the masses of Muslim converts who accepted Islam under a variety of pressures, all which have been analysed by Ja'far-I Makkī, was in fact no better than that of Hindus. Nevertheless, the Chishti Khanqahs did offer consolation, peace and nourishment to the thousands of Muslims who crowded the towns. From the time of the Khurasanian, Abu Said, khanqahs were rendezvous for artisans and merchants. All khanqahs in India followed this Khurasanian tradition for the mutual benefit of both sufis and their visitors. Merchants at this time were continually undertaking hazardous journeys to distant countries, while engaged in risky commercial ventures. Nevertheless, the network of Chishtiyya, Suhrawardiyya and Firdawsiyya Khanqahs in India and those of the Kubrawiyya and of other orders in Kashmir, offered greatly needed psychological comfort to merchants and other travellers during this period. The ceremonies and other anniversaries celebrate in khanqahs development into significant cultural institutions and were eagerly awaited by both the poor and affluent alike. Sufism gave birth to a very wide range of mystic symbolism and became an indispensable part of Persian poetry. This poetry was not only an expression of the mystic live of a thirsty soul seeking an intuitive understanding of God, but an avenue for emotions and feelings which would otherwise have never been expressed due to the fury of the orthodox, social inhibitions and political repression. Although this form of poetry gradually tended to degenerate as it became conventionalized and developed grotesque language, erotic obsessions, and imitative and repetitive thinking, nevertheless it served to manifest the personal emotions and judgements of individual sufis.

Sufi poetry written in Hindi language added a new dimension to Indian mysticism and a new lyrical and colourful way by which to achieve an ecstatic state. The subtle refinement of Hindi music, combined with Persian conversions and artistry, gave fresh meaning and depth to Indian sufi thought. Hindi language writing offered to sufis at that time a spiritual satisfaction they could then share with Hindu bhaktas, whose spirits equally thirsted for the higher reaches of Reality. The Hindis sufi poets and the bhaktas rebelled against all forms of religious formalism, orthodoxy, falsehood, hypocrisy, and stupidity and tried to create a new world in which spiritual bliss was the all-consuming goal. They were unconcerned with the idea of achieving any form of union between the two religions and instead tended to work within their respective religious communities for an understanding of the spiritual and social values of each other. The Ghazalian tradition in Sufism in India did inculcate hostility towards philosophy. The sufi movement tended to promote gullibility and credulity and discourage self-reliance. Most sufi khanqahs urged their disciples to pursue hard manual labour to crush the lower self, but unlike medieval Christian monasteries they did not invent labour saving devices, for example in a field like agriculture. The continual flow became a source of degeneration to khanqahs and led to the gradual dependence of their inmates on the state, merchants, and the nobility. The most serious threats to the survival of Sufism were the presumptuous and preposterous claims of sufi charlatans and impostors. The latter exploited the influence of Sufism, and the popular passion for the occult and thaumaturgy, to their own advantage. Their poetry and music promoted immoral practices, the use of drugs and the practice of homosexuality. Such developments shocked genuine and spiritually gifted sufis, however, they faced all challenges with an awareness of the magnitude of these problems and worked for the eradication of evil from society and a minimization of the hardships experienced by the people through practical wisdom, rather than their mystical intuition. Sufis in this period also sheltered both the politically and socially persecuted at the risk of their own popularity or reprisals from the government at the same time helping Muslims to stabilize their emotions.

The mystical trend in Islam is called Tasawwuf and is an act of devoting oneself to a way of life aimed at achieving a mystical union with God. Broadly speaking, it can be described as an intensification of Islamic faith and practice. In general, Sufis have always looked upon themselves as true Muslims, who take most seriously God's call to find proof of His existence in His creation, that is, both in the world spread in front of them and the self. They talk about the importance of reconciling the shariah and the tariqa. They lay stress on one's inner life, contemplation of one's actions, spiritual development, and cultivation of the soul. They acknowledge the fact that God, both in His essence and His attributes, can be approached through faith alone, and this is the way of the majority of the faithful. However, they assume that there are also other ways of knowing Him and those are not open to all. Thus, He may be known through intellectual endeavour, which is the way of the philosophers, but this way certainly falls short of its goal. And He may be known through a direct experience (which the Sufis claim for themselves). The direct, mystical experience of God is the most fulfilling way of knowing Him. However, not everyone may travel this path. Only some are called to it and even fewer attain their goal. The Truth (Al Haqq is veiled and can be accessed through His help alone. Though Allah is Al Zahir (The Evident), He is also Al Batin (The Hidden), as well as Al Fattah (The Opener). The Sufis trace the origin of Tasawwuf to the sayings and practice of the Prophet. Even before receiving the revelation, the Prophet used to spend days and nights in solitary meditation in the cave of Hira' near Makkah. It was on one such occasion that he saw an apparition in the form of an angel who asked him to recite a verse. The Prophet said he could not read, that he was illiterate (ummi) but after the insistence of the angel he recited after him a sentence, which was the first revelation of the Qur'an (96: 1- 5). It is for this reason that the Sufis attach such great importance to meditation and dhikr. Dhikr and meditation were the forms of the Prophet's prayers before his prophethood. The Sufis also emphasize the Prophet's self-imposed poverty, contempt of wealth and luxurious living, as well as his fasts, night vigils and additional prayers. The Companions of the Prophet faithfully followed his footsteps and lived simple lives. The Pious Caliphs refused to indulge themselves even in ordinary comforts, despite having the wealth of the whole Islamic world at their disposal. They considered the love of wealth as one of the greatest obstacles in the path of their devotion to God. Like the other branches of Islamic learning, Sufism too believes that the true knowledge is the knowledge of God, and it is passed down from a master to a disciple. The master's oral instructions give life to the articles of faith. Thus, the master's fundamental concern is to shape the character of the disciple and help him in attaining his goal, which is to come near to God and become one with Him. This concept of pirimuridi relationship emphasizes the personal dimension of the relationship between the Divine and the human.

We also see further what is **'Tasawwuf in Today's world'.** Sufism (Tasawwuf) ought to be just as important today as it has ever been throughout its long history. Being a way of purifying the soul a necessity for each new generations, its role should never with changing times and circumstances. Yet, paradoxically, although it still has millions of adherents, as a form of religion, it is in a state of decline. This is because the traditional form of Tasawwuf, as we now know, it is embroidered by tales of miracles and mysticism, and to find support for its ideology, it relies upon doubtful analogies. But the scientific mind is skeptical of analogies and is impatient with mysticism. There is also the question of Sufism being heart-based, the heart in ancient times being regarded as the seat of thought and emotion. But now modern science has shown the heart to be nothing but an organ which controls the circulation of the blood, and it has been conceded that it is the mind which is the centre of both thought and emotion. This being so, Tasawwuf should now be developed as a mind-based philosophy. It will thus have a much stronger attraction for educated minds. The need of the hour, therefore, is to modernize Sufism, couching it in the contemporary idiom and explaining its ideology in a way that should address the present-day individual, whose major concern is as much with intellectual development as it is with purification of the soul. That is why Tasawwuf should necessarily be linked with real events and its objectives expressed in a scientific manner. Its attraction will this reach far beyond the poor, the distressed, the under-educated and the downtrodden who at present make up the bulk of its following. Even in a modern country like Egypt, the adherents of Sufism largely fall into the category of the underprivileged. One constituent of present-day Sufism which may appeal to the modern mind is the practice of meditation. But it should be borne in mind that meditation, which began to be favoured by the Sufis under the influence of local yogic practices, should be discounted for the simple reason that it fails to awaken the human mind. In any case, medication is practiced more to relieve stress and promote relaxation than to attain great spiritual heights. Likewise, the practice of including a state of ecstasy by means of special exercises is not a part of authentic Sufism, because it has nothing to do with that spiritual development which is the actual aim of Sufism.

Formerly, people used to go to Sufis to learn the spiritual aspects of their religion and to be trained in spirituality. But now the situation has changed.

One reason for this is that at present there are very few genuine Sufis in the Khanqahs. This has led to Tasawwuf existing today in a degenerated form. For example, nowadays people do visit dargahs, supposedly to satisfy their spiritual feelings. But in actuality, all that they accomplish is to meet Sufis pirs in order to ask for their blessings and then go and prostrate themselves at Sufi graves. All this represents Sufism in a diluted if not distorted form. In ancient times a Sufi was revered on account of his great spiritual achievement. But, now Gaddis (seats) have been formed in the name of past Sufis and anyone who acquires such a seat, mostly as a matter of heredity, is acknowledged as a Sufi. These Sufis who have acquired gaddis in this way carry out no new research and produce no new books, for no rethinking or soul-searching is allowed. How then can Tasawwuf develop and face other disciplines of the modern age? Whereas in ancient times Tasawwuf was a living discipline, now it is largely ritual-based and as such has become stagnant. This, more than anything else, has led to the erosion of true Tasawwuf. However, we do find some reform and development in certain Sufi organizations which, to a great extent, eliminate miracles and ecstasy as parts of Sufism and which look with disfavour upon 'shrine worship'. Fazlur Rahman in his well-known book, Islam, has called this orientation towards reform 'neo-Sufism'. Reform in Sufism has been long overdue, for it had adopted so many indigenous rituals and practices that it had lost its original character altogether. For example, in the Indian context, it had adopted various yogic practices, including the inducement of ecstasy through loud music and song. All this went against the spirit of Islam. This ecstasy element has taken another form in Turkey where its practitioners are called 'whirling dervishes'. They go on dancing in circular movements until they enter a trance-like state. According to Islam we have come into this world for the purpose of God-realization, not for self-realization. Since the basis of Aryan religions was self-realization, what they held for man was a part (ansh) of God. This concept crept into Sufi thought. The Sufis started different kinds of yoga practices in the form of exercises which were believed to aid self- realization. This, according to them, amounted to God realization.

In this way several Sufi orders had diverged a long way from the path of the Shariah. Ultimately, there arose a strong movement in different parts of the world to bring Sufism closer to the Shariah, the Naqshbandiyas being foremost among its promoters. These new orders were also more organized than their predecessors. One reason for the revival of these Sufi orders in the twentieth century was colonialism, under which the Muslims suffered from an identity crisis. For most Muslims, interaction with the West during the colonial period was too great a culture shock to bear. Political power, their greatest support, had gone. Now they needed something to pin their hopes on. In this state of helplessness, the Khanqahs, Zawiyas (shrines) came to their rescue. In the hope of finding solace in spirituality, they thronged to these shrines and Sufi pirs. The pirs gave them incantations to recite on a rosary; and this was supposed to solve all of their problems. Novetzke takes observation further by showing how the textual archive of bhakti historically relates to performers (singers and exegetes of bhakti poetry attributed to saints' men of experience!) and their audiences. The devotional song-poems, often with deep mystical and pedagogical tint, were composed by saint-poets who often came from the lower and illiterate social strata. The songs increasingly became part of the folk poetical repertoire of devotion, at least since the last centuries of the first millennium. In the following millennium, they became widespread. These, with respect to the classical period from the 12th to 17th centuries, were compositions that were often transmitted orally and written down only later by those who transmitted the memory of the saints' devotional expressions as a part of their professional engagement mostly by the performers themselves. However, thanks to the performances and popularity of the poems themselves, the dynamics of the oral-written with respect to the poems' contents, shared motifs and even attributed authorship have hardly been lessened up to current times. Today the early written forms of such fluctuant poems are known from the performers' notebooks ('bāḍa' in Marathi) that served as sources of their later printed editions (gatha). These, in creating the kernel of bhakti's historiographical data, got accompanied by hagiographies, another set of handwritten texts composed out of narrative, both oral and written material.

However, Novetzke argues that even the hagiographical texts, while seemingly of just narrative character, are not bereft of connection to performance, because at least some of them display traces of being used and their texts organized to serve the performance, thus becoming in his words 'the literary fossils of performance'. Now all of this suggests that bhakti, as we know it from pre-modern times, developed along the collective lines of performers audiences. The latter functioned as networks often mapped onto trade and pilgrimage routes, as well as within the dynamics of sharers of experience and experiencers. The social act of performance that could be intensified by making pilgrimages to sites devoted to bhakti saints had a peculiar character of openness and sharing. It wasn't restricted to the stage, as it were, although that might have been the case too, but also carried across the streets of devotional centers and banks of rivers, or at crossroads where the performers and the public met. Such spatial encoding as well as unfolding of performance clearly constituted a different public sphere than the modern politically derived public arena glued by the print media, literacy, collective demands, and instruments of community representation. Moreover, the bhakti groups acted rather as temporary unified publics even if periodical festivals may have regulated their gatherings. Temporality, along with the spatial dimension of the bhakti-gathering, sharing, and experiencing, in turn, makes it an event. The religious content that it shared then can hardly be fixed to anything like a religious canon, text or clear set identity as suggested by the modern reconceptualization of religion. Finally, the performing/receiving social bodies for also bhakti's linguistic meaning is rooted in participation can hardly hide the communication aspect of their togetherness. Indeed, it was during the performance that the sought experience of the divine, and generally religious emotion, was invoked and communicated. Moreover, others were invited to join in. Importantly, the performance, while uniting the devotees in a common endeavour, is essentially also an experience for both the audience and the performers.

Muslim Marathi Sufi saints has a viewpoint on creation of Love, which is also needed to understand through a learning from Quran and Hadith. Since our main concern is to examine Muslim Marathi Sufi saints on divine love, Unity, devotion, destroying the practicing the superstitious practices. We shall considerably widen the scope of our survey of Muslim Marathi Sufi saints' views on divine love, Unity, devotion, destroying the practicing the superstitious practices. Hence, we shall look roots of Muslim Marathi Sufi saints and learning on creation of love which is mentioned in the Quran, and the Hadith (traditions which go back to the Prophet), theology, philosophy, and Sufism. The first two sourced do not supply us with much material on love. One can discern mainly on three issues. Firstly, the nomos motif occurs once in a manifest way, but many times through the notion that God loves the righteous and hates the wicked, that is, he loves those who carry out his commandments, say: If you love God, follow me and God will love you, and forgive your sins' (Quran 3.31) 'God loves not the evildoers' (Quran 3.134). 'God loves the good-doers' (Quran 3.140). Secondly, man's love for God is conditioned by God's love for man God is conditioned by God's love for man. '......God will assuredly bring a people he loves, and who love him...' (Quran 5.54) ; and lastly an identification of belief in God more ardently' (Quran 2.165). God appears as either lover or beloved in Quran 85.14: 'And he is the all-forgiving, the all-loving (wadūd).' Wadūd can be interpreted to mean either lover, if we regard the adjective wadūd as nomen agentis (fail), or beloved. It is obvious that such scanty material, at least concerning the plain meaning of the Quranic verses, could not be the sources of the great theories of divine love which were developed later in Islam. The Hadith adds to the Quran some other ideas, but also here the information is very limited. The love for God appears as a condition of belief. Asked what belief is, Prophet Muhammad answers: 'Belief means that God and his messenger are beloved by you more than anything else'. Thus, belief is described in terms of love. In one tradition the order to love God which is most prevalent in the Bible appears associated with its reason: 'Love God, because of the favours he bestows on you, and love me [that is Prophrt Muhammad], because God loves me.' Another Biblical notion is the statement that whoever loves God experience affliction. Moreover, the lover of God is not afraid of death, for it causes him to meet God. Abraham is the model of such ardent love. The Prophet is said to have prayed as follows: 'O God give me your love, and the love of those who love you, and the love which makes me come close to you and makes your love beloved to me more than cold water'. We shall see that these traditions have no influence on al-Ghazālī's theory of love, however he brings them forward to comply with his usual order of writing by which he opens each of his books in the Ihyā' with fragments of evidence from the Qur'ān the Hadith.

Looking to the theological aspect, it is not withstanding Quranic verses and traditions whose literal meanings indicate that God his creatures, some groups of theologians such as the Jahmites, Mu'tazilites and some Asharites who denied God's love, identified his love with his will or benefaction. Concerning the interpretation of God's love, the Ash'arite theologian al-Juwaynī (d. 478/1085) introduces two views. At first, God's love and contentment means his benefaction. 'God loves a person' (ahabba allāh abdan) does not mean feeling sympathy with or inclination toward a man but granting favours to him. And man's love for God is expressed through obedience to him. This is because God is too exalted to incline to man or to be the object of man's inclination. Al-Juwaynī seems to say that God's inclination would indicate that he lacks something, a notion which cannot be conceived of God who is perfect. On the other hand, man's inclination would infringe on God's transcendence held by the theologians. Al-Ghazālī reasons that the objection of the theologians to divine love is based on a doctrine which says that an entity which resembles nothing, and nothing resembles it cannot be the object of love. The Ash'aritr theologian al-Bāquillāni explains that since there is no change in God's essence, it is impossible to ascribe to him feelings which enjoin changes in one's essence. Other side, God's love is explained as his will. However, this will call love and contentment when it relates to a favor best word in man, and when it relates to punishment afflicting man, it is called anger. It is worth nothing that Sufis were persecuted for their theory of love. Ibn Taymiyya does not accept this view. He argues that the identification of love with will denies God one of his attributes, and results in God's love of injustice for everything in the world is willed by him. For theories of love in Ibn Taymiyya and other Hanbalite scholars the reader should consult Bell's excellent work. We would like, however, to cite Bell's table in which he shows the difference between the Hanbalites, who represent the nomos motif on the one hand, and the Ash'arites on the other who identify God's love with his will. For will Bell uses the Greek word thelema. As for the philosophical material, there are two basic works which underpin an introduction to al-Ghazālī and al-Dabbāgh's treatises on divine love. Firstly, the thirty-seventh epistle of Rasāil Ikhwan al-safā called Fimāhiyyat al-ishq (On the Essence of Love), and another is Ibn Sīnā's Risāla fīl-ishq (An Epistle on Love). The first Arabic philosopher al-Khindī wrote a treatise on love, but it is not extant. There are some scattered notes on the theme in the famous Neoplatonic work called the Theology of Aristotle, which is actually an Arabic version of parts of Plotinus' Enneads. These notes concentrate on the issue of beauty. The beauty of a material thing is inferior to the beauty of its idea. Beauty originates in the form, not in the matter, consequently, it exists also in immaterial substances. Since bodily beauty derives from the beauty of the soul, the latter is superior to the former. Also, the internal beauty of a human being, the beauty of character and disposition is preferable to external beauty. The degree of beauty increases according to its place in the cosmic hierarchy of beings. Hence, God is the most beautiful. Just as the beauty of immaterial beings is superior to the beauty of material beings, so love for the former, which is intellectual love for the former, which is intellectual love (true love), is preferable to love for the latter. Love is regarded in this work as an eternal force and moreover, the high world is identical with love. Also, in al-Fārābī is found no theory of love, only scattered reference. According to him, the form of love exists in the one, and drives from the one in an emanative manner. The one himself is the common object of the love of all beings, although each being has an object of love which is higher than itself in the cosmic hierarchy. Love for the first causes human beings to reach a certain amount of conjunction with the separate intellects. In the human sphere, love makes people be connected to and harmonized with each other.

Furthermore, detailed, and composite theories of Islamic mystic love have appeared only since the tenth/fourth century. Before them mainly utterances and poems on love are encountered. Partial theories exist, but only rarely. However, these already advance notions, such as the reasons of love for God, and the preparatory means to achieve love. What characterizes almost all writers is the central place they assign to love for God in the mystical life. It is impossible to be exhaustive in surveying such materials. Therefore, only the notions expressed by salient Sufi figures who are acknowledged to have influenced later generations. In my opinion, it is most appropriate to begin with Rābi'a al-Adawiyya, the most famous woman mystic in Islam. One of the first Sufis who created a synthesis between the religious ordinances and mysticism and who, on some significant points, influenced al-Ghazālī, is al-Harith ibn Asad-al-Muhāsibī. He reportedly held that the beginning of love for God is obedience to him (awwal al-mahabba al-tā'a), which is the expression of the nomos motif. However, in what is reminiscent of the agape motif, al-Muhāsibī stated that this kind of love derives from God's love for man, for God makes people know him and shows them how to obey him, although he does not need them. In his view, firm love for God means always remembering him and his favors in the heart and mentioning them on the tongue, thus encouraging great intimacy (uns) with him, and breaking off anything which separates man from him. He defines the love for God as intense longing (shiddat al-shawq) for him. In the last quarter of the fourth/tenth century treatises on Sufism characterized by Orthodoxy appeared. Among these was Kitāb-al-ulma' fi'l-Tasawwuf written by Abū Nasr al-Sarrāj. This is a trustworthy exposition of Sufic tenets by a Sufi who attained a high rank in practical Sufism.

The core of al-Sarrāj's discussion of divine love is his own tripartite division of this state which is corroborated by the statements of other Sufis. The love of the common people (mahabbat al-āmma) derives from God's doing good to them and having compassion on them. It is an inborn disposition in man to love his benefactor. In this context, al-Sarrāj cites several Sufis authorities who have dealt with love. The first is Sumnūn ibn Hamza nicknamed 'the Lover' (al-muhibb) who, according to al-Hujwīrī, regards love as the basis of the way to God and superior to gnosis. Asked what divine love is, Sumnun an answered that it is pure friendship (safa al-wudd) accompanied with continuous remembrance of God, for whoever loves something mentions it many times. This type of love is conditioned by such speech. Sahl ibn 'Abdallāh al-Tustarī supplements remembrance of God with agreement and obedience to him and to his messenger (the nomos motif) and the pleasantness of intimate conversation with God, meaning prayer. Moreover, this is the state of the veracious and truthful people (al-sādiqīn wa'l-mutahaqquqīn) which originates in the heart's contemplation (nazar al-qalb) of God's self-sufficiency, greatness, power, and knowledge. Thus, one loves God because of his attributes and not because of his actis for the sake of man. As a disinterested love it obliges aman to uncover the secrets of God (hatk al-astār wa-kashf al-asrār) to know him properly. This view is expressed by Abu la-Husayn al-Nūrī who probably introduced the use of the word 'ishq' into 'Sufism'. Likewise, Ibrahim al-Khawwas states that love is effacement of one's will, attributes and needs. It seems to me that by this statement he means turning to God alone and thinking only about him without paying attention to one's desire and without asking anything from him. Additionally, the love of the righteous and gnostic (al-siddiqīn wa'l-arifīn) which results from their knowledge of God's pre-existent and uncaused love for them (qadīm hubb allāh bi-lā 'illa). We are reminded of the agape motif according to which God's love for man derives from his eternal attribute of love which in turn causes man to love God without basing his love on personal reasons. To describe this kind of love, al-Sarraj brings forward Dhū al-Nūn al-Misri's statement to the effect that pure love means the omission of love from the heart and the organs so that all things will be in God and for the sake of him. Thus, Dhū al-Nūn seems to say that man is not aware of the state of love, for he is so absorbed in contemplation of God.

Another work of moderate Sufism is Abū Tālib al-Makkī's Qūt al-qulūb (The food of the Hearts) which influenced al-Ghazālī to a great extent. Al-Makkī considers love for God one of the highest stations (maqāmāt) of the gnostics. It is a favor bestowed initially by God on his sincere servants, and this favor causes them to love God. This is not love in the meaning of agape, God's spontaneous love, for al-Makkī clearly points out that God loves the pure people and those who repent, but not all the people, among them the evildoers. His view is reminiscent of the Biblical view. It is worth nothing that love as God's favor is inconsistent with Prophet Muhammad's ordinance to love God, for ordinance connotes man's endeavours, whereas favor connotes gift. Al-Makkī fails to reconcile different, inconsistent, and sometimes contradicting traditions on love. According to al-Makkī, each believer in God loves him and the measure of the believer's love depends on the degree of his belief. Basing himself on Qur'ān 2.165 'Those that believe love God more ardently', he concludes that as belief increases, love increases; that is, love has different ranks the highest of which applies to those who imitate God's attributes such as knowledge, compassion, tolerance and so on. However, he does not define clearly what he means by belief, and moreover, elsewhere he seems to contradict himself when stating that belief is conditioned by love meaning that one cannot believe in God unless one loves him. A compilation of early Sufic view on love for God accompanied with may poems and stories is a later work (Lawāmi anwār al-qulūb) composed by Abū al-Maālī 'Azīzī ibn 'Abd al-Malik al-Jīlī al-Shyadhala. Although his principal theme is divine love, the author sometimes uses illustrative example from profane love. The real meaning of love id frequently stated as obedience and total submission to God, and as absolute devotion to him in such a manner that love to anything other than God is considered idolatry (shirk). 'Man has to prefer the beloved to anything else and to leave everything except the beloved' (īthār al-mahbūb alā al-kull wa-tark al-kull illā al-mahnūb). Hence, one of the truest signs of love is the continuance of the remembrance of God. Also love means to feel intimacy (uns) and to rejoice (surūr) with the beloved alone. God's love for man is a perpetual favor which causes man to love God. Passing away from one's consciousness (fanā) occupies relatively a very marginal place. On the basic of Qur'anic verses, the author counts ten conditions for man's love for God (shurut al-mahabba), such as repentance, purity, prayer, justice, forbearance, without giving any rationale for his list and its hierarchy. Strangely enough in the list of the ten principal elements of love (arkan al-mahabbe), he again mentions piety (taqwā) and for bearance (sabr) which appear in the list of the conditions. Another inaccuracy occurs at the end of the book in which al-Shaydhala enumerates ten degrees (marātib) of love, each containing three stations (manāzil) and love occupies the eighth degree.

In this book I have tried to discuss the public engagement of a local group of Muslim performers descendants of a locally revered holy man that participate in the vibrant and centuries old mainstream regional religious tradition labelled as Warkari. Their engagement, even if it is possible to interpret in terms of the religious market but very much because such is the form of their religious environment, or perhaps the network of experienced and experiencers, does not primarily reveal itself through demand but through the offer symbolized by their calls for participation, perhaps akin to advertising. Such engagement is conditioned by the economic means of its agents that frame the strategies of communicating the divine message of their saintly ancestor. This mutual relationship, with all its vicissitudes and possibly conflicts along the centuries, also creates conditions where religious belief and practice can be thought of in the framework of the religious collective with its firm public presence.

In conclusion, bhakti, and a local bhakti tradition (parampara) which is organized under the network of regional (Maharashtrian) followers of bhakti (Warkaris). The family whose involvement in 'communicating the divine' I want to introduce one of the great examples here is the descendants of Shaikh Muhammad from Shrigonda a proverbial Maharashtrian saint-poet who shared his religious experience prevalently in Marathi, a dominant vernacular of Western India. The participation of various Muslim figures in vernacular bhakti culture is a well-known phenomenon mirrored in other South Asian regions. Having its beginnings in precolonial times, it stems from the engagement of Muslims in the devotional practice and idiom of vernacular religiosity that may also be termed as lived, or local, Islam. Compositions of Shaikh Muhammad have been classified under the rubric of bhakti literally by all authors engaging with his life and poetical testimony and I also subscribe to this view. It has been popularized and legitimized also by the upholders of Maharashtrian bhakti tradition themselves who included some of Shaikh's poetry into the most popular compilation of bhakti compositions in the Marathi vernacular space Sakala santa gatha.

Other important factors related to the person of Shaikh Muhammad that are to be heeded in the context of this article are his religious message and identity. With respect to the former, the dominant standpoint adopted by Shaikh is a monistic one pertaining to regional interpretations of advaita Vedanta found also in the texts of his other Warkari predecessors and fittingly called advaita-bhakti by Ramachandra Ranade. If bhakti provided Shaikh with the means of expressing the emotional aspect of his religiosity, via bhakti-performance, the philosophical monism adopted perhaps during his socialization to local religious ways allowed Shaikh to cross the space of Islamic theology that postulates a difference between God and his creation. This is the reason for some viewing Shaikh as a convert to Hinduism and generally adopting Hindu ways of life. It also suggests why most of his current and past followers are Warkaris. However, from Shaikh's writings a more complex personality emerges than only that of a Warkari bhakti saint-performer. He also appears to be well-versed in yogic-siddha practices and philosophy and shares them with his audiences. Additionally, but importantly, a later document coming from the third generation after Shaikh claimed him to be also a Qadiri Sufi. With respect to his religious identity, then, any interpretation seeking a clear divide between the 'Islamic' and the 'Hindu' flattens such complexity derived from pre-modern South Asian discourse, where understanding of collective belonging was far from the unified social bodies imagined as nations, or for that matter, religions. Today Shaikh's descendants the two distant cousin lineages continue to live in Ahmednagar and Bid districts of Maharashtra, in the Shrigonda and Aashti talukas respectively.[50] The saint's heritage, indeed, proved to be a divisive force in the family over the past more than three hundred and fifty years. Currently, there exist two of his graves, one in the taluka town of Shrigonda, where he had evidently stayed, and the other in Vahira village (Aashti), where certainly for a long time reside his descendants.[51] Historically, we know nothing concrete on why there are two graves, nor why the family split into two cousin-branches caring after the respective graves and adopting different narratives with respect to their saintly ancestor as well as to their own past. However, this history of the family division is a topic of itself. To the present study, it would be enough to note that today, but not necessarily in past, part of the Shrigondian branch in contrast to the majority of his Shrigondian devotees opts to see him as a Sufi whereas the Vahiran branch, to whom we will soon turn, claims Shaikh to be a Muslim saint who joined the Warkaris. Doubtless, the main center of Shaikh's cult is Shrigonda. There, inside a tomb, is located his more popular grave, together with the grave of his wife. There also, calculated according to the Shaka Hindu calendar, in the month of Phalgun (corresponding to February/March) takes place the annual ceremony commemorating his death that is preceded by seven days of ritual reading (parayan) of Dnyanadev's Dnyaneshvari and the joyful singing of poetry composed by

Warkari saints, including Shaikh. There are also other periodic ceremonies organized during the year (like Shaikh's birthday when his Yogasangram is read) including some (like Muharram) which are not directly connected to Shaikh but still participants gather at the precincts of his tomb. Throughout the year, various spots in Shrigonda are marked by images of Shaikh Muhammad, as is his tomb 'dargah' nowadays renamed 'mandir' (temple). All of this may be understood also in terms of 'communicating the divine'. News of locally popular events within a taluka are spread via accessible and current means from printed posters to online notifications. Notably, the organizers of most of these activities and events, as well as the work behind the images and posters, are predominantly Shaikh's local, and mostly Warkari- Vaishnava, followers. The role of Warkaris in organizing various religious activities and in shaping their public form is visibly pronounced. This is accentuated by the periodic accommodation of Warkari pilgrims within the tomb's compound, as well as by participation of many Shrigondians in pilgrimages. Those Shaikh's descendants who prefer a different, Sufi, narrative pertaining to the saint is somewhat marginalized from these public-cum-religious societal engagements.

However, discussing such marginalization would take us elsewhere, so let me leave it for some other occasion. Throughout the year, Shrigonda serves as a hub for devotions directed towards Shaikh, whether in the performative manner or as ritual of offerings, prayers and wishes. Muhammad Baba, as he is colloquially called, is after all too many of his followers a miracle-working helper and sustainer of happiness and success in their lives, and to Shrigondians a patron deity (Grāma devatā) of their little town. Compared to Shrigonda, Vahira would seem like a poorer relative, and in economic terms this is certainly true. A small village of about one-and-a-half thousand inhabitants located approximately 50 kms northeast of Shrigonda in a dry rural area, it is in many aspects no match for the vibrant taluka center. It is also possible to claim that the village, with respect to written, academic or other materials on Shaikh, has been thoroughly marginalized. Most of the above authors have not paid close attention to the fact that there is a different grave of Shaikh, nor that today it is precisely here (and in one case nearby) where most of Muslim transmitters of Shaikh's bhakti identity reside. In contrast to Shrigondians, Vahirans unanimously opt to follow the popular and prevalent Warkari understanding of Shaikh and his religious message epitomized in a line attributed to the saint: 'Śekh Mahaṃmad avindha, tyāce hṛdayī Govinda' Shaikh Muhammad is a Muslim, but in his heart dwells Govinda. By Vahirans I refer to three broader families of cousin brothers Abdul, Jabbar and Shubas who take care of the grave of Shaikh within the precincts of the small Muslim cemetery on the north-western outskirts of the village.

All three of them are known to be performers well linked to the networks of Warkari-Vaishnava public events (like ritual reading of the saints works parāyaṇ, or performances of devotional songs accompanied by narrating stories from saints' lives and explaining their philosophic-cum-religious ideas kīrtan). They are also the leaders of their respective pilgrim- groups that visit places related to widely popular Warkari saints during festivals devoted to them. Abdul leads the group annually visiting Alandi, the place associated with the founder of the Warkari tradition, Dnyanadev. Shubas leads a group that visits Paithan, the place associated with Eknath, another popular saint of the Warkaris, and Jabbar takes his followers to Pandharpur, a sacred town of the Warkaris that is the seat of Viththal-Vishnu. Apart from participating in Warkari religious events and venerating Vitthal-Vishnu, in whom they see the manifestation of the world's creator, the God of the Quran, the brothers also claim that they follow the basic tenets of the Islamic faith, such as prayer (namāz). Being a Muslim in this rural environment where socialization into a religious community is conditioned by having a saintly ancestor clearly also involves social ties, rather than just the ideally imagined Islamic belief and practice. However, being a descendant of one of the most popular saints of the wider Ahmadnagar region does create great social capital for the Vahira's cousin brothers. They are known to be 'maharajs (mahārājas)', which is an appellative denoting in this case wise men of religious pursuits whom others respect. It is also quite commonly used for a variety of persons engrossed in some kind of religious or generally respected public activity, and in our context almost ubiquitously for performers of bhakti saint-poetry. Being a 'maharaj' does bring one a respectable social status in rural society still ruled by the hierarchies of traditional social relationships, for instance being arbitrator in local arguments and being sought as adviser or for blessings for newborns or newlyweds, all because of one's intense engagement in religious matters. Such status is necessarily strengthened by the much wider social contacts that performers and keepers of the bhakti tradition have due to their frequent travelling while participating at devotional programs and festivals organized in Maharashtra's prominent religious centers.

Performing is also a chance for limited additional income to the rather poor livelihood gained from farming in the dry lands of the maharajs' permanent residence. It is also a traditional way of moving through the interstitial spaces of social, commercial, and devotional enterprises, to which festivals and performances certainly belong. Now, the bhakti performance of the noted Muslim maharajs, often a life-long engagement, is not only an important factor in building up their social prestige locally, but it also provides an avenue for them to communicate their understanding of what religion is, what role the Shaikh's devotional message plays there, and how their own experience of it can become the experience of their audiences. Doing this makes them a part of the religious market in sociological terms, and also presupposes certain strategies of invitations shared with their audiences akin to advertisement. Having limited economic means to employ modern communication technologies, which are increasingly seen all over South Asia, they resort to written texts and orally shared announcements. However simple this may seem, behind lies hidden a pattern that captures the mechanism of combining oral and printed ways of communication noted earlier. A hybrid way combining print media and the spoken word is advertising news of a public event through a simple printed poster. It is used for common, more numerous, events, which distinguishes it from the larger-size posters made only on greater occasions. I am far from estimating precisely how widespread the form of announcement through a simple printed poster is regarding bhakti performers in Maharashtra in general, for it would need more specific research than what I have done. Yet, as far as my own findings about Vahira maharajs are concerned, even if there may possibly be others who can link maharajs' ways of publicity to other media. However, importantly, and perhaps paradoxically too, the simple posters are not widely seen on and made for display! One reason for this is that there are not too many places in the rural countryside or in provincial small towns where they could be effectively displayed, such as a network of public boards. The posters bearing information on bhakti events may be to some limited extent found near or in the compounds of temples, or at public places such as town state transport bus stations. But displaying the poster is not, as far as I can say, the most popular way of letting others know about the bhakti event even if in the towns one may meet with a few larger size posters prior to the major religious events. This is because performers and their acquaintances share the news and invitations mainly personally, including those made into posters.[56] That of course does set the limits to, and overall does not prevent, wider publicity of shared information. Another reason is that in the rural setting there are no set distribution strategies nor precisely designed channels of distribution. But a far more important reason for personal involvement in spreading information is that often the performances are periodic events set by the calendric dates related to various festivals.

Hence it is not just the fact that the event will take place that is shared but who will take part in it and what will be the personal structure of the event. The poster, then, serves as a kind of reminder as well as a tangible manifestation of and assurance about the bhakti-performance's presence and continuity. Another peculiar factor that seemingly puts this kind of publicizing aside from commercial advertisement is that it relates to a non-commercial event (performance). Even if there is a commercial aspect to it the performers do get some reward for their performance the reward, including benefits like free use of a performance venue, food and lodging for the performers, etc., is generally given voluntarily. When greater celebrations (like birthday of a saint, or commemoration of his/her death) of which maharajs' performance makes only a part the whole event is obviously more commercial. Such celebrations include stalls of vendors, food stalls and its organizers collect donations from visitors. Yet attending the performance itself is free. The poster that I want to introduce as an example of how communication with the wider bhakti publics takes place in the rural Maharashtrian setting announces and details the nine-day pilgrimage conducted by Jabbar-maharaj in November 2012. Called "Pāyī Diṇḍī Sohḷā", it informs others about and, in a way, asks them to join Jabbar's group of followers in the 39th continuation of the annual walking on foot from Vahira across several towns and villages down to the center of the Warkaris' devotionthe city of Pandharpur. Such a 'header' situates the event under the care of a Warkari deity, its saints and within the visual world of Warkari -Vaishnava symbolism. The family of Muslim Warkaris is introduced right below. After announcing that to conduct the pilgrimage (vārī) "the diṇḍī of the gem of saints Śekh Mahaṃmad- mahārāj" from the "sacred land of Vahira" (Śrī kṣhestra Vāhirā) will start on the chosen day, comes the text that places the family within what may be called local Warkari temporal and genealogical coordinates. This is achieved by claiming that "in the 16th century in the land of Bhārat that is wholly purified by the touch of saints' feet who spread the Bhāgavata dharma, there appeared the great Śhaikh Mahaṃmad and the ninth generation of his descendants, namely Jabbār, Rājū and Baṇḍū mahārājs"also honorifically called "those who follow devotees of Hari [i.e., Vishnu]" (Hari-bhakta parāyaṇ) started this pilgrimage event (diṇḍī sohḷā)". Jabbar-maharaj is also introduced as the pilgrim group leader. Below this comes the list of all localities from where the pilgrims–cum-performers (ṭāḷkarī, literally those who clap hands or cymbals to the rhythm) of Jabbar's group come. This is followed by practical information on the itinerary of pilgrims and important people. A list of the performers who will perform at each of the nine stops is given, as well as a list of performers who form the core of Jabbar-maharaj's group, as well as of organizers of the whole pilgrimage group. The special announcement of Jabbar's own performance in Pandharpur is also included. In a separate section are listed the sponsors of the whole pilgrimage event. At the bottom of this complex poster, a tribute is paid to administrative representatives of Vahirans, who from their position of office holders give the event official support. Finally, the same is done for all the Vahira devotees. The last piece of information the poster provides is reference to the printing office located in Miraj gaon, a little town some 19 kms south of Vahira, where the printout of the poster was created. There can obviously be many aspects highlighted after reading through the poster briefed above. What can be clearly seen is that this rural pilgrimage is a complex and well-organized event which concerns not only its main protagonists but also many other people who help make it happen. It reveals details of how the bhakti is a collective and public endeavor well networked to different supporters, powerholders, local performers and, above all, audiences. So, if bhakti historically appears as a phenomenon that finds its expression especially in sharing (of texts, motifs, practices, moods, emotions), observing its current form suggests continuation with the past. Also, and this again connects to the mechanics of sharing traced in the past even if this comparatively little 'sohla' makes for a non-commercial event based on voluntary support, it is not devoid of its socio-economic aspect. The participation of people coming from a variety of social strata that include commoners, local officials and sponsors certainly creates social capital for all involved, especially the organizers, as well as provides space for circulation of items needed by the pilgrims.

To access the untold story of bhakti, it would be worth explaining the economy of this rural network in greater detail as well as detail its relation to power structures, but my data does not allow me to do this. Yet, this small-scale collaboration behind the devotional and doubtless honest goals of its protagonists may suggest what enterprise may be behind such a great pilgrimage gathering as when groups, some of which count their members in the hundreds and thousands, from all over Maharashtra gather in Pandharpur. But regarding what is communicated and how, the poster and indeed many other similar posters representing similar groups reveals a clear link between the pre-print pre-formalized practice of sharing knowledge and experience, and its modern-to-current development that employs newer ways of 'technologizing the word', to use the famous phrase of Walter Ong. Clearly and historically, the texts and hence knowledge embodied in bhakti get produced in the shared environments between the performers and publics, as Novetzke, Callewart and Hawley suggest, as well as get memorized and recalled situations (like the production of this posters' 'header', or for the purpose of the performance itself). Yet there is another layer to the whole process. The idea of the divine experience that manifests itself in as well as draws its texture and textuality from the shared songs and internalized meanings reaches the consumer irrespective of his technical literacy. Rather, it is the consumer's cultural literacy "the 'content-schemata' of the knowledge that is in fact translinguistic, i.e., beyond the abstract sense of the words" that is significant. Similarly, during the performance and this is very much the cultural practice the experience gets articulated somewhere between the participants and the performers.

Therefore, the technological and modern mode of 'communicating the divine' that has often been coded to text matters much less than the intended meaning of conveying the intersubjective experience. Such relationship is also considered a meritorious way of social engagement, whether it comes with the song, text, or narrative. It conveys not only the experience but the merit that stems from the latter, a process which Stark in the context of printed text refers to as "the traditional concept of cultivation of the mind". It is because of awareness of this how-to-gain-an-experience and putting it into practice that the poster the call to experience may be just delivered and not displayed, for displaying would anticipate reading and distance, whereas delivering anticipates the participation. It is a sort of adjusting (if you like, mimicry of) the printed message that in turn cannot be advertisement in solely commercial terms but is akin to it.

Another possible reading of such a call is with respect to the social conditions of keeping the religious identity of its conveners. As the call gets printed and imprinted in the minds of Warkaris, the local ways of understanding the social worth of maharajs gets publicly articulated. This, in turn, is linked to what has been academically termed as religious syncretism lived, localized or hybrid Islam. In her study of visualization of different objects and themes related to South Asian Muslims, Sandria Freitag observes that their 'visual vocabulary' provides Muslims with a 'notion of shared membership within this ostensible group'. My material shows that the sharing could take a trajectory that is perhaps not ostensible yet speaks for Muslims. Although the presented poster along with Shaikh Muhammad's texts, beliefs and practices of his descendants and followers may be interpreted as an example of how anything that, from the essentialist point of view, represents Islam has been marginalized if not completely erased, it begs the question of what would be the purpose of searching for such an Islam if the local Muslim Maharaj's do not consider it necessary. Even if hardly known in detail, what should be taken into consideration is rather the more than three hundred and fifty years of history of the family keeping the local Muslim identity that is rooted in the testimony of their saintly ancestor. Perhaps this is a tradition that gets articulated through and amended by the voices of the others (i.e., Warkaris), but Maharaj's do not seem to mind being the subject of the other voice, because this is what they experience and what they invite others to hear. This might be certainly called a peculiar local way of being a Muslim. But with respect to hundreds of years of the family tradition, isn't it that the older forms of religious identity, those that hardly fit its modern reconceptualization, such as Warkari Muslims, maintain their existence, perhaps, precisely because they, apart from engaging with the current models communicating their presence at the wider world of South Asian religious market, also maintain the older ways of communication rooted in the past. In contrast to identity that is marketable, the experience that their identity offers hardly has such a quality. True, bhakti can also become a divisive force when it is portrayed in a way that 'serves the constituency of a particular public' that allows for (such as in this very instance) participation of Muslims at Hindu events and opens possibilities to play their own role in the cult whose followers are the Hindu majority. Times are constantly changing. The situation is not the same at every time. Change is inevitable. So, the era in which Sufism emerged or the golden age of poetry and philosophy is no more. Like other medieval tools, Sufi tools seem unrealistic and dreamy in today age. It is true that in today age there is no room left for such passionate seekers, no faith and belief of that time. So, there may be a few Sufi seekers today, or a few very few people who believe in their doctrines, but in general it can be said that in today's age it is difficult and rare to see people like Sufis and high morals like them. Despite this, the breadth of the influence of Sufi philosophy cannot be denied. His way of thinking has influenced a very large population. In Arabic, Persian, Dakhini and Urdu literature, these influences can be seen step by step.

Among literature books in other languages, especially Hindi and Sindhi literature has influence on learning. To some extent, to a lesser extent, Marathi and Dakhani literature is no exception. Sufi ideology, like other ideologies that make man human in a fast-paced, fast-paced, fast-paced technique of communicating with people, is in flux today. In summary, the importance of the study of Sufi poetry and philosophy cannot be underestimated under any circumstances. Emphasis on the heart should be understood as the basic spirit of Sufism. Sadhana Or devotion sometimes takes the form of spiritualism or mysticism. Sufis have emphasized on purification of the mind for sadhana or devotion. A collection of some moral virtues is necessary for purification of the mind. The most beautiful thoughts on all these things will appear in Sufi literature. The struggle against the obstacles in the path of sadhana and the worldly forms of idolatry, caste system, caste discrimination, Hindu-Muslim animosity, shraddha, worship, etc. There is a mixture of nirguna bhakti with them. Sufis were high class seekers. Spiritual tools are best expressed in voice. Such a beautiful depiction of spiritual separation and reunion is simply not found in any other literature of the world. The eternal, moral, and spiritual virtues that he has commanded will be useful to every society for a long time to come. They have disregarded the external treatment of the tool. This was as a result of the social conditions of the time. They felt that these external treatments were a form of extravagance and were exploiting the vitality of the masses. Classes are being formed on the pretext of religion. Therefore, opposes extra-terrestrials, pointing to the basic moral and spiritual principles that are equally admirable in all religions. The Sufi view was realistic.

Spread over Asia and from there to Southeast Asia. Sufism is truly a beacon, in the light of which everyone sees right way without any discrimination. Its liquidity has neither rigidity nor shrinkage. It cannot be bound by country, caste, or religion. This is a natural tendency, an emotion. Whose omnipresence, like Brahma, pervades the entire universe. So, wherever the message of Sufism reached, no one welcomed it? The message is also of love, and it is also divine! The God of the Sufis is not Khuda, Rama, Krishna or any other noun with specific attributes related to any one caste or religion. He does not sit in any place, does not incarnate, and does not run the Jagarhat from anywhere like a ruler. It is a vast force, which can be called by any specific name. Where is the ruler like, who can be called by any specific name. We are not all different from him. That is our source. So, Hindus, Muslims, Christians, Jains, Buddhists, Parsis and Sikhs are all nominal differences. Everyone's goal is to reach the same place by different means and that is to become one with their original creator. Whether the chanting was done with the help of a rosary or avoided, whether the worship was taking place in a temple, or whether the worship was performed in a mosque, or anywhere else in any form, or whether the penance was performed in private, or whether Samadhi was performed, but this pride. Whether it is a dream in the middle of a masjid or whether one performs penance in solitude or attains samadhi, but the ultimate goal of all this is the same. His name can be self-realization, liberation from the world, enlightenment, reunion, Nirvana, or attainment of God. The only difference is in the name. Not in the intuition. So, after developing Aryanism in Iran, Iraq, etc., when Sufism entered India, it put itself in the mold here. By adopting such useful remedies in devotion, he conveyed the message of divine love and showed that it is through this love that we can get a glimpse of the cosmic soul. God's name can be self-realization, liberation from the world, enlightenment, reunion, Nirvana, or attainment of God. The only difference is in the name. Not in the intuition. So, after developing Aryanism in Iran, Iraq, etc., when Sufism entered India, it put itself in the mold here. By adopting such useful remedies in devotion, he conveyed the message of divine love and showed that it is through this love that we can get a glimpse of the cosmic soul. In his absence, not only we but you, Pananpan, atom-molecules all get disturbed.

In Sufism, there is something other than God. So, there are no differences of country, religion, caste etc. The whole human race is one. The essence of the truth of the world is one human religion and the whole universe is one country. So, it is foolish to argue in the name of country, religion, or caste. It is a violation of humanity and a gross violation of divine commandments. Inspired by this sentiment, Sufis used Persian, Hindi, Sindhi, Dakhni, Urdu and Marathi etc. heard the same message of love through all languages. It is here that man comes to the same level and settles down, and in the absence of darkness, walks on the path of light and departs towards his Beloved Lord. All the Mahatmas in the world are really Sufis. They sing the same raga on different strings of devotion in different countries, costumes, and languages over time. All the Mahatmas like Rama, Krishna, Buddha, Mahavira, Nanak, Isa, Musa, Ibrahim, and Prophet Muhammad etc. came with the same message and that message was to sever ties with this mortal world and meet the cosmos. It is not found in places of worship like temples and mosques as well as in places of pilgrimage like Kaaba-Kashi. God resides in the pure heart of the devotee. Therefore, disgusted with the world, one should seek him there (with a pure mind) only by loving him. The same message has been preached by thousands of saints like the above apostles and great men, and the same message will continue to be heard in the future. The cosmopolitanism that Sufism has taught alongside divine love is a boon not only for human society but for all living beings. The great virtues of kindness, forgiveness, empathy, and cooperation are the followers of cosmopolitanism. There is no room for violence, untruth, stigma, and other misconduct in their goodwill. So, the heart of the cosmopolitan is always pure, and he is the true lover of God. Thus, Sufism can be called cosmopolitanism because the essence of Sufi philosophy is the essence of the universe. Its umbrella is the same everywhere. So here everyone is the same. No one is high-low. Different sects, sects consider others as strangers, but this stranger is also considered as ours. Though as a Sufi today it seems to have passed away; but in the world, peace envoys and peace activists propagate the same sentiment, and the same path of love is being touted under different names of remedies. That's right because where is the peace without it? In the realm of love beyond discrimination, peace spreads its legs and sleeps firmly and securely and stays happy. Other than that, everything is noisy. It is a barren desert, full of war, strife, and destruction. Psychologists have concluded that love is more or less present in everyone in one form or another. So, everyone has a sense of cooperation. Apart from mental disorders like anger, malice, etc., animals also want happiness and peace. This price has always been and always will be. The usefulness of Sufism in the future lies in the fact that it will continue to teach the animals of love and peace, directly or indirectly, under the same name or some other name, to the restless and perplexed creatures. We all know that, by name, will continue to teach lessons of love and peace. We all know that the feeling inherent in Sufism is universal and everlasting. So, there is no purpose to the dictionary. In the future, whenever there will be love-propaganda, peace-efforts, organization-work and cooperation-statement, there will be a sense of Sufism at work. He must also be a Sufi in all forms of love-preacher, peace founder, organizer, and collaborator, whether he be a Peer (saint-Mahatma) or a prophet, a saint-man, or an incarnate great man. That is lasting peace in the world, can only be achieved through the path of love.

In the journey of Sufism, we see three major departures. 1. Arabia, 2. Iran and 3. India. We can call this the departure of Sufism. Sufism inspired karma in Arabia based on knowledge and devotion. The implication of the Karmamarga here is that the Sufis, by eliminating (destroying) the distinctions between the high and the low and the untouchables and the untouchables, brought about unity among them instead of the differences between Hindus and Muslims. Monotheism is a great gift of the Sufis. Besides, they Bhagwat gave a spiritual interpretation of the mystical romance of Dharma and embellished Hindi literature with the help of mysticism and mysticism. Marathi Muslim Saints literature has become very rich due to the unique influence of Sufi ideology on bhakti marga poetry and literature. Guidance for the attainment of formless, nirguna without erasing the embodied form in devotional poetry is the result of the expressive style of Sufism. Nominal forms that suit this style are symbols of all-pervading power. The expression of this symbolic meaning is helpful, so it is accepted. Or Economics has given the advantage of paving Marathi Muslim Saints literature the way for the attainment of the formless without abandoning the traditional Sakarupasana. Ancient boundaries, however, were not violated, and thought prevailed. The same ideology emerged in modern Marathi and Dakkhani poetry in the form of shadowism and mysticism. This added to the beauty of Marathi and Dakkhani poetry. Instead of narrowness, hesitation, control, the influence of this ideology led to the rise of generosity, comprehensiveness, tolerance, and freedom in Marathi and Dakkhani literature and can be expected to happen in the future as well.

It is with the help of Sufi insight that the divine light is revealed in the heart in the form of unity. Influenced and developed by various ideologies in Arabia, Syria, Egypt (Egypt), Persia (Iran) and Spain, Sufism did not give up its vast heart and re-entered India and taught love to all with the same generosity. The usefulness of the brilliant principles of Sufi philosophy inspired others. Poets like Kabir, Meera, Shaikh Mohmmad etc. seem to be taking refuge in the pervasiveness of the influence of Sufism. Modern day shadowism, mysticism and mysticism, but to some extent, to some extent, seem to be the same. Its influence on Urdu and Dakkhani literature is undeniable. In fact, it is the truth that always and everywhere exists in one form or another. In Marathi, Dakhani and Hindi literature, Sufism has taken the saints of knowledge on the one hand and the saints of love on the other under the umbrella of its influence. Nirguna Nirakar Brahma cannot be the subject of devotion and Saguna-Sakar becomes personal as Ishwar Rama-Krishna etc. are incarnated in different forms. So, it becomes the center of sectarianism and causes unrest, strife, and animosity. The Sufis, being followers of the path of love, made the formless Brahmas their own by accusing them of virtues. Due to this belief, love-symptom devotion is also possible, and the stench of sectarianism cannot come. In fact, it is useless to be distracted by imagining God as a lover and making oneself his lover. It is just a symbol. Because of this, it must be acknowledged that in the worship of love, husband and wife are not really important at all. This is an array of tools; But the goal is the same and that is to establish oneness with God through love. Sufi philosophy is as useful as Sufi poetry is beautiful. Because the solution to world peace is in cosmopolitanism and that cosmopolitanism is the epitome of divine love, the shades of which are abundantly visible to us in love-loving Marathi, Dakhani, Urdu and Hindi literature & quote. Due to the existence of religions, sects, countries, provinces and districts, animosity, enmity, strife, and hatred towards each other seem to have increased among the people. We are walking through this dark period. If there is one thing that the world desperately needs today, it is the ray of love. It was he who published the life of this friend of God, the Sufi seeker. They had gone so deep on the path of love that there was no way back from there. It is the only way to meet East and West. We have seen that Sufi saints spread and continued their teaching all over India since beginning of the 12th century. Alauddin Khilaji won Devagiri Dynasty, further to the downfall of Devagiri Dynasty, the number of Sufi saints seems to have increased in Maharashtra. Sufi saints had achieved a very good command on philosophical and ideological unity with the existing Warkari and Bhakti Marg sects in Maharashtra. At the same time, Sufi saints have found refuge with the local warlords who existed in various parts of Maharashtra. These Maratha chiefs were in the service of various Muslim rulers and in charge of the Jahagiri and their traditional Patilkis (Patilki means the honorable position offered for a person and it becomes the head of village. Since ancient times the village head played an important role in the running of the village and the person in that role was involved in maintaining law and order as well as solving social problems.) These Maratha chiefs ruled their kingdom in these areas call Jahagiri. These Maratha chiefs cared for all people and nurtured inter- religious harmony among all, because of this people like the ruler, they had laid the foundation for Hindu saints and Sufi saints to be their gurus. Naturally, the general people also showed respect for all Hindu saints and Muslim Sufi saints. Since the time of Shivaji's grandfather, the respect for Sufi saints has remained unaffected in Maharashtra. During that time, that love and faith of the people of Maharashtra towards Sufi saints observed to be increasing day by day. Not only that, but in many places the Guru between the Warakari sect and the Sufi sect has gone beyond the differences, came together and appear to be uniform. All these devotional readings and reflections of Sufi scriptures are still in practice in villages from year to year. Such a close relationship seems to have been forged in the land of Maharashtra through the adoption of Muslim Sufi saints in their various compositions of poetry, the message of unity, Yogasadhana, poems, etc. Initially, the saints came here from outside and over time they their next generations remained and settled in Maharashtra. Among such Muslim Sufi saints of Maharashtra, Shah Murtuza Bahamani, Ambar Hussain, Aalam Khan, Shaikh Sultan, Shaikh Chand Qadiri, and Shaikh Muhammad Shrigondekar are well-known saints, and their compositions and poetry are still studied today. From all these texts, we will find many learning examples those are useful to humanity, such as compassion, forgiveness, peace, opposition to racial inequality, doctrine of equality, blind faith, opposition to undesirable superstitions, simple living, high thinking, social unity, etc. The work of all these saints is incomparable. The Sufi tradition started outside India to bring happiness to humanity and the principle of love, which spreads all over the world, seems to have taken root in the soil and transformed it into a big tree. At a time when human values are declining, if we study on the poetry of these Sufi saints and try to apply their teachings in our daily lives, it will not take long for us to change the world and all humans, and their values will create an equality.

Appendices

Appendix 1

Various Definition of Religion

- **Patrick H. McNamara**: 'Try to define religion and you invite an argument'.
- **American Heritage Dictionary**: "Belief in and reverence for a supernatural power recognized as the creator and governor of the universe; A particular integrated system of this expression; The spiritual or emotional attitude of one who recognizes the existence of a superhuman power or powers".
- **John Ayto: Dictionary of Word Origins**: "Latin religio originally meant obligation, bond. It was probably derived from the verb religare 'tie back, tie tight' ... It developed the specialized sense 'bond between human beings and the gods, and from the 5th century it came to be used for 'monastic life' ... 'Religious practices' emerged from this, but the word's standard modern meaning did not develop until as recently as the 16th century".
- **Jalalu'l-Din Rumi**: The lamps are different, but the light is the same.
- **Thomas Hobbes**: To say that [God] hath spoken to [someone] in a dream, is no more than to say he dreamed that God spake to him!
- **Immanuel Kant**: Religion is the recognition of all our duties as divine commands.
- **Ludwig Feuerbach**: Religion is a dream, in which our own conceptions and emotions appear to us as separate existences, being out of ourselves.
- **E. B. Tylor**: Belief in spiritual things.
- **Frederich Nietzsche**: God is dead. God remains dead. And we have killed him. "What is it: is man only a blunder of God, or God only a blunder of man?
- **Emile Durkheim**: ...A unified system of beliefs and practices relative to sacred things, that is to say, things set apart and forbidden beliefs and practices which unite into one single moral community called a Church all those who adhere to them.

- **Emile Durkheim #2**:Religion is only the sentiment inspired by the group in its members, but projected outside of the consciousness that experiences them, and objectified.
- **James G. Frazer:** Religion is a propitiation or conciliation of powers superior to man which are believed to direct and control the course of Nature and of human life.
- **Alfred North Whitehead**: Religion is what an individual does with his solitariness.
- **William James**: The very fact that they are so many and so different from one another is enough to prove that the word 'religion' cannot stand for any single principle or essence but is rather a collective name.
- **Harriet Martineau**: Religion is the belief in an ever-living God, that is, in a Divine Mind and Will ruling the Universe and holding moral relations with mankind.
- **Rudolph Otto**: Religion is that which grows out of, and gives expression to, experience of the holy in its various aspects.
- **George Bernard Shaw**: There is only one religion, though there are hundreds of versions of it.
- **Sigmund Freud**: Religion is comparable to childhood neurosis.
- **John Dewey**: The religious is any activity pursued on behalf of an ideal end against obstacles and in spite of threats of personal loss because of its general and enduring value.
- **Karl Marx**: Religion is the sigh of the oppressed creature... a protest against real suffering... it is the opium of the people... the illusory sun which revolves around man for as long as he does not evolve around himself.
- **Paul Tillich**: Religion is the state of being grasped by an ultimate concern, a concern which qualifies all other concerns as preliminary and which itself contains the answer to the question of the meaning of life.
- **Friedrich Schleiermacher**: The essence of religion consists in the feeling of absolute dependence.
- **Spiro**: An institution consisting of culturally patterned interaction with culturally postulated superhuman beings.
- **Bradley**: Religion usually has to do with man's relationship to the unseen world, to the world of spirits, demons, and gods. A second element common to all religions ... is the term salvation. All religions seek to help man find meaning in a universe which all too often appears to be hostile to his interests. The world salvation means, basically, health. It means one is saved from disaster, fear, hunger, and a meaningless life. It means one is saved for hope, love, security, and the fulfilment of purpose.

- **J. Miltion Yinger**: Religion is a system of beliefs and practices by means of which a group of people struggle with the ultimate problem of human life.
- **Clifford Geertz**: Religion is (1) a system of symbols which acts to (2) establish powerful, persuasive, and long-lasting moods and motivations in [people] by (3) formulating conceptions of a general order of existence and (4) clothing these conceptions with such an aura of factuality that the moods and motivations seem uniquely realistic.
- **Hick**: Religion constitutes our varied human response to transcendent Reality.
- **Livingston**: Religion is that system of activities and beliefs directed toward that which is perceived to be of sacred value and transforming power.
- **Swidler**: An explanation of the meaning of life and how to live accordingly.
- **Wallace**: Religion is a set of rituals, rationalized by myth, which mobilizes supernatural powers for the purpose of achieving or preventing transformations of state in man or nature.
- **Cunningham, et al.**: Religion signifies those ways of viewing the world which refer to (1) a notion of sacred reality (2) made manifest in human experience (3) in such a way as to produce long-lasting ways of thinking, feeling, and acting (4) with respect to problems of ordering and understanding existence.
- **Horton**: An extension of the field of people's social relationships beyond the confines of a purely human society. One in which human beings involved see themselves in a dependent position vis-a-vis their non-human alters.
- **Otto Rank**: All religion springs, in the last analysis, not so much from fear of natural death as of final destruction.
- **R. Forrester Church**: Religion is 'our human response to being alive and having to die…'.
- **Robert Bellah**: '…a set of symbolic forms and acts that relate man to the ultimate conditions of his existence.'
- **Ernest Becker:** 'Culture itself is sacred, since it is the 'religion' that assures in some way the perpetuation of its members.' 'Culture is in this sense 'supernatural,' and all systems of culture have in the end the same goal: to raise men above nature, to assure them that in some ways their lives count in the universe more than merely physical things count.'
- **H. Smith:** 'Wherever people live, whenever they live, they find themselves faced with three inescapable problems: how to win food and shelter from their natural environment (the problem nature poses), how

to get along with one another (the social problem), and how to relate themselves to the total scheme of things (the religious problem). If this third issue seems less important than the other two, we should remind ourselves that religious artifacts are the oldest that archaeologists have discovered'.

- **Schmidt, et al.**: 'Religions, then, are systems of meaning embodied in a pattern of life, a community of faith, and a worldview that articulate a view of the sacred and of what ultimately matters'.
- **Aldous Huxley**: 'Religion is the price we pay for being intelligent, but not as yet intelligent enough'.

Appendix 2

List of Sufi Saints in the World

A

- **Abu al Hasan ash-Shadhili** known as Shaikh al Shadhili (1196-1258A.D.) an influential Moroccan Islamic scholar and Sufi, founder of the Shahdhili Sufi order.
- **Ameer Muhammad Akram Awan** (1934-2017A.D.) lived, preached, gave spiritual training, and buried at Dar-ul-Irfan Munara, Pakistan, was the 12th Shaikh of Silsila Naqshbandia Owaisiah and writer of several books and Tafaseer of the Holy Qur'an.
- **Abdallah ibn Alawi al-Haddad** (1634-1720A.D.), buried in Hadhramaut, the author of several books on Dhikr.
- **Abdullah Shah Ghazi** (720-773A.D.), buried in Clifton, Karachi.
- **Abdul Waahid Bin Zaid** (died 711A.D.), great early sufi Shaikh buried in Iraq.
- **Abdul Khaliq Ghijaduvani** (died 1179A.D.), buried in Bukhara, one of the Khwajagan of the Naqshbandi order.
- **Abdul Qadir Gilani** (1077-1166A.D.), buried in Baghdad, founder of the Qadiriyya Sufi order.[3][4]
- **Abdul Razzaq Gilani** (1134-1207A.D.), buried in Baghdad, son of Abdul Qadir Gilani, promoted the Qadiriyya order.
- **Abu Ishaq Shami** (10 June 852-940A.D.), buried on Mount Qasiyun, founder of the Sufi Chishti Order.
- **Abū-Sa'īd Abul-Khayr** (967-1049A.D.), buried in Miana, Turkmenistan, poet who innovated the use of love poetry to express mystic concepts.
- **Abu al-Abbas al-Mursi** (1219-1287A.D.), buried in Anfoushi, one of the four master saints of Egypt.
- **Abul Hasan Hankari** (1018-1093A.D.), buried in Baghdad, noted scholar and miracle worker.
- **Adam Khaki** - also known as Khaki Pir, period early 14th century, buried in Badarpur, Assam, took part in the Conquest of Sylhet and preached at Badarpur.
- **Afaq Khoja** (1626-1694A.D.), Also known as Khwaja Hidayat Allah, buried in Xinjiang, opposed the Chagatai Khanate's attempt to enforce Yassa law on Muslims.

- **Ahamed Muhyudheen Noorishah Jeelani** (1915-1990A.D.), buried in Hyderabad, India, founder of the Nooriya sufi order.
- **Ahmed Raza Khan Barelvi** (1856-1921A.D.), buried in the Bareilly Sharif Dargah, reformer in British India).
- **Ahmad Ghazali** (1061-1123 or 1126A.D.), buried in Qazvin, younger brother of the more famous Al-Ghazali, reasoned that as God is absolute beauty, to adore any object of beauty is to participate in a divine act of love.
- **Ahmad al-Tijani** (1737-1815A.D.), buried in Fez, Morocco founder of the Tijaniyyah order.
- **Ahmadou Bamba** (1853-1927A.D.), buried next to the Great Mosque of Touba, lead a pacifist struggle against the French colonial empire.
- **Ahmad Yasawi** (1093-1166A.D.), buried in the Mausoleum of Khoja Ahmed Yasawi, poet, founder of Turkish Sufism.
- **Akshamsaddin** (1389 Damascus -1459A.D.), buried in Göynük, tutor and advisor to Sultan Mehmed the Conqueror.Founder of Shamsiyya Bayramiyya Sufi order.
- **Akhundzada Saif-ur-Rahman Mubarak** (1925-2010A.D.), buried in Lahore, founder of the Saifia Sufi order.
- **Al-Busiri** (1211-1294A.D.), buried in Alexandria, poet, author of the Qasida Burda.
- **Ali Wasif** (1929-1993A.D.), buried in Lahore, was a teacher, writer, poet, and Sufi saint from Pakistan.
- **Ajami-al-Habib** (7th or 8th century March 738A.D.), buried in Basra.
- **Abu Bakr al-Aydarus** (1447-1508A.D.), buried in Aden, the patron saint of Aden, credited with introducing Qadiri Sufism to Ethiopia and coffee to the Arab world.
- **Ahmad al-Badawi** (1200-1276A.D.), buried in Ahmad Al-Badawi Mosque, most popular saint in Egypt.
- **Al-Ghazālī** (1058 Tous, Iran-19 December 1111A.D.), buried in Tous, Iran, considered a Mujaddid, author of The Revival of the Religious Sciences and The Incoherence of the Philosophers, influenced early modern European criticism of Aristotelian physics.
- **Al-Hallaj Or Mansoor Hallaj** (858- 26th March 922 A.D.), imprisoned and executed after requesting 'O Muslims, save me from God' and declaring 'I am the Truth'.
- **Ali al-Hujwiri** (14 August 1009-1072/77A.D.), buried in Lahore, Pakistan, author of Kashf-al Mahjoob, spread Sufism throughout the Indian Subcontinent.[5]
- **Ali-Shir Nava'i** (1441-1501 A.D.), buried in Herat, author of Muhakamat al-Lughatayn and founder of Turkic literature.

- **Abu al-Hassan al-Kharaqani** (963-1033A.D.), illiterate mystic who influenced Avicenna, Rumi, and Jami.
- **Al-Qushayri** (986-1072A.D.), buried in Nishapur, author who distinguished four layers of Quranic interpretation and defended the historical lineage of Sufism.
- **Alauddin Sabir Kaliyari** (21 February1196-16 March 1291 A.D.), buried near Haridwar, founder of the Sabiriya branch of the Chishti order.[6]
- **Amir Khusro** (1253-1325A.D.), buried in the Nizamuddin Dargah, influential musician, considered the 'father of Urdu literature'.[7]
- **Amir Kulal** (1277 Bukhara -28 November 1370A.D., Sokhar), buried near Bukhara, taught Amir Timur and Baha' al-Din Naqshband.
- **Attar of Nishapur** (1145-1221A.D.), buried in the Mausoleum of Attar of Nishapur, author of The Conference of the Birds and the hagiographic Tazkirat al-Auliya.
- **Azan Faqir** (Born 1610 Baghdad-17th century), buried in Sivasagar near the Brahmaputra River, reformer who stabilized Islam in the Assam region.[8]
- **Abd al-Karīm al-Jīlī** (1365-1424 A.D., expounded on the works of Ibn Arabi)
- **Abu Al Fazal Abdul Wahid Yemeni Tamimi** (Junaidia order Born 2 December 953 A.D. Baghdad, died at Baghdad).
- **Abdul Aziz bin Hars bin Asad Yemeni Tamimi** (Born 929 A.D. at yemen, died yemen).
- **Abu al-Najib Suhrawardi** (Born in 1097A.D., Suharward, Iran, and died in 1168 Baghdad).
- **Abu Bakr Shibli** (Born in 861A.D., Samarra, Iraq and died 946 AD, Baghdad).
- **Ahmad Zarruq** (Born 7th June 1442, Morocco, and died 1493, Misrata, Libiya).
- **Abdul Qadeer Siddiqui (Maulavi Mohammed)**'Hasrat'(Born1870 and died in 1962A.D. Hyderabad).

B

- **Baba Fakruddin** (1169-1295A.D., buried in Penukonda).[9]
- **Baba Kuhi of Shiraz** (948-1037A.D.).
- **Baba Shadi Shaheed** (17th century, first Chib Rajput to convert to Islam, married a daughter of Babur).
- **Sheikh Bedreddin** (1359-1420A.D., buried in Istanbul in 1961, revolted against Mehmed I).
- **Baha' al-Din Naqshband** (1318-1389A.D., buried in Bukhara, founder of the Naqshbandi order).

- **Balım Sultan** (1517/1519A.D., buried in Nevşehir Province, co-founder of the Bektashi Order).
- **Bahauddin Zakariya** (1170-1267A.D., buried in the Shrine of Bahauddin Zakariya, spread the Suhrawardiyya order through South Asia)[10]
- **Bande Nawaz** (1321-1422A.D., buried in Gulbarga, spread the Chishti Order to southern India).[11]
- **Baqi Billah Khwaja** (1564-1605A.D., buried in Delhi, spread the Naqshbandi order into India).[12]
- **Bawa Muhaiyaddeen** (1986A.D., founder of the Bawa Muhaiyaddeen Fellowship in Philadelphia).
- **Bayazid Bastami** (874/5-848/9A.D., buried in Shrine of Bayazid Bostami, noted for his ideas on spiritual intoxication).
- **Bibi Jamal Khatun** (1639 or 1647A.D., lived in Sehwan Sharif, sister of Mian Mir).[13]
- **Bodla Bahar** (1238-1298A.D., buried in Sehwan Sharif, features in the miracle stories of Lal Shahbaz Qalandar).
- **Bu Ali Shah Qalandar** (1209-1324A.D., buried in Panipat).[14]
- **Bulleh Shah** (1680-1757A.D., buried in Kasur, regarded as 'the father of Punjabi enlightenment').

D

- **Dara Shikoh** (1615-1659A.D., brother of king Aurangzeb, author of Majma-ul-Bahrain).[15]
- **Daud Bandagi Kirmani** (1513-1575A.D., buried in Shergarh, Punjab).[16]
- **Dawūd al-Qayşarī** (1260-1350A.D., Kayseri,Turkey).
- **Dawud Tai** Abu Sulaiman Dawud-Ibn-Nusair-al-Tai (777-782 A.D.).
- **Dhul-Nun al-Misri** or zul Nun (Born in 796A.D.,Akhmim,Egypt and died 859 A.D., Cairo, Egypt).

F

- **Fakhr ad-Din ar-Razi** (Born in 1149A.D. Shahr-e-Rey and died 5th April 1210A.D., Herat, Afaganistan).
- **Fariduddin Ganjshakar** (1188-1280 A.D., buried in the Shrine of Baba Farid, Pakpattan, Pakistan and developed Punjabi literature through poetry).[17]
- **Fuzûlî** (1494-1556 A.D., considered one of the greatest poets of Azerbaijani literature).

G

- **Ghulam Ali Dehlavi** (1743-1824 A.D., buried in Delhi).
- **Ghousi Shah** (1893-1954 A.D., buried in Hyderabad).
- **Gül Baba** (1541 A.D., buried in Tomb of Gül Baba, esoteric author and patron saint of Budapest).

H

- **Hazrat khawaja Mohammad** baba Sufi hamd Ali shah r.a Bhanpur Sharif district-dindori state-madhya pradesh India.
- **Hafez** (1315-1390A.D., buried in Tomb of Hafez, highly popular antinomian Persian poet whose works are regularly quoted and even used for divination).
- **Haji Huud** (1025-1141A.D., buried in Patan, Gujarat, helped spread Islam in India).[18]
- **Hacı Bayram-ı Veli** (1352-1430A.D., buried in Ankara, founder of the Bayramiye order).
- **Haji Bektash Veli** (1209-1271A.D., buried in the Haji Bektash Veli Complex, revered by both Alevis and Bektashis).
- **Hasan al-Basri** (642-728A.D., buried in Az Zubayr, highly important figure in the development of Sunni Sufism).
- **Hazrat Babajan** (1931A.D., buried in Pune, master to Meher Baba)
- **Hamadani** Mir Sayyid Ali (1314-1384A.D., buried in Khatlon Region, spread the Kubrawiya order throughout Asia)[19]

I

- **Iraqī** Fakir-Al- Din- Ebrahim (Born in 1213A.D., Hamedan, Iran, and died on 30th November 1289 Damascus, Syria).[20]
- **Ibrahim Niass** (Born on 8th November 1900, Kaolack Senegal and died on 26th July 1975A.D., London).
- **Ibrahim Ibn Adham** also called Ibrahim Balkh-(Born on 13th May 718A.D., Balkh, Afghanistan and died in 777 A.D. Arabia).
- **Ibn Arabi** (Born on 26th July 1165 A.D.,Murcia, Spain and died on 16th November 1240A.D., Dmascus, Syria).
- **Ibn Ata Allah** Al Iskandari (1260-1309A.D., Alexandria, Egypt, Cairo).
- **Imam Ali-ul-Haq** (925-971A.D., burried in Sialkot).
- **Ibrahim al-Dasuqi** (1255-1296A.D., buried in Desouk, founder of the Desouki order).
- **İbrahim Hakkı Erzurumi** (1703-1780A.D., buried in Tillo, astronomer and encyclopaedist, first Muslim author to cover post-Copernican astronomy).

- **Imadaddin Nasimi** Greatest Turkic Mystical poet (Died 1417A.D., Aleppo.).
- **Ismail Haqqi Bursevi** (1653-1725A.D., buried in Bursa, author noted for esoteric interpretations of the Quran).
- **Ismail Qureshi al Hashmi** (Born in 1260A.D. Multan, Pakistan and died in 1349A.D. Prayagraj, kashi).

J

- **Jalaluddin Surkh-Posh Bukhari** (Born in 1199A.D., Bukhara-Died 20th May 1292, Uch sharif, Pakistan).[21]
- **Jamal-ud-Din Hansvi** (Born in 1187A.D. Ghazani, Afaganistan - Died 1260A.D., India).
- **Jabir ibn Hayyan** (721-813A.D., Tous, Iran).
- **Ja'far al-Sadiq** (Born on 20th April 702A.D., Medina, Saudi Arabia - Died 14th December 765A.D. Medina).
- **Jahanara Begum Sahib** (Born on 23rd March 1614A.D., Ajmer - 16th September 1681A.D., Delhi).[15]
- **Jahaniyan Jahangasht** (Born on 19th January 1308A.D., Uch Sharif, Pakistan and died on 3rd February 1384A.D., Uch Sharif)
- **Jamī** (Born on 7th November 1414A.D., Kharjerd, Khorasan and died on 9th November 1492 A.D., Herat)
- **Junayd of Baghdad** (830-910A.D., Baghadad)

K

- **Khwaja Abdullah Ansari** (10th May 1006-1088A.D., Herat, Afaganistan).
- **Khwaja Ghulam Farid** (Born on 25th November 1845A.D., Chacharan and died on 24th July 1901 A.D., buried in Mithankot, Pakistan).
- **Khan Jahan Ali** (1369 at Delhi- 25th October 1459 A.D. Bangladesh).

L

- **Lal Shahbaz Qalander** (Born in 1177A.D. Maiwad, Kandahar and died on 19th February 1274A.D. shehwan, Pakistan).[22]

M

- **Mirza Mazhar Jan-e-Janaan** (1699-6th January 1781A.D.,Delhi).
- **MuMuhammad Noor Maharvi** (Born on 2nd April 1746A.D. and died on 3rd August 1793A.D., Bahawalnagar, Pakistan).
- **Muhammad Jaunpuri** (Born on 9th September 1443A.D., Jaunpur and died on 23rd April 1505 A.D. Farah, Afghanistan).

- **Muhammad al-Jazuli** (1404-1465A.D., Marrakesh, Morocco).
- **Maruf Karkhi** (Born in 750A.D., Baghdad and died at Baghdad).
- **Machiliwale Shah** also known as Syed Kamalullah Shah (Died 8th September 1932).
- **Magtymguly Pyragy** (Born at Hajji Qushan, Iran, Died 1797, Golestan, Iran).
- **Mahmoodullah Shah** (1st November 1945-26th September 2016A.D.,Battal, Pakistan).
- **Mahmud Hudayi** (1541-1628A.D.,Turkey).
- **Meher Ali Shah** (14th April 1859-11th May 1937A.D.,Pakistan Golra).
- **Mian Mir** (Born on11th August 1550A.D., Sindh, Pakistan and died on 11th August 1635A.D. Lahore)[23]
- **Mian Muhammad Bakhsh** (1830-22nd January 1907A.D., Khari Sharif).
- **Muhammad Suleman Taunsvi** (Born in 1770A.D., Balochistan and died in 1850A.D., Taunsa, Pakistan).
- **Mohammad Yousuf Abu al - Tartusi** (21st August 1016-28th October 1055A.D., Tartus, Syria).
- **Mubarak Makhzoomi** (Born 26th January 1013- Died at Baghdad).[24]
- **Muhammad Al-Makki** (Born in 1145 A.D., Mecca and died in 1246A.D., Sindh, Pakistan).
- **Muhammad ibn Tayfour Sajawandi** 12th century Islamic Scholar).
- **Muhammad Ilyas Attar Qadri** (Born 12th July 1950A.D., Karachi, Pakistan).
- **Mustafa Gaibi** or Gaibija -17th century dervish from Ottoman Bosnia.
- **Mushtaq Ali Shah** (?-1792 A.D.)
- **Makhdoom Ali Mahimi** (1372-1431 A.D.)[25]
- **Mohamed ben Issa** (1467-1526 A.D., buried in Meknes, founder of the Aissawa order).
- **Moinuddin Chishti** (1141-1230 A.D., buried in the Ajmer Sharif Dargah, spread the Chishti order throughout India).[26]
- **Muhammad ibn Ali at-Tirmidhi** (Born 824 C.E. - Died 9th October 892 C.E.).

N

- **Nadir Ali Shah** (Born in1897A.D., Gandaf, Pakistan and died on 8th October 1974 Sehwan, Pakistan).
- **Najm al-Din Razi** (1177-1256A.D.).
- **Nājm ūd-Dīn Kubrā** (1145-1221A.D., Turkmenistan).
- **Nasir Khusraw** (Born in 1004A.D.,Qabodlyon, Tajikistan and died in 1088 Badakshan, Afaghanistan).

- **Nathar Wali** (Born in 969 A.D., Antolia and died -1038 AD Tiruchirapalli).
- **Niamatullah Shah** (Born 1330A.D., Aleppo, Syria, Died- 1431-Iran).
- **Nasiruddin Chiragh Dehlavi** (Born -1274 AD, Ayodhya, Died – 13rd September 1356 Delhi)[27].
- **Nizamuddin Auliya** (Born -9th October 1238, Budaun, -Died 3rd April 1325 Delhi) (1238-1325 A.D.)[28]

O

- **Omar Khayyám** (Born on 18th May 1048, Neyshabur, Iran and died on 4th December 1131A.D., Neyashabur).
- **Osman Fazli** was a Jelveti Sufi spiritual guide in 17th century Ottoman Empire.
- **Otman Baba** (1378-1478A.D.,Haskovo, Bulgaria).

P

- **Pir Baba** (Born in 1431A.D., Fargana, Uzbekistan and died in 1502A.D., Buner, Pakistan).[29]

Q

- **Qasim ibn Muhammad ibn Abu Bakr** (655-725A.D., place of burial, Karbala).
- **Qutb ad-Dīn Haydar** (Died in 1221A.D., buried in Zava, Khurasan).
- **Qutb ūd-Dīn Shīrāzī** (Born in October 1236A.D., Kazerun, and died on 7th February 1311A.D., Tabriz, Iran).
- **Qutbuddin Bakhtiar Kaki** (Born in 1173A.D.,Osh, Kyrgyzstan and died in 1235A.D., New Delhi).[30]

R

- **Rabbānī** (1564-1624A.D.)[31]
- **Rabia Basri** (713- 801A.D., Basara, Iraq).
- **Rahman Baba** (1632-1706A.D., Peshawar, Pakistan).
- **Rukn-e-Alam** (26th November 1251- 3rd January 1335A.D., Multan Pakistan)[32]
- **Rumi** (Born on 30th September 1207A.D., Balkh, Afaghanistan and died 17th December 1273A.D., Koriya, Turkey).

S

- **Saadī** (Born in 1210A.D., Shiraz, Iran and died at Shiraz).
- **Sachal Sarmast** (Born in 1739A.D., Daraza Sharif Pakistan and died on11th April 1827).

- **Shah Maroof Khushabi** (Born at Pakpattan, Khushab, 16th century).
- **Shah Sulaimān Nūri** (1508-1604A.D.,Pakistan).
- **Sidi Boushaki** (Born -1394A.D.,Thenia, near Algiers and died in 1453A.D.)
- **Sahl al-Tustari** (Born in 818A.D., Shoostar, Iran and died 896A.D., Basara, Iraq).
- **Salim Chishti** (1478 -1572A.D., Fatehpur Sikri)[33]
- **Salman al-Farisī or Salman the Persian** (568-653A.D., C.E. Kazerun, Persia).
- **Sanai** (Born 1080A.D., Ghazani and died 1131/1141A.D. Ghazani).
- **Sarı Saltuk** (Born at Bukhara, died at Balbadag, Romania).
- **Sarmad Kashani** (Born in 1590A.D., Armenia and died in 1661A.D., Delhi)[34]
- **Semnanī** (1308-1405A.D.)[35]
- **Shah Abdul Latif Bhittai** (Born in 1689 /1690 Hala Haweli, Sindh and died 21st December 1752A.D.)
- **Shah Badakhshi** (1584-1661A.D.)[36]
- **Sayed Badiuddin** (Born 1050A.D., Aleppo, Syria and died at Makanpur, Kanpur)
- **Shah Gardez** (1026-1152A.D.)[37]
- **Shah Hussain** (Born 1538A.D., Lahore, Pakistan and died 1599A.D. Lahore).[38]
- **Shah Jalal** (Born on 25th May 1271A.D.,Konya, Turkey and died on 15th March 1346/ 1347A.D.)[39]
- **Shah Mustafa** (Born at Baghdad and died on 14th January 1336 chandrapur-modern days moulvibazar, Bangaladesh 1336 A.D.).
- **Shah Jalal Dakhini** (Born 25th May 1271 Konya, Turkey – Died 15th March 1346 Sylhet, Bangaladesh 1476 A.D.)
- **Shah Amanat** (Born at Bihar sharif - 1809A.D.)
- **Shah Paran** (Born at Hadhramaut-Died at Sylhet Bangaladesh,14th century Sufi saint).[40]
- **Shamas Faqir** (Born in 1843A.D., Habba Kadial, Srinagar, and died in 1901A.D., Budgam, Kashmir).
- **Shāms-i Tabrizī** (1185-1248A.D., Khoy, Iran).
- **Shaikh Edebali** (1206-1326A.D., Bilecik, Turkey).
- **Shah Syed Muhammad Nurbakhsh Qahistani** (21st August 1552 -18th May 1654A.D.).
- **Syed Ahmad Ullah** (Born on 14th January 1826A.D., Fatikchhari, Bangaladesh and died on 23rd January 1906 Maizbhandar, Darbar Sharif).
- **Syed Ahmad Sultan** (12th-century, 1120-1174A.D., Dera Gazi Khan, Pakistan).

- **Syeh Galib - Galib Mehmed Esad Dede** (1757- 3 January 1798A.D., Istanbul).
- **Syed Abdul Rehman Jilani Dehlvi** (Born in 1615 A.D., Hama, Syria and died in Delhi).
- **Sayyid Ali Hamadani** (Born 22nd October 1314A.D., Hamedan, Iran, and died in 1384A.D., Kunar, Afaghanistan).
- **Soch Kraal** (1782-29th November 1854A.D., Pulwama).
- **Sufi Barkat Ali** Ludhianwi 27th April 1911A.D., Ludhiana, India and died 26th January 1997 Dasuha, Pakistan).
- **Shahab-al-Din Abu Hafs Umar Suhrawardi** (1145-1234A.D. Baghdad, Iraq).
- **Shaykh Syed Mir Mirak Andrabi** (1515-1582A.D. Srinagar)
- **Sari-al-Saqati** - Early Muslim sufi saint of Baghdad, Born 776 A.D.
- **Sultan Bahu** (Born on 17th January 1630A.D., Shorkot, Pakistan and died 1st March 1691A.D., Jhang, Pakistan).
- **Sultan Walad** (Born on1st May 1226A.D. Karaman Turkey and died on 12th November 1312A.D., Konya, Turkey).
- **Shah Farid-ud-Din Baghdadi** (1551-1733 A.D., and died at Kishtwar, Kashmir).
- **Sadr al-Din al-Qunawi** (1207-1274A.D., Persian Philosopher).
- **Safi-ad-din Ardabili** (1252-12th September 1334 Adrabil).
- **Shah Abdul Latif Bhittai** (Born on 18th November 1689A.D., Hala Pakistan and died on 1st January 1752A.D., buried in the Shrine of Shah Abdul Latif Bhittai).
- **Shah Waliullah Dehlawi** (1703-1762 A.D., buried in Munhadiyan, author noted for anti-Shia and anti-Hindu works and 21st February 1703 Muzaffanagar, Died 20th August Delhi).

T

- **Tajuddin Muhammad Badruddin** (Born on 27th January 1861, Kamptee, Nagpur).
- **Telli Baba** (Died on 17th August 1925A.D., Nagpur).

U

- **Usman Harooni** (6th May 1107-3rd December 1220A.D., at Khorasan).

W

- **Waris Shah** (Born on 23rd January 1722A.D., Jandiala Sher Khan and died in 1798A.D., Malaka Hans, Pakistan).
- **Waris Ali Shah** (1819-5th April 1905A.D., Dewa, Barabanki, India).

Y

- **Yahya bey Dukagjini** (Born in1498A.D., Pijevija, Montenegro and died in 1582 Zvornik, Bosnia, Ottoman poet and military figure).
- **Yahya Efendi** (1494-1571A.D.,Istanbul, Turkey).
- **Yahya Maneri** (also known as Makhdoom Sharfuddin Ahmed) (1263-January 1381A.D., Maner, Patna).[41]
- **Yunus Ali Enayetpuri (R.)** (Born on 10th September 1886A.D., Enayatpur East Pakistan, and died in 1951A.D. Sirajganj, Bangaladesh).
- **Yunus Emre** (Born1238A.D. Sivrihisar and died in 1328A.D., Turkey).
- **Yusuf Hamdani** (1062-1141A.D., buried in Merv).

Z

- **Zahed Gilani** (1216A.D.-1301A.D., Iranian Grandmaster of the famed Zahediyeh Sufi order).

References

1. Schimmel, Annemarie *(1975)*. Mystical Dimensions of Islam. *Chapel Hill: University of North Carolina Press. p.* 346. ISBN 0-8078-1271-4.
2. Radtke, B., 'Saint', in: Encyclopaedia of the Qur'ān, General Editor: Jane Dammen McAuliffe, Georgetown University, Washington, D.C.
3. Biographical encyclopaedia of Sufis: Central Asia and Middle East by N. Hanif, 2002, p. 123.
4. The Sultan of the saints: mystical life and teaching of Shaikh Syed Abdul Qadir Jilani, Muhammad Riyāz Qādrī, 2000, p. 24.
5. Pnina Werbner (2003). Pilgrims of Love: The Anthropology of a Global Sufi Cult. C. Hurst & Co. p. 4.
6. Dr. Harbhajan Singh (2002). Sheikh Farid. Hindi Pocket Books. p. 11. ISBN 81-216-0255-6.
7. E.G. Browne (1998). Literary History of Persia.
8. The Brahmaputra Beckons. Brahmaputra Beckons Publication Committee. 1982. p. 39. Retrieved 2008-09-05.
9. Jagadish Narayan Sarkar. Thoughts on Trends of Cultural Contacts in Medieval India. p. 41.
10. Z.H.Sharib (2006). The Sufi saints of the Indian subcontinent. Munshirm Manoharlal Pub Pvt Ltd.
11. Urs-e-Sharief of Khwaja Bande Nawaz in Gulbarga from tomorrow Archived 2008-06-12 at the Wayback Machine 'The Hindu', Nov 27, 2007.
12. 'Article on KhwajaBaqi Billah'. Archived from the original on 2010-06-27. Retrieved 2009-11-15.
13. Ernst, Carl W. (1997). The Shambhala Guide to Sufism. Boston: Shambhala.p. 67. ISBN 978-1570621802.

14. 'Dargah of Bu-Ali-Shah-Qalandar'. Archived from the original on 2010-03-14. Retrieved 2009-11-08.

15. Schimmel, Annemarie (1997). My Soul Is a Woman: The Feminine in Islam. New York: Continuum. p. 50. ISBN 0-8264-1014-6.

16. Muntakhab-ut-Tawarikh', Vol II and III, by Abdul Qadir bin Mulik Shah Al-Badaoni (Translated into English by R.A. Ranking in 1894).

17. Sandeep Singh Bajwa. 'Baba Fariduddin Mas'ud' Archived from the original on 2009-10-07. Retrieved 2009-11-08.

18. 'Haji Huud' (Oct. 1, 2001). Published in Al Ashraf: 17–20.

19. G. M. D. Sufi. 'The Spread of Islam in Kashmir'. Archived from the original on 2007-04-19. Retrieved 2009-11-09.

20. William C. Chittick. 'Erāqī, Fakr-Al-Dīn Ebrāhīm'. Encyclopedia Iranica. Archived from the original on 2015-11-17. Retrieved 2015-11-17.

21. Muhammad Dawood. 'Jalaluddin Surkh-Posh Bukhari'. Archived from the original on 2010-03-15. Retrieved 2009-11-08.

22. Sarah Ansari (1971). Sufi Saints and State Power: The Pirs of Sind, 1843-1947. Vanguard Books.

23. K J S Ahluwalia (May 2006). 'Spot the Emperor in the Story of Fakir Mian Mir'. The Times of India. Archived from the original on 2012-02-11. Retrieved 2009-11-15.

24. Gibb, H.A.R.; Kramers, J.H.; Levi-Provencal, E.; Schacht, J. (1986) [1st pub. 1960]. Encyclopaedia of Islam. Volume I (A-B) (New ed.). Leiden, Netherlands: Brill. p. 69. ISBN 9004081143.

25. S Ahmed Ali (2002-12-22). 'On Urs, Mumbai police keep tryst with Sufi saint'. Archived from the original on 2005-04-22. Retrieved 2009-11-13.

26. Neeti M. Sadarangani. Bhakti poetry in medieval India. p. 60.

27. 'Chisti Saints'. Archived from the original on 2009-06-01. Retrieved 2009-11-09.

28. Originally compiled by Amir Hasan 'Alā' Sijzī Dehlawī; English translation with introduction and historical annotation by Ziya-ul-Hasan Faruqi. (1996). Fawa'id Al-Fu'ad Spiritual and Literary Discourses of Shaikh Nizammuddin Awliya. South Asia Books. ISBN 8124600422.

29. 'Hazrat Pir Baba (Rahmatullahi Allaih)'. www.pirbaba.org. Archived from the original on 29 October 2017. Retrieved 4 May 2018.

30. N. Hanif. Biographical encyclopaedia of Sufis. p. 321.

31. Aziz Ahmad, Studies in Islamic Culture in the Indian Environment, Oxford University Press, 1964, p.189

32. 'History Of Multan'. Archived from the original on 2008-12-04. Retrieved 2009-11-08.

33. Carl W. Ernst; Bruce B. Lawrence (2002). Sufi martyrs of love: the Chishti Order in South Asia and beyond. New York: Palgrave Macmillan. p. 98. ISBN 1403960275.

34. Gupta, M.G. (2000). Sarmad the Saint: Life and Works (Revised ed.). MG Publishers. ISBN 81-85532-32-X.
35. Carl W. Ernst; Bruce B. Lawrence (2002). Sufi Martyrs of Love: The Chishti Order in South Asia and Beyond. New York: Palgrave Macmillan. ISBN 1403960267.
36. Tasadduq Husain (Jul-Aug 2002). 'The Spiritual Journey of Dara Shukoh'. Social Scientist. 30 (7/8): 54–66. doi:10.2307/3518151. JSTOR 3518151.
37. Dramk Durrani (1989). 'Central Asian Saints of Multan'. Area Study Centre (Central Asia), University of Peshawar.
38. Lal, Mohan. (2006) Encyclopaedia of Indian literature. Vol. 5, Sahitya Akademi, Delhi, p. 3940. ISBN 81-260-1221-8
39. Karim, Abdul (2012). Shah Jalal (R). In Islam, Sirajul; Jamal, Ahmed A. (eds.). Banglapedia: National Encyclopedia of Bangladesh (Second ed.). Asiatic Society of Bangladesh. Archived from the original on 2015-07-07. Retrieved 2016-05-09.
40. Kānunago, Sunīti Bhūshaṇa (1988). A History of Chittagong. Dipankar Qanungo. Dipankar Qanungo. p. 476. Retrieved 2009-11-07.
41. Masood Ali Khan, S. Ram., ed. (2003). Encyclopaedia of Sufism. New Delhi: Anmol Publications. ISBN 8126113111.

Note: Wikipedia is referred for mentioning the birthdates and death related information for all the Sufi saints.

Appendix 3

Female Sufis

There is a significant contribution by female sufis in the development of early Sufism. Women continued to play an important role in the movement both as sufis and as the mothers of leading sufis. The progeny of Adam should adopt piety and obedience to God whether they be men or women. Among those mentioned, some are as follows.

1.   Ā'ishah al-Bāʿūniyyah

ʿĀ'ishah bint Yūsuf al-Bāʿūniyyah (عائشة بنت يوسف الباعونية, died the sixteenth day of Dhū al-Qaʿdah, 922/1517) was a Sufi master and poet.[1] She is one of few medieval female Islamic mystics to have recorded their own views in writing and she "probably composed more works in Arabic than any other woman prior to the twentieth century". 'In her the literary talents and Ṣūfi tendencies of her family reached full fruition".[2] She was born and died in Damascus. In 919/1513, ʿĀ'ishah and her son moved from Damascus to Cairo, returning to Damascus in 923/1517. ʿĀ'ishah's goal may have been to secure the career of her son. On the way, their caravan was raided by bandits near Bilbeis, who stole their possessions, including ʿĀ'ishah's writings. It appears that in Cairo, she and her son were hosted by Maḥmūd ibn Muḥammad ibn Ajā (b. 854/1450, d. 925/1519), who was personal secretary and foreign minister to the Mamluk sultan al-Ashraf Qansuh al-Ghuri (d. 922/1516). Ibn Ajā helped ʿAbd al-Wahhāb find work in the chancery and helped ʿĀ'ishah enter into Cairo's intellectual circles; ʿĀ'ishah went on to write him 'several glowing panegyrics'. In Cairo, ʿĀ'ishah studied law and was granted license to lecture in law and to issue fatwas (legal opinions); "she gained wide recognition as a jurist".[3] ʿĀ'ishah left Cairo in 922/1516, with her son and Ibn Ajā, and alongside al-Badr al-Suyūfī (c. 850–925/1446–1519), al-Shams al-Safīrī (877–956/1472–1549), and several other noted scholars, was granted an audience with Sultan Qansuh al-Ghawri in Aleppo shortly before his defeat at the Battle of Marj Dabiq: 'an extraordinary event befitting her exceptional life', ʿĀ'ishah then returned to Damascus, where she died in 923/1517. ʿĀ'ishah "inherited an independence of mind and outlook which is seen in her companionship with her men contemporaries on equal terms". Thus she was a close friend of Abu 'l-Thanā' Maḥmūd b. Ajā, who was the final ṣāḥib dawāwīn alinshā' of the Mamluk era, and corresponded, in verse, with the Egyptian scholar 'Abd al-Raḥmān al-'Abbāsī (b. 867/1463, d. 963/1557).[2] 'It is quite apparent from biographies of 'Ā'ishah and from her own comments in her writings that she was highly regarded as a pious woman and Sufi master'.

2. Aïsha Al-Manoubya

Aïsha Al-Manoubya (Arabic: عائشة المنوبية, 'Ā'isha al-Mannūbiyya), also known by the honorific Al-Saida ('saint') or Lella ('the Lady') (1199–1267 A.D.), is one of the most famous women in Tunisia, and a prominent figure in Islam. 'Ā'isha was known for her Sufism and good deeds. She was the supporter and student of Sidi Bousaid al-Baji and Abul Hasan ash-Shadhili. Her presence as a woman on the high level of education and advocacy activity and charity event was very unusual in her time. In popular memory, 'Ā'isha represents a powerful and respected saint. One of the souks of the Medina of Tunis, "Souk Al-Saida Al-Manoubya", was named after her.[4] A few kilometres from the Medina, a gourbiville takes her name.[5] Al-Manoubya used to retire to pray in that neighbourhood.[6] The inhabitants of Manouba built a second mausoleum to commemorate 'Ā'isha under the name of 'The Mausoleum of Al-Saida Al-Manoubya' in her birthplace area.[7] That mausoleum is very famous and has a big value in the Tunisian national heritage and history. It was vandalised and burned after the Tunisian Revolution, on 16 October 2012.[8][9][10][11]

3. Samiha Ayverdi

Samiha Ayverdi (25 November 1905 – 22 March 1993) was a Turkish writer and Sufi mystic. She was the sister of architect and historian Ekrem Hakki Ayverdi. Samiha Ayverdi was born in Istanbul to Fatma Meliha Hanim and Ismail Hakkı Bey, an Ottoman military official. She studied at Süleymaniye Kiz Numune Mektebi and among other things, learned French and read about philosophy and Islamic mysticism. She became a follower and later official successor of Sufi thinker Kenan Rifai, who became a major influence in her work.[12] In 1938, she published her first novel titled Aşk Budur and followed it with over 30 novels and short story collections.[13] Ayverdi died on 22 March 1993 and is buried at the Merkezefendi Cemetery in Zeytinburnu, Istanbul.

4. Rābi'a al-'Adawiyya al-Qaysiyya

Rābi'a al-'Adawiyya al-Qaysiyya (Arabic: رابعة العدوية القيسية) (714/717/718-801 A.D.)[14] was an Arab Sunni Muslim saint and Sufi mystic.[15] She is known in some parts of the world as, Hazrat Bibi Rabia Basri, Rabia Al Basri or simply Rabia Basri.[16] However, after the death of her father, famine overtook Basra. She parted from her sisters. Rabia went into the desert to pray and became an ascetic, living a life of semi-seclusion. She is often cited as being the queen of saintly women,[5] and was known for her complete devotion in the form of 'pure unconditional love of God'. As an exemplar among others devoted to God, she provided a model of mutual love between God and His creation; her example is one in which the loving devotee on earth becomes one with the Beloved.[17]

She prayed: "O Lord, if I worship You because of Fear of Hell, then burn me in Hell; If I worship You because I desire Paradise, then exclude me from Paradise; But if I worship You for Yourself alone, then deny me not your Eternal Beauty".[18]

Often noted as having been the single most famous and influential renunciant women of Islamic history, Rābi'a was renowned for her extreme virtue and piety. A devoted ascetic, when asked why she performed a thousand ritual prostrations both during the day and at night, she answered: "I desire no reward for it; I do it so that the Messenger of God, may God bless him and give him peace, will delight in it on the day of Resurrection and say to the prophets, 'Take note of what a woman of my community has accomplished". She was intense in her self-denial and devotion to God. She never claimed to have obtained unity with Him; instead, she dedicated her life to getting closer to God.[19] As an explanation of her refusal to lift her head toward the heavens [to God] as an act of modesty, she used to say: "Were the world the possession of a single man, it would not make him rich ... Because it is passing away".[4] She was the one who first set forth the doctrine of Divine Love known as Ishq-e-Haqeeqi[20] and is widely considered to be the most important of the early renunciant, one mode of piety that would eventually become labelled as Sufism.

5. Sitt al-Ajam

Sitt al-Ajam was a 13th century Sufi mystic from Baghdad. Her main merit was writing a commentary on ibn Arabi's Mashahid. Her full name is Sitt al-Ajam bint al-Nafis b. Abu l-Qasim.[21] In the history of female Muslim scholars two women are to be found bearing the same name. Fatima Mernissi argues that the Arabic term sitt literally means 'lady' and has been often attributed to women of power. However, with some exceptions, she listed three names beginning with sitt: one is Sitt al-Ajam not connected with the issue of politics at all. According to her, Sitt al-'Ajam is a fiqh scholar who lived in the 14th century in Damascus.[22] The name can be confused with Sitt al-'Ajam bint al-Nafis (the subject of this article), a 13th century Sufi woman whose thoughts on ibn Al-Arabi were transmitted by her husband.[23] Sitt al-'Ajam confessed in her book that she had a vision of ibn Al-Arabi who came to her and asked her to write a commentary on his book Mashāhid al-asrār al-qudsiyya wa matāli' al-anwār al-ilāhiyya (The Witnessing of the Holy Mysteries and the Rising of the Divine Lights). She explained in her words: "I closely examined his name and his biography, for a way to draw from him the definition [for my state], but I found that the similarity between us is in receiving the very same "hātimī gifts", that leads to attraction (jadhb). This, despite not having the same state of distinction, nor following the same path, nor having the same life; [the] similarity is [only] that of character and of [divine] bestowal, which is the privilege of the saints (Auliya). Thus, his luminous form could not but be witness to the knowledge of union that exists between us".

References

1. Qutbuddin, Tahera. 'Women Poets' Archived 2014-02-07 at the Wayback Machine, in Medieval Islamic Civilisation: An Encyclopedia, ed. by Josef W. Meri, 2 vols (New York: Routledge, 2006), II 865-67 (p. 866).

2. Khalidi, W. A. S. 'AL-BĀ'ŪNĪ', in The Encyclopaedia of Islam, new edn by H. A. R. Gibb and others (Leiden: Brill, 1960-2009), I 1109-10 (p. 1109).

3. Stewart, Devin J. 'Degrees, or Ijaza', in Medieval Islamic Civilization: An Encyclopedia, ed. by Josef W. Meri, 2 vols (New York: Routledge, 2006), I 201-204 (p. 203), citing Najm al-Gazzi, al-Matba'ah al-Amirikaniyah, 1945-58, pp. 287-92.

4. Slyomovics, Susan (5 November 2013). The Walled Arab City in Literature, Architecture and History: The Living Medina in the Maghrib. Routledge. ISBN 9781135281267.

5. Ferjani, Chérif. 'La Rehabilitation Dun Gourbiville: Satda-Manmou-la A Tuns' (Pdf).

6. Pacione, Michael (18 October 2013). Problems and Planning in Third World Cities (Routledge Revivals). Routledge. ISBN 9781134519910.

7. 'Salafists In Tunisia Target Sufi, The Mystics of Islam'.

8. "Thirty-Four Mausoleums in Tunisia Vandalized Since the Revolution - Tunisia Live". Tunisia Live. 24 January 2013. Archived from the original on 19 March 2017. Retrieved 18 March 2017.

9. "Saida Manoubia, Tunisia's only female Sufi saint, attracts followers".

10. "Salafist Arsonists Target Tunisian Heritage Sites". Al-Monitor. 31 January 2013.

11. "Unesco condemns the destruction of the Saida Manoubia Mausoleum | Islamopedia Online". islamopediaonline.org. Archived from the original on 26 August 2016. Retrieved 18 March 2017.

12. Hibri, Azizah (1982). Women and Islam. Pergamon Press. p. 145. ISBN 978-0-08-027928-2.

13. Mitler, Louis (1988). Contemporary Turkish writers: a critical bio-bibliography of leading writers in the Turkish Republican Period up to 1980. Indiana University. p. 50. ISBN 978-0-933070-14-1.

14. Margaret Smith (1995). Encyclopedia of Islam, 2nd ed., Vol. 8, 'Rābi'a al-'Adawiyya al-Qaysiyya'. Brill. p. 354–56.

15. Smith, Margaret (2010). Rabi'a The Mystic and Her Fellow-Saints in Islam. Cambridge University Press. p. 252. ISBN 9781108015912.

16. Hanif, N. (2002). Biographical Encyclopaedia of Sufis: Central Asia and Middle East. Sarup & Sons. p. 108–10. ISBN 9788176252669.

17. Khawar Khan Chrishti, Saadia (1997). Hossein Nasr, Seyyed (ed.). Islamic Spirituality Foundations. New York: Crossroads. p. 208–10.

18. Willis Barnstone; Aliki Barnstone (1992). A book of women poets from antiquity to now By. Schocken Books, Inc. p. 90. ISBN 978-93-82277-87-3.

19. Barbara Lois Helms, Rabi'a as Mystic, Muslim, and Woman.

20. Margaret Smith, Rabi'a: The Mystic and Her Fellow-Saints in Islam, Cambridge Library Collection, 1928.

21. Ibn 'Arabi. Contemplation of the Holy Mysteries. C. Twinch and P. Beneito, transl. Oxford: Anqa Publishing, p. 12

22. Mernissi, F. (1993). The Forgotten Queens of Islam. Polity Press: UK, p.19-20

23. Saeyyd, A. (2013). Women and the Transmission of Religious Knowledge in Islam. Cambridge University Press, p.193.

Appendix 4

Buddhism directive on Bhakti

Bhakti is a remarkable feature and tendency of human existence having to do with one's devoted involvement with a person, object, deity, or an inspired bhakti is a poignant word coined in the Eastern tradition of Indian thought to represent the love-laden and authentic living of philosophy and the loving experience of religion. The terms Bhagavat and Bhagavan, which share the root bhaj with bhakti, were especially reserved for the most superior deities. It is interesting to note that the incarnated Lords that appears in the Bhagavad-Gita, as well as the Buddha and Mahavira, were addressed as Bhagavan (the blessed one, the grand dispenser, or Vibhakta) by their respective followers.[1] It is generally believed by that this concept of bhakti originated in Hinduism and that it was this bhakti movement of Hinduism which had finally brought the decline of Buddhism in India. While there may be some truths in its effect on Buddhism, however, the facts are not so straight forward. In fact, so far as bhakti is concerned, it originated in Buddhism and Jainism long before Hinduism. It may be said that bhakti movement and the neo-Vaishnavism in India arose not only with the influence of Buddhism but at the expense of Buddhism. In a way, it may be said that Hinduism banished Buddhism from India and took from it the jewel of bhakti along with other Buddhist elements and institutions as its own. Bhagavad-Gita is the first explicit affirmation of theism in Vedic thought. Believed to be composed between 3rd century BC and 2nd century A.D., the Gita is an epoch-making creation of Hinduism which gives a summary of insights obtained hitherto by Vedic and Upanisadic philosophical quest. It fuses into a meaningful synthesis the Vedic cult of sacrifice (yajna), the Upanisadic speculations about Brahman-atman relation, the theism of the Bhagavata cult, and the Samkhya and Yoga systems. In the Bhagavad-Gita, bhakti is not only given a new legitimacy, but it also pervades the whole theistic insight of the Gita. Bhagavad-Gita also absorbed some Buddhist elements in its composition.

The bhakti Movement

In the medieval period, there was fresh rise of the bhakti movement in India, a new form of Hinduism which was the basis of neo-Vaishnavism that arose. bhakti became the faith of the masses that also tried to defy the Brahmanical supremacy of the caste system. The impetus for this new bhakti movement came from the Dravidian (Harappan) culture in South India that evolved in a process to claim for a world the liberal values of love and equality in its access to God so far confined to the Brahmanical rituals or the secret Upanishadic knowledge attainable only by the Brahmins and the high caste Hindus with exclusive knowledge of Sanskrit. The popular aspects of this movement took the shape of several mystical and passionate expressions of bhakti, which were represented on the Vaishnavite side by the Alvars, and on the Saivite side by the Nayanars. They were south Indian poet-saints between the 6th and 9th centuries A.D. They espoused 'emotional devotion' of bhakti to Vishnu-Krishna and Siva in their songs of longing, ecstasy, and service. These were like the singing of the Tantric Buddhist Charyagitis in Eastern India. A vast amount of bhakti literature sprang in south Indian culture that has contributed to the establishment and sustenance of bhakti culture that rooted itself in devotion as the path for salvation.[2]

This bhakti movement in South India basically sets the tone and trend of its propagation in rest of India in the modern period. The Bhagavata Purana of late ninth century and early tenth century marks the culmination of the bhakti ideal in its emotional form and renders in Sanskrit the religion of the Alvars.[3] We may mention here also of the influence created by Narada bhakti Sutra, a 10th century creation which has given the philosophical impetus to bhakti as an alternate Hindu path for salvation. It showed that philosophy should not only be objective and explain things but must also be subjective to explore the possibilities of higher spiritual living. The period between the 13th and 17th century are important when we see a transformation so great in the religious and cultural life of India that it seemed a spiritual revolution was under way.[4] Here we may say that in the bhaktivad, or the 'bhakti revolution' that developed, Hinduism finally found a voice for the masses which was not found strongly in the Bhagavad-Gita nor even found in any of the earlier Hindu philosophers such as Shakaracharya, Ramanujam, Madhava and others.

By 15th century A.D., we see the appearance of several saints in various provinces of India to carry the gospels of the new faith to the masses by rendering the Sanskrit Puranas into regional languages. As such different saints came up with their own separate beliefs, philosophy and practices based on his or her outlook, understanding and inspiration. The bhakti sects did not arise out of any original teaching or through conversion, rather they evolve as and when historical conditions were conducive to their growth intermeshed with castes to articulate their aspirations. Hence the variation in belief and practice and the lack of consciousness of an identity of a religion across the subcontinent plane.[5]

bhakti also arose outside on Hinduism. Sikhism is a purely monotheistic religion influenced by the bhakti movement. In its practice of bhakti, it is like Assam Vasihnavism.

Sufi is a sect of Islam which was very much influenced by the bhakti movement. Singing of bhajans and dancing formed important parts of this worship and different bhakti religions developed different types of bhajans with dance and singing with prayers: Kirtans in Hindu temples, Nam in Assam Namhors, Gurbani at Gurdwara, Qawalli at a Sufi Dargah etc. Many Hindu temples in India employed deva-dasis (female slave dancers of the deity) inside the temple. Apart from being overwhelmingly ritualistic, the worships tended to be intensely emotional. To, quote historian Toynbee, "Hinduism despoiled a senile Buddhist philosophy to acquire for itself the weapons with which it drove its philosophical rival out of their common homeland in the Indic world".[6] It was as if Hinduism beat Buddhism in its own game, the game of bhakti. However, to understand the bhakti movement in India, it is necessary to understand the background of Hinduism in general and Vaishnavism in India. In Buddha's time in the 6th century B.C., there was no separate religion known as Hinduism. The prevailing religion was known as Brahmanism that had already absorbed many belief systems from the prevailing pre-Aryan Harappan (Dravidian) system such as the worship of Siva (Pashupati) as a personal God, along with the belief in Karma, Reincarnation and the practice of Yoga meditation and we may presume the concept of bhakti. The common religion that we call Hinduism today is in fact an outgrowth of this ancient Brahmanism by assimilation of many of the Buddhist elements. "And much of what we nowadays call 'Hinduism', such as the centrality of the gods Siva or Vishnu, the ideas of Sankara's Advaita Vedanta, the themes of the Bhagavad-Gita, Tantric practices, and so on developed after the time of the Buddha".[7]

In the Vedic literature we first see the term bhakti explained as an alternate path of salvation in the Bhagavad-Gita which, we may note is a post Buddhist creation. The term bhakti is not to be found in any of the earlier ancient Hindu Sanskrit scriptures, such as the Vedas or the Upanishads, although some Hindu scholars claim to find traces of the concept of bhakti in these scriptures. According to R. G. Bhandarkar, the Bhagavad-Gita owes its origin of bhakti to the stream of thought which began with the Upanishads and culminated in the rise of Buddhism and Jainism.[8] In the Upanishad the term Guru bhakti as well as an explicit theism emerges in the last passage of the Svetasvatara Upanishad, and that is the only passage that contains the first usage in Vedic literature of the term bhakti in the devotional sense.[9] However, the Upanishads being restricted only to the higher castes, bhakti was never propagated to the masses as religious ethos by the Upanisadi sages.

In India, bhakti remains narrowly understood both historically and philosophically. It is often narrowly understood as an expression of theism by many scholars merely as the bhakta's devotion for his Bhagavan, a subject-object relationship, and thus absent in non-theistic religions like Buddhism and Jainism. In Hinduism sometimes, this theistic bhakti is also represented as narrow personal love between man and woman. Swami Vivekananda who may be considered as the spokesperson of Hinduism for the modern Indians, writes, "The story (of Radha and Krishna) simply exemplifies the true spirit of a bhakta, because no love in the world exceeds that existing between a man and woman".[10] Bhakti has much broader and spiritual meaning. In this wider context, the concept of bhakti was already was in vogue in religious circles when the Buddha appeared in the scene. Bhakti is generally more befitting for the non-Aryans who has the proper humility as opposed to the high caste Aryans engaged in the practice of Yajna. In our opinion bhakti originated amongst the non-Aryan Dravidians of Harappa culture for their devotion to God Siva before the Aryans arrived in India, like it did a second time amongst the non-Aryan Dravidian Alvars a thousand years later. Brahmanism (the Vedas, the Upanishad) and Buddhism and Jainism all, embraced bhakti along with other non-Aryan concepts such a Karma and Reincarnation etc in their religions.

In Buddhism bhakti towards the Buddha became the main force for movement and spread of Buddhism. This ancient form of bhakti was not only a part catalyst in the formation of Buddha's new world view, but bhakti continues to pervade the dharma of the Buddha's early doctrinal period as well as in Mahayana developments.[11] Buddhists were also exhorted to exercise bhakti in the form of karuna (empathy) not only towards fellow subjects of the dukkha (unsatisfactoriness) of existence, but also toward all beings. bhakti as the practice of love, as the existential rather than metaphysical approach as the fusion of the abstract truth with ideal ways, the doctrine (dharma) and its abiding presence in its adept practitioners (arhats) comes into and pervades Buddhism well before the arrival of Mahayana. It was the ancient form of bhakti that made Buddhism a living philosophy as well as a philosophical religion. In the dharma of the Buddha, the fusion between nirguna (abstract) and saguna (concrete) bhakti takes place. Buddha defined both bhakti and dharma precisely in terms of their essential as well as relevant philosophical meaning and implications. Both saguna and nirguna bhakti are exemplified in the Buddha's Parinirvana Sutta (Sutra) as explained by R. Raj Singh in his book 'bhakti and Philosophy'. In his Parinirvana Sutta the Buddha proclaimed to the bhikkhus thus:

Whether the Buddhas arise, O bhikkhus, or whether the Buddhas do not arise, it remains a fact and the fixed and necessary constitution of being that all constituents are transitory...that all its constituents are dukkha (pain) ... and all its elements are anatta (soul-less). This fact a Buddha discovers and masters, and when he has discovered and mastered it, he announces, teaches, publishes, proclaims, discloses, minutely examine, makes it clear, that all the constituents of being are ...transitory... dukkha ...and anatta. Explained by Singh, "In other words, while the Buddha reminds Mahasthavir Ananda that he has nothing more spectacular to say to the Order (Sangha) over and above what he has already been 'teaching, minutely explaining and making clear' for over forty-five years, he is exhorting his disciples to rise above the 'saguna bhakti' (devotion to a being with attributes i.e. a personal lord) to a 'nirguna bhakti' (devotion of an attribute less Being) of the dharma itself. While he did not recommend getting rid of personal devotion toward the elders, saints, arhats, and sramanas, which was and continues to be embedded in the culture of India, he asked his bhikkhus to be self-reliant and 'lamps unto themselves' and let dharma be their guide, refuge, and teacher, after their embodied teacher is gone. He asked them to rise above mere 'saguna bhakti' for human beings are more in need of internal lawfulness than external teachings. This also reflects the emphasis on the 'individual quest' that has endeared Buddhism forever to thoughtful minds beyond sectarianism and national boundaries.

In Buddhism, bhakti is not a separate or alternate path as prescribed in the Bhagavad-Gita where four alternate paths of salvation are prescribed. In Buddhism, pure bhakti without knowledge (dharma) and work (karma) will simply bring attachment which will not bring joy and salvation but will bring pain at separation. Thus, Buddhism prescribes the three jewels together: Buddha (bhakti), dharma (knowledge) and Sangha (karma). It also shows the exemplification of saguna and nirguna bhakti in Buddhism: "Buddham sharanam Gachchhami" (saguna bhakti), "Dharmmam sharanam Gachchhami" (nirguna bhakti), "Sangham Sharanam Gachchhami" (saguna bhakti). It is interesting to note that Assam Vaishnavism also, like Buddhism and unlike the Bhagavad-Gita, prescribes this three vastus (jewels) together: Guru (bhakti), Nam (knowledge) and bhakat (karma). Later with the development of Mahayana Buddhism, the bhakti element was given a higher status when Buddha was elevated to be a God, a Savior. The Buddha never approved worshiping of him as God for salvation. Man's salvation, according to him, lay not in prayer and worship but through his works through his own right efforts and wisdom. Later however Mahayana Buddhism turned the human Buddha into an eternal and supreme deity presiding over the world, and people began to pray and worship him so that he might guide them to salvation. Now salvation started to depend on devotion and fervent prayer, and people began to worship the image of the Buddha to stimulate feeling and meditation. Mahayana became popular and powerful owing to this devotional aspect. Another important feature to be noticed in Mahayana Buddhism is that its characters, the Bodhisattvas are enjoined to perform good deeds and pass the merit earned thereby on to all sentient beings to awaken their Bodhi hearts. It is likely that when the idea of service to others (pararthatva) was emphasized in Mahayana Buddhism, the practice was introduced as a token of the spirit of self-abnegation and detachment. Some people believe that this Buddhist practice of dedicating merit to others has influenced the Gita's teaching that action should be dedicated to God.

The original development of the bhakti in the Buddhist culture is also attested by many other scholars. According to Trevor Ling, the conception of bhakti most probably grew in Buddhism prominently with the erection of various Buddhist stupas in reverence for the Buddha from the 3rd century B.C. In Asoka's time various Buddhist stupas were erected to preserve and revere the remains of the Buddha. "Together with the growth and influence of Buddhism, there went a growth of non-priestly beliefs and customs. Perhaps the most significance of these was the cult of veneration of stupas, the stone or brick cairns in which were enshrined the reliquary remains of great men and heroes. …… It was this, associated as it was with Buddhism, which more than anything else marks the beginning of the characterization of the Buddhist movement in religious terms. By Asoka's time the seeds of the attitude of bhakti or reverential, loving devotion, had been sown, seeds which in later centuries were to bloom luxuriantly in the worship by lay people not only of the Buddha, Gotama, but of countless other potential Buddhas, or Bodhisattvas, heavenly beings of such exalted and potent spirituality that they were in function and status indistinguishable from gods".[12] According to Edward Thomas, "But for the laymen a new type of religion arose. It may in its origin have not been Brahmanical at all, but it finally became absorbed in Hinduism. In this type, we find an exclusive devotion (bhakti) to one God, a personal being who promises salvation to all that faithfully worship him. We have no evidence to place the contact of such religions with Buddhism earlier than the second century B.C. It is also from that period that we find archaeological evidence for the existence of the religion of bhakti, and it is also from that time that the worship of bodhisattvas appears in Buddhism". [13]It seems probable that the Buddhist Tantric system had crystallized into a definite form by the end of the third century A.D.[14] Spiritual prayer songs were written which were recited with dance. At the beginning of the fifth century, the early Mahasanghikas created a fourth pitaka called the Dharani Pitaka which is a collection of mantric formula, mudras, and mandalas, and thus another 'yana', the Dharaniyana, sprung into existence from the school of Buddhism. The idea of dharani (one that holds) of the main theme of a prayer is the one that is repeated throughout the song so that the singers can grasp and remember the meaning of the prayer better. Later, it is from

Buddhism, that Hinduism absorbed this bhakti element of prayer with dharani in its practice and philosophy.

Most of the beautiful literary works were destroyed by Brahmanic oppression. Fortunately, some of these works were preserved in Tibet from which these are being recovered now painstakingly. We also lost many valuable books on Mahayana Buddhism composed in India. One such valuable book was titled 'Bodhisattvacharyavrtara' by Shantideva who an eighth century Buddhist master at the monastic university of Nalanda. The book was a guide for all showing how bhakti needed to be practiced becoming a Bodhisattva. A Bodhisattva is one who is ready to become a Buddha but one who is holding his Buddhahood so that he can teach others through his compassion how to become a Buddha. The book was translated from Sanskrit to Tibetan and Chinese and Japanese and had great influence in those countries. We however do not find any reference of the book in India. The book was recently translated into English by Stephen Batchelor with the grace of Dalai Lama in 1979 titled, "A Guide to the Bodhisattva Way of Life".

Rabindranath Tagore also referred to another instance in England where a Japanese Buddhist was quoting about Buddhism the way he believed it. "This world is real; this is not unreal or sunya. This life is real. This is not a dream. We Buddhist believe in a first because who is all powerful, all wise and all compassionate. This world is the expression of that great wise and we see his manifestation in all life." Tagore admitted that that view of Buddhism expressed may not be for all sects of Buddhism, but it showed how Buddhism had spread so wide in different cultures and have so much divergent beliefs that we are not aware of. In India, it was the non-Aryan Dravidians who originated the bhakti concept with their worship of Siva. Buddhism, Jainism, and the Upanishads, all absorbed the concept from them. However, it was Buddhism that made it a popular movement with its absence of the caste system and took it to the general Indian population. Rabindranath Tagore seems to summarize the situation as follows: "It was in Buddhism first that the concept arose that a man can be seen with such extreme respect; and it is possible that the idea of treating Jesus Christ as a savior incarnation might have been borrowed from Buddhism. It is this reincarnation theory and the bhaktivad of Buddhism that Vaishnavism borrowed from Buddhism and propagated in India." In fact, Vaishnavism borrowed many other elements from Buddhism. Tagore continued: "But is not its Buddhism that has nourished Vaishnavism, the religion of love that sprung from the Dravida and flowed all over India? We have seen how the Vaishnav deities have replaced the Buddhist deities in Buddhist temples, and how the footprints of the Buddha have been taken over and considered as the footprints of Vishnu. Not only that, but the Buddhist ceremonies also such as the Ratha yatra has been taken over by the Vaishnavites as their own". All these go to show that Buddhism has contributed immensely to its propagation of bhakti as a religion of the people not only to Hinduism but to Christianity also. Overall, it may be said however that bhakti at a fundamental level is essentially a human experience, and it cannot be confined to a particular tradition.

References

1.   R. Raj Singh - bhakti and Philosophy - Lexington Books, (2006) p.1.

2.   A Brief Background of Tamil Culture: The Tamil society was dominated mostly by the Buddhist and Jain religions till at least about the 3rd century A.D. In fact, the period (300 B.C. to 300 A.D.) is known as the 'Sangam' period in Tamil culture; 'Sangam' being a term derived for the Buddhist term 'Sangha, denoting the assembly of monks. During this Sangam period, there were a vast number of Buddhist (as well as Jain) authors who composed very rich Tamil literature of the liberal humanistic theme. Amongst these, Silappatikaram, Manimekhalai and Kundalakesi are considered as Tamil epics of which the Manimekhalai is considered as a Buddhist epic. These authors, perhaps influenced by their monastic faiths, wrote books based on moralistic values to illustrate the futility of secular pleasures which was the essence of Buddhism and Jainism. The influence of Buddhism and Jainism is easily noticeable in it. From the 6th century onwards, new writers came forward to carry the tradition of creating bhakti poems. "(Religious Movements in South Asia 600-1800 Ed David N Lorenzen)".

3.   R. Champak Lakshmi - Religious Movement in South Asia - Article: From Devotion and Dissent to Dominance " The bhakti of the Tamil Alvars and Nayanars" p. 52.

4.   R. Raj Singh, p. 17.

5.   Romila Thapar 'Syndicated Moksha' - Seminar 313 (September 1985) – p. 16.

6.   Toynbee - A Study of History - p. 544.

7.   Paul Williams - Buddhist Thoughts - Rutledge; 2nd edition 2011- p. 8.

8.   N. Aiyaswami Sastri -Article-Approach to Hinduism - 2500 Years of Buddhism Ed P.V. Bapat p. 299.

9.   R. Raj Singh, p. 11.

10. Swami Vivekananda - Lectures from Colombo to Almora - 'Speech – Bhakti' – p. 305.

11. R. Raj Singh, p. 24.

12. Trevor Ling -The Buddha – p. 166.

13. Edward Thomas - History of Buddhist Thought, p. 199.

14. N. Aiyaswami Sastri, p. 300.

Appendix 5

Sufi Sampradaya

The major Sufi sects and their Sadguru tradition say that the Sufi sect entered India in the last years of the twelfth century AD. It should be noted here that in the development of Sufism, well-known seekers became disciples and as a result, different sects and sub-sects were formed. These sects then gradually spread to other countries. Sects were named after different Sufi seekers. The nature of these sects became clear by the twelfth century A.D. According to the Sufis, these different sects originated with Islam. In the first years of the Hijri year, in both Mecca and Medina, forty-five (45) people each came together and formed a party and took an oath of allegiance to the Prophet Muhammad. Almost all Sufi sects trace their origins back to the Prophet Muhammad and associate themselves with Ali, the fourth deputy in-charge (caliph) after the apostles. Abu Bakr and Ali had organized their forces during the lifetime of the apostles, and they were leading their forces. It was a kind of promise. In the early days, groups of seekers used to move from one place to another. In time, it came to be known as Attarik (Path) or Khanvad (Family). These are now called sects. The teachings or special rites of the early founders of the sect were passed on to the next generation of disciples. Thus began the tradition of discipleship among the sects. Murshad or Peer (Sadguru) in the sect is the successor of the pioneer. This Murshad or Peer is the head of that sect. It is believed that the evolution of all Sufi sects took place from the four Peers. But there is a difference of opinion as to who the four Peers were.

According to some, the names of these four peers are as follows,

1. Murtuza Ali (son-in-law of the apostles),
2. Ali appointed his successor, Khwaja Hassan Basri,
3. Hassan nominated by his successor Khwaja Habib Hazmi and
4. Abdul Wahid bin Zaid Krifi. The names of the above four peers are not universal.

Fourteen (14) khanbadas (families) were formed from the above four peers. In fact, these fourteen sects are made up of Hasan Basri disciples, three major Sufi sects - Chishti, Qadri and Suharwardi - are associated with Hasan Basri, and the fourth major sect, Naqshbandi, is associated with Abu Bakr. Due to the extraordinary importance of the Sadguru tradition in the Sufi sadhana.

1. Chishti sect,
2. Qadri sect,
3. Suharwardi sect and
4. The Sadguru tradition of the four major Sufi sects in India, the Naqshbandi Sampradaya, is being continued.

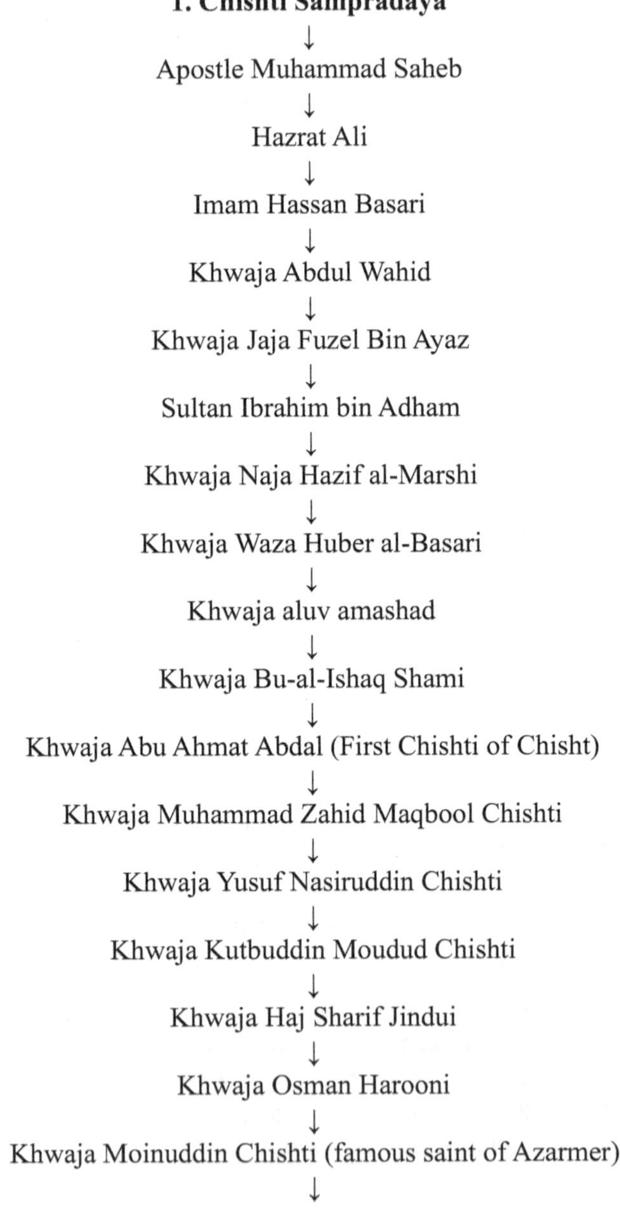

1. Chishti Sampradaya

↓

Apostle Muhammad Saheb

↓

Hazrat Ali

↓

Imam Hassan Basari

↓

Khwaja Abdul Wahid

↓

Khwaja Jaja Fuzel Bin Ayaz

↓

Sultan Ibrahim bin Adham

↓

Khwaja Naja Hazif al-Marshi

↓

Khwaja Waza Huber al-Basari

↓

Khwaja aluv amashad

↓

Khwaja Bu-al-Ishaq Shami

↓

Khwaja Abu Ahmat Abdal (First Chishti of Chisht)

↓

Khwaja Muhammad Zahid Maqbool Chishti

↓

Khwaja Yusuf Nasiruddin Chishti

↓

Khwaja Kutbuddin Moudud Chishti

↓

Khwaja Haj Sharif Jindui

↓

Khwaja Osman Harooni

↓

Khwaja Moinuddin Chishti (famous saint of Azarmer)

↓

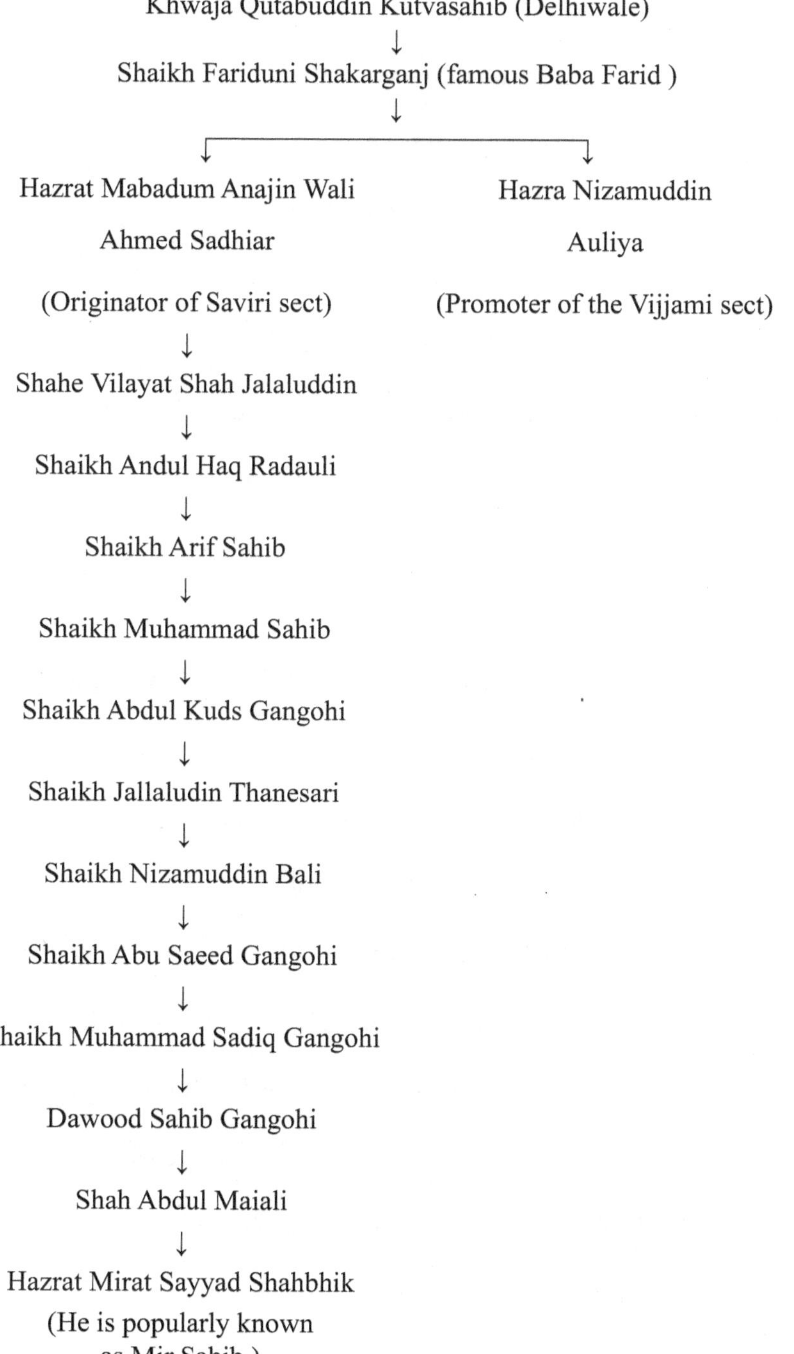

Khwaja Qutabuddin Kutvasahib (Delhiwale)
↓
Shaikh Fariduni Shakarganj (famous Baba Farid)
↓
Hazrat Mabadum Anajin Wali
Ahmed Sadhiar
(Originator of Saviri sect)
↓
Shahe Vilayat Shah Jalaluddin
↓
Shaikh Andul Haq Radauli
↓
Shaikh Arif Sahib
↓
Shaikh Muhammad Sahib
↓
Shaikh Abdul Kuds Gangohi
↓
Shaikh Jallaludin Thanesari
↓
Shaikh Nizamuddin Bali
↓
Shaikh Abu Saeed Gangohi
↓
Shaikh Muhammad Sadiq Gangohi
↓
Dawood Sahib Gangohi
↓
Shah Abdul Maiali
↓
Hazrat Mirat Sayyad Shahbhik
(He is popularly known
as Mir Sahib.)
Hazra Nizamuddin
Auliya
(Promoter of the Vijjami sect)

2. Kadari Sampraday: Satguru Tradition

↓

Preshit Muhammad Aheb

↓

Ali Ibn Abi Talib

↓

Shaikh Hasan Basari

↓

Shaikh Hebib ajmi

↓

Shaikh Dawud Tai

↓

Shaikh Maruf Kakhi (second)

↓

Shaikh Abdullah Siri Sakthi

↓

Shaikh bul Qasim Junaid Bagdadi

↓

Shaikh Abu Bakr Abduma Shivali

↓

Shaikh Abul Fazal Abdul Wahid Bin Andul Aziz Al Taymi

↓

Shaikh Anul Farah Tartusi

↓

Shaikh Abul Hassan Ali bin Muhammad bin Yusuf Al Qashi Alhankari

↓

Shaikh Anu Saeed Al - Mubarak Al Makhjumi

↓

Gausul Samdani Mehboob Subhani Sheikh Abduru Qadar Jilani

↓

Shaikh Tajuddin Abu Bakar Abdurzak bin Abdul Qadar Jilani

↓

Imaduhdin Saleh Nakstra bin Shaikh Tajuddin Abu Bakr Abdurandzak

↓

Shaikh Shahbuddin Ahmed bin Shaikh Imaduddin Abi Saleh Nastra

↓

Shaikh Shahanuddin Ahmed bin Shaikh Shahabuddin Ahmed

↓

Shaikh Shamsuddin Muhammad in Shaikh Sharfuheen Ishyya

↓

Shaikh Alauddin Ali bin Shaikh Shamsuhoon Muhammad

↓

Shaikh Badrudin bin Shaikh Alauhin Ali
↓
Shaikh Shahabuddin Ali Al Abwas Ahmed bin Shaikh Badruddin Hasan
↓
Shaikh Abdul Basit bin Shaikh Shahbadin Abi Al Abbas Ahmed
↓
Shaikh Qasam bin Shaikh Andul Basit
↓
Shaikh Muhammad bin Shaikh Qasam
↓
Shaikh Ahmed Binsheikh Muhammad Al - Hamvi
↓
Syed Shah Abdul Latif Qadri Laubali
↓
Shaikh Ali Sufi
↓
Shaikh Fariuddin Sufi
↓
Sayyed Ali Sufi Bukhari
↓
Sayyed Fariduddin Bukhari
↓
Sayyed Ali Bukhari
↓
Sayyed Muhibuddin Badshah Bukhari
↓
Sayyed Hussain Bukhari
↓
Sayyed Khwaja Ahmed Bukhari
↓
Sayyed Muhammad Padshah Bukhari
↓
Abul Hassanat Sayyed Abdusha

3. Suharvadi Sampradaya: Sadhguru Parampara
↓
Preshit Muhammad Saheb
↓
Ali Murtuja Ibn Abi Talia
↓
Shaikh Hasan Basari

↓

Shaikh Khawaja habib ajmi

↓

Shaikh Khawaja Dawud Tai

↓

Shaikh Abu Mahfouz Khawaja Maruf's kakhari

↓

Shaikh Siri Sakati

↓

Shaikh Junaid Baradadi

↓

Khawaja Mamshad Dinori

↓

Khawaja Shaikh Ahmed Asanwad Dinori

↓

Shaikh Abu Muhammad Amvia

↓

Shaikh Kaji Wajih Uddin

↓

Shaikh Ziauddin Abdul Najeeb Abdul Qahir Suharwadi

↓

Shaikh Shahnurin Suhswardi

↓

Shekhul Islam Kutbe Alam Bahauddin Zakriya Multani

↓

Shaikh Samardin

↓

Shaikh Ahmed Mashuk

↓

Shaikh Rkanuddin

↓

Shaikh Hamiduddin

↓

Sayyed Jalaluddin Makhdoome Jahania
Saeed Burhanuddin Kutb Alam

↓

Shaikh Moses

↓

Saeed Haji Abdul Wahab

↓

Baba Dawud Khaki

↓

Syed Jhulan Shah
↓
Meeran Muhammad Shah
↓
Shah Jamal
↓
Shah Daula Daryai
↓
Shaikh Jan Muhammad
↓
Shaikh Muhammad Ismail
↓
Shaikh Hassan Lalu

4. Nakshbandi Sampradaya: Sadhguru Parampara
↓
Preshit Muhammad Saheb
↓
Abu Bakra Assddik
↓
Imam Qasim bin Muhammad bin Abu Bakr
↓
Imam Zafar Sadiq
↓
Khawaja Bayzid Vistami
↓
Khawaja abulhasan kharkani
↓
Khawaja Abul Qasim Guragani
↓
Khawaja Abu Ali Farmadi
↓
Khawaja Abu Yusaf Hamdani
↓
Khwaja Abdul Khalin Ghazdwani
↓
Khawaja Muhammad Arif Revkari
↓
Khawaja Mahmud Al Rai Faganvi
↓
Khawaja Ali Ramitni

↓

Khawaja Muhammad Baba Sammasi

↓

Khawaja Sayvad Amir Kalal

↓

Khawaja Sayyed Bahuheen Nakshband

↓

Khawaja Aladdin Attar

↓

Khawaja Muzammad Yakub Charakhi

↓

Khawaja Nasiruddin Ubaidulla Ahrar

↓

Khawaja Muhammad Shafurddin Jahid

↓

Maulana Muhammad Darvesh

↓

Maulana Khawajagi Muhammad Amkingi

↓

Khawaja Muhammad Bakivijjah Berang

↓

Mehboob Samdani Imam Rabyani Muhid Alifsani Shaikh
Ahmed Fasuki Sarkhindi

↓

Khawaja Muhammad Masoom

↓

Shaikh Saifurin

↓

Hafiz Muhammad Muhsin Dihalvi

↓

Sayyed Noormuhammad Badauni

↓

Shammudin Hajibua Arif Vigyan Purchase Mita Mazhar Jaane Janan

↓

Shah Abdulla Gulam Ali Shah

↓

Arif Billah Shah Sadullah

↓

Haji Dost Muhammad Kandhari

↓

Muhammad Usman Kulachi

Special Instructions: It is possible to have a double (twin-facing) of the above family tree. If you read it down from bottom to top then it described disciple-tradition, and the satguru/sadhguru tradition is proved by reading from the top to bottom.

Fourteen Khanwadas (Family):

There are two branches of the fourteen Khanwadas of the Sufi sect. The founder of the first branch is Khwaja Habib Azmi, while the founder of the second branch is Abdul Wahid bin Jind. The first branch consists of a total of nine (9) sects, while the second branch consists of the remaining five (5) sects. The list is as follows

Chauda Khanwade (Family, Sect)
Khanaja Hasan Basri

1. Founder Khwaja Habib Azmi   2. Founder Abdul Wahid Zaid

Branch 1	Branch 2
1 Habibian	10. (1) Zaidian
2. Taifurian	11. (2) Ayazian
3. Karkhian	12. (3) Adhimiyan
4. Saktiyan	13. (4) Habirian
5. Junaidian	14. (5) Chishtian
6. Kazrunian	
7. Tusian	
8. Suharvardian	
9. Fidosian	

Appendix 6

Varkari Sampraday

The Varkari is a sampraday (religious tradition) based in western India, where Marathi is the dominant language, particularly in the state of Maharashtra. The Varkaris are distinguished by a devotional (bhakti) focus on the deity Vitthal, two major annual pilgrimages to Viṭṭhal's chief temple in the town of Pandharpur, and a textual corpus consisting of Marathi compositions by sant-kavi or 'saint-poets'. The word varkari literally means 'one who does vari (pilgrimage)', and pilgrimage to Pandharpur has been essential for the tradition's form since the 18th century, at least. The Varkaris observe no centralized institutional authority, and initiation into the sampradaya is facilitated by an unofficial network of independent local religious leaders (called maharajs or buvas). Women and men of all castes may join The Varkari Sampraday, although most Varkaris come from agrarian, non-Brahman backgrounds. Varkari pilgrimages, festivals, and other programs are nonrestricted public events, which makes identifying exactly what Varkaris do and believe more challenging than in the cases of stricter, more institutionally defined sampradays. This has led to confusion about how the term 'Varkari' is used. In its most restricted, sectarian sense, a Varkari is a person who has taken a minimal set of vows before a religious leader to regularly make the vari and to live by a particular code of conduct. In its general, descriptive sense, the term applies to anyone who joins the pilgrimage to Pandharpur regardless of sectarian allegiance. In its most diffuse sense, the word is sometimes used imprecisely to refer to Marathi bhakti Literature and cultural heritage generally, since the Varkaris have long comprised the largest religious Sampradaya of the region. However, this maximal use of the term overlooks major differences between the Varkaris and the Mahanubhav Sampraday another Marathi bhakti tradition whose history, theology, literature, and practices are very distinct.[1] The terminology is further complicated by the thorough incorporation of Varkari poetry and hagiography into 20th century Maharashtrian political and social discourses that were independent of the Varkari Sampraday. 'Varkari' in this chapter is used in its restricted, sectarian sense while acknowledging that the tradition's borders are porous, and its influence extends far beyond its sectarian membership.

History

The Varkari Sampraday's decentralized character and the region's fragmentary historical record make it difficult to attain a comprehensive view of how the Varkaris changed through the centuries, but some key points can be observed. Although Vitthal worship and the annual pilgrimage to Pandharpur are now essential features in the Varkari tradition, their historical roots clearly precede the Varkaris (Vaudeville, 1996). Copperplate inscriptions from the 5th century mention Pandharpur, and Sanskrit Mahatmyas describe the town as a location of both tirthas and kṣetras ('fields'; sacred areas that are pilgrimage destinations) unrelated to Vitthal, who is not mentioned as being in Pandharpur until the 12th century. Important scholars have argued that Vitthal's origins probably lie in the folk traditions of nomadic herders in the region who conceptualized him in relation to "hero stones" that memorialized men who had died while protecting the community's cattle.[2] Temples and stone inscriptions between the 12th and 15th centuries document the patronage by Hoysala rulers in what is now northern Karnataka, and the Kannada bhakti poetry of the Haridasa Sampraday reveals a strong devotion to Vitthal. The Vitthal temple at Pandharpur is first mentioned in a stone inscription from 1189 A.D. and a set of inscriptions between 1273 A.D. and 1277 A.D. record that the temple enjoyed the patronage of Ramachandra, the last of the Marathi-speaking Yadava (Devgiri) kings, and his famous minister Hemadri. It is also clear that by the 12th century, if not earlier, Vitthal had become incorporated into a broader Vaiṣṇava mythology, particularly by linking him to the legends in the Padmapuraṇa and Skandapuraṇa about Kṛiṣṇa coming to Pandharpur.[3] Observing this pre-Varkari background of Pandharpur and Vitthal is helpful for appreciating the divergence of interests between Varkari pilgrims and (non-Varkari) Brahmans who manage the Vitthal temple.[4]

According to tradition, the saint-poets Dnyandev and Namdev (13th century) initiated or formalized the annual pilgrimage to Pandharpur and thereby founded the Varkari Sampraday, and several poems attributed to them appear to support this view. However, based on the historical evidence available, it is impossible to rule out the possibility that this is a later interpretation of Varkari history and that the poetry in question was attributed pseudonymously later.[5] Datable manuscripts of hagiographical accounts of Namdev and Dnyandev demonstrate that a pilgrimage to Pandharpur was clearly well established by the early 17th century[6], though its exact route(s) and nature are not detailed. Several important historical developments in the Varkari tradition in the last two centuries also merit attention. At the turn of the 19th century, some of the major modern Varkari sub-traditions (phaḍs, lit. 'camps') were founded at Dehu, Alandi, and elsewhere. These groups, which gathered around local Varkari leaders whose traditions are passed on through blood or spiritual lineages, were instrumental in shaping the modern organizational form of the Varkari pilgrimage. On the literary side, it is clear from the poetry of the saint-poets, hagiographies, and the notebooks of kirtan performers that the performance of the saint-poets' compositions has long been an essential practice in the sampraday. At the end of the 19th century, editors began collecting and publishing anthologies of individual Varkari saint-poets poetry that was scattered among performers notebooks, and a single compilation of all this poetry was published for the first time in 1908 A.D. the Sakaḷa Santa Gatha '(Collection of Poems of All Saint-Poets)'. This anthology, which was endorsed by the influential Varkari leader Nana Maharaj Sakhre in Alandi, was reprinted many times and effectively became the 'standard' printed edition of Varkari poetry within the tradition. In terms of practice, as the pilgrimages to Pandharpur continued to grow in the 20th century, the hometowns of many saint-poets also developed as major Varkari pilgrimage destinations on festival days commemorating their respective saint-poets.

Key Figures

The Varkari Sampraday from at least the 16th century onward, and probably earlier, importantly incorporates the diverse voices of many saint-poets of Vitthal. Primary among these, four key devotees tend to be highlighted: Jñandev or Dnyanesvar ; 13th century), Namdev (13th–14th Century), Eknath (16th Century), and Tukaram (17th Century). The Varkaris also revere other saint-poets who come from a variety of sociocultural backgrounds as well. For example, there are female saint-poets: Muktabai (13th Century), the younger sister of Dnyandev; Janabai, an orphaned devotee of Namdev (13th-14th Century); and Bahiṇabai, a Brahman devotee of Tukaram (17th Century). The Varkaris revere an 'untouchable' saint-poet, Chokhameḷa (13th-14th Century), along with his poetically gifted family members, and a notable Muslim devotee, Shaikh Muhammad (16th-17th Century). Several minor low-caste Varkari saint-poets are remembered for using metaphors based on their trades to express their devotion to Vitthal: Sena the barber, Narhari the goldsmith, Savata the gardener, and Gora the potter. The Varkaris also revere several saint-poets whose songs are not recorded in Marathi, especially Surdas, Mira Bai, Rohidas (Ravidas), and Kabir, who are all of northern Indian origin. In addition to the writings of the saint-poets, hagiographical stories about them play important roles in the Varkari tradition. Many compositions attributed to various saint-poets refer to and praise other saint-poets.

A late, popular example of this is Bahinabai's use of a metaphor of a temple to illustrate the contributions of the saint-poets: Dnyandev laid the foundation, Namdev expanded it, Eknath erected columns, Tukaram became the temple's pinnacle (kalas), and Bahinabai's flag of bhakti flutters at the top. Thus, the saint-poets' own poetry, permeated by memories of other figures in the tradition, reinforces the cohesion of the larger tradition. The first hagiographies of Varkari figures appear in the work of Namdev, attributed to the 13th century, and extant in manuscripts from as early as the 16th century. These hagiographies were of Namdev's purported contemporaries Dnyandev and his siblings and Chokhamela, for example. In addition, Janabai composed hagiographical accounts of many of the same figures, and of Namdev as well. In the 17th and early 18th centuries, hagiographies about the saint-poet Eknath were composed by descendants in his familial and spiritual lineages. In the late 18th century, scattered individual hagiographies like these were gathered into compendia that could be called 'collective hagiographies', which constitute the hagiographical corpus of the Varkari Sampraday as it is largely remembered today. In the process of drawing stories together, the collective hagiographers also smoothed out and shaped the stories to cohere well in a generally Vaishnava framework. The most influential of these was a Brahman Varkari named Mahipati (1715–1790 A.D.), who wrote four massive volumes containing stories about hundreds of Marathi and North Indian saint-poets.[7] His Bhaktavijay (Victory of the Bhaktas) and the Bhaktalilamrut (Essence of the Divine Play of the Bhaktas) became the standard sourcebooks for Varkari hagiography, both in Marathi and in English translation.[8]

Belief and Practices

The 'essence' of the Varkari ethos its ethics and morality, its customs and conventions aren't standardized or regulated by any text, authority, or charismatic central leader. In general, the tradition's beliefs and practices are conveyed through the interpretation of the songs and actions attributed to the various Varkari saint-poets. In this context, some basic, though not necessarily ubiquitous, commonalities emerge. All Varkaris share a devotion of Vitthal, and all Varkaris understand Pandharpur to be the home of Vitthal. Not all Varkaris equally admire or revere the various saint-poets; however, most commonly accept the centrality of the four key saint-poets, and often many more besides those four mentioned above. In addition, most Varkaris revere Rukmin Vitthal's chief wife, as well as his other wives. Radha is conspicuously absent from Varkari lore despite the tradition's deep Krisnaite character. Given the large Varkari presence in rural western

India, many aspects of the Varkari tradition are tied to agricultural rhythms and customs.[9]

Varkaris generally espouse a theologically informed equality among castes, genders, and subcultures, although in practice many Varkari social structures are constituted along caste, gender, and regional lines such as in the organization of pilgrim groups called diṇḍ.[10] Female figures have central and consistent positions in the panoply of Varkari saint poets, and an ethics of equality is regularly promoted in the song-poems and hagiography of the saint-poets. On pilgrimage and at kirtan performances, Varkaris tend to observe a division between men and women. For example, at Varkari kirtan performances, men and women sit separately on opposite sides of the ground (most kirtan performances are held outdoors or in large tents). But customs are changing, and one now occasionally sees women in traditionally male Varkari roles (e.g., as kirtan performers and musicians). Within the cultural context of predominately rural Maharashtra, where most Varkaris live, the rhetoric of egalitarianism and fellowship is an important but moderated aspect of the tradition. Several other details about the Varkaris have become regarded as characteristic of the tradition, due to the work of the prominent scholarly interpreter S.V. Dandekar (commonly known as Sonopant Dandekar). S.V. Dandekar was a Brahman philosophy professor from Pune who became a Varkari in the early 20th century, founded an important spiritual lineage in Alandi, and published an extensive overview of the tradition that has informed most scholarship on the living varkari Sampraday.[11]

In modern times, the Varkari Sampraday has comprised a vast number of devotional sub-traditions (phaḍs or sampradays) of widely varying sizes that centered on male Varkari leaders maharajs). Some maharajs belong to familial lineages that were established in earlier generations, others claim spiritual (guru-disciple) lineages, and others arise by simply attracting a group of followers. Most claim to have had an immediate vision (sakṣhatkar) of one or another saint-poet, through meditation or in a dream. Most maharajs have undertaken years of training either with elder Varkari maharajs or at training schools such as the Varkari Shikshan Sanstha in Alandi. Such training includes studying the saint-poets' writings and learning how to perform kirtans. These maharajs are vitally involved in organizing groups of Varkaris to make pilgrimages to Pandharpur or to important saint-poets' temples on festival days. The maharajs also play the small but important role of hearing the vows of people who want to formally join the sampradaya and placing a necklace of 108 tulsi beads (a tulsimala) around the newly initiated Varkari's neck. However, as the Varkari Sampraday's borders are quite porous, non-Varkaris freely join in Varkari activities, and nothing precludes independently minded Varkaris from taking vows without a maharaj. When people want to formally join the Varkari Sampraday, they usually go to a maharaj and make a set of vows that include maintaining a vegetarian diet, speaking the truth, doing variat least once each year, repeating a mantra such as 'Ram kṛiṣṇa hari', and keeping Viṭṭhal in mind throughout their daily routines.[12] After they take these vows, the maharaj places on their neck the tulsimala, which they are told to wear continuously for the rest of their lives as an external mark that they are Varkaris. During pilgrimage, festivals, and other public events, Varkaris also regularly apply on their foreheads a ṭilaka (sectarian mark) consisting of a narrow, tan-colored vertical U made of sandalwood paste (gopichandan), inside which are placed a black dot of fragrant black powder (buka) below and a saffron dot above. While there is no official dress code for vari and other Varkari events, in practice Varkari men tend to wear a simple white cotton kurta paijama or dhoti and a white Gandhi cap, much like many would wear in their villages. Similarly, women wear their everyday colorful sarees (Marathi. saḍi), and on pilgrimage many carry (often balanced on their heads) a small metal container with a tulsi plant with them to Pandharpur.

The Vari

More than in any other practice, Varkaris are traditionally defined by their commitment to participate in at least one of the biannual pilgrimages to Pandharpur, called the vari. Although technically vari is a common noun in Marathi that could be used for any walking pilgrimage, in practice it connotes the Varkari pilgrimages. The larger of the two-yearly pilgrimages culminates on the 11th day of the first half of the month of aṣhadh (Jun–Jul), while the smaller of the two pilgrimages occurs in the month of karttik (Oct–Nov). Pilgrims come from most parts of Maharashtra (with the curious exception of the Konkan coastal region) following routes established by local traditions, and they travel mainly with groups (diṇḍis) that are organized by or on behalf of local maharajs. Some small independent groups and individuals make the pilgrimage without a maharaj, although even they tend to remain somewhat near a larger group to avail themselves of organized local hospitality at rest stops.

Groups who live far away may set out 40 or more days in advance to arrive in Pandharpur at the most auspicious time. At some point along the way, many groups join palanquins (palkhis) that set out from the towns of various saint-poets. These palkhis (nowadays mostly carried in highly decorated wagons pulled by bullocks) hold reproductions of the sandals (padukas) of a given saint poet. As the palkhis and their diṇḍis proceed to Pandharpur, residents of the places through which the various processions pass interact with the palkhis by touching them and giving some offering and receiving moments of darshan and prasad. The two largest palkhis in the pilgrimage, by far, are those of Dnyandev and Tukaram, which regularly bring hundreds of diṇḍis and hundreds of thousands of pilgrims with them from Alandi and Dehu, respectively. These two palkhis are so large, in fact, that they are sometimes mistaken for the vari itself rather than correctly recognized as its two largest branches. Their prominence, high degree of organization, and accompanying conveniences such as water tankers, doctors, mobile canteens, tea sellers, and even mobile bookshops now regularly attract many pilgrims and diṇḍ is from across Maharashtra and beyond who travel to Alandi and Dehu to join them. At the same time, dozens of other palkhis such as the Eknath palkhi from Paithan walk on their own distinct routes to Pandharpur, interacting more freely with local communities because of their smaller sizes.

In these smaller palkhis and diṇḍ is, it is customary for people along the path to give food, water, and tea to the Varkaris. When the palkhis approach Pandharpur, a palanquin devoted to Namdev (who is considered a resident of Pandharpur and therefore not on pilgrimage) comes out to greet them. All the major palkhis gather in the nearby town of Vakhri and proceed, one after another, into Pandharpur. Varkaris who cannot walk the pilgrimage (due to injury or lack of time) may take special bus services to the outskirts of Pandharpur but traveling on foot is still regarded as most desirable, as the journey is valued as much as the destination in completing the vari.

Literature and Viewpoint

The Varkari Sampraday makes extensive use of several performative media to express its devotional and ethical positions. The primary medium of all the saint-poets is the short poem (more accurately, a song-poem) that is composed in one of the flexible Marathi forms called ovi or abhanga. The Varkari saint-poets are remembered to have been vocal performers of their compositions, and each 'song-poem' is a performance. As pilgrims sing and chant the poetry of the saint-poets while walking to Pandharpur and in kirtans, they consciously participate in traditions that the saint-poets themselves are remembered to have done. In addition to these short poetic forms, some of the Varkari saint-poets composed renderings or "transcreations" of major Sanskrit texts. The aforementioned Dnyneshvari is the most famous example of this pattern, followed by Eknath's large commentary on the 11th skandha (book) of the Bhagavatapuraṇ a, Eknath's rendering of the Ramayana, as well as Marathi translations of portions the Mahabharata that are attributed Namdev under the name Viṣhṇudas

Nama (who may have been a later "Namdev" of the 16th cent.). While highly revered by Varkaris and drawn upon as foundational texts by kirtan performers, these works represent a more difficult textual genre that tends to be more studied more by maharajs and kirtan performers. The distinction between the saint-poets' short poetry and their transcreative compositions is insightful for considering a specifically 'Varkari' philosophy or set of doctrines. Although a good deal of philosophical argumentation and positioning occurs in the transcreative works, the goal of the saint-poets' popular short poetry was precisely to speak to audiences without such philosophical training. One of the distinctive features of Varkari thought is the tendency to hold together saguṇa and nirguṇan understanding of God. The transcreative works endorse nondualist positions (drawing on both Advaita Vedanta and Kashmir Shaivism), while the short poetry consistently emphasizes devotion to Viṭṭhal. In effect, Varkari literature allows saguṇa and nirguṇa notion to continue without conflicting with each other or offering a grand explanation of how they fit together. Varkari thought tends to be much more focused on bhakti in people's daily lives than on engaging in abstract philosophical argumentation.

Kirtan

The Varkari tradition has many expressive performance traditions, but the most ubiquitous is kirtan.[13] Kirtan as it is performed in Maharashtra is both unique in the subcontinent and central to the Varkari Sampraday. This song-sermon-dance event is one of the main ways in which Varkari literature is transmitted orally and reinterpreted in each new context. The tradition remembers Namdev as the first kirtankar (kirtan performer), and almost every saint-poet is credited with being an outstanding performer as well. Although the precise form certainly has changed through history, contemporary Varkari kirtan follows a relatively set pattern. At the center of the performance is the kirtankar, who may be a full-time professional performer but is more often a maharaj. Supporting him musically are a small group of (traditionally male) Varkaris who play brass hand cymbals (ṭal) in unison, following remarkably complex rhythms, as well as a man who plays a simple stringed instrument with between one and four strings (conventionally called viṇa in Marathi, or ektar in Hindi) that he plucks to maintain a singing pitch, and a man who plays a double-headed barrel drum (called a pakhvaj or mṛdanga). The kirtankar begins by leading the musicians and congregation in several simple bhajans (devotional songs) in which two or three main lines are repeated in a call-and-response format. The kirtankar then introduces a selected song-poem or passage from a longer composition by one of the main Varkari saint-poets and offers some introductory comments (in spoken voice, not sung). One or more bhajans are sung, and the kirtankar returns to his selected theme to discuss in greater detail the contemporary ethical and practical implications of the saint-poet's composition. This is interspersed with and followed by more bhajans or chanting of Vitthal's name, sometimes at length as the kirtankar and audience enter ecstatic states, after which the kirtan ends. Kirtans are a mainstay of every Varkari event and festival, and they are regularly organized for their own sake as well throughout the year. While most Varkari kirtankars are male, there are many female kirtankars in the allied genre called naradiya kirtan, which is also popular in Marathi contexts.

Varkari and Modern Society

Interpretations of the Varkari Sampraday over the last 150 years in the larger scope of Marathi society have been extremely mixed, as the tradition came to be perceived as an important element to be extolled (or rejected) in the struggle for Indian independence and nationhood and the creation of a Marathi speaking state (Maharashtra) in 1960. In this way, the Varkari Sampraday has affected modern Maharashtrian history while becoming in many ways separated from the public discourse about the region. The interpretation of the Varkari Sampraday became a central component in political and social movements in 20th century western India. M.G. Ranade (1961) argued that the Varkari saint-poets from the 16th century onward vitally unified Hindus in western India and prepared the way for the establishment of regional self-rule under the Maratha king Shivaji. Likewise, Ranade thought the Varkari saint-poets could be a source of inspiration for the Indian struggle for independence from the British. In contrast, the influential Marathi historian V.K. Rajvade dismissed the Varkari Sampraday as too passive, other-worldly, and uninterested in politics to be useful for the struggle toward independence. As noted earlier, the Varkaris freely accept people of all castes to the tradition and have often regularly denounced caste distinctions in religious and spiritual matters. The social implications of this spiritual egalitarianism have been much more complex. Several prominent leaders in early Dalit movements around the turn of the 20th century attempted to revive enthusiasm about the Mahar saint-poet Cokhameḷ a as a way of mobilizing their Dalit communities.

However, broader social discriminations against "untouchables" persisted; for example, the Vitthal Temple in Pandharpur prohibited "untouchables" from entering until 1947. Not surprisingly, some social reformers judged the Varkari Sampraday to be ineffective for thoroughgoing social reform. mahatma Jyotiba Phule and Dr. Bhimrao Ambedkar both openly discouraged their low-caste and 'untouchable' communities from joining the Varkaris.[14] Perhaps due to these patterns of interpreting the Varkaris and appropriating the saint-poets into a non-sectarian Marathi "spirituality," with a few exceptions[15] the living Varkari Sampraday consequently has received relatively little scholarly attention in the 20th and 21st centuries. Nonetheless the tradition shows no signs of diminishing but rather appears to be growing with each decade.

References

1. Feldhaus, 1983, 1984; Feldhaus & Tulpule, 1992.
2. Deleury, 1960; Dhere, 2011.
3. Reenberg Sand, 1990; Novetzke, 2005.
4. Reenberg Sand, 1987.
5. Kiehnle, 1992; Novetzke, 2003.
6. Novetzke, 2008.
7. Keune, 2007; Novetzke, 2008.
8. Abbott et al., 1935, 1980, 1981, 1982.
9. Youngblood, 2003.
10. Karve, 1988.
11. Dandekar, 1927; Bahirat & Bhalerav, 1972.
12. Bahirat & Bhalerav, 1972.
13. Novetzke, 2008; Schultz, 2012.
14. O'Hanlon,2002; Rao, 2009.
15. Youngblood, 2003; Keune, 2012.

Note: 'Varkari' and 'Warkari', both the words carried the same meaning and mentioned in various books, articles, published literatre.

Appendix 7

Sufi Interpreters of Yogic Practices

The foregoing remarks on the study of religion expand on a problem that has dogged the modern study of religion since its inception. As I have argued elsewhere, since the beginning of Orientalist scholarship over two centuries ago, it was an unquestioned assumption that Sufism was somehow derived from Hinduism, so it was not Islamic at all. This conceit has endured through the nineteenth century until recent times. In Zaehner's words, 'Muslim mysticism is entirely derivative'.[1] Orientalists and romantics alike agreed that mysticism must always and inevitably derive from India. The lack of historical evidence for this assumption demands that one seek elsewhere for an explanation of what one scholar has called 'Indomaniac zeal'. In part, no doubt, there was some attraction in the elegance and simplicity found in theories of cultural diffusion from a single source. One typical example of the romantic Orientalist interpretation of Sufism was E. H. Palmer's 1867 translation of an important thirteenth-century Persian text by Aziz al-Din Nasafi, which Palmer entitled Oriental Mysticism. "Steering a mid-course between the pantheism of India on the one hand and the spiritual of the on other, the Sufis culture is the religion of beauty. Sufiism is really the development of the Primaeval Religion of the Aryan race".[2] Arguments used to support this contention wavered between focusing on yogic practice and the philosophical doctrines of Vedanta as the essence of Indian mysticism. As Jonathan Z. Smith has commented, it is as if the only choices the comparativist has are to assert either identity or uniqueness, and that the only possibilities for utilizing comparisons are to make assertions regarding dependence. In such an enterprise, it would appear, dissimilarity is assumed to be the norm; similarities are to be explained either as the result of the 'psychic unity' of humankind, or the result of 'borrowing'.[3] If we are to avoid these essentialist dichotomies, the polythetic approach to religion is extremely helpful. No longer is it necessary to attack or defend arguments of influence or authenticity, since it is now possible to acknowledge freely that numerous examples of hybrid and multiplex symbols, practices, and doctrines can be at work in any religious milieu. Nevertheless, it is still worthwhile to dissect essentialist and orientalist interpretations of religion, particularly when they take the form of what literary critics call 'strong mis-readings', in which a theorist triumphantly proposes a revolutionary explanation based on newly detected alleged sources and origins. What, then, is the data regarding the relationship between Sufism and yoga, apart from a priori assumptions about Oriental mysticism? In a recent study, I have traced the history of the single text, 'The Pool of Nectar', which, in multiple versions and translations, made available to Muslim readers certain practices associated with the Nath yogis and the teachings known as hatha yoga (in standard North Indian pronunciation, yogis are called yogis).[4] These practices include divination by control of breath through the left and right nostrils, summoning female spirits that can be identified as yoginis, and performing meditations on the chakra centres accompanied by recitation of Sanskrit mantras.

All this material was increasingly Islamised over time, in a series of translations into Arabic, Persian, Ottoman Turkish, and Urdu. This remarkable text, and several other examples that I will mention, make it abundantly clear that in certain Sufi circles there was an awareness and use of practices that can be considered yogic (although the question of defining yoga, and the perspective from which it may be identified, still needs to be clarified). Contrary to Orientalist expectations, however, Sufi engagement with yoga was not to be found at the historical beginnings of the Sufi tradition, and it was most highly developed, unsurprisingly, in India.[5] Moreover, the knowledge of yoga among Indian Sufis gradually became more detailed over time. The most exact accounts of hatha yoga in Sufi texts, using technical terms in Hindi, occur in writings from as late as the nineteenth century, although these texts typically juxtapose yoga materials along-side Sufi practices without any real attempt at integration or synthesis. The Sufi interest in hatha yoga was very practical and did not (with certain notable exceptions) engage with philosophical texts of Vedanta or other Sanskritic schools of thought.[6]

The preceding summary of the Pool of Nectar translations has just introduced a few technical terms that will remain methodologically problematic if we do not pause for some basic attempts at historical and descriptive definition. What do we mean by Sufism and yoga? 'Sufism' is by its nature an outsider's term, belonging to the Enlightenment catalogue of ideologies and creeds identified as 'isms'. As such, it inevitably stands in tension with the insider vocabulary of spiritual vocations and ethical ideals of the Sufi tradition.[7] Historically, what we call Sufism may be considered a typical and prominent trend in most Muslim societies, gradually crystallising as a self-conscious movement in the ninth and tenth centuries. Despite the strong emphasis upon the Quran and the Prophet Muhammad in Sufi thought and practice, Sufism has been disassociated from Islam in both Orientalist scholarship and modern Muslim reformist polemics for the past two hundred years, so that now it is a highly contested subject. Sufism can refer to a wide range of phenomena, including scriptural interpretation, meditative practices, master-disciple relationships, corporate institutions, aesthetic and ritual gestures, doctrines, and literary texts. As a generic descriptive term, however, Sufism is deceptive. There is no Sufism in general. All that we describe as Sufism is firmly rooted local contexts, often anchored to the very tangible tombs of deceased saints, and it is deployed in relation to lineages and personalities with a distinctively local sacrality. Individual Sufi groups or traditions in one place may be completely oblivious of what Sufis do or say in other regions.

'Yoga' is a term that may be even harder to define. Georg Feuerstein maintains that "Yoga is like an ancient river with countless rapids, eddies, loops, tributaries, and backwaters, extending over a vast, colourful terrain of many different habitats".[8] Some regard it mainly as a philosophy linked to important Sanskrit texts, particularly Patanjali's 'Yoga Sutras'. For others, yoga signifies primarily meditative ascetic practices frequently associated with the god Shiva in Hindu teachings, though yoga is also widespread in Buddhist and Jain contexts. The yogic material that the Sufis mostly encountered was a highly specialised tradition called hatha yoga (literally, 'the yoga of force'), associated with charismatic figures of the tenth to twelfth centuries, especially Matsyendranath and Gorakhnath. The lineage that preserves the hatha yoga teachings is known collectively as the Nath siddhas (adepts) or Kanphata ('split-ear') yogis, due to the distinctive wooden inserts and large rings they put in their ears during initiation.[9]

The early Nath yogis were associated with the erotic practices of Kaula Tantrism, and prominent in their pantheon are the feminine deities known as yoginis or female yogis. Hatha yoga has a much more complicated psycho-physical set of techniques than the classical yoga of Patanjali, and it is presented with a minimum of metaphysical explanation. Special practices include manipulation of subtle physiology including psychic centres called chakras, retention of semen, pronunciation of syllabic chants or mantras with occult efficacy, and the summoning of deities. Despite their ascetic emphasis on sexual restraint, the Kanphata yogis have become over the past millennium a recognisable caste.[10] Yet, in the attempt to provide even such brief descriptions of both Sufism and yoga, we are faced with an especially challenging problem arising from the gap between scholarly analyses of the history of religions and the way in which these traditions are appropriated in the global marketplace of contemporary thought, especially under the rubric of New Age spirituality.

Although the scholarly Orientalist argument about Sufism and yoga addressed issues of authenticity and dependence related to anxieties about Islam and the relegation of mysticism to India, the attraction of both Sufism and yoga today rests primarily on the extent to which both traditions can be seen as transcending any religious definition. The accelerating distrust of authority that still marks the legacy of the Enlightenment values experience over doctrine and authenticity over institutional approval.[11] The most popular forms of Sufism in Europe and America are those that minimise or ignore any form of Islamic identity. Rumi is the best-selling poet in America precisely because he is seen as going beyond all religions. With yoga the definitional problem in relation to religion is even more severe. Yoga is often seen as the very basis of all spirituality, or alternatively as a physical technique for stress reduction that can be embraced by anyone regardless of religious affiliation. According to some estimates, over five million Americans practice yoga, and in most cases they do so in settings (physical education etc.) that downplay or ignore any connection whatever with Hindu religious traditions.

A quick survey of recent library acquisitions on the topic of yoga yields a series of titles that emphasise its universal accessibility on 'yoga for Americans', 'yoga for all' and inevitably. Glossy magazines on yoga are available at supermarket counters, and newspapers describe the yoga fashion accessories available for today's yoginis.[12] So when we use the term yoga now, it carries multiple burdens the sublime philosophy of transcendence associated with Patanjali, the intricate and esoteric psycho-physical system of the Nath yogis, and the mass marketing category of yoga as the generic basis of mysticism in all religions. Modern scholarship is not immune from these grandiose concepts of yoga.[13] When one turns to the historical context for the encounter of Sufism and yoga, it is a curious coincidence that the arrival of Sufis in India took place not long after the Nath or Kanphata yogis became organised, that is by the beginning of the thirteenth century. While ascetic orders certainly had existed in India for many centuries, the Nath's appear to have had a remarkable success at this time. The Nath yogis did not observe the purity restrictions of Brahminical ritual society and were free to drop in for meals at Sufi hospices, which in turn were open to all visitors. While hardly representative of 'Hindu' culture, the yogis were perhaps the only Indian religious group with whom Sufis had much in common. This was also an encounter between two movements that shared overlapping interests in psycho-physical techniques of meditation, and which competed to some extent for popular recognition as wonder-workers, healers, and possessors of sanctity.[14] Moreover, in a country where cremation was the preferred funeral method, both groups practiced burial; Sufi tombs, to the untutored eye, must have fit the model of the lingam shrines or samadhis set up over yogis, who were customarily buried in the lotus position.[15] Similarity, between yogis and Sufis extended to the point that the heads of Nath yogi establishments became known by the Persian term pir, the common designation for a Sufi master. While it is sometimes suggested that this name was adopted defensively to deter

Muslim rulers from wiping the yogis out,[16] from the historical evidence it seems clear that many Muslim rulers were quite familiar with the characteristic specialities of yogis, and it is striking that the Mughals in became patrons of yogi establishments.[17] Acculturation by the yogis to selected Islamicate norms seems a more likely reason than the presumption of religious persecution for the yogis' adoption of such a title.[18]

The theoretical problem with the Orientalist influence model is that, even in cases where Sufis clearly recognise a particular technique (such as breath control) as being associated with Indian yogis, this does not explain the significance of the practice as adapted by Sufis. Recently, Jürgen Paul returned to the influence model to inquire into the case of Naqshbandi Sufis in Central Asia. Using what he calls a phenomenological comparison, he proposed a concept of Indian influence based on deliberate study, consideration, and adoption of religious practices such as vegetarianism, celibacy, and breath control. There seems to have been a clear awareness among these Naqshbandis that breath control, a central technique at least since the time of Baha' al-Din Naqshband (1390 A.D.), was also common among Indian yogis. Paul therefore concludes that these Central Asian Sufis were "inspired by non-Muslim Indian mystical techniques".[19] Yet the significance of this breath control technique would seem to be affected by the fact that, among these Naqshbandis, breath control invariably was used to accompany dhikr recitation formulas in order to make this meditation continuous, with a focus on such typically Islamic chants such as la ilaha illa Allah (there is no god but God). In other words, if breath control was used to enhance the effect of Islamic meditation formulas, to what extent can it be considered "inspired by non-Muslim Indian mystical techniques?".

Another example raises questions about the influence model, in this case concerning a major systematisation of Sufi psycho-physical meditative practice. Ala-al-Dawla Simnani (1336 A.D.) was one of the chief figures in the Kubrawi Sufi order in Central Asia, whose vast literary output was matched by his extensive activities in training disciples. Heir to an already highly developed system of meditation established by his teacher Nur al-Din Isfarayini (1317 A.D.) and others, Simnani incorporated earlier practices and articulated a spiritual method of considerable subtlety, based on interior visualisation of seven subtle centres (latifa,pl.lata'if) within the body, each associated with a particular prophet and a colour.[20] The system of seven subtle centres developed by Simnani underwent further evolution in India in the Naqshbandi order, from the fifteenth through to the late nineteenth century, resulting in a new assignment of six subtle centres to particular parts of the body. A typical version of the Naqshbandi subtle centres puts the heart (qalb) two fingers below the left breast, the spirit (ruh) two fingers below the right breast, the soul (nafs) beneath the navel, the conscience (sirr) in the middle of the breast, the mystery (khafi) above the eyebrows, and the arcanum (akhfa) at the top of the brain.[21] One could argue that the Naqshbandi -Kubrawi system has a certain similarity with the yogic concept of seven chakras or subtle nerve centres located along the region of the spine, although some of the Sufi centres are clearly unconnected with the spinal region. Both systems include visualisation of appropriate colours and sometimes images in particular bodily locations, so that one might assume either that the Sufi practices were based on earlier unspecified Indian yoga techniques, or that figures like Simani would have been interested in contemporary yogis.

From his biography, however, it appears that Simnani, much against his inclination, was forced to engage in disputations with Buddhist monks at the court of the Mongol ruler Arghun; in these debates, Simnani showed considerable theological hostility to the Buddhists. Although they were probably from Mahayana schools with highly developed yogic techniques of their own, Simnani showed no interest in discussing meditation practices with them.[22] Recent research has shown that there was considerable practical variation among Sufis in the number of subtle centres, the colours assigned to each subtle centre, and even their physical locations in the body. Arthur Buehler has described the adjustable Naqshbandi system of subtle centres as "a heuristic device for the disciple to develop a subtle body or a subtle field with which to travel in non-material realms".[23] Similar variations occur within hatha yoga practices.[24] Despite their comparability, however, the Sufi techniques do not seem to have any intrinsic relation with the psycho-physiology of yoga, and they rarely make reference to the characteristic yogic descriptions of subtle nerves (nadis), the breaths, the sun and moon symbolism, or the kundalini. In addition, Sufi texts contain a multileveled prophetology and mystical Quranic exegesis tied to each of the seven subtle centres, so that distinctive Islamic symbolisms are embedded in the system. As will be indicated below, some Naqshbandi Sufis like Ahmad Sirhindi showed explicit hostility toward the practices of yogis and Brahmins.

Major manuals of Sufi contemplative practice from remoter areas, such as Miftah al-falah or The Key to Salvation, by the Egyptian Sufi master Ibn of Alexandria (1309 A.D.), make no reference to any identifiable Indian yoga technique. Judgments about sources and influences of such practices necessarily ignore the significance accorded them in Sufi interpretations. Enamul Haq, who argued for the yogic origin of the Naqshbandi subtle centres, was forced to explain away the differences by begging the question, calling the Sufi system "quite imperfect and immature ...due to the ignorance of Ata' Allah[25] anatomical knowledge of the Sufis who were far inferior to the Indian Yogis with respect to the scientific knowledge of human body". [26] This being said, it is striking to see a very late Urdu text that makes explicit comparison between the Naqshbandi system of subtle centres and the yogic chakras. After giving a lengthy description of a six-centre version of the Naqshbandi method, Ghawth Ali Shah Qalandar Qadiri (1880 A.D.) remarked in conversation that "These six subtle centres are also in the Sannyasi teaching, the six lotuses (k'hat kanwal) or six chakras, according to the Yoga shastra". He then enumerated these six lotuses according to a complex yogic scheme that includes a different number of petals for each lotus, which are ordered according to the Sanskrit alphabet; these are depicted in a diagram included in the published version of his discourses, in the form of a long-stemmed plant with groups of petals bunched together at the level of each lotus. In the upper right corner of the diagram, there is also a drawing of a throne-like platform, with a marginal note on the diagram reading, "Here the student must visualise his guru or pir sitting on the throne, [thinking that] from the treasury of hidden emanation, an ocean of light has poured over my heart". In the brief comment that follows this diagram, Ghawth Ali Shah remarked, "The method of this practice is that through visualization one should transfer each [Sanskrit] letter from the petal to the inside of the stem. Having imagined the stem as a single great river, after reaching the brahmanda [the chakra at the crown of the skull], one transfers [the letter] above. When all the letters are collected above, then in due order the subtle centres become active, and the entire body becomes luminous". [27]

This account shows a remarkably detailed knowledge of yoga, gained probably through contact with nineteenth-century yogis, rather than from the vaguely titled book mentioned in this passage (when the transcriber of these discourses inserted the description of the lotuses and their petals, he introduced it only as coming from 'a certain sage' [kisi gyani]). Although Ghawth Ali Shah just a pose the Naqshbandi subtle centres and the yogic chakras as similar, this late comparison does not attempt to bridge the conceptual and technical gap between the two meditative systems. This kind of comparison is more a testimony to the author's willingness to bring in the evidence of Indian sages as external confirmation of doctrines and practices based on traditional Islamic sources. [28] In recent times, Naqshbandi Sufi leaders in northern India have taken significant steps to spread their teachings among Hindu disciples, including several Hindu masters who explain the Naqshbandi cosmology with terms from classical hatha yoga. These Naqshbandi branches (centred particularly on Kanpur) constitute what is in effect a new Sufi-based school of yoga, known as Ananda-yoga. Particularly important practices of these groups include silent recitation of the name Allah to awaken the chakras. The overall doctrine of the identity of the microcosm and the macrocosm, common to both Islamicate and Indic traditions, permits a wide-ranging series of analogies between Sufi notions of subtle centres with yogic chakras.[29] This recent development, which inverts the Orientalist view of the relation between Sufism and yoga, is a striking indication of the way in which the history of religion can defy the expectations of essentialism. Keeping in mind these cautions about the comparative approach, we can briefly survey here some important examples of how Sufis appropriated or interpreted yogic practices, with attention to the most important text, The Pool of Nectar.

The earliest sources, from the fourteenth century, depict Sufis with a range of reactions to the teaching and practices of the yogis, ranging from sceptical criticism to frank admiration. On the critical side, Sharaf al-Din Maneri (1381 A.D.), for instance, felt that contemporary yogis did not understand the full meaning of the sayings that they had inherited.[30] The Chishti saint Burhan al-Din Gharib (1337 A.D.) believed that a certain yogi of his acquaintance used fraudulent alchemical techniques and supplemented these with drugs and the assistance of spirits.[31] Some Sufis criticised yogic practices such as meditation and ascetic exercises, on the grounds that in themselves they were devoid of spiritual grace; following the prescribed Islamic religious duties was much more beneficial. Such was the position, not surprisingly, of the doctrinally emphatic Naqshbandi Sufi, Shaikh Ahmad Sirhindi (1624 A.D.), who regarded yogis, Brahmins, and other non-Muslim ascetics (such as Plato and other ancient Greek philosophers) as irremediably misguided.[32] Likewise, a Sufi teacher in India named Muhammad Muhyi-al-Din displayed considerable ambivalence when a disciple questioned him in 1748 A.D. about the divination techniques for estimating the end of one's life, as explained in an early version of The Pool of Nectar known as the Kamrubijaksa. 'This is the practice of the Yogis', he replied, 'this is not an activity of the community of Muhammad. Nevertheless, it is correct'.[33] All the same, considerable evidence shows that Sufis commented with interest on yogic techniques and concepts, and many of them seem also to have been familiar with versions of The Pool of Nectar. The Chishti master Nizam al-Din Awliya' (1325 A.D.) found one yogi's concept of bodily control impressive, and he was also intrigued by yogic accounts of the effect of different days of the month on the conception of children (until his master indicated to him that he would live a celibate life). His disciple Nasir al-Din Chiragh-i Dihli (1356 A.D.) commented in passing on the yogic practice of breath control in comparison to that practiced by Sufis:

"The essence of this matter is restraint of breath, that is, the Sufi ought to hold his breath during meditation. As long as he holds his breath, his interior is concentrated, and when he releases his breath, the interior is distracted, and it destroys his momentary state .... Therefore, the Sufi is he whose breath is counted. The adept is the master of breath; this has but a single meaning. The accomplished yogis, who are called siddha in the Indian language, breathe counted breaths." [34] Nasir al-Din's disciple Muhammad al-Husayni Gisu Daraz (1422 A.D.) felt that breath control as essential for Sufi disciples. In a manual of discipline composed in 1404, here marked, "Following the habit of stopping the breath, as is done among the yogis, is necessary for the disciple, but not everyone can do it to the extent that those people can. Those who follow this habit must completely abstain from association with women. Diminution of intake of food and drink permits the performance of required and supererogatory prayers in the case of one of fixed abode, and the traveller retains mobility. One should avoid idle talk. If control becomes habitual, many thoughts can be banished; thought is natural to the carnal soul." [35]

Nonetheless, Gisu Daraz was extremely careful to limit the extent to which yogic practice as acceptable. "Except for breath control, which is the specialty and support of the yogis, it is necessary for the disciple to avoid all their other kinds of practices. These two points which I have written respecting the yogis are also incumbent on [advanced] Sufis."[36] Another Chishti, Ashraf Jahangir Simnani (1425 A.D.), is credited by his biographer with a victory over a yogi, and he was also familiar with mantras of the Naths used for purposes of curing snakebite and similar purposes, which he regarded as magical charms (afsun).[37] The later Chishti master Abd al-Quddus Gangohi (1537 A.D.) was probably more familiar with the yoga of the Naths than anyone else in that order. He wrote Hindi verses on the subject under the pre-name 'Alakhdas' or 'Servant of the Absolute'. It is in connection with al-Quddus that we find the earliest external reference to the Arabic version of The Pool of Nectar, which he is said to have taught to a disciple, Sulayman Mandawi, in the late fifteenth century, in exchange for instruction in Qur'anic recitation.[38] He also composed a treatise called Rushd nama or The Book of Guidance with considerable yogic content.[39] Later masters the Chishti order such as Nizam al-Din Awrangabadi (1729 A.D.) and Hajji Imdad Allah (1899 A.D.) continued to include descriptions of yogic mantras in Hindi alongside Arabic dhikr formulas, together with explicit accounts of yogic postures (although the latter account tends to be much abbreviated). In this way Nizam al-Din Awrangabadi gave a brief account of yogic mantras in his lengthy survey of Sufi meditative practices, Nizam al-qulub or The Order of Hearts:

"Recollection (dhikr) in the Hindi language. Towards the sky [say] "tūn", and towards oneself [say] "hūn", though some also [say] "hūn" towards the heart. Or one says to the right, "uhi hi", and to the left, "wuhi hi". Or one says to the right, "inhāntūn", to the left, "inhāntūn", towards the direction of prayer (qibla), "inhāntūn", towards heaven, "uhāntūn". In the heart one strikes "inhāntūn", though some say towards the ground, "inhāntūn", towards heaven, "uhāntūn", and in the direction of the heart, "inhāntūn". Another recollection (dhikr) in the Hindi language. One sits cross-legged just like the position of the yogis. One turns the head and eye toward heaven and recites this recollection one thousand times or recites it even more. In the end a world favors one's wishes. One says this very word: "uhi uhi". But one of the eighty-four postures (Hindi baithak) has been selected as having the benefit and special quality of all the postures, and it is as follows. One sits cross-legged and brings up both feet, placing the sole of the left foot beneath the genitals, and holding the right foot near it. Then one looks at the stomach and brings the breath up and collects it at the naval and takes it toward the back. One closes the mouth and holds the tongue firmly on the palate. Then one practices magical imagination (wahm), that is, one internally thinks, "uhi hi", and one remains hungry and without sleep. If he remains three days together without food or sleep, and remains occupied with this practice, he attains an unconsciousness that produces in him the unveiling of hidden things. He then returns to consciousness or becomes enraptured and intoxicated (majdhub u mad'hush).[40]

This account of yogic mantras from the fifteenth chapter of this survey of dhikr techniques resembles the Hindi chant of Farid al-Din Ganj-i Shakkar, the only Hindi chant that Muhammad Ghawth (discussed below) included in his Arabic meditation manual, The Five Jewels.[41] Although it is said that Nizam al-Din Awrangabadi had contact with living yogis, he generally prefers to cite yogic practice via Sufi authorities and texts deriving from different Sufi orders.[42] Along with the Chishtis, it is probably the Shattari Sufis who most integrated yoga into their practice without any hesitation, giving particular emphasis to the mantra.[43] Though the historical origins of this Sufi order are obscure, it seems that it was introduced to India by Abd Allah Shattari (1485 A.D.), the first Sufi to use that name. The same order is known as the Ishqiyya or Bistamiyya in Iran and Central Asia. The latter name points to the association of the Shattaris with the Iranian Sufi Abu Yazid al-Bistami, one of the most powerful early representatives of the ecstatic form of Sufism. There are, on the other hand, traditions that link the Shattaris with the Qadiri order, which trace its origin to the master of sober Sufism, Junayd of Baghdad (910 A.D.). The characteristic meditative practice of repetition of the Qur'anic names of God (dhikr, plural adhkar) formed a prominent part of 'Abd Allah Shattari's teaching, through only fragments of his written work have surved.[44] Certainly in the work of Shaikh Baha' al-Din Shattari (1515 A.D.) there is evidence of an interest in Indian spiritual practices; his work Risala-i Shattariyya or The Shattari Treatise contains repetitions of divine names in Hindi, alongside the divine names in Arabic and Persian. The fourth and last chapter is entitled "On various Arabic, Persian, and Hindi adhkar, with attention to certain methods (suluk) of the yogis and their adhkar, which they recite with magical imagination (wahm), the sentences that they recite in meditation, and other incantations (da'awat) related to them". Shattari's teaching, though only fragments of his written work have survived.[45] Thus by the beginning of the tenth/sixteenth century, a member of the Shattari order was able to produce a systematic account of yogic mantras and visualisation practices, assimilated and even incorporated into the conceptual structure of Sufi tradition.[46]

In conclusion, how can we meaningfully situate Sufism and yoga, in the light of the preceding discussion? Let us sum up the evidence. Indian Sufis and Nath yogis regarded each other as distinguishable groups, with overlapping interests in psycho-physical discipline and with often competing roles as spiritual leaders. While some yogic practices were to a certain extent compatible with Sufi disciplines, it is historically impossible to derive one entire system from the other. Different Indian Sufi groups, particularly the Chishti and Shattari orders, incorporated certain yogic practices into their repertory of techniques, but this addition did not fundamentally alter the character of existing Sufi practices; Hindi mantras, for instance, were infrequent in Sufi texts and clearly subordinate to Arabic formulas of Qur'anic origin. The Pool of Nectar was probably the most important single literary source for the diffusion of knowledge about yoga through Islamicate languages. Sufis and yogis alike both felt the need periodically to take account of the other group, and this acknowledgement took the form of competing narratives, including conversion stories, liminal figures like Baba Ratan the hadith scholar, pseudonymous Sufi authorship of yogic texts, and the identification of primordial yogis with the esoteric prophets of Islam. The repeated insistence on the identification of Sufi and yogic themes reveals a stubborn sense of difference. All these observations suggest that we must find a way to describe this sense of difference without essentialism. If it is true that Sufis assimilated and adapted certain yogic practices, to what extent did Sufis show resistance to incorporating yoga into their own worldview? I would suggest that we can answer this question best by dividing the material into three separate categories: yogic practices, yogis as individuals belonging to an identifiable group, and the abstract notion of yoga as a religious doctrine. With regard both to yogic practices and yogis as individuals, there is a variable spectrum among Sufis, ranging from complete appropriation of certain yogic material (breath control, chants, meditation techniques, yogis, and even goddesses) to wary approval and even complete rejection; it is not possible to reduce this range of reactions to a single formula. A critical issue for assessing this process of assimilation is the character of the strategies of translation that Sufis adopted to present the Indic data in Islamicate garb. Our most notable text, The Pool of Nectar, presents a number of identifications between Islamic and Indic personalities; in addition to the identification of the three yogis with Islamic prophets, we are also told that Brahma is Abraham, and Moses is Vishnu. A brahmin is equivalent to a Muslim scholar (– alim), and a yogi is an ascetic (murtad). Equivalents are also provided for a couple of minor practices; the Hindi term japa or counted prayer is equivalent to prayer.[47] Yet, some extremely important yogic terms are entirely missing from this account. In all this Sufi literature discussing practices of the yogis, the term yoga is scarcely ever mentioned.[48] Likewise, the extremely important technical terms mantra, yantra (diagram), and chakra are not spelled out or mentioned, although the phenomena to which they refer are described at length and in detail with numerous examples. All these critical terms for yogic practice have been completely subordinated to Islamicate categories and represented by Arabic terms; mantra is replaced by dhikr, yantra by shakl (shape), chakra by mawda (place), and yoga itself by riyada (asceticism). Only with the benefit of Indological resources, which were unavailable to premodern readers of The Pool of Nectar and kindred texts, can we plausibly restore the Indic originals. While there seems to be a clear recognition among Sufis of the existence of the Nath Yogis as a sociological group, and of their practices as distinctive, the discursive tradition of Sufi teaching was powerful enough to make the independent existence of something called yoga irrelevant precisely because yogic practices could be assimilated into a Sufi perspective without much effort. In short, there is no Sufi concept of yoga as a separate system. It would probably be safe to say that there was likewise no hatha yoga concept of Sufism as a separate entity. The highly abstract language of essentialism contributes nothing to our understanding of this phenomenon of historical difference. The old Orientalist debate about yoga as the source of Sufism was based on a "strong misreading", denying the apparent significance of a tradition by triumphant announcement of origins and influences detected only by modern scholars. Anxieties about textual authority, and about the very existence of Islam, continue to fuel such grandiose projects, as one can see in the recent attempt of 'Christoph Luxenburg' (a pseudonym) to unveil the Qur'an as a text, not written in Arabic, but in Syriac, in this way proposing that the entire Islamic tradition is based on a faulty reading of a Christian lectionary. Luxenburg's announcement that the 'white-eyed' virgins of the Qur'an are white raisins was considered important enough to be featured on the front page of the New York Times, which does not often happen with large German tomes on Semitic philology.[49] Meanwhile, the New Age essentialism views Sufism and yoga as forms of spirituality that contest for the position of the mysticism that is most authentic, because it is least authoritative. Despite their appeals to the history of religions, neither of these approaches is particularly historical. Against such strong misreading's, and their quest to find the essential origins of religion either in debunked sacred texts or in a bland universalism, we can offer alternate forms of interpretation. Wendy Doniger favours a more provisional form of categorisation: "An appropriate metaphor, I think, for the network of diffused narratives with no common origin is not the family tree that folklorists used to favor, but rather a banyan tree, which must have an original root but sends down so many subsequent roots from its branches (other variants) that one can no longer tell which was the original. The pattern of banyan roots is rather like a Venn diagram of family resemblances, or the web of an invisible spider."[50]

In this sense, polythetic approaches to categorising religious traditions offer a flexibility and an attention to historical difference that is not held hostage to the all-or-nothing comparativist constructions of source and influence. For religious studies scholars, an important task for the future will be to explain these non-essentialist interpretations of religion in a way that can be relevant to the broader public spheres beyond the academy.

References

1. R. C. Zaehner, Mysticism Sacred and Profane: An Inquiry into some Varieties of Praeternatural Experience (New York, 1961), p. 160.

2. E. H. Palmer, Oriental Mysticism: A Treatise on Sufiistic and Unitarian Theosophy of the Persians (London, 1867; eprint ed., London, 1969), pp. x–xi. Palmer dedicated this treatise to Napoleon III, whom he described as a great patron of "European Orientalism".

3. Smith, Drudgery Divine, p.47.

4. Ernst, "Islamization of Yoga".

5. To gauge the relative importance of these yoga practices for Sufism considered broadly, I would point to a cent encyclopedia article on Sufism, in which I devoted two sentences to yoga; see "Tasawwuf" Richard Martin (ed.), Encyclopedia of Islam and the Muslim World (New York, 2003), 2, pp.684–690.

6. For the larger context of this translation movement, see Carl W. Ernst, "Muslim Studies of Hinduism? A Reconsideration of Persian and Arabic Translations from Sanskrit", Iranian Studies, 36 (2003), pp. 173–195.

7. Ernst, Shambhala Guide to Sufism, Chapter1.

8. Georg Feuerstein, Yoga: The Technology of Ecstasy (Los Angeles, 1989).

9. David Gordon White, The Alchemical Body: Siddha Traditions in Medieval India (Chicago, 1996); George Weston Briggs, Gorakhnath and the Kanphata Yogis (Calcutta, 1938; reprinted Delhi, 1980), pp. 179–250; Shashibhusan

Das Gupta, Obscure Religious Cults (3rd ed., Calcutta, 1976), pp. 191–210, 392–398; Feuerstein, Yog a, pp.277–302.

10. Daniel Gold and Ann Grodzins Gold, "The Fate of the Householder Nath", History of Religions, 24 (1984), pp. 113–132.

11. "The modern age conflates authoritarianism with authority, hence, tends to suspect the latter (and its poetic epresentatives) as in fact embodying the former. Only when the notion of authority becomes a pejorative social term can anxiety concerning it spread to other areas like literature and criticism" (Renza, "Influence", p. 197).

12. Sara Steffens, "Yoga Baring: Find your Inner Fashionista with Exercise Gear", Raleigh News & Observer, 15 March 2004.

13. Frits Staal, Exploring Mysticism: A Methodological Essay (Berkeley, 1975).

14. For a stimulating sociological comparison of Hindu and Islamic asceticism, Marc Gaborieau, "Incomparables ou vrais jumeaux? Les renonc,ants dans l'hindousime et dans Islam", Annales: Histoire, Sciences Sociales, 57 (2002), pp. 71–92.

15. Briggs, Gorakhnath and the Kanphata Yogis, pp.39–40; Mircea Eliade, Yoga: Immortality and Freedom, trans. Willard Trask (Princeton, NJ, 1989), pp. 422–423.

16. G. S. Ghurye, Indian Sadhus (Bombay, 1964), p. 139, argues protective dissimulation from the proximity of Yogi shrines and pilgrimage sites to Muslim population centres and the alleged conversion of two shrines at Gorakhpur into mosques by Ala » al-Din Khalji (d. 1316) and Awrangzeb (d. 1707). And B. N. Goswamy and J. S. Grewal, The Mughals and the Yogis of Jakhbar, Some Madad-i-Ma – ash and Other Documents (Simla, 1967).

17. On Sufi terms in yogi centres, see V eronique Bouillier, Ascetes et Rois: Un Monastere de Kanphata Yogis au Nepal (Paris, 1997), pp. 91–93.

18. Jurgen Paul, "Influences indiennes sur la naqshbandiyya d'Asie centrale?", Cahiers d'Asie Centrale, 1–2 (1996), pp. 203–217. In a similar vein, William S. Haas observed that the dhikr technique of the Algerian Rahmaniyya order "has as its centre a thoroughly elaborated technique of breathing, obviously of Indian origin", and so he speculated that the nineteenth-century founder of the order must have gone to India; see "The Zikr of the Rahmanija-Order in Algeria: A Psycho-physiological Analysis", Moslem World, 33 (1943), pp. 16–28, citing p. 18.

19. Henry Corbin, En Islam iranien: Aspect's spirituals et philosophiques, vol.3,

20. Les Fid'eles d'amour, Shīisme et soufisme, Biblioth'eque des Id'ees (Paris, 1972), pp. 275–355; N ūruddī in Abdurrahm an-i Isfarāyinī, Le R'ev'elateur des myst eres: Kāshif al-Asrār, ed. and trans. Hermann Landolt (Paris, 1986), "Etude Preliminaire", pp. 38–49.

21. Muhammad Dhawqi Shah, Sirr-i dilbaran (4th printing, Karachi, 1405/1985), pp. 298–299.

22. Jamal J. Elias, The Throne Carrier of God: The Life and Thought of Ala-ad-dawla as-Simnani (Albany, 1995), pp. 18, 26; for Simnani's concept of subtle substances or centres, see pp. 79–99.

23. Arthur Frank Buehler, Sufi Heirs of the Prophet: The Indian Naqshbandiyya and the Rise of the Mediating Sufi Shaykh, Studies in Comparative Religion (Charleston, SC, 1998), p. 112; cf.pp.103–116 for a full account of the latifa system.

24. Agehananda Bharati, The Tantric Tradition (Garden City, N.Y., 1970).

25. Ibn-Ata' Allah al-Sikandari, Miftah al-falah wa misbah al-arwah (Egypt, 1381/1961); Ibn Ata' Allah, The Key Salvation and the Lamp of Souls, trans. Mary Ann Koury Danner (Cambridge, 1996).

26. Muhammad Enamul Haq, A History of Sufi-ism in Bengal, Asiatic Society of Bangladesh Publication no. 30 (Dacca, 1975), p. 139. This study, based on a 1937 dissertation, relies to a considerable extent on older Orientalist literature.

27. Gul Hasan Qadiri, Tadhkira-i ghawthiyya (Delhi, 1298/1881), pp. 148–150. This section is omitted from the English translation of this text, Gul Hasan, Solomon's Ring: The Life and Teachings of a Sufi Master, trans. HasanAskari (London, 1998), but see pp. 185–193 for "Encounters with Hindu Sages".

28. See the brief section entitled "Conversation with Mahapurusa Sannyasi Mata", ibid., pp. 139–144 (trans. Askari, pp. 155–160), which acts as a Hindu supplement to four lengthy chapters on the divine unity based on the Qur'an, hadith, and Sufi authorities (pp. 22–139). Other passing references to yogic practices discussed by Ghawth Ali Shah are found on pp. 52 (a mantra with translation), 332 (Hindi verses ascribed to Amir Khusraw on the anahita or unstruck sound).

29. Thomas D¨ahnhardt, "La scienza sufica dei centri sottili presso una scuola contemporanea di yoga", Asiatica Venetiana, 2 (1997), pp. 19–29; id., Change and Continuity in Indian Sufism: A Naqshbandi Mujaddidi Branch in the Hindu Environment (New Delhi, 2002).

30. Simon Digby, "Encounters with Yogis in Indian Sufi Hagiography", unpublished paper presented at the Seminar on Aspects of Religion in South Asia, University of London, January 1970, p.6.

31. Carl W. Ernst, Eternal Garden: Mysticism, History, and Politics at a South Asian Sufi Center, SUNYSeriesin Muslim Spirituality in South Asia (Albany, 1992), p. 328, n.361.

32. Ahmad Sirhindi, Maktubat-i imam-i rabbani (2 vols., Karachi, 1392/1972; reprint ed., Istanbul, 1977), I, p. 130 (letter 52); I, p. 366 (letter 221); I, p. 394 (letter 237); I, p. 666 (letter 313); II, p. 157 (letter 55).

33. Kamrubijaksa, Pakistan National Museum, Karachi, MS 1957–1060/18–1, fol.2b (marginal comment).

34. Nasir al-Din Mahmud Chiragh-i Dihli, Khayr al-majalis, comp. Hamid Qalandar, ed. Khaliq Ahmad Nizami, Publication of the Department of History, Muslim University, no. 5, Studies in Indo-Muslim Mysticism, 1 (Aligarh, 1959), pp. 59–60 (session 12).

35. Gisu Daraz, Khatima-i adab al-muridin al-ma–ruf bi-khatima, Urdutrans.Mu–in al-Din Darda'i (Karachi, 1976), no. 168, p.158.

36. Ernst, Eternal Garden, pp.90–91.

37. Ashraf Jahangir Simnani, Lata'if-i ashrafi, comp. Nizam Gharib Yamani (2 vols., Delhi, 1295/1878), II, p. 396.

38. Simon Digby, "Abd Al-Quddus Gangohi (1456–537 A.D.): The Personality and Attitudes of a Medieval Indian Sufi", Medieval India, A Miscellany, III (1975), pp. 1–66, citing p. 36, equivalent to Rukn al-Din Quddusi, Lata'if-I Quddusi (Delhi, 1311/1894), p. 41, anecdote 5. From this source it is known that – Abd al-Quddus composed a Risala-i qudsi, possibly in answer to Mandawi's questions on the yogic text, and a manuscript of this text is preserved in Lahore; cf. Muhammad Bashir Husayn, Fihrist-i makhtutat-i Sherani (Lahore, 1969), II, p. 224, no.1236. On examination, however, the manuscript turns out to be a conventional Sufi treatise with no reference to ogic practices. On Sulayman Mandawi (d. 945/1538–9, reportedlyagedover150), whose Qur'anic recitation was inspired by the Prophet and Ali during his fifty years of austerities in Mecca, see Mandawi, pp. 243–244.

39. For bibliographic references S.A.A.Rizvi,"SufisandNˆatha Yogis in Mediaeval Northern India (XII to XVI Centuries)", Journal of the Oriental Society of Australia, 7 (1970), pp. 119–133, citing p. 132, quoting Rukn al-Din's Lata'if-i Quddusi,p.41; id., A History of Sufism in India, vol.I, Early Sufism and its History in India to 1600 A.D.(Delhi,1978), p. 335;S.C.R.Weightman,"The Text of Alakh Bani", in R. S. McGregor (ed.), Devotional literature in South Asia: Current research, 1985–8 (Cambridge, 1992), pp. 171–178. Gangohi's knowledge of yoga is discussed at length by Digby in "Abd Al-Quddus".

40. Nizam al-Din Awrangabadi, Nizam al-qulub (Delhi, 1309/1891–2), p. This text is discussed in detail in Ernst and Lawrence, Sufi Martyrs of Love, Chapter 2.

41. Oral commentaries on these Hindi mantras, suggesting a simple mystical interpretation: "uhānn" resembles modern Hindi for "you are there", while "inhāntūn" sounds like "you are here", so the chant would underscore the presence of God everywhere. Thanks to the late Prof. M. R. Tarafdar for this suggestion.

42. K. A. Nizami, Tarikh-i mashayikh-i Chisht (Delhi, 1985), V, pp. 174–175; cf. Digby, "–Abd al-Quddus", p. 51. In the Kashkul-i Kalimi (Delhi, n.d.), Shah Kalim Allah (p. 30) describes the single most efficacious of the 84 postures of yoga according to Shaykh Baha' al-Din Qadiri (Shattari?), and he explains the yogi "unstruck sound" (pp. 40–41) with reference to the comments of Miyan Mir of Lahore (Qadiri) and Shaykh Yahya Madani (Chishti).

43. See Khaliq Ahmed Nizami, "The Shattari Saints and Their Attitude towards the State", Medieval India Quarterly, III (1950), pp. 56–70; Syed Hasan Askari, "A Fifteenth Century Shuttari Sufi Saint of North Bihar", Proceedings of the 13th Indian History Congress (1950), pp. 148–157; M. M. Haq, "The Shuttari Order of Sufism in India and its Exponents in Bengal and Bihar", Journal of the Asiatic Society of Pakistan, 16 (1971), pp. 167–175;S.A.A.Rizvi,A History of Sufism in India (Delhi, 1983), II, pp. 151–173.

44. Abd al-Haqq Muhaddith Dihlawi al-Bukhari, Akhbar al-akhyar fi asrar al-abrar, ed. Muhammad Abd al-Ahad (Delhi, 1332/1913–4), p. 176. Two manuscripts reportedly containing works by – – Abd Allah Shattari are Risala-I Abd Allah Shattari, MS Khudabakhsh Library, Patna: and Tawba wa dhikr, an anonymous treatise containing sayings Hallaj and – Abd Allah Shattari, MS Karachi, National Museum 1965–210–21, cit. Ahmad Munzawi, Fihrist-I-Mushtarak-i Nuskha-ha-yi Khatti-i Farsi-i Pakistan (Islamabad, 1363/1405/1984), III, p. 1365, no.2447.

45. Baha' al-Din ibn Ibrahim al-Ansari Shattari, Risala-i Shattariyya, MS297/61 no. 318, Osmania University, Hyderabad, available as microfilm 1018, Middle East collection, University of Chicago, fols. 2a–3a. Unfortunately, this copy lacks the fourth chapter. The use of the term imagination (wahm) is characteristic of The Pool of Nectar (ch. VII).

46. See Eth ′e, no. 1913, col.1060; numerous other copies are found in libraries in India and Pakistan. See also the undated work by Ishaq (a disciple of one Abd al-Rahman Shattari), titled Ma'rifat-i anfas, MS873(i) Persian (suppl. cat. I), Asiatic Society, Calcutta, which Dara N. Marshall described as "a Persian version of a Hindu tract metaphysics"; Mughals in India, A Bibliography (Bombay, 1967), no. 728, p.207. From the title, The Knowledge of Breaths, it appears to deal with breath control.

47. Ernst, "Islamization of Yoga", Chart 4, for these translations.

48. Shah Kalim Allah in passing refers to the postures of yoga (baithak-i jog) and mentions "the endless sound (sawt-i sarmadi), which in yoga (jog) they call an a hid [anahita]" (Kashkul-i Kalimi, pp.30, 39). But these mentions of yoga (jog) are extremely rare.

49. New York Times (2 March 2002). Luxenburg's book was also the subject of an article in Newsweek (25 July 2003), which was banned in Pakistan. For a critical review of Luxenburg's book, see Franc‚ois de Blois in Journal of Qur'anic Studies, 5 (2003), pp. 92–97. For the importance of the debunking of the Qur'an as a theme in recent Euro-American culture, see Ernst, Following Muhammad, Chapter 3.

50. Doniger, The Implied Spider, p.139. For a Venn diagram-style description of Chishti Sufism, see Ernst and Lawrence, Sufi Martyrs of Love, pp.2–4.

Appendix 8
Interface of Qawwali in Sufism

Hindustani classical music is the style of Indian classical music found throughout the northern Indian subcontinent. It is a tradition that originated in Vedic ritual chants and has been evolving since the twelfth century CE. Music was first formalized in India in connection with preserving the shruti texts, primarily the four [1] Vedas. The formal aspects of the chant are delineated in the Sama Veda, with certain aspects, for example, the relation of chanting to meditation, elaborated in the Chandogya Upanishad (ca. eighth century BC). Priests involved in these ritual chants were called samans and several ancient musical instruments such as the conch (shankh), lute (veena), flute (bansuri), trumpets and horns were associated with this and later practices of ritual singing.

In the Sanskritic tradition, the Sama Veda outlined the ritual chants for singing the verses of the Rig Veda, particularly for offerings of soma. It proposed a tonal structure consisting of seven notes. The most important text on music in the ancient canon is Bharata's Natya Shastra, composed around the third century. Narada's Sangita Makarandha treatise, from about 1100 A.D., is the earliest text where rules like those of current Hindustani classical music can be found. Jayadeva's Gita Govinda from the twelfth century was perhaps the earliest musical composition sung in the classical tradition. In the thirteenth century, Sharngadeva composed the Sangita Ratnakara, which has names such as the turushkatodi ('Turkish todi'), revealing an influx of ideas from Islamic culture. Much of the musical forms innovated merged with the Hindu tradition, and were composed in the popular language of the people (as opposed to Sanskrit) in the works of composers like Kabir or Nanak and became a part of a larger Bhakti tradition, which strongly related to the Vaishnavite movement and remained influential across several centuries; notable figures include Jayadeva (eleventh century), Vidyapati (1375 A.D.), Chandidas (fourteenth to fifteenth century) and Meerabai (1555–1603 A.D.). Jayadeva's Gita Govinda delineates the love of Krishna for Radha, the milkmaid, his faithlessness, and subsequent return to her, and is taken as symbolical of the human soul's straying from its true allegiance but returning at length to the god which created it.

The advent of Islamic rule under the Delhi Sultanate, and later the Mughal Empire, over northern [2] India caused considerable cultural interchange. This spurred the fusion of Hindu and Muslim ideas to bring forth new forms of musical synthesis like qawwali and khyal in addition to tarana, tappa, thumri and ghazal. The Bhakti poets eulogize the 'madhurya' aspect of Lord Krishna's personality as they see in it a metaphor for the union of the individual with the cosmic, the prakriti principle merging with the purusha (Khullar 2003) which resonates with the Sufi concept of seeker and sought and blends seamlessly with the existing repertoire of music, philosophy, and language. The most influential musician of the Delhi Sultanate period was Amir Khusro (1253–1325 A.D.), sometimes called the father of modern Hindustani classical and Sufi music. A composer in Persian, Turkish, Arabic as well as Braj Bhasha, he is credited with systematizing many aspects of Hindustani music. He created the qawwali genre, which fuses Persian melody and beat on a dhrupad-like structure. He is also credited with inventing instruments such as the sitar and tabla and introducing them into the system of music during his lifetime

Qawwali: A Vehicle for Obtaining Ecstasy and Marifat

Comparable to the Greek concept of gnosis, marifat indicates an inner knowledge not attainable by normal means. The words (kalam) set in the music create an intangible interplay between form and content, dwelling on certain words to give them a wider context, creating great depth in the apparently simple language of certain Sufi texts. The qawwal often dwells on one phrase or sentence, indicating both the obvious and hidden content by emphasizing and repeating various words and syllables, taking the audience into the discovery of hitherto not obvious meanings till all meanings are disclosed. A spinning wheel thus changes from a household instrument into the wheel of life, or the wheel of hope, depending on the shift of emphasis in one sentence (Nayyar 1988). It is often this element that transcends linguistic barriers. Qawwali shares with mystical Islam, the belief that knowledge can be imparted through entertainment (Nayyar 1988).[3] One of the objectives of a qawwali and the qawwali singer is to induce trance in a group of listeners in a communal ritualized setting (Nayyar 1988). The receptiveness of the listeners, although connected with intention and readiness to go into trance, rests on cultural mechanisms as opposed to natural forces all too often credited with a mysterious power beyond explanation.

The discontinuity of individual existence is complemented with the continuity of musical culture. The skill of the qawwal is severely tested before an audience not familiar with these concepts, but a master is able to move entire audiences to a hal, even if they do not understand a single word. Regular attendees of qawwali sessions often use the concept of travel when they speak of their experience during a qawwali. They feel as if they are travelling to another domain or plane, called hal, literally 'state of mind', and is often used to denote musically induced ecstasy. This ecstasy can range from rhythmic moving of the head, dreamy dancing, to such extremes as violent convulsions of the body, depending on the person affected. The society around the individual accepts this ritualized loss of control and no stigma is attached to this state; and after recovery, the individual carries on as if nothing had happened (Nayyar 1988). The last stage of hal is fana, the closest analogue of which is the Buddhist concept of nirvana. In this stage, the plane of worldly consciousness is dissolved and the ultimate union with the eternal is achieved. Occasionally, cases of death during a qawwali session have been recorded, and it is believed that the one who dies in such a manner has achieved fana. Saint Hazrat Qutubuddin Bakhtiar Kaki is said to have died in 1236 while in a musical trance induced by a qawwali.

1.   The All-male Nature of Qawwali

From the early beginnings of Islam, the public sphere was an exclusively male domain. Women did participate in scholarship and even warfare in extraordinary conditions, but the realm of worship, at best, permitted equal but separate action. Women were allowed to enter the sanctum sanctorum of a Sufi pir's dargah. However, a music religious gathering had only men, and this remains predominant to this day. Some notable exceptions have started appearing with the advent of women qawwals like Abida Parveen and Reshma. According to Eaton, the bulk of folk poetry written by the Sufis of Deccan was sung by village women while engaged in various household chores. There are several versions of charkha-nama (while spinning cotton) and chakki-nama (while grinding grain), as also lun-nama (lullaby), shadi-nama (marriage songs) and suhagan-nama (married women songs). It may be noted here that the first three activities are of a mundane but rhythmic nature and the Sufi verses could be sung to their rhythm.

2.   Language of Qawwali

Initially, the Persian language or Farsi with its rich literary tradition of mysticism became rapidly identified with Islam and Sufism in South Asia. However, the languages of South Asia Purbi (the language of Bihar) and Braj Bhasha were freely used by Amir Khusro in his compositions. Traditional qawwali starts with an invocation in Farsi, moving to Punjabi or Urdu and moving further eastwards with Hindi and/or Purbi. This west to east transition reflects the transitional link in keeping with the missionary form of qawwali for the propagation of Islam in South Asia, building bridges between linguistic and cultural regions. Deccan Urdu and Bengali are used in those parts in lieu of Braj or Purbi. In Bengal, Lalon Fakir (1774–1890 A.D.) is an iconic figure of religious tolerance whose songs have [4] inspired and influenced many poets and social and religious thinkers, including Ravindranath Tagore Nobel laureate and national poet of India, especially West Bengal and Kazi Nazrul Islam, the national poet of Bangladesh, amongst others. Lalon Fakir is also regarded as the founder of the baul music of Bengal. Bauls constitute a heterogeneous syncretic religious sect and a musical tradition. Most members are Vaishnava Hindus and Sufi Muslims[5]. At times when language is likely to be a barrier in connecting with the audience, the qawwals rely heavily on the musical form and rhythm to convey the concepts, achieve a trance, and induce ecstasy. Veteran qawwals achieve this with a high degree of success. A fine example would be Nusrat Fateh Ali Khan Saheb achieving this with Western audiences and achieving critical acclaim. In fact, the reason for the sudden recent popularity of qawwali beyond the borders of South Asia is this ability of mature qawwals to alter the consciousness of the audience in a display of skill and virtuosity amongst non-native and multicultural audiences. For an audience that cannot understand the content/lyrics of the qawwali, the use of rhythm is the basic matrix through which the variation and pitch of the voice is the unique musical experience that brings about a spiritual experience.

3.   The Setting and Seating of Qawwals

A usual qawwali traditionally takes place at the shrine of a saint or at the meeting place of a Sufi order. The usual day for performance at a shrine is a Thursday. A major performance usually takes place at the annual festival (urs; literally, the passing of a spiritual leader from his finite body to the eternal) of a shrine. Several qawwals sing/perform in honour of the pir whose urs is being celebrated. A muqabala or competition can be assumed to have begun at these urs as all qawwals attempt to do their best for the pir during the urs. Traditionally, it is a pious religious performance shorn of any technical support or showmanship. Everyone, both the qawwals and the audience, sit on the ground cross-legged in a courtyard facing the shrine. Even if the audience is large, traditionally, no microphones are used and the qawwals strong voice rings clearly across the courtyard to the audience. Also, traditionally, the master singer called mohri sits in the middle, facing the dargah directly, as if addressing the pir. The tabla player sits just behind him, while the prompter (with the books and manuscripts for the words of the mystic singing) sits behind him slightly to the left shoulder. The mohri is usually flanked on both sides by two singers with harmoniums, daflis and manjiras (avazia), while the rest of the chorus is aligned on both sides in two rows, with the better singers up front. Often, another good singer sits to the left of the avazia. This singer has sufficient knowledge of musical theory and supports the lead singer. The creation of the 'backup' singer was prompted by the fact that qawwal groups were often a leading pair of brothers or a father-and-son duo. Usually, everyone sits a little behind the lead singer as a mark of respect. There is an undefined hierarchy, usually on account of skill, seniority and/or birth, and those lower in hierarchy would typically sit behind those higher in hierarchy. This is often referred to as qayada. However, this is undergoing some change with the inclusion of technology (microphones, sound mixers, etc.) for stage performances and studio recordings. Keeping the audience experience in perspective, placing, and positioning of singers and instruments is undergoing changes.

4. The Performance

Qawwali in South Asia is usually performed by a group of about eleven performers (traditionally, the number was odd, but this number is changing in present times). It is reminiscent of the pir mureed/guru shishya system of imparting knowledge and leading towards enlightenment. According to Chand Nizami, the original style of performing a qawwali was only voice and tali (hand clapping) and only in shrines and hospices. Over a period, some folk music instruments came into the performance, possibly a spillover from those used during bhajans and kirtans.[6] The qawwali starts with the alap, that is, only the lead singer invoking God, Prophet and the pir through a mystical couplet, and is marked by complete silence from other members of the group and audience, setting the atmosphere for the ecstatic experience that qawwali creates. This period is used by the performers to scan the audience for sensitized individuals or group of individuals who can be addressed with ease. Gathering the momentum of the first stage, the qawwals launch themselves into the main body of the qawwali, in which rhythm is introduced with a moderate tempo. The tempo is slowly increased, and the audience is carefully observed. Any line or musical mode that touches the audience or the master of ceremonies is repeated with renewed fervour to induce trance.

5. Musical Instruments

The rhythm is provided by hand clapping (tali) and percussion instruments, that is, the two-sided drums (dholak and /or pakhwaz) and/or a pair of drums (tabla) have been the traditional accompaniments of folk music all over the Indian subcontinent. Small hand-held cymbals (khanjira) and dafli, a drum with cymbals, are also often used during the rendition of qawwali. Harmoniums are also now a permanent fixture of the qawwali, often played by the lead singer himself. Occasionally, the stringed instrument, sarangi, also makes an appearance. In fact, minimal local/traditional instruments are the accompaniments.

6. Apparel and Behaviour

However, there is a strict religious dress code and behaviour code during the performance of Sufi music globally. Traditional performers typically dress in black or white-coloured loose traditional clothes along with head dress. Other sober colours such as grey or brown are often used by seniors. A green scarf/kaffieh is allowed too. Some of the younger traditional singers from India have started using a red jacket, inspired from film apparel, that is frowned upon by the seniors.[7] The women performers of Sufi music from Iran wore a flowing blue garment that revealed only their faces and hands. The groups from Turkey, Morrocco, Tunisia and Egypt made it clear to the audience that it was a religious performance and appropriate decorum was expected from the audience.

In conclusion with the success of Nusrat Fateh Ali Khan, Junoon and Shergill, large-scale public performances of the genre began, and the subgenre techno-qawwali has come into existence. Techno-qawwali is a qawwali or lengthy lyrics set in funky music with heavy beats. This genre/subgenre of music is very popular with young people in the twenty-first century. It needs to be noted that the median age for the population of India and Indian subcontinent is under 30 years. [8] While the majority population is young and identifies with the techno-qawwali, traditional qawwalis in the dargahs continue to be performed following all the rules of a spiritual rendition. But, in recent times, as the qawwals are invited to sing/perform outside the shrine, they are flooded with requests to sing/ perform qawwalis of choice, filmi qawwali and/or techno-qawwali, by the audience who neither know the differences between the genres nor care. While the older generation of qawwals do not usually oblige, the younger ones often do due to economic pressures and the need to encash on the current popularity of qawwali and Sufi music. In the Islamic world, Sufi music of the region is not used in films since it is regarded as sacred and not to be mixed up with films that are purely for entertainment. 'Sama' (whirling dervishes) is an important cultural offering of Turkey and is often showcased abroad and for the uninitiated. But the audience is informed about its sacred antecedents in advance and told to maintain the decorum befitting a sacred ritual. No audience requests of any kind are entertained.[9] It may be said with a fair degree of surety that Sufi music, though a genre which has deep spiritual and religious antecedents, has never had any fixed form of performance. It was always a collective rendition of philosophical verses in the local language, set to local music, as could be found from the varying style of rendition by the various groups from across the Islamic world. In India, it adapted to the Hindustani classical music, changing its own form into qawwali, goma, dammal, baul fakiri, etc., as well as deeply influencing the entire genre of Hindustani classical music in a way that it is difficult to differentiate the two definitively. The Master of Music called 'pandits' if they were Hindus and 'ustads' if they belonged to the Islamic faith performed the genres seamlessly, singing the praise of the Lord of the other's faith without the smallest hesitation for centuries, creating a syncretic culture of Hindustani music in which the philosophical verses of either faith were set and embellished by their individual talent. In the current context, Sufi music has adapted to the popular culture of techno and pop music. It is a natural progression of the philosophical thoughts and popular music of the times. While the qawwals do so due to economic reasons and to ride the current wave of popularity of Sufi music, it is however just a natural progression in the consumption of Sufi music which has throughout set philosophical verses in common language and to popular music of the people. Studying the effect of this new wave of fusion would make another study later, mapping the effect that the music has had on the philosophical verses and vice versa, of the effect the philosophical verses have had on the currently popular heavy metals music. However, without doubt, Sufi music is achieving its traditional purpose of binding diverse people together with the message of peace and universal brotherhood through philosophical verses set in language and music well known to and well understood by them.

References

1. Retrieved 29 June 2013, http://www.omenad.net/page.php?goPage=%2 Farticles%2FBSV_samintro.htm.
2. Retrieved 29 June 2013, https://en.wikisource.org/wiki/The_Encyclopedia_ Americana_(1920)/Jayad.
3. Available at http://www.osa.co.uk/qawwali_history.html.
4. Interview of a baul–fakiri–qawwali music group from Bangladesh with the first author in 2012.
5. (Encyclopaedia Britannica Online, 2007; The Times of India 2010).
6. Interview of Chand Nizami who is the at the Nizamuddin shrine, New 2012.
7. Interview of Ahmed Sidi who is the author in New Delhi, 6 February 2013, and observation attires during the various performances during the research period.
8. Available at http://thebollywoodzone.com/qawwalis-are-back-as-techno-qawwali/.
9. Interview of Ahmet Erdogam, manager Turkish Sama Group, Turkey, by the author in New Delhi, 7 March 2012.

Appendix 9

The Contribution of Sufis to Peace

The contribution of the Indian Sufis to society lies in their sincere and dedicated struggle to find a unity for the heterogeneous elements that make up its totality. They appreciated the multi-racial, multi-religious and multilingual pattern of Indian society and, to use Rabindranath Tagore's words, 'set at naught all differences of men, by the overflow of their consciousness of God'. For them God was not a logical abstraction of unity, but a living reality who can be approached through the service of mankind. Their efforts were, therefore, directed towards the creation of a healthy social order free from dissensions, discords, and conflicts. It was a herculean task, but they undertook it as a divine mission. In love, faith, toleration, and sympathy they found the supreme talisman of human happiness. Shaikh Nizam-u'd-din Auliya often cited in his assemblies a remark of Shaikh Abu Said Abul Khair (ob. 1049) that though there were myriads of routes and roads leading to God, none was quicker and more effective than bringing happiness to the hearts of men. Ibn Battuta found in Damascus a trust which existed for providing balm to afflicted hearts.

The Sufi weltanschauung was based on three basic postulates which determined their attitude towards God, man, and society. All people are the children of God on earth (الخلق عيال الله) . The Sunnan-i-Abu Da'ud reports that the Prophet used to pray at night: 'Oh God! I bear witness that all they (أنا أشهد أن العباد كلهم اخوة) creatures are brothers. Sadi said that the reason for human brotherhood was that all human beings were made of the self-same clay and were as interdependent on each other as the limbs in the human body. Once Dara Shukoh asked Shah Muhibb-ullah of Allahabad, a distinguished saint of the Chishti order, if religion permitted making a distinction between a Hindu and a Muslim. The saint's emphatic reply was 'no'. To strengthen his point further he said the Prophet was sent as a 'Blessing for all Mankind' (رحمت للعالمين) and therefore no distinction could be made between one individual, and another based on religion (Maktubat-i Shah Muhibbullah, MS). Shaikh Hamid-u'd-din Nagauri, a distinguished disciple of Khwaja Mu'in-ud-din Chishti of Ajmer, did not permit his disciples to use the categories of kafir and momin as the basis of any social discrimination. Shaikh Abdul Quddus of Gangoh, a renowned Chishti saint of the sixteenth century, thus admonished his disciples in a letter: "Why this meaningless talk about the believer, the kafir, the obedient, the sinner, the rightly guided, the misdirected, the Muslim, the pious, the infidel, the fire worshipper? All are like beads in a rosary". (Maktubat, p. 205)

It would be vain and whimsical to think that they did not believe in their religious identity. While firmly adhering to the basic principles of their faith, they did not carry this difference to social relationships. Their toleration was the toleration of a spiritually powerful man who, while jealous of the frontiers of his own faith, admires other forms of thought and behaviour. When Shaikh Nizam-u'd-din Auliya saw Hindu's bathing in the river Jamuna and singing devotional songs, he said, هر قوم راست راهے دينے و قبلہ گاہے (Every people have their own path, their own religion and centre of worship). A whole world of religious broad-mindedness and tolerance is epitomized in this hemistich which came to be frequently cited inside and outside the khanqahs of medieval saints. Iqbal considered the following verse of Amir Khusro as the best illustration of religious toleration: (O you! who sneer at the idolatry of the Hindu, learn also from him how worship is done.)

The spirit of toleration, as Gibbon has remarked and Iqbal has approvingly quoted, springs from very different attitudes of the mind of man. There is the toleration of the philosopher, to whom all religions are equally true; of the historian, to whom all are equally false; and of the politician, to whom all are equally useful. There is the toleration of the man who tolerates other modes of thought and behaviour because he has himself grown indifferent to all modes of thought and behaviour. There is the toleration of the weak man who, on account of sheer weakness, pockets all kinds of insults heaped on things or persons whom he holds dear. It is obvious that these types of tolerances have no ethical value. On the other hand, they unmistakably reveal the spiritual impoverishment of the man who practises them. True toleration is begotten of intellectual breadth and spiritual expansion. (Islam and Ahmadism). The Sufis' toleration was an expression of confidence in their faith. For them all people were the children of God on earth and any social discrimination was a negation of the true spirit of faith.

The second foundational principle of the Sufi approach and ideology was their firm faith in تخلقوا باخلاق الله (adopt the ways of God). It meant that the aim of human life is to reflect in one's own thought and activity the attributes of God. Perfection in human life could be reached only by expressing in one's life more and more divine qualities. God's way is that He extends his bounties to all the pious and the sinner, the believer, and the non-believer, the high and the low. When the sun rises, it gives light and warmth to all living beings; when it rains, all benefit from the showers; the earth keeps its bosom open for all. Maulana Abul Kalam Azad calls it the mark of Rububiyat and thus explains its spirit:'The strangest thing about this scheme of Providence, though the most patent, is the uniformity and harmony underlying it. The method and manner of providing means of sustenance for every object of existence are the same everywhere. A single principle is at work in all things. The stone may appear different from the fragrant flower, but the two receive sustenance in the same way, and are granted growth in the same style'[1]

The Sufis identified service of God with the service of man. Shaikh Junaid Baghdadi was quoted in the mystic circles of Delhi as saying that he found God among the poor people in the streets of Medina. Bibi Fatima Sam, a very respected mystic woman of medieval India whose hut in Delhi attracted people from far and near, used to say that the divine reward for giving a piece of bread and a glass of water to the hungry was greater than offering thousands of genuflexions of prayer and keeping thousands of fasts (Ma'arij-ul-Walayat, MS). Shaikh Nizam-ud-din Auliya classified devotion to God into two categories: taat-i lazmi and taat-i muta'addi. Taat-i lazmi consisted of prayers and penitences that an individual performed; the taat-i muta'addi consisted in helping the needy and the poor and feeding the hungry. He told his disciples that the reward of taat-i-muta' addi was greater than that of obligatory prayers. Sadi, the famous Persian poet, echoed the same sentiments when he said:

طریقت بجز خدمت خلق نیست / به تسبیح و سجاده و دلق نیست (Higher spiritual life is nothing but service of humanity, it is not (chanting) the rosary, (remaining on the) prayer carpet or (wearing) coarse garments.)

The third foundational principle of Sufi ideology was their faith in the Unity of Divine revelation, which paved the way for contact with people of diverse faiths and denominations. Commenting on this concept in the light of the Quran, Maulana Azad remarks: The Quran points out that the tragedy of man has laid in his effort to make distinction between prophets or in his accepting some and rejecting others. Its attitude is summed up in the following verse: Say: We make no difference between them (prophets of God), and we are Muslims resigned to God (3:78).[2]

This basic approach opened the doors of deeper ideological contact and communication with people of different faiths and put an end to 'all notions of exclusiveness which had hitherto prevailed among mankind assigning divine blessings and favours to one's own community'.[3]

Amir Khusro, who had delved deep into the Hindu religious literature, said: هند اگرچه در طریقی که ما در آنیم نیست (Though Hindus do not believe in the religion in which we do, in many matters they and we believe in the same thing). [4] Mirza Mazhar Jan-i-Janan believed in the divine character of the Vedas. Works like Bahr-ul-Hayat, Jawahir-i Khamsa and Marj-us-Bahrain could never have come into existence without being inspired by this basic ideological position. The Upanisads, which contain the earliest exposition of pantheistic philosophy, inspired Muslim mystic thought in many ways. Toynbee has very correctly observed that the missions of the higher religions are not competitive but complementary. If the unity of Divine Revelation is accepted, it would automatically lead to this attitude of mind and soul. The Sufis not only preached it but practised it and helped in pulling down the barriers between various religious groups. Shah Niaz Ahmad of Bareilly thus declared the essential unity of all religions:

یہ سب ادیان و ملل ہیں شاخ ہائے یک درخت

اک جڑ سے ہیں نکلی ڈالیاں سب پھوٹ پھوٹ (All these religions and faiths are branches of the same tree, they have sprouted from one and the same root). The difference in the religious accents of different faiths was thus explained by him:

طوطی جو ہو دستاں سرا سو سو طرح سے دے نوا

ہر دم نئی بولے صدا اور ہے وہاں منقار اک (When the bird-nightingale starts its melodious songs, it raises hundreds of notes, it splashes a new tune every moment, but it comes from the same throat, the same beak.)

The songs of the bhakti saints reverberate with such ideas. A south Indian folk song thus echoes feelings of universal peace and brotherhood: Into the bosom of the one great sea, Flow streams that come from hills on every side., Their names are various as their springs, and thus, in every land do men bow down To one great God, though known by many names.[5] Chaitanya, Kabir, Guru Nanak, Namadev, Pipa, Sen and others familiarized themselves with the cosmopolitan ideas of the Sufi cult and broadcast them in their respective regions. All religions have three essential elements metaphysical, institutional, and social, i.e., a conception of a Supreme Being, rituals, and a code of ethics. The code of ethics assumes two forms: personal morality and social ideal. Richard Gregory in his Religion in Science and Society and Salter in his Ethical Religion have considered these as the central themes of any religious enquiry. After having surveyed the march of humanity in space and time, Toynbee has concluded that the practical test of a religion, always and everywhere, is its success or failure in helping human souls to respond to the challenges of suffering and sin.

The Sufis in India have played the same role. They lived during the lower strata of society and identified themselves with the problems and perplexities of the people. Shaikh Hamid-u'd-din Sufi lived in Suwal, a small village of Nagaur, like Rajasthani peasants, mixed with people of all castes and creeds and adopted vegetarian habits. Shah Waliullah, in a very illuminating chapter on urban life and organization in his Hujjat Allah al-Baligha, advocates the peaceful integration of all the components of society and their harmonious functioning to achieve human well-being. In fact, peace and goodwill between human beings was the end all and be all Sufi endeavours. A visitor presented a pair of scissors to Shaikh Farid Ganj-i Shakar, but he refused to accept them, saying: 'Give me a needle: I sew, I do not cut.'

The Sufi saints were anxious to create in society the harmony of a perfect orchestra. Their principle was to return hatred with love, violence with affection. Shaikh Nizam-u'd-din Auliya used to recite the following verse of Shaikh Abu Sa'id Abul Khair as his motto in life: هر که مارا رنجه دارد درراحتش بسیار باد (Whoever causes grief to us, may his life get more and more happiness.) A non-violent approach, sympathy with the weak and the downtrodden and consciousness of a divine mission to bring happiness to the hearts of men characterized the efforts of the Sufi saints of India. They did not indulge in criticism of other customs or practices. They disliked linguistic chauvinism and regarded all languages as different vehicles for the communication of feelings. They helped in the development of regional languages Bengali, Punjabi, Marathi, and so on. They were instrumental in the rise of a common lingua franca. The earliest sentences of Hindi were spoken in the khanqahs. In the matter of language, their approach was: سخن کز بهر دیں گوئی چه عبرانی چه سریانی (When you are talking about faith what does it matters it whether the words you utter in prayer are Hebrew or Syriac?) Their approach towards human relationships is neatly expressed in the imagery of eyes: (Learn from the eyes the way to develop unity and oneness. The two eyes appear different, but their vision is one.)

Sufi Thinkers:

The Sharia-guided mystic influence of Sufis produced the Muslim thinkers like Shaikh Ahmad Sirhindi, Shah Wali Ullah, Sayied Ahmad Barelavi, Karamat Ali, Sir Sayed Ahmad Khan, Allama Iqbal and Maulana Maududi. They used the mystic philosophy befitting to the political exigencies of the time for revival of political supremacy of Islam. Of them the Sufis like Sirhindi and Wali Ullah, who politicised the mystic ideology for political domination of Islam. They were projected as Islamic reformists for purifying Islam from any extraneous influences. They conveyed the political aspect of Islam to Muslim masses so aggressively that it created a permanent imprint on their psyche. It is therefore said that the Sufi Islamists saved the Islam but failed to save the downfall of Mughal Empire.

The mission of Shaikh Sirhindi popularly known as Mujaddid was to purify Islam from the influence of Akbar with a view to counter his policy of 'the Hindu wielding the sword of Islam' and 'Peace with all'. Unhappy with the regime of Emperor Akbar for withdrawal of Jejia tax imposed on the Hindus, Sirhindi made hectic effort to purge Islam of all extraneous influences. He viewed Hindu mystics like Guru Nanak and

Sant Kabir contemptible, as they did not follow Sharia. With contempt against old schools of mysticism for tolerance, Sirhindi condemned the reign of Akbar for his 'broadmindedness' and policy of 'peace with all'. Propagating against the contemporary socio-cultural situation Sirhindi, felt that the attitude of Akbar "sullied the purity of Islam and the political social and cultural life of Muslims".[6] During the closing years of Akbar reign, when his son Salim had revolted against him, Sirhindi spread the virus of communalism with some success 'in the beginning of Jehangir's reign'. He strongly criticised freedom of worship granted to the Hindus. Hate-Hindu syndrome was so deep in him that 'death of Akbar (1605) filled Shaikh Ahmad with hopes that the pristine purity of Islam would be implanted in India'.[7] "Misguided and greedy Ulama, he (Sirhindi) believed, were responsible for the alleged downfall of Islam in Akbar's regime". With his strong contempt against Shia and the Hindus, Sirhind wrote several letters to the nobles in the court of Jehangir for guiding the emperor on the path of Shariat, and for removal of Qafirs (Shias and Hindus) from the administration. He was dead against any honourable status of Hindus in Islamic government. Sirhind wanted the religious freedom enjoyed by the Hindus during Akbar regime to be curbed. Enraged with his too much interference in administration, Jehangir imprisoned him in Gwalier [8] but released him after one year. Sirhind not only "injected communal virus into the body politic of the country but also generated hatred, mutual distrust and discord among the various sections of Muslims". Despite this anti-Hindu tirade of Sirhindi, Maulana Abul Kalam Azad in 1919 eulogiged the role of Mujaddid (Sirhind), 'who did not see eye to eye with the policy of state'.

Shah Wali Ullah, a prominent Muslim thinker of eighteenth century who shaped the destiny of Indian Muslims was also a Sufi of Naqshbandi order. His contempt against the Hindus was identical to Shaikh Ahmad Sirhindi. The rise of two Hindu rebellious groups namely Marathas and Jats against the Muslim rulers in 1750s stirred the mystic spirit of Wali Ullah and he invited Ahmad Shah Abdali, the Afghan ruler to invade India to save the Muslims from the subjugation of Hindus. While formulating the contours of his mystical ideology, he transformed the Islamic mysticism to a theo-political concept for supremacy of Islam and for political power to the Sunnis. Wali Ullah started a tradition of reformed Sufism in which Islamic mysticism was far superior to other form of mystic philosophy. His reform in Sufi cult made the spirituality of Islam subservient to Political Islam. His doctrine for internal unity of Muslims through complete adherence to pure Islam was only to fight against the infidels and for reestablishment of assertive Islamic political power. His ideology had no scope to accommodate any order of non-

Islamic mysticism, which he regarded unhealthy. He tried to comb out all the foreign influences, such as neo-platonism and Vedantism from Islamic mysticism. Carving out a new path for Sufism he became an active Islamist with a sole objective for resurgent Sunni political power in Delhi.[9] Bridging the gulf between the Islamic clerics and Sufis, Wali Ullah infused new vigour in practice of Naqshbandi Sufi order. He synthesised the disciplines of the three major Sufi orders namely Qadari, Chishti and Naqshbandi with a view to unite the Muslim society against the Hindus. Like Shaikh Ahmad Sirhind he was also against the presence of Hindu employees in the administration of Muslim rulers as he viewed it detrimental to the purity of Islam. His attempt was to purify Islam from the mystic influence of Hinduism. Under the influence of Serhindi whose belief that Islam is a complete way of life stirred the Muslims to retrieve the medieval glory of the faith in this sub-continent. The exclusivist Ideology of Wali Ullah, which sowed the seed of Muslim separatism in South Asia had nothing to do with the secular intellectual approach towards spiritualism. Against the total rejection of Sufism by his contemporary radical Islamist Wahhab of Saudi Arabia, Waliullah used his mystic ideology for political domination of the Muslims in the region.

However, the spirit and aim of both were for adherence to pure Islam. He was the main guiding source for Muslims after the decline of Islamic rule in Indian subcontinent. Contrary to the commonly viewed Sufi tradition he was not receptive to the spiritual tradition of local Hindus in any form. His main spiritual concerns if any was for revival of Islamic India. The Muslim ruler under the influence of the doctrine of Shah Wali Ullah patronised Islamic learning and "took away the administrative and economic power that had passed into the hands of Hindus". [10] "For Shah Wali Ullah, the decline of Mogul political power and the spiritual decadence of Indian Islam were closely related.[11] Sayyid Ahmad Barelavi, a disciple of Abd al Aziz, (the son of Shah Wali Ullah) continued the tradition of Waliullah by synthesising the three major Sufi orders[12]. He launched armed jehad against the non-Muslims but was killed in the battle of Balkot against Sikh leader Ranjit Singh. Karamat Ali, a disciple of Sayed Ahmad Barelavi further developed the ideology for purifying Islam from the influences of Hindu custom and tradition. "His work largely paved the way for the establishment of the organisation which has more recently been developed under the name of Ahl-I-Hadith".[13] It was a neo-Sufi concept of Islam interpreted by Shah Wali-Ullah. The leaders of Deoband movement were also under the influence of both Wali Ullah and Wahhab and accordingly they resisted against the British and were critical of Aligarh movement because of its leader Sir Sayed

Ahmad being loyal to it. Protracted struggle with the concept of greater jehad was the basic creed of Deoband movement, which is a synthesis of Wahhab and Wali Ullah. Deobandis extreme austere approach towards Wahhab and harsh condemnation of the much popular practice of Sufism in India are being viewed as a totally anti-Sufi movement. Ahmad Riza Khan Barelavi (1856-1921), the founder of Barelavi movement was the defender of traditional Sufi movement but Mohammad Ilyas, a pietistic missionary group though, appropriated the ethical emphasis of Sufism rejected its ritual, metaphysics, and sainthood.[14]

The concept of Tawhid (Unity in God), which is the real formulation of Sufism suggests that Islamic mysticism has no difference with the formulations of other non-Islamic faiths about the oneness of God. On this basis Sufism became popular in India during the period of Muslim rule. But when the Sufis supported the Muslims in their political conflict with the Hindus and played important role in conversion of indigenous people to Islam, it gave birth to politicisation of religion, which generated communal tension between the two major religious communities. The movement for purifying Islam from extraneous influences, which was launched by the Sufis like Saikh Ahmad Sirhindi and Shah Wali Ullah was against the spiritual doctrine of 'Tawhid' (Unity in God). Creating a far-reaching impact on the psyche of Indian Muslims it continues to keep the Muslim mass away from the modern global changes. Sufism in India has commonly been viewed as a secular attempt for eternal quest of the soul for its direct experience of the ultimate Superpower. For centuries the Hindus accepted Sufi shrines as symbol of communal harmony. Many of them have been offering prayers in Sufi shrines without any reservation but this liberal gesture has not been reciprocated Muslims. Had Sufism as commonly been viewed as an attempt to adapt Islam in Hindu tradition, the philosophy of two-nation theory would not have emerged. The Hindu revivalist movement like Arya Samaj was a reaction to politicisation of the doctrine of Sufism, which widened the gap of mistrust between the two major religious communities of South Asia.

Contrary to the common perception that Sufism tried to unify the Hindu-Muslim spirituality for a communal harmony, the political Islamists of Sufi background used the doctrine of Tawhid to accelerate the process of Muslim separatism in Indian subcontinent. Their movements were the by-products of Sufi tradition of Islam.[15] They were basically the mystics for the political domination of Islam activists. The basic creed of mystic movements is unity of God irrespective of religious connotation. Unity of God denotes social unity and universal brotherhood. But these political mystics not only divided the society based on religion, but their doctrine created a permanent Hindu-Muslim conflict in the region. The spirit of mysticism is to resolve any dilemma confronting the society. But Sufi movement failed to resolve confronting Hindu-Muslim dilemma in Indian society. In practice they launched a movement for systematic dehumanisation of Islam and negated the concept of Islamic spiritualism of Tawhid (Unity of God).

References

1. Tarjuman ul Quran, Eng. tr. Vol. I, p. 24.
2. Tarjuman, Eng. ul Quran, Eng. tr. Vol. I, p.78.
3. Tarjuman, ul Quran, Eng. tr. Vol. I, p. 8.
4. Nuh Sipihr, p.163.
5. Gover, The Folksongs of Southern India, p.165.
6. History of Sufism in India by Saiyied Athar Abbas Rizvi, Volume 2, 1992, Page 212.
7. Sufism in India by Saiyied Athar Abbas Rizvi, Volume 2, 1992, Page 204.
8. A History of Sufism in India by Saiyid Athar Abbas Rizvi, Vol. II, 1972, Page 178.
9. A History of Sufism in India, Vol. II, Rizvi, Page 259.
10. Islamic Mysticism in India by Nagendra Kumar Singh, Page 185.
11. The Sufi Orders in Islam by J. Spencer Trimingham, Oxford, 1971, Page 196.
12. The Sufi orders in Islam by Spencer Trimingham, Oxford, 1971, Page 129.
13. Indian Islam by Murray T Titus, 1979, Page 186.
14. M.A. Haq - The Faith Movement of Maulana Ilyas, London, 1972 - Quoted from Encyclopaedia of Islam Vol. X, page 336.
15. Article by K. A. Nizami.

Appendix 10

Glossary of Sufi Terms and Phrases

A

- **'abd, abid** : devotee; dependent; servant; one who is conscious of his/her dependence on Allah
- **abdal** : substitute; one who has traded his own self for Allah
- **abraar** : best of believers; goodness; righteous; virtuous
- **Abu Bakr As-Siddiq** : first Khalifa after the Prophet (peace be upon him)
- **Abul Alemeyin** : Father of Two Banners, a title of Hz. Ahmed er Rifai
- **Abul Arca (or Beynennas):** Father of the Lame, a title of Hz. Ahmed er Rifai
- **adab** : etiquette; manners
- **adhan (azan)** : call to prayer
- **afidah** : plural of fuad
- **Ahl al Kitab, Ahle Kitab** : People of the Book or Scripture
- **Ahl al Tariqa, Ahle Tariqa** : People of the path; Sufis
- **Ahlullah** : People of Allah
- **Ahl al Suffa, Ahle Suffa** : Sufis during the time of Muhammad (pbuh)
- **ahwal** : lit. 'states', pl. of hal, a transitory mystical state.
- **Akbar** : Greatest or Greater than great (Allah)
- **akhfa** : very deeply hidden; the deepest part of the heart; sirr 'ul-asrar
- **akhir** : last; latter
- **'alam-i jabbarut** : the world or realm of the archangels
- **'alam-i kasrat** : the world or realm of multiplicity (kinetic energy)
- **'alam-i lahut** : the world or realm of the essence of Allah
- **'alam-i mulk** : the world or realm of creation
- **'alamin** : worlds; realms
- **'alam-i ruh** : the world or realm of the spirit
- **'alam-i wahdat** : the world or realm of oneness (potential energy)
- **Alayhi salaam** : 'Peace be upon him' (abbr., pbuh)
- **Alayhis-salat was-salaam** : 'Upon Him be blessing and peace'
- **Alhamdulillah** : 'All praise and gratitude be to Allah'
- **Ali Ibn Abu Talib** : fourth and last of the righteous Khalifas after Prophet Muhammad (pbuh)
- **Allahu Akbar** : 'Allah is Greater than great'

- **alim :** knower, in a scholarly sense
- **amaana :** object given for safekeeping; trust
- **anfus :** plural of nafs
- **ansar :** helpers
- **Aqim al salat :** 'Establish a system of connection and devotion to Allah' (command)
- **'aql :** the rational mind; intellect
- **aqtab :** plural of qutb
- **aqtab-i erbaa :** qutbs of all time, a very high spiritual station reached by only four human beings, among whom are Hz. Abdul Qadir Geylani and Hz. Ahmed er Rifai
- **arhul :** plural of ruh
- **arif :** spiritual knower; gnostic
- **arsh :** throne; the place of origin; stage from which Allah makes decisions; command post
- **Asma ul Husna:** The 99 Names (Attributes) of Allah, which are used individually or together in zikr
- **asr :** passing time; declining day; isha in the afternoon
- **As-salaamu alaykum (var. salaam alaykum, salaamun alaykum):** 'Peace be upon you'
- **As-salaamu alaykum wa rahmatullah wa barakatuhu :** 'Peace be upon you, and Allah's mercy and blessings'
- **Astaghfirullah, tubtu illallah, we na'aytu qalbi an masiwa'llah:** "Allah forgive me, please cleanse my heart of everything but You."
- **A'uzu billahi minashaitan al rajim, bismillah Al Rahman Al Rahim:** 'I seek refuge in Allah from Satan, who is cast out. In the name of Allah, The Source of Mercy, The One Who Acts with Mercy.'
- **awliya :** protecting friends of Allah; saints; guardians (pl. of wali)
- **awwal :** first; former
- **'awwam :** common people; the masses
- **ayat :** sign; portent; lesson; message; proof; revelation; verse; evidence
- **'ayn al yaqin :** sure knowledge gained through observation and experience

B

- **bala :** adversity in the form of a trial or test
- **baqa :** the state of 'subsistence'; continuing awareness through Allah.
- **baraka :** blessing; grace
- **bast :** expansion
- **batin :** inner
- **bayat, biat :** pledge; promise; initiation into a Sufi order
- **bayt :** house; sanctuary

- **Baz al-Ashab, Al, Bazul Eshep** : The White Falcon; title of Hz. Abdul Qadir Geylani (Arabic, Turkish)
- **biat** : see bayat
- **bid'a** : harmful religious innovation
- **Bismillah Al Rahman Al Rahim** : 'In the name of Allah, The One Who Acts with Mercy, The Source of Mercy'

D

- **dede** : lit., grandfather; an elder dervish with spiritual standing within the order
- **dergah** : Sufi center
- **dervish** : lit., poor one; formal member of an order; murid who has attained a certain level of maturity
- **dhawq** : lit., taste; perceptivity gained through divine grace.
- **din** : way of doing righteous deeds; way of life; religion; path of righteousness to Allah
- **dua** : prayer; supplication; invocation of Allah's favors
- **dunya** : material world
- **dzan** : assumption; good dzan is to assume the best or to give the benefit of the doubt

F

- **fajr** : dawn; salat just before dawn
- **fana** : annihilation; spiritual cessation of ego-awareness
- **fanafullah** : dissolving in Allah
- **fardz** : compulsory religious rule
- **fatiha, Al** : Opening sura of the Qur'an
- **fi'il-i Muhammad** : the example Muhammad (pbuh) projected in living according to Allah's wishes; Muhammad's (pbuh) implementation of sharia
- **firdaws** : paradise
- **fitna** : corruption; dissension between parties; trouble; disharmony; mischief-making; disorder; rebellion; planting the seeds of trouble
- **fuad** : spiritual heart as perception points within a human being
- **Furqan** : Criterion of Right and Wrong

G

- **Gavsul Azam, Ghawth-i Azam** : lit., The Greatest Help(er), a title of Hz. Abdul Qadir Geylani
- **ghafla** : heedlessness; mindlessness; ignorance
- **ghaib** : unseen
- **ghayba** : backbiting
- **Ghawth** : Helper; very high station in spiritual hierarchy

H

- **Habibullah** : Beloved of Allah; Muhammad (pbuh)
- **hadith** : tradition; saying attributed to, or anecdote regarding Prophet Muhammad (pbuh), according to traditional eyewitness accounts
- **hadith qudsi** : holy hadith
- **hadrah** : lit., presence; a gathering for the practice of zikr often accompanied with movement
- **haidar** : The ornamental vest worn by a dervish
- **Haj** : Pilgrimage to Mecca
- **haji** : pilgrim
- **halal** : permissible by Islamic law
- **Hal-i Muhammad** : the spiritual state of Muhammad (pbuh); Muhammad's direct knowledge of Allah
- **halka** : lit., circle; a group which gathers to practice or study Sufism, usually a shaykh and murids.
- **halvet** : spiritual retreat
- **haqiqa** : the state of knowing absolute truth
- **haqq** : truth
- **haqq al yaqin** : truth received directly from Allah; sure knowledge
- **haram** : unlawful
- **hawa** : lust; desire; whim
- **Hazrat, Hazreti (abbr., Hz.)** : honorific title
- **hidaya** : guidance
- **hikma** : wisdom
- **himmah** : force of heart; decisiveness
- **Hu** : third-person pronoun (without gender) used in reference to Allah and in invocation to Allah during zikr

I

- **'ibad** : plural of 'abd
- **ibada** : act of worship; devotion
- **ijaza** : permission; license to teach tasawwuf (Sufism)
- **ijtihad** : deduction; the process of reasoning through which one draws conclusions about a subject
- **ilah** : God; deity; a revered higher power to whom one adheres and appeals for help
- **ilm** : knowledge
- **ilm al ladun** : divine knowledge received directly from Allah
- **ilm al yaqin** : knowledge through research, written or verbal communication
- **iman** : faith; belief; that which you accept to be the truth

- **indallah** : nearness to or being in the presence of Allah
- **insan** : human being
- **insan-i kamil** : mature human being
- **Insha Allah, inshallah** : God willing
- **iqam al salat** : the establishment of prayer and connection to Allah
- **irada** : the quality of spiritual aspiration
- **irfan** : gnosis; direct perception of Reality
- **irshad** : guidance; direction
- **isha** : evening; salat in the evening
- **ishq** : love; passion; ardent desire
- **islam** : surrender; submission
- **istidraj** : to lead on; a test of sincerity by forestalling the consequences of wrong action
- **ittiqa** : watching for Allah's good pleasure with one's deeds; guarding oneself from evil or harm; not offending Allah in one's actions

J

- **jalal** : wrath; power
- **jamal** : mercy; beauty
- **jahri** : in a hearable voice; loud
- **jihad** : struggle; effort; holy war
- **jihadul-akbar** : the greater struggle, i.e., the fight against one's nafs
- **jinn** : unseen being with consciousness and abilities similar to humans

K

- **Ka'aba** : The Sanctuary; Inviolable Place of Worship; Mosque in Mecca
- **kalima** : word; speech; saying; command; science
- **Kalima Tawhid** : Utterance of Oneness ("La ilaha illa Hu" ["There is no god but Him"])
- **kamil** : mature
- **Kanz-i Makhfi:** Secret Treasure (Allah)
- **kashf** : observation; spiritual understanding
- **khafi** : hidden; subtle
- khalifa : representative; deputy; murid licensed by his/her shaykh to teach tasawwuf; designated successor of a particular shaykh
- **khas** : special; designated; destined
- **khawas** : people of rare distinction
- **Kitab** : Book; Scripture; established and applied knowledge; laws and regulations
- **Kitabin Mubin, Kitabi al Mubin** : Clear Book (of references); Book that Makes Everything Clear; established knowledge; scientific fact
- **kursi** : throne

L

- **La ilaha illallah:** 'There is no god but God'
- **La maqsudu illallah :** 'There is no goal other than Allah'.
- **lataif :** spiritual perception points within a human being
- **Laylat Al Qadr :** Night of Power, a holy night of special prayer during the month of Ramadan
- **Laylatul Mi'raj :** Prophet Muhammad's (pbuh) mystical Night Journey
- **liqa :** joining

M

- **maasiwa :** other than Allah
- **Ma'bud :** Object of devotion (Allah)
- **maghfira :** pardon
- **maghrib :** west; sunset; salat just after sunset
- **mahabba :** love; attraction
- **maqam :** station; place; position; state of spiritual development
- **maqam mahmud :** praised station
- **ma'rifa :** direct knowledge of Allah
- **mashallah :** what Allah wants (and happens)
- **masjid :** lit., place of prostration; mosque; place of worship
- **Masjid Al Aqsa, Al :** The Farthest Mosque; mosque in Jerusalem
- **mawla :** protector; guardian; master; lord
- **mawlana, mevlana :** spiritual teacher; our lord
- **meydan :** lit., 'field' or 'meeting place'; place where zikr is held
- **meydan-ji :** elder dervish who helps other students learn the proper customs and procedures in a meydan
- **Mi'raj :** Night Journey of the Prophet (pbuh); the type of 'ascension' that may be experienced by advanced Sufis
- **M'iraj ul Ma'nawiy :** Spiritual Journey
- **mihdi :** one who is guided
- **mihrab :** niche in the wall which shows the direction of prayer
- **mu'adh dhin, muezzin :** one who calls people to praye
- **muhabbest :** lit., attracted one; someone attracted to an order
- **muhib :** one who loves
- **muhasibi :** lit., rendering account; taking stock of one's actions
- **Muhyiddin :** Reviver of the Way of Doing Righteous Deeds (Religion); a title of Hz. Abdul Qadir Geylani
- **mukhlas :** sincere and dedicated one who chooses Allah as his/her goal
- **mulk :** sovereignty; domain; realm
- **mu'min :** accepter of the truth; believer; acknowledger
- **muraqabaa :** meditation practiced in solitude; watching over carefully

- **murid** : lit., directed one; a person who has accepted a spiritual teacher; Sufi student
- **murshid** : teacher of the Sufi path, a title usually reserved for the head of an order
- **musbaha** : string of prayer beads; rosary; also known as tasbih
- **Muslim** : one who surrenders; submitter; one who is willing to accept and make peace with Allah's laws and regulations

N

- **naas** : humanity
- **nabi** : prophet
- **nafs** : lit., breath; self; person; egoistic or animalistic nature
- **Nafs-i Ammara** : Dominant Nafs; the first of seven main levels of nafs attained in the process of Sufi purification
- **Nafs-i Lawwama** : Blaming Nafs; the second of seven main levels of nafs attained in the process of Sufi purification
- **Nafs-i Mardziyya** : Satisfying Nafs; the sixth of seven main levels of nafs attained in the process of Sufi purification
- **Nafs-i Mulhama** : Inspired Nafs; the third of seven main levels of nafs attained in the process of Sufi purification
- **Nafs-i Mutmaina** : Tranquil Nafs; the fourth of seven main levels of nafs attained in the process of Sufi purification
- **Nafs-i Radziyya** : Satisfied Nafs; the fifth of seven main levels of nafs attained in the process of Sufi purification
- **Nafs-i Safiyya** : Purified Nafs; the seventh of seven main levels of nafs attained in the process of Sufi purification
- **na'im** : bliss; delight
- **namaz** : formal Islamic worship that is observed five times daily
- **ni'ma** : favor; blessing; grace; kindness; benefit; comfort; pleasure; delight
- **niyyah** :intention
- **nur** : light

P

- **pir** : spiritual ancestor; founder of a Sufi tariqa; living principal of a Sufi tariqa
- **Pir-i Dastgir** : lit., 'Who Takes by the Hand', a title of Hz. Abdul Qadir Geylani
- **postaki, post** : sheepskin used as the seat of the shaykh in the traditional Sufi zikr ceremony

Q

- **qabd, qabz** : contraction; deflation
- **Qaddasa Allahu sirrahu** : 'May Allah sanctify his secret'
- **qahr** : wrath
- **qalb** : heart
- **Qalu Balaa** : covenant at the beginning of creation between the souls and Allah
- **qana'at** : contentment
- **Qawl-i Muhammad** : what Allah said through Prophet Muhammad (pbuh); sharia
- **qiblah** : direction turned to during prayer, which is geographically towards the Ka'aba in Mecca
- **Qur'an, Koran** : lit., lecture or recitation; revelation from Allah to Prophet Muhammad (pbuh) over a period of 23 years and compiled into a volume of 114 suras, or chapters
- **Qur'an-i Karim, Qur'an al Karim** : Generous Qur'an
- **qurb** : nearness; closeness
- **qutb** : lit., pole; a person of extremely high spiritual level who acts as administrator in the spiritual hierarchy of the world; human conduit of spiritual power from Allah, through whom it is distributed in the world.
- **Qutbul Azam** : Greatest Qutb, a title of Hz. Abdul Qadir Geylani
- **Qutbul Rabbani** : Divine or Devout Qutb, a title of Hz. Abdul Qadir Geylani

R

- **Rab** : Lord; Master; Allah
- **rabbi** : My Lord
- **Rabita** : purposeful spiritual connection; heartfelt connection
- **Rabbil 'alamin** : Lord of the worlds, realms, generations
- **rahbar** : lit., conductor; spiritual guide
- **rahma** : mercy; grace
- **rakat** : A unit of ritual prayer including standing, bowing, sitting, and prostrating
- **raqsh** : dancing
- **rashid** : maturity; wisdom
- **rasul** : messenger
- **rida** : contentment; good pleasure; satisfaction; approval
- **rijal** : person who is faithful to his or her vows under all circumstances
- **rijal al ghaib** : saint who can see remotely or travel through time and space in the service of Allah
- **rizq** : sustenance

- **ruh** : soul; spirit
- **ruhsat** : concession or permission given by a shaykh to perform a certain practice or organizational function
- **ruhul aminu** : trusted spirit
- **ruhul jismani:** : corporeal soul
- **ruhul quds** : holy spirit
- **ruhul seyrani** : moving soul
- **ruhul sultani** : kingly soul
- **ru'yah** : lit., vision, esp. of a spiritual nature

S

- **sabr** : patience
- **sadaqa** : charity; alms
- **sadr** : chest; heart; innermost self
- **sadr Latifa** : place in chest area equivalent to the heart chakra of Indian tradition
- **sahaba** : companions of Prophet Muhammad (pbuh)
- **sahv** : lit., sobriety; the condition of the mature practitioner who has returned to normative consciousness after sukr
- **sajda** : prostration
- **sajjada** : prayer rug
- **salaam** : peace
- **Salaam alaykum** : 'Peace be upon you'
- **salat** : worship; prayer; formal Islamic worship that is observed five times daily; making connection to Allah; namaz
- **salat al asr** : afternoon prayer
- **salat al fajr** : morning prayer
- **salat al isha** : night prayer
- **salat al maghrib** : sunset prayer
- **salat al zuhr** : noontime prayer
- **salawat** : invocation of peace and blessings upon Prophet Muhammad (pbuh)
- **salik** : lit., traveler; spiritual seeker
- **Salla Allahu 'alayhi wa salaam:** 'May Allah's peace and blessings be upon him', spoken or written after Muhammad's name
- **sama, sema** : turning; revolving; a spiritual concert or zikr accompanied by music and sometimes turning (whirling)
- **samawat** : heavens
- **shafi** : intercessor
- **sharia** : the body of Islamic religious canons; injunctions attributed to Prophet Muhammad (pbuh) regarding proper behavior for Muslims

- **shaykh** : lit., elder; appointed master in a Sufi order or tariqa
- **shirk** : attributing partners to Allah
- **shirk-e khafi** : hidden shirk
- **siddiq** : truthful and loyal one
- **sifat** : attribute
- **silm** : peace; submission
- **Silsila** : lit., chain; the lineage of a Sufi tariqa descending from Prophet Muhammad (pbuh), through Ali Ibn Abu Talib or Abu Bakr (may Allah be pleased with them). The chain of transmission includes all murshids of the order up to the present.
- **Silsiletil Zehep** : Golden Chain (Turkish), the spiritual lineage of Hz. Abdul Qadir Geylani
- **sirr** : secret; mystery
- **Sirr-i Muhammad** : Secret of Muhammad; haqiqa
- **sirr 'ul-asrar** : secret of secrets; akhfa
- **soffreh** : cloth spread on the floor used for meals
- **Subhan Allah** : 'Exalted is Allah' (Free from all defects)
- **Subhana Rabbi Al A'la** : 'Glory to my Lord the Highest'
- **subhat** : lit., association; spiritual affiliation
- **Sufi** : lit., wearer of wool or person of the bench; member of a tariqa
- **Sufism** : process of attaining closeness to the Creator through love, which is attained by purification of the nafs; tasawwuf
- **sultan** : king
- **Sultanul Awliya** : King of the Saints, a title of Hz. Abdul Qadir Geylani
- **suluk** : journey; the life-path of a spiritual seeker
- **sukr** : mystical intoxication, often accompanying wajd or fana
- **sunna** : the observed behavior of Prophet Muhammad (pbuh)

T

- **tafakkur** : reflection; contemplation
- **tafakkarun** : those who contemplate
- **tafsir** : scholarly interpretation; explanation
- **tahajjud** : special prayer during the night
- **taj ;** lit., crown; hat worn by a dervish
- **tajalli** : The state of irridation, epiphany, or theophany
- **takbir** : great word (Allahu Akbar [God is Greater than great])
- **taqwa** : self-vigilance; following the guidelines of Allah; devotion
- **talib** : candidate or aspirant to formal membership in a Sufi order
- **talqin** : inculcation; the practice of deliberate mental self-conditioning
- **tariqa** : lit., way to; path; order of Sufism founded by a recognized member of a silsila

- **tasarruf** : Allah's executive power
- **tasawwuf** : system of spiritual cleansing known in the West as Sufism
- **tasbih** : glorification; repeating the Names of Allah with the help of prayer beads; prayer beads
- **taslim** : surrender
- **tawba** : repentance
- **tawhid** : unity and oneness of God, the direct perception of central tenet of Islam, Allah's absolute singularity
- **ta'wil** : deep, authoritative interpretation
- **tawakkul** : complete trust in and reliance upon God alone
- **tekke (Turk.)** : lit., corner; dervish gathering place, synonymous with khaniqah (Pers.) and zawiya (Ar.)

U

- **Ummul Kitab** : The Mother or Totality of Knowledge of our universe
- **urs** : anniversary of the death of a Sufi saint, which is celebrated as their day of union with Allah
- **Uzkurullah** : 'Remember (make zikr of) Allah'

V

- **verd** : litany of praises; incantation prior to zikr

W

- **wahdat** : unity
- **Wahdat al Wujud** : Oneness of Being; the absolute non-duality of existence
- **wahy** : divine revelation; inspiration; suggestion; indication; saying something in a whisper
- **wajd** : state of ecstasy
- **wajh** : countenance; face; essence; attention
- **wakil** : trustee; representative; guardian; advocate; keeper; representative of a shaykh, lower in rank than a khalifa
- **wali** : protecting friend of Allah; guardian; saint; also, wali ul Allah; Sufi of a high spiritual level
- **waliyyan-murshid:** teacher who guides and protects
- **Watan Asli** : lit., Our Motherland; the face of Muhammad (pbuh)
- **wazifa** : repetition of names or attributes of Allah given as a practice prescribed to the murid; personal zikr
- **wudu** : ritual ablution, or washing, performed before salat

Y

- **yaqin** : certainty

Z

- **Zabur** : Psalms
- **zakir** : one who chants in the liturgy, also known as qawwal
- **zahir** : outer
- **zakat** : poor due; alms
- **zat** : essence; person
- **zikr** : lit., remembrance; reminder; the Sufi practice of repeating the Names of Allah
- **zuhr** : noon; salat around noontime

Reference

https://www.aqrtsufi.org/index.html

Bibliography

Chapter 1

1. The buddha and his Dhamma – Dr. Ambedkar Writings and Speeches Vol II.
2. 'Religion - Definition of Religion by Merriam-Webster'. Retrieved 16 December 2019.
3. Morreall, John; Sonn, Tamara (2013). 'Myth 1: All Societies Have Religions'. 50 Great Myths of Religion.
4. Wiley-Blackwell. pp. 12–17. ISBN 978-0-470-67350-8.
5. Before Religion: A History of a Modern Concept. Yale University Press ISBN 978-0-300-15416-0.
6. James, William (1902). The Varieties of Religious Experience. A Study in Human Nature. Longmans, Green, and Co. p.31.
7. Durkheim, Emile (1915). The Elementary Forms of the Religious Life. London: George Allen & Unwin
8. Tillich, P. (1957) Dynamics of faith. Harper Perennial; (p. 1).
9. Vergote, A. (1996) Religion, Belief and Unbelief. A Psychological Study, Leuven University Press. (p. 16).
10. James, Paul & Mandaville, Peter (2010). Globalization and Culture, Vol. 2: Globalizing Religions. London: Sage Publications.
11. Faith and Reason by James Swindal, in the Internet Encyclopaedia of Philosophy.
12. African Studies Association; University of Michigan (2005). History in Africa. 32. p. 119.
13. 'The Global Religious Landscape'. 18 December 2012. Retrieved 18 December 2012.
14. 'Religiously Unaffiliated'. The Global Religious Landscape. Pew Research Center: Religion & Public Life. 18 December 2012.
15. James, Paul (2018). "What Does It Mean Ontologically to Be Religious?". In Stephen Ames; Ian Barns; John Hinkson; Paul James; Gordon Preece; Geoff Sharp (eds.). Religion in a Secular Age: The Struggle for Meaning in an Abstracted World. Arena Publications. pp. 56–100 and Social & Cultural Anthropology. New York: Oxford University Press. p. 124. ISBN 978-0-19-285346-2.
16. Linell E. Cady, "Loosening the Category That Binds: Modern 'Religion' and the Promise of Cultural Studies," Converging on Culture: Theologians in Dialogue with Cultural Analysis and Criticism, edited by Delwin Brown, Sheila Greeve Davaney, and Kathryn Tanner, (Oxford: Oxford University Press, 2001).

17. Charlton T. Lewis and Charles Short, religion A Latin Dictionary. Retrieved June 8, 2021.

18. George A. Lindbeck, Nature of Doctrine (Louisville: Westminster/John Knox Press, 1984), 33.

19. Rudolf Otto, The Idea of the Holy John W. Harvey, (Translator) (Oxford University Press, 1958, ISBN 0195002105).

20. Winston King, "Religion," Encyclopaedia of Religion, edited by Lindsay Jones. Vol. 11. 2nd ed. (Detroit: Macmillan Reference USA, 2005), 7692-7701.

21. Encyclopaedia Britannica. Retrieved June 8, 2021.

22. Abraham & Aquino 2017; "a recent defence of religious faith without belief, Schellenberg 2017

23. The Routledge Companion to Theism (Taliaferro, Harrison, & Goetz 2012).

24. The Dictionary of Philosophy of Religion, Taliaferro & Marty 2010: 196–197; 2018, 240].

25. The Evolution of Religion Author(s): Shailer Mathews Source: The American Journal of Theology, Jan. 1911, Vol. 15, No. 1 (Jan. 1911), pp. 57-82 Published by: The University of Chicago Press Stable URL: https://www.jstor.org/stable/3155275].

26. This is a slightly modified definition of the one for "Religion" in the Dictionary of Philosophy of Religion, Taliaferro & Marty 2010: 196–197; 2018, 240.

27. Mikael Stenmark's "Competing conceptions of God: the personal God versus the God beyond being" (2015)

28. Buckareff & Nagasawa 2016; Diller & Kasher 2013; and Harrison 2006, 2012, 2015).

29. Van Inwagen 1998; for a defence see Taliaferro 2002, Kwan 2013, and Swinburne 1979; for general treatments see Sorensen 1992 and Gendler & Hawthorne 2002.

30. Judaism | Definition, Origin, History, Beliefs, & Facts. Encyclopaedia Britannica. Retrieved 10 January 2021.

31. *Mittal, Sushil (2003). Surprising Bedfellows: Hindus and Muslims in Medieval and Early Modern India.* Lexington Books. p. 103. ISBN 978-0-7391-0673-0.

32. J.O. Awolalu (1976) What is African Traditional Religion? Studies in Comparative Religion Vol. 10, No. 2. (Spring, 1976)Pew Research Center (2012) The Global Religious Landscape. A Report on the Size and Distribution of the World's Major Religious Groups as of 2010. The Pew Forum on Religion & Public Life.
Central Intelligence Agency. "Religions". World Factbook. Retrieved 3 January 2013.
Buckley, Jorunn Jacobsen (2002), The Mandaeans: ancient texts and modern people (PDF), Oxford University Press, ISBN 978-0-19-515385-9.

33. Asatrian, Garnik S.; Arakelova, Victoria (3 September 2014). The Religion of the Peacock Angel: The Yezidis and Their Spirit World. Routledge. ISBN 978-1-317-54429-6.

34. Açikyildiz, Birgül (23 December 2014). The Yezidis: The History of a Community, Culture and Religion. I.B. Tauris. ISBN 978-0-85772-061-0.

35. Selected Papers of Beijing Forum 2010 Religious Harmony: A Fresh Concept in the Age of Globalization by Wang Zuo'an / Procedia - Social and Behavioural Sciences 77 (2013) 210 – 213.

36. Philosophy of Religion (Stanford Encyclopaedia of Philosophy) First published Mon Mar 12, 2007; substantive revision Tue Jan 8, 2019.

Chapter 2

1. William C. Chittick (2009). "Sufism. Ṣūfi Thought and Practice". In John L. Esposito (ed.). The Oxford Encyclopedia of the Islamic World. Oxford: Oxford University Press.

2. Carl W. Ernst (2004). "Tasawwuf". In Richard C. Martin (ed.). Encyclopedia of Islam and the Muslim World. MacMillan Reference USA.

3. William C. Chittick (2009). "Sufism. Sūfī Thought and Practice". In John L. Esposito (ed.). The Oxford Encyclopedia of the Islamic World. Oxford: Oxford University Press.

4. Massington, L.; Radtke, B.; Chittick, W. C.; Jong, F. de.; Lewisohn, L.; Zarcone, Th.; Ernst, C.; Aubin, Françoise; Hunwick, J. O. (2012) [2000]. "Taṣawwuf" In Bosworth, C. E.; van Donzel, E. J.; Heinrichs, W. P. (eds.). Encyclopaedia of Islam, Second Edition. 10. Leiden: Brill Publishers. doi:10.1163/1573 3912 islam COM 1188. ISBN 978-90-04-11211-7.

5. Rashid Ahmad Jullundhry, Qur'anic Exegesis in Classical Literature, New Westminster: The Other Press, 2010. ISBN 9789675062551.

6. The Naqshbandi Sufi Tradition Guidebook of Daily Practices and Devotions, Muhammad Hisham Kabbani, Shaikh Muhammad Hisham Kabbani, 2004.

7. "Sufism in Islam". Mac.abc.se. Archived from the original on April 17, 2012. Retrieved 13 August 2012.

8. The Bloomsbury Companion to Islamic Studies by Clinton Bennett.

9. "Origin of sufism–Qadiri". Sufi Way. 2003. Archived from the original on 27 January 2021. Retrieved 13 August 2012.

10. Abdurahman Abdullahi Baadiyow (2017). Making Sense of Somali History: Volume 1. Adonis & Abbey Publishers. ISBN 9781909112797.

11. Carl W. Ernst (2003). "Tasawwuf [Sufism]". Encyclopedia of Islam and the Muslim World.

12. Taking Initiation (Bay'ah). Naqshbandi Sufi Way.

13. Muhammad Hisham Kabbani (June 2004). Classical Islam and the Naqshbandi Sufi tradition. Islamic Supreme Council of America. ISBN 9781930409231.

14. "Taking Initiation (Bay'ah) The Naqshbandiyya Nazimiyya Sufi Order of America: Sufism and Spirituality". Naqshbandi.org. Retrieved 2017-05-12.

15. Shaikh Tariq Knecht (2018-11-09). Journal of a Sufi Odyssey. Tauba Press. ISBN 9781450554398.

16. "Khalifa Ali bin Abu Talib - Ali, The Father of Sufism - Alim.org". Retrieved 27 September 2014.

17. Brown, Jonathan A.C. (2014). Misquoting Muhammad: The Challenge and Choices of Interpreting the Prophet's Legacy. Oneworld Publications. ISBN 978-1780744209. Retrieved 4 June 2018.

18. Nancy Emara (2002-08-30). "Sufism": A Tradition of Transcendental Mysticism". IslamOnline.net. Archived from the original on July 24, 2009.

19. Massignon, Louis. Essai sur les origines du lexique technique de la mystique musulmane. Paris: Vrin, 1954.

20. Imam Birgivi, The Path of Muhammad, WorldWisdom, ISBN 0-941532-68-2.

21. "Dr. Jonathan AC Brown - What is Sufism?". youtube.com. 13 May 2015.

22. Michael S. Pittman Classical Spirituality in Contemporary America: The Confluence and Contribution of G.I. Gurdjieff and Sufism Bloomsbury Publishing ISBN 978-1-441-13113-3.

23. Trimingham, J. Spencer (1998). The Sufi Orders in Islam. Oxford University Press. ISBN 978-0-19-512058-5.

24. Faridi, Shaikh Shahidullah. "The Meaning of Tasawwuf". masud.co.uk. Retrieved 2017-05-12.

25. For the pre-modern era, see Vincent J. Cornell, Realm of the Saint: Power and Authority in Moroccan Sufism, ISBN 978-0-292-71209-6; and for the colonial era, Knut Vikyr, Sufi and Scholar on the Desert Edge: Muhammad B. Oali Al-Sanusi and His Brotherhood, ISBN 978-0-8101-1226-1.

26. Leonard Lewisohn, The Legacy of Medieval Persian Sufism, Khaniqahi-Nimatullahi Publications, 1992.

27. Seyyed Hossein Nasr, Islam: Religion, History, and Civilization, HarperSanFrancisco, 2003. (Ch. 1).

28. Dina Le Gall, A Culture of Sufism: Naqshbandis in the Ottoman World, 1450–1700, ISBN 978-0-7914-6245-4.

29. Arthur F. Buehler, Sufi Heirs of the Prophet: The Indian Naqshbandiyya and the Rise of the Mediating Sufi Shaikh, ISBN 978-1-57003-783-2.

30. A.J. Arberry, Sufism: An Account of the Mystics of Islam (London: George Allen & Unwin, 1950).

31. A.J. Arberry, Sufism: An Account of the Mystics of Islam (1950).

32. J.S. Trimingham, The Sufi Orders in Islam (Oxford: Clarendon Press, 1971).

33. L.E. Schmidt, "The Making of Modern 'Mysticism'," Journal of the American Academy of Religion 71, 2 (2003).

34. See e.g., H. Dabashi, Truth and Narrative: The Untimely Thoughts of 'Ayn-al-Qud-at al-Hamadh an (London: Routledge, 1999) and L. Massignon, The Passion of al-Hall-aj: Mystic and Martyr of Islam, 4 vols (Princeton: Princeton University Press, 1982 [1922]).

35. A. Hammoudi, Master and Disciple: The Cultural Foundations of Moroccan Authoritarianism (Chicago: University of Chicago Press, 1997).

36. I.M. Lewis, Saints and Somalis: Popular Islam in a Clan-Based Society (Lawrenceville: The Red Sea Press, 1998)

37. N.S. Green, "Between Heidegger and the Hidden Imam: Reflections on Henry Corbin's Approaches to Mystical Islam," in M.R. Djalili, A. Monsutti & A. Neubauer (eds), Le Monde turcoiranienen question (Paris: Karthala, 2008).

38. W.C. Chittick, Sufism: A Short Introduction (Oxford: Oneworld Publications, 2000), C.W. Ernst, The Shambhala Guide to Sufism (Boston: Shambhala, 1997), and A. Schimmel, Mystical Dimensions of Islam (Chapel Hill: University of North Carolina Press, 1975).

39. For an excellent case study of the inner workings of tradition in one Sufi brotherhood, C.W. Ernst & B.B. Lawrence, Sufi Martyrs of Love: The Chishti Order in South Asia and Beyond (New York: Palgrave Macmillan, 2002).

40. N.S. Green, "The Religious and Cultural Roles of Dreams and Visions in Islam," Journal of the Royal Asiatic Society 13, 3 (2003).

41. S.T. Katz, "The 'Conservative' Character of Mystical Experience," in Katz (ed.), Mysticism and Religious Traditions (Oxford: Oxford University Press, 1983).

42. M. Mole, Les Mystiques musulmans (Paris: Presses Universitaires de France, 1965), my translation.

43. S.T. Katz, "Mystical Speech and Mystical Meaning," in Katz, Mysticism and Language (New York: Oxford University Press, 1992).

44. E. Shils, Tradition (Chicago: University of Chicago Press, 1981).

45. E. Shils, Tradition (University of Chicago Press, 1981).

46. E. Shils, Tradition (Chicago: University of Chicago Press, 1981).

47. E. Shils, Tradition (University of Chicago Press, 1981).

48. A.J. Arberry, Sufism: An Account of the Mystics of Islam (1950)

49. For critical evaluations of the historiography of Sufism, N.S. Green, "Making Sense of 'Sufism' in the Indian Subcontinent: A Survey of Trends," Religion Compass (Wiley-Blackwell Online, 2008); A. Knysh, "Historiography of Sufi Studies in the West," in Y.M. Choueiri (ed.), A Companion to the History of the Middle East (Oxford: Wiley-Blackwell, 2005); and D. Le Gall, "Recent Thinking on Sufis and Saints in the Lives of Muslim Societies, Past and Present," International Journal of Middle East Studies 42, 4 (2010).

50. On this Sufi lexicon, N.S. Green, "Idiom, Genre and the Politics of Self-Description on the Peripheries of Persian," in N.S. Green & M. Searle-Chatterjee (eds), Religion, Language and Power (New York: Routledge, 2008)

51. G. Ogén, "Did the Term Sufi Exist before the Sufis?" Acta Orientalia (Copenhagen) 43 (1982).

52. G. Ogén, "Did the Term Sufi Exist before the Sufis?" Acta Orientalia (Copenhagen) (1982).

53. R.A. Nicholson, "A Historical Enquiry Concerning the Origin and Development of Sufism," Journal of Royal Asiatic Society (1906).

54. E. Key Fowden, "The Lamp and the Wine Flask: Early Muslim Interest in Christian Asceticism," in A. Akasoy, J.E. Montgomery & P.E. Pormann (eds), Islamic Crosspollinations: Interactions in the Medieval Middle East (Cambridge: E.J.W. Gibb Memorial Trust, 2007); H. Kilpatrick, "Monasteries

Through Muslim Eyes: The Diyarat Books," in D. Thomas (ed.), Christians at the Heart of Islamic Rule: Church Life and Scholarship in 'Abbasid Iraq (Leiden: Brill, 2003); and F. Rosenthal, Greek Philosophy in the Arab World: A Collection of Essays (Aldershot: Variorum, 1990).

55. M. Smith, Studies in Early Mysticism in the Near and Middle East (London: The Sheldon Press, 1931). On earlier claims of Indian influences, see T. Duka, "The Influence of Buddhism on Islam," Journal of the Royal Asiatic Society (1904) and M. Horten, Indische Strömungen in der Is lamischen Mystik (Heidelberg: O. Harrassowitz, 1927–28).

56. Julian Baldick, Mystical Islam (London: LB. Tauris, 1989); O. Livne-Kafri, "Early Muslim Ascetics and the World of Christian Monasticism," Jerusalem Studies in Arabic and Islam 20 (1996); and A. Vööbus, History of Asceticism in the Syrian Orient: A Contribution to the History of Culture in the Near East (Louvain: Secrétariat du Corpus SCO, 1958).

57. M. Smith, Studies in Early Mysticism in the Near and Middle East (London: The Sheldon Press, 1931).

58. L. Kinberg, "What is Meant by Zuhd?" Studia Islamica 61 (1985) 27–44 and C. Melchert, "The Transition from Asceticism to Mysticism at the Middle of the Ninth Century CE," Studia Islamica 83 (1996).

59. M. Molé, Les mystiques musulmans (Paris: Presses Universitaires de France, 1965)

60. J. Baldick, "The Legend of Râbi'a of Basra: Christian Antecedents, Muslim Counterparts," Religion 20 (1989).

61. J. Baldick, "The Legend of Râbi'a of Basra: Christian Antecedents, Muslim Counterparts," Religion 20 (1990). For a fuller and more traditional account, M. Smith, Râbi'a the Mystic and her Fellow-Saints in Islâm (Cambridge: The University Press, 1928).

62. For attempts to alternatively uncover the earliest historical data and the biographical tropes of these figures, see J. Chabbi, "Fudayl ibn 'Ayyâd, un précurseur du hanbalisme (187/803)," Bulletin d'Études Orientales de l'Institut Français de Damas 30 (1978) and M. Cooperson, "Ibn Hanbal and Bishr-al-Hafi: A Case-Study in Biographical Traditions," Studia Islamica 86, 2 (1997).

63. M. Bonner, Aristocratic Violence and Holy War: Studies in the Jihad and the Arab-Byzantine Frontier (New Haven: American Oriental Society, 1996).

64. Muslim World 97, 2 (2007).

65. M.Cooperson, Al-Ma'mun (Oxford: Oneworld, 2005) and J.A. Nawas, "A Reexamination of Three Current Explanations for al-Ma'mun's Introduction of the Mihna," International Journal of Middle East Studies 26, 4 (1994).

66. On the notion of 'constitutional' and 'autocratic' blocs, see W.M. Watt, Islamic Philosophy and Theology (Edinburgh: Edinburgh University Press, 1962).

67. For different approaches to the problem of early Sufi controversialism, G. Böwering, "Early Sufism between Persecution and Heresy," in F. de Jong 8c B. Radtke (eds), Islamic Mysticism Contested (Leiden: Brill, 1999) and B. Radtke, "Warum ist der Sufi Orthodox?" Der Islam 71, 2 (1994).

68. On debates about whether Hadith should actually be allowed to be written down, see M. Cook, "The Opponents of the Writing of Tradition in Early Islam," Arabica AA (1997) and G. Schoeler, The Oral and the Written in Early Islam (New York: Routledge, 2006).

69. L. Massignon, Essay on the Origins of the Technical Language of Islamic Mysticism (Notre Dame: University of Notre Dame Press, 1997 [1922]) and P. Nwiya, Exégése Coranique et Langue Mystique (Beirut: Dar el-Machreq Editeurs, 1970).

70. J. Baldick, "The Legend of Râbi'a of Basra: Christian Antecedents, Muslim Counterparts," Religion 20 (1989).

71. On the earliest surviving evidence of Sufi interpretations of the Quran, G. Böwering, The Mystical Vision of Existence in Classical Islam (Berlin: Walter de Gruyter, 1980) and K.Z. Sands, Sûfî Commentaries on the Qur'ân in Classical Islam (London: Routledge, 2006).

72. The fullest study of Muhasibi remains J. van Ess, Die Gedankenwelt des Hârit al-Muhâsibî anh and von übersetzungen aus seinen Schriften dargestellt und erläutert (Bonn: Selbstverlag des Orientalischen Seminars der Universitát Bonn, 1961); for the best synthesis in English, L. Librande, "Islam and Conservation: The Theologian-Ascetic al-Muhâsibî," Arabica 30, 2 (1983). On his opponents, G. Picken, "Ibn Hanbal and al-Muhasibi: A Study of Early Conflicting Scholarly Methodologies," Arabica 55, 3 (2008).

73. On Muhasibi as a non-Sufi, see Baldick (1989).

74. S. Sviri, "The Self and its Transformation in Sufism, With Special Reference to Early Literature," in D.D. Shulman 8c G.G. Stroumsa (eds), Self and Self-Transformation in the History of Religions (Oxford: Oxford University Press, 2002).

75. The fullest study is N. Saab, "Mystical Language and Theory in Sufi Writings of al-Kharrâz," unpublished PhD thesis, Yale University, 2004. On the Epistles, see Nwiya (1970).

76. J. Baldick, "The Legend of Râbi'a of Basra: Christian Antecedents, Muslim Counterparts," Religion 20 (1989).

77. Abu Sa'id al-Kharraz, The Book of Truthfulness (Kitâb al-Sidq), trans. A. J. Arberry (Calcutta: Oxford University Press, 1937), citing Quran XVIII: 110.

78. Abu Sa'id al-Kharraz, The Book of Truthfulness (Kitâb al-Sidq), trans. A. J. Arberry (Calcutta: Oxford University Press, 1937).

79. Nwiya (1970). On the discussion of Friendship (wilaya) in the writings of Kharraz and his contemporaries, B. Radtke, "The Concept of Wilâya in Early Sufism," in L. Lewisohn (ed.).

80. Nwiya (1970) On the discussion of Friendship (wilaya) in the writings of Kharraz and his contemporaries, B. Radtke, "The Concept of Wilâya in Early Sufism," in L. Lewisohn (ed.), Classical Persian Sufism: From its Origins to Rumi (London: Khaniqahi Nimatullahi Publications, 1993).

81. For a full elucidation of Tustari's thought, Böwering (1980).

82. C. Melchert, "Basran Origins of Classical Sufism," Der Islam 83 (2006).

83. J. Chabbi, "Remarques sur Ie Développement Historique des Mouvements Ascétiques et Mystiques au Khurasan," Studia Islamica 46 (1977); on the various designations in use.

84. G. Ogén, "Did the Term Sufi Exist before the Sufis?" Acta Orientalia (Copenhagen) 63 (1982).

85. C.E. Bosworth, "The Rise of the Karâmiyyah in Khurasan," Muslim World 50 (1960), W. Madelung, Religious Trends in Early Islamic Iran (Albany, N.Y.: Persian Heritage Foundation, 1988) and M. Malamud, "The Politics of Heresy in Medieval Khurasan: The Karramiyya in Nishapur," Iranian Studies 17 (1994).

86. For the fullest accounts, see B. Radtke, Al-Hakîm at-Tirmidî: Ein Islamischer Theosoph des 3./9. Jahrhunderts (Freiberg: K. Schwarz, 1980) and Sviri (1993).

87. B. Radtke & J. O'Kane (trans.), The Concept of Sainthood in Early Islamic Mysticism: Two Works by Al-Hakim al-Tirmidhi (Richmond: Curzon Press, 1996).

88. The autobiography is translated in Radtke & O'Kane (1996).

89. Radtke & O'Kane The Concept of Sainthood in Early Islamic Mysticism: Two Works by Al-Hakim al-Tirmidhi (1996).

90. J. Paul, The State and the Military: The Samanid Case (Bloomington: Indiana University, Research Institute for Inner Asian Studies, 1994) and Tor (2009).

91. M. Malamud, "Sufi Organizations and Structures of Authority in Medieval Nishapur," International Journal of Middle East Studies 26, 3 (1994).

92. For a recent version of the critique, the comments on Malamud (1994) in Melchert, "Competing Movements" (2001).

93. Melchert "Competing Movements" (2001).

94. Malamud "Sufi Organizations and Structures of Authority in Medieval Nishapur," International Journal of Middle East Studies 26, 3 (1994).

95. G. Böwering, "The Qur'an Commentary of al-Sulami," in W. Hallaq &; D. Little (eds), Islamic Studies Presented to Charles J. Adams (Leiden: EJ Brill, 1991) and F.S. Colby, "The Subtleties of the Ascension: al-Sulamî on the Mi'râj of the Prophet Muhammad," Studia Islamica, 94 (2002).

96. F. Meier, "Khurasan and the End of Classical Sufism," in Meier, Essays on Islamic Mysticism and Piety (Leiden: Brill, 1999).

97. Most famously, A.J. Arberry, Sufism: An Account of the Mystics of Islam (London: George Allen &; Unwin, 1950) and J.S. Trimingham, The Sufi Orders in Islam (Oxford: Clarendon Press, 1971). For the most thorough reassessment of the contrast as it relates to the master/disciple relationship, see L. Silvers-Alario, "The Teaching Relationship in Early Sufism: A Reassessment of Fritz Meier's Definition of the Shaikh al-Tarbiya and the Shaikh al-Ta'lîm," Muslim World 93 (2003).

98. F. Meier, "Khurasan and the End of Classical Sufism," in Meier, Essays on Islamic Mysticism and Piety (1999).

99. For translations, Abu Nasr al-Sarraj, The Kitáb al-Luma' fi'1-Tasawwuf of Abú Nasr 'Abdallahb. 'Ali al-Sarráj al-Ṭúsi (trans. R.A. Nicholson) (London: Luzac & Co., 1914); Abu Bakr al-Kalabadhi, The Doctrine of the Ṣûfîs (trans. AJ. Arberry) (Lahore: Sh. Muhammad Ashraf, 1966); Abu'l-Qasim alQushayri, Al-Qushayri's Epistle on Sufism (trans. A.D. Knysh) (Reading: Garnet Publishing, 2007); and Ali bin Uthman al-Hujwiri, The Kashf al Mahjúb: The Oldest Persian Treatise on Súfism (trans.R.A. Nicholson) (London: Luzac & Co., 1936).

100. Ibn al-Husayn al-Sulami, The Way of Sufi Chivalry (trans. T.B. al-Jerrahi) (London: East West Pub lications, 1983). On the subsequent development of this sub-tradition, see L. Ridgeon, Morality and Mysticism in Persian Sufism: A History of Sufi-Eutuwwa in Iran (London: Routledge, 2009).

101. J.A. Mojaddedi, The Biographical Tradition in Sufism: The Tabaqat Genre from al-Sulami to Jami (Richmond: Curzon Press, 2001). For translated selections from later Sufi biographies, see J. Renard (ed.), Tales of God's Friends: Islamic Hagiography in Translation (Berkeley: University of California Press, 2009).

102. On the presentation of Junayd's life by the biographers Abu Nu'aym alIsfahani (d.1038) and 'Abd al-Rahman Jami (d.1492), see J.A. Mojaddedi, "Junayd in the 'Hilyat al-Awliyâ' and the 'Nafahat al- Uns'," in Renard (2009). University Press, 2005) and F. Sobieroj, Ibn HafîfAš-Ðîrâzî und seine Schrift zur Novizenerziehung (Kitâb al-Iqtiṣâd): Biographiche Studiën, Edition und Ubersetzung (Beirut: Franz Steiner Verlag, 1998).

103. D. Aigle, "Un Fondateur d'Ordre en Milieu Rural: Le Cheikh Abû Ishâq de Kâzarûn," in Aigle (ed.), Saints Orientaux (Paris: De Boccard, 1995). For Kazaruni's biography, see F. Meier (ed.), Die Vita des Scheich Abū Isḥāq alKāzarūmī in der Persischen Bearbeitung (Leipzig: Kommisionsverlag F.A. Brockhaus, 1948).

104. C.E. Bosworth, "An Early Persian Sufi: Shaikh Abū Sa'īd of Mayhanah," in R. M. Savory &;D.A. Agius (eds), Logos Islamikos: Studia Islamica in Honorem Georgii Michaelis Wickens (Toronto: Pontifical Institute of Medieval Studies, 1984), T. Graham, "Abu Sa'id ibn Abi'l-Khayr and the School of Khurasan," in Lewisohn (1993) and R.A. Nicholson, Studies in Islamic Mysticism (Cambridge: Cambridge University Press, 1921).

105. A.G. Ravan Farhadi, "The Hundred Grounds of 'Abdullāh Ansârî of Herat (d.448/1056): The Earliest Mnemonic Sufi Manual in Persian," in Lewisohn (1993).

106. On developments in the theory of sama' in Abu Sa'id's lifetime, especially by Qushayri (d.1074) in Khurasan, Avery (2004).

107. For a translation of the later of the two, Mohammad Ibn-e Monawwar, Les Étapes Mystiques du Shaikh Abu Sa'id: My stères de la Connaissance de I'Unique (trans. M. Achena) (Paris: Desclée De Brouwer, 1974).

108. The expression belongs to Trimingham (1971), p.71. The influential decline model is most clearly outlined in Trimingham (1971).

109. al-Hujwiri (1936), pp.68–69, 234–235.

110. On the links of many Sufis to the most "traditionalist" wing of Sunni Islam, G. Makdisi, "The Hanbali School and Sufism," in Makdisi, Religion, Law and Learning in Classical Islam (Aldershot: Variorum, 1991) and Melchert, "Hanábila" (2001).

111. For contrasting readings of Suhrawardi as mystic or philosopher, see M. Amin Razavi, Suhrawardi and the School of Illumination (Richmond: Curzon Press, 1997) and H. Ziai, Knowledge and Illumination: A Study of Suhrawardī's Hikmat al-Ishrâq (Atlanta: Scholars Press, 1990).

112. L.R. Netton, "The Neoplatonic Substrate of Suhrawardi's Philosophy of Illumination: Falsafa as Tasawwuf," in L. Lewisohn (ed.), The Legacy of Medieval Persian Sufism (London: Khanaqah Nimatullahi Publishing, 1992) and J. Walbridge, The Leaven of the Ancients: Suhrawardî and the Heritage of the Greeks (Albany: State University of New York Press, 1999).

113. On later Sufi light mysticism, H. Corbin, The Man of Light in Iranian Sufism (Boulder: Shambhala, 1978) and J.J. Elias, "A Kubrawî Treatise on Mystical Visions: The Risâla-yi Nûriyya of 'Ala' ad- Dawla as-Simnânî," Muslim World 83, 1 (1993), pp.68–80.

114. Shihâboddîn Yahya Sohravardî, Le Livre de la Sagesse Oriëntale (trans. H. Corbin) (Paris: Gallimard, 1986).

115. R.D. Marcotte, "Reason ('Aql) and Direct Intuition (Mushahada) in the Work of Shihab al-Din Suhrawardi (d.1191)," in T. Lawson (ed.), Reason and Inspiration in Islam: Essays in Honour of Hermann Landolt (London: LB. Tauris, 2004).

116. W.M. Thackston (trans.), The Mystical and Visionary Treatises of Suhrawardi (London: Octagon Press, 1982). For an interpretation of the symbolism of two of the treatises, G. Webb, "An Exegesis of Suhrawardi's The Purple Intellect ('Aql-i Surkh)," Islamic Quarterly 26, 4 (1982), pp.194–210 and A.K. Tuft, "Symbolism and Speculation in Suhrawardf the Song of Gabriel's Wing," in P. Morewedge (ed.), Islamic Philosophy and Mysticism (New York: Caravan, 1981)

117. C.W. Ernst, Ruzbihan Baqli: Mysticism and the Rhetoric of Sainthood in Persian Sufism (Rich mond:Curzon Press,1996).

118. Carl W. Ernst (2003). "Tasawwuf [Sufism]" (1996), p.118.

119. Carl W. Ernst (2003). "Tasawwuf [Sufism]" (1996), p.20.

120. J.G. Katz, Dreams, Sufism, and Sainthood: The Visionary Career of Muhammad al-Zawāwī (Leiden: E.J. Brill, 1996).

121. On Ibn 'Arabi's life, C. Addas, Quest for the Red Sulphur: The Life ofIbn 'Arabi (Cambridge: Islamic Texts Society, 1993). On his connections to Spanish and North African Sufis, see G. Elmore, "Poised Expectancy: Ibn al-'Arabī s Roots in Sharq al-Andalus," Studia Islamica 90 (2000), pp.51–66 and A. Shafik, "Los Šādiliyya e ibn 'Arabī tras las huellas de Abū Madyan," Revista de Ciencias de las Religiones 14 (2009), pp.117–132. For Ibn al'Arabi's own account of his teachers in Spain, see Ibn 'Arabi, Sufis of

Andalusia: The Ruh al-Quds and al-Durrah al-Fakhirah of Ibn Arabi (trans. R.W.J. Austin) (London: George Allen & Unwin, 1971).

122. Ibn al-'Arabī, The Meccan Revelations: Selected Texts of al-Futūhāt alMakkiya (trans. M. Chodkiewicz, W.C. Chittick & J.W. Morris) (New York: Pir Press, 2002).

123. On medieval discussion over the finality of Muhammad's message, see Y. Friedmann, Prophecy Continuous: Aspects of Ahmadi Religious Thought and its Medieval Background (Berkeley: University of California Press, 1989), chapter 2 8c.

124. S.H. Bashier, Ibn al-'Arabī's Barzakh: The Concept of the Limit and the Relationship between God and the World (Albany:State University of New York Press, 2004).

125. W.C. Chittick, The Sufi Path of Knowledge: Ibn al-'Arabi's Metaphysics of Imagination (Albany: State University of New York Press, 1989).

126. S. Akkach, "The World of Imagination in Ibn 'Arabi's Ontology," British Journal of Middle Eastern Studies 24, 1 (1997), pp. 97–113 and H. Corbin, Creative Imagination in the Sūfism of Ibn al-'Arabl (Princeton: Princeton University Press, 1969).

127. W.C. Chittick, Imaginal Worlds: Ibn al-'Arabi and the Problem of Religious Diversity (Albany: State University of New York Press, 1994).

128. On his critics, see A.D. Knysh, Ibn 'Arabi in the Later Islamic Tradition: The Making of a Polemical Image in Medieval Islam (Albany: State University of New York Press, 1999).

129. W.C. Chittick, "Notes on Ibn al-'Arabi's Influence in the Indian Sub-Continent," Muslim World 82 (1992), pp.218–241; J. Clark, "Early BestSellers in the Akbarian Tradition: The Dissemination of Ibn 'Arabi's Teaching through Sadr al-Din al-Qunawi," Journal of the Muhyiddin Ibn 'Arabi Society 33 (2003); V.J. Cornell, Realm of the Saint: Power and Authority in Moroccan Sufism (Austin: University of Texas Press, 1998), chapters 6 &c 7; L. Lewisohn Beyond Faith and Infidelity: The Sufi Poetry and Teachings of Mahmud Shabistari (Richmond: Curzon Press, 1995); and RJ.A. McGregor, Sanctity and Mysticism in Medieval Egypt: The Wafā' Sufi Order and the Legacy oflbn 'Arabī (Albany: State University of New York Press, 2004).

130. Amid the voluminous literature on Rumi, the outstanding survey is F.D. Lewis, Rumi: Past and Present, East and West (Oxford: Oneworld, 2000).

131. For alternative approaches to the definition and emergence of the brotherhoods, J.M. Abun-Nasr, Muslim Communities of Grace: The Sufi Brotherhoods in Islamic Religious Life (Columbia University Press, 2007), chapter 3 &c 4, C.W. Ernst &c B.B. Lawrence, Sufi Martyrs of Love: The Chishti Order in South Asia and Beyond (New York: Palgrave Macmillan, 2002), chapter 1 and J.S. Trimingham, The Sufi Orders in Islam (Oxford: Clarendon Press, 1971), chapter 2 8c 3.

132. L. Fernandes, The Evolution of a Sufi Institution in Mamluk Egypt: The Khanqah (Berlin: Klaus Schwarz, 1988), Y. Tabbaa, The Transformation of

Islamic Art during the Sunni Revival (Seattle: University of Washington Press, 2001) and E.S. Wolper, Cities and Saints: Sufism and the Transformation of Urban Space in Medieval Anatolia (University Park: Pennsylvania State University Press, 2003).

133. On women as patrons in this period, see R.S. Humphreys, "Women as Patrons of Religious Architecture in Ayyubid Damascus," Muqarnas 11 (1994), pp.35–54 and E.S. Wolper, "Princess Safwat al- Dunyā wa al-Dîn and the Production of Sufi Buildings and Hagiographies in Pre-Ottoman Anatolia,".

134. D.F. Ruggles (ed.), Women, Patronage and Self-Representation in Islamic Societies (Albany: State University of New York Press, 2000).

135. On the popular preaching as a means of social influence for Sufis and others, J.P. Berkey, Popular Preaching and Religious Authority in the Medieval Islamic Near East (Seattle: University of Washington Press, 2001).

136. M. Milson (trans.), A Sufi Rule for Novices: Kitāb Ādāb al-Murīdīn of Abū al-Najīb al-Suhrawardl (Cambridge: Harvard University Press, 1975).

137. On his relationship with the caliph, A. Hartmann, "La Conception Gouvernementale du Calife an-Nasir li-Din Allah," Orientalia Suecana 22 (1973), pp.52–61. On his overall career, seeE.S. Ohlander, Sufism in an Age of Transition: 'Umar al-Suhrawardl and the Rise of the Islamic Mystical Brotherhoods (Leiden: Brill, 2008), chapter 2.

138. For translations, R. Gramlich (trans.), Die Gaben der Erkenntnisse des 'Umar as-Suhrawardī ('Awārif al-Ma'ārif) (Wiesbaden: Steiner, 1978) and Shahāb-u'd-DIn 'Umar b. Muhammad Suhrawardi, The 'Awārif-u'l-Ma'ārif (trans. H. Wilberforce Clarke) (Lahore: Sh. Muhammad Ashraf, 1973). Note that the latter translation is of a later Persian recension.

139. Ohlander (2008), chapters 3 & 4.

140. J.J. Elias, "The Sufi Robe (Khirqa) as a Vehicle of Spiritual Authority," in S. Gordon (ed.), Robes and Honor: The Medieval World of Investiture (New York: St. Martin's Press, 2000).

141. Ohlander (2008), chapters 3 & 4.

142. On Chishti Sufism as a vehicle of Muslim 'integration' with Hindus, M. Alam, The Languages of Political Islam (London: Hurst, 2004), chapter 3.

143. For overviews of the brotherhood's history, H. Algar, "The Naqshbandi Order: A Preliminary Survey of its History and Significance," Studia Islamica 44 (1976), pp.123–152 and I. Weismann, The Naqshbandiyya: Orthodoxy and Activism in a Worldwide Sufi Tradition (London: Routledge, 2007).

144. J. Paul, "Solitude within Society: Early Khwajagani Attitudes toward Spiritual and Social Life," in P.L. Heck (ed.), Sufism and Politics: The Power of Spirituality (Princeton: Markus Wiener Publishers, 2007).

145. D. DeWeese, "Khojagani Origins and the Critique of Sufism: The Rhetoric of Communal Uniqueness in the Manaqib of Khoja 'Ali 'Azizan Ramitani" in F. De Jong &; B. Radtke (eds), Islamic Mysticism Contested: Thirteen Centuries of Controversies and Polemics, ed. Frederick and Bernd (Leiden: E.J. Brill, 1999), pp.492–519.

146. D. DeWeese, "The Mashā'ikh-i Turk and the Khojagan: Rethinking the Links between the Yasawî and Naqshbandî Sufi Traditions," Journal of Islamic Studies 7, 2 (1996), pp.180–207.

147. T. Zarcone, "Le mausolée de Baha al-Din Nakshband a Bukhara (Uzbekistan)," Journal of Turkish Studies 19 (1995), pp.231–244.

148. On the latter regions in this period, see D. Ephrat, Spiritual Wayfarers, Leaders in Piety: Sufis and the Dissemination of Islam in Medieval Palestine (Cambridge, MA: Harvard University Press, 2008), E. Geoffroy, Le Soufisme en Egypte et en Syrie sous les Derniers Mamelouks et les Premiers Ottomans: Orientations Spirituelles et Enjeux Culturels (Damascus: Institut Francais de Damas, 1995) and R. McGregor 8c A. Sabra (eds), Le Développement du Soufisme en Égypte a I' Époque Mamelouke (Cairo: Institut Francais d'Archéologie Oriëntale, 2006).

149. Trimingham (1971), p.70: "This development into orders, and the integral association of the saint cult with them, contributed to the decline of Sufism as a mystical Way." For a more sympathetic survey of the evolution of Islamic sainthood, see J. Renard, Friends of God: Islamic Images of Piety, Commitment and Servanthood (Berkeley: University of California Press, 2008).

150. M. Fierro, "The Polemic about the Karāmāt al-Awliyā' and the Development of Sūfism in al-Andalus (Fourth/Tenth-Fifth/Eleventh Centuries)", Bulletin of the School of Oriental and African Studies 55, 2 (1992), pp.236–249.

151. For contrasting positions on whether we can speak of 'sanctity' in Islam, J. Baldick, Mystical Islam (London: LB. Tauris, 1989), pp.7–8 and F.M. Denny, "God's Friends: The Sanctity of Persons in Islam," in R. Kieckhefer &c G.D. Bond (eds), Sainthood (Berkeley: University of California Press, 1988). For a fuller comparative survey, N. Amri 8c D. Gril (eds), Saint et Sainteté dans le Christianisme et I'Islam: Le Regard des Sciences de I'Homme (Paris: Maisonneuve &c Larose, 2007).

152. On such shared shrines and practices, see M. Ayoub, "Cult and Culture: Common Saints and Shrines in Middle Eastern Popular Piety", in R.G. Hovannisian &c G. Sabagh (eds), Religion and Culture in Medieval Islam (Cambridge: Cambridge University Press, 1999) and J.W. Meri, The Cult of Saints Among Muslims and Jews in Medieval Syria (Oxford: Oxford University Press, 2002).

153. L. Halevi, Muhammad's Grave: Death Rites and the Making of Islamic Society (New York: Columbia University Press, 2007) and C. Robinson, "Prophecy and Holy Men in Early Islam", in J. Howard-Johnston 8c P.A. Hayward (eds), The Cult of the Saints in Late Antiquity and the Middle Ages (Oxford: Oxford University Press, 1999).

154. For of a study of such guides, pilgrims and the literature surrounding them, see C.S. Taylor, In the Vicinity of the Righteous: Ziyāra and the Veneration of Muslim Saints in Late Medieval Egypt (Leiden: Brill, 1999). For translations from a wide range of hagiographies themselves, J. Renard (ed.), Tales of

God's Friends: Islamic Hagiography in Translation (Berkeley: University of California Press, 2009).

155. Ernst (1992), R. Marefat, "Beyond the Architecture of Death: The Shrine of the Shah-i-Zindah in Samarkand" (unpublished Ph.D. dissertation, Harvard University, 1991) and Taylor (1999).

156. Indian and Egyptian examples, Currie (1989) and Hallenberg (2005).

157. M. Chodkiewicz, Seal of the Saints: Prophethood and Sainthood in the Doctrine of Ibn 'Arabī (Cambridge: Islamic Texts Society, 1993) and M. Takeshita, Ibn 'Arabī's Theory of the Perfect Man and its Place in the History of Islamic Thought (Tokyo: Institute for the Study of Languages and Cultures of Asia and Africa, 1987).

158. R. Amitai-Preiss, "Sufis and Shamans: Some Remarks on the Islamization of the Mongols in the Ilkhanate," Journal of the Economic and Social History of the Orient 42, 1 (1999), pp.27–46, V.F. Minorsky, "A Mongol Decree of 720/ 1320 to the Family of Shaikh Zahid," Bulletin of the School of Oriental and African Studies 16 (1954), pp.515–527 and L.G. Potter, "Sufis and Sultans in Post-Mongol Iran", Iranian Studies 27, 1–4 (1994), pp.77–102.

159. S.S. Blair, "Sufi Saints and Shrine Architecture in the Early Fourteenth Century", Muqarnas 7 (1990), pp.35–49 and L. Golombek, "The Cult of Saints and Shrine Architecture in the Fourteenth Cen tury," in D.K.Kouymjian (ed.), Near Eastern Numismatics, Iconography, Epigraphy and History: Studies in Honour of George C. Miles (Beirut: American University of Beirut, 1974).

160. E.J. Grube, "Il-Khanid Stucco Decoration: Notes on the Stucco Decoration of Pir-i Bakran," in G. Scarcia (ed.), Isfahan: Quaderni del Seminario di Iranistica, Uralo-Altaistica e Caucasologia (Venice: La Tipografica, 1981), pp.88–96.

161. Z.A. Desai, "The Major Dargahs of Ahmadabad," in Troll (1989), C.-P. Haase, "Shrines of Saints and Dynastic Mausolea: Towards a Typology of Funerary Architecture in the Timurid Period," Cahiers d'Asie Centrale 3–4 (1997) and M.E. Subtelny, "The Cult of 'Abdullah Ansari under the Timurids," in A. Giese &c J.C. Biirgel (eds), Gott ist Schbn und Er Liebt die Schönheit: Festschrift fur AnnemarieSchimmel (Bern: Peter Lang, 1994).

162. F. Çagman 8c Z. Tanmdi, "Manuscript Production at the Kāzarūnī Orders in Safavid Shiraz", in S.R. Canby (ed.), Safavid Art and Architecture (London: British Museum Press, 2002), p.44.

163. For fuller discussion, see Safi (2006), chapter 5.

164. On this overlapping process, N.S. Green, "Stories of Saints and Sultans: Remembering History at the Sufi Shrines of Aurangabad", Modern Asian Studies 38, 2 (2004), pp.419^46.

165. N.S. Green, "Blessed Men and Tribal Politics: Notes on Political Culture in the Indo-Afghan World", Journal of the Economic and Social History of the Orient 49, 3 (2006), pp.344–360 and Hartmann (1973).

166. M.S. Siddiqi, The Bahmani Sufis (Delhi: Idarah-i Adabiyat-i Delli, 1989), chapter 3 and G. Yazdani, Bidar: Its History and Monuments (London: Oxford University Press, 1947), pp.114–148.

167. A. Karamustafa, "Early Sufism in Eastern Anatolia", in Lewisohn (1993) and I. Mélikoff, Hadji Bektach, un Mythe et ses Avatars: Genése et Évolution du Soufisme Populaire en Turquie (Leiden: Brill, 1998). For the counter-argument, see A. Karamustafa, "Origins of Anatolian Sufism", in A. Yas, ar Ocak (ed.), Sufism and Sufis in Ottoman Society: Sources, Doctrine, Rituals, Turuq, Architecture, Literature and Fine Arts, Modernism (Ankara: Turkish Historical Society, 2005), pp.67–95.

168. R. Foltz, "The Central Asian Naqshbandi Connections of the Mughal Emperors", Journal of Islamic Studies 7, 2 (1996), pp.229–239.

169. For an Anatolian case study in a slightly later period, see S. Faroqhi, "Agricultural Crisis and the Art of Flute-Playing: The Worldly Affairs of the Mevlevi Dervishes", Turcica 20 (1988), pp.43–70.

170. Carl W. Ernst (2003). "Tasawwuf [Sufism]" (1996), chapter 10.

171. M.P. Connell, "The Nimatullahi Sayyids of Taft: A Study of the Evolution of a Late Medieval Iranian Sufi Tariqah" (unpublished PhD dissertation, Harvard University, 2004), pp.166–170.

172. On the links between several generations of Simnani's family and the Khwarazmian and Mongol elite, J. Elias, The Throne Carrier of God: The Life and Thought of 'Ala' ad-Dawla as-Simndnï (Albany: State University of New York Press, 1995), chapter 2.

173. S. Digby, "The Sufi Shaikh and the Sultan: A Conflict of Claims to Authority in Medieval India," Iran 28 (1990), pp.71–81.

174. D. DeWeese, Islamization and Native Religion in the Golden Horde: Baba Tükles and Conversion to Islam in Historical and Epic Tradition (University Park: Pennsylvania State University Press, 1994), chapters 3 &; 4.

175. C. Mayeur-Jaouen, "Maîtres, Cheikhs et Ancêtres: Saints du Delta a l' Époque Mamelouke", in McGregor &; Sabra (2006).

176. A. Singer, "Ethnic Origins and Tribal History of the Timuri of Khurasan", Afghan Studies 3–4 (1982), pp.65–78.

177. M.F. Köprülü, Influence du Chamanisme Turco-Mongol sur les Ordres Mystiques Musulmans (Istanbul: Imp. Zellitch Freères, 1929) and T. Zarcone, "Interpénétration du Soufisme et du Chamanisme dans l'Aire Turque," in D. Aigle, B. Brac de la Perrière &; J.-P. Chaumeill (eds), La Politique des Esprits: Chamanismes et Religions Universalistes (Nanterre: Société d'Ethnologie, 2000).

178. R. Jones, "Ten Conversion Myths from Indonesia", in N. Levtzion (ed.), Conversion to Islam (New York: Holmes &; Meier Publishers, 1979).

179. For Morocco, India and Palestine respectively, see Cornell (1998), chapter 2, Digby (2004) and Ephrat (2008), chapter 3.

180. R.M. Eaton, "Sufi Folk Literature and the Expansion of Indian Islam", History of Religions 14 (1974), pp.117–127.

181. On Syria and India, see Meri (2002) and H. van Skyhawk, "Nasîruddîn and Âdinâth, Nizâmuddîn and Kâniphnâth: Hindu-Muslim Religious Syncretism in the Folk Literature of the Deccan", in H. Bruckner, L. Lutze &c A. Malik (eds), Flags of Fame: Studies of South Asian Folk Culture (Delhi: Manohar, 1993).

182. Wolper (2003), chapters 3 & 4.

183. For an overview of Yezidi history, P.G. Kreyenbroek, Yezidism: Its Background, Observances, and Textual Tradition (Lewiston: Edwin Mellen Press, 1995).

184. For more discussion of the Sufi lexicon, N.S. Green, "Idiom, Genre and the Politics of Self- Description on the Peripheries of Persian," in Green &c SearleChatterjee (2008).

185. For an overall survey up to circa 1500, J.T.P. de Bruijn, Persian Sufi Poetry: An Introduction to the Mystical Use of Classical Persian Poems (Richmond: Curzon, 1997)

186. Dick Davis, "Sufism and Poetry: A Marriage of Convenience?" Edebiyat 10, 2 (1999), pp.279–292.

187. Dick Davis, "Sufism and Poetry: A Marriage of Convenience?" Edebiyat 10, 2 (1999)

188. J.T.P. de Bruijn, "The Qalandariyyát in Persian Mystical Poetry," in Lewisohn (1992).

189. J.T.P. de Bruijn, Of Piety and Poetry: The Interaction of Religion and Literature in the Life and Works of Hakīm Sanā'ī of Ghazna (Leiden: Brill, 1983).

190. On the cosmological models that Sufis borrowed from earlier philosophers, S.H. Nasr, An Introduction to Islamic Cosmological Doctrines: Conceptions of Nature and Methods Used for its Study by the Ikhwān al-Safā, al-Bîrûnî and Ibn Sînâ (Albany: State University of New York Press, 1993).

191. For a study of Persian texts written the wake of the Mongol invasion in the safety of Anatolia, W.C. Chittick, Faith and Practice of Islam: Three Thirteenth Century Sufi Texts (Albany: State University of New York Press, 1992)

192. Najm al-Dîn Râzî, The Path of God's Bondsmen from Origin to Return (trans. H. Algar) (Delmar: Caravan Books, 1982).

193. B.B. Lawrence, Notes Prom a Distant Flute: The Extant Literature of PreMughal Indian Sufism (Tehran: Imperial Irani an Academy of Philosophy, 1978)

194. For one fourteenth century Indian Sufi letter collection, Sharafuddin Maneri, The Hundred Letters trans. P. Jackson (New York: Paulist Press, 1980).

195. On this process, see Green, "Idiom, Genre and the Politics of Self-Description on the Peripheries of Persian", in Green 8c Searle-Chatterjee (2008).

196. For the two most important, A. Behl, "The Magic Doe: Desire and Narrative in a Hindavi Sufi Romance, circa 1503", in R.M. Eaton (ed.), India's Islamic Traditions, 711–1750 (Delhi: Oxford University Press, 2003) and Manjhan, Madhumalati, trans. A. Behl 8c S. Weightman (Oxford: Oxford University Press, 2000).

197. M.F. Köprülü, Early Mystics in Turkish Literature (London: Routledge, 2006), chapters 5 8c 6.

198. T. Halman (ed.), Yunus Emre and his Mystical Poetry (Bloomington: Indiana University Turkish Studies, 1989) and Köprülü (2006), chapter 9.

199. A. Karamustafa, "Early Turkish Islamic Literature", section 10 of article "Turk," The Encyclopaedia of Islam, 3rd edition (Leiden: Brill, 2007), vol. 10, pp.715–716

200. Lewis (2000), pp.239–240. On the Arabic-script Greek poems, P. Burguière &c R. Mantran, "Quelques Vers Grecs du XIIIe Siècle en Caractères Arabes", Byzantion 22 (1952), pp.63–80.

201. M.U. Menon, Ibn Taimïya's Struggle against Popular Religion (The Hague: Mouton, 1976).

202. For the debate about whether Ibn Taymiyya was a Sufi, G. Makdisi, "Ibn Taymiyya: A Sufi of the Qādirîya Order," American Journal of Arabic Studies 1 (1973), pp.118–129 and F. Meier, "The Cleanest About Predestination: A Bit of Ibn Taymiyya," in Meier, Essays on Islamic Mysticism and Piety (Leiden: Brill, 1999), note 9, pp.317–318. Thanks to Ahmet Karamustafa for this reference.

203. E. Landau-Tasserson, "The 'Cyclical Reform': A Study of the Mujaddid Tradition," Studia Islamica 70 (1989), pp.79–117.

204. N.S. Green, "Tribe, Diaspora and Sainthood in Afghan History," Journal of Asian Studies 67, 1 (2008), pp.171–211.

205. G. Veinstein (ed.), Syncr'étismes et hérésies dans l'orient Seljoukide et Ottoman (XIVe-XVIIIe siécles) (Louvain: Peeters, 2005).

206. On Mamluk institutional patronage, H. Hallenberg, "The Sultan Who Loved Sufis: How Qâytbây Endowed a Shrine Complex in Dasûq," Mamluk Studies Review 4 (2000), pp.147–158.

207. N. Clayer, "Des agents du pouvoir ottoman dans les Balkans: Les Helvetis," Revue du monde musulman et de la Méditerranée 66 (1992), pp.21–30 and B.G. Martin, "A Short History of the Khalwati Order of Dervishes," in N.R. Keddie (ed.), Scholars, Saints, and Sufis: Muslim Religious Institutions since 1500 (Berkeley: University of California Press, 1972).

208. Z. Yürekli, "A Building between the Public and Private Realms of the Ottoman Ruling Elite: The Sufi Convent of Sokollu Mehmed Pasha in Istanbul," Muqarnas 20 (2003), pp.159–185.

209. E. Geoffroy, Le Soufisme en Egypte et en Syrië sur les derniers Mamelouks et les premiers Ottomans (Damascus: Institut Francais de Damas, 1995), pp.128–135.

210. N. Clayer, Mystiques, état et société: Les Halvetis dans l'aire balkanique de la fin du XVe sieècle aè nos jours (Leiden: E.J. Brill, 1994), pp.113–179 and A. Layish, "Waqfs and Sufi Monasteries in the Ottoman Policy of Colonization: Sultan Selim's Waqf of 1516 in Favour of Dayr alAsad," Bulletin of the School of Oriental and African Studies 50, 1 (1987), pp.61–89.

211. S. Faroqhi, "The Tekke of Had Bekta§: Social and Economic Activities," International journal of Middle East Studies (1986), pp.112–113.

212. S. Faroqhi, "The Tekke of Had Bekta§: Social and Economic Activities," International journal of Middle East Studies 7, 2 (1976), pp.183–208.

213. Faroqhi (1976) and K. Kreise, "Medresen und Derwischkonvente in Istanbul: Quatitative Aspekten," in J.-L. Bacqué-Grammont &c P. Dumont (eds), Economies et soci' ét' és dans l'Empire ottoman (Paris: CNRS, 1983).

214. Karamustafa, God's Unruly Friends: Dervish Groups in the Later Middle Period 1200–1550 (Salt Lake City: University of Utah Press, 1994), chapter 6. 21. Le Gall (2005), pp.167–172.

215. D. Terzioğlu, "Sufi and Dissident in the Ottoman Empire: Niyāzî-i Misrî (1618–1694)" (unpublished PhD dissertation, Harvard University, 1999). Clayer (1994), p.79.

216. Clayer (1994), pp.113–142 and C. Kafadar, Between Two Worlds: The Construction of the Ottoman State (Berkeley: University of California Press, 1995), pp.62–90.

217. On the Ottoman interpretation oighaza and its distinction from formal jihad, M.D. Bonner, Jihad in Islamic History: Doctrines and Practice (Princeton: Princeton University Press, 2006), pp.144–149.

218. S. Faroqhi, "Seyyid Gazi Revisited: The Foundation as Seen through Sixteenth and Seventeenth- Century Documents," in Faroqhi, Peasants, Dervishes and Traders in the Ottoman Empire (London: Variorum Reprints, 1986) and M. Kiel, "Ottoman Urban Development and the Cult of a Heterodox Sufi Saint: San Saltuk Dede and Towns of Isakce and Babadağ in the Northern Dobruja," in Veinstein (2005).

219. J.K. Birge, The Bektashi Order of Dervishes (London: Luzac Oriental, 1994); S. Faroqhi, Der Bektashi-Orden in Anatolien (vom späten fünfzehnten Jahrhundert bis 1826) (Vienna: Verlag des Instituts für Orientalistik, 1981); A. Karamustafa, "Kalenders, Abdals, Hayderis: The Formation of the Bektasiye in the Sixteenth Century," in H. Inalcik &c C. Kafadar (eds), Süleyman the Second and his Time (Istanbul: Isis Press, 1993); and A. Popovic &c G. Veinstein (eds), Bektachiyya: études sur l'ordre mystique des Bektachis et les groupes relevant de Hadji Bektach (Istanbul: Les Editions Isis, 1995).

220. I. Mélikoff, Hadji Bektach: Un mythe et ses avatars (Leiden: E.J. Brill, 1998).

221. I. Mélikoff, "Qui était Sari Saltuk? Quelques remarques sur les manuscrits du Saltukname," in C. Heywood and C. Imber (eds), Studies in Ottoman History in Honour of Professor V. L. Ménage (Istanbul: Isis Press, 1994). Thanks to Ahmet Karamustafa for pointing me to the agriculturalist dimension. Mélikoff (1998), pp.145–161.

222. S. Faroqhi, "The Tekke of Had Bekta: Social and Economic Activities," International journal of Middle East Studies, p.206.

223. M. Balivet, Islam mystique et revolution armée dans les Balkans Ottomans: Vie du cheikh Bedreddin, le "Halláj des Turcs," 1358/59–1416 (Istanbul: Isis Press, 1995).

224. Ahmet Karamustafa for pointing me to the agriculturalist dimension.Mélikoff (1994), p.70.

225. V. Minorsky, "The Poetry of Shah Isma'il," Bulletin of the School of Oriental and African Studies 10, 4 (1942).

226. M. Bloch, The Royal Touch: Sacred Monarchy and Scrofula in England and France (London: Routledge &c Kegan Paul, 1973 [1924]) and E.H. Kantorowicz, The King's Two Bodies: A Study in Mediaeval Political Theology (Princeton: Princeton University Press, 1957).

227. The objection is raised by Julian Baldick, in Mystical Islam (London: LB. Tauris, 1989), p.124.

228. S. Faroqhi, "The Tekke of Had Bekta§: Social and Economic Activities," International journal of Middle East Studies, (1976) p.206.

229. Bashir (2006), p.240.

230. M. Balivet, Islam mystique et revolution armée dans les Balkans Ottomans: Vie du cheikh Bedreddin, le "Halláj des Turcs," 1358/59–1416 (Istanbul: Isis Press, 1995).

231. I. Beldiceanu-Steinherr, "La Règne de Selîm Ier: Tournant dans la vie politique et religieuse de l'empire Ottoman," Turcica 6 (1975), pp.34–48 and G. Veinstein, "Les premières mesures de Bâyezîd II contre les kizilba°," in Veinstein (2005).

232. M.M. Mazzaoui, The Origins of the Safawids: Ši'ism, Sūfisrn, and the Gulāt (Wiesbaden: Franz Steiner, 1972), chapter 4.

233. Arjomand (1981), p.7 and Bashir (2006), p.249.

234. R. Foltz, "The Central Asian Naqshbandiyya Connections of the Mughal Emperors," Journal of Islamic Studies 7, 2 (1996), pp.229–239.

235. W.M. Thackston (trans.), The Baburnama: Memoirs of Babur, Prince and Emperor (Washington, D.C.: Freer Gallery of Art, 1996), p.327.

236. S. Digby, "Dreams and Reminiscences of Dattu Sarvani, a Sixteenth Century Indo-Afghan Soldier," Indian Economic and Social History Review 2 (1965), pp. 178–194 and N.S. Green, "Blessed Men and Tribal Politics: Notes on Political Culture in the Indo-Afghan World," Journal of the Economic and Social History of the Orient 49, 3 (2006), pp.344–360.

237. Abū'l Fazl, Ā'īn Akbarī, ed. H. Blochmann, 2 vols (Calcutta: Asiatic Society of Bengal, 1875), vol. 2, pp.207–225.

238. A. Husain, "The Family of Shaikh Salim Chishti during the Reign of Jehangir," in K.A. Nizami (ed.), Medieval India: A Miscellany, vol. 2 (Delhi: Asia Publishing House, 1972).

239. K. Rizvi, "'Its Mortar Mixed with the Sweetness of Life': Architecture and Ceremonial at the Shrine of Safī al-dīn Ishāq Ardabīlī during the Reign of Shâh Tahmâsb I," Muslim World 90, 3–4 (2000), pp.323–352 and A. Petruccioli, "The Geometry of Power: The City's Planning," in M. Brand &; G.D. Lowry (eds), Fatehpur Sikri (Bombay: Marg Publications, 1987).

240. LA. Khan, "The Nobility under Akbar and the Development of his Religious Policy, 1560–80,".

241. Journal ofthe Royal Asiatic Society 1, 2 (1968), pp.29–36.

242. P. Hardy, "Abul Fazl's Portrait of the Perfect Padshah: A Political Philosophy for Mughal India - or a Personal Puff for a Pal?" in C.W. Troll (ed.), Islam in India: Studies and Commentaries, vol. 2 (Delhi: Vikas, 1985) and J.F. Richards, "The Formulation of Imperial Authority under Akbar and Jahangir," in idem, (ed.), Kingship and Authority in South Asia (Delhi: Oxford University Press, 1988).

243. C.G. Lingwood, "Jami's Salaman va Absal: Political Statements and Mystical Advice Addressed to the Aq Qoyunlu Court of Sultan Ya'qub (d. 896/1490)," Iranian Studies AA, 2 (2011), pp.175–191.

244. A.H. Morton, "The Chúb-i Tariq and Qizilbásh Ritual in Safavid Persia," in J. Calmard (ed.).

245. S.A.A. Rizvi, Shāh W'ah Allāh and his Times: A Study of Eighteenth Century Islam, Politics and Society in India (Canberra, Maèrifat Publishing House, 1980), p.80.

246. M. Alam &; S. Subrahmanyam, "Frank Disputations: Catholics and Muslims in the Court of Jahangir (1608–11)," Indian Economic and Social History Review A6, A (2009), pp.457–511.

247. Alam & Subrahmanyam (2009), pp.476, 487.

248. M. Alam, "The Mughals, the Sufi Shaikhs and the Formation of the Akbari Dispensation," Modern Asian Studies 43, 1 (2009), pp.135–174.

249. N.S. Green, Indian Sufism since the Seventeenth Century: Saints, Books and Empires in the Muslim Deccan (London: Routledge, 2006), chapter 1.

250. M.Alam, "Assimilation from a Distance: Confrontation and Sufi Accommodation in Awadh Society," in R. Champakalakshmi &; S. Gopal (eds), Tradition, Dissent and Ideology: Essays in Honour ofRomila Thapar (Delhi: Oxford University Press, 1996) and H. van Skyhawk, "Nasīruddîn and Âdinâth, Nizâmuddîn and Kâniphnâth: Hindu-Muslim Religious Syncretism in the Folk Literature of the Deccan," in H. Bruckner, L. Lutze &; A. Malik (eds), Flags of Fame: Studies of South Asian Folk Culture (Delhi: Manohar, 1993).

251. M.Alam, "The Pursuit of Persian: Languages in Mughal Politics," Modern Asian Studies 32, 2 (1998), pp.317–349 and Green (2008).

252. T. Kamran, "Some Prominent Strands in the Poetry of Sultan Bahu," in S. Singh 8c I.D. Gaur (eds), Sufism in Punjab: Mystics, Literature and Shrines (Delhi: Aakar Books, 2009), C. Shackle, "Styles and Themes in the Siraiki Mystical Poetry of Sind," in H. Khuhro (ed.), Sind through the Centuries (Karachi: Oxford University Press, 1981) and T.K. Stewart, "In Search of Equivalence: Conceiving the Muslim-Hindu Encounter through Translation Theory," History of Religions 40, 3 (2001), pp.260–287.

253. S. Digby, "Before Timur Came: Provincialization of the Delhi Sultanate through the Fourteenth Century," Journal of the Economic and Social History of the Orient 47, 3 (2004), pp. 298–356.

254. R.M. Eaton, The Rise of Islam and the Bengal Frontier, 1204–1760 (Berkeley: University of California Press, 1993), chapter 9.

255. M.S. Siddiqi, "The Ethnic Change at Bidar and its Influence (AD 1422–1538)," in A.R. Kulkami, M.A. Nayeem & T.R. de Souza (eds), Mediaeval Deccan History: Commemoration Volume in Honour of Purshottam Mahadeo Joshi (Bombay: Popular Prakashan, 1996), pp.41–43.

256. Ahmad (1972), p.210, Persian text only.

257. R.M. Eaton, The Rise of Islam and the Bengal Frontier, (1973), p.52.

258. Kenneth R. Hall, "Upstream and Downstream Unification in Southeast Asia's First Islamic Polity: The Changing Sense of Community in the Fifteenth Century 'Hikayat Raja-Raja Pasai' Court Chronicle," Journal of the Economic and Social History of the Orient 44 (2001), pp.198–229; see especially pp.203 and 208–209.

259. R. Jones, "Ten Conversion Myths from Indonesia," in N. Levtzion (ed.), Conversion to Islam (New York: Holmes &c Meier, 1979). M. C. Ricklefs, Mystic Synthesis in Java: A History of Islamization from the Fourteenth to the Early Nineteenth Centuries (Norwalk: East Bridge, 2006), pp.21–25.

260. A.H. Johns, "Islamization in Southeast Asia: Reflections and Reconsiderations with Special Reference to the Role of Sufism," Southeast Asian Studies 31, 1 (1993), pp.43–61.

261. For variant evidence on Fansuri's biography and death date, V.I. Braginsky, "Towards the Biog raphy of Hamzah Fansuri: When Did Hamzah Live? Data from his Poems and Early European Accounts," Archipel 57, 2 (1999), pp.135–175 and C. Guillot &c L. Kalus, "La stèle funéraire de Hamzah Fansuri," Archipel 60 (2000). On Fansuri's travels in their larger regional context, see P.G. Riddell, Islam and the Malay-Indonesian World: Transmission and Responses (London: C. Hurst &c Co., 2001).

262. C. Guillot &c L. Kalus, "La stèle funéraire de Hamzah Fansuri," Archipel 60 (2000) pp.18–19.

263. S.M.N Al-Attas, The Mysticism of Hamzah Fanṣūrī (Kuala Lumpur: University of Malaya Press, 1970). On Fansuri's language, see Al-Attas (1970), pp.142–175.

264. J. Paul, "Forming a Faction: The Himāyat System of Khwaja Ahrar," International Journal of Middle East Studies 23, 4 (1991), pp.533–548. For fuller exploration of the socio-political entrenchment of the brotherhood, see Paul, Die Politische und Soziale Bedeutung der Naqsbandiyya in Mittelasien im 15. Jahrhundert (Berlin: W. de Gruyter, 1991). M. Subtelny, Timurids in Transition: Turko-Persian Politics and Acculturation in Medieval Iran (Leiden: Brill, 2007), chapter 6.

265. Paul, "Forming a Faction: The Himāyat System of Khwaja Ahrar," International Journal of Mid dle East Studies 23, 4 (1991), p.541.

266. J. Gross, "Authority and Miraculous Behavior: Reflections on Karāmāt Stories of Khwâja 'Ubaydullâh Ahrâr," in L. Lewisohn (ed.), The Heritage of Sufism: The Legacy of Medieval Persian Sufism (1150–1500), vol. 2 (New York: Khaniqahi Nimatullahi Publications, 1992).

267. T. Zarcone, "Sufism from Central Asia among the Tibetans in the 16–17th Centuries," Tibet Jour nal 20, 3 (1995), pp.96–114.

268. S. Kugle, Rebel Between Spirit and Law: Ahmad Zarruq, Sainthood, and Authority in Islam (Bloomington: Indiana University Press, 2006), pp.85–88.

269. M. El Mansour, "Saints and Sultans: Religious Authority and Temporal Power in Pre-Colonial Morocco," in K. Masatoshi (ed.), Popular Movements and Democratization in the Islamic World (London: Routledge, 2006). V.J. Cornell, Realm of the Saint: Power and Authority in Moroccan Sufism (Austin: University of Texas Press, 1998), p.271.

270. M. Garcia-Arenal, "La conjunction du sufisme et du sharifisme au Maroc: le Mahdi comme sauveur," Revue du monde musulman et de la Mediterranée 55–56 (1990), pp.233–256.

271. J. Cornell, Realm of the Saint: Power and Authority in Moroccan Sufism, ISBN 978-0-292-71209-6, pp.257–271.

272. M. Garcia-Arenal, "Mahdi, Murabit, Sharif: L'Avènement de la dynastie Sa'dienne," Studia Islamica 71 (1990), pp.77–113.

273. J. Cornell, Realm of the Saint: Power and Authority in Moroccan Sufism, ISBN 978-0-292-71209-6, pp.261–271.

274. J. Cornell, Realm of the Saint: Power and Authority in Moroccan Sufism, ISBN 978-0-292-71209-6, pp.248–249.

275. F. Rodriguez-Manas, "Agriculture, Sufism and the State in Tenth/Sixteenth Century Morocco," Bulletin of the School of Oriental and African Studies 59, 3 (1996), pp.450–471.

276. R. Ensel, Saints and Servants in Southern Morocco (Leiden: Brill, 1999).

277. J.O. Hunwick, "Religion and State in the Songhay Empire, 1464–1591," in I. M. Lewis (ed.), Islam in Tropical Africa (Oxford: Oxford University Press, 1966). N. Grandin, "La shádhiliyya au soudan nilotique du nord: Notes sur la tradition du xvie au xixe siècle," in E. Geoffroy (ed.), La Voie Soufie des Shadhilis (Paris: Maisonneuve &c Larose, 2005), p.208.

278. P.M. Holt, "Holy Families and Islam in the Sudan," in idem., Studies in the History of the Near East (London: Routledge, 1973), pp.121–134 and N. McHugh, Holymen of the Blue Nile: The Making of an Arab-Islamic Community in the Nilotic Sudan, 1500–1850 (Evanston: Northwestern University Press, 1994), pp.70–85.

279. R.S. O'Fahey, "Islamic Hegemonies in the Sudan: Sufism, Mahdism and Islamism," in L. Brenner (ed.), Muslim Identity and Social Change in Sub-Saharan Africa (Bloomington: Indiana University Press, 1993), p.23.

280. N. McHugh, Holymen of the Blue Nile: The Making of an Arab-Islamic Community in the Nilotic Sudan (1994), pp.57–70.

281. N. McHugh, Holymen of the Blue Nile: The Making of an Arab-Islamic Community in the Nilotic Sudan (1994), pp.116–128.

282. Frontiers of Ottoman Studies: State, Province, and the West (London: LB. Tauris, 2005). Zilfi (1986), p.252.

283. J.J. Curry, "Defending the Cult of Saints in 17th Century Kastamonu: Omeral Fu'adi's Contribu tion to the Religious Debate in Ottoman Society," in C. Imber 8c K. Kiyotaki (eds), Frontiers of Ottoman Studies: State, Province, and the West (London: LB. Tauris, 2005). Zilfi (1986), p.267.

284. R. Peters, "The Battered Dervishes of Bab Zuwayla: A Religious Riot in Eighteenth Century Cairo," in N. Levtzion &; J.O. Voll (eds), Eighteenth Century Renewal and Reform in Islam (Syracuse: Syracuse University Press, 1987), pp.94–95.

285. R. Chih, "Cheminements et situation actuelle d'un ordre mystique réformateur: la Khalwatiyya en Égypte (fin XVe siècle a nos jours)," Studia Islamica 88 (1998), pp.181–201.

286. R. Chih "Cheminements et situation actuelle d'un ordre mystique réformateur: la Khalwatiyya en Égypte (fin XVe siècle a nos jours)," Studia Islamica (1998), pp.186–187.

287. Delong-Bas (2004), p.84.

288. A.J. Newman, "Sufism and Anti-Sufism in Safavid Iran: The Authorship of the Hadīqua al-Shī'a Revisited," Iran 37 (1999), pp.95–108.

289. A. Papas, Soufisme et politique entre Chine, Tibet et Turkestan: Étude sur les Khwajas Naqshbandis du Turkestan oriental (Paris: J. Maisonneuve, 2005), pp.90–102.

290. T. Zarcone, "Le Mathnavî de Rûmî au Turkestan Oriental et au Xinjiang," in V. Bouillier 8c C. Servan-Schreiber (eds), De I'Arabie a I'Himalaya: Chemins croisés en hommage a Marc Gaborieau (Paris: Maisonneuve &c Larose, 2004). Murata (2000), p.26.

291. Y. Friedmann, Shaikh Ahmad Sirhindī: An Outline of his Thought and a Study of his Image in the Eyes of Posterity (Delhi: Oxford University Press, 2000).

292. Friedmann, Shaikh Ahmad Sirhindī: An Outline of his Thought and a Study of his Image in the Eyes of Posterity (2000), pp.94–95.

293. S. Chandra, "The Religious Policy of Aurangzeb during the Later Part of his Reign Some Con siderations," Indian Historical Review 13, 1–2, (1986–87), pp.88–101.

294. N. Katz, "The Identity of a Mystic: The Case of Sa'id Sarmad, a Jewish-Yogi Sufi Courtier of the Mughals," Numen 47 (2000), pp.142–160.

295. Green (2006), chapter 3 and Rizvi (1980), chapter 7.

296. M.K. Hermansen, "Contemplating Sacred History in Late Mughal Sufism: The Case of Shāh Walī Allâh of Delhi," in Lewisohn & Morgan (1999).

297. J.M.S. Baljon, Religion and Thought of Shāh Walī Allāh Dihlawī, 1703–1762 (Leiden: E.J. Brill, 1986). A. Schimmel, And Muhammad is his Messenger: The Veneration of the Prophet in Islamic Piety (Chapel Hill: University of North Carolina Press, 1985), chapter 11.

298. R.S. O'Fahey & B. Radtke, "Neo-Sufism Reconsidered," Der Islam 70, 1 (1993), pp.52–87.

299. J. Malik, "Muslim Culture and Reform in 18th Century South Asia," Journal of the Royal Asiatic Society 13, 2 (2003), pp. 227–243, p.233.

300. Dargah Quli Khan, Muraqqa'-e-Delhi: The Mughal Capital in Muhammad Shah's Time, trans. C. Shekhar &; S.M. Chenoy (Delhi: Deputy Publications, 1989).

301. A. Schimmel, Pain and Grace: A Study of Two Mystical Writers of Eighteenth Century Muslim India (Leiden: E.J. Brill, 1976), p.202.

302. Braginsky (1999), p.149. For discussion on whom Davis was actually referring to, see Guillot & Kalus (2000), p.15.

303. T. Gibson, Islamic Narrative and Authority in Southeast Asia: From the 16th to the 21st Century (New York: Palgrave Macmillan, 2007), pp.41–42Gibson (2007), p.42.

304. A.H. Johns (trans.), The Gift Addressed to the Spirit of the Prophet (Canberra: Australian National University, 1965).

305. G.W.J. Drewes, "Nūr al-Dīn al-Rānīrī's Charge of Heresy against Hamzah and Shamsuddin from an International Point of View," in CD. Grijns & S.O. Robson (eds), Cultural Contact and Textual Interpretation (Leiden: KITLV, 1986).

306. A.H. Johns (trans.), The Gift Addressed to the Spirit of the Prophet (Australian National University) (1993), pp.53–58.

307. A. Azra, The Origins of Islamic Reformism in Southeast Asia: Networks of Malay-Indonesian and Middle Eastern 'Ulama' in the Seventeenth and Eighteenth Centuries (Honolulu: University of Hawaii Press, 2004) and R.S. O'Fahey, 'Small World': Neo-Sufi Interconnexions between the Maghrib, the Hijaz and Southeast Asia," in S.S. Reese (ed.), The Transmission of Teaming in Islamic Africa (Leiden: Brill, 2004).

308. C. Greyling, "Schech Yusuf: The Founder of Islam in South Africa," Religion in Sou Cornell (1998), pp.230–231.

309. J. El-Adnani, Ta Tijaniyya, 1781–1881: Tes origines d'une confr'erie religieuse au Maghreb (Rabat: Marsam, 2007), pp.121–123.

310. A.D.O. Abdellah, "Le 'passage au suï: Muhammad al-Hafiz et son heritage," in J. L. Triaud &c D. Robinson (eds), Ta Tijâniyya: Une confrérie musulmane a la conquête de I'Afrique (Paris: Karthala, 2000).

311. M. El Mansour, Morocco in the Reign of Mawlay Sulayman (Wisbech: Middle East &c North African Studies Press, 1990), chapter 4.

312. D.P.V. Gutelius, "The Path is Easy and the Benefits Large: The Nāsiriyya, Social Networks and Economic Change in Morocco, 1640–1830," Journal of African History 43, 1 (2002), pp.27^9.

313. A. McDougall, "The Economics of Islam in the Southern Sahara: The Rise of the Kunta Clan," Asian and African Studies 20, 1 (1986), pp.45–60.

314. D.P.V. Gutelius, "Sufi Networks and the Social Contexts for Scholarship in Morocco and the Northern Sahara, 1660–1830," in Reese (2004). Karrar (1992) and K. Vikor, "Sufi Brotherhoods in Africa," in N. Levtzion &c R.L. Pouwels (eds), The History of Islam in Africa (Oxford: James Currey, 2000). 172. Karrar (1992), pp.21–24.

315. Karrar (1992), pp.25–26.

316. N. McHugh, Holymen of the Blue Nile: The Making of an Arab-Islamic Community in the Nilotic Sudan (1994), pp.111–115.

317. Karrar (1992), pp.44–47; N. McHugh, Holymen of the Blue Nile: The Making of an Arab-Islamic Community in the Nilotic Sudan (1994), pp.136–141.

318. Abdellah "Le 'passage au suï: Muhammad al-Hafiz et son heritage," in J.-L. Triaud &c D. Robinson (eds), Ta Tijâniyya: Une confrérie musulmane a la conquête de I'Afrique (2000), pp.78–83.

319. M. Hiskett, The Sword of Truth: The Tife and Times of the Shehu Usuman Dan Fodio (Evanston: Northwestern University Press, 1973). L. Brenner, "Muslim Thought in Eighteenth Century West Africa: The Case of Shaikh 'Uthman b. Fudi," in Levtzion & Voll (1987), pp.55–59.

320. P.-A. Claisse, Les Gnawa marocains de tradition loyaliste (Paris: L'Harmattan, 2003). H. Basu, Habshi-Sklaven, Sidi-Fakire: Muslimische Heiligenverehrung im westlichen Indien (Berlin: Das Arabische Buch, 1994). V. Crapanzano, The Hamadsha: A Study in Moroccan Ethnopsychiatry (Berkeley: University of California Press, 1973), pp.32–35.

321. J.M. Abun-Nasr, Muslim Communities of Grace: The Sufi Brotherhoods in Islamic Religious Life (New York: Columbia University Press, 2007), chapter 8.

322. A. Iloliev, The Ismā'īlī-Sufi Sage of Pamir: Mubārak-i Wakhānī and the Esoteric Tradition of the Pamiri Muslims (Amherst: Cambria Press, 2008), pp.89, 95–96.

323. Green (2011); M.F. Laffan, Islamic Nationhood and Colonial Indonesia: The Umma below the Winds (London: Routledge Curzon, 2003), O'Fahey (2004).

324. M. Sedgwick, Saints and Sons: The Making and Remaking of the Rashīdi Ahmadi Sufi Order, 1799–2000 (Leiden: Brill, 2005).

325. M. Laffan, "The New Turn to Mecca: Snapshots of Arabic Printing and Sufi Networks in Late 19th Century Java," Revue des mondes musulmans et de la Méditerranée 124 (2008), pp.113–131.

326. Abu-Manneh, "The Naqshbandi-Mujaddidi and the Bektashi Orders in 1826," in Abu-Manneh, Studies on Islam and the Ottoman Empire in the 19th century (1826–1876) (Istanbul: Isis Press, 2001).

327. Abu-Manneh, "The Naqshbandiyya-Mujaddiyya in Istanbul in the Early Tanzimat Period," (2001), p.66.

328. A. Houráni, "Shaikh Khalid and the Naqshbandi Order," in. M. Stern, A. Houráni 8c V. Brown (eds), Islamic Philosophy and the Classical Tradition (Columbia: University of South Carolina Press, 1972).

329. Abu-Manneh, "The Naqshbandiyya-Mujaddiyya in Istanbul in the Early Tanzimat Period," (2001), p.69.

330. Abu-Manneh, "The Naqshbandiyya-Mujaddiyya in Istanbul in the Early Tanzimat Period," in Abu-Manneh (2001), pp.106–107.

331. I. Weismann, "Sufism and Law on the Eve of Reform: The Views of Ibn 'Abidin," in I. Weismann &c F. Zachs (eds), Ottoman Reform and Muslim Regeneration: Studies in Honour ofButrus Abu-Manneh (London: LB. Tauris, 2005).

332. T. Eich, Abū'l-Hudā aṣ-Ṣayyādī: eine Studie zur Instrumentalisierung sufischer Netzwerke und genealogisch er Kontroversen im sp'ätosmanischen Reich (Berlin: Klaus Schwarz, 2003).

333. T. Eich, Abū'l-Hudā aṣ-Ṣayyādī: eine Studie zur Instrumentalisierung sufischer Netzwerke und genealogisch er Kontroversen im sp'ätosmanischen Reich (2003), pp.53–69.

334. A. Ghazal, "Sufism, Ijtihād and Modernity: Yusuf al-Nabhânî in the Age of 'Abd al-Hamīd II,," Archivum Ottomanicum 19 (2001), pp.239–272; Weismann (2001a).

335. A. Ghazal, "Sufism, Ijtihād and Modernity: Yusuf al-Nabhânî in the Age of 'Abd al-Hamīd II,," (2001), pp.264–269.

336. I. Weismann, Taste of Modernity: Sufism, Salafiyya, and Arabism in Late Ottoman Damascus (Leiden: Brill, 2001b), chapter 7.

337. Sirriyeh (1999), chapter 4 and Weisman (2001b).

338. A. Azra, "The Transmission of al-Manar's Reformism to the Malay-Indonesian World: The Cases oial-lmam and al-Manir," Studia Islamika 6, 3 (1999) pp.75–100.

339. E. Daniel, "Theology and Mysticism in the Writings of Ziya Gökalp," Muslim World 67, 3 (1977), pp.175–184 and Sirriyeh (1999), pp.116–117.

340. B. Silverstein, "Sufism and Governmentality in the Late Ottoman Empire," Comparative Studies of South Asia, Africa and the Middle East 29, 2 (2009), pp.171–185.

341. H. Küçük, "Sufi Reactions against the Reforms after Turkey's National Struggle: How a Nightingale Turned into a Crow," in T. Atabaki (ed.), The State and the Subaltern: Modernization, Society and the State in Turkey and Iran (London: LB. Tauris, 2007).

342. R. Gramlich, Die schiitischen Derwischorden Persiens, 3 vols (Wiesbaden: Kommissionsverlag Steiner, 1965–1981), vol. 1, pp.27–43 and L. Lewisohn, "An Introduction to the History of Modern Persian Sufism," Bulletin of the School of Oriental and African Studies 61 (1998), pp.437–464 and 62 (1999), pp.36–59.

343. M. Miras, La Methode spirituelle d'un maître du soufisme iranien, Nur AliShah (Paris: Editions du Sirac, 1973), pp.319–331.

344. R. Patai, Jadīd al-Islām: The Jewish "New Muslims" of Meshhed (Detroit: Wayne State University Press, 1997), chapter 3.

345. H. Algar, Religion and State in Iran, 1785–1906: The Role of the Ulamain the Qajar Period (Berkeley: University of California Press, 1969), pp.105–106.

346. N.S. Green, "A Persian Sufi in British India: The Travels of Mirza Hasan Safi 'Ali Shah (2011), chapter 4.

347. N.S. Green, "A Persian Sufi in British India: The Travels of Mirza Hasan Safi 'Ali Shah (1251/1835–1316/1899)," Iran: Journal of Persian Studies 42 (2004), pp.201–218.

348. N.S. Green, "Mirza Hasan Safi 'Ali Shah: A Persian Sufi in the Age of Printing," in L. Ridgeon (ed.), Religion and Politics in Modern Iran (London: LB Tauris, 2005).

349. Van den Bos (2002).

350. N.S. Green, "Defending the Sufis in Nineteenth Century Hyderabad," Islamic Studies 47, 3 (2009), pp.327–348.

351. N.S. Green, "Mystical Missionaries in Hyderabad State: Mu'in Allah Shah and his Sufi Reform Movement," Indian Economic and Social History Review 41, 2 (2005), pp.45–70.

352. D.B. Edwards, "The Political Lives of Afghan Saints: The Case of the Kabul Hazrats," in G.M. Smith 8c C.W. Ernst (eds), Manifestations of Sainthood in Islam (Istanbul: Isis Press, 1993).

353. D.B. Edwards, "The Political Lives of Afghan Saints (1993), p.172.

354. D.B. Edwards, "The Political Lives of Afghan Saints (1993), p.176.

355. M.H. Sidky, "'Malang,' Sufis, and Mystics: An Ethnographic and Historical Study of Shamanism in Afghanistan," Asian Folklore Studies, 49, 2 (1990),

pp.275–301 and B. Utas, "The Naqshbandiyya of Afghanistan on the Eve of the 1978 Coup d'etat," in Özdalga (1999).

356. M. Centlivres-Demontin, "Un corpus de risala du Turkestan afghan," in N. Grandin 8c M. Gaborieau (eds), Madrasa: La transmission du savoir dans Ie monde musulman (Paris: Editions Arguments, 1997).

357. M. Gilsenan, "Trajectories of Contemporary Sufism," in E. Gellner (ed.), Islamic Dilemmas: Reformers, Nationalists and Industrialization (Berlin: Mouton, 1985) and F. de Jong, "Aspects of the Political Involvement of Sufi Orders in Twentieth-Century Egypt (1907–1970): An Exploratory Stock Taking," in G.R.Warburg 8c U.M. Kupferschmidt (eds), Islam, Nationalism, and Radicalism in Egypt and the Sudan (New York: Praeger, 1983).

358. Ewing (1997), chapter 2 and A. Schimmel, Gabriel's Wing: A Study into the Religious Ideas of Sir Muhammad Iqbal (Leiden: E.J. Brill, 1963).

359. C. Lindholm, "Prophets and Firs: Charismatic Islam in the Middle East and South Asia," in P. Werbner &c H. Basu (eds), Embodying Charisma: Modernity, Locality and the Performance of Emotion in Sufi Cults (London: Routledge, 1998).

360. K.P. Ewing, "The Politics of Sufism: Redefining the Saints of Pakistan," Journal of Asian Studies 42, 2 (1983), pp.251–265.

361. Rozehnal (2007), pp.103–112.

362. M. van Bruinessen, "Saints, Politicians and Sufi Bureaucrats: Mysticism and Politics in Indonesia's New Order," in M. van Bruinessen Sc J. Day Howell (eds), Sufism and the 'Modern' in Islam (London: LB. Tauris, 2007).

363. J. Day Howell, "Sufism and the Indonesian Islamic Revival," Journal of Asian Studies 60, 3 (2001), pp.701–729.

364. J. Gross, "The Polemic of 'Official' and 'Unofficial' Islam: Sufism in Soviet Central Asia," in de Jong Sc Radtke (1999).

365. M.E. Louw, Everyday Islam in Post-Soviet Central Asia (London: Routledge, 2007) and B.G. Privratsky, Muslim Turkistan: Kazak Religion and Collective Memory (London: Routledge, 2001).

366. V. Schubel, "Post-Soviet Hagiography and the Reconstruction of the Naqshbandi Tradition in Contemporary Uzbekistan," in Ozdalga (1999), pp.77–79.

367. S. Mardin, "The Naqshibendi Order of Turkey", in M.E. Marty &c R.S. Appleby (eds), Fundamentalisms and the State: Remaking Polities, Economies, and Militance (Chicago: University of Chicago Press, 1993) and M. Hakan Yavuz, Islamic Political Identity in Turkey (Oxford: Oxford University Press, 2003), chapters 6–8.

368. T. Michel, "Sufism and Modernity in the Thought of Fethullah Giilen," Muslim World 95, 3 (2005), pp.341–358.

369. B. Balci, Missionnaires de I'Islam en Asie centrale: les écoles turques de Fethullah Gülen (Paris: Maisonneuve et Larose, 2003).

370. M. Gilsenan, "Some Factors in the Decline of Sufi Orders in Modern Egypt," Muslim World 57 (1967), pp.11–18 and P. Pinto, Mystical Bodies: Ritual, Experience and the Embodiment of Sufism in Syria (unpublished Ph.D. dissertation, Boston University, 2002).

371. S. Schielke, "On Snacks and Saints: When Discourses of Order and Rationality Enter the Egyptian Mawlid," Archives de Sciences Sociales des Religions 135 (2006), pp.117–140.

372. K. Arai, "Combining Innovation and Emotion in the Modernization of Sufi Orders in Contemporary Egypt," Middle East Critique 16, 2 (2007), pp.155–169.

373. J. During, "Sufi Music and Rites in the Era of Mass Reproduction Techniques and Culture," in Özdalga (1999).

374. A.N. Hamzeh &c R.H. Dekmejian, "A Sufi Response to Political Islamism: Al-Ahbash of Lebanon," International Journal of Middle East Studies 28, 2 (1996), pp.217–229.

375. M. Mahmoud, "Sufism and Islamism in the Sudan," in D. Westerlund &c E.E. Rosander (eds), African Islam and Islam in Africa: Encounters between Sufis and Islamists (London: Hurst, 1997).

376. D.B. Cruise O'Brien, "Charisma Comes to Town: Mouride Urbanization, 1945–1986," in D.B. Cruise O'Brien 8c C. Coulon (eds), Charisma and Brotherhood in African Islam (Oxford: Clarendon Press, 1988).

377. J. Copans, "Mourides des champs, mourides des villes, mourides du telephone portable et de l'internet: Les renouvellements de l'économie politique d'une confrérie," Afrique contemporaine 194 (2000), pp.24–33.

378. S. Bava, "De la 'baraka aux affaires': ethos économico-religieux et transnationalité chez les migrants sénégalais mourides," Revue europ'eenne des migrations internationals 19, 2 (2003), pp.1–13.

379. B.F. Soares, "Saint and Sufi in Contemporary Mali," in van Bruinessen 8c Howell (2007).

Chapter 3

1.   The History of British India by James Mill (1817).

2.   Thapar, Romila (1978), Ancient Indian Social History: Some Interpretations (PDF), Orient Blackswan, archived from the original (PDF) on 14 February 2015, retrieved 14 February 2015 Part 1, p. 19, 20.

3.   Michaels, Axel (2004), Hinduism. Past and present, Princeton, New Jersey: Princeton University Press.

4.   Heehs, Peter (2002), Indian Religions: A Historical Reader of Spiritual Expression and Experience, New York: New York University Press, ISBN 978-0-8147-3650-0, p. 39.

5.   Wright, Rita P. (2009). The Ancient Indus: Urbanism, Economy, and Society. Cambridge University Press. ISBN 978-0-521-57219-4, p. 281–282.

6.   Ratnagar, Shereen (April 2004). "Archaeology at the Heart of a Political Confrontation the Case of Ayodhya" (PDF). Current Anthropology. 45 (2): 239–259. JSTOR 10.1086/381044. S2CID 149773944.

7.   Marshall, John, ed. (1931). Mohenjo-Daro and the Indus Civilization: Being an Official Account of Archaeological Excavations at Mohenjo-Daro Carried Out by the Government of India Between the Years 1922 and 1927. p. 48–78 London: Arthur Probsthain.

8. Possehl, Gregory L. (2002). The Indus Civilization: A Contemporary Perspective. Rowman Altamira. ISBN 978-0-7591-1642-9. p. 141–156.

9. Possehl, Gregory L. (2002). The Indus Civilization: A Contemporary Perspective. Rowman Altamira. ISBN 978-0-7591-1642-9, p. 141–144.

10. Srinivasan, Doris (1975). 'The so-called Proto-Śiva seal from Mohenjo-Daro: An iconological assessment'. Archives of Asian Art. 29: p. 47–58.

11. Srinivasan 1997, Srinivasan, Doris Meth (1997). Many Heads, Arms and Eyes: Origin, Meaning and Form in Multiplicity in Indian Art. Brill. ISBN 978-90-04-10758-8, p. 180–181.

12. Sullivan 1964. Srinivasan, Doris Meth (1997). Many Heads, Arms and Eyes: Origin, Meaning and Form in Multiplicity in Indian Art. Brill. ISBN 978-90-04-10758-8.

13. Hiltebeitel, Alf (2011). 'The Indus Valley 'Proto-Śiva", Re-examined through Reflections on the Goddess, the Buffalo, and the Symbolism of vāhanas'. In Adluri, Vishwa; Bagchee, Joydeep (eds.). When the Goddess was a Woman: Mahabharata Ethnographies – Essays by Alf Hiltebeitel. Brill. ISBN 978-90-04-19380-2, p. 399–432.

14. Vilas Sangave (2001). Facets of Jainology: Selected Research Papers on Jain Society, Religion, and Culture. Mumbai: Popular Prakashan. ISBN 978-81-7154-839-2.

15. Zimmer 1969, Zimmer, Heinrich (1969). Campbell, Joseph (ed.). Philosophies of India. Princeton University Press. ISBN 978-0-691-01758-7, p. 60, 208–209.

16. Thomas McEvilley (2002) The Shape of Ancient Thought: Comparative Studies in Greek and Indian Philosophies. Allworth Communications, ISBN 1-58115-203-5.

17. Possehl, Gregory L. (2002). The Indus Civilization: A Contemporary Perspective. Rowman Altamira. ISBN 978-0-7591-1642-9., p. 141–145.

18. McIntosh 2008, McIntosh, Jane (2008). The Ancient Indus Valley: New Perspectives. ABC-CLIO.ISBN 978-1-57607-907-2. p. 286–287.

19. Marshall, John, ed. (1931). Mohenjo-Daro and the Indus Civilization: Being an Official Account of Archaeological Excavations at Mohenjo-Daro Carried Out by the Government of India Between the Years 1922 and 1927, p. 67.

20. Possehl, Gregory L. (2002). The Indus Civilization: A Contemporary Perspective. Rowman Altamira. ISBN 978-0-7591-1642-9, p. 18.

21. Thapar, Romila (1978), Ancient Indian Social History: Some Interpretations (PDF), Orient Blackswan, archived from the original (PDF) on 14 February 2015, retrieved14 February 2015 Part 1, p. 85.

22. McIntosh 2008, McIntosh, Jane (2008). The Ancient Indus Valley: New Perspectives. ABC-CLIO. ISBN 978-1-57607-907-2, p. 275–277, 292.

23. Possehl, Gregory L. (2002). The Indus Civilization: A Contemporary Perspective. Rowman Altamira. ISBN 978-0-7591-1642-9, p. 152, 157–176.

24. McIntosh 2008, McIntosh, Jane (2008). The Ancient Indus Valley: New Perspectives. ABC-CLIO ISBN 978-1-57607-907-2, p. 293–299.

25. Mudumby Narasimhachary, ed. (1976). Āgamaprāmāṇya of Yāmunācārya. Issue 160 of Gaekwad's Oriental Series. Oriental Institute, Maharaja Sayajirao University of Baroda.

26. Grimes, John A. (1996). A Concise Dictionary of Indian Philosophy: Sanskrit Terms Defined in English. SUNY Press. ISBN 9780791430682.

27. The Modern review: Volume 28. Prabasi Press. 1920.

28. Kanchan Sinha, Kartikeya in Indian art and literature, Delhi: Sundeep Prakashan (1979)

29. John Keay. India: A History, Grove Press, p. 14.

30. J.P. Mallory and D. Q. Adams, Encyclopedia of Indo-European Culture (1997), p.308.

31. K. Zvelebil, Dravidian Linguistics: An Introduction, (Pondicherry: Pondicherry Institute of Linguistics and Culture 1990), p. 81.

32. Krishnamurti Krishnamurti, Bhadriraju (2003), The Dravidian Languages, Cambridge University Press, ISBN 0-521-77111-0, p. 6.

33. Larson 1995, Larson, Gerald (1995). India's Agony Over Religion. SUNY Press. ISBN 978-0-7914-2411-7. p. 81.

34. Harman, William P. (1992). The sacred marriage of a Hindu goddess. p. 6.

35. Chopra, Pran Nath (1979). History of South India. S. Chand.

36. Bate, Bernard (2009). Tamil oratory and the Dravidian aesthetic: democratic practice in south India. Columbia University Press.

37. A. Kiruṭṭinan (2000). Tamil culture: religion, culture, and literature. Bharatiya Kala Prakashan, p. 17.

38. Embree, Ainslie Thomas (1988). Encyclopedia of Asian history: Volume 1. Scribner. ISBN 9780684188980.

39. Thiruchandran, Selvy (1997). Ideology, caste, class, and gender. Vikas Pub. House.

40. Manickam, Valliappa Subramaniam (1968). A glimpse of Tamilology. Academy of Tamil Scholars of Tamil Nadu. p. 75.

41. Lal, Mohan (2006). The Encyclopaedia of Indian Literature, Volume 5 (Sasay to Zorgot). Sahitya Akademi, ISBN 8126012218, p. 4396.

42. Shashi, S. S. (1996). Encyclopaedia Indica: India, Pakistan, Bangladesh: Volume 100. Anmol Publications.

43. Subramanium, N. (1980). Śaṅgam polity: the administration and social life of the Śaṅgam Tamils. Ennes Publications.

44. Stephanie W. Jamison and Michael Witzel in Arvind Sharma, editor, The Study of Hinduism. University of South Carolina Press, 2003, page 65.

45. History Of Ancient India (portraits of a Nation), 1/e By Kamlesh Kapur.

46. Hindu Spirituality: Vedas Through Vedanta, Volume 1 edited by K. R. Sundararajan, Bithika Mukerji, p. 382.

47. I Am Proud to Be A Hindu By J. Agarwal, p. 46.

48. Hinduism: An Alphabetical Guide By Roshen Dalal, p. 41.

49. Nigal, S.G. Axiological Approach to the Vedas. Northern Book Centre, 1986. ISBN 81-85119-18-X, p. 81

50. Indian sociology through Ghurye, a dictionary By S. Devadas Pillai, p. 285.

51. Encyclopædia Britannica, Other sources: the process of 'Sanskritization'.

52. Deussen, Paul (1966) Philosophy of the Upanishads. New York: Dover Publications. ISBN 9780486216164.

53. Deussen, Paul (1966) Philosophy of the Upanishads. New York: Dover Publications. ISBN 9780486216164, p. 51.

54. Neusner, Jacob (2009), World Religions in America: An Introduction. Westminster John Knox Press. ISBN 978-0-664-23320-4, p. 183.

55. Melton, J. Gordon; Baumann, Martin (2010), Religions of the World, Second Edition: A Comprehensive Encyclopedia of Beliefs and Practices, ABC-CLIO, ISBN 978-1-59884-204-3, p. 1324.

56. Mahadevan, T.M.P (1956), Sarvepalli Radhakrishnan (ed.), History of Philosophy Eastern and Western, George Allen & Unwin Ltd, p. 57.

57. von Glasenapp 1999, von Glasenapp, Helmuth (1999). Jainism: An Indian Religion of Salvation. Delhi: Motilal Banarsidass, ISBN 81-208-1376-6, p. 16.

58. Dr. Kalghatgi, T. G. 1988 In: Study of Jainism, Prakrit Bharti Academy, Jaipur.

59. S. Cromwell Crawford, review of L. M. Joshi, Brahmanism, Buddhism and Hinduism, Philosophy East and West (1972).

60. Pratt, James Bissett (1996), The Pilgrimage of Buddhism and a Buddhist Pilgrimage, Asian Educational Services, ISBN 978-81-206-1196-2, p. 90.

61. Upadhyaya, Kashi Nath (1998), Early Buddhism and the Bhagavadgītā, Motilal Banarsidass, ISBN 978-81-208-0880-5, p. 103–104.

62. Hajime Nakamura, A History of Early Vedānta Philosophy: Part 1. Reprint by Motilal Banarsidass Publ., 1990, p. 139.

63. Mary Pat Fisher (1997) In: Living Religions: An Encyclopedia of the World's Faiths I.B.Tauris: London ISBN 1-86064-148-2.

64. The Life of Buddha as Legend and History, by Edward Joseph Thomas.

65. The Progress of Insight Visuddhinana katha. Ven Mahasi sayadaw, translated by Nyanaponika Thera. 1994, ISBN 955-24-0090-2.

66. Rādhākrishnan, S. (1996), Indian Philosophy, Volume II, Oxford University Press, ISBN 0-19-563820-4.

67. Radhakrishnan & Moore 1967, C.A. (1967), A Sourcebook in Indian Philosophy, Princeton University Press, ISBN 0-691-01958-4, p. xviii–xxi.

68. Radhakrishnan & Moore 1967, C.A. (1967), A Sourcebook in Indian Philosophy, Princeton University Press, ISBN 0-691-01958-4, p. 227–249.

69. Chatterjee & Datta 1984, Chatterjee, S.; Datta, D. (1984), An Introduction to Indian Philosophy (8th ed.), University of Calcutta, ASIN: B0007BFXK4 p. 55.

70. Durga Prasad, History of the and hras up to 1565 A. D., p. 116.

71. National Geographic January 2008, VOL. 213, NO. 1 'The flow between faiths was such that for hundreds of years, almost all Buddhist temples, including the ones at Ajanta, were built under the rule and patronage of Hindu kings'.

72. The rise of Buddhism and Jainism. Religion and Ethics - Hinduism: Other religious influences. BBC. 26 July 2004. Retrieved 21 April 2007.

73. Andrea Nippard. 'The Alvars' (PDF). Archived from the original (PDF) on 3 December 2013. Retrieved 20 April 2013.

74. Battuta's Travels: Delhi, capital of Muslim India Archived 23 April 2008 at the Wayback Machine

75. Director (Research Services Division). 'Ritual and reform in the research' Retrieved 23 July 2020.

76. Venkatesh, Karthik (12 November 2016). 'A brief history of the Bhakti movement'. Livemint. Retrieved 23 July 2020.

77. 'Culture And Heritage - Medieval History - Bhakti Movement - Know India: National Portal of India'. knowindia.gov.in. Retrieved 23 July 2020.

78. 'Kabir in His Time, And Ours'. The Wire. Retrieved 7 January 2021.

79. Encyclopedia Britannica. Retrieved 23 July 2020.

80. M. R. Sakhare, History and Philosophy of the Lingayat Religion, Prasaranga, Karnataka University, Dharwad.

81. Omvedt, Gail. Buddhism in India: Challenging Brahmanism and Caste. 3rd ed. London/New Delhi/Thousand Oaks: Sage, 2003. pages: 2, 3–7, 8, 14–15, 19, 240, 266, 271.

82. Thomas Pantham; Vrajendra Raj Mehta; Vrajendra Raj Mehta (2006), Political Ideas in Modern India: thematic explorations, Sage Publications, ISBN 0-7619-3420-0.

83. 'Plea in SC to remove 'socialist' and 'secular' words from Constitution's preamble | India News - Times of India'. The Times of India.

84. 'Plea in SC seeks to remove words 'socialist', 'secular' from Constitution's preamble-India News, First post'. First post. 29 July 2020.

85. 'Preamble To The Indian Constitution'. www.legalserviceindia.com. Retrieved 23 February 2021.

86. Olivelle, Patrick. 'Moksha | Indian religion'. Encyclopedia Britannica. Retrieved 6 January 2021.

87. Basu, Durga Das (2013). Introduction to the Constitution of India (21 ed.). LexisNexis. p. 124. ISBN 978-81-803-8918-4.

88. Samirah Majumdar, '5 Facts About Religion in India', Pew Research Center, June 29, 2018.

89. Thomas, Maria. 'Kumbh Mela, the world's largest religious festival, begins in India'. Quartz India. Retrieved 5 January 2021.

90. P. 225 Essential Hinduism By Steven Rosen.

91. Pechilis, Karen; Raj, SelvJanuary 2013 (2013). South Asian Religions: Tradition and Today. Routledge. ISBN 9780415448512.

92. '10 Countries with the Largest Muslim Populations, 2010 and 2050'. Pew Research Center's Religion & Public Life Project. 2 April 2015. Retrieved 7 February 2017.

93. Diplomat, Akhilesh Pillalamarri, The. 'How South Asia Will Save Global Islam'. The Diplomat. Retrieved 7 February 2017.

94. The sacred and the feminine: imagination and sexual difference By Griselda Pollock, Victoria Turvey Sauron., p. 80,81.

95. Satish Chandra, Medieval India; From Sultanate to the Mughals, vol-I, p.235.

96. Carl W. Ernst, Shambhala Guide to Sufism, New Delhi, 1997. Amit Dey, 'Sufism in India' in Abakshay (a bilingual journal), 2004.

97. Satish Chandra, Medieval India; From Sultanate to the Mughals, vol-I, p. 237.

98. Amalendu De, Theological Discourses in Indian History, Presidential Address, 2003-04, The Asiatic Society, Kolkata.

99. S Nurul Hasan, Religion, State and Society in Medieval India, New Delhi, 2005, p.72.

100. Satish Chandra, Medieval India; From Sultanate to the Mughals, vol-I, p.257.

101. Saiyid Athar Abbas Rizvi, A History of Sufism in India, vol-I, New Delhi, 1986 (Reprint) p.239.

102. Satish Chandra, Medieval India; From Sultanate to the Mughals, vol-I, pp. 239-40.

103. Amalendu De, Theological Discourses, p.9.

104. Chandra, Medieval India, for information about individual sufi saints of south asia see N.Hanif, Biographical Encyclopaedia of Sufis; South Asia, New Delhi, 2000, p.239-40.

105. Arthur Buehler, Sufi Heirs of the Prophet: The Indian Naqshbandiyya and the Rise of the Mediating Sufi Shaykh, South Carolina, 1998. Amit Dey, The Image of the Prophet in Bengali Muslim Piety: 1850-1947, Kolkata, 2005.

106. Satish Chandra, Medieval India; From Sultanate to the Mughals, vol-I, p.240.

107. Abdul Haqq Dihlawi, Akhbarul Akhyar, (in Persian), p.47.

108. Another Persian text entitled Fawaid ul Fuad (p.180) confirms that Shaikh Jalaluddin was the disciple of Shaikh Shihabuddin. Noted medievalist Khaliq Ahmad Nizami, in his Tarikh Mashaikh i Chisht (in Urdu, vol-I, Delhi, 1980,) has provided a genealogy of the Suhrawardi order, p.179.

109. Abdul Karim, Social History of the Muslims in Bengal, Dacca, 1959, p.95, Abdul Karim, Corpus of Arabic and Persian Inscriptions of Bengal, Chittagong, 1992, p.348, Muhammad Enamul Haq, A History of Sufism in Bengal, Dhaka, 1975, pp.146, 160-168, Shek Subhodaya, edited by Sukumar Sen, Calcutta, 1927, cited by Enamul Haq, in his History of Sufism, p.160 ff.

110. Amir Hasan Sijzi, Fawaid ul Fuad, Lucknow, 1885, p.236.

111. Abdul Karim, Social History, Sijzi, Fawaid ul Fuad, Lucknow, 1885 p.94.

112. Abid Ali Khan, Memoirs of Gaur and Pandua, edited by H.E.Stapleton, Calcutta, 1931, pp.97-106.

113. Ghulam Hussain Salim, Riyaz us Salatin, Bibliotheca Indica, 1898 A.D., p.94-95, cited by A Karim, Social History of the Muslims, p.94.

114. Abid Ali Khan, Memoirs of Gaur and Pandua, edited by H.E.Stapleton, Calcutta, 1931 Memoirs, p.100.

115. Abid Ali Khan, Memoirs of Gaur and Pandua, edited by H.E.Stapleton, Calcutta, 1931, p.102

116. Sunita Puri, Advent of Sikh Religion; A Socio-Political Perspective, New Delhi, 1993, Chapter 4. 23

117. Amit Dey, Sufism in India, Kolkata, 1996, p.22-25.

118. Richard M. Eaton, Sufis of Bijapur; 1300-1700; Social Roles of Sufis in Medieval India, (First published in 1978), New Delhi, 1996.

119. Simon Digby, Sufis and Soldiers in Awrangzeb's Deccan, New Delhi, 2001.

120. Buehler, Heirs of the Prophet, p.82-97.

121. Z.A.Desai, "The Major Dargahs of Ahmadabad" in Christian W. Troll edited, Muslim Shrines in India, New Delhi, 2004 (Second edition), p. 76-97.

122. A comprehensive picture of factionalism and intrigues that accentuated the decline of the Mughal Empire during the eighteenth century has been provided in Satish Chandra's book entitled Parties and Politics at the Mughal Court.

123. Desai's article "Dargahs of Ahamadabad" in Troll edited Muslim Shrines, p.92.

124. Vide, Ruqaiyyah Waris Maqsood, A Basic Dictionary of Islam, New Delhi, 1998, rpt. 2000, p.71. Muslim ambivalence towards some ritual dynamics associated with Sufism is reflected in the above paragraph.

125. Muhammad Zuber Qureshi, "The Library of Hazrat Pir Muhammad Shah at Ahmadabad," in C.W.Troll edited, Islam in India: Studies and Commentaries, vol. 2, New Delhi, 1985, p.282-300. Cited in Z.A.Desai's article mentioned above.

126. Desai's article "Dargahs of Ahamadabad" in Troll edited Muslim Shrines," p.93.

127. Amit Dey, Image of the Prophet, chapters 2 and 3. How the advent of print in Muslim society posed a serious threat to the institution of Sufism has been dealt with in chapter 2 of my book.

128. Makhdoom Sabri, Concise Twentieth Century Dictionary; Urdu into English, Delhi, 2001, p.409.

129. Desai's article "Dargahs of Ahamadabad" in Troll edited Muslim Shrines" p.94. 24

130. Amit Dey, Image of the Prophet, chapter 1. For a list of Persian texts on Sufism see Amit Dey, Sufism, chapters 1 and 2.

131. Desai's article "Dargahs of Ahamadabad" in Troll edited Muslim Shrines", p.94.

132. Bengali book entitled Upakule Juganta: Sholo Satak, Portuguese Abhighat O Asiar Banijyer Punarbinyas, Kolkata, 1999, p.18-21.

133. Neeru Misra edited, Sufis and Sufism; Some Reflections, New Delhi, 2004, See Iqbal Sabir's article 'Impact of Ibn Arabi's Mystical thought...'

134. Dr. Raziuddin Aquil's lecture. Delivered at the Department of History, University of Calcutta, on 27 March 2006.

135. Dey, Terence P. (1982). The Conception of Punishment in Early Indian Literature. Ontario: Wilfrid Laurier University Press. ISBN 0-919812-15-5. Image of the Prophet, Chapter 4.

136. Dey, Terence P. (1982). The Conception of Punishment in Early Indian Literature. Ontario: Wilfrid Laurier University Press. ISBN 0-919812-15-5. Sufism, Chapter 1.

137. Afghans and Islam in Medieval North India. New Delhi, 2007. Written by Dr. Amit Dey, Professor of History, Calcutta University, for Sripat Singh College Seminar Volume. 2016.

138. Abdullah Jawadi Amuli. 'Dhikr and the Wisdom Behind It' (PDF). Translated by A. Rahmim. Retrieved 2020-02-08.

139. Hakim Moinuddin Chisti The Book of Sufi Healing, ISBN 978-0-89281-043-7.

140. 'The Naqshbandi Way of Dhikr'. Archived from the original on 1997-05-29. Retrieved 26 August 2015.

141. Touma 1996, p.162.

142. 'What is Remembrance and what is Contemplation?'. Archived from the original on 2008-04-15.

143. 'Muraqaba'. Archived from the original on 2015-06-09.

144. Muhammad Emin Er, Laws of the Heart: A Practical Introduction to the Sufi Path, ISBN 978-0-9815196-1-6, p. 77.

145. Hussain, Zahid (22 April 2012). 'Is it permissible to listen to Qawwali?'. The Sunni Way. Retrieved 12 June 2020.

146. Desai, Siraj (13 January 2011). 'Moulana Rumi and Whirling Zikr'. ask mufti. Retrieved 12 June 2020. However, later on this Simaa' was modernized to include dancing and music, thus giving rise to the concept of 'whirling dervishes. This is a Bidah and is not the creation of orthodox Sufism.

147. Darul Ma'rifa. p. 396.

148. Hashiyah at-Tahtaawi. Al-Ilmiyya. p. 319.

149. 'The Sema of the Mevlevi'. Mevlevi Order of America. Archived from the original on 2012-12-21. Retrieved 2009-03-26.

150. Desai, Siraj (13 January 2011). 'Moulana Rumi and Whirling Zikr'.

151. Murad, Abdul Hakim. "Music in the Islamic Tradition." Cambridge Muslim College Retreat. May 18, 2017.

152. Rabbani, Faraz (25 December 2012). "Listening to Islamic Songs with Musical Instruments". Seekers Guidance. Retrieved 12 June 2020.

153. 'Is Music Prohibited in Islam?'. My Religion Islam. Retrieved 12 June 2020.

154. Muhammad-Ibn-Adam (14 April 2004). 'Music and Singing - A Detailed Article'. Darul Ifta. Leicester.

155. Muhammad bin Mubarak Kirmani. Siyar-ul-Auliya: History of Chishti Silsila (in Urdu). Translated by Ghulam Ahmed Biryan. Lahore: Mushtaq Book Corner.

156. Nizamuddin Auliya (31 December 1996). Fawa'id al-Fu'aad: Spirtual and Literal Discourses. Translated by Z. H. Faruqi. D.K. Print World Ltd. ISBN 9788124600429.

157. Nusrat Fateh Ali Khan: National Geographic World Music. 2013-03-20. Archived from the original on 2013-03-20. Retrieved 2018-10-09.

158. John Renard, Friends of God: Islamic Images of Piety, Commitment, and Servanthood (Berkeley: University of California Press, 2008); Idem, Tales of God Friends: Islamic Hagiography in Translation (Berkeley: University of California Press, 2009).

159. Radtke, B.; Lory, P.; Zarcone, Th.; DeWeese, D.; Gaborieau, M.; Denny, F.M.; Aubin, Françoise; Hunwick, J.O.; Mchugh, N. (2012). "Walī". In P. Bearman; Th. Bianquis; C.E. Bosworth; E. van Donzel; W.P. Heinrichs (eds.). Encyclopaedia of Islam (2nd ed.). Brill. doi:10.1163/1573-3912 islam_COM_1335.

160. B. Radtke, Drei Schriften des Theosophen von Tirmid̲, ii (Beirut-Stuttgart, 1996), pp. 68-69.

161. Titus Burckhardt, Art of Islam: Language and Meaning (Bloomington: World Wisdom, 2009), p. 99.

162. "Popular Sufi leader in Morocco dies aged 95". gulfnews.com. Retrieved 2020-12-30.

163. Staff Writer (2018-03-28). 'Confreries: A Crossroads of Morocco's Literary and Spiritual Diversity'. Morocco World News. Retrieved 2020-12-30.

164. Gardet, L. (2012). 'Karāma". In P. Bearman; Th. Bianquis; C.E. Bosworth; E. van Donzel; W.P. Heinrichs (eds.). Encyclopaedia of Islam (2nd ed.). Brill. doi:10.1163/1573-3912_islam_COM_0445.

165. Jonathan A.C. Brown, 'Faithful Dissenters', Journal of Sufi Studies 1 (2012), p. 123.

166. Anup Tanya, Sufi CULTS and evolution of Medieval Indian Culture, ICHR, Mongraph Series a Northern Book Centre, Darayaganyi, New Delhi, p. 01.

167. Farid-al- Din, Tazkirat- ul-Awliya, (Ed.), by RA. Nicholson (London), 1905, and Leiden, 1907, Part I, 1905, p. 37.

168. Annie Marie, Schimmel, (1975), Sufism in Indo-Pakistan, Mystic Dimension of Islam, Chapel Hill, p. 346.

169. Annie Marie, Schimmel, (1975), Sufism in Indo-Pakistan, Mystic Dimension of Islam, Chapel Hill op. cit., p. 345.

170. M. Michael Hamilton, (2007), Lost History: The Enduring Legacy of Muslim Scientist Thinkers, Artist, Washington, p. 7.

171. A. Zaziuddin, (2007), Sufism Culture of Politics, Oxford University Press, New Delhi, p. 9.

172. Susan Bayly, (2004), Saints Goddesses and Kings, Cambridge University Press, p. 137.

173. Ellison Banks Findly, (1993), Nurjahan, Empress of Mughal India, Oxford University Press, p. 208.

174. Evelyn, Underwill, (1911), Mysticism, London, p. 462.

175. T. Umar Sadiq, Sufi Movement in Tamil Nadu: A Historical Perspective, unpublished Ph.D. Thesis, (2014), Bharathithasan University, India, p. 111.

Chapter 4

1.   Alam M. 'The Languages of Political Islam'. India 1200 – 1800.

2.   History of the Rise of Mahomedan Power in India, Vol. II, p 250–25.

3.   Allama Prabhu - Sherwani, H. K. The Bahmani's of the Deccan. An objective study, p. 213. For Mrtyunjay - DEVĻE, S. R. (ed.). Sri Bhaktavijaya [The Victory of the Devotees], pp. 397–401 and for Ramdas and king Shivaji -

Abbott. J. E. The Poet-Saints of Maharashtra, No. 8. Ramdas, pp. 50–63, 109–112.

4. Veer, P. Religious Nationalism. Hindus and Muslims in India.

5. Note: The Marathas, as a warrior caste-group, whose different clans proved to be tremendously successful in the Deccan in military, political, social, and economic terms roughly from 17th to early 19th century, should not be confused with all Marathi speakers.

6. Elliot, H. M. Sir Henry Elliot's Original Preface. In Elliot, H. M., Dowson, J. (transl. and ed.). The History of India as Told by Its Own Historians: The Muhammadan Period, pp. xv–xxvii.

7. A movement (1956 – 1960) that demanded the creation of the Indian state of Maharashtra on linguistic grounds as a separate state for Marathi speakers.

8. Deshpande, P. Creative Pasts. Historical Memory and Identity in Western India, 1700 – 1960.

9. One of its results is easily seen in the statues of Chhatrapati-Shivaji that are literally dotted around on the map of Maharashtra (and the Marathi areas of the adjoining states). On the politics of memory in Maharashtra see Jasper, D. of Relics and Living Traditions: Creating heritage in Maharashtra. In Deak, D. Jasper D. (ed.). Rethinking Western India: The Changing Contexts of Culture, Society, and Religion, p 105–119.

10. Some insight may be gained by comparing the number of works that cover many aspects of the pre-Maratha Marathi Deccan with the writings particularly on the Marathas. Starting from Grant Duff's magnum opus through the works of V. K. Rajwade, D. V. Potdar, G. H. Khare, V. S. Bendre, G. S. Sardesai, or outside Maharashtra, Sir Jadunath Sarkar, up to comparatively recent authors such as A. R. Kulkarni, and to certain extent also current analysts, it seems that the Maratha world looms much larger than the one which is assumed to precede it.

11. The detailed analysis of different discursive layers that framed this past to be engaged with in the terms of collective identities is found in Deshpande P. Creative Pasts. Historical Memory and Identity in Western India, 1700 – 1960. A good attempt to explain the complex world of pre-colonial political and cultural alliances that were far from the idea of timeless nations can be found in Fischel R. S. Local States in an Imperial World Identity, Society and Politics in the Early Modern Deccan.

12. Clothey F. W. Religion in India. A Historical Introduction, p. 8.

13. Recent positive deviations from this trend - Sohoni, P. The Architecture of a Deccan Sultanate: Courtly Practice and Royal Authority in Late Medieval India; Haidar N. N. Sardar M. Sultans of Deccan India, 1500 -1700.

14. A good example of how misleading such an effort may be is found in the brilliant study by Mcleod W. H. The Hagiography of the Sikhs. In Callewaert W. M. Snell R. (ed.). According to Tradition (Hagiographical Writing in India), p 15–41.

15. Truschke A. Culture of Encounters: Sanskrit at the Mughal Court; Pollock S. The Language of the Gods in the World of Men. Sanskrit, Culture and

Power in Pre-Modern India; Guha S. Mārgī, Deśī, Yāvanī: High Language and Ethnic Speech in Maharashtra. In Kotani H. et al. (ed.). Mārga. Ways of Liberation, Empowerment, and Social Change in Maharashtra, p 129–146.

16. Consider in this context Pushkar Sohoni's idea of "vernacular as a space" and that "vernacular or localized worldviews operated through a continuum of tongues". Sohoni P. Vernacular as a space: writing in the Deccan. In South Asian History and Culture, 2016, Vol. 7, No. 3, p. 264.

17. See for instance Gosavi R. Rā. (ed.). Śrī Sakalasantagāthā [Songs of all the Saints]. The historical precursor of Sakalasantagāthā was Navanīt published by pandit Parashurampant Godbole as early as 1854.

18. Ernst C. W. Eternal Garden (Mysticism, History and Politics in South Asian Sufi Center); Novetzke Ch. L. Religion and Public Memory. A Cultural History of Saint Namdev in India; Keune Jon M. Eknāth Remembered and Reformed: Bhakti, Brahmins, and Untouchables in Marathi Historiography. Green, Nile. Indian Sufism Since the Seventeenth Century. Saints, books, and empires in the Muslim Deccan; Naregal, Veena. Language and Power in pre-colonial western India: Textual hierarchies, literate audiences, and colonial philology. In Indian Economic and Social History Review, 2000, Vol. 37, No. 3, p 259–294.

19. Voll J. O. Islam as a Special World-System. In Journal of World History, 1994, Vol. 5, No. 2, p 213–226.

20. Pagdi S. Sūfī sampradāy. Tattvadnyān āṇi kārya [The Sufi Tradition. Principles and Practice].

21. Vakil A. Sūfī sampradāyāce antaraṅg [The Heart of the Sufi Tradition].

22. Ahmad A. Studies in Islamic Culture in the Indian Environment, p 140–200. Studies in Indology and Medieval Indian History (Prof. G. H. Khare Felicitation Volume), p 173, 189.

23. For more on this in the context of syncretism Ernst C. W., Stewart T. Syncretism. In Mills M. A., Claus P. J., Diamond S. (ed.). South Asian Folklore. An Encyclopedia, p 586–588.

24. Ḍhere R. C. Musalmān marāṭhī santkavī [Muslim Marathi Saint-Poets]; Ḍhere R. C. Ekātmatece śilpakār [The Forgers of Unity]; Pathan Y. M. Musalmān (sūfī) santāñce marāṭhī sāhitya [Marathi Literature of the Muslim (Sufi) Saints].

25. In literary Indo-Persian tradition qalandars are called 'perpetually intoxicated' (damādam mast qalandar) for they drove the 'intoxication' (sukr) trend of Sufism to extremity.

26. Al-Hujwiri cites as an example of malāmatī's typical behaviour an event from Ibrahim b. Adham's life, as narrated by him: 'On one occasion I was in a ship where nobody knew me. I was clad in common clothes and my hair was long, and my guise was such that all the people in the ship mocked and laughed at me. Among them was a buffoon, who was always coming and pulling my hair and tearing it out and treating me with contumely after the manner of his kind. At that time, I felt entirely satisfied, and I rejoiced in my garb. My joy reached

its highest pitch one day when the buffoon rose from his place and super me minxit [urinated on me]' (al-Hujwiri 1992: 68).

27. The other ancestor of the Qalandariyya movement is Hasan al-Juwaliqi (died 1322) who established the first cloister (zāwiya) of qalandars in Egypt.

28. Despite great loss of blood, Nasiruddin Chiragh-i-Dihli survived. In accordance with the moral principles of the Chishtis he forgave the qalandar who had made the attempt on his life and even paid him twenty tankās in compensation for the 'damage', since the clumsy murderer had got wounded with his own knife. At the saint's urgent request Sultan Firoz Shah did not take any measures against Turab, confining himself to his banishment from Delhi.

29. The Hyderis of Khurasan derived from Qutbuddin Hyder, a disciple of the above-mentioned Muhammad b.Yunus as-Sawaji. Ibn Battuta considered Hyderis, Jalalis and the 'Iraqian Ahmadiyya (Rifa'iyya) to be related groups.

30. Members of the Turkish fraternity Bektashiyya used to wear on their chest similar stones, called taslīm-tash as a token of humility or submission to the will of God.

31. According to Nizamuddin Awliya: 'During the Mongol onslaught, the infidels of Chinghiz Khan turned toward India. At that time Qutb uddin counseled his friends, "Flee, for these people will overpower you!" "What are you talking about?" they asked him. "They have brought a dervish along with them," he explained, "and they have kept him hidden. That dervish is coming (here) now. In a dream I have wrestled with that same dervish, and he threw me to the ground. The truth of the matter is that they also will overpower you, so flee!" Having said this, he himself retired into a cave and did not reappear. And what he had predicted came to pass' (Amir Hasan 1992: 101).

32. Barani believed that the bloodshed and unlawful execution of Sidi Maula called down divine retribution on Sultan Jalaluddin Khalji. The event was the watershed and was followed by an unprecedented dust storm and a severe drought and famine throughout his reign.

33. According to the anecdote, narrated in the chronicle of the seventeenth century Tārīkh-i Dā'ūdī, the founder of the empire of the Great Mughals, Babur visited Sikandar Lodi's court with a shaven head and in the company of qalandars. The Sultan of Delhi supposedly recited to the guest a verse of Hafiz, to the effect that a shaven head did not make one a qalandar. Babur countered it in verse, that a crown on one's head had not yet made anybody a true ruler. This legend nevertheless stands testimony to the status held by qalandars in the beginning of the sixteenth century.

34. Babamatita, Vol. II, Trans. by A.G. Beverldge p 481-82.

35. Baburnama Vol-II, p – 480.

36. Tripathi - Rise and fall of the Mughal Empire, p 20.

37. Babamai Ra Vol XI, p 476.

38. Mirat-i-Sikandari Eng. Trans., p 101.

39. Baburnama, Vol II, p 483-84.

40. Habibullah - Foundation of riusliir rule in India.

41. Mohd. Habib and K.A. Nizami - Comprehensive History of India, Vol. V, p 138.

42. Elliot and Jowson History of India as told by its own Historian, Vol. ll, p 251.

43. Comprehensive History of India Vol. V, p 138.

44. Tara Chand - Influence of Islam on Indian Culture, p 101.

45. A.L. Srivastava medieval Indian Culture.

46. Yusuf Husain - Glimpse of medieval Indian Culture p. 33.

47. M. Rahman - Islamic Culture (Sufism and Islam), 1927 p 641-42.

48. Rahtrtan - Islamic Culture (Sufism and Islam.) 1927 p 64.

49. Mir Valliuddin - What is Sufism (Islamic Culture), Voi.20 (1946), Vol.1-4, p 371-72.

50. Mir Valllud'ain What is Sufism (Islamic Culture) Vcl.20 (1946) Vol 4, p.375.

51. Mir Valliuddin - What is Sufism (Islamic Culture), Voi.20 (1946), Vol.1-4, p 373-74.

52. B.L. Uniya Life and Culture in Medieval India p 334.

53. Vivek Bhattacharya - The Spirit of Indian Culture (Saints of India), p 209.

54. R.P. Tripathi - Rise and fall of the Mughal Empire p 350.

55. Tarild-i-Feroz shahi Afif, p 363.

56. Fawaid-ul-Fuad, Slyarul Auliya p.60.

57. Khbarul Akhara pp.26.

58. Tara Chand – Influence of Islam on Indian Culture, 176.

59. L. Shrivastava Medieval Indian Culture, p 97.

60. Garierson - Bhakti marga.

61. Tarachand - Influence of Islam on Indian culture, H.100

62. Macauliffa - The Sila, Vol. VI, p 102.

63. M. P. Srivastava - Society and Culture in Medieval India p 61.

64. A.L. Srivastava - Medieval Indian Culture, p 65.

65. Prem Lata - Mystic saints of India, p. 114.

66. R. G. Bhandarker – Vaishnaviatr, Salvism and other minor Religiousism, p 83.

67. Bhakti ttiaktinal A.L. Srivastava Medieval Indian Culture, p 63.

68. Ramoharitnanas Gita press, Gorakhpur, ed. 2020, p 56.

69. Kari Ram Gupta -> History of the Sikh Gurus p. 81.

70. P. Srivastava - Society and Culture in Medieval India p 86.

71. Tarachand - Influence of Islam on Indian Culture p 182.

72. Bahirat, B.P. Sadhu shaikh Muhammad', in Mahadwaar, Santancha Maharashtra (Special Volume), No.5, Parandeka Baba Edi., Kolhapur, Shake 1886, pp. 25-27; See, Wagale, S.C. Edi., Yogsangram, Mumbai; Bendre, V.C. Edi., Yogsangram, Mumbai, 1961; Dhere, R.C., Muslim Marathi Saint Kavi, pp. 84-117; Khanolkar G.D. Edi., Marathi Vangmay Kosh, Volume I, p. 380; Carl W. Ernst, Admiring the Works of the Ancients: The Ellora Temples as Viewed by Indo-Muslim Authors', in Beyond Turk and Hindu: Rethinking Religious Identities in Islamicate South Asia, Edi. By David Gilmantin & Bruce B. Lawrence, University Press of Florida, Florida. p.114; Bendre, V.S., Shaikh Muhammadbaba Yanche Kavitasamgrah, Mumbai, 1961, p.115.

73. Maktubat-e-Mujaddid, book I, letter 221.

74. For early Sufism and the development of Sufi orders see for example, A History of Sufism in India, Vol. I, S.A.A. Rizvi, Munshiram Manoharlal Publishers Pvt. Ltd., New Delhi, 1978.

75. The Faith and Practice of AI-Ghazali tr. W.M. Watt, Oneworld Publications, Oxford, 1953, 1994, pp 56-57; the above book consists of a translation of Deliverance from Error (Al-Munqidh min adDalal), which is largely autobiographical, and The Beginning of Guidance (Bidayat al-Hidayah) from The Revival of the Religious Sciences (Ihya''Ulum ad-Din). For a translation of the complete Ihya''Ulum ad-Din, see also Imam Ghazali's Ihya Ulum-id-Din, tr. Maulana Fazul-ul-Karim, Sind Sagar Academy, Lahore, 1971.

76. Abu Nasr 'Abdallah bin 'Ali al-Sarraj al-Tusi, the Kitab al-Luma' fi 'I-Tasawwuf ed. R.A. Nicholson, London, 1914 and 1963. The title can be translated as The Book of Flashes. This book has also been translated into Urdu by Sayyid Asrar Bukhari Kitab al-Luma', Lahore: Islamic Book Foundation, 1984.

77. For a description of the 'stages', with references to al-Sirraj and Sufi writers later than al-Siraj, see for example: The Persian Sufis by C. Rice, Ltd., London, 1964; S. H. Nasr, Sufi Essays, London 1972; and others.

78. Dabistan-i-i-iagahib p 186, Tarachand - Influence of Islam on Indian Culture, p 147.

79. Mohd. Hidayatullah - Kabiff of Hindu Muslim Unity, p 125 – 126.

80. Shailesh Zaidi, S. A. Rizvi Alakhbani p 78.

81. S. A. A. Risvi - A History of Sufism in India, Vol. ll p 410.

82. S. A. A. Rizvi - A History of Sufism in India Vol. I, p 392-393.

83. K.A. Misami Shatter! saints and their attitude towards State (Medieval India Quarterly)Vol.1 (1950) No.2, p.58.

84. Prem Lata - Mystic Saints of India (Ramanuja), p 115 Vivek Bhattacharya 'The Spirit of Indian Culture', (States of India), p 293-294.

85. Tarachand - Influence of Islam on Indian Culture p 190

Chapter 5

1. The Maloji kings had two sons, Shahaji and Sharifji, by the grace of a pir named Shah Sharif. You will find a detailed description of this in the Annual Minutes of the Board of Research in the History of India, 1916, p. 1180 to 193.

2. Salma Ahmed Farooqui (2011). A Comprehensive History of Medieval India: From Twelfth to the Mid-Eighteenth Century. Dorling Kindersley India. p. 314–. ISBN 978-81-317-3202-1.

3. V. B. Kulkarni (1963). Shivaji: The Portrait of a Patriot. Orient Longman. p. 27.

4. The Islamic path: Sufism, and society, in India, Saiyid Zaheer Husain Jafri, Helmut Reifeld – 2006 p. 211.

5. Kosambi, Meera (editor); Laine, James (2000). Intersections :socio-cultural trends in Maharashtra. London: Sangam. p. 62. ISBN 9780863118241. Retrieved 28 July 2017.

6.　Gazetteer of the Bombay Presidency: Ahmednagar. Printed at the Government Central Press. 1884.

7.　The Islamic path: Sufism, and society in India, Saiyid Zaheer Husain Jafri, Helmut Reifeld – 2006 p.174.

8.　Kosambi, Meera (editor); Laine, James (2000). Intersections : socio-cultural trends in Maharashtra. London: Sangam. p. 62. ISBN 9780863118241. Retrieved 28 July 2017.

9.　Asgharali Engineer (1989). Communalism and communal violence in India: an analytical approach to Hindu-Muslim conflict. Ajanta Publications (India), p. 182. ISBN 978-81-202-0220-7. Retrieved 30 March 2013.

10.　Richard M. Eaton; Munis D. Faruqui; David Gilmartin; Sunil Kumar (7 March 2013). Expanding Frontiers in South Asian and World History: Essays in Honour of John F. Richards. Cambridge University Press. p. 263–264. ISBN 978-1-107-03428-0.

11.　Bhave, Y.G. (2000). From the death of Shivaji to the death of Aurangzeb : the critical years. New Delhi: Northern Book Centre. p. 19. ISBN 9788172111007.

12.　Farooqui Salma Ahmed (2011). A Comprehensive History of Medieval India: Twelfth to the Mid-Eighteenth Century. Pearson. p. 315. ISBN 9788131732021.

13.　V. B. Kulkarni (1963). Shivaji: The Portrait of a Patriot. Orient Longman.

14.　Marathi book Shivkaal (Times of Shivaji) by Dr V G Khobrekar, Publisher: Maharashtra State Board for Literature and Culture, First edition 2006. Chapter 1.

15.　Salma Ahmed Farooqui (2011). A Comprehensive History of Medieval India: From Twelfth to the Mid-Eighteenth Century. Dorling Kindersley India. p. 314, ISBN 978-81-317-3202-1.

16.　Richard M. Eaton (17 November 2005). A Social History of the Deccan, 1300 -1761: Eight Indian Lives. 1. Cambridge University Press. p. 128 - 221. ISBN 978-0-521-25484-7.

17.　Mehta 2005, p. 7; Laine 2011, p. 8-9.

18.　Sarkar, Shivaji and His Times 1920, p. 26.

19.　Ranohandra Shukla - Hindi Sahitya Ka Itihaa (Hindi), p 87.

20.　Tulpule S.G. & Anne Feldnaus, A Dictionary of Old Marathi, New York, 2000, p. xi; Sumit Guha, Transitions and Translations: Regions, Power & Vernacular Identity in the Dakhan, 1500-1800, Comparative Studies of South Asia, Africa & the Middle East, 24:2, 2004. p.23-31; George Michell & Mark Zebrowski, The New Cambridge History of India, 1:7 Architecture and Art of the Deccan Sultanates, Edited Volume, Cambridge, 1999, pp. 5-9; Munis Faruqi & Vasudha Dalmiya, Religious Interactions in Mughal India, OUP, New Delhi, 2012, p.107.

21.　Pathan, Y.M. Dr. (2011) Contribution of Muslim Saint Poets to Medieval Marathi Literature, Maharashtra Rajya Sahitya Sanskriti Mandal, Mumbai, pp.12-13; Purnanad Charitra (Marathi), Hanuman Atmaja, Line No. 16:265; R.C.Dhere, (1967) Musalman Marathi Sant Kavi (Marathi), Padmgandha Pub. Pune, p. 9 - 43.

22. Shaikh Musak Rajjak, Sufism, Marathi Bhakti Movemet and Eknath's Hindu-Turk Samvad', in Sufism:A Selebration of Love, Edited by Ajeet Caur, Refaqat Ali Khan, Prof. [Edi.](2012), FOSWAL, New Delhi, p. 216-225; Shaikh Musak Rajjak, Bhakti Cults in Medieval Marathwada and Sufism, in Samshodhak Quarterly Journal, Rajwade History Research Institute, Dhule, p. 40-51.

23. Shah Murtuza Bahamani, Mrutunjaya' (Marathi) Edi. By Dr. Shaikh Julfi, Guru Prakashan, Nagpur, p. 17-49; Maharashtra Saarswat, Fifth Edition, V.L. Bhave & Tulpule S.G. Edi., Popular Prakashan, Mumbai, 1963, p. 249, 782.

24. Shah Murtuza Bahamani, Avindh Punjikaran Kosh (Manuscript collection) at Shri Samarth Vangdevata Mandir, D.S. Joshi Collection, Rajwade Institute, Dhule; Pathan, Y.M. Dr. (2011) Contribution of Muslim of Muslim Saint Poets to Medieval Marathi Literature, Mumbai, p. 47; Prakashdeep:15, in Manuscript Collection at V.K. Rajwade Samshodhan Mandal, Dhule, Maharashtra.

25. Saiyid Ali Tabataba, Burhan-i-Mathir, Tami Press, Delhi, 1936; Sherwani H.K. & P.M. Joshi Edi. (1973) History of Medieval Deccan (1295-1724), Vol. II. Government AP Press, p. 166; The Articulation of Islamic Space in the Medieval Deccan, Richard M. Eaton, in Meenakshi Khanna (Edi.) (2012) Cultural History of Medieval India, Social Science Press, New Delhi, pp. 127-144; Chandorkar, G.K. Maharashtra Kavya Suchi, Pune, p. 36; Mr. Dhere, Ekaatmateche Shilpkar (Marathi), Manjul Prakashan, Pune, 1991, p. 38-45; Dr. Y.M.Pathan, p. 11-52.

26. 26. Interesting list of Marathi texts in Saraswati Mahal Library: Part I. Vedanta class, serial number 49, class number 374. (Three other manuscripts numbered 50, 51, 52 belong to 'Amberhuseni'.) Prof. A. Of Priyolkar has printed the first two chapters of 'Amberhuseni' in the October 1954 issue of 'Marathi Research Magazine' and a single excerpt from the ninth and eighteenth chapters in the January 1963 issue.

27. The saga of Sri Ramavallabhadas: Collector- Subrav Gopal Ubhaykar. p. 294.

28. Maloji and Shahji: Vasudev vaman khare p. 22.

29. Ekatmatache shilpakar author Ra. Chi Dhere, Majul prakashan, pune, 1994, p. 42.

30. Marathi Vagmayacha itihas, part 1, Author Dr. S. G. Malshe, marathi sahitya parishad, pune parkashan, 1982, p. 178.

31. 'Musalmanachi juni Marathi Kavita' Prof. A.K.Priyolkar, Marathi Sansodhak Mandal, Mumbai 1965, p.16.

32. Priyolkar, A.K. Prof., Musalmananchi Juni Marathi Kavita, Mumbai, 1965, p. 13-16; Dhere, R.C., Ekaatmateche Shilpkaar, Manul Prakashan, Pune, 1994, p. 38-45; Carl W. Ernst, Eternal Garden: Mysticism, History and Politics at a South Asian Sufi Center, Second Edition. New Delhi:2004; Amberhussaini, 2nd Adhyay, Edited Text, Maharashtra Samshodhan Patrika Quarterly Journal, Marathi Sahitya Mandal, Dadar, Mumbai, Oct. 1954, p. 9-15; Husainambari Manuscript, Tanjor Sarswati Mahal Library, 1575, Balaji Bad Collection No. 49, Tamilnadu; Dhere, Ramchandra Chintaman, Musalman Marathi Santkavi, Pune, 1967, p. 42-49.

33. Dhere, R. C. (1994) Ekatmateche Shilpkaar, Manjul Prakashan, Pune, p.51-63.

34. Aawalikar, Pandit, Dr. (1964) June Wangmay: Nawe Samshodhan, Dharwad, Karnataka, p. 260; Marathi Poem Manuscripts of Aalamkhan at: 1) Aalamkhan Padsamgrah, Shree Govindraj Baba Maharaj Samshtan, Gulbarga, 2) Shri Samarth Wangdevata Mandir, Dhule, Maharashtra State, Ref. Mss. 376, 1152, 3) Bharat Itihaas Samshodhan Mandal, Pune, Annual Report, Shak 1837, p. 280; Moholkar, V.S. Editor (1991) Nagesh Darpan, Nagesh Pub. House, Solapur, p. 164.

35. Pathan, U.M., Musalman Santanche Marathi Sahitya, Maharashtra Rajy Sahitya Aani Samskriti Mandal, Mumbai, 2011, p.196.

36. Saints of Tukaram Maharaj, come. C. Bedai, Moj Prakashan, Mumbai. 1958, p. 58-61.

37. The sculptor of unity, Dr. R. C. Dhere, Manjul Prakashan, Pune. 1994, p. 80-82.

38. Three research essays, Dr. Brahmananda Deshpande, Introduction Publications, Aurangabad, 1982, p. 28-30

39. Dr. Dhere, R.C., Ekatmateche Shilpkaar, p. 60; Manuscript of Shaikh Sultan, No. 1733, Shree Samarth Vangdevata Mandir, Dhule; Tulpule, S.G., Maharashtra Sarswat, Vth Edition, Popular Prakashan, Mumbai, 1963, p. 618.

40. Khanolkar G. D. (1970) Marathi Literature Encyclopeadia, Volume I, Maharashtra Rajya Sahitya Samskriti Mandal, Mumbai, p. 449; Dr. Dhere R.C.(1963) Eknathaachi guruparmpara, Indrayini Publication, Pune, p. 5-13; Bendre V.S. (1958) Shaikh Muhammad Baba Shrigondekar: Tukaram Maharaj Yanche Saint Sangati, Mumbai, p. 50-82.

41. "Santkavi Shaikh Mohammad: Ek chikitsak Abhyas", Dr.Bhima Modale, 1998, Unpublished book, Pune University, p. 294.

42. Etakmateche Shilpakar, p. 92.

43. Maharashtra – Saraswat, Bhave – Tulpule, 5th Edition, 1963, Popular Prakashan, Mumbai, p. 831.

44. Shaikh Mohammad Shrigondekar's 'Kavitasangrah" Vol 2, Shri. V.C. Bendre, p. 25,26,27.

45. Shaikh Mohammad Shrigondekar's writing named 'Yogsangram" Shri. V.P. Viachand Dalichand Desai, Shrigonda, 1973, p. 5.

46. Marathi Vagmayacha etihas, vol 2, Part 1, Dr..S.G.Malshe, Marathi Sahitik Parishad Prakashen, Pune, p. 619-20

47. Muslamanachi Old Marathi Kavta, Prof. A.K. Proyolkar, Marathi Sanshodhan Mandal, Mumbai 1965, p. 20.

48. Prachin Marathi Vagmayacha Itihas, Vol 2, Dr. A.N. Deshpande, Venus Publication, Pune, p. 145.

49. 'Shrisakalsantgatha', S.D.K.Thaware, Usamanabad, 1990, p. 300-01.

50. 'Sakalsantgatha' Editor D.K. Thaware Publication, Vasantrao Nagade Usmanabad p. 270-72.

51. SamarthVagdewata Mandir, Dhule, Badank (old script book), number 10, 82, 135 and 166.

52. Marathi Research Paper, year 10, Number 3, p.30

53. This book was first written by Ganapat Krishnaji etc. (1870). It was later published by Pandharinath Vinayak Pathak at Jagadishwar Press, Mumbai.

54. Sir Monier Monier-Williams, Dvaita, A Sanskrit-English Dictionary: Etymologically and Philologically Arranged with Special Reference to Cognate Indo-European Languages, Oxford University Press (Reprinted: Motilal Banarsidass), ISBN 978-8120831056, p. 507.

55. Jeaneane D. Fowler (2002). Perspectives of Reality: An Introduction to the Philosophy of Hinduism. Sussex Academic Press. p. 340–343. ISBN 978-1-898723-94-3.

56. Gopal, Madan (1990). K.S. Gautam (ed.). India through the ages. Publication Division, Ministry of Information and Broadcasting, Government of India. p. 79.

Dara Shikoh 137, 336

dargāh 205, 212, 213, 214

Dattatraya 299, 300

Daulatabad 245, 249, 267, 269, 274, 275, 276, 284, 285, 286, 287

Dayal xxv, 231, 235

Deccan 126, 174, 178, 199, 200, 201, 202, 203, 205, 222, 244, 245, 251, 268, 269, 270, 272, 273, 275, 281, 283, 285, 288, 290, 291, 292, 296, 397, 437, 442, 456, 458, 459, 460, 464, 465

Delhi 100, 108, 124, 125, 138, 168, 170, 173, 174, 175, 177, 178, 194, 196, 197, 208, 210, 211, 216, 217, 222, 224, 226, 244, 246, 247, 248, 249, 252, 254, 255, 258, 259, 270, 281, 303, 336, 337, 338, 340, 341, 342, 345, 390, 392, 393, 394, 395, 401, 404, 408, 436, 437, 438, 441, 442, 445, 452, 453, 454, 455, 456, 457, 458, 461, 463, 464, 465

dervishes 5, 118, 143, 192, 208, 210, 212, 213, 214, 215, 216, 221, 304, 308, 400, 457

Devagiri Dynasty 327

devotional xvii, xviii, 40, 103, 126, 137, 167, 168, 169, 188, 191, 193, 194, 219, 232, 233, 238, 244, 261, 263, 266, 267, 272, 288, 292, 309, 315, 318, 321, 326, 328, 353, 355, 368, 372, 374, 375, 403

Dhacca 225

dharma 37, 161, 320, 354, 355

Dhere R.C 245, 466

dhikr 42, 51, 63, 67, 76, 83, 84, 111, 134, 154, 191, 192, 207, 211, 253, 281, 306, 382, 386, 387, 389, 391, 394

Dhikr 191, 306, 333, 457

din-e-ilahi 123, 124

divine xiv, 2, 3, 4, 8, 15, 16, 17, 25, 26, 27, 28, 30, 31, 32, 35, 40, 42, 44, 52, 62, 67, 71, 72, 90, 91, 123, 136, 138, 159, 161, 166, 185, 187, 188, 190, 191, 193, 207, 209, 213, 226, 238, 249, 258, 260, 263, 265, 300, 310, 311, 313, 314, 315, 317, 321, 324, 325, 326, 329, 334, 349, 387, 392, 402, 403, 404, 406, 413, 414, 421, 461

dnyan 227

Dnyaneshwar xxv, 168, 199, 237, 238, 240, 243, 244, 275, 278, 287

Dnyaneshwari 269

Dnyaneshwari. 272

Dnyansagar 272, 287, 298

Dravidian xxiii, 158, 159, 352, 353, 354, 452

Dutt 290

Dyandev xvii

E

earth xiv, 13, 99, 175, 184, 186, 188, 192, 264, 348, 402, 403

Egypt 57, 64, 66, 89, 91, 92, 95, 97, 98, 102, 118, 130, 131, 134, 141, 145, 147, 149, 152, 153, 215, 224, 307, 326, 333, 334, 336, 337, 392, 400, 433, 435, 449, 450, 461

Egyptian 23, 37, 59, 66, 154, 158, 347, 383, 436, 450

Eknath xvii, xviii, xxv, 199, 243, 244, 272, 283, 284, 285, 286, 287, 293, 294, 295, 297, 318, 370, 371, 374, 465

Eknathi Bhagawat 285

energy xiv, 411

essence xiii, xiv, 4, 12, 25, 46, 161, 185, 188, 191, 196, 221, 229, 235, 239, 306, 311, 324, 330, 358, 371, 378, 385, 411, 421, 422

Europe 26, 36, 53, 54, 57, 114, 118, 120, 125, 141, 145, 146, 154, 381

European expansion 146

F

faith xv, xvi, 2, 5, 8, 23, 30, 38, 39, 41, 59, 90, 121, 133, 145, 151, 170, 172, 175, 176, 185, 186, 188, 189, 191, 196, 209, 221, 223, 225, 226, 228, 233, 237, 244, 251, 265, 267, 272, 287, 291, 292, 296, 299, 301, 306, 318, 323, 327, 332, 351, 352, 401, 402, 403, 404, 406, 408, 414, 423, 424

fanā 314

Fatehpur Sikri 123, 182, 341, 441

First World War 145, 148, 149

G

Gabriel 27, 87, 432, 449

Ganpati janma 284

About the Author

Dr. Kiran Paithankar is an Indian author and has been a reader, researcher of various subjects which includes majorly History, Philosophy, Ayurveda, Astrology, Alternative and traditional medicines, literature, ancient languages, and script for more than 30 years. He is an informational guide for Ph.D. students and a spiritual astrologer and Philosopher. He is personal quest to unearth the meaning of sufi Muslim saints of Maharashtra from there's literature wisdom. Dr. Paithankar had a successful career as a physician (Alternative and Ayurvedic Medicines) and business professional in Mumbai. He always makes effective time management on continue his reading and becoming expert about Sufism. Professionally, he is Chief Executive officer (CEO) of well-known company named 'SHOGAI Healthcare Pvt Ltd.' which is based at Badlapur in Maharashtra, and have positions as 'Director' at 'Clinomatrix solutions' and 'Step High career Counselling Services and Abhived Publications' at Mumbai. He is linguistic person and learned Persian language from 'IRAN Culture House, Mumbai' and completed certification and Diploma in Persian Language in year 2014 from Mumbai University. He successfully completed 'Doctor of Philosophy (Ph.D.) from Indian Board of Alternative Medicines, Calcutta in year 2010. He was awarded with 'Dhanwantari Award' in the international conference arrange by Indian Board of Alternative Medicines, Calcutta in 2010.

More from the author

The research book entitled as "The Efficacy of Guduchi Oil when administered in patients with ear disease (copy righted) is published by Author in 2011. Various aticles on Ayurvedic Medicines are published in the well-known newspaper named 'PUDHARI' in Mumbai (Thane) region of Maharashtra Mumbai in year 2009. A completed Magazine written as a Annual special edition named "Diwali Pahat" year 2009. The national seminar held on 23-24 February 2016 on "Persian, Marathi and other Indian languages: Linguistic and Literary Relations" by Persian department, University of Mumbai. Author has presented research paper on 'Influence of Persian Language on Konkani Language (Gomantakiy)'. Parsiana is the international, semi-monthly, English magazine published from Mumbai covering a wide range of knowledge and related topics on literature and Persian languages. In the magazine issue release on 7th March 2016, Volume 38, number 15, the article on 'Through the Persian Prism' which talks about the influence of Persian Language on Indian Languages into a 'Literary Category'. Unpublished work includes 'Marathi translation of 'Aramaic inscriptions' of King Ashoka, and 'An introduction of Tripitaka in Marathi language and the ongoing research work consist of 'Origin of Vedic Sanskrit and old Persian language and it's script' and 'Influence of Vedic Sanskrit and old Persian language on Indian Tribal languages'.

9 789355 221179